CONTEMPORARY LINGUISTICS

An Introduction

CONTEMPORARY LINGUISTICS

An Introduction

William O'Grady and Michael Dobrovolsky
University of Calgary

U.S. Edition prepared by
Mark Aronoff
State University of New York at Stony Brook

St. Martin's Press
New York

Senior Editor: Mark Gallaher
Associate Editor: Kim Richardson
Project Editor: Elise Bauman
Production Supervisor: Julie Power
Text Design: Bill Smith Studios
Cover Design: Celine Brandes/Photo Plus Art

Library of Congress Catalog Card Number: 88-60559
Copyright © 1989 by St. Martin's Press, Inc. Adapted from
Contemporary Linguistic Analysis,
published in Canada by Copp Clark Pitman, Ltd.

Manufactured in the United States of America.
321
fed

For information, write:
St. Martin's Press, Inc.
175 Fifth Avenue
New York, NY 10010

ISBN: 0-312-01878-9

Acknowledgment

The spectrographs on pp. 416–417 first appeared
in Peter Ladefoged's *A Course on Phonetics,*
Harcourt Brace Jovanovich, Inc. Reprinted by
permission.

PREFACE

I have taught Introductory Linguistics almost every semester for the last fifteen years. It is still a greater source of pleasure for me than any other course. This is especially true after the final exam, when a handful of students tell me that because of the course they now see not just the complexity of the language but some of the orderliness of its complexity.

In all these years of teaching Introductory Linguistics, I have never found a textbook that lived up to the subject matter. I tried all the usual introductory texts, as they appeared, as well as readers, workbooks, and various combinations, but none of them satisfied me. I began to long for the old days of Gleason and Hockett and the even older days of Bloomfield's *Language*.

Yet even if the old days and the old books were as good as I remembered them, they still would not be representative of what linguists today know and believe or of how they proceed in their analysis of language. Maybe, I decided, I would have to write a linguistics text myself. To that end, I had begun tentative discussions with a textbook publisher, when I received a call from New York: an editor at St. Martin's Press wanted to know whether I had any interest in working on an introductory linguistics textbook. She went on to explain that two linguists in Canada had put together a new text that had taken the country by storm. St. Martin's wanted to publish a U.S. edition, and they needed help in revising the original.

I agreed to have a look at it, not mentioning either my long-standing dissatisfaction with the current crop of textbooks or my skepticism toward yet another. But when the book arrived, I was pleasantly surprised. What I read really was a fine introductory textbook: comprehensive, up-to-date, and readable without being condescending. It was also a book that could be adapted to many different audiences and many different course designs. Yes, I wanted very much to work on this book. I have done so, and the results now lie before you.

This U.S. edition retains all that I found so praiseworthy in the Canadian original, while incorporating new material to make this a genuinely American textbook. The specifically Canadian factual material has been deleted or replaced (although not where the Canadian example served its pedagogical purpose as well as another might), and some specifically American material has been added or substituted, especially in the revised chapter on language in social contexts, where American dialects and sociolinguistic phenomena have been given center stage. The morphology and syntax chapters have been revised extensively to reflect up-to-date American research, and a new chapter on computational linguistics, written expressly for this edition, has been added. Most other changes have been editorial in nature, so that the theoretical stance of this edition is basically the same as that of its precursor. In particular, the intent of the original edition to allow students and instructors the option of covering specialized linguistic concerns along with traditional basic concepts has been maintained. Throughout the text, asterisks mark sections that might be considered advanced or "too contemporary," allowing them to be easily treated as optional.

I would like to thank a number of people who helped immensely in the preparation of the American edition of this book. Virginia Clark (University of Vermont), Kyle Johnson (UCLA), and Jennifer Peterson (University of Wisconsin) provided a host of valuable suggestions and comments, without which my job would have been significantly more difficult. At St. Martin's, Nancy Perry talked me into the project, Kim Richardson held my hand, and Elise Bauman guided me through the traumas of proof preparation. Three graduate students at Stony Brook, Marcia Haag, Su-i Chen, and Yi-Lin Yin, provided crucial assistance in the preparation of the text and the Instructor's Manual. Thank you all.

Mark Aronoff

PREFACE TO THE CANADIAN EDITION

Thanks to the application of rigorous analysis to familiar subject matter, linguistics provides students with an ideal introduction to the kind of thinking we call "scientific." Such thinking proceeds from an appreciation of problems arising from bodies of data, to hypotheses that attempt to account for those problems, to the careful testing and extension of these hypotheses. But science is more than a formal activity. One of the great pleasures offered introductory students of linguistics is the discovery of the impressive body of subconscious knowledge that underlies language use. This book emphasizes the extent of this knowledge as well as the scientific methodology used in linguistic analysis.

As the title suggests, we have attempted an introduction to linguistics as it is practiced at this stage in the development of our discipline. While we do not ignore or reject other fruitful approaches to linguistics, we have taken the generative paradigm as basic for two reasons. First, generative linguistics provides a relatively coherent and integrated approach to basic linguistic phenomena. Phonetics, phonology, morphology, syntax, and semantics are viewed within this framework as perhaps in no other as fully integrated and interrelated. Secondly, the generative approach has been widely influential in its application to a broad range of other linguistic phenomena over the past twenty years.

The extent of our "contemporariness" has been limited by the inevitable compromise between the need to present basic concepts and the demands of sophisticated and competing recent approaches. In many cases, early versions of our chapters were judged "too contemporary" by instructors who were not specialists in the subfields in question. This led to substantial revisions and a somewhat more traditional approach to certain issues than was originally intended. Where possible, however, later sections of the chapters are used to present more contemporary material. In this way, we have attempted to provide what is promised by the title—an introductory text that provides a solid grounding in basic linguistc concepts, but one that also prepares the student to go on to current work in the discipline. For this reason, the student is introduced to multi-leveled phonology (in preparation for further tiered analyses), allophonic/morphophonemic distinctions (in preparation for lexical phonology), interaction among components of the grammar (in preparation for a more extended modular approach), word formation rules in morphology, and examples of parametric variation in syntax.

To the extent possible, we have attempted to integrate the basic mechanisms outlined in the first five chapters of the book into our discussion of phenomena in later chapters. Thus, our discussion of semantics, historical linguistics, first and second language acquisition, and neurolinguistics draws to some degree on the notions presented in our introduction to generative grammar.

No textbook can be all things to all users. We hope that this book will provide students not only with a springboard to the realm of scientific linguistic analysis, but also with a greater appreciation for the wonder of human language, the variety and complexity of its structure, and the subtlety of its use.

William O'Grady
Michael Dobrovolsky

CONTENTS

Preface   vi

Chapter 1 Language: A Preview
William O'Grady and Michael Dobrovolsky   1
    1.1   Creativity   1
    1.2   Grammar and Linguistic Competence   4
    1.3   Specialization   9
    Summing Up   10
    Sources   11
    Recommended Reading   11
    Questions   11

Chapter 2 Phonetics: The Sounds of Language
Michael Dobrovolsky   13
    2.1   Phonetic Transcription   14
         Segments   14
    2.2   The Sound-Producing System   15
         The Lungs   15
         The Larynx   16
         Glottal States   16
    2.3   Sound Clauses   17
         Vowels and Consonants   17
         Glides   18
    2.4   Consonant Articulation   18
         The Tongue   18
         Places of Articulation   19
    2.5   Manners of Articulation   20
         Oral versus Nasal   21
         Stops   21
         Fricatives   22
         Affricates   23
       *Voice Lag and Aspiration   24
         Liquids   25
         Syllabic Liquids and Nasals   26
         American Glides   26
    2.6   Vowels   26
         Simple Vowels and Dipthongs   27
         Basic Parameters for Describing Vowels   27
         Tense and Lax Vowels   29
       *Nasal Vowels   30
    2.7   Phonetic Transcription of American English
         Consonants and Vowels   31

* 2.8 Other Vowels and Consonants   32
        Vowels   32
        Consonants   33
    2.9 Suprasegmentals   35
        Pitch   36
        Length   39
        Stress   39
    2.10 Coarticulation   40
        Ease of Articulation   40
        Articulatory Processes   41
* 2.11 Classes and Features   44
        Major Class Features   46
        Place Features   47
        Manner Features   48
        Vowel Features   49
Summing Up   50
Sources   50
Recommended Reading   50
Appendix: Articulatory/Feature Representation of English
Consonants   51
Questions   51

Chapter 3 Phonology: The Function and Patterning of Sounds
    Michael Dobrovolsky   54
    3.1 Phonotactics: Segments in Sequence   55
        Some English Phonotactics   55
        Accidental and Systematic Gaps   56
        Phonotactics and Borrowed Forms   56
    3.2 Segments in Contrast   57
        Minimal Pairs and Sets   57
        Language-Specific Contrasts   57
    3.3 Phonetically Conditioned Variation: Phonemes and
        Allophones   59
        Complementary Distribution   59
        Phonemes and Allophones   60
        The Reality of Phonemes   61
        Phonemes and Natural Classes   62
        Nasal Vowels   63
        Vowel Raising   63
        Language-Specific Patterns   64
        Free Variation   66
    3.4 Phonetic and Phonological Transcription   66
    3.5 Features and Tones   67
        The Role of Features   67
        Tones and Their Representation   69
* 3.6 Above the Segment: Syllables   70
        Defining the Syllable   70

Setting up Syllables   71
Syllabic Phonology   73
* 3.7   Derivations and Rules   75
Derivations   75
The Form and Notation of Rules   76
Features, Segments, and Syllables   77
* 3.8   Representing Processes   77
Assimilation   77
Deletion   79
Epenthesis   79
Stress as a Process   80
Processes: A Last Word   81
* 3.9   Rule Application   81
Free Rule Application   81
Ordered Rule Application   81
Summing Up   82
Sources   82
Recommended Reading   83
Appendix: Hints for Solving Phonology Problems   83
Questions   84

Chapter   4   Morphology: The Study of Word Structure
*Videa P. De Guzman, William O'Grady, and
Mark Aronoff*   89
4.1   The Minimal Meaningful Units of Language   90
Free Forms   90
Words   90
Signs and Morphemes   91
4.2   Morphology   91
Identifying Morphemes and Allomorphs   92
Free and Bound Morphemes   93
Word Structure   93
4.3   Word Formation   100
Derivation   100
Compounding   103
Other Word Formation   106
4.4   Inflection   107
Properties of Inflection   108
*Nominal Inflection   110
*Verbal Inflection   114
4.5   Morphology and Phonology   116
Morphophonemic Rules   116
Deriving Allomorphs   117
Conditioned Allomorphs   117
Conditioning by Morphological Class   119
Abstract Underlying Representations   120
Summing Up   122

Sources   122
Recommended Reading   122
Questions   123

Chapter 5 Syntax: The Study of Sentence Structure
William O'Grady and Daniel Finer   126
5.1   Syntactic Categories   127
Lexical Categories   127
Phrasal Categories   128
Recursion   134
Sentence Structure   135
5.2   Phrase Structure Rules   136
The S Rule   136
The NP Rule   137
The VP Rule   138
Modal Auxiliaries   139
5.3   Lexical Insertion   139
Subcategorization   140
More Ambiguity   141
5.4   A Generative Grammar   142
5.5   Transformational Rules   143
Inversion in Yes-No Questions   143
Particle Movement   144
Deep Structure and Surface Structure   146
5.6   Embedded Clauses   148
Verb Complements   148
Adverbial Clauses   149
5.7   *Wh* Questions   151
Wh Movement   151
Wh Movement in Verb Complements   152
Long Distance Movement   153
* 5.8   Relative Clauses   154
Wh Movement Again   154
* 5.9   Islands   155
5.10   Some Cross-Linguistic Variation   158
Syntactic Categories   158
Korean Phrase Structure   159
Selayarese Phrase Structure   160
Question Formation in Tamil   161
Inversion in French and Spanish   162
*Passive Structures   163
Summing Up   166
Sources   166
Recommended Reading   166
Questions   167

Chapter 6 Semantics: The Study of Meaning *William O'Grady*   169
 6.1 Meaning 169
  Word Meaning 169
  Semantic Relations among Words 171
  Semantic Relations Involving Sentences 173
 6.2 Syntactic Structure and Interpretation 174
  Structural Ambiguity 174
  *Thematic Roles 176
  *The Interpretation of Reflexive Pronouns 179
 6.3 Other Factors in Sentence Interpretation 180
  Pragmatics 181
  Presuppositions 181
  Speech Acts 182
 6.4 Language, Meaning, and Thought 183
  The Sapir-Whorf Hypothesis 184
 Summing Up 186
 Sources 186
 Recommended Reading 186
 Questions 187

Chapter 7 Historical Linguistics *James M. Anderson*   189
 7.1 The Nature of Language Change 189
  Systematicity of Language Change 190
  Triggers of Linguistic Change 191
 7.2 Sound Change 193
  Phonetically Conditioned Sound Change 193
  Non-phonetically Conditioned Sound Change 197
  Phonetic versus Phonological Change 197
  Ordering of Sound Changes 200
 7.3 Morphological Change 200
  Addition and Loss 201
  The Loss of Case 201
  Analogy 202
 7.4 Syntactic Change 203
  Word Order 203
  Inversion 204
 7.5 Lexical and Semantic Change 204
  Borrowing 205
  Semantic Change 206
 * 7.6 The Spread of Change 207
  Diffusion through the Language 207
  Diffusion through the Population 209
 7.7 Language Reconstruction 210
  Cognates 210
  *Techniques of Reconstruction 211
  *Internal Reconstruction 214
  The Discovery of Indo-European 214

Summing Up   216
Sources   217
Recommended Reading   218
Questions   218

Chapter 8 The Classification of Languages
Aleksandra Steinbergs   223
    8.1   Structural versus Genetic Relationships   223
    8.2   Structural Classification   225
    Phonology   225
    Morphology   229
    Syntax   231
    Explaining Universals   233
    8.3   Genetic Classification   235
    The Indo-European Family   236
    Some Other Families   239
    8.4   The Americas   246
    Language Isolates   248
Summing Up   249
Sources   249
Recommended Reading   249
Questions   250

Chapter 9 Brain and Language *Sook Whan Cho*   253
    9.1   The Human Brain   253
    Cerebral Dominance   254
    9.2   Brain and Language   255
    The Left Hemisphere   255
    The Language Centers   257
    Aphasia   259
    9.3   The Critical Period Hypothesis   263
    Supporting Evidence   263
    Counter-Evidence   264
    The Case of Genie   264
Summing Up   266
Sources   266
Recommended Reading   267
Questions   267

Chapter 10 Language Acquisition: The Emergence of a Grammar
Sook Whan Cho and William O'Grady   269
    10.1   The Study of Language Acquisition   270
    Methods   270
    10.2   Phonological Development   271
    Babbling   272
    Early Phonetic Processes   272
    Production versus Perception   275
    Developmental Order   275

10.3 Morphological Development   276
      A Developmental Sequence   276
      Morphophonemic Rules   278
      Word Formation Rules   279
10.4 Development of Word Meaning   280
      The Acquisition of Word Meaning   280
      Spatial and Dimensional Terms   283
10.5 Syntactic Development   284
      The One-Word Stage   284
      The Two-Word Stage   284
      The Telegraphic Stage   285
      Later Development   286
10.6 Determinants of Language Acquisition   288
      The Role of Imitation and Correction   289
      The Role of Parental Speech   290
      The Role of Cognitive Development   291
    *The Role of Inborn Knowledge   292
Summing Up   294
Sources   295
Recommended Reading   296
Questions   297

Chapter 11 Second Language Acquisition *Christine Laurell*   299
11.1 Questions and Issues   300
      The Optimal Age Issue   300
      The Role of Linguistic Input   301
      The Language Learning Environment   302
      Comparing L1 and L2 Acquisition   303
*11.2 The Study of Second Language Acquisition   304
      Phonological Development   305
      Morphological Development   305
      Syntactic Development   307
11.3 Methods of Analysis   309
      Contrastive Analysis   309
      Error Analysis   310
11.4 The Learner   312
      Language Learner Strategies   312
      Cognitive Style   314
      Personality   315
11.5 Teaching Methodologies   317
      Grammar Translation Method   317
      Direct Method   317
      Audiolingual Method   318
      Communicative Language Teaching   318
11.6 The Immersion Approach   320
      Total Immersion   321
      Partial Immersion   321
Summing Up   322

Sources   322
Recommended Reading   323
Questions   324

Chapter 12 Language in Social Contexts
            Ronald H. Southerland and Frank Anshen   326
            12.1   Fundamental Concepts   326
            12.2   Dialectology   327
                    Methods   327
                    English in North America   329
            12.3   Social Differentiation of Language   331
                    The Social Stratification of English   332
                    Language and Sex   335
                    Politics and Language   339
            12.4   Special Languages   341
                    Slang   341
                    Argots and Play Languages   341
                    Sublanguages   343
            12.5   Mixed Languages   344
                    Pidgins   344
                    Creoles   346
            12.6   Speech Situations   349
                    Register   351
                    Forms of Address   352
            Summing Up   354
            Sources   354
            Recommended Reading   356
            Questions   356

Chapter 13 Writing Systems *James M. Anderson*   358
            13.1   Types of Writing   358
                    Logographic Writing   358
                    Syllabic Writing   359
                    Alphabetic Writing   359
            13.2   The History of Writing   359
                    Pictograms   360
                    From Pictogram to Ideogram   360
                    From Pictogram to Logogram   361
                    From Logogram to Syllabary   364
                    From Syllabary to Alphabet   367
          *13.3   Some Non-European Writing Systems   371
                    Chinese Writing   371
                    American Scripts   372
                    Korean Writing   373
                    African Scripts   375
                    Indian Scripts   375

13.4   English Spelling   376
     Irregularities   376
     Obstacles to Reform   377
13.5   Impact on Reading   379
Summing Up   380
Sources   381
Recommended Reading   381
Questions   382

Chapter 14   Animal Communication   *Michael Dobrovolsky*   383
14.1   Nonvocal Communication   383
14.2   Communication Structure   384
     Organization   385
     Kinds of Tokens   386
     Token Structure   387
     A View of Animal Communication   388
14.3   The Bees   389
     The System   389
     Bees and Humans   390
14.4   The Birds   392
     The System   392
     Birds and Humans   394
14.5   Nonhuman Primates   395
     Prosimian Communication   396
     Monkeys   396
     Gibbons, Baboons, and Chimpanzees   398
14.6   Testing Nonhuman Primates for Linguistic
     Ability   400
     Some Experiments   400
     Nonsigning Experiments   401
     The Clever Hans Controversy   403
     The Great Ape Debate   404
     Implications   405
14.7   Comparing Communication Systems: Design
     Features   406
     The Features   406
Summing Up   409
Picture Credits   410
Sources   410
Recommended Reading   411
Questions   411

Chapter 15   Computational Linguistics   *Judith Klavans*   413
15.1   Computational Phonetics and Phonology   415
     The Talking Machine: Speech Synthesis   415
     Speech Recognition or Speech Analysis   419

15.2　Computational Morphology　　420
　　　Morphological Processes　　420
　　　Some Problems in Computational Morphology　　423
15.3　Computational Syntax　　424
　　　Natural Language Analysis　　424
　　　Natural Language Generation　　430
15.4　Computational Lexicology　　431
15.5　Computational Semantics　　436
　　　Pragmatics　　438
15.6　Practical Applications of Computational
　　　Linguistics　　439
　　　Indexing and Concordances　　439
　　　Text Retrieval　　441
　　　Machine Translation　　441
　　　Speech Recognition　　443
　　　Speech Synthesis　　444
Summing Up　　445
Recommended Reading　　445
Questions　　445

Glossary　　448
Language Index　　471
Index　　475

CONTEMPORARY LINGUISTICS
An Introduction

1 LANGUAGE
A Preview

*The gift of language is the single human trait
that marks us all genetically, setting us
apart from the rest of life.*

Lewis Thomas, *The Lives of a Cell*

Language is many things—a system of communication, a medium for
thought, a vehicle for literary expression, a social institution, a matter
for political controversy, a factor in nation building. All normal human
beings speak at least one language, and it is hard to imagine much significant
social or intellectual activity taking place in its absence. Each of us, then,
has a stake in understanding how language is organized and how it is used.
This book provides a basic introduction to **linguistics**, the discipline that
studies these matters.

1.1 CREATIVITY

What is human language? What does it mean to "know" a language? To
answer these questions, it is first necessary to understand the resources that
a language makes available to its **native speakers**, those who have acquired
it as children in a natural setting. The scope and diversity of human thought
and experience place great demands on language. Because communication
is not restricted to a fixed set of topics, language must do something more
than provide a package of ready-made messages. It must enable us to produce and understand new words, phrases, and sentences as the need arises.
In short, human language must be **creative**—allowing novelty and innovation
in response to new experiences, situations, and thoughts.

Despite this creative potential, language use is subject to very specific
rules and constraints. This can be illustrated by a relatively simple phenomenon in English: the process that creates verbs (words naming actions) from
nouns (words naming things).

1. *a) beach* the boat
   b) ground the airplane
   c) powder the aspirin
   d) knife the man
   e) spear the fish
   f) orphan the children

As the following sentences show, there is a great deal of freedom to innovate in the formation of such verbs.

> 2. *a*) He *wristed* the ball over the net.
>   *b*) She would try to *stiff-upper-lip* it through.
>   *c*) She *Houdini'd* her way out of the locked closet.

However, there are also rules limiting this freedom. For instance, a new verb is rarely coined if a word with the intended meaning already exists. Although we say *shelve the books* to mean 'put the books on the shelf', we do not say *hospital the patient* to mean 'put the patient in the hospital'. This is presumably because the well-established verb *hospitalize* already has the meaning that the new form would have.

There are also special constraints on the meaning and use of particular subclasses of these verbs. One such constraint involves verbs that are created from time expressions such as *summer* and *holiday*.

> 3. *a*) Julia *summered* in Paris.
>   *b*) Kent *wintered* in Mexico.
>   *c*) Martine *holidayed* in France.
>   *d*) They *honeymooned* in Hawaii.

While the sentences in *3* are all acceptable, not all time expressions can be used in this way. (Throughout this book an asterisk is used to indicate that a sentence is unacceptable.)

> 4. *a*) *Jerome *midnighted* in the streets.
>   *b*) *Andrea *nooned* at the restaurant.
>   *c*) *Philip *one o'clocked* at the airport.

The foregoing examples show that when a verb is created from a time expression, it must be given a very specific interpretation—roughly paraphrasable as 'to be somewhere for the period of time X'. Thus, *to summer in Paris* is 'to be in Paris for the summer', *to holiday in France* is 'to be in France for the holidays', and so on. Since *noon* and *midnight* express points in time rather than periods of time, they cannot be used to create verbs of this new class.

Constraints are essential to the viability of the creative process. If well-established words were constantly being replaced by new creations, the vocabulary of English would be so unstable that communication could be jeopardized. A similar danger would arise if there were no constraints on the meaning of new words. If *winter in Hawaii* could mean 'make it snow in Hawaii' or 'wish it were winter in Hawaii' or any other arbitrary thing, the production and interpretation of new forms would be chaotic and would subvert rather than enrich communication.

This rule-governed creativity characterizes all levels of language, including the way in which sounds are combined to form words. The forms in *5*, for instance, are recognizable as possible names for new products or inventions.

5. *a*) prace
   b) flib
   c) traf

Such forms contrast with the patterns in 6, which simply do not have the "sound" of English words.

6. *a*) psarp
   b) nbik
   c) ftra

This shows that part of our subconscious knowledge of English includes a set of constraints on possible sequences of sounds.

Still other constraints determine how new words can be created from already existing forms with the help of special endings. Imagine, for example, that you learn that there is a word *soleme* (used perhaps for a newly discovered atomic particle). As a speaker of English, you then automatically know that something with the properties of a soleme can be called *solemic*. You also know that to make something solemic is to *solemicize* it, and you call this process *solemicization*. Further, you know that the *c* is pronounced as *s* in *solemicize* but as *k* in *solemic*. Without hesitation, you also recognize that *solemicize* is pronounced with the stress on the second syllable. (You would say *soLEmicize*, not *SOlemicize* or *solemiCIZE*.)

Nowhere is the ability to deal with novel utterances in accordance with rules more obvious than in the production and comprehension of sentences. Apart from a few fixed expressions and greetings, much of what you say, hear, and read in the course of a day consists of sentences that are novel to you. In conversations, lectures, newscasts, and textbooks you are regularly exposed to novel combinations of words, the expression of unfamiliar ideas, and the presentation of new information. Such is the case with the sentences you have just read. While each of these sentences is no doubt perfectly comprehensible to you, it is extremely unlikely that you have ever seen any of them before.

This ability to deal with novel utterances does not ensure that you can understand or use any imaginable combination of words. You would not ordinarily say a sentence such as *7a*, although *7b* would be perfectly acceptable.

7. *a*) *He brought a chair in order to sit on.
   b) He brought a chair to sit on.

Or, to take another example, *8a* is well formed—if bizarre—but *8b* is gibberish.

8. *a*) The pink kangaroo hopped over the talking lamp.
   b) *Pink the the talking hopped kangaroo lamp over.

As with other aspects of language, your ability to produce and comprehend sentences is subject to limitations.

1.2 GRAMMAR AND LINGUISTIC COMPETENCE

As we have seen, speakers of a language know a system that enables them to create and understand novel utterances. This unconscious knowledge, which is often labeled **linguistic competence**, constitutes the central subject matter of linguistics and of this book. In attempting to describe linguistic competence, linguists construct a **grammar**, which is an explicit system of elements and rules needed to form and interpret sentences. All languages have a grammar consisting of the components listed in Table 1.1. Linguists use the term *grammar* in a rather special and technical sense. To appreciate the central role of this notion in current linguistic analysis, it is necessary to set aside a number of common fallacies and misconceptions.

Table 1.1 The components of a grammar

Component	Function
Phonetics	the articulation and perception of speech sounds
Phonology	the patterning of speech sounds
Morphology	word formation
Syntax	sentence formation
Semantics	the interpretation of words and sentences

Fallacy 1: Only some languages have grammars.

It is not unusual to hear the remark that some unfamiliar language—Pennsylvania Dutch, Navaho, or Chinese—"has no grammar." Given our definition of grammar, such a statement is obviously not true. Since all human languages are spoken, they must have phonetic and phonological rules; since they all have words and sentences, they also must have a morphology and a syntax; and since these words and sentences have systematic meanings, they obviously must have a semantic component as well. Clearly, all human languages have grammars.

Unfamiliar languages sometimes appear to have no grammar because their grammatical systems may be very different from those of better-known languages. In Walbiri (an aboriginal language of Australia), for example, the relative ordering of words is so free that the English sentence *The two dogs now see several kangaroos* could be translated by the equivalent of any of the following strings of words.

> 9. *a*) Dogs two now see kangaroos several.
>   *b*) See now dogs two kangaroos several.
>   *c*) See now kangaroos several dogs two.
>   *d*) Kangaroos several now dogs two see.
>   *e*) Kangaroos several now see dogs two.

While Walbiri may not restrict the order of words in the way English does, it does have other types of rules. One such rule places the ending *lu* on the word for 'dogs' to indicate that it names the animals that do the seeing rather than the animals that are seen. This allows speakers of Walbiri to signal that the dogs see the kangaroos rather than vice versa. In English, this information is conveyed by placing *the two dogs* in front of the verb and *several kangaroos* after it. Rather than showing that Walbiri has no grammar, such differences simply demonstrate that it has a grammar unlike that of English in certain respects. This important point is applicable to all differences among languages: there are no languages without grammars, merely languages with different types of grammatical systems.

Fallacy 2: Some languages have grammars that are radically simpler or more "primitive" than those of other languages.

Although it is not uncommon to hear reports of languages with very simple or "primitive" grammars, such claims are untrue. The grammars of all languages are essentially equal in terms of overall complexity. Once again, however, it is easy to be misled by a superficial examination of the facts. For instance, one might think that English is somehow simpler or more primitive than French since it has no rule to vary the form of the word *the* when the noun is plural.

> 10. *le* livre   *les* livres
>   'the book'   'the books'

A case constructed on a single example such as this is misleading since there are also grammatical contrasts that are found in English, but not French. For example, English makes use of changes in the form of the verb to distinguish between an action that is currently taking place and a general tendency.

> 11. *a*) He is listening to music.
>   *b*) He listens to music.

In French, both meanings are expressed by the same form of the verb (*Il écoute la musique*) and, where necessary, words like *now* and *usually* are used to distinguish between current and habitual actions.

This example illustrates a general point. The fact that one language may lack a rule or contrast found in another does not indicate that it has a simpler or more primitive grammar. Elsewhere in its grammar, we can expect to find rules and contrasts not present in the other language.

In some cases, these rules and contrasts may be quite unlike those found in the familiar languages of Europe. For example, in Hua, a language spoken by about three thousand people in a remote area of Papua New Guinea, a contrast between two interpretations for English *we* is made in the form of the verb.

> 12. *a*) rmu'e
>   'We (= you and I) have descended.'
>   *b*) rmune
>   'We (= you, I, and someone else) have descended.'

Hua uses the ending *'e* to indicate 'we' in the sense of 'you and I' and *ne* for the sense 'you, I, and someone else'. No such contrast exists in English. Each language has its own set of rules and contrasts.

Fallacy 3:   People must be taught the grammatical rules of their language.

There is a widespread belief that grammatical rules are mastered through schooling and that some speakers of a language "do not know their grammar." Such an attitude is as ill-founded as the belief that some languages do not have grammars. Since all language use requires knowledge of sound patterns, rules for word and sentence formation, and principles of semantic interpretation, it is clear that speakers of a language must have knowledge of its grammar. It is equally clear that this knowledge is not acquired through formal education. Consider your pronunciation of the past tense ending written as *-ed* in the following words.

13. *a*) hunted
    b) slipped
    c) buzzed

Note that whereas you say *id* in *hunted,* you say *t* in *slipped* and *d* in *buzzed.* If you heard a new verb, say *flib*, you would form the past tense as *flibbed* and pronounce the ending as *d*. This is surely not the result of training. In fact, it is unlikely that this phenomenon has ever been drawn to your attention. Rather, it is knowledge that you gained subconsciously in the course of the language acquisition process.

Consider another example. Speakers of English know whether or not a pronoun in certain structures may refer to a particular person. In sentence *14*, for example, the pronoun *he* cannot refer to *John* but must refer to someone else.

14. He knows that John left.

However, if we reverse the positions of the words *John* and *he*, then the sentence becomes ambiguous. The pronoun can now refer either to *John* or to someone else.

15. John knows that he left.

The difference between *14* and *15* is so obvious that no elementary grammar book ever mentions it. As a native speaker of English, you know intuitively that a pronoun preceding a noun cannot normally refer to the person or thing designated by that noun. Once this is pointed out, you become conscious of the difference.

Examples like these can be multiplied indefinitely, but by now the general point should be clear. The grammatical rules needed to produce and understand sentences are, for the most part, subconscious and are acquired without the help of instruction or training.

Fallacy 4:   Grammatical rules are supposed to be "logical."

A common misconception about grammatical rules holds that they should somehow conform to the rules of logic. This is usually taken to mean that, at the very least, linguistic rules and structures should not contradict common sense. In reality, there is little reason to think that grammatical rules are like this. If they were, we would use *sheeps* and *foots* as the plural of *sheep* and *foot*. Since we use the *-s* ending in the vast majority of other cases (*cats, dogs, cars, houses,* and *books*), it would surely make sense to mark the plural in the same way throughout the language. Evidently, something other than logic is shaping the grammar in these cases.

A favorite example of those who argue that grammatical rules should reflect logic involves structures such as *I didn't see nothing,* which contain two negatives—*n't* and *nothing.* Such structures, they claim, cannot be grammatical since the two negatives cancel each other out, giving a meaning that is the precise opposite of what is intended. However, it can be argued just as persuasively that two negatives reinforce each other, thereby strengthening the negation. Presumably this happens in the speech of those who use double negatives as well as in the many languages, such as Spanish, that obligatorily employ such patterns of negation.

> *16.* Juan no vió nada.
>   John not saw nothing
>   'John didn't see anything.'

The lesson to be learned from these examples is that language has its own system of rules whose workings need not reflect particular conventions of logic or common sense.

Fallacy 5:   Grammars deteriorate with the passage of time.

It is now a well-established fact that all languages are constantly undergoing change. Some of these changes are relatively minor and occur very quickly (for example, the addition of new words such as *patriation, yuppie, biosphere, byte,* and *prioritize* to the vocabulary of English). Other changes have a more drastic effect on the overall form of the language and typically take place over a long period of time.

The formation of negative structures in English has undergone this type of change. Prior to 1200, English routinely used double negative constructions, placing *ne* before the verb and a variant of *not* after it.

> *17. a)* Ic ne seye not.   ('I don't say.')
>   *b)* He ne speketh nawt.   ('He does not speak.')

By 1400 or thereabouts, *ne* was used infrequently. Typically, *not* occurred by itself after the verb.

> *18. a)* I seye not the wordes.
>   *b)* We sawe nawt the knyghtes.

It was not until several centuries later that English adopted its current practice of allowing *not* to occur after only certain types of verbs (such as *do, have,* and *will*).

> *19. a)* I will not say the words.   (vs. I will say not the words.)
>   *b)* He did not see the knights.   (vs. He saw not the knights.)

These very drastic modifications illustrate the extent to which grammatical rules change over time. Whereas the structures exemplified in *18* are archaic by today's standards, the constructions in *17* sound completely foreign to most speakers of modern English.

Through the centuries, concern has frequently been expressed about the deterioration of English and other languages. In 1710, for example, Jonathan Swift (author of *Gulliver's Travels*) lamented "the continual Corruption of our English Tongue." Among the corruptions to which Swift objected were contractions such as *he's* for *he is,* although he had no objection to *'tis* for *it is.*

In the nineteenth century, Edward S. Gould, a columnist for the New York *Evening Post,* published a book entitled *Good English; or, Popular Errors in Language,* in which he accused newspaper writers and authors of "sensation novels" of ruining the language by introducing "spurious words" like *jeopardize, leniency,* and *underhanded.* To this day, the tradition of prescriptive concern about the use of certain words continues in the work of such popular writers as Edwin Newman and John Simon, who form a kind of self-appointed language police.

The view that languages attain a state of perfection at some point in their history and that subsequent changes lead to deterioration and corruption is rejected by modern linguistics. The fact that *it's* is now entirely accepted while *'tis* has fallen out of use has affected neither the overall complexity of English nor its adequacy as a medium of communication. Moreover, since there is no external standard of logic with which grammars must comply (see fallacy 4), there are simply no grounds for claiming that one set of grammatical rules is somehow perfect or inherently superior to another.

This does not deny the importance of clear expression in writing and speech. Such skills are quite rightly an object of concern among educators. However, the difficulties that arise in this area do not stem from the fact that grammars change over time. Problems of self-expression occur in all cultures and all times, regardless of the language's stage of historical development.

Fallacy 6: Grammars differ from each other in unpredictable ways.

At first glance, the well-known differences among human languages would seem to suggest that there are no limits on the type of linguistic systems that human beings can acquire and use. In fact, it is now understood that underlying obvious differences in sound patterns, vocabulary, and word order, there are important grammatical principles and tendencies shared by all human languages.

One such principle involves the manner in which sentences are negated. With unlimited variation, one would expect to find that the equivalent of English *not* could occur in a wide range of positions in the languages of the world. Thus, we might expect each of the following possibilities to occur with roughly equal frequency.

20. *a*) Not Pat is here.
    b) Pat not is here.
    c) Pat is not here.
    d) Pat is here not.

As it happens, the first and fourth patterns are very rare. In virtually all languages, negative elements such as *not* either immediately precede or immediately follow the verb.

The relative ordering of other elements is also subject to constraints. Without such constraints, we would expect that a basic statement such as *Dogs like bones* could be expressed by each of the orders in *21* in a roughly equal number of languages.

21. *a*) Dogs like bones.
    b) Dogs bones like.
    c) Like dogs bones.
    d) Like bones dogs.
    e) Bones like dogs.
    f) Bones dogs like.

In reality, most languages adopt one of the first three orders for basic statements. The fourth and fifth orders are found in a handful of languages, and the sixth pattern is not used as the dominant order for basic statements in any language. The absence of such combinations is not accidental. Rather, it reflects the existence of constraints that limit variation among languages.

This is not an isolated example. As later chapters will show, many grammatical categories and rules are universal. This suggests that the properties of language reflect deeper facts about the structure and organization of the human mind. Herein lies much of the fascination and importance of linguistic analysis.

1.3 SPECIALIZATION

There is every reason to believe that humans have a special capacity for language that is not shared by other creatures. The evolutionary adaptation of certain physiological mechanisms for linguistic ends has occurred only in humans. The so-called speech organs (the lungs, larynx, tongue, teeth, lips, palate, and nasal passages) did not originally evolve for speech; rather, they were—and still are—directly concerned with ensuring the physical survival of the organism. But each nonlinguistic use of these organs is paralleled by a linguistic use unique to humans. Table 1.2 compares the linguistic uses of the major speech organs with their primary survival functions in humans and other mammals.

In humans, these organs have all become highly specialized for linguistic ends. The vocal folds, for example, are more muscular and less fatty in humans than in nonhuman primates such as chimpanzees and gorillas. Because of a highly developed network of neural pathways, they also respond more precisely to commands from the brain. The same extensive set of neural pathways allows a high degree of control over other speech organs, such as the tongue, palate, and lips. Such control exceeds anything found in even our closest primate relatives.

There are additional indications of the evolution of linguistic vocalization. Unlike the breathing of survival respiration, speech breathing shows higher lung pressure and a longer exhalation time than respiration. Abdom-

Table 1.2   Dual functions of the speech organs

Organ	Survival function	Speech function
Lungs	to exchange CO_2, oxygen	to supply air for speech
Vocal folds	to create seal over passage to lungs	to produce voice for speech sounds
Tongue	to move food back to throat	to articulate vowels and consonants
Teeth	to break up food	to provide place of articulation for consonants
Lips	to seal oral cavity	to articulate vowels and consonants

inal muscles that are not normally employed for respiration are brought into play in a systematic and refined manner in order to maintain the air pressure needed for speech. Again, a specialized, extensive set of neurological controls exclusive to humans makes this type of breathing possible.

In other words, the human capacity for speech is superimposed on already existing biological structures. Evolution has produced a refinement both in degree and in kind through a long interplay between the demands of language and the development of the human speech-producing apparatus.

We know considerably less about the evolutionary specialization for nonvocal aspects of language such as word formation, sentence formation, and the interpretation of meaning. Nonetheless, it is clear that some sort of evolutionary specialization must have occurred. As we will see in Chapter 9, specific parts of the brain are associated with each of these linguistic activities. Moreover, the brain areas in question have no counterparts in other species. These facts suggest that the human brain is specially structured for language, and that species with different types of brains will not be able to acquire or use the types of grammars associated with human language. After devoting most of this book to the study of grammatical phenomena in human language, we will, in Chapter 14, return to the question of whether comparable linguistic systems occur in other species.

Summing Up

Human language is characterized by **rule-governed creativity**. Speakers of a language possess a **grammar**, a mental system of elements and rules that allows them to form and interpret familiar and novel utterances. The grammar governs the articulation, perception, and patterning of speech sounds, the formation of words and sentences, and the interpretation of utterances. Contrary to popular belief, all languages have grammars that are roughly equal in complexity and are acquired subconsciously by their speakers. The existence of such linguistic systems in humans is the product of unique anatomical and cognitive specialization.

Sources

The discussion of word creation is based on an article by Eve Clark and Herb Clark, "When Nouns Surface As Verbs" in *Language* 55 (1979). The Walbiri data are based on K. Hale's article "Person Marking in Walbiri" in *A Festschrift for Morris Halle,* edited by S. Anderson and P. Kiparsky (New York: Holt, Rinehart and Winston, 1973). The data on Hua come from an article by John Haiman, "Hua: A Papuan Language of New Guinea" in *Languages and Their Status,* edited by T. Shopen (Cambridge, Mass.: Winthrop Publishers, 1979). The Gould book is cited in Dennis Baron's *Grammar and Good Taste* (New Haven: Yale University Press, 1982). The data on the positioning of negative elements within sentences in human language come from an article by O. Dahl, "Typology of Sentence Negation" in *Linguistics* 17:79–106 (1979).

Recommended Reading

Clark, Eve and Herb Clark. 1979. "When Nouns Surface As Verbs." *Language* 55:767–811.

Farb, Peter. 1975. *Word Play: What Happens When People Talk*. New York: Bantam Books.

Matthei, Edward and Thomas Roeper. 1983. *Understanding and Producing Speech*. Glasgow: Fontana.

Questions

1. Part of linguistic competence involves the ability to recognize whether novel utterances are acceptable. Consider the following sentences and determine which are possible sentences in English.

   a) Jason's mother left himself with nothing to eat.
   b) Miriam is eager to talk to.
   c) This is the man that I took a picture of.
   d) Colin made Jane a sandwich.
   e) Is the dog sleeping the bone again?
   f) Wayne prepared Zena a cake.
   g) Max cleaned up the garden.
   h) I desire you to leave.
   i) The toad gulped down it.
   j) That you likes liver surprises me.

2. Which of the following forms are possible in English?

   a) mbood   e) sproke
   b) frall   f) flube
   c) coofp   g) worbg
   d) ktleem   h) bzarn

3. Imagine you are developing new names for products. Create four new English words for these products.

4. The following sentences contain verbs created from nouns. Establish a meaning for each of these new verbs.

   a) We punk-rocked the night away.
   b) He dog-teamed his way across the Arctic.
   c) We MG'd to Oregon.
   d) We Concorded to London.
   e) He Khaddafi'd the American Embassy.
   f) He Kareemed his way to the basket.
   g) We Greyhounded to Chicago.
   h) We'll have to Ajax the sink.
   i) She Windexed the windows.
   j) You should Clairol your beard.
   k) Let's carton the eggs.

5. Using the examples in the preceding exercise as a model, create five new verbs from nouns. Build a sentence around each of these new verbs to show its meaning.

2 PHONETICS
The Sounds of Language

Heavenly labials in a world of gutturals
Wallace Stevens

We do not need to speak in order to use language. Language can be written, recorded mechanically, and even produced by computers in limited ways, but speech remains the primary way we encode it. As we saw in Chapter 1, humans are anatomically specialized to speak, and our species spoke long before we began to write language down. Because language and speech are so closely linked, we begin our study of language by examining the inventory and structure of the sounds of language. This branch of linguistics is called **phonetics**.

Human languages display a wide variety of sounds, called **phones** or **speech sounds**. There are a great many speech sounds, but not an infinite number of them. Certain sounds that humans are capable of producing with the vocal tract do not occur in speech—the sound made by inhaling through one corner of the mouth, for instance, or the ''raspberry'' produced by sticking out the tongue and blowing hard across it. Equally ''exotic-seeming'' sounds do occur in human languages, such as the clicking made by drawing the tongue hard away from the sides of the upper molars or the sound made by constricting the sides of the throat while breathing out. The class of possible speech sounds is not only finite, it is universal. A portion of the total set will be found in the inventory of any human language. Any human, child or adult, can learn how to pronounce these sounds, regardless of racial or cultural background.

There are two ways of approaching phonetics. One way studies the physiological mechanism of speech production. This is known as **articulatory phonetics**. The other, known as **acoustic phonetics**, deals with the physics of speech sounds. It examines the physical properties of speech sounds as they are determined and measured by machines, and attempts to deduce the acoustic basis of speech production and perception. Both approaches are indispensable to an understanding of phonetics. This chapter focuses on articulatory phonetics, but also makes some reference to the acoustic properties of sounds and to acoustic analysis.

2.1 PHONETIC TRANSCRIPTION

Since the sixteenth century, efforts have been made to devise a universal system for transcribing the sounds of speech. The best-known system, the **International Phonetic Alphabet (IPA)**, has been developing since 1888 (see Table 2.1). The goal of this system of transcription is to represent each sound of human speech with a single symbol. These symbols are enclosed in brackets [ ] to indicate that the transcription is phonetic and does not represent the spelling system of a particular language. For example, the sound spelled *th* in English *this* is transcribed as [ð] (pronounced *eth*, as in *weather*). IPA transcription uses this symbol to write the sound in whichever language it is heard, whether it is English, Spanish, Turkmen (a Turkic language spoken in Central Asia and written with the Cyrillic alphabet), or any other. The use of a standardized international phonetic alphabet enables linguists to transcribe languages consistently and accurately. In North American usage, though, some phonetic symbols differ from those employed by IPA transcription. For example, the sound heard at the beginning of the English word *shark* is transcribed as [ʃ] in IPA, but usually as [š] in North America. These differences will be noted where relevant.

Table 2.1 Use of [ð] in the International Phonetic Alphabet

Language	Spelling	IPA	
English	this	[ðɪs]	
Spanish	boda	[bɔða]	'wedding'
Turkmen	aдak	[aðak]	'foot'

Segments

A phonetic alphabet represents speech in the form of **segments**, or individual speech sounds like [p], [s], or [m]. This may seem to be a natural thing to do, but anyone who hears a new language for the first time finds it hard to break up the flow of speech into the individual sounds that make up words. Even when we hear our own language spoken, we do not focus our attention on individual sounds as much as we do on the meanings of words, phrases, and sentences. Still, all speakers of a language can identify the sounds of their language. Linguistic knowledge makes it possible to break down a stream of speech into its component parts, one of which is sound segments.

What makes segmental phonetic transcription a "natural" way of transcribing speech is the relative invariance of speech sounds. It is impossible to represent all variants of human speech sounds, since no one says the same sound in exactly the same way twice. Nonetheless, the sounds of speech remain invariant enough from language to language for us to transcribe them consistently. A *p* sound is much the same in English, Russian, or Uzbek. The fact that when producing a *p* sound, English speakers press their lips together but Russian speakers draw theirs slightly inward does not make the sounds different enough to warrant separate symbols. But the sounds *p* and *t* are distinct enough from each other in languages the world over to be consistently transcribed with separate symbols.

2.2 THE SOUND-PRODUCING SYSTEM

Sound is produced when air is set in motion. Think of the speech production mechanism as consisting of an air supply, a sound source that sets the air in motion, and a set of filters that modifies the sound in various ways. The air supply is provided by the lungs. The sound source is in the **larynx**, where the vocal cords are located. The filters are the organs above the larynx: the tube of the throat between the oral cavity and the larynx, which is called the **pharynx**; the oral cavity; and the nasal cavity. These passages are collectively known as the **vocal tract** depicted in Figure 2.1.

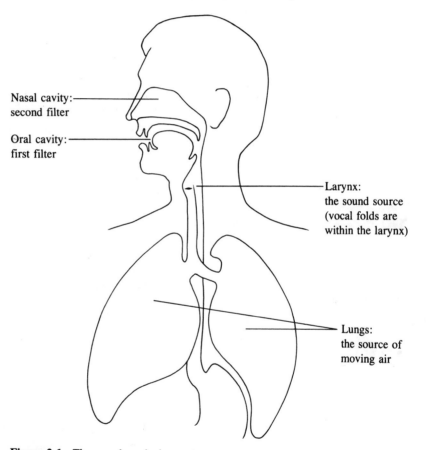

Nasal cavity: second filter

Oral cavity: first filter

Larynx: the sound source (vocal folds are within the larynx)

Lungs: the source of moving air

Figure 2.1 The sound producing system

The Lungs

In order to produce the majority of sounds in the world's languages, we take air into the lungs and then expel it during speech. (A small number of sounds are made with air as it flows into the vocal tract.) A certain level of air pressure is needed to keep the speech mechanism functioning steadily. The pressure is maintained by the action of various sets of muscles coming into play during the course of an utterance. The muscles are primarily the **intercostals** (the muscles between the ribs) and the **diaphragm** (the large sheet of muscle that separates the chest cavity from the abdomen).

The Larynx

As air flows out of the lungs up the **trachea** (windpipe), it passes through a boxlike structure made of cartilage and muscle, the larynx (commonly known as the voice box or Adam's apple). Several fine sheets of muscle line the inner wall of the larynx. A set of these flare outward, forming the paired folds known as the **vocal folds** or **vocal cords**. The vocal folds can be pulled apart or drawn closer together, especially at their back or posterior ends, where each is attached to a small cartilage. As air passes through the space between them, which is called the **glottis**, different glottal states are produced, depending on the positioning of the vocal folds.

Glottal States

Though the vocal folds may be positioned in a number of ways, three primary glottal states underlie much speech production.

Voiceless Sounds When the vocal folds are pulled apart as illustrated in Figure 2.2, air passes directly through the glottis. Any sound made with the vocal folds in this position is said to be **voiceless**. You can confirm a sound's voicelessness by touching your fingers to the larynx as you produce it. You will not feel any vibration from the vocal folds being transmitted to your fingertips. The initial sounds of *fish, sing,* and *house* are all voiceless.

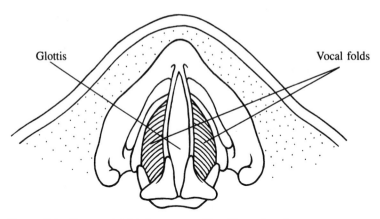

Glottis   Vocal folds

Figure 2.2 The vocal folds in open position (from above)

Voiced Sounds When the vocal folds are brought close together, but not tightly closed, air passing between them causes them to vibrate, producing a state called **voicing**. (See Figure 2.3, where the movement of the vocal folds during voicing is indicated by the wavy line.) You can determine whether a sound is voiced in the same way you determined voicelessness. By lightly touching the fingers to the larynx as you produce an extended version of the initial sounds of the words *zip* or *vow*, or any vowel, you can sense the vibration of the vocal folds within the larynx.

Whisper Another glottal state produces a **whisper**. Whispering is voiceless, but, as shown in Figure 2.3, the vocal folds are adjusted so that the anterior

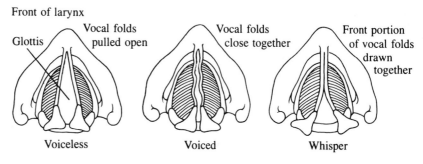

Figure 2.3 Vocal fold states

(front) portions are pulled close together, while the posterior (back) portions are apart.

2.3 SOUND CLASSES

The sounds of language can be grouped into classes, based on the phonetic properties that they share. You have already seen what some of these properties can be. All voiced sounds, for example, form a class, as do all voiceless sounds. The most basic division among sounds is into two major classes, **vowels** and **consonants**. Another class of sounds, the **glides**, shares properties of both vowels and consonants. Each of these classes of sounds has a number of distinguishing features.

Vowels and Consonants

Vowels and consonants can be distinguished on the basis of differences in articulation, as well as acoustically and functionally.

Consonantal sounds, which may be voiced or voiceless, are made with a narrow or complete closure in the vocal tract. The airflow is either blocked momentarily or restricted so much that noise is produced as air flows past the constriction. Vowels are produced with little obstruction in the vocal tract and are generally voiced.

As a result of the difference in articulation, consonants and vowels differ in the way they sound. Vowels are more sonorous than consonants—that is, we perceive them as louder and longer lasting than consonants.

The greater sonority of vowels allows them to form the basis of **syllables**. A syllable can be defined as a peak of sonority surrounded by less sonorous segments. For example, the words, *a* and *go* each contain one syllable, the word *water* two syllables, and the word *telephone* three syllables. In counting the syllables in these words, we are in effect counting the vowels. A vowel is thus said to form the **nucleus** of a syllable. "Syllabic Liquids and Nasals" (page 26) will show that certain types of consonants can form syllabic nuclei as well.

In *1*, the initial sounds of the words in the left column are all consonants; those on the right are all vowels.

1. t̲ake   a̲bove
      c̲art   a̲t
      f̲eel   e̲el
      jump   i̲t
      t̲hink   u̲gly
      b̲ell   o̲pen

Table 2.2 sums up the differences between the two classes presented here.

Table 2.2 The major differences between consonants and vowels

Vowels	Consonants
• Are produced with relatively little obstruction in the vocal tract	• Are produced with a narrow or complete closure in the vocal tract
• Are more sonorous	• Are less sonorous
• Are syllabic	• Are generally not syllabic

Glides

A type of sound that shows properties of both consonants and vowels is called a glide. Glides may be thought of as rapidly articulated vowels; this is the auditory impression they produce. Glides are produced with an articulation like that of a vowel. However, they move quickly to another articulation, as do the initial glides in *yet* or *wet*, or quickly terminate, as do the word-final glides in *boy* and *now*.

Even though they are vowellike in articulation, glides function as consonants. For example, glides can never form the nucleus of a syllable. Since glides show properties of both consonants and vowels, it is no wonder that the terms semivowel or semiconsonant are used interchangeably with the term glide.

2.4 CONSONANT ARTICULATION

Airflow is modified in the oral cavity by the placement of the tongue and the positioning of the lips. These modifications occur at specific places or points of articulation. The major places of articulation used in speech production are outlined in this section. Figure 2.4 provides a midsagittal section or cutaway view of the vocal tract, on which each place of articulation has been indicated.

The Tongue

The primary articulating organ is the tongue. It can be raised, lowered, thrust forward or drawn back, and even rolled back. The sides of the tongue can also be raised or lowered.

Phonetic description refers to five areas of the tongue. The **tip** is the narrow area at the front. Just behind the tip lies the **blade**. The main mass

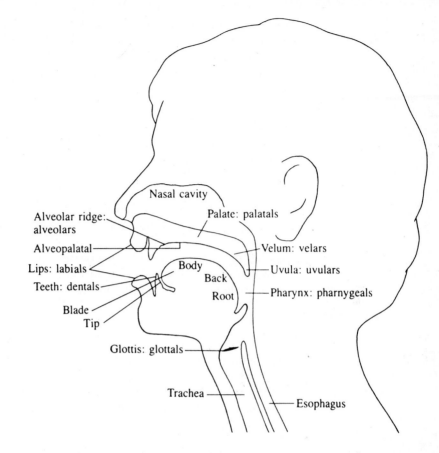

(Places of articulation are listed, followed by a term used to describe sounds made at the place. Areas of the tongue are also provided.)

Figure 2.4 The vocal tract

of the tongue is called the **body**, and the hindmost part of the tongue that lies in the mouth is called the **back**. The **root** of the tongue is contained in the upper part of the throat.

Places of Articulation

Each point at which the airstream can be modified to produce a different sound is called a **place of articulation**. Places of articulation are found at the lips, within the oral cavity, in the pharynx, and at the glottis.

Labial Any sound made with closure or near closure of the lips is said to be **labial**. Sounds involving both lips are termed **bilabial**; sounds involving the lower lip and upper teeth are called **labiodentals**. English includes the bilabials heard word-initially in *peer*, *bin*, and *month*, and the labiodentals heard initially in *fire* and *vow*.

Dental Some phones are produced with the tongue placed against or near the teeth. Sounds made in this way are called **dentals**. If the tongue is placed between the teeth, the sound is said to be **interdental**. Interdentals in English include the initial consonants of the words *this*, *thy*, and *thing*. (Some English speakers produce *s* and *z* as dentals.)

Alveolar Within the oral cavity, a small ridge protrudes from just behind the upper front teeth. This is called the **alveolar ridge**. The tongue may touch or be brought near this ridge. Alveolar sounds are heard at the beginning of the following English words: *top*, *deer*, *soap*, *zip*, *lip*, and *neck*.

Alveopalatal and Palatal Just behind the alveolar ridge, the roof of the mouth rises sharply. This area is known as the **alveopalatal** area (**palatoalveolar** in some books). The highest part of the roof of the mouth is called the **palate**, and sounds produced with the tongue on or near this area are called **palatals**. Alveopalatal consonants are heard in the following English words: *show*, *measure*, *chip*, and *judge*. The glide heard word-initially in *yes* is a palatal glide.

Velar The soft area toward the rear of the roof of the mouth is called the **velum**. Sounds made with the tongue in this position are called **velars**. Velars are heard in English at the beginning of the words *call* and *guy*, and at the end of the word *hang*. The glide heard word-initially in *wet* is called a **labiovelar**, since the tongue is raised near the velum and the lips are rounded at the same time.

Uvular The small fleshy flap of tissue known as the **uvula** hangs down from the velum. Sounds made with the tongue near or touching this area are called **uvulars**. English has no uvulars, but the *r* sound of standard French is uvular.

Pharyngeal The area of the throat between the uvula and the larynx is known as the pharynx. Sounds made through the modification of airflow in this region by retracting the tongue or constricting the pharynx are called **pharyngeals**. Pharyngeals can be found in many dialects of Arabic, but not in English.

Glottal Sounds produced by adjusting the glottal opening to states other than voicing or voicelessness are called **glottals**. The sound at the beginning of the English words *heave* and *hog* is made at the glottis.

2.5 MANNERS OF ARTICULATION

The lips, tongue, velum, and glottis can be positioned in different ways to produce different sound types. These various configurations are called **manners of articulation**.

Oral versus Nasal

A basic distinction in manners of articulation is between **oral** and **nasal** phones. Oral sounds are produced with air flowing through only the mouth. The velum, however, can be lowered to allow air to pass through the nasal passages, producing a sound that is nasal. Both consonants and vowels can be nasal, in which case they are generally voiced. The consonants at the end of the English words *sun*, *sum,* and *sung* are nasal. For many speakers of English, the vowels of words such as *can't* and *wink* are also nasal.

Stops

Stops are made with a complete and momentary closure of airflow through the oral cavity. In the world's languages, stops are found at bilabial, dental, alveolar, palatal, velar, uvular, and glottal points of articulation.

In English, bilabial, alveolar, and velar oral and nasal stops occur as shown in Table 2.3. Note that [ŋ] does not occur word-initially in English. The glottal stop is commonly heard in English in the expression *uh-uh*, meaning 'no'. The two vowels in this utterance are each preceded by a momentary closing of the airstream at the glottis. The *t* before [n] in words like *button* and *written* is pronounced as a glottal stop by most American English speakers. In some dialects, the glottal stop is also commonly heard in place of the [t] in a word like *bottle*. The glottal stop is often spelled with an apostrophe (*bo'l*); its standard phonetic transcription is [ʔ].

Table 2.3 English stops and their transcription

Bilabial	Transcription	
Voiceless	span	[p]
Voiced	ban	[b]
Nasal	man	[m]
Alveolar		
Voiceless	stun	[t]
Voiced	dot	[d]
Nasal	not	[n]
Velar		
Voiceless	scar	[k]
Voiced	gap	[g]
Nasal	wing	[ŋ]

A Grid for Stops Table 2.4 presents a phonetic grid on which the stop consonants of English are ranged horizontally according to point of articulation. As you can see, each stop, with one exception, has voiced and voiceless counterparts. The glottal stop is always voiceless. It is produced with the

Table 2.4 English stop consonants

	Bilabial	Alveolar	Velar	Glottal
Voiceless	[p]	[t]	[k]	[ʔ]
Voiced	[b]	[d]	[g]	
Nasal	[m]	[n]	[ŋ]	

vocal folds drawn firmly together, and since no air can pass through the glottis, the vocal folds cannot be set in motion.

Fricatives

Fricatives are consonants produced with a continuous airflow through the mouth. They belong to a large class of sounds called **continuants** (a class that also includes vowels and glides), all of which share this property. The fricatives form a special class of continuants; during their production, they are accompanied by a continuous audible noise. The air used in their production passes through a very narrow opening, resulting in turbulence, which causes the noise.

English Fricatives English has voiceless and voiced labiodental fricatives at the beginning of the words _fat_ and _vat_, voiceless and voiced interdental fricatives word-initially in the words _thin_ and _those_, alveolar fricatives word-initially in _sing_ and _zip,_ and a voiceless alveopalatal fricative word-initially in _ship_. The voiced alveopalatal fricative is rare in English. It is the first consonant in the word _azure,_ and is also heard in the words _pleasure_ and _rouge_. The voiceless glottal fricative of English is heard in _hotel_ and _hat_.

Special note must be taken of the alveolar fricatives [s] and [z]. There are two ways that English speakers commonly produce these sounds. Some speakers raise the tongue tip to the alveolar ridge and allow the air to pass through a grooved channel in the tongue. Other speakers form this same channel using the blade of the tongue; the tip is placed behind the lower front teeth. Still others pronounce these sounds as dentals. The symbols for English fricatives are given in Table 2.5.

Table 2.5 The transcription of English fricatives

Glottal state	Point of articulation	Transcription
	Labiodental	
Voiceless	fan	[f]
Voiced	van	[v]
	Interdental	
Voiceless	thin	[θ]
Voiced	then	[ð]
	Alveolar	
Voiceless	sun	[s]
Voiced	zip	[z]
	Alveopalatal	
Voiceless	ship	[š]
Voiced	azure	[ž]
	Glottal	
Voiceless	hat	[h]

A Grid for Fricatives Table 2.6 presents a grid on which the fricative consonants of English are ranged according to point of articulation. As in Table

2.5, dentals are not distinguished from alveolars, since most languages have sounds with either one or the other point of articulation, but not both. Note that North American [š] and [ž] correspond, respectively, to IPA [ʃ] and [ʒ].

Table 2.6   English fricatives

	Labiodental	Interdental	Alveolar	Alveopalatal	Glottal
Voiceless	[f]	[θ]	[s]	[š]	[h]
Voiced	[v]	[ð]	[z]	[ž]	

Affricates

When a stop is released, the tongue moves rapidly away from the point of articulation. Some noncontinuant consonants show a slow release of the closure; these sounds are called **affricates**. English has only two affricates, both of which are alveopalatal. They are heard word-initially in <u>church</u> and <u>jump</u>, and are transcribed as [č] and [ǰ], respectively.

A Grid for Affricates   Table 2.7 presents the two English affricates. Note that North American [č] and [ǰ] correspond to IPA [tʃ] and [dʒ], respectively.

Table 2.7   English affricates

	Alveopalatal
Voiceless	[č]
Voiced	[ǰ]

Stridents and Sibilants   The beginning of this chapter noted that acoustic as well as articulatory criteria are sometimes used in describing speech sounds. An acoustic criterion comes into play to describe fricatives and affricates. These sounds are subdivided into two types, some of which are distinctly louder than others as they are articulated. These noisier fricatives and affricates are called **stridents** (see Table 2.8). Their quieter counterparts, which have the same or nearly the same place of articulation, are labeled nonstrident.

Strident sounds that are relatively higher in pitch than other stridents have a hissing quality. In English, these sounds are [s], [z], [š], [ž], [č], and [ǰ]. They are known as **sibilants**.

Table 2.8   Strident and nonstrident fricatives and affricates in English

Articulation	Strident	Nonstrident
Labiodental	[f], [v]	(none in English)
Alveolar	[s], [z]	[θ], [ð] (Interdental)
Alveopalatal	[š], [ž]	(none in English)
	[č], [ǰ]	

*Voice Lag and Aspiration

After the release of some voiceless stops in English, you can sometimes hear a lag or brief delay before the voicing of a following vowel. Since the lag in the onset of vocalic voicing is accompanied by the release of air, the traditional term for this phenomenon is **aspiration**. It is transcribed with a small raised [ʰ] after the aspirated consonant. Table 2.9 provides some examples of aspirated and unaspirated consonants in English. Note that the sounds that show both aspirated and unaspirated varieties are all voiceless stops. In other languages, fricatives and affricates may also be aspirated or unaspirated. (Some vowel symbols are introduced here as well.)

Table 2.9 Aspirated and unaspirated consonants in English

Aspirated		Unaspirated	
[pʰæt]	pat	[spæt]	spat
[tʰʌb]	tub	[stʌb]	stub
[kʰowp]	cope	[skowp]	scope

Figure 2.5 shows how aspiration of a voiceless consonant takes place. At the moment the consonant is begun, the glottis is open. When the closure for the consonant is released, the glottis is not yet closed enough to permit voicing to begin; after a short delay, measurable in milliseconds, voicing begins. The short delay before voicing begins is known as aspiration. The

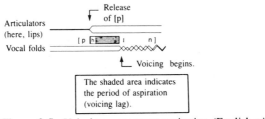

Figure 2.5 Voiceless consonant aspiration (English *pin*)

length of the lag varies from language to language and even from speaker to speaker within a given language. In Figures 2.5 to 2.7, the term *articulators* refers specifically to the lips. The raised tongue involved in the production of [n] is not indicated. Figures 2.6 and 2.7 show the relation between articulation and voicing for unaspirated and voiced consonants. The unaspirated consonant, such as the [p] of English *spin*, shows voicing starting very soon

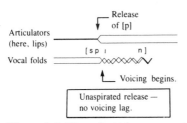

Figure 2.6 Unaspirated consonant production (English *spin*)

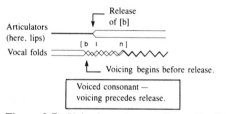

Figure 2.7 Voiced consonant release (English *bin*)

after release. The voiced initial [b] of English *bin* shows voicing starting just before the release of the bilabial articulation. In Figure 2.7, note how voicing precedes the release of the labial articulators.

Liquids

Among the sounds commonly found in the world's languages are *l* and *r* and their numerous variants. They form a special class of consonants known as **liquids**. Liquids are continuants, but the vocal tract obstruction formed when producing them is not as great as it is for the fricative consonants.

Laterals Varieties of *l* are called **laterals**. As laterals are articulated, air escapes through the mouth along the lowered sides of the tongue. When the tongue tip is raised to the dental or alveolar position, the dental or alveolar laterals are produced. Both may be transcribed as [l].

Because laterals are generally voiced, the term *lateral* used alone usually means 'voiced lateral'. Still, there are instances of voiceless laterals in speech. The voiceless dental or alveolar lateral is written with an additional phonetic symbol, called a diacritic. In this case, the diacritic is a circle beneath the symbol: [l̥]. Voiceless laterals can be heard in the pronunciation of the English words *please* and *clear*.

English *r*'s Numerous varieties of *r* are also heard in the world's languages. This section describes the types found in English.

The *r* of English, as it is spoken in the United States and Canada, is made either by curling the tongue tip back into the mouth or by bunching the tongue upward and back in the mouth. This *r* is known as a **retroflex** *r* and is heard in *ride* and *car*. It is transcribed as [r] in this book. IPA transcription favors [ɹ] for this sound, though it also offers the symbol [r].

Another sound commonly identified with *r* is the **flap**. The flap is produced when the tongue tip strikes the alveolar ridge as it passes across it. It is heard in the North American English pronunciation of *bitter* and *butter*, and in some British pronunciations of *very*. It is commonly transcribed as [D] and is generally voiced.

Table 2.10 presents the laterals, *r*, and flap of English.

Table 2.10 English liquids

			Dental/alveolar
Laterals	voiced		[l]
	voiceless		[l̥]
R's	retroflex	voiced	[r]
		voiceless	[r̥]
	flap		[D]

Syllabic Liquids and Nasals

Liquids and nasals are more resonant than other consonants and in this respect are more like vowels than are the other consonants. In fact, they are so vowellike in their resonance that they can function as syllabic nuclei. When they do so, they are called **syllabic liquids** and **syllabic nasals** (see Table 2.11). Syllabic liquids and nasals are found in many of the world's languages, including English. In transcription, they are usually marked with a short diacritic line underneath. Unfortunately for beginning linguistics students, North American transcription is not always consistent here. The syllabic r sound heard in words like *bird* and *her* is transcribed as a vowel-*r* sequence: [ər]. This is because many linguists hear this sound not as a consonant but as a vowel with 'r-coloring'. (The vowel symbol is presented in ''Basic Parameters for Describing Vowels'' on page 27.) The IPA symbol for this sound is [ɚ]. In spite of the slight asymmetry in transcription, this book will retain the North American transcription practice.

Table 2.11 Syllabic liquids and nasals in English

Syllabic		Nonsyllabic	
bottle	[baDl̩]	lift	[lɪft]
funnel	[fʌnl̩]	pill	[pʰɪl]
bird	[bərd]	rat	[ræt]
her	[hər]	car	[kʰar]
button	[bʌtn̩]	now	[naw]
rhythm	[rɪðm̩]	mat	[mæt]

American Glides

The two glides of English are the *y*-glide [y] of *yes* and *boy*, and the *w*-glide [w] of *wet* and *now*. The [y] of North American transcription corresponds to [j] in IPA transcription.

The [y] is a palatal glide whose articulation is virtually identical to that of the vowel [i] of *see*. You can verify this by pronouncing a [y] in an extended manner; it will sound very close to an [i]. The glide [w] is made with the tongue raised and pulled back near the velum and with the lips protruding, or **rounded**. For this reason, it is sometimes called a labiovelar. The [w] corresponds closely in articulation to the vowel [u] of *who*. This can be verified by extending the pronunciation of a [w]. Some speakers of English also have a voiceless labiovelar glide, transcribed [ʍ], for *wh* in words like *which* (but not in *witch*), *when*, *where*, and *wheel*.

2.6 VOWELS

Vowels are sonorous, syllabic sounds made with the vocal tract more open than it is for consonant and glide articulations. Different vowels are produced by varying the placement of the body of the tongue and shaping the lips. The shape of the cavity can be further altered by protruding the lips to produce rounded vowels, or by lowering the velum to produce a nasal vowel. Finally, vowels may be tense or lax, depending on the degree of vocal tract constriction during their articulation.

Simple Vowels and Diphthongs

English vowels are divided into two major types, **simple vowels** and **diphthongs**. Simple vowels do not show a noticeable change in quality. The vowels of *pit, set, cat, dog, but, put* and the first vowel of *suppose* are all simple vowels. Diphthongs are vowels that exhibit a change in quality within a single syllable. English diphthongs show changes in quality that are due to tongue movement away from the initial vowel articulation toward a glide position. This change in vowel quality is clearly perceptible in words such as *say, buy, cow, ice, lout, go,* and *boy*. The change is less easy to hear, but present nonetheless, in the vowels of words such as *heat* and *lose*. Table 2.12 presents the simple vowels and diphthongs of English. The diphthongs are transcribed as a vowel-glide sequence.

Table 2.12 Simple vowels and diphthongs of American English

Simple vowel		Diphthong	
pit	[ɪ]	heat	[iy]
set	[ɛ]	say	[ey]
cat	[æ]	buy	[ay]
pot	[ɑ]	cow	[aw]
but	[ʌ]	lose	[uw]
dog	[ɔ]	grow	[ow]
put	[ʊ]	boy	[ɔy]
suppose	[ə]		

There is still a great deal of discussion among linguists on the subject of diphthongs. English vowels that show a change in quality are considered diphthongs as long as the change in quality follows the vowel nucleus. But words such as *yes* and *yak* are considered to begin with a glide that is not an integral part of the vocalic nucleus. However, in transcribing other languages (Finnish, for example), sounds such as [yɛ] and [wo] are considered to be diphthongs. This book follows the established practice of treating the diphthongs presented in Table 2.12 as unit vowels, and the initial two sounds of words such as *yes* and *yak* as distinct segments.

Basic Parameters for Describing Vowels

Vowel articulations are not as easy to feel as consonant articulations at first, since the vocal tract is not narrowed as much. To become acquainted with vowel articulation, alternately pronounce the vowels of *he* and *pot*. You will feel the tongue move from a **high** front to a **low** back position. Once you feel this tongue movement, alternate between the vowels of *pot* and *pat*. You will feel the tongue moving from the low back to low front position. Finally, alternate between the vowels of *he* and *who*. You will notice that in addition to a tongue movement between the high front and high back position, you are also rounding your lips for the [uw]. Figure 2.8 shows a midsagittal view of the tongue position for the vowels [iy], [ɑ], and [uw] based on X-ray studies of speech.

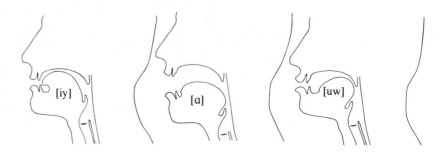

Figure 2.8   Tongue position and transcription for three English vowels

Vowels for which the tongue is neither raised nor lowered are called **mid** vowels. The front vowel of English *made* or *fame* is mid, front, and unrounded. The vowel of *code* and *soak* is mid, back, and rounded. In the case of diphthongs, the articulatory descriptions refer to the tongue position of the vowel nucleus. The vowels presented so far are summed up in Table 2.13. Note that in describing the vowels the articulatory parameters are presented in the order *height, backness, rounding*.

Table 2.13 Basic phonetic parameters for describing American English vowels

heat	[iy]	high, front, unrounded
fate	[ey]	mid, front, unrounded
mad	[æ]	low, front, unrounded
sun	[ʌ]	mid, back, unrounded
Sue	[uw]	high, back, rounded
boat	[ow]	mid, back, rounded
cot	[ɑ]	low, back, unrounded

Tongue positions for these vowels are illustrated in Figure 2.9. The trapezoid corresponds roughly to the space within which the tongue moves, which is wider at the top of the oral cavity and more restricted at the bottom. Since many books distinguish between central and back vowels, the traditional term *central* is supplied in parentheses.

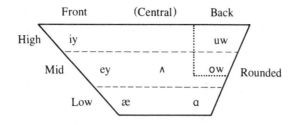

Figure 2.9 Basic tongue positions for English vowels

Tense and Lax Vowels

All the vowels illustrated in Figure 2.9 except [æ] and [ʌ] are tense: they are produced with a greater degree of constriction of the tongue body or tongue root than are certain other vowels. Some vowels of English are made with roughly the same tongue position but with a less constricted articulation: they are called lax vowels. Table 2.14 provides examples from English comparing tense and lax vowels.

Table 2.14 Tense and lax vowels in English

	Tense		Lax
heat	[iy]	hit	[ɪ]
mate	[ey]	met	[ɛ]
(no tense partner)	---	mat	[æ]
(no tense partner)	---	cut	[ʌ]
(no tense partner)	---	Canada	[ə]
shoot	[uw]	should	[ʊ]
coat	[ow]	(caught	[ɔ] in some dialects)

The difference in one pair of vowels illustrated in Table 2.14 is not obvious at first. Both the vowel [ʌ] in *cut, dud, pluck,* and *Hun,* and the vowel [ə] of *Canada, about, tomahawk,* and *sofa* are lax. The vowel of the second set, labeled **schwa,** is called a **reduced** vowel; it is characterized by very brief duration as well as being lax.

The vowel [ɔ] is heard before *r,* as in the words *more* and *torn,* and is heard in the diphthong of *boy.* It is also heard in some American dialects and is widespread in British, Australian, and New Zealand English in words like *caught* and *law.* In other American and most Canadian dialects, both members of pairs like *caught* and *cot* are pronounced with the vowel [ɑ] or [a].

There is a test that helps determine whether vowels are tense or lax. In English, monosyllabic words spoken in isolation do not end in lax vowels. We find *see, say, Sue, so,* and *saw* in English, but not *s*[ɪ], *s*[ɛ], *s*[æ], *s*[ʊ], or *s*[ʌ]. The schwa frequently appears in unstressed positions in words like *sof*[ə] and *Canad*[ə]. It should be pointed out—especially for those who think their ears are deceiving them—that many speakers hear these vowels not as [ə] but as [ʌ].

The representation of vowels and their articulatory positions (Figure 2.9) is expanded in Figure 2.10 to include both tense and lax vowels.

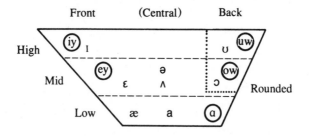

Figure 2.10 Tense and lax vowels (Tense vowels are circled.)

***Diphthongs** Two English vowels occur with either a *y*-glide or a *w*-glide component (see Table 2.15). The low back lax unrounded vowel [a] is heard in the diphthong [ay], as in *buy*, and in the diphthong [aw], as in *cow*. In some varieties of English, the vowel [ʌ] forms part of the diphthong [ʌy], as in *mice*, and the diphthong [ʌw], as in *mouse*. Like all English diphthongs, these diphthongs are tense.

Table 2.15 Diphthongs with varying glide components

eyes	[ay]	ice	[ʌy]
tied	[ay]	tight	[ʌy]
loud	[aw]	clout	[ʌw]
down	[aw]	doubt	[ʌw]

Figure 2.11 places these diphthongs on the articulation chart, completing the inventory of English vowels.

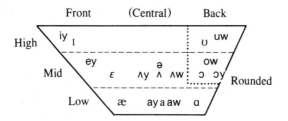

Figure 2.11 English vowels

*Nasal Vowels

Nasal vowels, like nasal consonants, are produced with a lowered velum. Air passes simultaneously through the oral and nasal cavities. Nasal vowels can be heard in English, French, Portuguese, Hindi, and a wide variety of other languages. They are often transcribed with a tilde [˜] over the vowel symbol as shown in Table 2.16.

Table 2.16 Some nasal vowels

English: win [wĩn]
French: pain [pɛ̃] 'bread'
Portuguese: sento [sẽntu] 'one hundred'
Polish: ząb [zɔ̃p] 'tooth'

2.7 PHONETIC TRANSCRIPTION OF AMERICAN ENGLISH CONSONANTS AND VOWELS

Tables 2.17 and 2.18 show the phonetic symbols for consonants and vowels commonly used to transcribe American English. To show how each symbol is used, one word is transcribed completely, and then some other words in which the same sound is found are given. You will notice that in the example words, the spelling of the sound may vary. Be careful of this when you transcribe words phonetically—the sound of a word, not its spelling, is what is transcribed! Remember also that most speakers do not use all these different sounds.

Table 2.17 Consonants

Symbol	Word	Transcription	More examples
[pʰ]	pit	[pʰɪt]	pain, upon, apart
[p]	spit	[spɪt]	spar, crispy, upper, Yuppie, culprit, bumper
[tʰ]	tick	[tʰɪk]	tell, attire, terror, Tutu
[t]	stuck	[stʌk]	stem, hunter, nasty, mostly
[kʰ]	keep	[kʰiyp]	cow, kernel, chord
[k]	skip	[skɪp]	scatter, uncle, blacklist, likely
[č]	chip	[čɪp]	lunch, lecher, ditch, belch
[ǰ]	judge	[ǰʌǰ]	germ, journal, budge, wedge
[b]	bib	[bɪb]	boat, liberate, rob, blast
[d]	dip	[dɪp]	dust, huddle, sled, draft
[D]	butter	[bʌDər]	madder, matter, hitting, writer, rider
[g]	get	[gɛt]	gape, mugger, twig, gleam
[f]	fit	[fɪt]	flash, coughing, proof, phlegmatic, gopher
[v]	vat	[væt]	vote, oven, prove
[θ]	thick	[θɪk]	thought, ether, teeth, three, bathroom
[ð]	though	[ðow]	then, bother, teethe, bathe
[s]	sip	[sɪp]	psychology, fasten, lunacy, bass, curse, science
[z]	zap	[zæp]	Xerox, scissors, desire, zipper, fuzzy
[š]	ship	[šɪp]	shock, nation, mission, glacier, wish
[ž]	azure	[æžər]	measure, rouge, visual, garage (for some speakers)
[h]	hat	[hæt]	who, ahoy, forehead, behind, José
[y]	yet	[yɛt]	use, few
[w]	witch	[wɪč]	wait, weird, queen
[ʍ]	which	[ʍɪč]	what, where, when (not all speakers have this phone)
[l]	leaf	[liyf]	loose, lock, alive, hail
[r]	reef	[riyf]	prod, arrive, tear
[ər]	bird	[bərd]	early, hurt, stir, purr, doctor
[m]	moat	[mowt]	mind, humor, shimmer, sum, thumb
[n]	note	[nowt]	now, winner, angel, sign, wind
[ŋ]	sing	[sɪŋ]	singer, longer, bank, twinkle

Table 2.18 Vowels

Symbol	Word	Transcription	More examples
[iy]	fee	[fiy]	she, cream, believe, receive, serene, amoeba, highly
[ɪ]	fit	[fɪt]	hit, income, definition, been (for some speakers)
[ey]	fate	[feyt]	they, clay, grain, gauge, engage, great, sleigh
[ɛ]	let	[lɛt]	led, lead, says, said, sever, guest, air
[æ]	bat	[bæt]	panic, racket, laugh, Vancouver
[uw]	boot	[buwt]	to, two, loose, brew, Louise, Lucy, through
[ʊ]	book	[bʊk]	should, put, hood
[ow]	note	[nowt]	no, throat, though, slow, toe, oaf, O'Conner
[ɔy]	boy	[bɔy]	loyal, coin
[ɔ]	bore	[bɔr]	oral, normal, caught, bought
[ɑ]	pot	[pɑt]	cot, father, rob
[a]	car	[kʰar]	bar, far
[ə]	roses	[rowzəz]	collide, afford, hinted, telegraph, (to) suspect
[ʌ]	shut	[šʌt]	other, udder, tough, lucky, was, flood
[ʌw]	shout	[šʌwt]	outer, (a) house, pout (for some speakers)
[ʌy]	ice	[ʌys]	fight, ripe, like, type (for some speakers)
[aw]	crowd	[krawd]	(to) house, plow, bough
[ay]	lies	[layz]	my, tide, thigh, buy

*2.8   OTHER VOWELS AND CONSONANTS

Up to this point, we have considered only the vowels and consonants of English. Many speech sounds found in English are heard in other languages. There are also many speech sounds found in the world's languages that are not heard in English. Since phonetic descriptions are universally valid, once you have mastered the basic articulatory parameters, it is not too difficult to describe and even to pronounce less familiar sounds. This section presents a number of speech sounds found in other languages.

Vowels

Front vowels, which in English are always unrounded, can also be rounded. A high front tense rounded vowel is heard in French *pur* 'pure', German *Bücher* 'books', and Turkish *düğme* 'button'. It is transcribed as [ü] in North America, but as [y] in IPA transcription—a difference that sometimes leads to confusion. A rounded high front lax vowel, [ᴜ̈], is heard in Canadian French *lune*, 'moon' and *duc* 'duke'. A rounded mid front tense vowel, transcribed [ö] (IPA [ø]), is found in French *peu* 'few' and German *schön* 'beautiful'. A rounded mid front lax vowel, transcribed [œ], is heard in French *oeuf* 'egg' and *peur* 'fear', German *örtlich* 'local', and Turkish *göl* 'lake'. Finally, an unrounded high central vowel, transcribed as [ɨ], is heard in Russian words like *bɨl* 'was', and Rumanian *mɨnă* 'hand'. These vowels, as well as other "exotic" ones, are found in many other languages as well. Table 2.19 illustrates the vowels presented in this chapter (UR = unrounded, R = rounded).

Table 2.19 Articulatory grid of vowels presented in this chapter

	Front		Central		Back	
	UR	R	UR	R	UR	R
High	i	ü	ɨ			u tense
	ɪ	ʊ				ʊ lax
Mid	e	ö	ə			o tense
	ɛ	œ	ʌ			ɔ lax
Low	æ	(lax)	a	(lax)	ɑ	(tense)

Consonants

The same stop consonants found in English are widespread in other languages. A few additional stops are introduced in this section.

Stops In many European languages, we find not alveolar [t], [d], and [n], but dental [t̪], [d̪], and [n̪]. Although this seems like a very slight difference in articulation, it can be readily observed in the speech of French, Spanish, or Italian speakers.

Other stop positions are common in the world's languages. Retroflex stops [ʈ] and [ɖ], pronounced with the tongue curled back as in English [r], are common in the languages of India. Serbo-Croatian has both a voiceless and voiced palatal stop in words like *ćasa* 'dish', and *đak* 'pupil'. These are transcribed as [c] and [ɟ], respectively. Inuktitut dialects show a voiceless and voiced uvular stop pair in words like *imaq* 'sea', and *ugsik* 'cow'. These are transcribed as [q] and [G], respectively. A nasal stop is also made at the palatal point of articulation, as in Spanish *año* 'year' (transcribed as [ñ] in North America and as [ɲ] in IPA) and at the uvula as well, where it is transcribed as [N]. Sounds found in English are set off in boxes in Table 2.20.

Table 2.20 Stops

	Bilabial	Alveolar	Dental	Retroflex	Palatal	Velar	Uvular	Glottal
Voiceless	[p]	[t]	[t̪]	[ʈ]	[c]	[k]	[q]	[ʔ]
Voiced	[b]	[d]	[d̪]	[ɖ]	[ɟ]	[g]	[G]	
Nasal	[m]	[n]	[n̪]	[ɳ]	[ñ]	[ŋ]	[N]	

Fricatives Other fricatives are found in the world's languages. A bilabial fricative, produced by drawing the lips almost together and forcing the airstream through the narrow opening, is found in many languages. The voiceless bilabial fricative [Φ] is heard word-initially in the Japanese word *Fuji* (the mountain). The voiced bilabial fricative [β] is found in Spanish in words like *deber* 'to owe'. A voiceless palatal fricative [ç] is found in Standard German; the word *ich* 'I' contains this sound. Velar fricatives are not found in English but are widespread in the world's languages. The voiceless velar fricative [x] is common in German and Russian. The composer Bach's name, pronounced in German, has a final voiceless velar fricative. A voiced velar fricative [ɣ] is commonly heard in Spanish words such as *agua* 'water'.

Table 2.21 presents a grid on which some common fricative consonants are ranged according to point and manner of articulation. Dentals are not distinguished from alveolars, as most languages have sounds with either one or the other point of articulation, but not both. Sounds found in English are set off in boxes.

Table 2.21 Fricatives

	Bilabial	Labio-dental	Inter-dental	Alveolar	Alveo-palatal	Palatal	Velar	Glottal
Voiceless	[Φ]	[f]	[θ]	[s]	[š]	[ç]	[x]	[h]
Voiced	[β]	[v]	[ð]	[z]	[ž]	[j]	[ɣ]	

Affricates Affricates are found at most points of articulation. In German, a voiceless labiodental affricate, transcribed [pᶠ], is heard at the beginning of the word *pferd* 'horse'. Some New York speakers have voiceless and voiced dental (or alveolar) affricates [tˢ] and [dᶻ] in words like *time* and *dime*.

Table 2.22 presents a grid including the two English affricates and some others commonly found in languages. Sounds found in English are again set off in a box.

Table 2.22 Affricates

	Labiodental	Alveolar	Alveopalatal	Velar
Voiceless	[pᶠ]	[tˢ]	[č]	[kˣ]
Voiced	[bᵛ]	[dᶻ]	[ǰ]	[gᵞ]

Liquids As with the stops, laterals may be dental as well as alveolar. Laterals can also be made with the tongue body raised to the palate. Such a sound is called a palatal lateral and is transcribed with the letter [ʎ]. It is heard in some pronunciations of the Spanish words *caballo* 'horse' and *calle* 'street', and in the Serbo-Croatian words *dalje* 'farther' and *ljudi* 'people'. The palatal lateral may also be voiceless, in which case it is transcribed as ([ʎ̥]).

Lateral fricatives are produced when a lateral is made with a narrow enough closure to be classified as a fricative. This sound is transcribed as [ɮ] when voiced and [ɬ] when voiceless. Lateral fricatives can be heard in many American Indian languages, in Welsh, and in many languages spoken in the Caucasus. Table 2.23 shows some examples of voiceless alveolar lateral fricatives from Welsh. Other types of *r* besides the retroflex and flap are also found. One is called a **tap**. It is not heard in North American English. Unlike the flap, which is made as the tongue rapidly passes across a point of articulation, the tap is made by rapidly touching the tongue tip to the back

Table 2.23 Voiceless alveolar lateral fricatives in Welsh

llan	[ɬan]	'clan'
ambell	[ambɛɬ]	'some'

of the teeth or the alveolar ridge. (The point of articulation is language-specific.) It should not be confused with a [d], which is a true stop. Stops are made with a brief articulatory closure, while a tap is a very rapid gesture of striking the point of articulation and pulling away. The tap is transcribed as [ɾ] in IPA, though it is often found transcribed as [r] on a language-specific basis. The tap is the variety of *r* heard in Spanish *pero* 'but' and *pájaro* 'bird'.

Other *r*-like sounds are widely heard in the world's languages. The **trill** is made by passing air over the raised tongue tip and allowing it to vibrate. Trills are commonly transcribed as [r̃]. They can be heard in the Spanish words *perro* 'dog' and *río* 'river', and the Italian words *carro* 'wagon' and *birra* 'beer'. A similar trilling effect can be made with the uvula, and is called a uvular trill. Its IPA transcription is [R].

A uvular *r* made without trilling is more commonly heard. This is the voiced *r* of Standard European French; it is also widespread in German. IPA transcription classifies this sound along with the fricatives. It is transcribed as [χ] when voiceless and as [ʁ] when voiced.

Table 2.24 presents the liquids. As before, sounds found in English are set off in boxes. The flaps, taps, and trills can be voiceless as well. Voicelessness for these sounds is usually indicated by a small open circle beneath the symbol, as in [r̥] or [R̥].

Table 2.24 Liquids

		Dental/Alveolar	Palatal	Uvular
Laterals:	voiced	[l]	[ʎ]	
	voiceless	[ɬ]	[ʎ̥]	
Lateral fricatives:	voiced	[ɮ]		
	voiceless	[ɬ]		
R's:	retroflex	[r]		
	flap	[D]		
	tap	[ɾ]		
	trill	[r̃]		[R]

Glides The schwa [ə] appears as a glide in certain forms of English. In these varieties, words like *here* and *door* are pronounced [hiyə̯] and [dɔə̯]. The curved line diacritic indicates that the schwa is a glide.

Other glides are found in the world's languages. The most commonly heard one is a glide made with the tongue position of [y] but with the lips rounded. It is transcribed as [ɥ] and can be heard in French words such as [ɥit] *huit* 'eight', [ɥil] *huile* 'oil', and [ɥitχ] *huitre* 'oyster'.

2.9 SUPRASEGMENTALS

All phones have certain inherent **suprasegmental** or **prosodic** properties that form part of their makeup no matter what their place or manner of articulation. These properties are **pitch**, **loudness**, and **length**. Pitch is the auditory property of a sound that enables us to place it on a scale that ranges from low to high. All sounds give a subjective impression of being relatively higher or lower in pitch. Pitch is especially noticeable in sonorous sounds like vowels, glides, liquids, and nasals. Even stop and fricative consonants convey different pitches. This is particularly obvious among the fricatives, as you can hear by extending the pronunciation of [s] and then of [š]; the [s] is clearly higher pitched. All sounds have some degree of intrinsic loudness as well or they could not be heard. Moreover, all sounds occupy a certain stretch of time—they give the subjective impression of length.

Pitch

Speakers of any language have the ability to control the pitch of vowels and sonorant consonants. This is accomplished by controlling the tension of the vocal folds and the amount of air that passes through the glottis. The combination of tensed vocal folds and greater air pressure results in higher voice pitch, while less tense vocal folds and lower air pressure results in lower voice pitch. Two kinds of controlled pitch movement found in human language are called **tone** and **intonation**.

Tone Languages A language is said to have tone or be a **tone language** when differences in word meaning are signaled by differences in pitch. Pitch of forms in tone languages functions very differently from the movement of pitch in a nontone language. When a speaker of English says *a car?* with a rising pitch, the form *car* does not mean anything different from the same form pronounced on a different pitch level or with a different pitch contour. In contrast, when the speaker of a tone language such as Mandarin pronounces the form *ma* [ma] with a falling pitch, it means 'scold', but when the same form (*ma*) is pronounced with a rising pitch, the meaning is 'hemp'. There is no parallel to anything like this is nontone languages, such as English and French.

   Some tone languages have distinct level tones. Sarcee, an Athapaskan language spoken in Canada, shows tones at high, mid, and low pitch levels. In Figure 2.12, the uppercase letters H, M, and L stand for high, mid, and low tones, respectively. A line drawn from the letter to the vowel indicates the pitch at which the vowel is spoken.

H	M	L
|	|	|
[miֽ] 'moth'	[miֽ] 'snare'	[miֽ] 'sleep'

Figure 2.12   Sarcee level tones

   Level tones that signal meaning differences are called **register tones**. Two or three register tones are the norm in most of the world's register tone languages, although as many as four have been reported for Mazateco (a language spoken in Mexico).

   In some languages, tones change pitch on single syllables. Moving pitches that signal meaning differences are called **contour tones**. In Mandarin, both register and contour tones are heard. Contour tones are shown by pitch level notation lines that converge above the vowel, as shown in Figure 2.13. In Figure 2.13, there is one (high) register tone. The other tones are all contour tones.

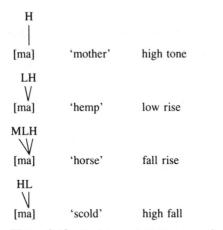

Figure 2.13   Register and contour tones in Mandarin

In other languages, tone may mark grammatical categories. In Bini, a language spoken in Nigeria, tone can signal differences in the tense of a verb (such as past versus present), as Figure 2.14 shows. Phonetic transcription for tones varies a great deal. In addition to the notation given above, tones can be marked by diacritics. Often the symbol [ˊ] represents a high tone and [ˋ] a low tone, so that the Bini words in Figure 2.14 are transcribed as

Figure 2.14   Tense and tone in Bini

[ì mà], [í mà], and [ì má], respectively. Contour tones are sometimes marked with a combination of the two, so that a word like Mandarin *horse* from Figure 2.13, which has a fall-rise, is represented as [mǎ].

While tones may seem exotic to native speakers of Western European languages, they are very widespread. Tone languages are found throughout North and South America, Sub-Saharan Africa, and the Far East.

Intonation Pitch movement in spoken utterances that is not related to differences in the word meaning is called intonation. It makes no difference to the meaning of the word *seven*, for example, whether it is pronounced with a rising pitch or a falling pitch. Intonation often serves to convey information of a broadly meaningful nature. For example, the falling pitch we hear at the end of a statement in English such as *Fred parked the car* signals that the utterance is complete. For this reason, falling intonation at the end of an utterance is called a terminal intonation contour. Rising or level intonation, on the other hand, often signals incompleteness. Rising or level intonations are heard in the nonfinal forms found in lists and telephone numbers as in Figure 2.15. In questions, as in Figure 2.16, final rising intonations

e e n^y   m e e n ^y   m i n e ^y   m o_e

two eight f o u r two f i v e one t h r e e

Figure 2.15 Rising nonterminal intonations

also signal a kind of incompleteness in that they indicate that a conversational exchange is not finished. However, English sentences that contain question words like *who, what, when,* and *how* (for example, *What did you buy?*) ordinarily do not have rising intonation. It is as if the question word itself is enough to indicate that an answer is expected.

Did you   have a n i c e   t i m e

Figure 2.16 Rising intonation in a question

Intonation is a very complex subject, and it has just been touched on here. Still, the overall falling pitch contour as a mark of completeness and a nonfalling contour as a mark of incompleteness is widespread in language, though the specific details of pitch level and pitch movement vary from language to language.

Intonation and Tone Tone and intonation are not mutually exclusive. Tone languages show intonation of all types. This is possible since the tones are not absolute but relative pitches. A tone is perceived as high if it is high relative to the pitches around it. As long as this relative difference is maintained, the pitch distinctions will also be maintained. Figure 2.17 shows this graphically. It represents the overall pitch of a declarative sentence in Igbo, a West African language with register tones. Note how an Igbo speaker clearly maintains the distinction among the pitch registers even as the overall pitch of the utterance falls. Each high tone is lower than the preceding high tone, but higher than the low tone that immediately precedes it. This phenomenon is known as **downdrift**.

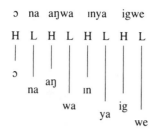

'He is trying to ride a bicycle.'

Figure 2.17 Tone and intonation—downdrift in Igbo

Length

In many languages, there are vowels or consonants whose articulation is held longer relative to that of other vowels and consonants. This phenomenon, known as length, is widespread in the world's languages. Length is indicated in phonetic transcription by the use of a colon [:] placed after the long segment.

Hungarian, German, Cree, and Finnish are a few of the many languages that show long and short vowels. Yap, a language spoken on the island of Yap in the Western Pacific, shows short and long vowels in pairs of words such as those in Table 2.25. Italian shows short and long consonants in pairs of words such as those in Table 2.26. Long and short consonants are found in many other languages, including Finnish, Turkish, and Hungarian.

Table 2.25   Short and long vowels in Yap

[θis]	'to topple'	[θi:s]	'(a) post'
[pul]	'to gather'	[pu:l]	'moon'
[ʔer]	'near you'	[ʔe:r]	'part of a lagoon'

Table 2.26   Short and long consonants in Italian

fato	[fatɔ]	'fate'	fatto	[fat:ɔ]	'fact'
fano	[fanɔ]	'grove'	fanno	[fan:ɔ]	'they do'
casa	[kasa]	'house'	cassa	[kas:a]	'box'

Stress

In any utterance, some vowels are perceived as more prominent than others. In a word such as *telegraphic* [tʰɛləgræfɪk], the two vowel nuclei that are more prominent than the others are [ɛ] and [æ]. Vowels perceived as relatively more prominent are **stressed**. Stress is a cover term for the combined effects of pitch, loudness, and length—the result of which is vowel prominence. In each language, the effect of these prosodic features varies. In general, English stressed vowels are higher in pitch, longer, and louder than unstressed ones. But this is not always the case. The example word *telegraphic* might just as well be pronounced with the stressed syllables lower than the unstressed ones. The important thing is that they be prominent with respect to the syllables around them, and this is usually accomplished by a relatively large shift in one or all of the three parameters—pitch, loudness, and length.

In some languages, the impression of vowel prominence results from an interaction of the prosodic parameters that is different from that found in English. In modern Greek, for example, syllables tend to be of equal length. Stress, therefore, is manifested by a change only in pitch and loudness and not in syllable length. Tone languages do not change the pitch level or contour of tones to mark stress. In many of these languages, relative prominence is marked by exaggerating the vowel length or pitch contour.

There are various ways to mark stress in phonetic transcription. North American transcription commonly uses an acute accent ['] placed over the vowel nucleus in question to mark the most prominent or **primary** stress, and a grave accent [`] to mark the second more prominent or **secondary** stress. (This should not be confused with the use of the same diacritics to mark tone in tone languages.) Stress can also be marked by placing numbers above the stressed vowels, usually ^{1} for a primary stress and ^{2} for a secondary stress. The word *telegraphic* is transcribed as either of the following:

2.   [tʰɛ̀ləgrǽfɪk]   or   [tʰɛ̀ləgrǽfɪk]

Since it is debatable whether any degrees of stress less than primary, secondary, and tertiary exist, this book will mark only primary and secondary stresses. Unmarked vowels have tertiary stress. Table 2.27 shows some differences in English stress placement. In the last four examples in the table, you can see that the quality of certain vowels varies depending on whether they are stressed or unstressed. This is common in English, Russian, and many other languages, but it is not universal.

Table 2.27 Differing stress placement in English

(an)	éxport	[ékspɔrt]	(to) expórt	[ɛkspɔ́rt]
(a)	présent	[prézənt]	(to) presént	[priyzént]
	télegràph	[tʰéləgræf]		
	telégraphỳ	[təlégrəfìy]		
	tèlegráphic	[tʰɛ̀ləgræfik)		

2.10 COARTICULATION

Speech production is not a series of isolated events. The process of articulation is a complex one, and many fine adjustments are carried out very rapidly as we speak. As a consequence, speech production often results in the articulation of one sound affecting that of another sound.

Ease of Articulation

You have seen how nasal sounds are produced with the velum lowered to allow air to pass through the nasal cavities. Raising and lowering the velum is not always precisely coordinated with other speech production activity.

Speakers often anticipate lowering the velum for nasal consonants and, consequently, produce a nasal vowel before a nasal consonant. Many English speakers do this when they pronounce words such as *bank* [bǽŋk] or *him* [hĩm] (see Figure 2.18). Another typical articulatory adjustment occurs when we pronounce the sound [k] before the vowel [iy] in English words such as *keys* and *keel*. The [k] we articulate before [iy] is pronounced with the back of the tongue so far forward it nearly touches the palate. It is scarcely a velar articulation at all for many speakers. The [k] we pronounce before the vowels [ɑ] and [o] in words such as *call* and *cold* is articulated further back and is a true velar. These adjustments are made in anticipation of the tongue position that will be needed for the vowel in question: front for [iy] and back for the [ɑ] and [o]. The [k] pronounced before the vowel [uw] in a word such as *cool* also shows lip rounding in anticipation of the following (back) rounded vowel.

```
Stop released,
velum begins
to lower for [ŋ].
   ↓
[  b  æ̃  ŋ  k  ]
          ↑
    Velum raises.
```

Figure 2.18 Coarticulation resulting in a nasal vowel

Articulatory adjustments that occur during the production of speech are called **processes**. Their cumulative effect often results in making words easier to articulate, and in this sense they are said to make speech more efficient. When speakers of English nasalize the vowel of *bank*, they do not delay lowering the velum until the exact moment the nasal consonant articulation is reached. Most English speakers begin lowering the velum for a nasal consonant almost as soon as they articulate the vowel that precedes it. In a parallel manner, when speakers pronounce [k] as more palatal in a word such as *key,* they are speaking more efficiently from the point of view of articulation since they are making a less drastic adjustment in moving from the articulation of a more palatal [k] to that of a high front vowel than they would make in moving from a velar [k] to a high front vowel. Even more drastically, a speaker of English who says [pr̥eyd] for *parade* is making a major adjustment that results in a more efficient articulation. The two syllables of a careful pronunciation of *parade* are reduced to one by dropping the unstressed vowel of the first syllable. The voicelessness of the initial stop is then carried on through the [r̥].

Articulatory Processes

Only a finite number of processes operate in language, though their end result is to produce a great deal of linguistic variability. This section surveys some of the most common of these processes.

Assimilation A number of different processes collectively known as **assimilation** result from the influence of one segment on another. Assimilation always results from a sound becoming more like another nearby sound in terms of one or more of its phonetic characteristics.

Progressive and Regressive Assimilation Nasalization of a vowel before a nasal consonant is caused by speakers anticipating the lowering of the velum in advance of a nasal segment. The result is that the preceding segment takes on the nasality of the following consonant. This type of assimilation is known as **regressive assimilation**, since the nasalization is, in effect, moving *backwards* to a preceding segment.

The nasalization of vowels following nasal consonants in Scots Gaelic is an example of **progressive assimilation**, since the nasality moves *forward* from the nasal consonant onto the vowel (see Table 2.28). It results from speakers not immediately raising the velum after the production of a nasal stop. Voicing assimilation is also widespread. For many speakers of English, voiceless liquids and glides occur after voiceless stops in words such as *please* [pl̥iyz], *proud* [pr̥awd], and *pure* [pyur]. These sounds are said to be devoiced in this environment. Devoicing is a kind of assimilation. Here, the vocal folds are not set in motion immediately after the release of the voiceless consonant closure. The opposite of devoicing is voicing. In Dutch, fricatives assimilate to the voicing of the stops that follow them, in anticipation of the voiced consonant. The element *af* [ɑf] 'off, over' is pronounced with a [v] in the words *afbelen* 'to ring off' and *afdeken* 'to cover over'.

Table 2.28   Progressive nasalization of vowels in Scots Gaelic

[mõ:r]	'big'
[nĩ]	'cattle'
[mũ]	'about'
[nẽ:l]	'cloud'

Assimilation for place of articulation is also widespread in the world's languages. Nasal consonants are very likely to undergo this type of assimilation, as shown in Table 2.29. The negative forms of each of these words is made with either *im* or *in*. In both cases, the form shows a nasal consonant that has the same place of articulation as the stop consonant that follows it: labial in the case of *possible* and *potent*, and alveolar in the case of *tolerable* and *tangible*. In informal speech, many English speakers pronounce words such as *inconsequential* and *inconsiderate* with an [ŋ] where the spelling shows *n*. Assimilation can also be heard in pronunciations such as

Table 2.29   Assimilation for place of articulation

possible	impossible
potent	impotent
tolerable	intolerable
tangible	intangible

Va[ŋ]*couver* and *i*[m]*fant*. Occasionally, it even crosses the boundaries between words. In rapid speech, it is not uncommon to hear people pronounce a phrase such as *in code* as [ɪŋkʰówd].

The preceding English example shows regressive assimilation in place of articulation. The example in Table 2.30, taken from German, shows progressive assimilation that again affects nasal consonants. In careful speech, certain German verb forms are pronounced with a final [ən], as in *laden* 'to

Table 2.30 Progressive assimilation in German

Careful speech		Informal speech	
laden	[la:dən]	[la:dn̩]	'to invite'
loben	[lo:bən]	[lo:bm̩]	'to praise'
backen	[bakən]	[bakŋ̩]	'to bake'

invite', *loben* 'to praise', and *backen* 'to bake'. In informal speech, the final [ən] is reduced to a syllabic nasal, which takes on the point of articulation of the preceding consonant. The diacritic line under the phonetically transcribed nasals indicates that they are syllabic. **Flapping** is a type of assimilatory process in which a voiceless alveolar stop is pronounced as a voiced flap between vowels, the first of which is generally stressed. This process is characteristic of American English in words such as *butter, writer, fatter, udder, wader, waiter,* and even phrases such as *(I) caught her*. The sound heard intervocally in these forms is the voiced flap [D] (discussed on page 34) and not the voiced stop [d]. Flapping is considered a type of assimilation since it results in voicing being maintained throughout a sequence of segments.

Dissimilation, the opposite of assimilation, results in two sounds becoming less alike in articulatory or acoustic terms. The resulting sequence of sounds is easier to articulate and distinguish. It is a much rarer process than assimilation. One commonly heard example of dissimilation in English occurs in words ending with three consecutive fricatives, such as *fifths*. Many speakers dissimilate the final [fθs] sequence to [fts], apparently to break up the sequence of three fricatives with a stop.

Deletion is a process that removes a segment from certain phonetic contexts. Deletion occurs in everyday rapid speech in many languages. In English, a schwa [ə] is often deleted when the next vowel in the word is stressed (see Table 2.31). Deletion also occurs as an alternative to dissimilation in a word such as *fifths*. Many speakers delete the [θ] of the final consonant cluster

Table 2.31 Deletion of [ə] in English

Slow speech	Rapid speech	
[pəréyd]	[pṛéyd]	parade
[kərówd]	[kṛówd]	corrode
[səpʰówz]	[spówz]	suppose

and say [fɪfs]. In very rapid speech, both [f] and [θ] are sometimes deleted, resulting in [fɪs].

Epenthesis is a process that inserts a vowel or a consonant segment within an existing string of segments. For example, in careful speech, the words *prince* and *wince* are pronounced [prɪns] and [wɪns]. It is common in casual speech for speakers to insert a [t] between the *n* and the *s* and pronounce the words [prɪnts] and [wɪnts].

This consonant epenthesis arises when speakers simultaneously maintain the stop closure of the nasal and anticipate the voicelessness of the *s*. The result is a [t]—a segment that is a stop and is voiceless, and that retains the alveolar point of articulation of both the *n* and the *s*.

In Japanese, a syllable may never contain two successive consonants, nor may a word end in any consonant but a nasal. When foreign words with consonant clusters or nonnasal final consonants are borrowed into Japanese, an epenthetic vowel (often *u*) is inserted between any sequence of two consonants and after a final consonant, thus creating a new and permissible syllable shape (see Table 2.32).

Table 2.32 Vowel epenthesis in Japanese

suturaiku	'strike'
kurabu	'club'
nekutai	'necktie'

Metathesis is a process that reorders a sequence of segments. Metathesis often results in a sequence of phones that is easier to articulate. It is common to hear metathesis in the speech of children, who often cannot pronounce all the consonant sequences that adults can. For example, English-speaking children pronounce *spaghetti* as *pesghetti* [pəskɛDiy]. In this form, the initial sequence [spə], which is often difficult for children to pronounce, is metathesized to [pəs].

The pronunciations of *prescribe* and *prescription* as *perscribe* and *perscription* are often-cited examples of metathesis in adult speech. In these cases, metathesis may facilitate the pronunciation of two consonant-*r* sequences in each word.

*2.11 CLASSES AND FEATURES

When processes apply in the course of speech, they generally affect **natural classes** of sounds. A natural class is a group of sounds such as nasals, vowels, liquids, fricative consonants, or stops, whose members share one or more phonetic characteristics. There are a limited number of natural classes in human language. By comparing the articulatory and acoustic properties of phones and the processes that they undergo, linguists have arrived at a set of **features** that represent the possible sounds of human language. Each feature represents an independently controllable aspect of speech production, or some acoustic property shared by a natural class. Most features have labels (which are stated in brackets) that reflect traditional articulatory terms such as [voice], [consonantal], and [nasal]. These features require little further description. A few features, described later in this section, have less familiar labels, such as [coronal] and [anterior]. From this point on, features will be used to describe classes of sounds. At the same time, we will continue throughout the book to use time-honored terms such as *consonant, glide,* and *obstruent* (consonants that are not glides, liquids, or nasals) in phonetic description. The traditional terminology will be maintained because it is still widely used in phonetic description.

Features are represented as **binary** properties of language. They are considered to be wholly present or wholly absent from the articulation of a sound. In binary representation, [+] means that a feature is present and [−] means it is absent. A segment is represented by lining up the features vertically and enclosing them in brackets to show their simultaneous production. The following example shows the feature representation for *p*.

3.
$$
p \\
\begin{bmatrix}
+ \text{ consonantal} \\
+ \text{ anterior} \\
- \text{ coronal} \\
- \text{ continuant} \\
- \text{ voice}
\end{bmatrix}
$$

Features identify classes of sounds, and processes operate on these classes. For this reason, we can use features to represent processes. Nasal assimilation in vowels, for example, applies in English to the entire class of vowels, not merely to one or two isolated members of the class. Using features to represent English nasal assimilation, we can state that all [+ syllabic] segments (the class of vowels) are [+ nasal] (nasal) before the class that is [− syllabic, + nasal] (the nasal consonants).

In addition to their value in making explicit the effects of processes, features enable us to distinguish among classes of sounds with many members. For example, the set of sounds [p], [t], [k], and [č] can be readily distinguished from the set [b], [d], [g], and [ǰ] by the feature [voice] alone (see Table 2.33). It will always take more features to describe any one member of a natural class than it takes to describe the whole class. For example, [p], [t], [s], and [č] are all [− voice], but [s] is also [+ continuant].

Table 2.33 Segments differing in a single feature

[− voice]	[+ voice]
[p]	[b]
[t]	[d]
[k]	[g]
[č]	[ǰ]

Since sounds share various features, they can belong to several classes at once. The sounds [b], [v], [z], and [g] are all [+ voice]. At the same time, [b] and [g] are [− continuant], while [v] and [z] are [+ continuant]. The vowels [iy] and [uw] are both [+ high], but only [uw] is [+ round], a feature that it shares with [ow]. Figure 2.19 illustrates some intersecting features of English vowels. There is no feature mid: mid vowels are expressed as [− high, − low]. There are also no features front or central. Central and back vowels are expressed as [+ back] and front vowels as [− back].

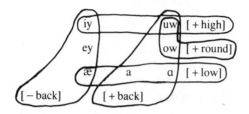

Figure 2.19 Intersecting features in English vowels

The next section presents and describes the features necessary to describe the sounds of English. Additional features will be introduced elsewhere in the book as needed.

Major Class Features

The first set of features accounts for differences among the major classes of segments: vowels, glides, and consonants.

[consonantal] This feature describes all sounds made with closure in the vocal tract greater than that needed for glides. The obstruents (stops, fricatives, and affricates), as well as liquids and nasals, are [+ consonantal].

[syllabic] This feature is characteristic of sounds that function as the nucleus of a syllable. This includes all vowels, as well as nasals and liquids when they function as syllable nuclei. Glides are never [+ syllabic].

[sonorant] All relatively noise-free sounds that can be sung on a held pitch are considered to be [+ sonorant]. This feature thus takes in vowels, glides, liquids, and nasals and excludes obstruent consonants.

[nasal] Consonants, vowels, or glides that are made with the velum lowered are all [+ nasal].

Combining these binary features enables us to describe the following classes of sounds: consonants, vowels, glides, syllabic consonants, liquids, and nasals. The matrix in Table 2.34 shows explicitly that each class of sounds is

Table 2.34 Major class features

	Obstruents	Vowels	Glides	Non-syllabic liquids	Non-syllabic nasals	Syllabic liquids	Syllabic nasals
[consonantal]	+	−	−	+	+	+	+
[syllabic]	−	+	−	−	−	+	+
[sonorant]	−	+	+	+	+	+	+
[nasal]	−	±	±	−	+	−	+

distinguished from the others by one or more binary feature values. The ± means that a class of sounds may be heard with either value: for example, vowels can be oral or nasal.

Place Features

The next set of features describes the places of articulation.

[anterior] Any sound articulated in front of the alveopalatal region is considered to be [+ anterior]. This includes the labial, dental, and alveolar sounds.

[coronal] Any sound articulated with the tongue tip or blade raised is [+ coronal].

These two features enable us to separate labials from dentals and alveolars and to distinguish the class of sounds made in front of the alveopalatal region from those made at or behind it as shown in Table 2.35. The following features characterize the placement of the body of the tongue, the area behind the tip and blade. These features, [high] and [back], are also used to describe vowels.

Table 2.35 Place of articulation features

	Labials	Dentals/ alveolars	Alveopalatals	Palatals/ velars
[anterior]	+	+	−	−
[coronal]	−	+	+	−

[high] Sounds produced with the tongue body raised are considered [+ high]. Palatal and velar sounds as well as high vowels are all [+ high].

[low] Vowels made with the tongue body distinctly lowered from a central position in the oral cavity are [+ low]. Both [h] and [ʔ] are [− low] since they are not made in the oral cavity.

[back] Any sound articulated behind the palatal region in the oral cavity is [+ back]. Both [h] and [ʔ] are [− back] since they are not made in the oral cavity.

We can now distinguish among the consonants produced behind the alveopalatal region. For English, we need only take note of the distinction among palatals, velars, and glottals, as shown in Table 2.36.

Table 2.36 Features for nonanterior consonants

	Palatals	Velars	Glottals
[high]	+	+	−
[back]	−	+	−

Manner Features

The next features characterize various manners of articulation. They enable us to distinguish among stops, fricatives, and affricates.

[continuant] Free airflow through the oral cavity means a sound is [+ continuant]; continuants thus include vowels, fricative consonants, glides, and *r*'s; for *l*, see the discussion of the feature [lateral]. Nasal stops are [− continuant] since the airflow is through the nasal passage, not the mouth.

[delayed release] Only affricate consonants such as [č] and [ǰ] are [+ delayed release]. This feature describes the slow release from a stop articulation typical of affricates.

[strident] This feature refers to what we may subjectively call the relative noisiness of both fricatives and affricates. It enables us to group certain fricatives and affricates together into a natural class. In English, [θ] and [ð] are [− strident], while [f], [v], [s], [z], [š], [ž], [č], and [ǰ] are [+ strident].

[voice] This feature refers to the state of the glottis. All [+ voice] sounds are voiced; all [− voice] sounds are voiceless.

[aspirated] This feature distinguishes unaspirated from aspirated consonants. It refers to a delay in the voicing onset of a voiced segment following the release phase of a voiceless consonant.

[lateral] This feature is used to distinguish the lateral liquids (varieties of *l*) from the nonlateral liquids (varieties of *r*). Both *l* and *r* may be considered to be [+ continuant] in English. In some languages, laterals pattern like noncontinuants, in others, like continuants.

The matrix in Table 2.37 presents the features needed to represent the consonants of English. Appended to this chapter on page 51 is a table that provides an articulatory grid of English consonants along with the features needed to describe them.

Table 2.37 Feature matrix for English consonants

	p	pʰ	b	m	t	tʰ	d	n	k	kʰ	g	ŋ	f	v	s	z	θ	ð	š	ž	č	ǰ	l	r	y	w	ʍ	h	ʔ
[syllabic]	−	−	−	−	−	−	−	−	−	−	−	−	−	−	−	−	−	−	−	−	−	−	−	−	−	−	−	−	−
[consonantal]	+	+	+	+	+	+	+	+	+	+	+	+	+	+	+	+	+	+	+	+	+	+	+	+	−	−	−	+	+
[sonorant]	−	−	−	+	−	−	−	+	−	−	−	+	−	−	−	−	−	−	−	−	−	−	+	+	+	+	+	−	−
[nasal]	−	−	−	+	−	−	−	+	−	−	−	+	−	−	−	−	−	−	−	−	−	−	−	−	−	−	−	−	−
[anterior]	+	+	+	+	+	+	+	+	−	−	−	−	+	+	+	+	+	+	−	−	−	−	+	+	−	−	−	−	−
[coronal]	−	−	−	−	+	+	+	+	−	−	−	−	−	−	+	+	+	+	+	+	+	+	+	+	−	−	−	−	−
[high]	−	−	−	−	−	−	−	−	+	+	+	+	−	−	−	−	−	−	−	−	−	−	−	−	+	+	+	−	−
[low]	−	−	−	−	−	−	−	−	−	−	−	−	−	−	−	−	−	−	−	−	−	−	−	−	−	−	−	−	−
[back]	−	−	−	−	−	−	−	−	+	+	+	+	−	−	−	−	−	−	−	−	−	−	−	−	−	+	+	−	−
[continuant]	−	−	−	−	−	−	−	−	−	−	−	−	+	+	+	+	+	+	+	+	−	−	+	+	+	+	+	+	−
[delayed release]	−	−	−	−	−	−	−	−	−	−	−	−	−	−	−	−	−	−	−	−	+	+	−	−	−	−	−	−	−
[strident]	−	−	−	−	−	−	−	−	−	−	−	−	+	+	+	+	−	−	+	+	+	+	−	−	−	−	−	−	−
[voice]	−	−	+	+	−	−	+	+	−	−	+	+	−	+	−	+	−	+	−	+	−	+	+	+	+	+	−	−	−
[aspirated]	−	+	−	−	−	+	−	−	−	+	−	−	−	−	−	−	−	−	−	−	−	−	−	−	−	−	−	−	−
[lateral]	−	−	−	−	−	−	−	−	−	−	−	−	−	−	−	−	−	−	−	−	−	−	+	−	−	−	−	−	−

Vowel Features

Some of the features used to describe consonants are also used to describe vowels. Remember that vowels are made by shaping the body of the tongue in various ways within the oral cavity. The tongue body features [high], [low], and [back] are used to describe the vowels in the same manner as presented in the traditional articulatory description. Two other important features must be introduced.

[round] This feature refers to vowels made with lip rounding, such as [ow] and [uw].

[tense] This feature characterizes vowels that are generally longer and made with a more constricted tongue position than that used for the lax vowels. It is used in English to distinguish between the sets of vowels that are otherwise described with the same features, such as [iy] and [ɪ], [ey] and [ɛ], [uw] and [ʊ], the former in each case being [+ tense] and the lax vowels being described as [− tense].

[reduced] This feature refers only to the vowel schwa [ə] and distinguishes it from [ʌ].

The matrix in Table 2.38 illustrates the application of the feature system to English vowels. All vowels are [+ syllabic], [− consonantal], and [+ sonorant]. Mid vowels are neither [+ high] nor [+ low]. Feature notation does not provide a convenient way to distinguish the diphthongs [ay] and [aw] from the other vowels. These diphthongs may be treated as vowel-glide sequences when using features.

Table 2.38 Feature matrix for English vowels

	iy	ɪ	ey	ɛ	æ	uw	ʊ	ow	ɔ	a	ɑ	ʌ	ə
[high]	+	+	−	−	−	+	+	−	−	−	−	−	−
[low]	−	−	−	−	+	−	−	−	−	+	+	−	−
[back]	−	−	−	−	−	+	+	+	+	+	+	+	+
[round]	−	−	−	−	−	+	+	+	+	−	−	−	−
[tense]	+	−	+	−	−	+	−	+	−	−	+	−	−
[reduced]	−	−	−	−	−	−	−	−	−	−	−	−	+

Universality The features presented here are not exhaustive, although they do account for all the consonants and vowels of English as well as a great number of other languages. They form part of a universal feature inventory, that is, an inventory of phonetic possibilities that linguists believe constitutes part of human linguistic ability.

Summing Up

The study of the sounds of human language is called **phonetics**. These sounds are widely transcribed by means of the **International Phonetic Alphabet**. The sounds of language are commonly described in **articulatory** and **acoustic** terms; they fall into three major types: **consonants**, **vowels**, and **glides**. Sounds may be **voiced** or **voiceless**, and **oral** or **nasal**. Consonants are produced at various **places of articulation**: **labial**, **dental**, **alveolar**, **alveopalatal**, **palatal**, **velar**, **glottal**, and **pharyngeal**. At the places of articulation, the airstream is modified by different **manners of articulation** and the resulting sounds are **stops**, **fricatives**, or **affricates**. Vowels are produced with less drastic closure and are described with reference to tongue position (**high**, **low**, **back**, and **front**), tension (**tense** or **lax**), and lip rounding (**rounded** or **unrounded**). Language also shows **suprasegmental** phenomena such as **tone**, **intonation**, and **stress**. A number of phonetic **processes** act on **natural classes** of sounds in speech, and these classes of sounds as well as the individual sounds that make them up can be described in terms of a finite set of **features**.

Sources

Information on the International Phonetic Alphabet can be obtained from the International Phonetic Association, University College, Gower Street, London WC1E 6BT, England. Sarcee data are from E.-D. Cook, ''Vowels and Tones in Sarcee'' in *Language* 47:164–79; Gaelic data are courtesy of James Galbraith. Bini data are adapted from Ladefoged (cited below). More detailed reading on the phonetics of English and other languages is reported below.

Recommended Reading

Catford, J. C. 1977. *Fundamental Problems in Phonetics*. Bloomington: Indiana University Press.

Delattre, P. 1965. *Comparing the Phonetic Features of English, French, German and Spanish*. Heidelberg: Julius Groos Verlag.

Fromkin, V. A., ed. *Tone: A Linguistic Survey*. New York: Academic Press.

Ladefoged, P. 1982. *A Course in Phonetics*. 2d ed. New York: Harcourt Brace Jovanovich.

Shearer, William M. 1968. *Illustrated Speech Anatomy*. Springfield, Illinois: Charles C. Thomas.

Appendix: Articulatory/Feature Representation of English Consonants

Place of articulation		Labial	Interdental	Alveolar	Alveopalatal	Velar	Glottal	
Manner of articulation	Glottal state	$\begin{bmatrix} +anterior \\ -coronal \end{bmatrix}$	$\begin{bmatrix} +anterior \\ +coronal \\ -strident \end{bmatrix}$	$\begin{bmatrix} +anterior \\ +coronal \\ (+strident) \end{bmatrix}$	$\begin{bmatrix} -anterior \\ +coronal \\ -high \end{bmatrix}$	$\begin{bmatrix} +back \\ +high \\ -low \end{bmatrix}$		
STOP [−continuant]	[−voice]	p		t		k	ʔ	[−sonorant]
	[+voice]	b		d		g		
FRICATIVE [+continuant]	[−voice]	f	θ	s	š		h	
	[+voice]	v	ð	z	ž			
AFFRICATE [+del rel]	[−voice]				č			
	[+voice]				ǰ			
NASAL [+nasal]	[+voice]	m		n		ŋ		$\begin{bmatrix} -syllabic \\ +consonantal \end{bmatrix}$
LIQUID Lateral [+lateral]	[+voice]			l [−strident]				[+sonorant]
Retroflex [−lateral]	[+voice]			r [−strident]				
GLIDE	[+voice]	w			y*	(w)		
$\begin{bmatrix} -consonantal \\ -syllabic \end{bmatrix}$	[−voice]	ʍ			$\begin{bmatrix} +high \\ -coronal \end{bmatrix}$	(ʍ)		

Major manner features — The glides [w] and [ʍ] are represented in parentheses as velars since they are both labia and velar (labiovelar). The features of labials are assigned to them.
* The glide [y] is, strictly speaking, a palatal.

Questions

* 1. After each of the following articulatory descriptions, write in phonetic brackets the sound described.

   Example: voiceless glottal fricative   [h]

   a) voiceless velar stop
   b) voiced labiodental fricative
   c) voiced alveopalatal affricate
   d) voiced palatal glide
   e) voiced velar nasal
   f) voiceless interdental fricative
   g) high back rounded lax vowel
   h) low front unrounded vowel

2. In which of the following pairs do the words show the same vowel quality? Which show different vowels? Mark each pair as *same* or *different*. Next, transcribe the vowels of each word. Be sure to include differences in vowel length in your transcription.

a)	back	sat	h)	hide	sigh
b)	weed	creep	i)	least	heed
c)	though	owe	j)	drug	cook
d)	luck	flick	k)	sing	wit
e)	ooze	deuce	l)	oak	own
f)	cot	coy	m)	lose	loose
g)	sell	sale	n)	reed	fear

3. Transcribe the following sets of words, indicating which voiceless stops are aspirated and which are not.

a)	tog	peel	spell	keg
b)	kid	stun	cord	pure
c)	attain	Oscar	accord	scold
d)	despise	cooler	astound	tone

4. Mark primary and secondary stresses (where present) on the following words. It is not necessary to transcribe them.

a)	sunny	f)	secrete	k)	secret
b)	central	g)	defy	l)	exceed
c)	blackboard	h)	summary	m)	summery
d)	Canada	i)	Canadian	n)	Canadianize
e)	(to) reject	j)	(a) reject	o)	immobility

5. Write the following English words in phonetic transcription. Pay particular attention to aspiration and nasalization.

a)	elbow	e)	sigh	i)	debt
b)	haul	f)	hulk	j)	wheeze
c)	juice	g)	explode	k)	remove
d)	thimble	h)	tube	l)	clinical

6. Circle each group of sounds that makes up a natural class in the following data. Be sure to indicate which feature or features define the class, as in the example.

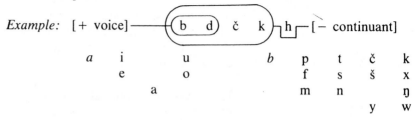

Example: [+ voice] —— (b   d) č   k   h [– continuant]

	a	i		u		b	p	t	č	k
		e		o			f	s	š	x
			a				m	n		ŋ
									y	w

7. Name the single feature that distinguishes the following pairs of sounds.

a)	[θ]:[ð]	f)	[s]:[š]
b)	[p]:[f]	g)	[ɪ]:[ĩ]
c)	[u]:[ʊ]	h)	[k]:[x]
d)	[i]:[e]	i)	[ʌ]:[ə]
e)	[b]:[m]	j)	[s]:[θ]

8. Complete the following feature matrices.

a)

	iy	ey	uw	ow
[consonantal]	−	−	−	−
[syllabic]	+	+	+	+
[high]	+	−		−
[low]			−	
[back]	−			+
[round]		−		

b)

	p	t	č	k
[consonantal]	+	+	+	+
[syllabic]	−	−	−	−
[continuant]	−			−
[anterior]		+		−
[coronal]				−
[voice]				

c)

	l	r	m	n	y
[consonantal]					
[syllabic]					
[sonorant]					
[nasal]					

9. Transcribe the following English utterances as you would say them in careful speech.

   a) Twenty sleek spotted snakes
   b) Wild whizzing witches which whoop and wail
   c) A big blue bug bit a big black bear.
   d) The sixth sheik's sixth sheep's sick.

10. Compare the careful speech and rapid speech pronunciations of the following English words and phrases. Then, name the process or processes that make the rapid speech pronunciation different from the careful speech. (Stress is omitted here.)

		Careful speech	Rapid speech
a)	in my room	[ɪn may ruwm]	[ɪm may ruwm]
b)	I see him	[ay siy hɪm]	[ay siy ɪm]
c)	okay	[owkʰey]	[owgey]
d)	balloons	[bəluwnz]	[bluwnz]
e)	sit down	[sɪt dawn]	[sɪDawn]
f)	my advice	[mayədvʌys]	[mayəvʌys]
g)	Scotch tape	[skač tʰeyp]	[kʰač steyp]

11. Find a fluent speaker of a language other than English and transcribe phonetically five sentences of that language. Do you encounter any sounds not dealt with in this chapter? Can you describe them phonetically?

3 PHONOLOGY
The Function and Patterning of Sounds

My voice goes after what my eyes cannot reach,
With the twirl of my tongue I encompass
words and volumes of words.

Walt Whitman

When we speak of linguistic knowledge, we often mean subconscious or implicit knowledge that speakers of a language cannot readily put into words. As pointed out in Chapter 1, English speakers know that forms like *slish* and *screk* are acceptable, while forms like *pnap* and *sdip* are not. Few people could state without considerable reflection what pattern, if any, governs the acceptability of some sequences and the unacceptability of others. This chapter deals with **phonology**, the component of a grammar made up of the categories and principles that determine how sounds pattern in a language. Phonologists attempt to make clear and explicit statements about the sound patterns of individual languages in order to discover something about the linguistic knowledge that people must have in order to use these patterns. Even more broadly, the study of phonology attempts to discover general principles that underlie the patterning of sounds in human language.

The search for sound patterns in language implies the existence of some basic elements or units that combine to make up these patterns. Three major units of analysis will be presented in this chapter. The smallest of these units is the **feature**, which was introduced in the previous chapter. Features may be thought of as the smallest building blocks of linguistic structure. A second element of phonological structure is the segment. We saw in the previous chapter how individual segments such as [p], [l], or [ə] are made up of features. Any reference to segments in this chapter assumes that they are composed of features. Segments, in turn, are combined to produce syllables such as *in, duc,* or *tion.* A syllable is a unit of linguistic structure that consists of a vowel (or vowellike sound) and any consonants that are associated with it. These units—feature, segment, and syllable—all form part of a speaker's linguistic knowledge.

The study of phonology thus views linguistic forms as composed of several levels of sound structure. Each level is composed of elements at the level beneath it. A word-sized unit such as *induction* is represented by the

Greek letter μ (*mu*). It consists of three syllables, each of which is abbreviated with the Greek letter σ (*sigma*). Each syllable is made up of a number of segments, and each segment, in turn, is composed of features. A representation of *induction* is given in Figure 3.1. (For purposes of illustration, just one feature is provided for each segment.) The following section examines the way in which segments pattern in sequence.

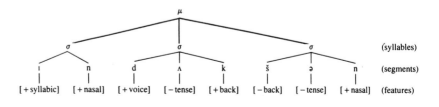

Figure 3.1 Phonological representation of *induction*

3.1 PHONOTACTICS: SEGMENTS IN SEQUENCE

Native speakers of any language intuitively know that certain words that come from other languages sound unusual. They often adjust the segment sequences of these words to conform with the pronunciation requirements of their own language. These speaker intuitions are based on a tacit knowledge of the permissible segment sequences of the speaker's own language. For example, English-speaking students learning Russian have difficulty pronouncing a word like *vprog* [fprɔk] 'value, good', since the sequence [fpr] is never found at the beginning of words in English. Since speakers typically adjust an impermissible sequence by altering it to a permissible one, many English speakers would pronounce the Russian word [fprɔk] as [fəprɔk] in order to break up the impermissible sequence *fpr* at the beginning of the word. **Phonotactics**, the set of constraints on how sequences of segments pattern, forms part of a speaker's knowledge of the phonology of his or her language.

Some English Phonotactics

Table 3.1 contains examples of the possible syllable-initial consonant sequences of English that contain a voiceless stop consonant. These sequences are all illustrated in word-initial position to make them easier to pick out.

Table 3.1 Initial consonant clusters in English

[pl]	please	[tl]	---	[kl]	clean
[pr]	proud	[tr]	trade	[kr]	cream
[pw]	---	[tw]	twin	[kw]	queen
[py]	pure	[ty]	tune (Southern)	[ky]	cute
[spl]	splat	[stl]	---	[skl]	sclerosis
[spr]	spring	[str]	strip	[skr]	scrap
[spw]	---	[stw]	---	[skw]	squeak
[spy]	spew	[sty]	stew (Southern)	[sky]	skewer

(Some details of pronunciation are omitted in the transcription.) These examples show that the first segment of a word-initial three-consonant cluster in English is always *s*; the second consonant in the series is always a voiceless stop, and the third is either a liquid or a glide. These sound patterns can be formally represented as shown in Figure 3.2. In this formalization, the crosshatch # indicates the boundary of a word, and the curly braces designate 'either/or'. The sounds in parentheses are not found in all combinations. Although there are twenty-four possible two- and three-consonant word-initial sequences in English containing a voiceless stop, not all of these combinations are exploited in the vocabulary of the language.

$$ \#\ \ s\ \ \left\{ \begin{array}{c} p \\ t \\ k \end{array} \right\} \left\{ \begin{array}{c} (l) \\ r \\ (w) \\ y \end{array} \right. \text{Vowel} $$

Figure 3.2   Possible initial three-consonant clusters in English

Accidental and Systematic Gaps

Some gaps in the inventory of possible English words include *smool, plick, sklop, flis, trok,* and *krif,* although none of these forms violates any phonotactic constraints on segment combination found in English. Gaps in a language's inventory of forms that correspond to nonoccurring but possible forms are called **accidental gaps**. Occasionally, an accidental gap will be filled in by the invention of a new word. The word *Kodak* is one such invented word. Borrowed words such as *Bic, Mazda,* and *Toyota* are readily accepted by English speakers as long as they conform to the phonotactic patterns of the language.

There are no English words that begin with #*stl*- or #*spw*-. The absence of these sequences is not accidental. These are precisely the combinations of sounds that would involve the same point of articulation for the second and third elements in the sequence. A constraint in English forbids the combining of two consonants with the same point of articulation at the beginning of a word if the first consonant is a stop. This naturally holds true for words that begin with just two consonants; *#*tl*- and *#*pw*- are not possible initial sequences in most English dialects. Gaps that result from the phonotactic constraints of a given language are called **systematic gaps**.

Phonotactics and Borrowed Forms

Borrowings from other languages into English must also be accommodated to these and other constraints. Many Greek words beginning with #*ps*- and #*pt*- have been absorbed into English, as the spellings of *psychology, psoriasis,* and *pterodactyl* attest. In all of them, the impermissible initial-consonant clusters *#*ps*- and *#*pt*- have been reduced to *s*- or *t*-.

It is important to emphasize that these particular constraints are language-specific—that is, they hold true for English, and they may or may not be found in other languages. Each language has a set of restrictions on how its sounds may combine. Speakers of Russian are quite accustomed to pronouncing syllable-initial consonant sequences such as *pt-*, *ps-*, and *fsl-*, as the examples in Table 3.2 show. Phonotactic constraints represent one kind of phonological knowledge. The next sections look at the phonological knowledge that enables speakers to distinguish among forms and to deal with the considerable phonetic variation found in speech.

Table 3.2   Some initial-consonant sequences of Russian

[psa]	'dog's'
[fslux]	'aloud'
[ptitsə]	'bird'

3.2 SEGMENTS IN CONTRAST

All speakers know which segments of their language **contrast**. Segments are said to contrast (or to be distinctive or be in opposition) when their presence alone may distinguish forms with different meanings from each other. The segments [s] and [z] contrast in the words *s̲ip* and *z̲ip*, as do the vowels of *hi̲t*, *ha̲te*, and *ho̲t*.

Minimal Pairs and Sets

The basic test for a sound's distinctiveness is called a minimal pair test. A minimal pair consists of two forms with distinct meanings that differ by only one segment found in the same position in each form. The examples [sɪp] *sip* and [zɪp] *zip* given previously form a minimal pair and show that the sounds [s] and [z] contrast in English.

Consonant Contrasts in English   A number of minimal pairs that demonstrate contrastive consonants for English are shown in Table 3.3. Remember that

Table 3.3 Contrasts among consonants in English

Obstruents									
tap	[p]			pat	[t]	chug	[č]	pick	[k]
tab	[b]			pad	[d]	jug	[ǰ]	pig	[g]

Continuants								
fat	[f]	thigh	[θ]	sip	[s]	mesher	[š]
vat	[v]	thy	[ð]	zip	[z]	measure	[ž]

Nasals							
sum	[m]			sun	[n]			sung	[ŋ]

Liquids and glides				
wet	[w]			yet	[y]
		leer	[l]	
		rear	[r]	

it is on the basis of sound and not spelling that minimal pairs are established. Pairs that show segments in nearly identical environments, such as *azure/ assure* or *author/either,* are called near-minimal pairs. They help to establish contrasts where no minimal pairs can be found.

It is possible for a larger group of contrasts, called a minimal set, to be established based on a series of minimal pairs. Table 3.4 shows a series of words that contrast only in their initial consonant. Such extended sets are

Table 3.4 A minimal set

tip	dip	[t]	[d]
sip	zip	[s]	[z]
ship	chip	[š]	[č]
lip	nip	[l]	[n]

not really necessary to establish the contrastiveness of a given sound. You may assume that two sounds contrast once a minimal pair or a near-minimal pair has been established. It is in fact rare to find minimal pairs for all distinctive sounds in all environments in a language, since the historical evolution of every language has led to some sounds being used more frequently than others, or being removed from some environments. For example, you will find no minimal pairs involving [h] and [ŋ] in word-initial or word-final position in English, because there are no words that begin with [ŋ] or end in [h]. It is also difficult to find minimal pairs in English that involve the sound [ž].

Vowel Contrasts in English Contrasts among English vowels can be established with a few minimal sets, as in Table 3.5. We will continue to assume, that English vowel-glide sequences like [iy], [uw], and [ow] are single vowels. From this perspective, we can say that the vowels [iy] and [ɪ], [ey] and [ɛ], and so on, contrast.

Table 3.5 Vowel contrasts in American English

beet	[biyt]	[iy]
bit	[bɪt]	[ɪ]
bait	[beyt]	[ey]
bet	[bɛt]	[ɛ]
bat	[bæt]	[æ]
cooed	[kʰuwd]	[uw]
could	[kʰʊd]	[ʊ]
code	[kʰowd]	[ow]
caught	[kʰɔt]	[ɔ]
cot	[kʰɑt]	[ɑ]
cut	[kʰʌt]	[ʌ]
lewd	[luwd]	[uw]
loud	[lawd]	[aw]
lied	[layd]	[ay]
Lloyd	[lɔyd]	[ɔy]

Language-Specific Contrasts

Contrasts are language-specific; sounds that are distinctive in one language will not necessarily be distinctive in another (see Table 3.6). For example, the difference between the two vowels [ɛ] and [æ] is crucial to English, as

Table 3.6   English and Turkish language-specific vowel contrasts

English	Turkish
Ben [bɛn]	[bɛn] 'I'
ban [bæn]	[bæn] 'I'

we can see from minimal pairs like *Ben* [bɛn] and *ban* [bæn]. But in Turkish, this difference in pronunciation is not distinctive. A Turkish speaker may pronounce the word for 'I' as [bɛn] or [bæn], and it will make no difference to the meaning. Conversely, sounds that do not contrast in English, such as long and short vowels, may be distinctive in another language. There are no minimal pairs of the type [bæt]:[bæːt] or [hɪt]:[hɪːt] in English. But in Serbo-Croatian, the pairs shown in Table 3.7 contrast. Establishing the contrasting segments in a language is one step in phonological analysis. There are many sounds in any language that never contrast with each other. Non-contrastive phonetic variation is extremely common in all languages. The following section deals with this major subject of phonological analysis.

Table 3.7   Serbo-Croatian short/long vowel contrasts

[grad]	'hail'	[graːd]	'city'
[duga]	'stave'	[duːga]	'rainbow'

3.3 PHONETICALLY CONDITIONED VARIATION: PHONEMES AND ALLOPHONES

Everyday speech contains a great deal of phonetic variation. Some of it is due to variation in articulation that arises from extralinguistic factors such as orthodontic work, fatigue, excitement, and gum-chewing. Such variation is not part of the domain of phonology. Much phonetic variation, however, is systematic. It occurs most often among phonetically similar segments and is conditioned by the phonetic context or **environment** in which the segments are found. That is, sounds are affected and altered by the phonetic characteristics of neighboring sounds. Every speaker has the ability to factor out this systematic variation in order to focus attention on only the relevant contrasts of the language.

Complementary Distribution

When first learning phonetic transcription, English speakers are often surprised that all the *l*'s they pronounce are not identical. In Table 3.8, the *l*'s

Table 3.8   Voiced and voiceless *l* in English

A		B	
blue	[bluw]	plow	[pl̥aw]
gleam	[gliym]	clap	[kl̥æp]
slip	[slɪp]	clear	[kl̥iyr]
flog	[flɑg]	play	[pl̥ey]
leaf	[liyf]		

in column A are voiced, while those in column B are voiceless (indicated here by a subscript ͜). Most speakers of English are unaware that they routinely produce this difference in articulation. The voicelessness of the *l*'s in column B is an automatic consequence of their phonetic environment. These consonants vary systematically in that all of the voiceless ones occur predictably after the class of voiceless stops. Since no voiced [l] ever occurs in the same phonetic environment as a voiceless one (and vice versa), we say that the two variants of *l* are in **complementary distribution**. The term *elsewhere* is used in Table 3.9 to indicate the wider distribution (occurrence in a greater number of different phonetic environments) of voiced [l]. It occurs after voiced stops, voiceless fricatives, and in word-initial position.

Table 3.9   Complementary distribution of [l] and [l̥] in English

	[l]	[l̥]
After voiceless stops	no	yes
Elsewhere	yes	no

In spite of these phonetic differences, native speakers consider the two English *l*'s to be instances of the same consonant, since they are phonetically similar, and the differences between them are systematic and predictable. This perception of sameness is supported by the fact that the two *l*'s never contrast in English. There are no minimal pairs like [pley] and [pl̥ey]. We can sum up the relationship that the two *l*'s bear to each other by stating that, for speakers of English, the two *l*'s are phonetically different but phonologically the same.

Phonemes and Allophones

The ability to group phonetically different sounds together into one class is shared by all speakers of all languages. This phonological knowledge is expressed formally as a level of phonological (as opposed to phonetic) representation called the **phonemic** level. Predictable phonetic variants that are phonetically similar and in complementary distribution are called **allophones**. These are grouped together into a phonological unit called a **phoneme**. A representation of this relationship is shown in Figure 3.3. The phonemic symbol for the class—generally the same symbol as the elsewhere variant—is placed between slashes, and the symbols for allophones are framed by phonetic brackets. Allophonic variation is found throughout language. Every speech sound we utter is an allophone of some phoneme and can be grouped

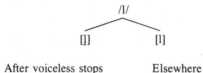

After voiceless stops   Elsewhere

Figure 3.3 The phoneme /l/ and its allophones in English

together with other, usually phonetically similar sounds, into a class that is represented by a phoneme on a phonological level of representation. Phonological analysis is largely concerned with discovering the phonemes of languages and accounting for allophonic variation.

A minimal pair test is a quick and direct way of establishing that two sounds belong to separate phonemes in a language. If the sounds contrast, they are members of different phonemes. But a minimal pair test is not the only way to discover the phonological inventory of a language. As noted in the previous section, historical accidents of their distribution prevent some sounds in a language from ever contrasting. In cases like these, we can establish the phonemic status of a sound by default. If the sound cannot be grouped together with any other phonetically similar sounds as an allophone of a phoneme, we may assume it has phonemic status. The following data help to illustrate this point.

> *1.* *ŋope   hope
> *ɲate   hate

We can see here the [h] and [ŋ] do not contrast in initial position in English. The following examples show that neither do they contrast in final position.

> *2.* long   *loh
> sing   *sih
> clang   *clah

These lists could be extended for pages, but a minimal pair involving [h] and [ŋ] could never be found in English. At the same time, [h] and [ŋ] are in complementary distribution. These facts do not mean that [h] and [ŋ] are allophones of one phoneme. Since they are so distinct phonetically, we assume that each one is a member of a separate phoneme.

The Reality of Phonemes

Phonemes are more than convenient symbols for groups of allophones. Phonemes represent a form of linguistic knowledge. Even though we never pronounce a phoneme, only its allophones, there is ample evidence that speakers mentally store the phonological system of their language in terms of phonemes. It is not surprising, for example, that English spelling uses only one letter for both [l] and [ɫ], since there is only one /l/ phoneme. Generally, spelling systems ignore phonetic variation that is nondistinctive.

Another demonstration of the reality of phonological versus phonetic distinctions lies in speech perception. Speakers of English often have a hard time hearing the phonetic difference between the voiced and voiceless allophones of /l/, because the difference is not contrastive. Allophonic differences are easily ignored in perception, even though they are systematically produced in the appropriate context. Phonologically relevant distinctions, such as that between /l/ and /r/ in the English words *lift* and *rift*, are never missed. Speakers of languages other than English sometimes find it difficult to distinguish between [r] and [l] when learning English if these two sounds are not contrastive in their language. In Japanese, for example, [l] and [r] are allophones of the same phoneme. It is not surprising that speakers of Japanese sometimes have difficulty making this distinction in English.

Phonemes and Natural Classes

Phonological analysis permits us to account for the great amount of phonetic variation in everyday speech. This systematic variation is widely extended within languages. Compare the English data in Table 3.10 with those in Table 3.8. The data show that the allophones of English /r/ pattern like those of

Table 3.10   Voiced and voiceless allophones of English /r/

	A		B
brew	[bruw]	prow	[pr̥aw]
green	[griyn]	trip	[tr̥ɪp]
drip	[drɪp]	creep	[kr̥iyp]
frog	[frɑg]	pray	[pr̥ey]
shrimp	[šrɪmp]		

English /l/. On the basis of this information, we can state that there is an /r/ phoneme in English with two allophones—one voiced, the other voiceless. But if we were to stop there, we would overlook an important point. The phonemes /r/ and /l/ belong to the same natural class of sounds: both are *liquids*. By taking this information into account, we can state a general fact about English.

   3. In English, liquids show voiceless allophones after voiceless stops and voiced allophones elsewhere.

A major goal of phonological description is the formulation of the most general statements possible. Reference to natural classes helps to accomplish this. Natural classes reflect the kind of phonological generalizations we can make about language. Additional data from English illustrate this point. The forms in Table 3.11 demonstrate that the contrasting glides /y/ and /w/ each

Table 3.11   Voiced and voiceless allophones of English glides

	A		B
beauty	[byuwDiy]	putrid	[pyuwtrɪd]
Duane	[dweyn]	twin	[tw̥ɪn]
Gwen	[gwɛn]	quick	[kw̥ɪk]
view	[vyuw]	cute	[kyuwt]
swim	[swɪm]		
thwack	[θwæk]		

pattern like the liquids. We can now extend the general statement even further.

> *4.* In English, liquids and glides show voiceless allophones after voiceless stops, voiced allophones elsewhere.

Clearly, phonemes and their allophones do not pattern piecemeal, but rather according to their membership in natural classes. In terms of the features that were introduced in Chapter 2, the liquids and glides form a natural class that can be expressed by the features [− syllabic, + sonorant, − nasal].

Nasal Vowels

The data in Table 3.12 provide a second illustration of allophonic variation in English. These examples contain both oral and nasal vowels. The nasal vowels each occur before (but not after) a nasal consonant. Furthermore,

Table 3.12 Oral and nasal vowels in English

bat	[bæt]	ban	[bãn]
sick	[sɪk]	sink	[sĩŋk]
fake	[feyk]	fame	[fẽỹm]
mat	[mæt]	Mack	[mæk]
new	[nuw] or	neat	[niyt]
	[nyuw]	maze	[meyz]

there are no minimal pairs in English that have contrasting oral and nasal vowels. Taken together, this evidence shows that each nasal vowel is an allophone of a vowel phoneme with an oral and a nasal vowel. Figure 3.4 presents this in diagram form. Only three vowels are given as examples, but

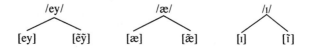

Figure 3.4 Oral and nasal allophones of some English vowels

the same relationship between oral and nasal vowels holds for all English vowels. Because of this, we can tentatively make the following statement.

> *5.* Vowels are nasal in English when they are followed by a nasal consonant.

Vowel Raising

A final example of allophonic variation is taken from English. In most Canadian and some American dialects, you can hear low and central vowel allophones. In Table 3.13, the vowels [ay] and [ʌy] are in complementary distribution. The [ay] occurs before voiced consonants or in word-final position, and the [ʌy] occurs before voiceless consonants. As shown in Figure

Table 3.13 Low and central vowel allophones in raising dialects

[ayz]	eyes	[ʌys]	ice
[layz]	lies	[lʌys]	lice
[trayd]	tried	[trʌyt]	trite
[trayb]	tribe	[trʌyp]	tripe
[hawz]	house (Verb)	[hʌws]	house (Noun)
[lawd]	loud	[lʌwt]	lout
[kaw]	cow	[skʌwt]	scout
[flay]	fly	[flʌyt]	flight

3.5, the two are allophones of a single phoneme /ay/. The same relationship holds between the vowels [aw] and [ʌw], which are allophones of /aw/. Again, we see this phonological fact reflected in everyday language use.

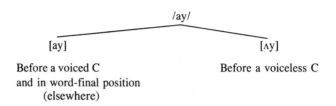

Figure 3.5 Allophones of /ay/ in raising dialects

Most speakers of raising dialects find it difficult to distinguish between these allophones, even when the difference is pointed out to them. This is because the difference is not contrastive. On the other hand, many people who speak varieties of English that do not have these allophones are very much aware of the distinction. To them, a Canadian speaker sounds markedly different, even though they may be confused about the nature of the difference.

> I don't agree he was an American. . . . Where all other English-speaking people pronounce OU as a diphthong, the Canadian . . . makes a separate sound for each letter. The word *about*, for instance, he pronounces as ab-oh-oot.
>
> Philip MacDonald, *The List of Adrian Messenger*

This phenomenon is sometimes referred to as Canadian raising, since the allophone [ʌy] has a higher vowel component than the elsewhere [ay].

Language-Specific Patterns

As with phonotactic constraints, the patterning of phonemes and allophones is language-specific. What we discover for one language may not hold true for another. It is not unusual for nasal vowel allophones to occur near a nasal consonant, but, as Table 3.14 shows, the patterning may vary from

Table 3.14 Nasal vowels in Scots Gaelic

[mõːr]	'big'
[nĩː]	'cattle'
[nẽːl]	'cloud'
[mũ]	'about'
[rũːn]	'secret'

language to language. Scots Gaelic has oral and nasal vowel allophones, but the general pattern here is different from that of English. Here we can state:

6. Vowels are nasal in Scots Gaelic when preceded or followed by a nasal consonant.

Malay, a language spoken in Malaysia and Singapore, presents another variation on the theme of nasal allophones. In Table 3.15, all vowels and glides

Table 3.15 Nasalization in Malay

[mẽw̃ãh]	'luxurious'
[mãỹãŋ]	'stalk'
[mãrah]	'scold'
[nãɛ̃ʔ]	'ascend'
[mə̃laraŋ]	'forbid'
[mãkan]	'eat'
[rumãh]	'house'
[kəreta]	'car'

following a nasal are predictably nasalized until an obstruent, liquid, or [h] is reached. For Malay the generalization is:

7. All vowels and glides following a nasal consonant and not separated from it by a nonnasal consonant are nasalized.

As was shown on page 59, a phonemic contrast in one language may not prove to be a phonemic contrast in another. This means that the relationship of phonemes to allophones may vary. A comparison of the contrasts among stops in English and Khmer (Cambodian), given in Table 3.16, illustrates this point. In both languages, aspirated and unaspirated phones can

Table 3.16 Stop phones in English and Khmer

English		Khmer	
[p]	[pʰ]	[p]	[pʰ]
[t]	[tʰ]	[t]	[tʰ]
[k]	[kʰ]	[k]	[kʰ]

be heard. In English, aspirated and unaspirated stops are allophonic; there are no contrasting forms like [pɪk] and [pʰɪk]. In Khmer, unaspirated and aspirated voiceless stops contrast, as shown in Table 3.17. The phonological contrasts of the two languages are different, even though the phones are not

Table 3.17 Khmer contrastive voiceless stops

[pa:]	'father'	[pʰa:]	'silk cloth'
[tu:]	'chest'	[tʰu:]	'relaxed'
[kae]	'to repair'	[kʰae]	'month'

(see Figure 3.6). These distributions are the same for the other voiceless stops in both languages. ("Syllabic Phonology" on page 73 deals with the distribution of the English voiceless stop allophones.)

	English		Khmer	
Phonemes		/p/	/p/	/pʰ/
Allophones	[p]	[pʰ]	[p]	[pʰ]

Figure 3.6 English and Khmer voiceless stop phonemes and allophones

Free Variation

Minimal pairs or near-minimal pairs help us establish which sounds contrast in a language; phonetic similarity and complementary distribution help us decide which sounds are allophones of one phoneme. But not all examples of variation among sounds can be dealt with through these approaches.

In some cases, phonetically similar sounds are neither in complementary distribution nor are they found to contrast. It is possible, nevertheless, to determine which phonemes these sounds belong to. A case in point is the variation in English voiceless stops when they are found in word-final position, as in the word *stop*. Sometimes, an English speaker releases the articulation of these sounds rather forcefully. Let us represent this with a diacritic sign [!]. At other times, the same speaker may keep the articulators closed for a moment after the articulation; the diacritic [-] can represent this. Some speakers may even coarticulate a glottal stop and produce the word as [stɑpʔ]. Thus, we can find at least three pronunciations of *stop*: [stɑp!], [stɑp-], and [stɑpʔ]. Since there is no difference in the meaning of these forms and since the final consonants are phonetically similar, we say that these three sounds are in **free variation**, and that they are all allophones of the phoneme /p/. The same pattern holds for the other voiceless stops of English.

3.4 PHONETIC AND PHONOLOGICAL TRANSCRIPTION

Having seen how nondistinctive properties of segments are factored out by phonological analysis, we can now compare the type of transcription used for phonological representation with phonetic transcription. Table 3.18 shows this difference for the classes of sounds in English that we have examined thus far. In the phonological transcription, voicelessness in liquids and glides and nasality in vowels are not indicated, since these properties

Table 3.18 Phonetic and phonological transcription

Phonetic transcription	Phonological transcription	
[pl̥aw]	/plaw/	plow
[kr̥iyp]	/kriyp/	creep
[kw̥ɪk]	/kwɪk/	quick
[bæ̃n]	/bæn/	ban
[pl̥ʌ̃m]	/plʌm/	plum
[tʰãỹm]	/taym/	time
[tʰʌyt]	/tayt/	tight
[tʰa:yd]	/tayd/	tied

are predictable. ("Syllabic Phonology" shows that aspiration is also an allophonic property of English voiceless stops.)

As Table 3.19 shows, the contrast between phonetic and phonological representation is even more striking for the Malay forms given earlier in Table 3.15. Here, nasalization of all vowel and glide segments is predictable and is therefore omitted from the phonological representation.

Table 3.19 Phonetic and phonological transcription of Malay nasal vowels

Phonetic transcription	Phonological transcription	
[mẽw̃ãh]	/mewah/	'luxurious'
[mãỹãŋ]	/mayaŋ/	'stalk'
[nãɛ̃ʔ]	/naɛʔ/	'ascend'

Although phonetic and phonological transcription commonly employ segments, segmental notation is itself a kind of shorthand (as pointed out in Chapter 2). Segments are composed of features—in phonological as well as phonetic representation. The next section takes up this aspect of phonology.

3.5 FEATURES AND TONES

Allophonic variation is represented as adjustments made in specific contexts to the features that make up segments. To see how this is done, we first examine the role of features in phonology.

The Role of Features

Since segments are composed of features, phonemic contrasts can be stated in a general way in terms of features. Each of these features is phonetically based and is independently controllable by the speaker. Table 3.3 showed that /p/ and /b/ contrast in English. Table 3.20 breaks these segments down into features. The only contrast between these segments resides in the feature [voice]. In phonological terms, we say that voicing is a **distinctive feature** of English.

Table 3.20 Feature representation of a contrast

p	b
+ consonantal	+ consonantal
− syllabic	− syllabic
− sonorant	− sonorant
+ anterior	+ anterior
− coronal	− coronal
− continuant	− continuant
− voice	+ voice

It is now a short step to note that the set of contrasts involving the otherwise identical pairs /p/ and /b/, /t/ and /d/, /k/ and /g/, /s/ and /z/, /š/ and /ž/, and /č/ and /ǰ/ are all manifestations of a single distinction involving the feature [voice]. The use of features enables us to make the simple statement that in English voicing is phonemic (contrastive), as shown in Table 3.21.

Table 3.21 Voiced-voiceless contrasts as a feature

p [− voice]	b [+ voice]
t	d
k	g
s	z
š	ž
č	ǰ

We can also represent the phonemic contrast between /t/ and /s/ in English with a single feature. In this case, the relevant difference is one of continuancy. Both /t/ and /s/ are voiceless and have an alveolar point of articulation. The fact that the tongue tip is used in the production of one sound and the tongue blade is used in the other is not relevant to any phonological distinction, and can therefore be ignored. The relevant distinctive feature is [continuant]. The same feature can be used to distinguish between /p/ and /f/, /b/ and /v/, and /d/ and /z/, as in Table 3.22. By systematically examining the phonemic contrasts of a language, we can extract the phonologically distinctive features and state the phonemic inventory in terms of these irreducible linguistic elements. Allophonic features such as aspiration and nasalization in English are those which are predictable and not part of the phonemic representation.

Table 3.22 Stop-fricative contrasts as a feature

p [− continuant]	f [+ continuant]
b	v
t	s
d	z

While feature representation may at first look more complex and clumsy than strictly segmental representation, it is in the long run very advantageous. Most allophonic variation can now be represented as the addition, loss, or change of a few features. The influence of the conditioning environment is also made more obvious with this type of representation, as shown in Section 3.8 of this chapter.

Tones and Their Representation

Tone languages show contrastive pitch on lexical items. Examples from Sarcee such as [mí̠l] 'moth' and [mì̠l] 'sleep' illustrated this in Chapter 2. A variety of descriptive notations have been developed to represent tone. One approach is to represent it on a separate level or **tier** of phonological description. Lines called **association lines** then link the tone to the appropriate vowel. A representation of the word *tunko* 'sheep' from Duwai, a language spoken in West Africa, is given in Figure 3.7. This type of representation

```
L H
| |
tunko
```

Figure 3.7   Representing tone

has the advantage of being able to show explicitly certain facts about tone languages. Tonal phenomena in Mende, another language spoken in West Africa, illustrate this. In Mende, there are certain polysyllabic forms that show the same tone on each syllable (in Table 3.23, the diacritic ´ indicates a high tone and the diacritic ` indicates a low tone). This type of notation

Table 3.23   High-tone and low-tone words in Mende

pélέ	'banana'
háwámá	'waistline'
kp̀akàlì	'tripod chair'

allows us to represent the tone as characteristic of an entire form (see Figure 3.8). The single underlying tone unit is associated with all vowels. Tones, like other phonological phenomena, are subject to conditioned variation. A

Figure 3.8   Tone as a word feature

good example of this comes from Duwai. In Duwai, many words show the tonal pattern LH (see Figure 3.9). When a word with an LH tonal pattern

```
L H                              L H
| |                              | |
kəvus      'warthog'             məri       'beard'


L  H                             L H
Λ  Λ                             | |
uudau      'mush'                tunko      'sheep'
```

Figure 3.9   Low-high tonal patterns in Duwai

is followed by a word with an L tone, the H tone of the first word becomes L (see Figure 3.10). This tonal change is a kind of assimilation, and parallels common processes of assimilation of segmental features. Here, it is tones, not segmental features, that are assimilating.

```
L  L   L                        L L  L
|  |   Λ                        | |  Λ
kəvus  bai  'it's not a warthog'   məri  bai  'it's not a beard'

L  L   L                        L  L   L
Λ  Λ   Λ                        |  |   Λ
uudau  bai  'it's not mush'        tunko  bai  'it's not sheep'
```

Figure 3.10 Tone assimilation in Duwai

*3.6 ABOVE THE SEGMENT: SYLLABLES

We now have established a segmental unit of phonological analysis called the phoneme. The examples of allophonic variation used thus far all result from conditioning by neighboring segments. The examples of allophonic variation in this section depend on conditioning that involves another level of phonological representation, the **syllable**.

Defining the Syllable

The syllable is made up of a syllabic nucleus, which is usually a vowel, and its associated nonsyllabic segments. Native speakers of a language demonstrate their awareness of this unit of phonological structure whenever they count syllables in a word. No English speaker would hesitate to say that the word *accident* has three syllables, and most speakers would feel confident that it could be broken up into the syllables /æk . sə . dənt/. One of the many interesting things about this awareness is the way in which it interacts with phonotactics. Speakers do not syllabify words in a way that violates the phonotactic constraints of their language. The word *extreme* /ɛkstriym/ would never be syllabified as /ɛ . kstriym/. Instead, syllabification complies with the phonotactic constraint presented in Figure 3.2 that prohibits English words from beginning with a sequence like *kstr* and results in the division /ɛk. striym/. In other words, three-consonant sequences follow the pattern outlined in Figure 3.2 not just in *word-initial* position but in *syllable-initial* position in English. You might wonder what prevents the forms in Table 3.24 from being syllabified as /ɛks.triym/, /əp.lɔd/, /diyk.layn/, /ɛks.pleyn/,

Table 3.24 Syllable-initial sequences in English

/ə . plɔd/	applaud
/diy . klayn/	decline
/ɛk . spleyn/	explain
/ɪm . prə . vayz/	improvise

and /ɪmp.rəv.ayz/, since these divisions do not violate any phonotactic constraints either. The next section outlines a procedure for establishing the association of consonants and vowels in syllables that provides an answer to this question.

Setting up Syllables

Each language defines its own syllable structure, although there are some general principles that interact with language-specific factors. The process for setting up syllables in a given language involves the following steps (see Figures 3.11–3.14).

Step a Each syllabic segment (usually a vowel) makes up a syllabic nucleus. To represent this, link a vowel to an N above it by drawing an association line, and then to a σ symbol above the N by drawing another association line.

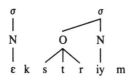

Figure 3.11

Step b The longest sequence of consonants to the left of each nucleus that does not violate the phonotactic constraints of the language in question is called the **onset** of the syllable. Link these consonants to an O and join it to the same syllable as the vowel to the right. Note that there is no onset in the first syllable of *extreme*.

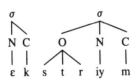

Figure 3.12

Step c Any remaining consonants to the right of each nucleus are called the **coda** and are linked to a C above them. This C is associated with the syllabic nucleus to its left.

σ σ
N C O N C
| | ∧ | |
ɛ k s t r iy m

Figure 3.13

Step d Syllables that make up a single form (usually a word) branch out from the symbol μ. Given this procedure, it is clear why words such as *applaud* and *explain* in Table 3.24 are syllabified the way they are. The permissible consonant clusters make up the onset of the second syllable, and not the coda of the first syllable.

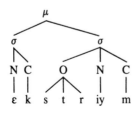

Figure 3.14

This procedure is used to syllabify forms in any language. A straight-forward example from Japanese demonstrates in more detail how this universal syllabification procedure works. In Japanese, syllables are always composed of an optional consonant followed by a vowel; the vowel nucleus may be followed by a nasal consonant (here represented as N, and not to be confused with the abbreviation for the syllabic nucleus). This is represented as follows (the parentheses indicate optionality):

8. Japanese syllable structure: (C) V (N)

The words in Figure 3.15 can be syllabified in the steps given earlier (Steps c and d have been collapsed here).

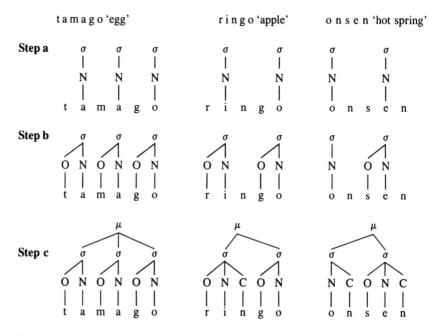

Figure 3.15 Syllabification in Japanese

Applying the same procedure to syllabify English words will yield different results because of the language-specific differences in phonotactic constraints. Figure 3.16 demonstrates the syllabification of the English words *slim, decline,* and *scratch.* With this method in mind, we can now consider the relevance of syllables to phonological description.

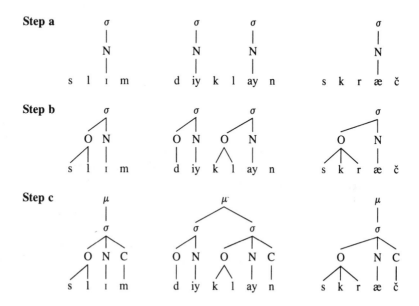

Figure 3.16 Syllabification in English

Syllabic Phonology

Syllables are considered units of phonological structure because they are relevant to stating generalizations about the distribution of allophonic features. The following data from English show the relevance of the syllabic level to phonological analysis. As Table 3.25 shows, the voiceless stops of English each have an aspirated and an unaspirated allophone. The distri-

Table 3.25 English aspiration

[pʰǽn]	pan	[spǽn]	span
[pʰéyn]	pain	[spéyn]	Spain
[pʰówk]	poke	[spówk]	spoke
[tʰówn]	tone	[stówn]	stone
[kʰɪn]	kin	[skín]	skin
[pʰʌt]	putt	[ʌ́pər]	upper
[əpʰán]	upon	[əpsét]	upset

bution of the feature [aspiration] can be stated generally by referring to syllable structure (see Table 3.26). The phonemic representations of the three English stops are unaspirated, since aspiration is a predictable feature. The

Table 3.26 Distribution of aspirated stops in English

Aspirated stops	Unaspirated stops
• Syllable-initial before a stressed vowel	Elsewhere: • Before a stressed vowel preceded by *s* • Before an unstressed vowel • Before a consonant

environments where aspiration occurs can be stated very generally by referring to syllable structure.

>   9. English voiceless stops are aspirated syllable-initially before a
>   stressed vowel.

This statement accounts for all the data in the left-hand column of Table 3.25, where voiceless stops appear syllable-initially before stressed vowels. No aspiration is found in the forms in the right-hand column since the voiceless stops appear either as the second member of the syllable onset (in *span, Spain, spoke, stone,* and *skin*) or syllable-initially but before an unstressed vowel, as in *upper*; or in a coda, as in *upset*.

English Long and Short Vowels English offers a second example of the phonological relevance of syllables. Length is a predictable feature of English tense vowels, as the examples in Table 3.27 show. (Since lax vowels show

Table 3.27 Long and short vowels in English

Long vowels		Short vowels	
bad	[bæ:d]	bat	[bæt]
Abe	[e:yb]	ape	[eyp]
phase	[fe:yz]	face	[feys]
leave	[li:yv]	leaf	[liyf]
tag	[tʰæ:g]	tack	[tʰæk]
brogue	[bro:wg]	broke	[browk]
		tame	[tʰẽỹm]
		meal	[miyl]
		soar	[sɔr]
		show	[šow]

less obvious length, only one is included in the examples. Stress is not indicated since it is irrelevant here.) English vowels show short allophones before voiceless consonants, before sonorant consonants, and in word-final position; they show long allophones before voiced nonsonorant consonants. As the examples in Table 3.28 show, this distribution is determined by syllable structure. The first-syllable vowels all precede voiced, nonsonorant consonants, but they are short since the voiced consonant is in the following syllable. In order for an English vowel to be long, it must be followed by a voiced consonant in the same syllable. The following generalization can now be made.

Table 3.28 Short vowels before voiced consonants in English

obey	[owbey]
redo	[riyduw]
regard	[riygard]
able	[eybl̩]
ogre	[owgər]

> *10.* English vowels are long when followed by a voiced nonsonorant (obstruent) consonant in the same syllable.

The use of syllabic representations in phonology often allows us to make more general statements about allophonic patterns in language than if we use only statements that do not make reference to syllable structure.

In the next section we turn our attention to the way in which statements of phonological patterning and distribution are formalized.

*3.7 DERIVATIONS AND RULES

Up to this point, we have established the existence of three units of phonological structure: the feature, the phoneme, and the syllable. We have also seen how general statements can be made that account for the presence of noncontrastive features. These statements make reference to conditioning by natural classes of sounds and sometimes by syllable structure. Current linguistics goes beyond making general statements in words about the distribution of predictable features. Specifically, it provides a way to link phonological and phonetic representations in a more formal manner.

The relationship between phonological and phonetic representation is formalized by assuming that the unpredictable features of the phonemic segment are basic or **underlying**. For our purposes, the terms *phonemic* and *underlying* mean the same thing. Phonetic forms are then **derived** by the use of **phonological rules**. Phonological rules are formalized versions of the general statements about the distribution of noncontrastive properties you were introduced to in Section 3.3. Rules derive phonetic representations (PRs), which are in phonetic transcription, from underlying representations (URs), which are in phonological transcription. In spite of the fact that underlying and derived representations are written as segments, all segments are understood to be composed of features.

Derivations

Phonetic forms are derived by setting up the underlying form and then allowing the rule or rules in question to operate where they are relevant. The derivation of three phonetic representations from underlying forms is shown in the diagram presented in Figure 3.17. Here, the underlying (phonemic)

UR	# bluw # blue	# pleyt # plate	# krawd # crowd
LGD	---	# pl̥eyt #	# kr̥awd #
V-length	---	---	# kr̥a:wd #
PR	[bluw]	[pl̥eyt]	[kr̥a:wd]

Figure 3.17 Three derivations

representation is on the top line; reading downward, each rule applies, and the underlying representation is adjusted as required. Where a rule fails to apply, the form remains unchanged; this information is conveyed by dashes. The resulting output then serves as the input to the following rule. In this example, two rules are applied. The first accounts for the voiceless allophones of liquids and glides, and the second for the long vowels. Here, LGD stands for liquid-glide devoicing, and V-length for vowel lengthening.

The Form and Notation of Rules

General statements about allophonic distribution are formalized as rules. Rules take the following form.

11. $A \rightarrow B / X \underline{\quad\quad} Y$

In this notation, *A* stands for the underlying representation, *B* for the change it undergoes, and *X* and *Y* for the conditioning environment. Either *X* or *Y* may be absent (null) if the conditioning environment is found only on one side of the allophone. The _____ (focus bar) indicates the segment undergoing the rule. The slash separates the statement of the change from the statement of the conditioning environment. This rule is read as *A becomes B between X and Y*. When this formalism is employed to state the liquid-glide devoicing rule of English, the result is as shown in Figure 3.18. This rule is read as follows:

12. Liquids and glides become voiceless after voiceless stops.

Certain abbreviations are commonly used in stating rules. A capital *C* (shown in Figure 3.18) represents the features [− syllabic, + consonantal];

$$\begin{bmatrix} - \text{ syllabic} \\ + \text{ sonorant} \\ - \text{ nasal} \end{bmatrix} \rightarrow [-\text{voice}] \ / \ \begin{matrix} C \\ \begin{bmatrix} - \text{ continuant} \\ - \text{ voice} \end{bmatrix} \end{matrix} \ \underline{\quad\quad\quad}$$

Figure 3.18 Liquid-glide devoicing in English

a capital *V* represents [+ syllabic, − consonantal] sounds—the vowels. Since these classes are frequently referred to in rules, the abbreviations save repetitious writing of features. Any other features needed to represent a given consonant or vowel are written under the *C* or *V* symbol. The rule of vowel lengthening in English makes reference to syllable structure.

13. English vowels are long when followed by a voiced nonsonorant consonant in the same syllable.

Stated in Figure 3.19 as a rule, an underlying short vowel is lengthened in the appropriate context. Note here that the onset of the syllable is irrelevant to the statement of the rule and so is not included in the formalization.

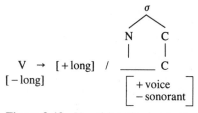

V → [+long] / _____ C
[−long]

Figure 3.19   Vowel lengthening in English

Rule and feature notation formally represents the fact that allophones have their origin in phonetic processes that arise in the course of speech. For example, the devoicing of liquids and glides in English is a typical process of assimilation. Rule notation shows explicitly how this change of [+ voice] to [− voice] occurs in a specific class of sounds following a class of sounds that is [− voice].

Features, Segments, and Syllables

The phonological units we have examined are related to each other by rules that act with reference to features, segments, or syllables. Clearly, the hierarchy of phonological structure is a dynamic one. The phonology of language is a set of processes that act on an inventory of features, segments, and syllables. In the next section, we will see in more detail how the rules that represent these processes are formulated.

*3.8   REPRESENTING PROCESSES

Chapter 2 outlined a number of processes that operate on features, segments, and syllables. In this section you will see how these processes are represented by phonological rules and derivations.

Assimilation

The processes collectively known as **assimilation** (see Chapter 2, Section 2.10) result in the changing of features due to the influence of nearby segments. Assimilation always results in a feature or features from one segment being adjusted to conform with a feature or features from a neighboring segment. Assimilation rules specify explicitly the manner in which articulations influence neighboring segments.

In the preceding section, we saw how to write the phonological rule of English that lengthens vowels when they are followed by a voiced obstruent in the same syllable. The rule of vowel nasalization in English is also a syllabic one. It states that a vowel nasalizes when it is followed by a nasal consonant in the same syllable. (For some speakers, the vowel must also be stressed.) The word *banker*, for example, is pronounced [bǽŋkər]. The rule for this regressive nasalization in English is stated in Figure 3.20. The progressive nasalization of vowels in Malay shown in Table 3.15 and stated in 7 can also be expressed by a rule. In Malay, vowels and glides that follow

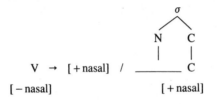

$$V \rightarrow [+\text{nasal}] \quad / \quad \underline{\hspace{2cm}} \quad C$$
$$[-\text{nasal}] \qquad\qquad\qquad\qquad [+\text{nasal}]$$

Figure 3.20 Vowel nasalization in English

a nasal segment are nasal. A nonnasal consonant breaks this string of nasal segments. To express this as a rule, we can use features to identify the class of sounds that includes vowels and glides. Since these sounds are all non-consonantal and (underlyingly) nonnasal, the features [− consonantal, − nasal] state the class (see Figure 3.21). We next look at the derivation of

$$\begin{bmatrix} -\text{consonantal} \\ -\text{nasal} \end{bmatrix} \rightarrow [+\text{nasal}] \quad / \quad [+\text{nasal}] \quad \underline{\hspace{2cm}}$$

Figure 3.21 Nasalization in Malay

the forms that undergo this rule. If we allow the rule to apply at the beginning of the form and work its way across from left to right, we see that each time a segment is nasalized, it provides the environment that allows the segment to its right to become nasalized. In this way, the rule can keep applying until there is no longer a suitable environment. (When applying a rule repeatedly to the same form, it is not necessary to write the form as many times as the rule applies. This is done in Figure 3.22 only for purposes of clarity.)

UR	# mewah # 'luxurious'	# məlaraŋ # 'forbid'
Nasalize	# mẽwah #	# mə̃laraŋ #
	# mẽw̃ah #	
	# mẽw̃ãh #	
PR	[mẽw̃ãh]	[mə̃laraŋ]

Figure 3.22 Derivation of nasalized forms in Malay

Assimilation and Alpha Notation Assimilation is often represented with a type of notation called *alpha notation*. Here, the Greek letters α,β (and any others that may be needed) are used to represent both feature values + and −. Whenever a Greek letter variable is used in a rule, it must have the same value wherever it occurs. For example, an alpha may be read as '+'. If it is, all other alphas in the same rule are to be read as '+'.

In French, consonant clusters must agree in voicing. If they do not, then the first consonant assimilates in voicing to the second. Thus, in a word like *absolu,* which was originally Latin, the *b* is pronounced as [p] because the following *s* is voiceless. If, however, the second consonant were voiced and the first voiceless, as in a cluster like *sb*, then the first would become voiced rather than voiceless, resulting in this case in [zb]. In other words, whatever the value for voicing of the second, + or −, the first must take on the same value. This generalization can be expressed easily with alpha notation, as in Figure 3.23.

$$[\text{-sonorant}] \longrightarrow [\alpha \text{ voiced}] / \underline{\hspace{1cm}} \begin{matrix} [\text{-sonorant}] \\ [\alpha \text{ voiced}] \end{matrix}$$

Figure 3.23 Alpha notation in an assimilation rule

In reading an alpha rule, the rule must be read twice, once with a plus value for the alpha, and once with a minus value. In more complex cases, other Greek letters may be used in the same way.

Deletion

The deletion of segments is a familiar phonological phenomenon, occurring in rapid speech in many languages. In English, there is a rule that (optionally) drops a schwa [ə] in syllables when it is followed by a stressed vowel, as in *police* [pl̥íys] and *parade* [pr̥é:yd]. Any number of consonants may intervene between the two vowels. The rule can be formalized as in Figure 3.24. Here, $C_\emptyset$ is an abbreviation for any number of successive consonants

$$\text{ə} \rightarrow \emptyset / \underline{\hspace{2cm}} C_\emptyset \begin{matrix} V \\ [\text{+stress}] \end{matrix}$$

Figure 3.24 Schwa deletion in English

from zero on up. The English schwa-deletion rule interacts with the constraint on possible consonant sequences. It automatically fails to apply when an impermissible sequence would result. There are no forms like *[ptʰéyDow] *potato* or *[dlíyt] *delete* (except in very, very fast speech).

Epenthesis

Epenthesis, like several of the processes we have already seen, is often sensitive to syllable structure. In Japanese, a syllable may never contain two successive consonants, nor may a syllable end in any consonant but a nasal. When any foreign words with syllable-internal consonant clusters or nonnasal final consonants are borrowed into Japanese, a new and permissible syllable shape must be created. When this syllable is created (by a rule that is not formalized here), a place is left for a syllabic nucleus (N). An epenthetic vowel (often the high back unrounded vowel [ɨ], which is spelled with *u* here) is inserted to fill this nucleus. The rule that inserts this vowel is presented in Table 3.29. This syllable-governed epenthesis is stated as a rule in Figure 3.25.

Table 3.29 Epenthesis in borrowings into Japanese

suturayku	'strike'
kurabu	'club'
nekutai	'necktie'

CHAPTER THREE

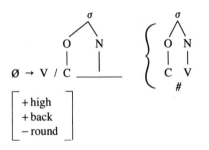

Figure 3.25 Vowel epenthesis in Japanese

Stress as a Process

Most languages exhibit stress, defined as the perceived prominence of one or more vowels over others in an utterance. Recall that stress is easily perceived in English in pairs of semantically related words such as the contrasting noun and verb pairs *présent* and *presént*, and *éxport* and *expórt*. Stress may be thought of as a process that assigns prominence to certain vowels in a word. Rules can be written to reflect its placement. A stress rule invariably begins with a formalization of the statement, 'a vowel becomes stressed' (see Figure 3.26).

V → [+stress]

Figure 3.26

The environments in which the stress rule applies are language-specific. In many languages, though, stress placement can be stated in a general way. In Finnish, the stress rule is straightforward, as the data in Table 3.30 show.

Table 3.30 Stress in Finnish

éno	'uncle'
póika	'boy'
mátala	'low'
súomalainen	'Finnish'

The Finnish stress rule stresses the first vowel of any word and is written as in Figure 3.27. In Swahili, stress invariably falls on the penultimate (next-to-last) syllable of words (see Table 3.31). The rule that stresses the penultimate vowel of any Swahili word is written as in Figure 3.28. You may assume that any monosyllabic word is also stressed. Apparently this is true in most of the world's languages.

V → [+stress] /# $C_\emptyset$ _____

Figure 3.27 Finnish stress rule

V → [+stress] / _____ $C_\emptyset V \, C_\emptyset$ #

Figure 3.28 Swahili stress rule

Table 3.31   Stress in Swahili

čúra	'toad'
čakúla	'food'
sikuzóte	'always'
ušikamáno	'adhesion'

Processes: A Last Word

Although the processes presented here are among the most common and widespread, there are other processes that occur in human language. The combined use of features and processes in phonological description reflects the dynamic nature of linguistic behavior. First, the use of features reflects a basic level of phonological activity—contrasts are taking place on the feature level, not on the level of whole segments. Secondly, the use of process notation and rule formalization reflects the realities of linguistic production, in which sounds are affected by the context in which they are pronounced.

*3.9   RULE APPLICATION

Given the use of features, rules, and processes as a means of representing phonology, another question arises: how are several rules applied to a given underlying form when these rules interact?

Free Rule Application

Recall that the English rule that aspirates stop consonants contains, as part of its environment, a stressed vowel (see page 73, "Syllabic Phonology"). It follows that a vowel stressing rule (which we will not formalize here) must apply to an underlying representation before the aspiration rule can apply. By simply allowing rules to apply until they succeed once, we can derive the correct forms of *connect* [kənɛ́kt] and *upon* [əpʰán], as in Figure 3.29. This type of application is called **free rule application**.

UR	# kənɛkt # connect	# əpɑn # upon
Aspiration	(cannot apply yet)	
Stress	# kənɛ́kt #	# əpán #
Aspiration	---	# əpʰán #
PR	[kənɛ́kt]	[əpʰán]

Figure 3.29   Free rule application in a derivation

Ordered Rule Application

There are cases in language that suggest that rule application can be more complex. In North American English, there is a rule of flapping that creates a voiced flap from underlying /t/ when the /t/ is between two vowels, the first of which is stressed. Thus, we find [hít] *hit*, but [híDər] *hitter,* and [bǽt] *bat,* but [bǽDər] *batter.* As you have seen on page 63, there is also a rule that raises the diphthong /ay/ to [ʌy] before a voiceless consonant in some dialects. (Compare the vowel of *ice* [ʌys] with that of *eyes* [a:yz], or *tight* [tʰʌyt] with *tide* [tʰa:yd], and so on.)

The flapping and raising rules interact in a very specific way. Since it creates a voiced segment, application of the flapping rule removes the context that allows the raising rule to apply (the commonly used expression is that it "bleeds" it). If we allow free rule application, the flapping rule might apply first, and the raising rule would then fail to apply, resulting in the phonetic form [ráyDər]. But in most raising dialects, the word *writer* is always pronounced [rʌyDər]. In this case, we must guarantee that the rules apply in the order *raising > flapping* in order to provide the correct output, as shown in Figure 3.30. Such rule ordering is called extrinsic ordering, since it must be set up by the analyst independently of a general principle like free rule application. The need for extrinsic rule ordering contradicts the notion that speakers simply apply the phonological rules of their language whenever possible.

UR	# raytər # writer
Stress	# ráytər #
Raising	# rʌyter #
Flapping	# rʌyDər #
PR	[rʌyDər]

Figure 3.30 Ordered rule application in a derivation

Summing Up

Phonology deals with the sequential and phonetically conditioned patterning of sounds in language. To account for this patterning, three units of phonological representation have been established—the **distinctive feature**, the **phoneme**, and the **syllable**. Phonemes are contrastive segmental units composed of distinctive features. Phonetically conditioned variants of phonemes are **allophones**.

Phonology is represented as a dynamic process that makes use of **underlying forms**, **phonological rules**, and **derivations** to formally represent allophonic variation. Sequential patterning is dealt with by rules of **phonotactics**.

The chapter also reviews the **processes** that are the basis of this patterned variation, and shows how the patterning of phonological units is based upon general principles that are applicable to the study of any human language.

Sources

A classic and still valuable presentation of phonemic analysis is found in H. A. Gleason, Jr.'s *An Introduction to Descriptive Linguistics* (New York: Holt, Rinehart and Winston, 1961). Tone data on Mende are from W. R.

Leben's "The Representation of Tone" and on Duwai from R. G. Schuh's "Tone Rules," both in *Tone: A Linguistic Survey,* edited by V. A. Fromkin (New York: Academic Press, 1978). Literature on syllabification is growing rapidly, and different analyses of syllable structure are available. One treatment can be found in J. Harris's *Syllable Structure and Stress in Spanish* (Cambridge, Mass.: MIT Press, 1983). The Malay data are adapted from Kenstowicz and Kisseberth (cited below) and additional examples are provided by S. L. Lee.

Data sources for problems are as follows: for Inuktitut, B. Harnum; for Yakut, *Grammatika Sovremennogo Jakutskogo Literaturnogo Jazyka* (Moskva: Nauka, 1982); for Mokilese, S. Harrison's *Mokilese Reference Grammar* (Honolulu: University of Hawaii Press, 1976); for Tamil, R. Radhakrishnan; for Gascon, R. C. Kelley's *A Descriptive Analysis of Gascon* (Amsterdam: Mouton, 1978); for Plains Cree, Y. Carifelle and M. Pepper.

Recommended Reading

Anderson, Stephen R. 1985. *Phonology in the Twentieth Century*. Chicago: University of Chicago Press.

Halle, Morris and G. N. Clements. 1983. *Problem Book in Phonology*. Cambridge, Mass.: MIT Press.

Hawkins, P. 1984. *Introducing Phonology*. London: Hutchinson.

Hyman, Larry M. 1975. *Phonology: Theory and Analysis*. New York: Holt, Rinehart and Winston.

Kenstowicz, Michael and Charles Kisseberth. 1979. *Generative Phonology*. New York: Academic Press.

Stampe, David. 1980. *A Dissertation on Natural Phonology*. New York: Garland.

Appendix: Hints for Solving Phonology Problems

The task of solving a phonology problem is made easier if certain facts, presented in this chapter and summarized here, are kept in mind.

1. Begin by looking for minimal pairs. These establish which segments are contrastive.
2. Allophones of a given phoneme are usually phonetically similar. Look for sounds that are phonetically similar and check to see whether they are in complementary distribution. The best way to do this is to list the environments.
3. If two potential allophones of one phoneme are in complementary distribution, you can be reasonably sure they are allophones of the same phoneme. Try to make a general statement about their distribution in terms of some natural phonological class. It may be helpful to set up a traditional phoneme-allophone diagram. (See Figure 3.3.)

4. Select one allophone as underlying. This is usually the allophone with the widest distribution (the elsewhere variant).

5. You should now be able to write a phonological rule that accounts for the predictable features of the other allophones. Your rule is probably correct if it describes a common linguistic process in terms of natural classes of sounds interacting with neighboring segments and/or syllabic structure.

You can assume that any segments are phonemic if there are no minimal pairs for them and if they cannot be shown to be allophones of a phoneme. The data simply did not provide minimal pairs.

Questions

Assume phonetic transcription of the data in all exercises.

1. English
   a) Discover the permissible word-final voiceless two-consonant sequences of English by expanding the following list.

(1) lap	[læp]	(7) lapped	[læpt]
(2) lit	[lɪt]	(8) lift	[lɪft]
(3) pack	[pʰæk]	(9) packed	[pʰækt]
(4) lapse	[læps]	(10) laughed	[læft]
(5) fits	[fɪts]	(11) fetch	[fɛč]
(6) trucks	[trʌks]	(12) fetched	[fɛčt]

   b) Are the permissible sequences the same as the word-initial ones?
   c) Formalize a general statement about the permissible voiceless word-final two-consonant sequences of English.

2. Inuktitut (Eastern) (Native Canadian)
   a) List the minimal pairs found in the following data.

(1) iglumut	'to a house'	(8) pinna	'that one up there'
(2) ukiaq	'late fall'	(9) ani	'female's brother'
(3) aiviq	'walrus'	(10) iglu	'house'
(4) aniguvit	'if you leave'	(11) panna	'that place up there'
(5) aglu	'seal's breathing hole'	(12) aivuq	'she goes home'
(6) iglumit	'from a house'	(13) ini	'place, spot'
(7) anigavit	'because you leave'	(14) ukiuq	'winter'

   b) On the basis of the list you have made, note all contrastive pairs of vowels.

3. Yakut (short vowels) (Yakut is a Turkic language spoken in northeast Siberia.)

(1)	bit	'mark'	(16) kur	'belt'
(2)	il	'peace'	(17) ol	'he'
(3)	taŋ	'to thread'	(18) büt	'end'
(4)	öl	'die'	(19) xatın	'woman'
(5)	tes	'try'	(20) uk	'insert'
(6)	sil	'saliva'	(21) tus	'directly'
(7)	köhün	'appear'	(22) kühün	'autumn'
(8)	sur	'grey'	(23) kem	'time'
(9)	ket	'dress'	(24) tıs	'paw'
(10)	ık	'wring'	(25) it	'shoot'
(11)	kim	'who'	(26) ot	'grass'
(12)	xotun	'woman'	(27) ıt	'dog'
(13)	tas	'carry'	(28) sor	'grief'
(14)	sıl	'year'	(29) toŋ	'frozen'
(15)	tüs	'descend'	(30) kir	'nibble'

a) Is there a minimal pair for each contrasting vowel?

b) What phonological phenomenon do the different forms for *woman* illustrate?

c) What phenomenon do the forms that mean *dog* and *shoot* illustrate?

d) Complete the feature matrix for the vowels of Yakut. Use only those features relevant to making phonological distinctions.

	i	e	. . .
[syllabic]			
[consonantal]			
[sonorant]			
[high]			
[low]			
[back]			
[round]			

4. English

The phoneme /g/ in English has a number of allophones. For many speakers, these allophones include *fronted g* [gʸ], articulated with the back of the tongue at or near the palate. Another is *rounded g* [gʷ], which is made with the lips rounded. Consider the distribution of both [gʸ] and [gʷ] in the following examples. Then answer the questions that follow.

(1)	[gɑt]	got	(7) [gʷu:wl]	ghoul
(2)	[ləgʷuwn]	lagoon	(8) [gʷuwf]	goof
(3)	[gluw]	glue	(9) [gʸi:yr]	gear
(4)	[tʰʌg]	tug	(10) [fyu:wg]	fugue
(5)	[gʸiys]	geese	(11) [gow]	go
(6)	[li:yg]	league	(12) [gliym]	gleam

a) State in words the distribution of each allophone.

b) Write a general statement that accounts for the distribution of the allophones.

c) Given the distribution of the allophones of /g/, which allophones of /k/ would you expect to find in forms like *cool, raccoon, keep,* and *quiche*? Why?

5. Rules

a) State the following rules in words.

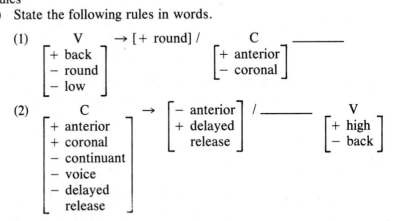

b) Write the following statements in rule and feature notation.
(1) Voiceless stops are voiced after glides, liquids, and nasals.
(2) Stress the second vowel from the beginning of a word.
(3) Word-final obstruents are voiceless.

6. Mokilese (Mokilese is an Austronesian language of the South Pacific.) Examine the following data from Mokilese carefully, taking note of where voiceless vowels occur.

(1)	pi̥san	'full of leaves'	(7)	uduk	'flesh'
(2)	dupu̥kda	'bought'	(8)	kaskas	'to throw'
(3)	pu̥ko	'basket'	(9)	poki	'to strike something'
(4)	ki̥sa	'we two'	(10)	pil	'water'
(5)	su̥pwo	'firewood'	(11)	apid	'outrigger support'
(6)	kamwɔki̥ti	'to move'	(12)	lujuk	'to tackle'

a) In Mokilese, [i̥] is derived from underlying /i/, and [u̥] is derived from underlying /u/. State in words the conditioning factors that account for this.

b) Using features, write a rule that accounts for the derived allophones.

7. Tamil (Tamil is a Dravidian language spoken in South India and Sri Lanka.) In the following Tamil data, some words begin with glides while others do not. The symbol [ɖ] represents a voiced retroflex stop and the diacritic [̪] indicates dentals.

Initial *y*-glide		Initial *w*-glide		No initial glide	
(1) yeli	'rat'	(6) woḍi	'break'	(11) arivu	'knowledge'
(2) yi:	'fly'	(7) wo:lay	'palm leaf'	(12) aiṇtu	'five'
(3) yilay	'leaf'	(8) wu:si	'needle'	(13) a:say	'desire'
(4) yeŋge:	'where'	(9) wuyir	'life'	(14) a:ru	'river'
(5) yiḍuppu	'waist'	(10) wo:ram	'edge'	(15) a:di	'origin'

a) The occurrence of these glides is predictable. Using your knowledge of natural classes, make a general statement about the distribution of the glides.

b) Assuming the glides are not present in the underlying representations, name the process that accounts for their presence in the phonetic forms.

c) Using features, write a rule using alpha notation that formalizes this process. Show the derivation of the forms for *fly* and *break*.

8. Gascon (Gascon is spoken in southwest France.)
The phones [b], [β], [d], [ð], [g], and [ɣ] are all found in Gascon, as the following examples show.

(1) bux	'you'		(11) aβe	'to have'
(2) bako	'cow'		(12) alaβets	'then, well'
(3) ūmbro	'shadow'		(13) saliβo	'saliva'
(4) breñ	'endanger'		(14) noβi	'husband'
(5) dilüs	'Monday'		(15) buðɛt	'gut'
(6) dïŋko	'until'		(16) ešaðo	'hoe'
(7) duso	'sweet'		(17) biɣar	'mosquito'
(8) gat	'cat'		(18) riɣut	'he laughed'
(9) guteža	'flow'		(19) dariɣa	'pull out'
(10) ēŋgwãn	'last'			

a) Which pairs among the phones [b], [β], [d], [ð], [g], and [ɣ] are the most phonetically similar? Support your claim with phonetic descriptions of the similar pairs.

b) List the environments in which the phones [b], [β], [d], [ð], [g], and [ɣ] are found.

c) Is there any evidence for grouping these pairs of sounds into phonemes? State the evidence for each pair.

d) Make a general statement about the patterning of the phonemes you have established.

e) Write a rule that accounts for the patterning you have discovered.

f) What are the underlying representations of the following forms?
(1) [puɣo]   (2) [deðat]   (3) [guβar]   (4) [ambud]

9. Plains Cree (Plains Cree is a Native Canadian language of the Algonquian family.)
The following data from Plains Cree show a number of different voiced and voiceless consonantal segments.

(1) niska	'goose'	(12) nisto	'three'
(2) kodak	'another'	(13) či:gahigan	'axe'
(3) asaba:p	'thread'	(14) a:dim	'dog'
(4) wasko:w	'cloud'	(15) mi:bit	'tooth'
(5) paskwa:w	'prairie'	(16) pime:	'lard'
(6) ni:gi	'my house'	(17) mide	'heart'
(7) ko:gos	'pig'	(18) o:gik	'these'
(8) tahki	'often'	(19) čihčiy	'finger'
(9) namwa:č	'not at all'	(20) wa:bos	'rabbit'
(10) ospwa:gan	'pipe'	(21) na:be:w	'man'
(11) mijihčiy	'hand'	(22) mi:jiwin	'food'

a)   Are [p] and [b] separate underlying phonemes, or can they be derived from one underlying phoneme? If you think they are separate phonemes, list data to support your case. If you think they are allophones, first state the conditioning factors in words, and then, using features, write a rule that accounts for their distribution.

b)   Do the same for [t] and [d], [k] and [g], and [č] and [ǰ].

c)   Can you make a general statement about the relationship among all the consonantal pairs whose distribution you have examined? If you can, write this statement as a rule using features.

d)   Show the complete derivation of the forms for (11) *hand,* (13) *axe,* and (15) *tooth.*

10. English
Some speakers of English have two types of [l]. One, called *clear l,* is transcribed as [l] in the following data. The other, called *dark l,* is transcribed as [ɫ]. Examine the data, and answer the questions that follow.

(1) [lʌyf]	life	(7) [pɪɫ]	pill
(2) [liyp]	leap	(8) [fiyɫ]	feel
(3) [lu:wz]	lose	(9) [hɛɫp]	help
(4) [iylowp]	elope	(10) [bʌɫk]	bulk
(5) [diylʌyt]	delight	(11) [sɔɫd]	sold
(6) [sliyp]	sleep	(12) [fʊɫ]	full

Are [l] and [ɫ] separate phonemes or allophones of the same phoneme? If you believe they are separate phonemes, answer question (a). If you believe they are allophones of the same phoneme, answer question (b).

a)   List the evidence that makes your case for considering [l] and [ɫ] as separate phonemes.

b)   State the distribution of [l] and [ɫ] in words.

c)   Which variant makes the best underlying form? Why?

d)   Can you make reference to syllable structure in your distribution statement? If you can, do so in rule form.

4 MORPHOLOGY
The Study of Word Structure

Llanfairpwllgwyngyllgogerychwyhndrobwllllantysiliogogogoch
(a town name in Wales)

How is it that we can use and understand words in our language that we have never encountered before? This is the central question of **morphology**, the component of a grammar that deals with the internal structure of words. If we are watching a television program about homelessness in American cities, for example, we may hear that many of the homeless are former mental patients who were released because of a policy of deinstitutionalization. An expert interviewed on the program may advocate reinstitutionalization as the only recourse for many of these people. Even if we have never heard these terms before, we understand quite effortlessly that they refer to the practices of releasing patients from hospitals for the mentally ill (*deinstitutionalization*) and returning them to these institutions (*reinstitutionalization*). We know this because we know what the word *institution* means, and we have an unconscious command of English morphology.

Morphology deals with the internal structure of complex words. The words of any language can be divided into two broad categories, **closed** and **open**, of which only the latter are relevant to morphology. The closed categories are the **function words**: **pronouns** like *you* and *she*; **conjunctions** like *and*, *if*, and *because*; **determiners** like *a* and *the*; and a few others. Newly coined or borrowed words cannot be added to these categories, which is why we say that they are closed. The categories of words that are open are the **major lexical categories**: **noun (N)**, **verb (V)**, **adjective (Adj)**, and **adverb (Adv)**. It is to these categories that new words may be added. Because the major problem of morphology is how people make up and understand words that they have never encountered before, morphology is concerned only with major lexical categories.

Each word that is a member of a major lexical category is called a **lexical item**. A lexical item can best be thought of as an entry in a dictionary or **lexicon**. The entry for each lexical item will include, in addition to its pronunciation (phonology), information about its meaning (semantics), to what lexical category it belongs, and in what syntactic environments it may occur (subcategorization).

As with any other area of linguistic theory, we must distinguish between general morphological theory that applies to all languages and the morphology of a particular language. General morphological theory is concerned with delimiting exactly what types of morphological rules can be found in natural languages. The morphology of a particular language, on the other hand, is a set of rules with a dual function. First, these rules are responsible for **word formation**, the formation of new words. Second, they represent the speakers' unconscious knowledge of the internal structure of the already existing words of their language.

In this chapter, we examine both word structure and word formation. We begin by identifying the minimal meaningful units of language.

4.1 THE MINIMAL MEANINGFUL UNITS OF LANGUAGE

In any science, one of the basic problems is to identify the minimal units, the basic parts out of which more complex units are constructed. Cells, molecules, atoms, particles—each is the minimal unit of some science. In language, we must distinguish the basic units of sound, which in themselves are meaningless, from the basic meaningful units, which are made up of individually meaningless sounds.

Words

Most people, if asked what the minimal meaningful units of language are, would have a ready answer—words. Indeed, of all the units of linguistic analysis, the **word** is the most familiar. In fact, its existence is taken for granted by most of us. We rarely have difficulty picking out the words in a stream of speech sounds or deciding where to leave spaces when writing a sentence. But what, precisely, is a word? A word need not have any special phonetic properties: some words bear stress but others do not; some words are set off by intonational cues but others are not. The two syllables in the following examples have exactly the same pronunciation even though they are separate words in the first case but part of the same word in the second case.

> *1.* a door   adore

It is also difficult to distinguish words from other linguistic units in terms of the types of meaning they express. *Bachelor* and *unmarried adult male*, for example, seem to have the same meaning, even though one is a word and the other a phrase. Similarly, *builder* and *someone who builds* mean about the same thing even though one is a word and the other a phrase.

Free Forms

Most linguists believe that the word is best defined in terms of the way in which it patterns syntactically. One widely accepted definition of this type is as follows:

> *2.* A word is a minimal free form.

A **free form** is an element that can occur in isolation and/or whose position with respect to neighboring elements is not entirely fixed. Thus, we would say that *hunters* is a word since it can occur in isolation (as in answer to the question, *Who are they?*) and can occur in different positions within the sentence, as *3* shows.

3. *a*) The hunters pursued the bear.
   b) The bear was pursued by the hunters.

In contrast, the units *-er* and *-s* do not count as words here since they cannot occur in isolation and their positioning with respect to adjacent elements is completely fixed. Thus, we cannot say **erhunts* or **serhunt*, only *hunters*.

The reference to *minimal* in *2* is necessary to ensure that we do not identify phrases such as *the hunters* as a single word. Although this unit can occur in isolation and can occupy different positions, it is not a minimal free form since it consists of two smaller free forms—*the* and *hunter*. (We know that *the* is a separate word because its positioning with respect to *hunters* is not entirely fixed; thus, another word can appear between the two, as in *the courageous hunters*.)

Signs and Morphemes

Words, though they may be definable as minimal free forms, are not the minimal meaningful units of language we are looking for, since they can often be broken down further. The word *hunters*, which as we have just seen can stand alone and is thus a free form, nonetheless consists of three meaningful parts: *hunt*, *er*, and *s*. The traditional term for these minimal meaningful units is **sign**. A more common term in linguistics is **morpheme**. Most linguistic signs are **arbitrary**, which means that the connection between the sound of a given sign and its meaning is purely conventional, not rooted in some property of the object for which the sign stands. For example, there is nothing about the sound of the word *frog* that has anything to do with frogs. We could just as appropriately use the word *gorf* to refer to those little green creatures, or [čiŋwa], which is the Mandarin Chinese word, or [plava], the Sanskrit word. The minimal meaningful units of language are not words, but arbitrary signs or morphemes.

4.2 MORPHOLOGY

There are two basic types of words in human language—simple and complex. **Simple** words are those that cannot be broken down into smaller meaningful units while **complex** words can be analyzed into constituent parts, each of which expresses some identifiable meaning. The word *houses*, for example, is made up of the form *house* and the plural marker *-s*, neither of which can be divided into smaller morphemes. While many English words consist of only one morpheme, others can contain two, three, or more (see Table 4.1).

Table 4.1 Words consisting of one or more morphemes

One morpheme	Two	Three	More than three
and			
boy	boy-s		
hunt	hunt-er	hunt-er-s	
hospital	hospital-ize	hospital-iz-ation	hospital-iz-ation-s
gentle	gentle-man	gentle-man-ly	gentle-man-li-ness

Identifying Morphemes and Allomorphs

A major problem for morphological analysis is how to identify the morphemes that make up words. Given our definition of the morpheme as the minimal meaning-bearing unit of language, this will involve matching strings of sounds with co-occurring features of meaning. As an example of this procedure, consider the small set of data from Turkish in Table 4.2. In Table 4.2, there is only one feature of meaning, plurality, that is present in all four cases. There is also only one string of sounds, /lar/, that is found in all four words. This suggests that /lar/ is the morpheme marking plurality in Turkish while /mum/ means 'candle', /top/ means 'gun', and so on. We would therefore predict that a single candle would be designated by the morpheme /mum/, without /lar/. This is correct.

Table 4.2 Some Turkish plurals

Turkish	
/mumlar/	'candles'
/toplar/	'guns'
/adamlar/	'men'
/kitaplar/	'books'

This is an unusually simple case, and many complications can arise. One such complication involves the fact that morphemes do not always have an invariant form. The morpheme used to express indefiniteness in English, for instance, has two forms—*a* and *an*.

4. an orange   a building
   an accent   a car
   an eel   a girl

The form *a* is used before words beginning with a consonant and the form *an* before words beginning with a vowel. The variant forms of a morpheme are called its **allomorphs**.

As another example of allomorphic variation, consider the manner in which you pronounce the plural morpheme *-s* in the following words.

5. cats
   dogs
   judges

Whereas the plural is pronounced as [s] in the first case, it is realized as [z] in the second, and as [əz] in the third. Here again, selection of the proper allomorph is dependent on phonetic facts. We will examine this phenomenon in more detail in Section 4.5.

Free and Bound Morphemes

The analysis of morphological structure is based on a number of fundamental contrasts. The first involves the distinction between a **free** morpheme, which can constitute a word by itself, and a **bound** morpheme, which must be attached to another element. The morpheme *house*, for example, is free since it can be used as a word on its own; plural *-s*, on the other hand, is bound.

The morphemes that are free or bound in English do not necessarily have the same status in other languages. For example, in Hare (an Athapaskan language spoken in Canada's Northwest Territories), words that indicate body parts are always bound to a morpheme designating a possessor. Table 4.3 shows the morphemes *fí* ('head'), *bé* ('belly'), and *dzé* ('heart'), each of which must be attached to a morpheme naming the possessor. (A high tone is marked by the diacritic ´.)

Table 4.3 Some bound forms in Hare

Hare		
sefí	'my head'	(never *fí)
nebé	'your belly'	(never *bé)
bedzé	'his heart'	(never *dzé)

Just as there are some free forms in English that are bound in other languages, so there are some bound forms in English that are free in other languages. Past tense, for example, is expressed by a bound morpheme (usually *-ed*) in English, but by the free morpheme *le* in Mandarin. (To simplify, tone is not marked in these examples.)

    6. a) Ta chi   le fan.
        He eat past meal
        'He ate the meal.'
      b) Ta chi   fan   le.
        He eat meal past
        'He ate the meal.'

As you can see from these examples, *le* is apparently not attached to the verb since it is separated from it by the direct object in *6b*.

Word Structure

Like sentences, complex words such as *builder* and *gentlemanly* have an internal structure. In this section, we will consider the categories and representations that are relevant to the analysis of word structure.

What sort of structure do complex words have? Let's look in some detail at the word *denationalization*. This word contains five morphemes: *de nation al ize ation*. *Nation* is a free morpheme, since it can stand alone as a word, while the rest are bound morphemes. But simply listing the parts of the word and whether they are free or bound does not tell us all there is to know about the structure of this word. The parts have to be put together in a particular way, with a particular arrangement and order. For example, none of these possible orders of the same five morphemes constitutes an English word:

7. *ationizalnationde
    *alizdeationnation
    *nationdeizational

In fact, of the 120 possible arrangements of these five morphemes, only one, *denationalization*, could be an English word. The order is so strict because each of the bound morphemes is an **affix**, a bound morpheme which not only must be bound, but must be bound in a particular position. Furthermore, each affix attaches only to a particular lexical category (either N or V or Adj), called its **base**, and results in a word of another particular lexical category. The negative affix *de-*, for example, attaches to verbs and forms other verbs:

8. ionize → deionize
    segregate → desegregate

Similarly, the affix *-al* forms adjectives from nouns, *-ize* forms verbs from adjectives or nouns, and *-ation* forms nouns from verbs.

Given these restrictions, the structure of the word *denationalization* can best be seen as the result of beginning with the simple free form *nation*, which we may call the **root** of the word, and adding affixes successively, one at a time, as follows:

9. nation
    national
    nationalize
    denationalize
    denationalization

The structure of the entire word may be represented by means of either a **set of labeled brackets** or a **tree diagram**. (Brackets and trees are also used to represent the structures of sentences, and are discussed more fully in

[[de[[[nation]$_N$ al]$_{Adj}$ ize]$_V$]$_V$ ation]$_N$

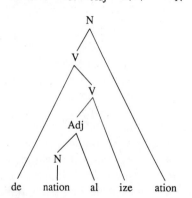

Figure 4.1

Chapter 5.) The two types of notation are for the most part interchangeable. Both are shown in Figure 4.1.

Some other representations of structures of English words are given in Figure 4.2. Such representations indicate the details of morphological structure. Where these details are irrelevant to the point being considered, it is traditional to use a much simpler system of representation that indicates only the location of the morpheme boundaries: *il-legal, hospital-ize*, and so on.

a

[[hunter]$_N$ s]$_N$

b

[[[hospital]$_N$ ize]$_V$ ed]$_V$

c

[[[hope]$_N$ less]$_{Adj}$]ness]$_N$

d

[mis[under[stand]$_V$]$_V$]$_V$

Figure 4.2

Stems A **stem** is the form to which an affix is added. In many cases, the stem will also be the root. In *books*, for example, the element to which the affix *-s* is added corresponds to the root. In other cases, however, an affix can be added to a unit larger than a root. This happens in words such as *hospitalized*, in which the past tense affix *-ed* is added to the stem *hospitalize*—a unit consisting of the root morpheme *hospital* and the suffix *-ize* (see Figure 4.3). In this case, *hospital* is not only the root for the entire word but also the stem for *-ize*. The unit *hospitalize*, on the other hand, is simply the stem for *-ed*.

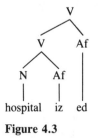

Figure 4.3

Types of Affixes It is possible to distinguish among several types of affixes in terms of their position relative to their stem. An affix that is attached to the front of its stem is called a **prefix** while an affix that is attached to the end of its stem is termed a **suffix**. Both types of affix occur in English, as Table 4.4 shows.

Table 4.4 Some English prefixes and suffixes

Prefixes	Suffixes
disappear	vividly
replay	government
illegal	hunter
inaccurate	distribution

A far less common type of affix, known as an **infix**, occurs within another morpheme. The data in Table 4.5, from the Philippine language Tagalog, contain two infixes, -*um*- and -*in*-. Often word-internal vowel or consonant replacement is confused with infixing. A change such as the one found in English *foot-feet* is not an example of infixing since there is no morpheme **ft*. As you see in Table 4.5, the form to which the Tagalog infix is added actually exists as a separate morpheme.

Table 4.5 Some Tagalog infixes

Root		Infixed form	
takbuh	'run'	tumakbuh	'ran'
lakad	'walk'	lumakad	'walked'
pili?	'choose'	pinili?	'chose'

In English, although infixing is not part of the normal morphological system, it does occur quite commonly with expletives, providing a kind of extra emphasis, as in the following examples:

10. guaran-damn-tee
       abso-bloody-lutely

Still another kind of affix varies according to the stem with which it occurs. It is called a **reduplicative** affix since its form duplicates all or part of the stem. Once again, Tagalog provides examples of this type of affixation (see Table 4.6). The reduplicative affix here is a copy of the first consonant-

Table 4.6 Some reduplicative affixes

Stem		Reduplicated form	
takbuh	'run'	tatakbuh	'will run'
lakad	'walk'	lalakad	'will walk'
pili?	'choose'	pipili?in	'will choose'

vowel sequence of the root. This is an example of **partial reduplication**. Full reduplication is the repetition of the entire word, as in the data in Table 4.7, from Turkish and Indonesian, respectively.

Table 4.7 Some examples of full reduplication

Turkish			
čabuk	'quickly'	čabuk čabuk	'very quickly'
yavaš	'slowly'	yavaš yavaš	'very slowly'
iyi	'well'	iyi iyi	'very well'
güzel	'beautifully'	güzel güzel	'very beautifully'
Indonesian			
oraŋ	'man'	oraŋ oraŋ	'all sorts of men'
anak	'child'	anak anak	'all sorts of children'
maŋga	'mango'	maŋga maŋga	'all sorts of mangoes'

Structure without Affixes When one word is formed from another, the structural relation between the two words is usually marked by means of an affix, as we have seen, but it is possible for one word to be formed from another without any affix.

Conversion, or **zero-derivation**, is probably the most frequent single method of forming words in English. It is especially common in the speech of children. Conversion creates a new word without the use of affixation by simply assigning an already existing word to a new syntactic category. In the case of the derived verbs in Table 4.8, there is no modification, whereas in the case of the derived nouns, there is a stress shift. Structurally, the derived forms remain simple in both instances even though they are new lexical items belonging to a syntactic category different from that of the source form. In the case of *father* and *butter*, for instance, the derived form is a verb capable of taking the normal past tense ending.

Table 4.8 Some examples of conversion

Noun	Derived verb	Verb	Derived noun
father	father	subjéct	súbject
butter	butter	contést	cóntest
ship	ship	survéy	súrvey
nail	nail	permít	pérmit
brush	brush	condúct	cónduct

> *11.* He fathered three children.
> He buttered the bread.

Conversion is usually restricted to unsuffixed words, although there are a few exceptions such as *propos-ition* (noun to verb), *refer-ee* (noun to verb), and *dirt-y* (adjective to verb).

Another device is **ablaut**, the replacement of a vowel with a different vowel (see Table 4.9). Ablaut was frequent in earlier stages of English and in related ancient languages. Vestiges remain in Modern English, though the process is no longer productive.

Table 4.9 Some examples of ablaut

Verb stem	Ablaut noun
sing	song
abide	abode
shoot	shot
sell	sale

Stress shift is used in English to mark the difference between related nouns and verbs. We have already seen some examples of this in Table 4.8.

Generally, the verbs have final stress, while the nouns have initial stress, as the further examples in Table 4.10 illustrate.

Table 4.10 Nouns and verbs that differ only in stress

Noun	Verb
cómbine	combíne
tórment	tormént
ímplant	implánt
rétest	retést

Nonaffixal morphology is common in other languages and may involve vocalic patterns or tone and other suprasegmental phonological features, sometimes in complex ways.

Word-Based Morphology In English, the base of a new word is almost invariably an already existing word. For this reason, we say that English morphology is **word-based**: words are built on words. As we saw in the case of the complex word *denationalization*, each affix is added successively to an English word.

There are, however, many English words whose stems, when the outer affixes are removed, are not existing English words. Consider the words *recalcitrant, horrible*, and *uncouth*. These are all English words, but when the affixes *re-, -ible*, and *un-* are removed, we are left with the stems **calcitrant, *horr*, and **couth*, which are not English words. In all three cases, the reasons for the anomaly are historical. *Recalcitrant* and *horrible* were borrowed in their entirety from Latin and French. Because the affixes *re-* and *-ible* were also borrowed, these words appear to have been formed by means of English morphology, although they were not. English has many words like these two, borrowed from the Romance languages, from which many productive English affixes have also been borrowed. Many of them have nonword stems for the same reason. *Uncouth* is not borrowed, but was formed many centuries ago from the then existing word *couth* (historically related to *can* and *know* and still found in some British dialects). Some time after *uncouth* was formed, *couth* disappeared from most dialects, including the standard, leaving *uncouth* stranded without a base. *Grateful* is another example of the same phenomenon. Words like *grateful* and *horrible* may be described as having bound stems; in any case, they can be explained as cases of historical accident. When we understand how such exceptional words arose, it remains true that all productive English word formation is word-based. Whether all languages are like English in this respect is still an open question.

Some Problematic Cases It is not always easy to determine a word's internal structure. In the case of words such as *cranberry* and *huckleberry*, it is tempting to assume that the root is *berry*, but this leaves us with the morphemes *cran-* and *huckle-*. These elements are obviously not affixes like *un-* or *re-* since they occur with only one root. At the same time, however, neither *cran-* nor *huckle-* can be considered a free morpheme since neither ever stands alone as an independent word. The status of such morphemes continues to be problematic for linguists, who generally classify them as exceptional cases (or refer to them as **cranberry morphemes**).

A slightly different problem arises in the case of words such as *receive, deceive, conceive,* and *perceive* or *remit, permit, submit,* and *commit.* The apparent affixes in these words do not express the same meaning as they do when they are attached to a free morpheme. Thus, the *re-* of *receive*, for example, does not have the sense of 'again' that it does in *redo* ('do again'). Nor does the *de-* of *deceive* appear to express the meaning 'reverse the process of' associated with the affix in *demystify* or *decertify*. Moreover, the other portions of these words (*ceive* and *mit*) have no identifiable meaning either.

Because they have no meaning, *ceive* and *mit* are not morphemes of a normal sort. However, they do have some interesting properties. For example, when certain suffixes are added to words ending in *ceive*, *ceive* quite regularly becomes *cept* (as in *receptive* and *deception*); similarly, *mit* becomes *miss* when the same suffixes are added (*permissive, admission*). These changes are not phonologically determined, since the *ss* does not occur before these suffixes in other words ending in *t* (*prohibitive, edition*). The changes must therefore be due to idiosyncratic properties of *mit* and *ceive*, similar to those of the morpheme *man*, whose plural is always *men* rather than the expected *mans* (*postmen, brakemen*, and so on). *Mit* and *ceive* are thus morphemes, although of a marginal type.

4.3 WORD FORMATION

A characteristic of all human languages is the potential to create new words. The categories of noun, verb, adjective, and adverb are open in the sense that new members are constantly being added. The two most common types of word formation are **derivation** and **compounding**, both of which create new words from already existing morphemes. Derivation is the process by which a new word is built from a base, usually through the addition of an affix. Compounding, on the other hand, is a process involving the combination of two words (with or without accompanying affixes) to yield a new word. The noun *helper*, for example, is related to the verb *help* via derivation; the compound word *mailbox*, in contrast, is created from the words *mail* and *box*.

Derivation

Derivation creates a new word by changing the category and/or the meaning of the base to which it applies. The derivational affix *-er*, for instance, combines with a verb to create a noun with the meaning 'one who does X', as shown in Figure 4.4.

Verb	Derived noun
[help]$_V$	[[help]$_V$ er]$_N$
[walk]$_V$	[[walk]$_V$ er]$_N$
[teach]$_V$	[[teach]$_V$ er]$_N$
[drive]$_V$	[[drive]$_V$ er]$_N$
[jump]$_V$	[[jump]$_V$ er]$_N$

Figure 4.4

Table 4.11 Some English derivational affixes

Affix	Change	Semantic effect	Examples
Suffixes			
-able	V → Adj	able to be X'ed	fixable
-ation	V → N	the result of X'ing	realization
-er	V → N	one who X's	worker
-ing	V → N	the act of X'ing	the shooting
	V → Adj	in the process of X'ing	the sleeping giant
-ion	V → N	the result or act of X'ing	protection
-ive	V → Adj	having the property of doing X	assertive
-ment	V → N	the act or result of X'ing	adjournment
-al	N → Adj	pertaining to X	national
-ial	N → Adj	pertaining to X	presidential
-ian	N → Adj	pertaining to X	Canadian
-ic	N → Adj	having the property of X	organic
-ize	N → V	put in X	hospitalize
-less	N → Adj	without X	penniless
-ous	N → Adj	the property of having or being X	poisonous
-ate	Adj → V	make X	activate
-ity	Adj → N	the result of being X	stupidity, priority
-ize	Adj → V	make X	modernize
-ly	Adj → Adv	in an X manner	quietly
-ness	Adj → N	the state of being X	happiness, sadness

Prefixes			
ex-	N → N	former X	ex-president
in-	Adj → Adj	not X	incompetent
un-	Adj → Adj	not X	unhappy
	V → V	reverse X	untie
re-	V → V	X again	rethink

English Derivational Affixes English makes very widespread use of derivation. Table 4.11 lists some examples of English derivational affixes, along with information about the type of base with which they combine and the type of category that results. The first entry states that the affix *-able* applies to a verb base and converts it into an adjective with the meaning 'able to be X'ed'. Thus, if we add the affix *-able* to the verb *fix*, we get an adjective with the meaning 'able to be fixed'.

Derivational Rules Each line in Table 4.11 can be thought of as a word formation rule that predicts how words may be formed in English. Thus, if there is a rule whereby the prefix *un-* may be added to an adjective *X*, resulting in another adjective, *unX*, with the meaning 'not X', then we predict that an adjective like *harmonious* may be combined with this prefix to form the adjective *unharmonious*, which will mean 'not harmonious'. The rule also provides a structure to the word, given in Figure 4.5.

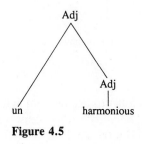

Figure 4.5

These rules have another function: they may be used to analyze words as well as to form them. Suppose, for example, that we come across the word *unharmonious* in a book on architecture. Even though we may never have encountered this word before, we will probably not notice its novelty, but simply use our unconscious knowledge of English word formation to process its meaning. In fact, many of the words that we encounter in reading, especially in technical literature, are novel, but we seldom have to look them up, relying instead on our morphological competence.

Multiple Derivations Derivation can create multiple levels of word structure, as shown in Figure 4.6. Although complex, *organizational* has a structure

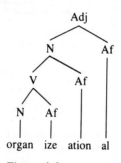

Figure 4.6

consistent with the word formation rules given in Table 4.11. Starting with the outermost affix, we see that -*al* forms adjectives from nouns, -*ation* forms nouns from verbs, and -*ize* forms verbs from nouns.

In some cases, the internal structure of a complex word is not obvious. The word *unhappiness*, for instance, could apparently be analyzed in either of the ways indicated in Figure 4.7. By considering the properties of the affixes *un-* and -*ness*, however, it is possible to find an argument that favors Figure 4.7a over 4.7b. The key observation here is that the prefix *un-* com-

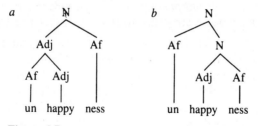

Figure 4.7

bines quite freely with adjectives, but not with nouns as shown in Table 4.12. (The advertiser's *uncola* is an exception to this rule and therefore attracts the attention of the reader or listener.) This suggests that *un-* must combine with the adjective *happy* before it is converted into a noun by the

Table 4.12 Distribution of *un-*

un + Adj	un + N
unable	*unknowledge
unkind	*unintelligence
unhurt	*uninjury

suffix -*ness*—exactly what the structure in Figure 4.7a depicts. The derivation of this word therefore proceeds in two steps. First, the prefix *un-* is attached to the adjective *happy*, resulting in another adjective (see Figure 4.8). The second step is to add the suffix -*ness* to this adjective (see Figure

4.9). We see, then, that complex words have structures consisting of hierarchically organized constituents arranged in accordance with explicit rules. The same is true of sentences, as we will see in the next chapter.

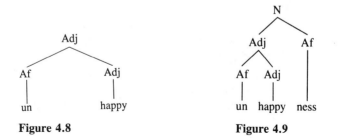

Figure 4.8   Figure 4.9

Compounding

In derivational word formation, we take a single word, the base of a word formation rule, and change it somehow, usually by adding an affix, to form a new word. The other way to form a new word is by combining two already existing words in a **compound**. *Blackbird, doghouse, seaworthy*, and *bluegreen* are examples of compounds.

Compounding is highly productive in English and in related languages such as German. It is also widespread throughout the languages of the world. In English, compounds can be found in all the major lexical categories—nouns (*doorstop*), adjectives (*winedark*), and verbs (*stagemanage*)—but nouns are by far the most common type of compounds. Verb compounds are quite infrequent. Among noun compounds, most are of the form noun + noun (N N), but Adj N compounds are also found quite frequently; V N compounds are rare. An example of each type is given in Figure 4.10. Compound adjectives are of the type Adj Adj or N Adj, as shown in Figure 4.11.

Although there are very few true compound verbs in English, this does not seem to be due to any general principles. In other languages, compound verbs are quite common.

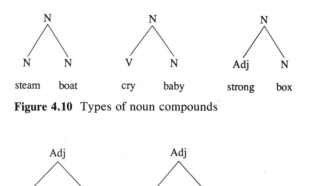

Figure 4.10 Types of noun compounds

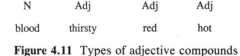

Figure 4.11 Types of adjective compounds

Structurally, two features of compounds stand out. One is the fact that the constituent members of a compound are not equal. In all the examples given thus far, the lexical category of the last member of the compound is the same as that of the entire compound. Furthermore, the first member is always a modifier of the second: steamboat is a type of boat; red-hot is a degree of hotness. In other words, the second member acts as the **head** of the compound, from which most of the syntactic properties of the compound are derived, while the first member is its **dependent**. This is generally true in English and in many other languages, although there are also languages in which the first member of a compound is the head.

The second structural peculiarity of compounds, which is true of all languages of the world, is that a compound never has more than two constituents. This is not to say that a compound may never contain more than two words. Three-word (*dog food box*), four-word (*stone age cave dweller*), and longer compounds (*trade union delegate assembly leader*) are easy to find. But in each case, the entire compound always consists of two components, each of which may itself be a compound, as shown in Figure 4.12. The basic compounding operation is therefore always binary, although repetition of the basic operation may result in more complex individual forms.

Compounding and derivation may also feed each other. The members of a compound are often themselves derivationally complex, and sometimes, though not often, a compound may serve as the base of a derivational affix. An example of each of these situations is given in Figure 4.13.

English orthography is not consistent in representing compounds since they are sometimes written as single words, sometimes with an intervening hyphen, and sometimes as separate words. However, it is usually possible to recognize noun compounds by their stress pattern since the first com-

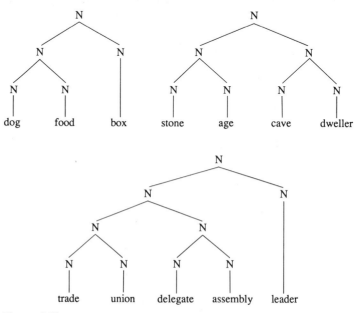

Figure 4.12

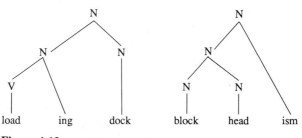

Figure 4.13

ponent is pronounced more prominently than the second. In noncompounds, conversely, the second element is stressed (see Table 4.13).

Although the exact types of compounds differ from language to language, the practice of combining two existing words to create a new word is very widespread, as Table 4.14 indicates.

Table 4.13 Compounds versus noncompounds

Compound word		Non-compound expressions	
greénhoùse	an indoor garden	greèn hoúse	a house painted green
bláckboàrd	a chalkboard used in classrooms	blàck boárd	a board that is black
wét sùit	a diver's costume	wèt suít	a suit that is wet

Table 4.14 Compounds from various languages

Mandarin		
tian-liang	tou-teng	di-zhen
day brightens	head aches	earth quakes
'dawn'	'headache'	'earthquake'
French		
un timbre-poste	une grand'mère	un coffre-fort
a stamp mail	a great mother	a box strong
'a postage stamp'	'a grandmother'	'a safe'
German		
Haus-friedens-bruch	Wort-bedeutungs-lehre	
house peace break	word meaning theory	
'trespass'	'semantics'	
Finnish		
lammas-nahka-turkki	elin-keino-tulo-vero-laki	
sheep skin coat	life's means income tax law	
'sheepskin coat'	'income tax law'	
Tagalog		
basag-ulo	agaw-buhay	hampas-lupaʔ
break-head	snatch-life	strike-ground
'a brawl/trouble'	'near death/dying'	'a vagabond'

Other Word Formation

Compounding and derivation through affixation are the most common word formation processes in English, but they are not the only ones. As the examples in this section indicate, there are various other ways to create new words.

Clipping is a process whereby a new word is created by shortening a polysyllabic word. This process, which seems especially popular among students, has yielded forms such as *prof* for *professor, phys-ed* for *physical education, ad* for *advertisement*, and *poli-sci* for political science. A number of such abbreviations have been accepted in general usage: *doc, auto, lab, sub, bike, porn, burger, condo*, and *prep*. The most common abbreviations occur in names—such as *Liz, Ron, Kathy*, and *Lyn*.

Acronyms are formed from the initial sounds or letters of a string of words, such as the name of an organization or a scientific expression. Some examples of acronyms include AIDS for acquired immune deficiency syndrome, NASA for National Aeronautics and Space Administration, radar for radio detecting and ranging, and snafu for situation normal all fouled up. Where the combined initial letters follow the pronunciation patterns of English, the string can be pronounced as a word, such as NATO (North Atlantic Treaty Organization). However, if it happens to be unpronounceable, then each letter is sounded out separately (RBI for run batted in, UNH for University of New Hampshire, NFL for National Football League). In other cases, even if the combined initials can be pronounced, it may be customary to sound out each letter, as in NIV for New International Version (of the Bible) or UCLA for the University of California at Los Angeles.

Blends are words that are created from parts of two already existing lexical items. Well-known examples of blends include *motel* from *motor hotel, brunch* from *breakfast* and *lunch, selectric* from *select* and *electric, telethon* from *telephone* and *marathon, dancercise* from *dance* and *exercise*, and *chortle*, coined by Lewis Carroll as a blend of *chuckle* and *snort*. Usually, the first part of one word and the last part of a second one are combined to form a blend. Sometimes, though, only the first word is clipped, as in *perma-press* for 'permanent-press'.

Backformation is a process whereby a word whose form is similar to that of a derived form undergoes a process of deaffixation. *Resurrect* was originally formed in this way from *resurrection*. Other backformations in English include *enthuse* from *enthusiasm, donate* from *donation*, and *orient* or *orientate* from *orientation*. A major source of backformations in English has been words that end with *-or* or *-er* and have meanings involving the notion of an agent, such as *editor, peddler, swindler*, and *stoker*. Because hundreds of words ending in these affixes are the result of affixation, it was assumed that these words too had been formed by adding *-er* or *-or* to a verb. By the process of backformation, this led to the conclusion that *edit, peddle, swindle*, and *stoke* exist as simple verbs.

Other Sources It is sometimes possible to create new words from names. For example, brand names sometimes become so widely used that they are accepted as generic terms (*kleenex* for 'facial tissue' or *xerox* for 'photocopy'). Scientific terms such as *watt*, *curie*, and *fahrenheit* provide examples of words derived from the names of individuals associated with the things to which they refer.

Finally, all languages have words that have been created to sound like the thing to which they refer. Examples of such **onomatopoeic** words in English include *buzz*, *hiss*, *sizzle*, and *cuckoo*. Since these words are not exact phonetic copies of the things to which they refer, onomatopoeic words with the same referents can differ from language to language (see Table 4.15).

Table 4.15 Onomatopoeia across languages

English	Japanese	Tagalog
cock-a-doodle-doo	kokekoko	kuk-kukauk
meow	nya	ŋiyaw
chirp	pi-pi	tiririt
bow-wow	wau-wau	aw-aw

4.4 INFLECTION

Virtually all languages have contrasts such as singular and plural, and past and present. These contrasts are often marked with the help of a morphological process called **inflection**. Instead of creating a new word as derivation or compounding does, inflection modifies a word's form in order to mark the grammatical subclass to which it belongs. In the case of English nouns, for instance, inflection marks the plural subclass by adding the affix *-s* (see Table 4.16). In the case of verbs, on the other hand, inflection marks a distinction between past and nonpast subclasses—usually by adding the suffix *-ed* to indicate the past tense (see Table 4.17).

Table 4.16 Plural inflection

Singular	Plural
apple	[[apple] s]
car	[[car] s]
dog	[[dog] s]

Table 4.17 Tense inflection

Present	Past
work	[[work] ed]
jump	[[jump] ed]
hunt	[[hunt] ed]

Because inflection applies after all word formation rules, the plural affix can be added to the output of derivation and compounding as well as to a simple noun (see Table 4.18). Similarly, tense affixes can be attached to the output of derivation and compounding as well as to simple verbs (see Table 4.19).

Table 4.18 Inflection of derived or compound nouns

Derived form	Compound
[[worker] s]	[[football] s]
[[creation] s]	[[outlaw] s]
[[kingdom] s]	[[blackboard] s]

Table 4.19 Inflection of derived or compound verbs

Derived form	Compound
[[hospitalize] d]	[[outwork] ed]
[[activate] d]	[[underestimate] d]

Properties of Inflection

Three criteria help distinguish between inflectional and derivational affixes. First, inflection does not change the grammatical category of the word to which it applies. This follows from the fact that inflection simply marks subclasses of already existing words; it does not create new words.

12. *a)* [[book]$_N$ s]$_N$
    b) [[work]$_V$ ed]$_V$

In contrast, derivational affixes characteristically change the category and/or the meaning of the form to which they apply and are therefore said to create a new word. As the forms in *13* show, *-ize* makes a verb out of a noun (*hospitalize*), *-ment* makes a noun out of a verb (*government*), *-al* makes an adjective out of a noun (*national*), and *-dom* creates a noun with an entirely new type of meaning.

13. *a)* [[hospital]$_N$ ize]$_V$
    b) [[govern]$_V$ ment]$_N$
    c) [[nation]$_N$ al]$_{Adj}$
    d) [[king]$_N$ dom]$_N$

A second property of inflectional affixes has to do with their positioning within the word. As the examples in *14* illustrate, a derivational affix must be closer to the root than an inflectional affix. (IA = inflectional affix; DA = derivational affix.)

14. neighbor hood s   *neighbor s   hood
      root   DA   IA   root   IA   DA

The positioning of inflectional affixes outside derivational affixes reflects the fact that inflection takes place after all word formation processes, including derivation.

A third criterion for distinguishing between inflectional and derivational affixes has to do with **productivity**, the relative freedom with which they can combine with stems of the appropriate category. Inflectional affixes typically have very few exceptions. The suffix -s, for example, can combine with virtually any noun that allows a plural form (aside from a few exceptions such as *oxen* and *feet*). In contrast, derivational affixes characteristically apply to restricted classes of stems. Thus, -*ize* can combine with only certain nouns to form a verb.

15. hospitalize   *clinicize
    terrorize   *horrorize
    crystalize   *glassize

In the case of verbs, matters are somewhat more complicated, since many English verbs have irregular or idiosyncratic past tense forms (*saw*, *left*, *went*, and so on). Nonetheless, the distribution of the inflectional affix -*ed* is still considerably freer than that of a derivational affix such as -*ment*, which combines with only certain verbs to give nouns. While all the verbs in Table 4.20 can take the regular past tense ending, only those in the first three rows are able to take the -*ment* suffix. With only eight inflectional affixes, English is not a highly inflected language. In some languages, inflectional affixes number in the dozens and encode many contrasts not represented in English. We will see examples of such languages in the next section.

Table 4.21 gives a complete list of productive English inflectional affixes.

Table 4.20 Compatibility with -*ment*

Verb ⟶ Past		Verb ⟶ Noun	
confine	confined	confine	confinement
align	aligned	align	alignment
treat	treated	treat	treatment
arrest	arrested	arrest	*arrestment
straighten	straightened	straighten	*straightenment
cure	cured	cure	*curement

Table 4.21 English inflectional affixes

Nouns	
plural -*s*	the book**s**
possessive -*'s*	John**'s** book

Verbs	
third person singular present -*s*	John read**s** well.
progressive -*ing*	He is work**ing**.
past tense -*ed*	He work**ed**.
past participle -*ed*	He has stud**ied**.

Adjectives and adverbs	
comparative -*er*	This one is small**er**. He arrived earl**ier**.
superlative -*est*	This one is the small**est**. He arrived earl**iest**.

*Nominal Inflection

In this section, we will consider three common types of contrasts that are expressed with the help of inflectional affixes on nouns.

Number is the morphological category that expresses contrasts involving countable quantities. The simplest number contrast consists of a two-way distinction between the **singular** (one) and the **plural** (more than one). This is the contrast found in the English inflectional system, where a noun takes the suffix -s if it refers to two or more entities. Even this basic distinction is not found in all languages, however. In Nancowry (spoken in India's Nicobarese Islands), for example, number is not marked on nouns at all. A sentence such as *16* is therefore ambiguous since *nɔ́t* 'pig' can refer to one or more pigs.

16. Sák   nɔ́t   ʔin   ciʔɔ́y.
    spear pig   the   we
    'We speared the pig(s).'

In Inuktitut, on the other hand, there is an obligatory three-way number contrast involving singular, dual (two and only two), and plural (more than two).

17. iglu   'a house'
    igluk   'two houses'
    iglut   'three or more houses'

Noun Class Some languages divide nouns into classes based on shared semantic and/or phonological properties. A well-known example of this involves what is sometimes called **gender classification**. In French, Italian, and Spanish, for example, nouns are either masculine or feminine while in German there are three subclasses: masculine, feminine, and neuter. In general, there is a correlation between the inherent sex of living things and the grammatical gender of the noun designating them. For example, in Italian, *fratello* 'brother' is masculine while *sorella* 'sister' is feminine. However, most inanimate nouns in gender languages are classified more or less arbitrarily. Thus, *lune* 'moon' is feminine in French while the corresponding German word *Mond* is masculine. Even some nouns referring to animate entities seem to be classified arbitrarily since German *Mädchen* 'young girl' is neuter, not feminine, and French *victime* 'victim' is feminine regardless of whether the person it refers to is male or female. Facts like these have led many linguists to use the more neutral term **noun class** rather than gender to refer to this type of contrast.

Noun class or gender can be marked in a variety of ways. In some languages, the form of the determiner varies depending on the class of the noun. Thus, Spanish uses the definite determiner *el* for masculine nouns and *la* for feminine ones; French uses *le* for the masculine subclass and *la* for the feminine subclass. In other languages, inflectional affixes rather than determiners can be used to indicate the gender subclass of the noun. Russian, for instance, uses one set of affixes for nouns in the feminine subclass and another set for nouns in the masculine subclass. The examples in Table 4.22 show the gender endings for nouns that head subject phrases.

Table 4.22 Russian gender endings

Noun		Ending	Class
dom	'house'	Ø	masculine
ulica	'street'	-a	feminine
čuvstvo	'sensation'	-o	neuter

Some languages have extremely elaborate systems of noun classification. The Bantu language Swati, for instance, makes use of prefixes to distinguish among more than a dozen noun classes, some of which are given in Table 4.23. (Tone is not represented in these examples.)

Table 4.23 Noun classification in Swati

Prefix	Example		Description of class
um(u)	um-fana	'boy'	persons
li	li-dvolo	'knee'	body parts, fruit
s(i)	si-tja	'plate'	instruments
in	in-ja	'dog'	animals
bu	bu-bi	'evil'	abstract properties
pha	pha-ndle	'outside'	locations

Case Still another type of inflectional contrast associated with nouns in many languages involves **case**—a category that encodes information about the syntactic role (subject, direct object, and so on) of an NP. In Modern English, this information is expressed largely through word order and the use of prepositions.

18. Bette composed a song on the bus.

In this sentence, the subject *Bette* occurs before the verb and the direct object *a song* appears after it, while the element expressing location (*the bus*) is preceded by the preposition *on*. In many languages, however, these distinctions are marked by inflectional affixes. As an illustration of this, consider Table 4.24, which presents the set of related nominal forms (called

Table 4.24 Turkish case

Case	Form
Nominative	ev
Accusative	ev-i
Dative	ev-e
Genitive	ev-in
Locative	ev-de
Ablative	ev-den

a **nominal paradigm** or **declension**) for the Turkish word *ev* 'house'. In general, the **nominative (Nom)** case (which is not overtly marked in Turkish) indicates the subject of the sentence; the **accusative (Ac)** the direct object; the **dative (Dat)** the indirect object or recipient; and the **genitive (Gen)** the possessor. The **locative (Loc)** marks place or location, and the **ablative (Abl)** marks direction away from. The following sentences illustrate the use of these forms.

19. a) Adam   ev-i   Ahmed-e   göster-di.
       man-Nom house-Ac Ahmed-Dat showed
       'The man showed the house to Ahmed.'

    b) Ev   -in   rengi   māvi.
       house-Gen color-Nom blue
       'The house's color is blue.'

    c) Adam   ev-de   kaldɨ.
       man-Nom house-Loc stayed
       'The man stayed in the house.'

    d) Adam   ev-den   čɨktɨ.
       man-Nom house-Abl went
       'The man went from the house.'

Table 4.25 Russian nominal paradigms

Masculine nouns (*dom*   'house')

	Singular	Plural
Nominative	dom	dom-ɨ
Genitive	dom-a	dom-ov
Accusative	dom	dom-ɨ
Dative	dom-u	dom-am
Locative	dom-e	dom-ax
Instrumental	dom-om	dom-ami

Feminine nouns (*ulica*   'street')

	Singular	Plural
Nominative	ulic-a	ulic-ɨ
Genitive	ulic-ɨ	ulic
Accusative	ulic-u	ulic-ɨ
Dative	ulic-e	ulic-am
Locative	ulic-e	ulic-ax
Instrumental	ulic-oy	ulic-ami

Neuter nouns (*čuvstvo*   'sensation')

	Singular	Plural
Nominative	čuvstv-o	čuvstv-a
Genitive	čuvstv-a	čuvstv
Accusative	čuvstv-o	čuvstv-a
Dative	čuvstv-u	čuvstv-am
Locative	čuvstv-e	čuvstv-ax
Instrumental	čuvstv-om	čuvstv-ami

The contrasts represented in the Turkish case system are intermediate in complexity compared to languages like Finnish, which has fifteen distinct case categories, and languages like Rumanian, which has only two contrasts. It is sometimes suggested that nouns in Modern English exhibit a maximally simple two-way contrast between the genitive (marked by -'*s*) and all other grammatical functions.

In many languages, number, gender, and case contrasts are combined into one ending, as the nominal paradigm for Russian in Table 4.25 shows. In this paradigm, a single ending is used to indicate the noun's number, gender, and case. Thus -*ov*, for example, is used to indicate that the noun belongs to the masculine gender, that it is plural, and that it functions as a genitive. A morpheme that encodes more than one grammatical contrast is called a **portmanteau** morpheme.

Some languages make use of case marking to encode grammatical contrasts quite unlike those found in familiar European languages. In the Australian language Yidin, for instance, the case-marking pattern groups together the subject of an intransitive verb and the direct object of a transitive verb (both of which receive a zero ending) while using a special marker (-*ngu*) for the subject of a transitive verb (see Figure 4.14). In this type of system, the case associated with the subject of the transitive verb (such as -*ngu* in Figure 4.14a) is called the **ergative**, while the case associated with the direct object (*tree*) and with the subject of an intransitive verb (*man* in Figure 4.14b) is called the **absolutive**.

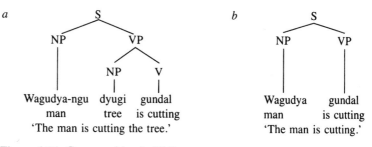

Figure 4.14 Case marking in Yidin

Ergative case marking is found in a small but varied set of languages, including Basque (Spain), Tagalog (in the Philippines), Georgian (in the Soviet Union), Inuktitut (in northern Canada and Greenland), and Halkomelem (on the west coast of Canada). Ergative case marking is far less common than the nominative-accusative pattern, which groups together the subjects of transitive and intransitive verbs, distinguishing them from direct objects. This is the pattern found in German, Russian, Turkish, Japanese, Korean, and many other languages. In the examples in Figure 4.15 from Tamil (a language spoken in South India and Sri Lanka), the subject of both a transitive and an intransitive verb takes the zero ending, while the direct object has the suffix -*ai*. (The internal structure of the NPs is not represented here.)

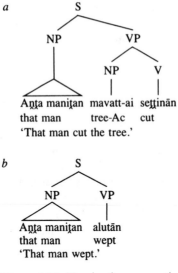

Figure 4.15 Nominative-accusative marking in Tamil

English nouns do not use case contrasts to distinguish between subjects and direct objects, although the genitive suffix -'s is used to mark the possessor role. However, pronouns exhibit a more elaborate set of contrasts.

20. Nominative: *They* laughed. *They* read the billboard.
    Accusative: Sue saw *them*.
    Genitive: Sue took *their* car.

Since the same form of the pronoun is used for the subject of a transitive verb as for the subject of an intransitive verb, we can say that these contrasts follow the nominative-accusative pattern.

*Verbal
Inflection

In this section, we consider some of the more common inflectional categories associated with verbs in the world's languages.

Person and Number Agreement A widely attested type of verbal inflection in human language involves **person**—a category that typically distinguishes among the first person (or speaker), the second person (or addressee), and the third person (anyone else). In many languages, the verb is marked for both the person and number (singular or plural) of the subject. A clear illustration of this is found in Finnish, which exhibits the contrasts in the present tense shown in Table 4.26. (The complete set of inflected forms

Table 4.26 Finnish verbal paradigm

	Singular		Plural	
First person	puhun	'I speak'	puhumme	'we speak'
Second person	puhut	'you speak'	puhutte	'you speak'
Third person	puhuu	'he, she, or it speaks'	puhuvat	'they speak'

associated with a verb is called a **verbal paradigm** or a **conjugation**.) Because the inflectional markers provide so much information about the person and number of the subject phrase, this element need not be overtly present in Finnish.

21. *a*) As-uu tässä.
         live - 3rd sg. here
         '[He] lives here.'
     b) As-un tässä.
         live - 1st sg. here
         '[I] live here.'

The optionality of the subject phrase is a common feature of languages with rich verbal inflection.

English has a much more impoverished system of person and number agreement in the verb, and an inflectional affix is used only for the third person singular in the present tense (see Table 4.27). Except for commands, English does not tolerate sentences without overtly expressed subjects.

22. *Spoke English.

Table 4.27 English verbal paradigm

	Singular	Plural
First person	I speak	we speak
Second person	you speak	you speak
Third person	he, she, or it speaks	they speak

Tense is the category that encodes the time of a situation with reference to the moment of speaking. The most fundamental and frequent tense contrasts involve past (prior to the time of speaking), present (at the time of speaking), and future (after the time of speaking). According to many traditional analyses, the English tense system is built around these three contrasts.

23. *a*) They played hockey.   (past)
     b) They play hockey.   (present)
     c) They will play hockey. (future)

In terms of inflectional morphology, however, English has only a two-way contrast between past (marked by the inflectional suffix *-ed* in regular verbs) and the nonpast (unmarked). Futurity is expressed by means of the free morpheme *will* (and *shall* in some dialects). In Spanish, on the other hand, inflectional endings are used to express a three-way past-present-future contrast.

24. *a*) Juan habl-ó bien
         'John spoke well.'
     b) Juan habl-a bien.
         'John speaks well.'
     c) Juan habl-ar-á bien.
         'John will speak well.'

The expression of tense in English is sometimes complicated by **suppletion**, the replacement of one root by another to express an inflectional contrast. Examples of this include the use of *went* as the past tense form of *go* and *was* or *were* as the past tense form of *be*.

Voice Still another grammatical contrast in verbal systems involves what has traditionally been called **voice**. The major function of this system is to indicate the role of the subject in the action described by the verb. In English, there are two voices. In the active voice, the subject denotes the actor or agent (in sentence *25*, the one who writes). In the passive voice, in contrast, the subject denotes a nonactor. As the following structures indicate, the English passive voice is expressed with the help of the verb *be* and a past participle (see Table 4.21).

25. An author writes books.

26. *a*) Books are written by an author.
    b) The author was given a royalty by the company.

In many languages, the passive voice is marked by a special bound morpheme rather than by an auxiliary verb. The following example is from Turkish, in which -*il* marks the passive.

27. Penǰere Hasan tarafɨndan ač   -ɨl   -dɨ.
    window Hasan   by   open Pass Past
    'The window was opened by Hasan.'

4.5 MORPHOLOGY AND PHONOLOGY

Chapter 3 of this book dealt with allophonic variation, rules that derive allophones from underlying (phonemic) representations. A second type of variation in language involves morphemes and their allomorphs. An example of allomorphic variation can be seen in the English plural morpheme, which has different allomorphs in the words *cat*[s], *dog*[z], and *match*[əz]. Like allophonic variation, this phenomenon is analyzed with the help of a single underlying representation from which the allomorphs can be derived. The rules that account for both allophonic and allomorphic variation make reference to phonetic environments, including syllable structure. There are, however, differences between allophonic and allomorphic variation, two of which are outlined in the following section.

Morphophonemic Rules

Rules that account for alternations among allomorphs (morphophonemic alternations) are called **morphophonemic** rules. The major differences between allophonic and morphophonemic rules can be summed up under two major points.

- Allophonic rules are exceptionless—they apply in the appropriate environment to all classes and forms in a language. There are, for example, no exceptions to a rule such as aspiration in English. In contrast, morphophonemic rules often show exceptions. They may, for example, apply to a limited class of forms, as in the case of the rule that changes final *f* to *v* in the plural of a few English words such as *knife* and *thief*. (We will examine this rule in more detail later in this section.)

- Morphophonemic rules often (but do not always) make reference to particular morphemes or morphological structures. This does not occur with allophonic rules.

Deriving Allomorphs

We derive allomorphs in much the same way as we derive allophones. An underlying representation (UR) is set up, and rules apply to derive all phonetic variants from the same underlying representation. Often, the underlying representation of the morpheme is the elsewhere allomorph—the one that occurs with the widest distribution.

Conditioned Allomorphs

The allomorphs of the English plural morpheme provide a good example of phonologically conditioned allomorphs.

English Plural Allomorphs The plural morpheme in English shows three-way variation in its allomorphs. The three allomorphs, /-s/, /-z/, and /-əz/, are distributed in a systematic manner, as Table 4.28 illustrates. The phonetic

Table 4.28 English plural allomorphs

Allomorph /-s/		Environment
tops	/tɑps/	Stems end in a voiceless
mitts	/mɪts/	consonant that is not
backs	/bæks/	both strident and
puffs	/pʌfs/	coronal.
baths	/bæθs/	

Allomorph: /-z/		Environment
cobs	/kɑbz/	Stems end in a vowel or a
lids	/lɪdz/	voiced consonant that is
lads	/lædz/	not both strident and
doves	/dʌvz/	coronal.
lathes	/leyðz/	
pins	/pɪnz/	
bums	/bʌmz/	
wings	/wɪŋz/	
teas	/tiyz/	
days	/deyz/	

Allomorph /-əz/		Environment
hisses	/hɪsəz/	Stems end in a consonant
buzzes	/bʌzəz/	that is both strident
crutches	/krʌčəz/	and coronal.
judges	/jʌǰəz/	
wishes	/wɪšəz/	

form of these allomorphs is determined by the segment that precedes them. Stems that end in a strident coronal (sibilant) consonant always appear with the /-əz/ allomorph. Stems that end in a vowel or a voiced consonant that is not both strident and coronal take the /-z/ allomorph, and stems that end in a voiceless consonant that is not both strident and coronal take the /-s/ allomorph.

A fundamental strategy of the linguist in selecting the underlying form (UF) of an allomorph is to choose the one with the widest distribution. Since the /-z/ allomorph occurs after all vowels as well as after most voiced consonants, it is chosen as basic. This choice results in underlying representations that show /-z/ after all stems, as in Table 4.29.

Table 4.29 Underlying representations of some English plurals

tops	tɑp-z	cobs	kɑb-z	hisses	hɪs-z
mitts	mɪt-z	lids	lɪd-z	buzzes	bʌz-z
				judges	ǰʌǰ-z

***Derivation** Once the underlying representations have been set up, the phonetic forms (PFs) can be derived. We can account for the allomorph /-əz/ by noting that whenever the underlying /-z/ appears after a stem that ends in a strident coronal consonant, a schwa is present. This reflects a general phonotactic constraint of English: a word cannot contain a sequence of strident coronals in the same syllabic coda. Such a sequence may occur across word boundaries in compound forms, such as *buzz saw* /bʌz sɔ/. It may even occur across syllable boundaries, as in *posture* /pɑsčər/ (/pɑščər/ for some speakers). But when a sequence of two coronal stridents occurs in a coda, it is broken up by the epenthesis of a schwa. (In effect, a new syllable is created.) It is possible to write a rule that inserts a schwa and breaks up the succession of a stem-final strident coronal consonant and the strident coronal /-z/ of the underlying representation, as in Figure 4.16. At this point, we can derive forms such as *matches*, *judges*, and so on. This is shown in Figure 4.17.

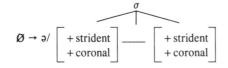

$$\emptyset \rightarrow \text{ə/} \begin{bmatrix} + \text{strident} \\ + \text{coronal} \end{bmatrix} \underline{\qquad} \begin{bmatrix} + \text{strident} \\ + \text{coronal} \end{bmatrix}$$

Figure 4.16 English schwa epenthesis

	UF	# m æ č - z #
Schwa epenthesis		# m æ č - ə z #
	PF	[mæčəz]

Figure 4.17 Derivation of English *matches*

It is now necessary to account for the appearance of [s] after voiceless consonants and [z] elsewhere. This is formalized in Figure 4.18. No rule is necessary for the /-z/ allomorph, which will now appear only in words where

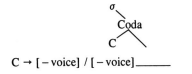

C → [– voice] / [– voice]_____

Figure 4.18 Voicing assimilation

the rules of voicing assimilation and schwa epenthesis have not applied. It is the elsewhere variant, the allomorph that appears where none of the restricted, rule-derived allomorphs appear. Figure 4.19 shows derivations of all three plural allomorphs. The ordering of the rules is crucial here. If voicing assimilation applied first, the plural ending of forms such as *match* and *hiss* would incorrectly end up as /mæčəs/ and /hɪsəs/, since the suffix would assimilate in voicing before epenthesis could apply. In the next section we see how these same rules for determining the plural allomorphs of English interact with another type of morphophonemic rule.

	UF	#bʊk-z#	#fɪb-z#	#mæč-z#
Schwa epenthesis		----	----	#mæč-əz#
Voicing assimilation		#bʊk-s#	---	---
	PF	[bʊks]	[fɪbz]	[mæčəz]

Figure 4.19 Derivations of English plural forms

Conditioning by Morphological Class

A second type of morphophonemic rule refers to a subclass of forms, rather than applying to all members of a class of forms. English plurals again provide the example.

Irregular English Plurals As Table 4.30 illustrates, English includes a limited class of words that show an alternating /f/ and /v/ in their plural forms. The alternating class is unproductive; new words with final /f/ entering English

Table 4.30 Alternating stem-final /f/ and /v/ in English

The /f/ — /v/ alternation (irregular forms)		No alternation (regular forms)	
wife	wives	whiff	whiffs
thief	thieves	chief	chiefs
leaf	leaves	fife	fifes
knife	knives	laugh	laughs

will not show this alternation. For example, speakers would pluralize a hypothetical new word *nif* as [nɪfs], not [nɪvz]. This suggests that each word in this class needs to be marked as undergoing a rule that voices its stem-final segment when the form is pluralized. Such a rule takes the form shown in Figure 4.20, in which it is labeled *Rule PL*. Information about rules that

Rule PL: f → v / _____ - z$_{plural}$

Figure 4.20 The f → v alternative rule for English

a form must undergo is included in its lexical entry. A form that undergoes Rule PL is marked as [+ Rule PL]. Forms that are not so marked are automatically assumed to be [− Rule PL]. Following a stem-changing rule such as Rule PL, the morphophonemic rule of voicing assimilation introduced in Figure 4.18 applies. Other relevant rules such as vowel lengthening apply as well. (Stress is not shown in Figure 4.21.) The allophonic rule of

	UF	# θiyf - z #$_{[+ Rule PL]}$	# čiyf - z #
f → v (Rule PL)		# θiyv - z #	---
Voicing assimilation		---	# čiyf - s #
Vowel lengthening		# θi:yv - z #	---
	PF	[θi:yvz]	[čiyfs]

Figure 4.21 Derivation of English *thiefs* and *chiefs*

vowel lengthening presented in Chapter 3 has also applied here to give the correct form of *thieves*.

   The underlying forms presented so far in this chapter are all very much unlike their phonetic representations. The next section takes up the implications of this kind of representation in more detail.

Abstract Underlying Representations

Underlying representations generally show some degree of difference from phonetic representations. There are no phonetic forms like [mɪtz], [bæθz], or [wayfz] in English, although such forms are found as underlying representations. Underlying representations are therefore said to be **abstract**. By an abstract representation, we mean one that is distinct from its phonetic realization. The greater the difference between the phonological and the phonetic representations, the more abstract the phonological representation is said to be.

Although morphophonemic URs can be very abstract, there is an advantage to this kind of representation. Employing abstract underlying representations enables us to make greater generalizations about the relationship among allomorphs. For example, we have just seen how two phonetically distinct forms of the root morpheme *thief* are derived from the same UR.

Abstraction and English Stems In English, we can derive the root of both *electri*[k] and *electri*[s]*ity* from one underlying form. This approach expresses the fact that English speakers recognize the two phonetic forms as variants of the same morpheme. Assuming that the underlying representation ends in *k*, we can write a morphophonemic rule that changes *k* to *s* before the suffix *-ity*, as in Figure 4.22. The variant of the stem that ends in *k* is

k → s / ____ + ɪtiy

Figure 4.22 English *k* to *s* fronting

chosen as underlying for two reasons. First, the stem *electri*[k] has a wider distribution than the allomorph *electri*[s]; it occurs in words such as *electrical* as well as in the unsuffixed form. Second, our proposed rule has the advantage of reflecting a natural process of fronting of final /k/ to [s] before the high front vowel of the suffix. It would be more difficult to find phonetic motivation for a rule that changes an /s/ to [k] in final position or before the suffix *-al*.

It is also significant that the rule must include morphological information—the identity of the suffix that triggers the change—since /k/ is not pronounced as [s] whenever it appears before the vowel [ɪ] in English. If it were, English speakers would automatically pronounce *kill* as *sill*, and *kick* as *sick*. Since they do not, we assume that the morphological information is a crucial determining factor in this rule.

The derivations of *electric* and *electricity* are given in Figure 4.23. The allophonic rule of flapping and the stress rule are also involved in this deri-

	UR	# iylɛktrɪk #	# iylɛktrɪk - ɪtiy #
Stress		# iylɛktrík #	# iylɛktrík - ɪtiy #
k → s rule		---	# iylɛktrís - ɪtiy #
Flapping		---	# iylɛktrís - ɪDiy #
	PR	[iylɛktrík]	[iylɛktrísɪDiy]

Figure 4.23 Derivation of *electric* and *electricity* in English

vation but are not formalized here. Our underlying form is rather abstract in the case of #iylɛktrɪk + ɪtiy#, but our rule has allowed us to represent an English speaker's knowledge that the stems *electri*[k] and *electri*[s] are allomorphs of the same morpheme.

Summing Up

This chapter is concerned with the structure of **words** in human language. Many words consist of smaller formative elements, called **morphemes**. These elements can be classified in a variety of ways (**free** vs. **bound**, **root** vs. **affix**, **prefix** vs. **suffix**) and can be combined in different ways to create new words. Two basic processes of word formation in English are **derivation** and **compounding**. Words may also be **inflected** to mark grammatical contrasts in **person**, **number**, **gender**, **case**, **tense**, and **voice**.

Although the processes of word formation may differ, all languages have the means to create new words and therefore exhibit the rule-governed creativity that is typical of human language.

Interaction between the phonological and morphological components of the grammar is reflected by the presence of allomorphs. The use of underlying representations and derivation by **morphophonemic** rule accounts for these morphophonemic alternations. In some cases, allomorphy is determined by the fact that only certain classes of forms undergo a given morphophonemic rule. Dealing with allomorphy leads to underlying representations, which in many instances are **abstract.**

Sources

The discussion of words and morphemes draws heavily on the classic treatments found in Gleason's *An Introduction to Descriptive Linguistics* (cited below) and C. F. Hockett's *A Course in General Linguistics* (New York: Macmillan, 1958). The problem of an underlying form for the plural suffix and of morphophonemic variation in general is discussed in Arnold Zwicky's article "Settling on an Underlying Form: The English Inflectional Endings" in *Testing Linguistic Hypotheses*, edited by D. Cohen and J. Wirth (New York: John Wiley and Sons, 1975).

Recommended Reading

Aronoff, M. 1976. *Word Formation in Generative Grammar*. Cambridge, Mass.: MIT Press.

Bauer, Laurie. 1983. *English Word-formation*. London: Cambridge University Press.

Gleason, H. 1955. *An Introduction to Descriptive Linguistics*. New York: Holt, Rinehart and Winston.

Matthews, P. H. 1974. *Morphology*. London: Cambridge University Press.

Questions

1. Each of the following words contains at least two morphemes. Draw the appropriate tree structure for each of these words. Do some of these words have bound stems?

a) unfair	g) disinfect	m) inane
b) employee	h) destroyer	n) unkempt
c) trial	i) presidency	o) possibility
d) lawless	j) original	p) professorial
e) stupidity	k) reliable	q) inconsiderate
f) idiotic	l) Americanize	r) deform

2. The following are examples of word formation from Chamorro, a language spoken in Guam and the Marianas Islands. What morphological devices are involved in these derivations? Can you state the rule of word formation in each case? Do any of the affixes have more than one allomorph?

   Verb to noun derivation

Verb root		Derived noun	
a) adda	'mimic'	aadda	'mimicker'
b) kanno	'eat'	kakanno	'eater'
c) tuge	'write'	tutuge	'writer'

   Verb to adjective derivation

Verb root		Derived adjective	
d) atan	'look at'	atanon	'nice to look at'
e) sanan	'tell'	sananon	'tellable'
f) guaiya	'love'	guaiyayon	'lovable'
g) tulaika	'exchange'	tulaikayon	'exchangeable'

   Adjective to adjective derivation

Adjective root		Derived intensive adjective	
h) nalang	'hungry'	nalalang	'very hungry'
i) dankolo	'big'	dankololo	'very big'
j) metgot	'strong'	metgogot	'very strong'
k) bunita	'pretty'	bunitata	'very pretty'

3. In Samoan, the plural form of the verb is formed from the singular form by means of a reduplicative affix. Compare the following forms. Formulate a general statement as to how the reduplicated forms in Samoan are formed.

	Singular		Plural	
a)	manao	'he wishes'	mananao	'they wish'
b)	matua	'he is old'	matutua	'they are old'
c)	malosi	'he is strong'	malolosi	'they are strong'
d)	punou	'he bends'	punonou	'they bend'
e)	atamaʔi	'he is wise'	atamamaʔi	'they are wise'

Given that *savali* means 'he travels', how would you say 'they travel'?
Given that *pepese* means 'they sing', how would you say 'he sings'?

4. The following words have all been formed by compounding, derivation, or both. Assign a tree structure to each of these words.

   a) football   i) deregulation   q) hockey match
   b) billboard   j) unlawfully   r) unacceptable
   c) unhindered   k) shortstop   s) goalie
   d) hurtful   l) ex-husband   t) blueprint
   e) attendance   m) city center   u) creationism
   f) misfire   n) discussion   v) spaceship
   g) apple picker   o) potato grower   w) incorruptible
   h) firefighter   p) ballad singing   x) potluck

5. The words in Column 2 have been created from the corresponding word or words in Column 1. Indicate the word formation process responsible for the creation of each word in Column 2.

	Column 1	Column 2
a)	automation	automate
b)	humid	humidifier
c)	head, hunter	headhunter
d)	combíne	cómbine
e)	typographical error	typo
f)	act	deactivate
g)	aerobics, marathon	aerobathon
h)	Mothers Against Drunk Driving	MADD
i)	curve, ball	curve ball
j)	perambulator	pram
k)	comb (Noun)	comb (Verb)
l)	imprínt	ímprint
m)	telephone, marketing	telemarketing

6. Determine whether the words in each of the following groups are related to one another by inflection or derivation.
   a) go, goes, going, gone
   b) discover, discovery, discoverer, discoverable, discoverability
   c) lovely, lovelier, loveliest
   d) inventor, inventor's, inventors, inventors'
   e) democracy, democrat, democratic, democratize

7. This chapter presented an argument in favor of the following structure for the word *unhappiness*. Using the same type of argument, justify tree structures for the words *unexceptional* and *rewasher*. (*Hint*: This will involve determining the type of syntactic category with which the affixes in these words can combine.)

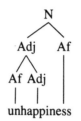

8. The following data provide the possible forms of the regular past tense morpheme of English.

   a) List the alternate forms of the past tense morpheme.

(1) walked	/wɔkt/	(12) heaved	/hiyvd/
(2) cracked	/krækt/	(13) wheezed	/wiyzd/
(3) flipped	/flɪpt/	(14) fined	/faynd/
(4) hissed	/hɪst/	(15) flitted	/flɪtəd/
(5) huffed	/hʌft/	(16) butted	/bʌtəd/
(6) hushed	/hʌšt/	(17) padded	/pædəd/
(7) munched	/mʌnčt/	(18) loaded	/lowdəd/
(8) drubbed	/drʌbd/	(19) collided	/kʌlaydəd/
(9) dragged	/drægd/	(20) allowed	/ʌlawd/
(10) jogged	/jɑgd/	(21) sowed	/sowd/
(11) fudged	/fʌjd/		

   b) Which alternate makes the best underlying form? Why?

   c) State in words the conditioning factors that account for the presence of the alternate forms of the past tense morpheme.

9. Vowel harmony is a process that results in all vowels of a word sharing a certain feature or features. Morphophonemic rules of vowel harmony are found in many languages.

   a) List the allomorphs of the plural morpheme in the following data from Turkish.

	Singular	Plural
(1) 'eye'	göz	gözler
(2) 'candle'	mum	mumlar
(3) 'gun'	top	toplar
(4) 'horse'	at	atlar
(5) 'sheath'	kɨn	kɨnlar
(6) 'thread'	ip	ipler
(7) 'rose'	gül	güller
(8) 'hand'	el	eller

   b) What phonological feature is shared by the vowels of both allomorphs of the plural?

   c) What phonological feature distinguishes the vowels of the allomorphs?

   d) Is it possible in this case to pick one allomorph as the best underlying form?

   e) Choose one allomorph as underlying, and write a rule that derives the other one from it. Provide derivations for the words for 'eye' and 'gun.'

5 SYNTAX
The Study of Sentence Structure

Noun-substantives, the names of things declare,
And adjectives, what kind of things these are . . .
A structure: and the toil of grammar's past.

Israel Tonge (c. 1680)

One of the underlying themes of this book is that language is a highly structured system of communication. Utterances are not formed by randomly combining linguistic elements. Rather, as you saw in Chapter 3, words consist of phonological units called syllables, which in turn are made up of segments and features. This chapter focuses on **syntax**, the system of rules and categories that allows words to be combined to form sentences.

The data that linguists use to study syntax consist primarily of judgments about the grammaticality of individual sentences. Roughly speaking, a sentence is considered **grammatical** if speakers judge it to be a possible sentence of their language. Example *1a* is not a possible sentence in English, although the same words can be combined in a different way to form the grammatical structure in *1b*.

> *1. a)* *house painted student a the
> *b)* A student painted the house.

Often, it is not obvious why a particular sentence has to be ungrammatical. Consider in this respect the following examples.

> *2. a)* Mike will leave tomorrow at 3:00 P.M.
> *b)* Will Mike leave tomorrow at 3:00 P.M.?
> *3. a)* Mike leaves tomorrow at 3:00 P.M.
> *b)* *Leaves Mike tomorrow at 3:00 P.M.?

While *2a* and *3a* mean essentially the same thing, only one of them has a question structure formed by reversing the order of the first two words. There is nothing logically wrong with sentence *3b*. Such structures are found in many human languages and, until a few centuries ago, were perfectly acceptable in English. For some reason, however, the rules that form sentences in Modern English do not allow this pattern.

In the following pages, we will use information about grammaticality to illustrate the workings of the syntactic component of the grammar. We will begin by considering the role of word classes in sentence formation. Next, we will examine the various types of rules that form sentences by arranging words into patterns appropriate to English. Finally, we will consider some basic syntactic phenomena in languages other than English.

5.1 SYNTACTIC CATEGORIES

The first step in syntactic analysis is the identification of the categories to which the words of a language belong. If words could not be assigned to a small group of categories, it would be very hard to learn or use a language. Each of the ten thousand or so lexical items in the average person's everyday spoken vocabulary would have its own set of properties that would have to be memorized—a rather daunting task.

Lexical Categories

Fortunately, such a feat of memory is unnecessary since large groups of words have very similar properties. These shared characteristics allow us to organize words into a relatively small number of **lexical categories** or classes (see Table 5.1). Four **major lexical categories** are typically recognized, namely **noun (N)**, **verb (V)**, **adjective (Adj)**, and **adverb (Adv)**. Membership

Table 5.1 Lexical categories

Major lexical categories		Examples
Noun	(N)	Pierre, butterfly, wheat, policy
Verb	(V)	arrive, discuss, melt, feel, remain
Adjective	(Adj)	good, tall, silent, old, expensive
Adverb	(Adv)	yesterday, silently, slowly, quietly, quickly
Minor lexical categories		Examples
Determiner	(Det)	the, a, this, these
Auxiliary verb	(Aux)	will, can, may, must, be, have
Preposition	(P)	to, in, on, near, at, by
Pronoun	(Pro)	he, she, him, his, her
Conjunction	(C)	and, or, but

in these categories is open in the sense that new words are always being added. There is also a group of **minor** or closed categories in which membership is restricted to a fixed set of elements already in the language. Minor lexical categories include **determiner (Det)**, **auxiliary verb (Aux)**, **preposition (P)**, **pronoun (Pro)**, and **conjunction (C)**. How are lexical categories defined? As noted previously, the words in each lexical category share certain properties. Some of these properties pertain to meaning. Nouns, for instance, typically name entities such as individuals (*Shawn, Marie*) and concrete and abstract things (*book, desk, policy*). Verbs, on the other hand, designate actions (*run, jump*), sensations (*feel, hurt*), and states (*be, remain*).

The meanings associated with nouns and verbs can be modified in various ways. The typical function of an adjective, for instance, is to designate a property or attribute that is applicable to the individuals and things named by nouns. Thus, adjectives such as *tall*, *old*, and *red* name properties that can be attributed to individuals and things. When we say *That building is tall*, we are attributing the property 'tall' to the building named by the noun.

Just as adjectives bear a special relationship to nouns, so adverbs typically name properties and attributes that can be applied to the actions, states, and sensations designed by verbs. In the following sentences, for example, the adverb *quickly* indicates the manner of Janet's leaving and the adverb *early* specifies its time.

> 4. *a*) Janet left quickly.
>   *b*) Janet left early.

Phrasal Categories

The members of each lexical category also share certain combinatorial properties. This means that they can combine with certain other types of words to form larger units.

Noun Phrases The words that we have grouped together as nouns can all combine with determiners and adjectives to form larger phrases such as the following:

> 5. *a*) the books
>   *b*) the controversial books

In *5*, the adjective *controversial* modifies the noun *books* while the determiner *the* indicates that the speaker has in mind a definite set of books. Such a group of words, called a **noun phrase** or **NP**, can be represented by either a tree structure or a set of labeled brackets. In Figure 5.1, each word is

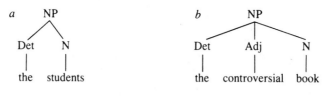

[NP [Det the] [N students]]   [NP [Det the] [Adj controversial] [N book]]

Figure 5.1

marked by the appropriate lexical category label and is shown to be part of a larger phrasal unit (NP). Evidence that NPs are syntactic units comes from the fact they can often be replaced by a single word such as the pronoun *they* or *it*. This is illustrated in *6*, where *they* replaces *the students* and *it* replaces *the controversial book*. (This is called a **substitution test**.)

> 6. *The students* read *the controversial book*, and then *they* returned *it* to the library. (*they = the students, it = the controversial book*)

Even though the sequence of words *the controversial book* is longer and contains more information than the single word *it*, both are NPs and both can occur in the same places in sentences. In fact, a pronoun can replace any NP, no matter how long or complex it may be. In 7, for example, *it* can replace the considerably longer NP:

> 7. *The controversial book that the teacher almost forgot to remind the students to return to the library* was banned by the committee.

From the syntactic point of view, a pronoun like *it* or *she* counts as a full NP, even though it would be listed in the dictionary as a pronoun only one word long (see Figure 5.2).

NP
|
N
|
it

[NP [N it]]

Figure 5.2

Note that the pronoun substitutes for the entire NP and not simply for the N, as shown in 8.

> 8. *a)* The students read *it*.
> *b)* *The students read the controversial *it*.

Prepositional Phrases The class of words making up the minor lexical category of preposition includes such items as *near*, *in*, *on*, *before*, and *after*. In terms of meaning, these words typically designate relations in space (such as *in*), time (such as *before*), or direction (such as *to* or *from*). A preposition combines with an NP to form a **prepositional phrase** or **PP** (see Figure 5.3).

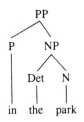

[PP [P in] [NP [Det the] [N park]]]

Figure 5.3

The substitution test confirms that *in the park* is a unit since it can be replaced by a single word in sentences such as 9.

> 9. The team practiced *in the park*, and Lisa trained *there* too.
> (*there* = *in the park*)

A second indication that *in the park* forms a phrase is that it can be moved as a single unit to different positions within the sentence. (This is called a **movement test**.) In *10*, for instance, *in the park* occurs at the beginning of the sentence.

 10. *In the park*, the team practiced for the championship game.

Verb Phrases The lexical category consisting of verbs has yet another set of combinatorial properties. As Figures 5.4 and 5.5 show, elements in this class can combine with NPs and/or PPs (among other categories) to form a

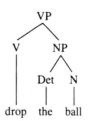

[VP [V drop] [NP [Det the] [N ball]]]

Figure 5.4

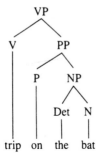

[VP [V trip] [PP [P on] [NP [Det the] [N bat]]]]

Figure 5.5

verb phrase or **VP**. We know that *drop the ball* and *trip on the bat* form syntactic units because they can be replaced by the single word *did*.

 11. *a*) The catcher *dropped the ball*, and the pitcher *did* too.
        (*did* = *dropped the ball*)
    b) The player *tripped on the bat* and the coach *did* too.
        (*did* = *tripped on the bat*)

Other Phrases Two other types of phrasal categories are commonly found in language. An adjective can combine with a **degree specifier** (**Spec**) such as *very*, *quite*, or *really* to form an **adjectival phrase** or **AdjP**, as in Figure 5.6. AdjPs can be replaced by the word *so* in structures such as *12*.

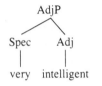

$[_{AdjP} [_{Spec} \text{very}] [_{Adj} \text{intelligent}]]$

Figure 5.6

> *12.* Linda is *very intelligent*, and Mark appears *so* too.
> (*so* = *very intelligent*)

Adverbial phrases (AdvPs) consist of an adverb and an optional specifier, as in Figure 5.7. AdvPs expressing times can usually be replaced by the word *then*.

$[_{AdvP} [_{Spec} \text{very}] [_{Adv} \text{quickly}]]$

Figure 5.7

> *13.* Jeremy arrived *very early*, and Cheryl arrived *then* too.
> (*then* = *very early*)

Other types of AdvPs cannot be easily replaced by a single word, but substitution by larger units is possible.

> *14.* Doug types *very quickly*, and Caroline types *that way* too.
> (*that way* = *very quickly*)

A small number of time expressions such as *yesterday*, *today*, and *now* are problematic for syntactic analysis. In terms of the meaning they express, such elements appear to be adverbs in that they provide information about the time of actions. In terms of form, however, these elements do not combine with specifiers such as *very*. For the purposes of this book, we will consider these expressions to make up an exceptional class of adverbs.

Intermediate Structures The substitution test that we used to justify the claim that NPs are syntactic units can also be used to show that there is a syntactic unit larger than an N but smaller than an NP. This new category is N′ (pronounced N-bar). It is sometimes also written as $\overline{\text{N}}$. An item that substitutes for N′ is the word *one*.

> *15.* *a)* This book is longer than that *one*. (*one* = *book*)
>   *b)* This book about Australia is longer than that *one* about New Guinea. (*one* = *book*)
>   *c)* This book about Australia is longer than that one. (*one* = *book*, or *book about Australia*)

Here we see that the word *one* can substitute for something the size of an N or something larger than an N but smaller than an NP. If we postulate N′ as a category intermediate between N and NP, we can think of these examples as involving the same kind of substitution. Another set of examples illustrating this is shown below.

16. a) This book is heavier than that *one*. (*one* = *book*)
    b) This book on the shelf is heavier than that one on the table. (*one* = *book*)
    c) This book on the table is better than that one. (*one* = *book*, or *book on the table*)

In general, we can think of the NP as initially branching in two directions, to *Det* and *N′*. *N′* can go directly to *N*, or it can branch to *N′* and something else, such as *PP*. At each level, *one* may substitute for *N′*. This is diagrammed in Figure 5.8.

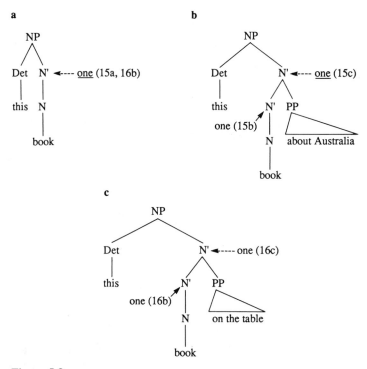

Figure 5.8

The substitutability of *one* in other cases involving adjectives shows that an AdjP can be a subconstituent of N′ (see Figure 5.9). That is, *one* may substitute for an AdjP + N sequence, as in *17a*. In fact, there is even more structure in this example, since *one* may also replace only *book*, as in *17b*.

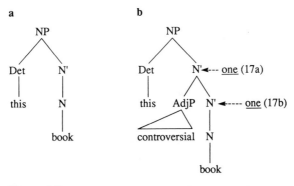

Figure 5.9

> 17. *a*) This controversial book is longer than that *one*. (*one = controversial book*)
>
> *b*) This controversial book is longer than this innocuous *one*. (*one = book*)

(Because this section is optional, the NPs diagrammed in the following sections do not reflect the N′ innovation discussed here.)

Heads As we have seen, each phrasal category is built around a lexical category—NP around N, VP around V, AdjP around Adj, and so on. The lexical category around which a phrasal category is built is called the **head** of that phrase. The head of a phrase has two distinctive properties. First, it is the one component of a phrase that is invariably present. Thus, it is not possible to have a VP without a verb, although it is possible to have such a phrase without an NP or a PP.

> 18. *a*) No NP: They [$_{VP}$ left early].
>
> *b*) No PP: They [$_{VP}$ left the room].
>
> *c*) No NP or PP: They [$_{VP}$ left].
>
> *d*) No verb: *They [$_{VP}$ the room]

Second, the type of meaning associated with the head is also associated with the phrase. Thus, just as the noun *girls* designates a group of individuals, so does the NP *the young girls*. Similarly, just as the verb *run* names an action, so does the VP *run to the store*.

This head—phrase relation can be expressed by using the variable X to stand for N, V, Adj, or P. Every XP contains an X as its head, and many of the properties of the X, as illustrated above in the previous paragraph, are shared by the XP. This way of looking at phrases leads us to expect that an XP will always have an X as its head. It should therefore come as a great surprise if we were to find a VP with something other than a V as its head—an N for instance.

> 19. *a*) [$_{VP}$ [$_{V}$ run] to the store]
>
> *b*) *[$_{VP}$ [$_{N}$ noun] to the store]

A system of phrase structure called X′ (X-bar) theory, incorporating the notion of head discussed here as well as intermediate-sized categories like the N′ discussed earlier, has been elaborated and applied in much recent work in syntactic theory.

Recursion

One very important property of any natural language is that it contains an indefinite number of possible sentences; given any grammatical sentence of the language, it is always possible to form a sentence that is longer. This property is called **recursion**, and it can be illustrated with notions introduced in this section. Take, for example, the NP in *16b*, *this book on the shelf*. Note that this NP contains a PP (*on the shelf*) as a subconstituent, and note further that this PP contains an NP (*the shelf*) as a subconstituent.

Now imagine that this NP itself contained a PP, *this book on the shelf in the corner*. Here we have a longer sentence, formed by the introduction of a PP into the NP, a reapplication of the procedure used to form the NP in Figure 5.10. The following general pattern is emerging: an NP may contain a PP which in turn contains an NP, which may contain a PP, and so on (see Figure 5.11). Were it not for the fact that the NP need not contain a PP, the sentence would never end.

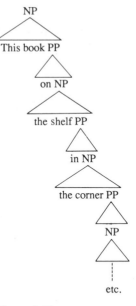

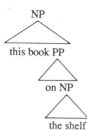

Figure 5.10   **Figure 5.11**

Recursion is exhibited in other parts of the syntax of a language. We have seen that AdjPs, for example, may contain the specifier *very*, as in the AdjP *very quiet*. We may also have an AdjP that contains two occurrences of *very* (*very, very quiet*), or three (*very, very, very quiet*), or in fact any number. Nor is there a numerical limit on the number of AdjPs that can occur inside NP, as in *the small, white poodle*, or *the very, very large, very black, quite silly, rather undignified bulldog.*

Sentence Structure

A **sentence (S)** consists of an NP and a VP, each of which can itself consist of other categories. This is illustrated in Figure 5.12. (For clarity of exposition, tree structures rather than labeled bracketing will be used to represent full sentences in many cases.) Tree structures such as Figure 5.12 express a fundamental insight of syntactic analysis. That insight is that sentences do not simply consist of strings of lexical categories. Rather, within any sentence, words are grouped together to form phrases, which then combine with each other to form still larger phrases, and so on. As we have seen, the presence of each phrasal unit can be verified with the help of substitution and movement tests.

Some Syntactic Relations Tree structures can be used to define various important syntactic notions. The points where category labels appear in Figure 5.12 are called **nodes**. One node is said to **dominate** another if there is a path in the tree from the first node down to the second. Thus, the S node in Figure 5.12 dominates all other nodes, while the NP node dominates only Det and N. Two or more categories that have the same node immediately above them are called **sisters**. In Figure 5.12, for example, each determiner and the noun to its right are sisters as are the verb and the NP and PP to its right. In contrast, the noun *player* and the verb *lost* are not sisters since they do not occur immediately beneath the same node.

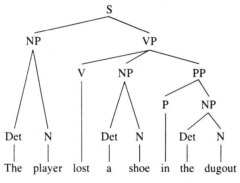

Figure 5.12

Dominance and sisterhood allow us to define the following important distinction between two structural positions in the sentence.

> *20.* **Subject**: the NP immediately dominated by S (it is the sister of VP)
> **Direct object**: the NP immediately dominated by VP (it is the sister of V)

When applied to Figure 5.12, these definitions identify *the player* as subject and *a shoe* as direct object. Frequent reference to subjects and direct objects is made in the remainder of this chapter.

Structural Ambiguity The grouping together of words into phrases reflects not only the syntactic organization of the sentence, but also the way in which word meanings are combined to give the meaning of the full sentence. Consider in this regard a sentence such as *Fast cars and motorcycles are dangerous*. This sentence can mean either that there is danger in fast cars and fast motorcycles or that there is danger in fast cars and any type of motorcycle. We can use tree structures to represent these two meanings by assuming that the phrase *fast cars and motorcycles* can be analyzed in either of the two ways shown in Figure 5.13. (*C* marks a conjunction, a minor lexical category whose members serve to join categories of the same type.) Figure 5.13a corresponds to the interpretation in which the property expressed by the word *fast* applies to both cars and motorcycles, while Figure 5.13b represents the interpretation in which only the cars are taken to be fast.

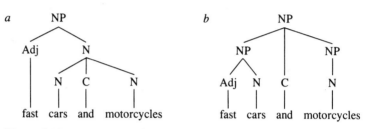

Figure 5.13

When the same string of words can be associated with more than one tree structure, it is said to be **structurally ambiguous**. We will consider this type of ambiguity in more detail in the chapter on semantics. For the time being, the important thing to note is that tree structures provide a natural way to represent this phenomenon.

5.2 PHRASE STRUCTURE RULES

Now that we have established the existence of syntactic structures consisting of lexical and phrasal categories, our next step must be to determine the rules that allow some combinations of words but not others. As noted in the introductory chapter, there is no numerical limit on the set of possible grammatical sentences in a language. It therefore makes no sense to think that speakers simply memorize all of the syntactic structures of their language. Rather, they must have access to a system of rules that enables them to form sentences as needed. Part of this system consists of **phrase structure rules**, which specify the grouping of lexical categories into phrases. A sample set of phrase structure rules is given in *21*.

21. a) S → NP   VP
       b) NP → (Det)   (AdjP)   N (PP)
       c) VP → V   (NP)   (PP)
       d) PP → P   NP
       e) AdjP → (Spec) Adj

The S Rule

Each arrow can be read as 'branches into,' 'consists of,' or 'is rewritten as.' Thus, the first phrase structure rule, called 'the S rule,' indicates that an S (sentence) branches into an NP and a VP (see Figure 5.14).

Figure 5.14

The NP Rule

The NP rule in *21b* is somewhat more complicated since it indicates that NPs can optionally contain a determiner, a PP, and an adjectival phrase in addition to an obligatory noun head. (As is the custom, optional elements are enclosed in parentheses.) This gives the eight possibilities exemplified in Figure 5.15. To simplify, N′ will not be used here, and the AdjPs in these examples consist of only an adjective head.

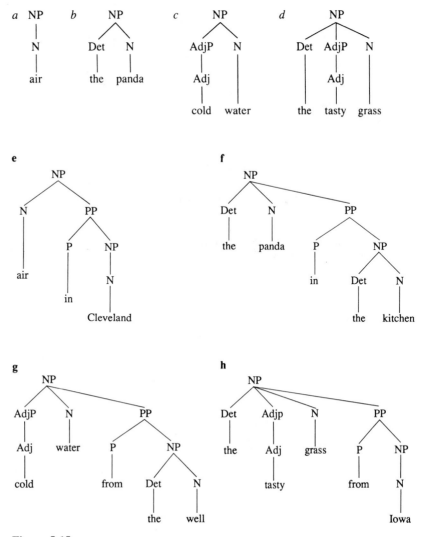

Figure 5.15

The VP Rule

A wide range of options is also allowed by *21c*, the VP rule. These options include the verb (the head) standing alone or accompanied by an NP, a PP, or both (see Figure 5.16).

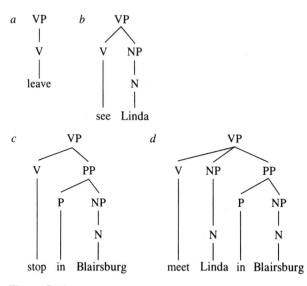

Figure 5.16

The phrase structure rules given in *21* also allow us to construct syntactic structures for entire sentences. Reconsider in this regard the syntactic structure in Figure 5.12, repeated here as Figure 5.17. In Figure 5.17, the S rule applies first—giving NP and VP. The NP rule then permits the *determiner-noun* sequence corresponding to *the player*. The VP rule allows the VP to branch into a verb (*lost*), an NP, and a PP. The NP rule can then be applied, giving the *determiner-noun* sequence corresponding to *a shoe*. The PP rule will give a preposition (*in*) and an NP. At this point, the NP rule can be used once again to yield the *determiner-noun* sequence corresponding to *the dugout*.

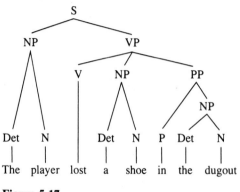

Figure 5.17

Modal
Auxiliaries

Now consider the following sentences.

> *22. a)* Mosquitoes will sting.
> *b)* The winds can shift.
> *c)* This grade may impress Holly.

These sentences all include **modal auxiliary verbs** such as *will, can, may,* and *must*, which express notions like permission, possibility, obligation, and futurity. These elements are called **auxiliary** or **helping** verbs because they must always occur with a regular or **main** verb in a complete sentence. The utterance *Ships must*, for instance, is not a complete sentence of English since it has no main verb.

A second type of auxiliary verb is found in sentences such as *23*.

> *23. a)* The boy has done the laundry.
> *b)* The boy is doing the laundry.

Auxiliary *have* and *be* can be used in conjunction with a modal to create complex patterns such as the one in *24*.

> *24.* The copilot must have been flying the plane.

In order to simplify, we will focus our attention here on modal auxiliaries, which are introduced by the rule in *25* and appear in structures such as Figure 5.18 (M = modal).

> *25.* S → NP (M) VP

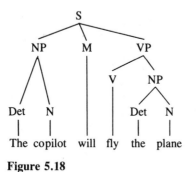

Figure 5.18

5.3 LEXICAL INSERTION

Having seen how phrase structure rules determine the arrangement of phrasal and lexical categories into sentences, we can now consider how individual words are inserted into syntactic structure. One obvious precondition for **lexical insertion** is a "match" between the word's syntactic category and the category of the node under which it is inserted. In Figure 5.19, for example, the determiner *The* occurs under the Det node, the noun

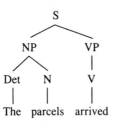

Figure 5.19

parcels under the N node, and the verb *arrived* under the V node. A match between the category of the lexical item and the node under which it is inserted does not always ensure a correct result. The section that follows deals with a second equally important condition on lexical insertion.

Subcate-gorization

Lexical insertion is also sensitive to the category of other phrases in syntactic structure. As Figure 5.20 shows, not just any verb can be inserted into the V position in a tree structure. The verb *arrive* cannot take a direct object

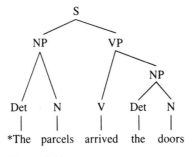

Figure 5.20

NP. That is, it cannot be inserted into a tree structure where it will have an NP as its sister. (Recall that the direct object NP is the sister of V.) In this, it differs from the verb *like*, which requires a direct object NP.

> 26. *a)* *The wrestlers like.
> *b)* The wrestlers like the fans.

Different again are verbs such as *study*, which can occur with or without a direct object.

> 27. *a)* The candidates must study.
> *b)* The candidates must study the problem.

These contrasts are captured by means of **subcategorization frames**, features that divide syntactic classes into subcategories by indicating the types of sister categories with which they can or must occur.

Verb Subcategorization The subcategorization frame − [__ NP] indicates that a verb cannot occur with a sister NP (a direct object). Such verbs are often called **intransitive**. The frame + [__ NP], in contrast, indicates that the verb requires a direct object. Such verbs are called **transitive**. Verbs (such as *study*) that optionally take a direct object have the subcategorization frame + [__ (NP)].

> 28. arrive: V,   − [__ NP]
>   like: V,   + [__ NP]
>   study: V,   + [__ (NP)]
>   hit: V,   + [__ NP]

Verbs may also be subcategorized for a sister PP. The verb *put*, for example, requires not only a sister NP but also a sister PP.

> 29. *a*) *Trevor put.
>   *b*) *Trevor put the glass.
>   *c*) *Trevor put on the table.
>   *d*) Trevor put the glass on the table.

In order to account for these facts, we will have to assume that *put* has the subcategorization frame + [__ NP PP] and that it can therefore be inserted only into structures such as Figure 5.21 in which it will have two sisters—an NP and a PP. Verbs whose subcategorization frames make no mention of PPs are assumed to allow such elements as optional sisters.

Figure 5.21

More Ambiguity

The condition that allows PPs as optional sisters of Vs predicts more structural ambiguity of the sort discussed earlier. Consider the following sentence.

> 30. Curly will hit the dog with the stick.

This sentence is ambiguous; it has two meanings. The first meaning can be paraphrased by using a relative clause: *Curly will hit the dog that is carrying the stick.* Here, the PP is modifying *the dog*. In the second interpretation, Curly will use the stick as a weapon, as in *Curly will use the stick to hit the dog.* Here, we might say that the PP is modifying the verb *hit*. (The first interpretation may be called the PP modifier interpretation, and the second, the instrument interpretation.) This ambiguity is a consequence of the optionality of PP both within the VP and within the direct object NP. That is, the PP *with the stick* may be mapped into either of two positions, daughter of VP or daughter of NP, as illustrated in Figure 5.22. In each case, the resulting structure is licensed by the set of phrase structure rules.

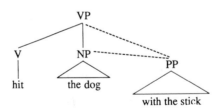

Figure 5.22

5.4 A GENERATIVE GRAMMAR

Table 5.2 summarizes the phrase structure rules proposed to this point as well as the syntactic categories and subcategorization frames for some of the words used in the examples in the preceding section. Table 5.2 provides

Table 5.2 A preliminary generative grammar

Rules	Lexical items	
	Examples	Syntactic categories and subcategorization frames
S → NP (M) VP	*the*	Det
NP → (Det) (AdjP) N (PP)	*in*	P
VP → V (NP) (PP)	*parcels*	N
PP → P NP	*arrive*	V, −[__ NP]
	put	V, +[__ NP PP]
	hit	V, +[__ NP]

an illustrative fragment of a **generative grammar**, a system of rules that forms or **generates** syntactic representations (tree structures) for all the grammatical sentences of a language. This approach to syntactic analysis was introduced to linguistics in the 1950s by Noam Chomsky, a linguist at the Massachusetts Institute of Technology. Since that time, many of the most influential syntactic analyses have made use of generative grammar in one form or another. For this reason, this approach constitutes the focus of our introduction to syntax.

A major objective of current linguistic research is to construct a grammar capable of generating all the grammatical sentences of a language and no ungrammatical ones. This research involves identifying the rules that allow speakers to determine which sentences of their language are well formed and which are not.

The syntactic rules considered up to this point are very incomplete. (There has been no mention, for example, of AdvPs in the phrase structure rules.) Instead of simply adding to the list of phrase structure rules, we will turn our attention to an entirely different type of syntactic rule, one that better illustrates the type of grammar that many linguists believe is associated with human language.

5.5 TRANSFORMATIONAL RULES

Although phrase structure rules generate a very wide range of patterns, there are syntactic phenomena that they cannot describe in an entirely satisfactory way. This section presents a number of these phenomena and discusses the changes that must be made in the grammar in order to accommodate them.

Inversion in Yes-No Questions

The following structures are called *yes-no* questions because the expected response is usually *yes* or *no*.

> 31. a) *Will* Tiffany leave?
> b) *Can* Joan scale this cliff?

Notice that the sentences in *31* have an auxiliary verb in initial position rather than after the subject NP, as in *32*.

> 32. a) Tiffany *will* leave.
> b) Joan *can* scale this cliff.

The former structures create a problem for the S rule (restated in *33*), which allows a modal auxiliary to occur only *after* the subject NP.

> 33. S → NP (M) VP

What changes must be made to accommodate *yes-no* questions? One possibility is a revision to the S rule along the lines indicated in *34*.

> 34. S → (M) NP (M) VP

Although *34* will allow a modal to occur either at the beginning of the sentence (as in *31*) or after the first NP (as in *32*), it can also incorrectly generate ungrammatical sentences such as *35*, in which modals occur in both positions.

> 35. a) *Can Tiffany will leave?
> b) *Will Joan can scale this cliff?

This problem can be overcome if we retain the original (and simpler) S rule outlined in *33* and add to the grammar an entirely new type of rule called a **transformation**. A transformation is a rule that applies to a syntactic tree to yield a new syntactic tree. In the case of *yes-no* questions, such a rule applies to the structure formed by the phrase structure rules to bring about the change stipulated in *36*, where 'Aux' equals any auxiliary, including modals.

> 36. Inversion:
> NP Aux
> 1　2 ⇒ 2　1

The left side of the transformation, called the **structural description**, states the input to the rule while the right side, called the **structural change**, designates the output. Thus, *36* indicates that Inversion applies to an *NP Aux* (auxiliary verb) sequence to bring about the change indicated by the numbers in the second line.

A sentence such as *Will Alex leave?* is generated by first using the usual phrase structure rules to form the tree in Figure 5.23a and then applying the Inversion rule. Since the modal *will* is a type of auxiliary verb, the Inversion rule will convert the tree in Figure 5.23a into the tree in Figure 5.23b. What is the advantage of using the Inversion transformation to help generate *yes-no* questions? For one thing, we now avoid the ungrammatical sentences in *35*. Since we can use the simple phrase structure rule in *33* to form the structure to which the Inversion rule applies, we can be sure that there will be only one modal auxiliary verb in each S.

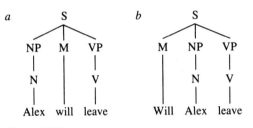

Figure 5.23

A second advantage of the transformational approach is that it allows us to capture the relationship between sentences such as those in *37*.

37. *a*) Alex will leave.
       b) Will Alex leave?

Sentence *37b* is the question form corresponding to *37a*. This fact is captured in our analysis since both sentences are formed by the same set of phrase structure rules. The difference between them is then attributed to the fact that the Inversion transformation has applied in the question structure.

Particle Movement

English includes numerous constructions such as the following:

38. *a*) Chris looked up the reference.
       b) Bob threw away the wrapper.
       c) Amy put down the hamster.

In these sentences, the words, *up*, *away*, and *down* are examples of **particles**. Although many of the words in this minor lexical category can also function as prepositions, it is important to keep the two categories separate. Unlike prepositions, particles appear immediately under the VP node rather than a PP node. This is reflected in the revised VP rule outlined in *39*, which yields the tree structure depicted in Figure 5.24.

39. VP → V (Prt) (NP) (PP)

A distinctive fact about particles is that their positioning is somewhat flexible. As you can see by comparing the sentences in *40* with those in *38*, the particle can occur either immediately after the verb or after the direct object NP.

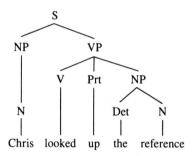

Figure 5.24

> 40. *a*) Chris looked the reference up.
> *b*) Bob threw the wrapper away.
> *c*) Amy put the hamster down.

In contrast, prepositions must always occur before an NP, as stipulated in the PP rule. Thus, we can *41a*, but not *41b*.

> 41. *a*) We sat near the stage.
> *b*) *We sat the stage near.

The flexible positioning of particles is accounted for by the following transformation, which applies optionally to the tree structure formed by the VP rule in *39*.

> 42. Particle Movement:
> V Prt NP
> 1   2   3 ⇒ 1 3 2

Applied to Figure 5.24, this movement transformation will yield the structure depicted in Figure 5.25 by reversing the order of the particle and the direct object NP. An advantage of this analysis is that it allows the same phrase structure rule to be used in the generation of both constructions containing a particle. This provides a way of capturing the fact that the two structures are variants of the same basic pattern and differ from each other only in terms of the positioning of the particle.

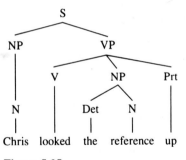

Figure 5.25

Deep Structure and Surface Structure

The preceding examples show how sentences are generated with the help of two distinct rule systems—phrase structure rules, which stipulate the internal structure of phrasal categories, and transformations, which modify tree structures by reordering the elements in specific ways. Because sentences are generated in these two major steps, it is possible to identify two levels of syntactic representation. The first is called **deep structure**. It results from insertion of lexical items into the tree structure generated by the phrase structure rules. As will be shown in the chapter on semantics, deep structure plays a very central role in the interpretation of sentences. The second level of syntactic structure is called **surface structure**. It results from the application of whatever transformations are needed to yield the final syntactic form of the sentence. Thus, the deep structure for the sentence *Can chimps count?* will be Figure 5.26a, while the surface structure will be Figure 5.26b. The first structure is the product of the usual phrase structure rules, while Figure 5.26b is formed by applying the Inversion transformation to Figure 5.26a.

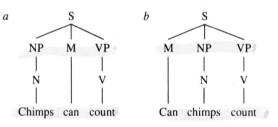

Figure 5.26

The set of steps or rule applications that results in the formation of a sentence is called a **derivation**. In sentences where the derivation does not include any transformations, the deep structure and surface structure will look alike. Thus, the sentence *Tourists will leave,* which does not undergo any transformations, will have a surface structure (final syntactic form) identical to its deep structure (the tree produced by the phrase structure rules).

Transformations can interact with each other and with the phrase structure rules to generate a wide range of sentences. An example of this interaction is given in Figure 5.27.

The diagram in Figure 5.28 helps represent the organization of the syntactic component of the grammar as it has just been outlined. As Figure 5.28 shows, the grammar makes use of different syntactic operations. Some of these operations are responsible for the formation of syntactic structure, others for the insertion of lexical items, and still others for the movement of categories within syntactic structure. As we have seen, these rule systems operate in conjunction with each other to generate grammatical sentences of English. In later sections of this chapter, we will see how these rules can be modified to generate an even wider range of English sentences and how they can be further modified to account for syntactic patterns in other languages as well.

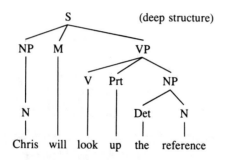

Particle Movement:

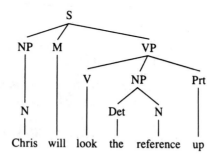

Inversion:

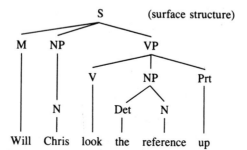

Figure 5.27 Interaction involving the Particle Movement and Inversion transformations

Phrase structure rules
↓
Insertion of lexical items
↓
DEEP STRUCTURE
↓
Transformational Rules
↓
SURFACE STRUCTURE

Figure 5.28 The syntactic component of the grammar

5.6 EMBEDDED CLAUSES

All human languages allow sentence-like constructions to be embedded within larger structures.

> 43. *a)* Anna said [that Eric made the sandwiches].
>   *b)* Anna asked [whether Eric made the sandwiches].
>   *c)* Anna wondered [if Eric made the sandwiches].

The bracketed phrases in *43* are called **complement clauses**. The larger clauses in which they occur are called **matrix** clauses. The grammar imposes no limit on the number of embedded clauses that can occur in a sentence. As *44* shows, we can easily put together a long string of complement clauses—notwithstanding the difficulty a reader may have comprehending the structure.

> 44. Heather said that Meghan remembered that the police officers thought that Gordon reported that. . . .

Complement clauses have the structure depicted in Figure 5.29. Words such as *that, if,* and *whether* are called **complementizers** (**COMPs**). These elements are attached to S to indicate that it is embedded within a larger structure. The category created by combining a complementizer with S is known as *S'* (pronounced *S-bar*).

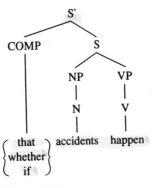

Figure 5.29

Verb Complements

All of the examples given in *43* involve complement clauses within the VP portion of the sentence. Such clauses are called complements of the verb or **verb complements**. In order to form these structures, we must revise the VP rule as indicated in *45* and add to the grammar the rule outlined in *46*. For the time being, assume that the COMP position can be filled by the words *that, whether,* and *if* or simply left empty (as in the sentence *He said he would leave*).

> 45. VP → V (Prt) (NP) (PP) (S')
> 46. S' → COMP S

Rule *45* allows several options. As before, the VP can consist of a verb (its head) followed by various optional elements. Crucially, however, we are now also able to have an S′ within VP. The simplest such case involves a structure such as Figure 5.30. By exploiting the option of expanding VP as V plus S′, we ensure the presence of a second S which, in turn, will provide a new VP. Since a VP can be expanded as V plus S′ (and so on, indefinitely), the grammar can now create an unlimited number of embeddings, as in *44*. As noted earlier, a rule that can reapply indefinitely in this way is said to be **recursive**.

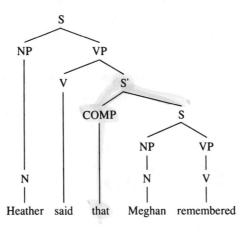

Figure 5.30

Not all verbs can take an S′ complement. The verb *criticize,* for instance, contrasts with *say* in this respect.

47. a) *Brett criticized [s′ that Leah laughed].
    b) Brett criticized Leah.

It seems that whereas *say* can head a VP that also includes an S′, *criticize* cannot. This is the type of contrast that is expressed by means of subcategorization frames. The verbs *say* and *criticize* will have subcategorization frames that differ in the following way with respect to S′ complements.

48. say: +[__ S′]
    criticize: −[__ S′]

The subcategorization frame for *say* indicates that it occurs with an S′ sister in its VP; conversely, the frame for *criticize* indicates that it cannot occur in this type of structure.

Adverbial Clauses

Verb complements should not be confused with the **adverbial clauses** exemplified in *49*.

49. a) The workers left [s′ after management complained].
    b) The workers left [s′ because management complained].

Adverbial clauses, which usually express notions such as 'before', 'after', 'while', and 'because', differ from complement clauses in a very important way. Whereas adverbial clauses can usually be moved to the beginning of the sentence, complement clauses cannot.

50. Adverbial clause: After management complained, the workers left.
51. Complement clause: *That management complained, the workers said.

Adverbial clauses are not sisters of the verb. Rather, they are attached directly to the matrix S. (We will assume that words such as *after* and *because* occur in the COMP position.) Adverbial clauses are introduced by the following phrase structure rule, a revised version of the original S rule.

52. S → NP (M) VP (S')

This rule will generate structures such as the one in Figure 5.31. In order to form the variant of this structure in which the adverbial clause occurs at the beginning of the sentence, we need only formulate the following transformation.

53. Adverbial clause movement:

$$\frac{\text{NP (M) VP}\quad\text{S}'}{1\qquad\quad 2}\Rightarrow 2\ 1$$

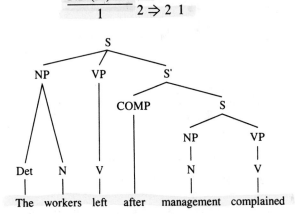

Figure 5.31

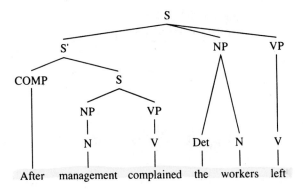

Figure 5.32

This transformation will apply to a structure such as Figure 5.31 to give Figure 5.32.

5.7 Wh QUESTIONS

Consider now the set of question constructions exemplified by *54*. These sentences are called **wh questions** because of the presence of a question word beginning with *wh*. (We are concerned here with a variant of English that does not use the *wh* word *whom*.)

> *54. a)* Who will politicians attract?
>   *b)* Who can voters trust in?

Wh Movement

Do the deep structures associated with *54a* and *54b* resemble the surface form of these sentences, or are they quite different? Most linguists take the position that the sentences in *54* must have the deep structures in Figure 5.33. We will assume that *wh* words like *who* and *what* are a type of noun

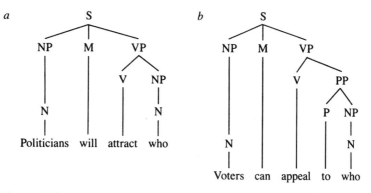

Figure 5.33

and that *wh* words like *which* and *whose* are a type of determiner. The NPs that contain these *wh* words in Figure 5.33 are *wh* phrases. An important argument in favor of these deep structures involves subcategorization. Consider in this regard the following sentences.

> *55. a)* *Politicians will attract.
>   *b)* *Voters can trust in.

The unacceptability of these sentences suggests that the subcategorization frames for *attract* and *in* must be $+[\_\_ \text{NP}]$. That is, *attract* and *in* can be inserted into deep structure only if they have a sister NP. Thus, the *wh* questions in *54* must have deep structures like those in Figure 5.33, in which the verb and the preposition each have an NP sister—the interrogative element *who*.

In order to convert these deep structures into the corresponding surface structures, the following movement transformation is used.

56. Wh Movement: Move a *wh* phrase into the COMP position.

According to this analysis, a sentence such as *Who will politicians attract?* would be formed in several steps, the first of which involves generation of the structure depicted in Figure 5.34. In order to generate Figure 5.34, we

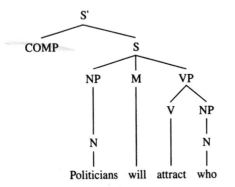

Figure 5.34

must assume that the phrase structure rule expanding S′ applies first, giving COMP and S. Although we have been assuming that the generation of single-clause sentences begins with the rule expanding S, nothing prevents the rule expanding S′ from applying first. Henceforth, we will assume that the S′ rule *invariably* applies first and that the COMP position is simply left empty in unembedded clauses.

Once the structure in Figure 5.34 has been generated, *Wh* Movement and Inversion can apply to yield Figure 5.35.

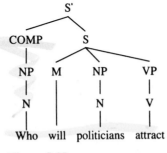

Figure 5.35

Wh Move-
ment in Verb
Complements

We have just seen that there is a transformational rule that moves *wh* phrases into COMP and that helps derive the surface structure in *57b* from the deep structure in *57a*.

57. *a)* Deep structure: [s′ [s The voters would choose who]].
    b) Surface structure: [s′ Who [s would the voters choose]].

Since embedded clauses also have a COMP, we would expect *Wh* Movement to be applicable within complement clauses as well. As the following example shows, this assumption is correct.

58. *a)* Deep structure: The senator knew [s′ [s the voters would choose who]].
    b) Surface structure: The senator knew [s′ who [s the voters would choose]].

Although *Wh* Movement can apply in embedded clauses, Inversion cannot. We have no sentences such as *59b* in English, derived from *59a* by applying Inversion in the embedded clause.

59. *a)* The lobbyists knew [what the senators would do].
    b) *The lobbyists knew [what would the senators do].

In order to avoid the formation of ungrammatical sentences such as *59b*, we formulate the following constraint on Inversion.

60. Inversion can apply only in an unembedded S.

This ensures that inversion can apply only in the topmost S in any tree structure and prevents the formation of ungrammatical sentences such as *59b*.

Long Distance Movement

Earlier in this section we saw *Wh* Movement applying inside the main clause, and we just saw examples of *Wh* Movement applying in embedded clauses. If we think of this transformation simply stated as "Move *wh* to COMP," we might expect to find cases where the *wh* phrase is inside a complement clause at deep structure, but in the top COMP node at surface structure. There are indeed examples like this.

61. *a)* Deep structure: [s′ [s The senators will believe [s′ [s the voters chose who]]]]
    b) Surface structure:
    [s′ who [s will the senators believe [s′ [s the voters chose ___]]]]

Similar examples may be constructed to show that this kind of *Wh* Movement, called **long distance movement**, is a fairly general property of English and other languages. In the examples that follow, the dash indicates the deep structure position of the *wh* word.

62. *a)* Who did the president say that the senators believed that the voters chose ___?
    b) Whose shoe did the newspaper report that the police commissioner had alleged that the detectives said that they had found ___ at the scene of the crime?

*5.8 RELATIVE CLAUSES

The transformation of *Wh* Movement plays a role in the formation of structure other than *wh* questions. Consider:

> *63. a)* Angela knows [NP the guitarists [S′ who Bryan hired]].
> *b)* Jay saw [NP the singer [S′ who Bryan spoke to]].

The bracketed S′s in *63*, called **relative clauses**, are embedded within an NP. As the following sentence shows, a sequence such as *the guitarists who Bryan hired* is a syntactic unit since it can be replaced by the pronoun *them*.

> *64.* Angela knows [NP the guitarists who Bryan hired], and I know them too. (*them = the guitarists who Bryan hired*)

Relative clauses provide information about the head of the NP in which they occur. In sentence *63a*, for example, the relative clause helps identify the guitarists by indicating that they are the people hired by Bryan.

Wh Movement Again

Relative clause structures resemble embedded *wh* questions in two respects. First, they begin with a *wh* word such as *who* or *which*. Second, there is an "empty" position within the sentence from which the *wh* phrase has apparently been moved. In sentences *63a* and *63b*, for instance, the NP position following the transitive verb *hire* and the preposition *to* is unfilled in surface structure.

These are the simplest relative clause structures for the grammar to generate, and we will briefly consider how this is done. The first step involves the formation of a deep structure such as Figure 5.36 with the help of the revised NP rule in *65*.

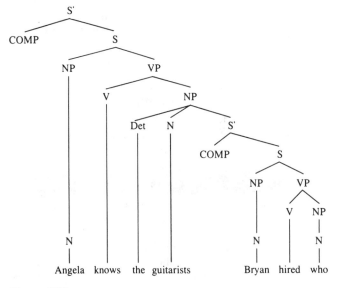

Figure 5.36

65. NP → (Det) (AdjP) N (S′)

The next step involves the application of the *Wh* Movement rule to give Figure 5.37. We see, then, that no new transformations are required to form relative clause structures such as *63a* and *63b*. Rather, these structures can be formed with the help of the same *Wh* Movement transformation that was independently required for *wh* questions.

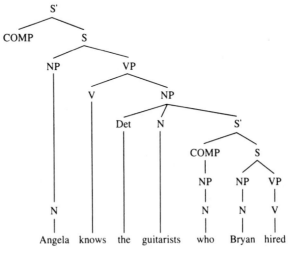

Figure 5.37

*5.9 ISLANDS

The distance, measured in terms of clause boundaries, that may intervene between the *wh* word in COMP and its deep structure position is in principle indefinite. That is, another longer sentence involving a longer movement can always be constructed that will be grammatical in the language. There is, however a sense in which a *wh* phrase can be moved "too far." In particular, there are environments out of which a *wh* item cannot be moved. Consider, for example, sentences similar to the examples in *62* with the deep structure shown in *66*. Note that here there are two *wh* phrases in the same embedded clause.

66. [s′ [s The commissioner might wonder [s′ [s the detectives found whose shoe at which house]]]]

Wh Movement may now apply to this deep structure, and two surface structures are possible if both *wh* phrases undergo movement. Either *wh* phrase may move to the top COMP, and the other may move to the lower COMP. Neither surface structure, however, gives a grammatical sentence.

67. *a)* *[S′ whose shoe [S might the commissioner wonder [S′ which

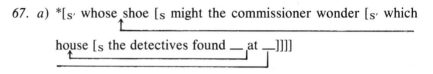

house [S the detectives found __ at __]]]]

b) *[S′ which house [S might the commissioner wonder [S′ whose

shoe [S the detectives found __ at __]]]]

Following are other cases with environments out of which movement is somehow prohibited. Here again the gap shows the deep structure position of the *wh* phrase.

68. *a)* *Who did the rumor that the tiger ate __ surprise the game warden?
    b) *Whose shoes did the commissioner reward the detectives who found __?

The tree configurations out of which movement is impossible are known as **islands**. It is important to note here that simple distance does not create an island. That is, the sort of movement illustrated in *68a* is fairly short compared to that shown in *62b*, yet it is the relatively short movement in this case that yields the ungrammatical sentence. It appears that there is a set of syntactic categories on structures that cannot intervene between the *wh* phrase in COMP and its deep structure position. In particular, NP and an embedded S′ that contains a *wh* phrase already in COMP appear to create islands. *Wh* Movement is thus sensitive to *structural* conditions, and without any notions of overall sentence structure (as built into our phase structure rules), we would be unable to explain why some sentences are grammatical and some are ungrammatical. Sentences involving movement out of an island are some of the more spectacularly ungrammatical cases illustrating the importance of structural notions in syntactic descriptions. The discovery that there are syntactic islands in turn allows us to state the rule of *Wh* Movement very simply: move *Wh* to COMP. If our theory of syntax did not specify the structure of sentences, or have a place for conditions on transformations, imagine how complex (and uninformative) our description of *wh* questions and relative clauses would be.

Let us return for a minute to an earlier example, repeated in *69*.

69. Curly will hit the dog with the stick.

We observed in this case that two structures could be assigned to this string of words; the main difference was whether or not the PP *with a stick* was internal to the direct object NP. If we replace the NP *the stick* with the *wh* phrase *what*, either of the following deep structures results.

70. *a)* [S′ [S Curly will [VP hit [NP the dog [PP with what]]]]]
    b) [S′ [S Curly will [VP hit [NP the dog] [PP with what]]]]

Observe that the *wh* phrase *what* is inside the direct object NP in *70a*. According to our notions of island, *Wh* Movement out of this position should be impossible. In *70b*, on the other hand, the *wh* phrase *what* is not contained in an island, so movement should be permitted. The result of these movements is shown in *71*.

71. *a)* *[s' What [s will Curly [vp hit [np the dog [pp with ___]]]]]

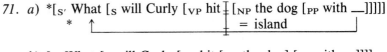

b) [s' What [s will Curly [vp hit [np the dog] [pp with ___]]]]

Figure 5.38 shows the equivalent tree structures.

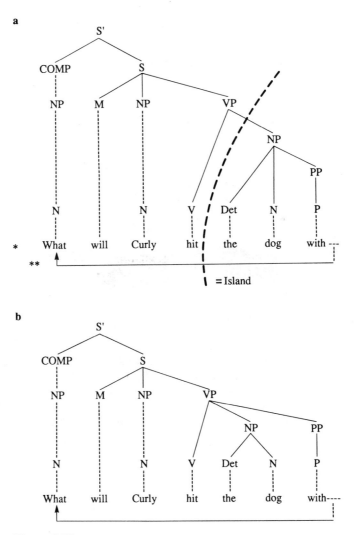

Figure 5.38

Our theory allows only one of these surface structures; only one structure can be assigned to the string of words *What will Curly hit the dog with,* while two can be assigned to *Curly will hit the dog with the stick.* There is a further prediction: since only one structure can be assigned to the string of words *What will Curly hit the dog with,* it cannot be ambiguous in the same way as the string of words *Curly will hit the dog with the stick.* Only one interpretation is possible with the *wh* question, and it is the one that corresponds to the instrument interpretation—an answer to this question will specify the item with which Curly will strike the dog. The answer will not give a further description of the dog; the PP modifier interpretation is blocked. Recall that this interpretation corresponds to the structure in which the PP is inside the NP. The *wh* question, however, cannot reflect this PP modifier structure because it would involve a movement of the *wh* phrase out of the island, which is prohibited. Only one interpretation is allowed because only one syntactic structure is allowed. Recognition of island phenomena in syntax can thus help to explain why certain structures are ungrammatical as well as why others are not ambiguous.

5.10 SOME CROSS-LINGUISTIC VARIATION

The generative grammar we have been considering is far from complete. There are many phenomena that we have not attempted to discuss, and there are many sentence types that could not be generated without quite extensive additions to the syntactic rules we have been working with. However, even in its incomplete form the grammar considered here contains a representative sampling of the syntactic devices that are found in English and other languages. In this section, we will examine a few phenomena from languages other than English and demonstrate how they can be analyzed within the framework of generative grammar.

Syntactic Categories

The syntactic categories outlined in this chapter make up a universal set that can be manifested in different ways in particular languages. As pointed out in Chapter 3, a similar phenomenon is found in phonology, where there is a universal inventory of potential distinctive features from which individual languages draw a subset. In the case of syntactic categories, only the contrast between nouns and verbs is found in all human languages. While the category of adjective is also very common, it is not universal. In many languages (Hausa, Japanese, Telugu, Hua, and Bemba), there are no adjectives and no direct translation for English sentences such as *72*.

72. The cat is hungry.

Instead, the concept 'hungry' is expressed with the help of a noun in structures like *73a* or a verb in structures like *73b*.

73. *a*) The cat has hunger.
     b) The cat hungers.

Even where languages adopt the same set of categories, the precise rules for sentence formation may differ. For example, both English and French have adjectives, but, in French, they generally follow rather than precede the noun.

> 74. la voiture rouge
>   the car red
>   'the red car'

Even more drastic differences in word order arise in the case of Korean, which consistently places heads in the final position within their phrase. Thus, the noun comes at the end of the NP, the verb at the end of the VP, and so on (see Figure 5.39). Because "prepositions" occur at the end of the

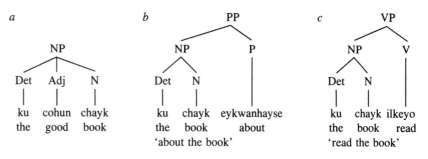

Figure 5.39 Examples of Korean word order

PP in Korean, they are called **postpositions**. (Korean examples are written in the traditional system of romanization.) Differences such as these reflect the positioning of the head within phrases, not the presence of an entirely new type of syntactic category. There are important cross-linguistic constraints on the ordering of heads within phrasal categories—a matter that is discussed in Chapter 8.

Korean Phrase Structure

The following two sentences provide another illustration of the way in which Korean differs from English in the word order it employs within phrasal categories.

> 75. *a)* Chun ku chayk poata.
>   Chun that book see
>   'Chun sees that book.'
>   *b)* Chun Bob-hako malhata.
>   Chun Bob with   speak
>   'Chun speaks with Bob.'

As in the earlier examples, the verb occurs at the end of the VP and the postpositions at the end of the PP. However, as in English, the subject NP typically occurs first in the sentence, and determiners precede nouns. We can account for these facts by formulating the following phrase structure rules for Korean.

76.   S → NP VP
       NP → (Det) N
       VP → (PP) (NP) V
       PP → NP P

These rules will generate structures such as Figure 5.40, corresponding to 75a. The important thing to recognize here is that although Korean employs

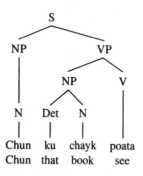

Figure 5.40

a word order different from that of English, its sentences still consist of phrasal and lexical categories organized in accordance with phrase structure rules. Beneath the obvious word order differences between English and Korean, then, there is a more fundamental similarity in the categories and rule types needed to generate syntactic structure.

Selayarese Phrase Structure

The following sentences from Selayarese (a language of Indonesia) exemplify a word order pattern that differs from both Korean and English.

77.   a) La?allei doe?   iñjo i Baso?.
          take   money the   Baso
          'Baso took the money.'
      b) Lataroi doe?   iñjo ri lamari   iñjo i Baso?.
          put   money the in cupboard the   Baso
          'Baso put the money in a cupboard.'
      c) nra?bai sapon-na.
          collapse house his
          'His house collapsed.'

Contrary to both English and Korean, the Selayarese subject NP occurs at the end of the sentence, and (again contrary to English and Korean) the determiner follows the noun inside the NP. The VP and PP, however, appear to follow the same pattern as their English counterparts. These facts can be expressed by the following set of phrase structure rules for Selayarese.

78. S → VP NP
NP → N (Det)
VP → V (NP) (PP)

Application of these rules will yield Figure 5.41 as the structure corresponding to *77b*.

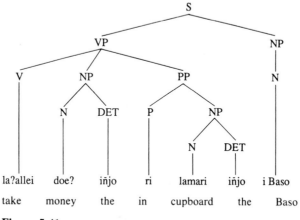

Figure 5.41

Even though the Selayarese word order here differs from earlier examples, the syntactic categories we have been using up to this point are still applicable. A further interesting feature, discussed in Chapter 8, emerges when we compare the rules for the phrasal categories in Korean and Selayarese. Beyond the word order differences, a generalization concerning the placement of the head within the phrase can be stated. That is, Korean is head-final within the phrase, and Selayarese is head-initial. Using the notions of X'-theory introduced previously, we can abbreviate much of the syntactic structure of these two languages as follows, using X to refer to N, V, and P.

79. *a*) Korean Phrase Structure (head-final)
XP → . . . X
b) Selayarese Phrase Structure (head-initial)
XP → X . . .

This contrast in phrase structure illustrates how languages can differ from each other while preserving a fundamental similarity. Here, Selayarese and Korean contrast along the lines of head-placement, but they are similar in that the head of the phrase is placed at one end or the other.

Question Formation in Tamil

Languages often differ from each other in the kinds of rules they use to form a particular sentence type. In Tamil (a Dravidian language of southern India and Sri Lanka), for example, *yes-no* question structures are formed without an Inversion transformation by simply adding the particle *a* to the end of the sentence. This is illustrated in *80*. (The diacritic ˙ indicates a dental point of articulation; the diacritic ‾ marks a long vowel; ḷ is a retroflex liquid.)

80. *a*) Muṭṭu paḷam parittān.
       Muttu fruit   picked
       'Muttu picked the fruit.'
    b) Muṭṭu paḷam parittān-ā.
       Muttu fruit   picked ?
       'Did Muttu pick the fruit?'

Instead of positing a question-forming transformation for Tamil, then, we would simply formulate the following phrase structure rule. (*Q* stands for the question particle *ā*.)

81. S → NP VP (Q).

Rule *81* will help generate the tree structure depicted in Figure 5.42, corresponding to sentence *80b*. (Like Korean, Tamil places the V at the end of

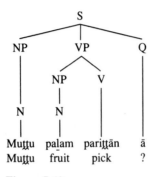

Figure 5.42

the VP.) Examples such as these show that languages can use very different means to express the same type of meaning. Whereas English can use a movement transformation (Inversion) to form *yes-no* questions, the equivalent structure in Tamil is formed exclusively by the phrase structure component of the grammar.

Inversion in French and Spanish

Languages may also differ from each other by adopting slightly different forms of the same basic transformational operation. A major difference between French and English, for instance, relates to the nature of the Inversion rule used in *yes-no* questions. Like English, French can form a question by moving an auxiliary verb leftward—as *82* illustrates.

82. *a*) Tu peux rester.
       'You can stay.'
    b) Peux-tu rester?
       'Can you stay?'

However, unlike English, French also allows Inversion to affect nonauxiliary verbs when the NP to the left is a pronoun. Thus *83b*, formed by moving the verb to the left of a pronominal subject, is acceptable.

83. *a)* Il sait.
    'He knows.'
    b) Sait-il?
    knows he
    'Does he know?'

However, a sentence derived by movement of a verb to the left of a non-pronominal subject, such as *84b*, is ungrammatical.

84. *a)* Jean sait.
    'John knows.'
    b) *Sait Jean?
    'Knows John?'

Still a different option is adopted in Spanish, where (simplifying somewhat) only a main verb can undergo Inversion.

85. *a)* Él ha partido.   Él partió.
    'He has left.'   'He left.'
    b) *Ha él partido?   Partió él?
    'Has he left?'   'Left he?'
86. *a)* Juan ha partido.   Juan partió.
    'John has left.'   'John left.'
    b) *Ha Juan partido?   Partió Juan?
    'Has John left?'   'Left John?'

The differences just outlined are reflected in the type of Inversion transformation used by each of these languages (see Table 5.3). Inversion provides

Table 5.3 Inversion rules in English, French, and Spanish

Inversion (English)	Inversion (French)	Inversion (Spanish)
NP aux	pronoun verb	NP main verb
1 2 $\Longrightarrow$ 2 1	1 2 $\Longrightarrow$ 2 1	1 2 $\Longrightarrow$ 2 1

an excellent example of how languages can differ from each other by adopting slightly different versions of essentially the same rule. Thus, English allows only auxiliary verbs to undergo Inversion, but places no restriction on the type of subject NP involved in this process. French, on the other hand, permits any type of verb to be inverted but only allows pronominal NPs to be involved in this process. Spanish, in contrast, places restrictions on the verbs that can undergo Inversion, but not on the subjects.

*Passive Structures

Consider now the pair of sentences in *87.*

87. *a)* The thieves took the painting.
    b) The painting was taken by the thieves.

Not only are these two sentences virtually identical in meaning, but also there is a systematic relationship between their structures. The NP functioning as direct object in *87a* (*the painting*) is the subject in *87b*, while the subject in *87a* (*the thieves*) occurs as part of the *by* phrase in *87b*. There are many other such pairs.

> 88. *a*) The dog chased the truck.
> *b*) The truck was chased by the dog.
> 89. *a*) The teacher praised Ginette.
> *b*) Ginette was praised by the teacher.

The *a* sentence in each pair is called **active** because its subject names the actor (the doer of the action designated by the verb). The *b* sentences are called **passive** in recognition of the fact that the subject does not name the actor (which appears in a PP headed by the preposition *by*). In English, passive structures are formed with the help of the auxiliary verb *be* and the so-called past participle form of a main verb. (Most English verbs take either *-ed* or *-en* as their past participle ending.)

A Passive Transformation The relationship between active and passive constructions in English has traditionally been captured by means of a transformation. Since the usual phrase structure rules already generate active constructions, the transformation is used to derive a passive sentence from its active counterpart. The transformation operations required to do this are stated in *90*. (Following the common practice, *-en* is used as the symbol for the past participle ending, although many verbs take the *-ed* ending or are irregular.)

> 90. Passivization:
> NP V (Prt) NP
> 1   2   3 $\Rightarrow$ 3 *be* 2 *en* by 1

The effect of these transformational operations is illustrated in Figure 5.43. As Figure 5.43 illustrates, the direct object NP in the active structure (*the painting*) appears as subject in the passive while the subject NP in the active structure (*the thieves*) occurs with the preposition *by* after the verb. In addition, a form of the auxiliary verb *be* is present in the passive construction as is the past participle ending *-en*. The tense of the auxiliary verb is identical to that of the verb in the active sentence.

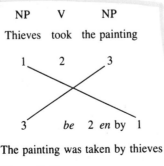

NP   V   NP
Thieves took   the painting
1   2   3

3   *be* 2 *en* by 1

The painting was taken by thieves

Figure 5.43

Universal Properties of Passivization Although almost all languages have passives, the formation of these structures does not always involve movement of NPs or addition of auxiliary verbs. In Tzotzil (a Mayan language of Mexico), for instance, NPs occur in the same position in active and passive constructions.

91. *a*) Lá snákan ti vīnike ti xpétule.
     seated   the man   the Peter
     'Peter seated the man.'
   b) Inákanat   ti vīnike yuʔun ti xpétule.
      was seated the man by   the Peter
      'The man was seated by Peter.'

In Mandarin, on the other hand, Passivization changes the positioning of NPs, but does not affect the form of the verb.

92. *a*) Zhu laoshi   piye-le wode kaoshi.
     Zhu professor marked my   test.
   b) Wode kaoshi bei Zhu laoshi   piye-le.
      my   test by Zhu professor marked
      'My test was marked by Professor Zhu.'

In some recent work, an attempt has been made to capture certain universal aspects of Passivization. Instead of indicating the changes in word order and the form of the verb brought about by Passivization, a statement is made about the effect of this process on the grammatical relations of subject and direct object. As noted previously, the phrase that bears the direct object relation in an active sentence functions as subject in the corresponding passive structure. Furthermore, the phrase that functions as subject in the active sentence appears with a special marker in the passive (in English, the preposition *by*) which signals that it names the actor but is no longer the subject of the sentence.

The relational changes associated with Passivization can be stated as follows. (The arrow here is read as 'becomes'; for convenience, we will use the English preposition *by* to represent the marker of a nonsubject actor.)

93. Passivization:
      Subject NP → *by* NP
  Direct object NP → Subject NP

Since the criteria used to identify subjects and direct objects differ from language to language, *93* can have correspondingly different effects. In English, where the direct object appears after the verb and the subject before it, a change in an NP's grammatical role also involves a change in its linear position. Thus, a deep structure direct object that becomes subject in surface structure appears to the left of the verb rather than to the right. In other languages, changes in grammatical relations may be marked in different ways—as the Tzotzil and Mandarin examples show. What all languages with passive structures have in common, however, is the pair of relational changes stated in *93*.

Summing Up

This chapter focuses on some of the fundamental devices involved in determining the **grammaticality** of sentences in human language. These devices seem to be of different types: there are **phrase structure rules**, which form the initial **tree structures**, **subcategorization frames**, which ensure compatability between words and the tree structures into which they are inserted to form a **deep structure**, and **transformations**, which can modify the structural configuration in various ways to produce a **surface structure**. Some constraints on the application of transformations were noted as well in the section on *islands*. Taken together, these devices make up an important part of linguistic competence in that they provide the basic ability to combine words into sentences in novel ways.

Although the precise rules for sentence formation differ from language to language, the same general type of syntactic devices, such as phrase structure rules and transformations, appear to be found in all human languages. This in turn suggests that all human beings are endowed with the same type of linguistic ability. This issue is described further in the chapter on language acquisition.

Sources

Transformational generative grammar was first proposed in the 1950s by Noam Chomsky, most notably in his monograph *Syntactic Structures* (The Hague: Mouton, 1957). Since that time, many other variants of transformational grammar have been proposed. For an overview of the development of transformational grammar, see F. Newmeyer's *Linguistic Theory in America* (New York: Academic Press, 1980). For an account of recent developments, such as X'-theory or islands, see the books by Baker, Radford, and van Riemsdijk and Williams (cited below). An alternate theory of syntactic structure is presented in the article on passivization by Perlmutter and Postal cited below. The data on the universal properties of Passivization come from this article.

Recommended Reading

Akmajian, Adrian and Frank Heny. 1975. *An Introduction to the Principles of Transformational Syntax*. Cambridge, Mass.: MIT Press.

Baker, C. L. 1978. *Introduction to Generative-Transformational Syntax*. Englewood Cliffs, N.J.: Prentice-Hall.

Perlmutter, David and Paul Postal. 1983. "Toward a Universal Characterization of Passivization." D. Perlmutter, ed., *Studies in Relational Grammar I*. Chicago: University of Chicago Press.

Radford, Andrew. 1983. *Transformational Syntax: A Student's Guide to Chomsky's Extended Standard Theory*. London: Cambridge University Press.

van Riemsdijk, Henk and Edwin Williams. 1986. *Introduction to the Theory of Grammar*. Cambridge, Mass.: MIT Press.

Questions

1. As you saw in the first section of this chapter, each word can be assigned to a lexical category. Examine the following sentences and indicate the lexical category of each word.
   a) The glass broke.
   b) He ran toward the red post.
   c) This tall tree gives good shade.
   d) He took out the garbage.

2. Verbs are divided into subcategories on the basis of the elements that they can or must take as sisters in deep structure. Determine whether each of the following verbs has the frame +[__ NP], −[__ NP], or +[__ (NP)].
   a) faint
   b) destroy
   c) retract
   d) speak
   e) clean

3. Following are some simple sentences from English, all of which can be formed by means of the phrase structure rules given in this chapter. Use the appropriate phrase structure rules to generate a tree for each of these sentences.
   a) The machine broke.
   b) The teacher put the answers on the board.
   c) A clever magician fooled the audience.

4. In this chapter, no attempt was made to formulate a phrase structure rule for AdvPs. Such a rule would have to allow for the following possibilities: *quickly/very quickly, late/very late*. On the basis of the following patterns, formulate an AdvP rule and make a revision to the VP rule so as to introduce AdvPs within the VP category.
   a) Leslie ate the donut (very) quickly.
   b) Zena talked to Gary (very) quietly.
   c) Richard learned French in school (quite) successfully.

5. The formation of many sentences involves the use of transformations. The derivation of the following sentences involves Particle Movement and/or Inversion. Show the deep structure and surface structure for each of these sentences.
   a) The wind knocked a vase over.
   b) Harry threw the rake away in the yard.
   c) Will the new owner hire Rob?
   d) Can the robot take the garbage out?

6. The following sentences involve the rule of *Wh* Movement in addition to the rules required by the sentences in the previous exercise. Show the derivation for each of these sentences.
   a) What can the debaters talk about?
   b) What could Celia give away?
   c) Who should the pro give a racket to?

7. The following sentences involve the rule of Passivization in addition to at least some of the transformations and phrase structure rules required by the sentences in the previous exercise. Show the derivation for each of these sentences.
   a) A valuable calculator was lost by the professor.
   b) Was a trophy presented by the committee?
   c) The container was thrown away by the girl.
   d) Who was the vintage Rolls driven by?

8. The following sentences all involve embedded clauses that are either complements of the verb or adverbial clauses. Identify the type(s) of embedded clause(s) in each sentence and use the necessary rules to derive these sentences.
   a) The reporter said that the accident injured a pedestrian.
   b) The reporter wrote the story after the accident injured a pedestrian.
   c) Because the accident injured a pedestrian, the reporter wrote the story.
   d) The reporter said that the pedestrian hit the curb before the car swerved.

9. Write the phrase structure rules required to generate these sentences from Japanese. (The endings *-ga* and *-o* indicate a subject and a direct object respectively and may be ignored for the purposes of this exercise.)
   a) Taroo-ga sono gakusei-o hihansita.
      Taroo   the   student   criticized
      'Taroo criticized the student.'
   b) Sono syoonen-ga isu   ni suwatta.
      the   boy   chair on sat
      'The boy sat on the chair.'
   c) Hanako-ga hon-o tukue ni oita.
      Hanako   book table on put
      'Hanako put the book on the table.'
   d) Etsuko-ga tuita.
      'Etsuko arrived.'

6 SEMANTICS
The Study of Meaning

*Indeed, it is well said, in every object there is
inexhaustible meaning.*

Thomas Carlyle

Up to this point in the book, the emphasis has been on the form of utterances—their sound pattern, morphological structure, and syntactic composition. In order for language to fulfill its communicative function, however, utterances must also attempt to convey a meaning or message. This chapter is concerned with **semantics**, the study of meaning in human language. We will examine four major issues in this field: (1) the nature of meaning, (2) the contribution of syntactic structure to the interpretation of sentences, (3) the role of nongrammatical factors in the understanding of utterances, and (4) the possible influence of language on thought.

6.1 MEANING

Long before linguistics existed as a discipline, thinkers were speculating about the nature of meaning. For thousands of years, this question has been considered central to philosophy. More recently, it has come to be important in psychology as well. Contributions to semantics have come from a diverse group of scholars, ranging from Plato and Aristotle in ancient Greece to Bertrand Russell in the twentieth century. Our goal in this section will be to consider in a very general way what this research has revealed about the meanings of words and sentences in human language.

Word Meaning

The basic repository of meaning within the grammar is the lexicon, which provides the information about the meaning of individual words relevant to the interpretation of sentences. We know very little about the nature of this type of meaning or how it should be represented. Nonetheless, it is worthwhile to review briefly some of the better-known proposals and their attendant problems.

Referents One well-known approach to semantics attempts to equate a word's meaning with the entities to which it refers—its **referents**. According to this theory, the meaning of the word *dog* corresponds to the set of entities (dogs) that it picks out in the real world. Although not inherently implausible, this idea encounters certain serious difficulties. For one thing, there is a problem with words such as *unicorn* and *dragon*, which have no referents in the real world even though they are far from meaningless. A problem of a different sort arises with expressions such as *the Prime Minister of Great Britain* and *the leader of the Conservative Party,* both of which refer (in 1989 at least) to Margaret Thatcher. Although these two expressions may have the same referent, we would not say that they mean the same thing. No one would maintain that the phrase *Prime Minister of Great Britain* could be defined as 'the leader of the Conservative Party' or vice versa.

Extension and Intension The impossibility of equating a word's meaning with its referents has led to a distinction between **extension** and **intension**. Whereas a word's extension corresponds to the set of entities that it picks out in the world, its intension corresponds to its inherent sense, the concepts that it evokes. Some examples are given in Table 6.1. Thus, the extension of *woman*

Table 6.1 Extension versus intension

Phrase	Extension	Intension
Prime Minister of Great Britain	Margaret Thatcher	leader of the majority party in Parliament
World Series champions (1988)	L.A. Dodgers	winners of the baseball championship
capital of California	Sacramento	city containing the state legislature

would be a set of real word entities (women) while its intension would involve notions like 'female' and 'human'. Similarly, the phrase *Prime Minister of Great Britain* would have as its extension an individual ('Margaret Thatcher'), but its intension would involve the concept 'leader of the majority party in Parliament'. The distinction between a word's intension and its extension does not allow us to resolve the question of meaning. It simply permits us to pose it in a new way: what is the nature of a word's inherent sense or intension?

One suggestion is that word meanings (intensions) correspond to mental images. This is an obvious improvement over the referential theory since it is conceivable that one might have a mental image of a unicorn or a dragon even if there are no such entities in the real world. Unfortunately, this idea encounters serious difficulties of another sort. For one thing, it is hard to conceive of a mental image for words like *nitrogen, 522,101, if, very,* and so on. Moreover, there seems to be no mental image for the meaning of the word *dog* that could be general enough to include Chihuahuas and Irish wolfhounds, yet still exclude foxes and wolves.

Semantic Features Still another approach to meaning tries to equate a word's intension with an abstract concept consisting of smaller components called **semantic features**. This componential analysis is especially effective when it comes to representing similarities and differences among words with related meanings. The feature analysis in Figure 6.1 for the words *man, woman, boy,* and *girl* illustrates this. An obvious advantage of this approach is that it allows us to group entities into natural classes (much as we do in phonology). Hence, *man* and *boy* could be grouped together as [+HUMAN, +MALE], while *man* and *woman* could be put in a class defined by the features [+HUMAN, +ADULT].

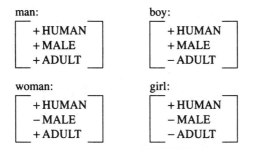

man:

    ⎡ +HUMAN ⎤
    ⎢ +MALE ⎥
    ⎣ +ADULT ⎦

boy:

    ⎡ +HUMAN ⎤
    ⎢ +MALE ⎥
    ⎣ −ADULT ⎦

woman:

    ⎡ +HUMAN ⎤
    ⎢ −MALE ⎥
    ⎣ +ADULT ⎦

girl:

    ⎡ +HUMAN ⎤
    ⎢ −MALE ⎥
    ⎣ −ADULT ⎦

Figure 6.1 Semantic feature composition for *man, woman, boy, girl*

Componential analysis gives its most impressive results when applied to sets of words referring to classes of entities with shared properties. As illustrated above, a few simple features will allow us to distinguish among subclasses of people—men, women, boys, and girls. Unlike phonological features, however, semantic features do not seem to make up a small, well-defined class, and it is often very hard to reduce word meanings to smaller parts. Can we say, for example, that the meaning of *blue* consists of the feature [+COLOR] and something else? If so, what is that other thing? Isn't it blueness? If so, then we still have not broken the meaning of *blue* into smaller features, and we are back where we started.

In other cases, it is unclear whether semantic features really provide any insights into the nature of the meaning they are supposed to represent. What value is there, for instance, in characterizing the meaning of *dog* in terms of the feature complex [+ANIMAL, +CANINE] so long as there is no further analysis of the concept underlying the feature [CANINE]? A similar objection could be made to the use of features like [HUMAN] and [MALE] to define *man* and *woman*.

Semantic Relations among Words

Despite the difficulties associated with determining the precise nature of meaning, it is possible to identify a number of important universal semantic relations relevant to the analysis of word meaning. Foremost among these are the relations of synonymy, antonymy, polysemy, and homophony.

Synonymy Words or expressions that have identical meanings are called **synonyms**. Although genuine synonymy is rare in human language, the pairs of words in Table 6.2 provide plausible examples of complete or near synonymy.

Table 6.2 Some English synonyms

youth	adolescent
automobile	car
remember	recall
purchase	buy
big	large

Antonymy Words or phrases that have opposite meanings are called **antonyms**. The pairs of words in Table 6.3 provide examples of antonymy.

Table 6.3 Some English antonyms

dark	light
male	female
hot	cold
up	down
in	out
come	go

Polysemy and Homophony When a word has two or more meanings that are at least vaguely related to each other, this is called **polysemy** (see Table 6.4).

Table 6.4 Some English polysemous words

iron	a type of metal	an instrument (made of iron) for pressing clothes
diamond	a precious stone	a baseball field (in the shape of a diamond)
leaf	a part of a tree	a sheet of paper

Homophones are words that have a single phonetic form but two or more entirely distinct meanings (see Table 6.5). In such cases, it is assumed that

Table 6.5 Some English homophones

bat	a winged rodent	a piece of equipment used in baseball
bank	a commercial lending institution	a small cliff at the edge of a river
club	a social organization	a blunt weapon
pen	a writing instrument	a small cage

there are two separate words with the same pronunciation (rather than a single word with two related meanings). Polysemy and homophony create **lexical ambiguity** in that a single word has two or more meanings. Thus, a sentence such as *1* could mean either that Liz purchased an instrument to write with or that she bought a small cage.

1. Liz bought a pen.

Of course, in actual speech the context usually makes the intended meaning clear. Thus, it is improbable that anyone would perceive ambiguity in a sentence such as *2*.

  2. He got a loan from the bank.

Semantic Relations Involving Sentences

Like words, sentences have meanings that can be analyzed in terms of their relation to each other. We consider three such relations here—paraphrase, entailment, and contradiction.

Paraphrase Two sentences with identical meanings are said to be **paraphrases** of each other. The following pairs of sentences provide examples of complete or near paraphrases.

  3. *a*) The police chased the burglar.
     b) The burglar was chased by the police.
  4. *a*) I gave the summons to Erin.
     b) I gave Erin the summons.
  5. *a*) It is unfortunate that the schooner lost.
     b) Unfortunately, the schooner lost.
  6. *a*) The game will begin at 3:00 P.M.
     b) At 3:00 P.M., the game will begin.

The *a* and *b* sentences in each of the above pairs are obviously very similar in meaning. Indeed, it would be impossible for one sentence in any pair to be true without the other also being true. Thus, if it is true that the police chased the burglar, it must also be true that the burglar was chased by the police. For some linguists, the fact that two sentences must either be both true or both false is an indication that they have the same meaning. However, you may notice that there are subtle differences in emphasis between the *a* and *b* sentences in *3* to *6*. For instance, it is natural to interpret *3a* as a statement about what the police did and *3b* as a statement about what happened to the burglar. Similarly, *6b* seems to place more emphasis on the starting time of the game than *6a* does. Some linguists feel that it would be inefficient for a language to retain two or more structures with absolutely identical meanings and that perfect paraphrases therefore do not exist.

Entailment A relation in which the truth of one sentence necessarily implies the truth of another, as happens in examples *3* to *6*, is called **entailment**. In the cases we have been considering, the entailment relation between the *a* and *b* sentences is mutual since the truth of either member of the pair guarantees the truth of the other. In some cases, however, entailment is asymmetrical. The following examples illustrate this.

  7. *a*) The police wounded the burglar.
     b) The burglar is injured.
  8. *a*) The house is red.
     b) The house is not white.

The *a* sentences in *7* and *8* entail the *b* sentences. If it is true that the police wounded the burglar, then it must also be true that the burglar is injured. However, the reverse does not follow since the burglar could be injured without the police having wounded him. Similarly, if it is true that the house is red, then it is also true that it cannot be white. Once again though, the reverse does not hold: even if we know that the house is not white, we cannot conclude that it must be red.

Contradiction Sometimes, the truth of one sentence entails the falsity of another. This is the case with the examples in *9*.

9. *a*) Charles is a bachelor.
   b) Charles is married.

If it is true that Charles is a bachelor, then it cannot be true that he is married. A relationship wherein the truth of one sentence entails the falsity of another sentence in this way is called a **contradiction**.

In this section, we have considered some of the major problems associated with the representation of word meaning as well as some basic semantic relations and contrasts involving words and sentences. Our next task must be to consider how speakers of a language are able to produce and understand meaningful utterances. Although much of the work in this area is quite complex, it is worthwhile to consider simplified versions of a few representative proposals.

6.2 SYNTACTIC STRUCTURE AND INTERPRETATION

The syntactic representations (tree structures) generated by the grammar are important not only for determining the form of sentences, but also for determining their interpretation. In this section, we will consider the relevance of syntactic structure to three aspects of sentence interpretation—the representation of structural ambiguity, the assignment of thematic roles, and the interpretation of reflexive pronouns.

Structural Ambiguity

As noted in the chapter on syntax, some sentences are ambiguous because their component words can be arranged into phrases in more than one way. This is called structural ambiguity and is to be distinguished from lexical ambiguity, which is the result of homophony or polysemy. Structural ambiguity is exemplified by phrases like *old men and women,* where we can take old to be a property of both the men and the women or of the men alone. These two interpretations or readings can be linked to separate tree structures, as Figure 6.2 shows. (C = conjunction.) Figure 6.2a corresponds to the reading in which *old* modifies *men* as well as *women*. This is shown by making the adjective a sister of the category that dominates both nouns. In Figure 6.2b, on the other hand, the adjective is a sister of only the N

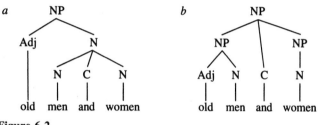

Figure 6.2

men, and this structure corresponds to the reading in which 'old' applies only to the men.

Another case of structural ambiguity is found in sentences such as *10*.

10. Nicole saw the people with binoculars.

In one interpretation of *10*, the people had binoculars when Nicole noticed them (the phrase *with binoculars* modifies the noun *people*), while in the other interpretation, Nicole saw the people by using the binoculars (the PP modifies the verb). These two readings can be represented as in Figure 6.3. In Figure 6.3a, the PP *with binoculars* combines with the N *people,* reflecting the first reading for this sentence. In Figure 6.3b, on the other hand, the PP is a sister of the verb and its direct object and is not linked in any special way to the N *people*.

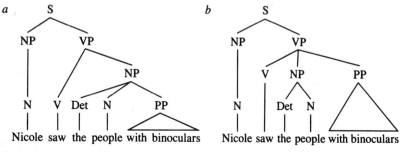

Figure 6.3

As a final example of this type of structural ambiguity, consider the compound *French history teacher,* which can refer either to a history teacher who is French or to a teacher of French history. These two readings can be associated with the trees depicted in Figure 6.4a and 6.4b, respectively.

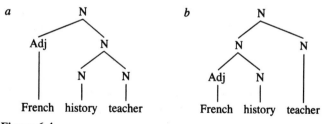

Figure 6.4

The three cases of structural ambiguity just outlined all have in common the fact that the two interpretations can be related to differences in the surface structure tree. Sometimes, however, ambiguity can be properly characterized only with the help of deep structure. Consider in this regard a sentence such as the following:

11. Who do you expect to play?

On one reading, 11 can be interpreted as a question about who your opponent will be (who you will play against) while on another, it asks who will be playing. Although it is difficult to see how the grouping of constituents in surface structure could reflect these different interpretations, consideration of the relevant deep structures provides the needed insight. The first reading corresponds to 12a, in which who appears as direct object of play. The second interpretation, on the other hand, is associated with the deep structure depicted in 12b, in which the wh word is subject of play. In both cases, Wh Movement will yield the sentence in 11. (See Section 5.7 of Chapter 5.)

12. a) You expect to play who.
    b) You expect who to play.

The fact that deep structure is needed to represent certain types of ambiguity provides interesting additional evidence for the view that there are at least two levels of syntactic structure—deep structure and surface structure.

*Thematic Roles

Part of semantic interpretation involves determining the roles that the referents of NPs play in the situation described by sentences. Consider in this regard the simple sentence in 13.

13. The senator sent the lobster from Maine to Nebraska.

It would be impossible to understand this sentence if we could not identify the senator as the person who is responsible for sending something, the lobster as the thing that is sent, and so on. The term **thematic role** or **semantic role** is used to describe the part played by a particular entity in an event. In most linguistic analyses, at least the thematic roles in Table 6.6 are rec-

Table 6.6 Thematic roles

The senator sent the lobster from Maine to Nebraska.		
Agent:	the entity who deliberately performs an action	*the senator*
Theme:	the entity undergoing a change of state or transfer	*the lobster*
Source:	the starting point for a transfer	*Maine*
Goal:	the end point for a transfer	*Nebraska*

ognized. (These definitions have been simplified somewhat.) The notion of transfer used in the definition of theme, source, and goal is intended to involve not only actual physical movement, but also changes in possession, as in 14, and identity, as in 15.

14. Terry gave the skis to Mary.
    agent   theme   goal

15. The magician changed the handkerchief into a rabbit.
    agent   theme   goal

Many semantic analyses recognize various other thematic roles, as shown in Table 6.7, to describe the NPs in sentences such as the following:

16. The astronomer saw the comet with a new telescope at the observatory.

Table 6.7 Some additional thematic roles

The astronomer saw the comet with a new telescope at the observatory.		
Experiencer:	the entity perceiving something	*the astronomer*
Stimulus:	the entity perceived	*the comet*
Instrument:	the entity used to carry out an action	*a new telescope*
Location:	the place at which an entity or action is located	*the observatory*

Thematic Role Assignment The lexicon includes information about the type of thematic role associated with particular verbs and prepositions. The entry for the verb *send,* for example, indicates that the subject NP expresses an agent, the direct object NP a theme, and so on. (By convention, the thematic role of the subject is written to the left of the dash and that of the direct object to the right.)

17. send
    NP __ NP (from NP) (to NP)
    agent theme   source goal

The lexical entries for the verbs *see* and *receive* include the following information about thematic roles.

18. see
    NP   __ NP
    experiencer stimulus

19. receive
    NP __ NP
    goal   theme

The entry for the preposition *near* would include the following piece of information.

20. near
    __ NP
      location

The thematic role that an NP receives is determined by its position in deep structure. Consider first a sentence such as *13*, repeated here as *21*, whose surface structure and deep structure are identical in the relevant respects.

21. The senator sent the lobster from Maine to Nebraska.

Here, the order of the NPs in deep structure is such that they can be linked in one-to-one fashion with the thematic roles mentioned in the lexical entry for *send* in *17*. A more interesting case involves sentences such as *22* in which the NP bearing the theme role (*what*) occurs at the beginning of the sentence rather than after the verb (the position corresponding to the theme role in the lexical entry).

22. What will the senator send from Maine to Nebraska?

Fortunately, this does not present a problem since the NP *what* will occur in the right position in deep structure to receive the theme role. As *23* shows, *what* occurs in direct object position prior to *Wh* Movement.

23. The senator will send what from Maine to Nebraska.

Deep Structure and Meaning The discovery of the relevance of deep structure to sentence interpretation had an important and lasting impact on linguistic theory, allowing formulation of the following hypothesis.

24. In sentences with the same deep structure, noun phrases will be associated with the same thematic roles.

This generalization is true not only for *wh* questions, but also for other pairs of sentences that share a deep structure. Consider the following:

25. *a)* Anton will throw the ball.
    b) Will Anton throw the ball?
       Anton = agent; *the ball* = theme
26. *a)* The boxer knocked out the champion.
    b) The boxer knocked the champion out.
       the boxer = agent; *the champion* = theme
27. *a)* Sandra received the book.
    b) The book was received by Sandra.
       Sandra = goal; *the book* = theme

The relevance of deep structure to the assignment of thematic roles is important for two reasons. First, it shows that syntactic structures not only represent the way in which words are organized into phrases, but also are relevant to semantic interpretation. Second, the fact that an NP's position in deep structure determines its thematic role provides additional evidence for the existence of this underlying level of syntactic structure. This, in turn, lends support to the claim that there must be at least two types of syntactic rules: phrase structure rules, which form the deep structure; and transformations, which convert it into surface structure.

*The Interpretation of Reflexive Pronouns

The interpretation of **reflexive pronouns** such as *himself, herself,* or *themselves* provides another example of the relevance of syntactic structure to semantics. Reflexive pronouns are considered to be a type of NP since they occur in the positions normally reserved for this type of syntactic category. In *28*, for instance, the reflexive pronoun *himself* occurs in the direct object position.

> 28. Jim hurt himself.

In order to interpret a reflexive pronoun, it is necessary to identify elsewhere in the sentence the NP that indicates its referent. In a sentence such as *28*, the referent of the reflexive pronoun *himself* is specified by the NP *Jim*. The NP to which a pronoun looks for its interpretation is called its **antecedent**.

Consider now the following two sentences.

> 29. *a)* [s Clare showed Alice a picture of herself].
>   *b)* [s Clare said [s Alice took a picture of herself]].

Most speakers of English find that the first sentence is ambiguous in that *herself* can have either *Clare* or *Alice* as its antecedent. Thus, the picture mentioned in *29a* could be of either Clare or Alice. Not so in *29b*. Here, *herself* can only take *Alice* as its antecedent. The reason for this contrast stems from the following principle.

> 30. The Same S Requirement: A reflexive pronoun and its antecedent must occur in the same S.

In *29a*, there are two NPs in the same S as the reflexive (*Alice* and *Clare*), either of which could be its antecedent according to *30*. The sentence is therefore ambiguous. In *29b*, in contrast, only one NP (*Alice*) occurs in the same S as the reflexive pronoun. The NP *Clare* occurs outside the embedded S in which *herself* occurs and therefore cannot serve as its antecedent. This shows that a feature of syntactic structure, the occurrence of clause boundaries, is crucial to the interpretation of sentences.

The C-Command Requirement A somewhat more abstract feature of syntactic structure enters into the interpretation of the reflexive pronoun in sentences such as *31*, which would be associated with the tree in Figure 6.5.

> 31. The boy's uncle admired himself.

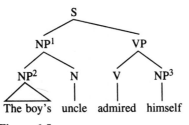

Figure 6.5

Although there are two NPs in the same S as *himself,* only one (*the boy's uncle*) can serve as antecedent for the reflexive pronoun. Thus, the person who was admired in *31* must have been the boy's uncle, not the boy. The principle needed to ensure this interpretation makes use of the notion **c-command**, which is defined as follows.

> *32.* The NP *x* c-commands the NP *y* if every category dominating *x* also dominates *y.*

A second constraint on the interpretation of reflexives is now formulated as follows.

> *33.* The C-Command Requirement: A reflexive pronoun must be c-commanded by its antecedent.

Now consider how this principle applies to the NPs *the boy* and *the boy's uncle* in structures such as Figure 6.5. There is only one category dominating the NP *the boy's uncle*—namely S. Since this category also dominates the reflexive, NP[1] c-commands *himself* according to our definition and can therefore serve as its antecedent. As we have already seen, the sentence has this interpretation. But what of the forbidden interpretation? The NP *the boy* (NP[2]) in Figure 6.5 is dominated by two categories—S and NP[1]. Each of these categories is circled in Figure 6.6. Since only the first of these categories also dominates the reflexive, NP[2] does not c-command *himself* and can therefore not serve as its antecedent. This is the desired result.

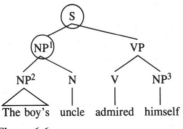

Figure 6.6

There is much more that can and should be said about the interpretation of pronouns. A more detailed examination of this very complex phenomenon would reveal the need for even more abstract principles referring to additional properties of syntactic structure. However, the examples we have already considered suffice to illustrate the crucial point in all of this; namely, that syntactic structure plays an important role in various aspects of semantic interpretation.

6.3 OTHER FACTORS IN SENTENCE INTERPRETATION

Syntactic structure is just one of the factors entering into sentence interpretation. In order to use a language appropriately, it is also necessary to understand how the grammar interacts with other systems of knowledge and belief. Several examples of this interaction are presented in this section.

Pragmatics

A major factor in sentence interpretation involves a body of knowledge that is often called **pragmatics**. This includes the speaker's and addressee's background attitudes and beliefs, their understanding of the context in which a sentence is uttered, and their knowledge of the way in which language is used to communicate information. As an example of this, consider the following pair of sentences.

34. a) The councilors refused the marchers a parade permit because they feared violence.
    b) The councilors refused the marchers a parade permit because they advocated violence.

These two sentences have identical syntactic structures, differing only in the choice of the verb in the second clause (*feared* in the first sentence vs. *advocated* in the second). Yet, the pronoun *they* is usually interpreted differently in the two sentences. Most people believe that *they* should refer to *the councilors* in 34a but to *the marchers* in 34b. These preferences seem to have nothing to do with grammatical rules. Rather, they reflect beliefs we have about different groups within our society—in particular, that councilors are more likely to fear violence than to advocate it.

The Cooperative Principle In many cases, pragmatic knowledge is put to even subtler uses in the interpretation of sentences. Suppose, for example, that a ship's captain makes the following entry in the log: *The first mate was not drunk tonight*. Although this statement says nothing about the first mate's condition on other nights, a reader is likely to infer that he has a problem with drunkenness. This inference does not follow from the literal meaning of the sentence, but rather from the way in which language is used to communicate. Ordinarily, the sentences we use are supposed to be informative and relevant. This is part of what has been called the **Cooperative Principle** for conversation. When an utterance appears to be uninformative or irrelevant, the listener (or reader) assumes that he or she is to draw a conclusion that can restore its informativeness and relevance.

In the example we are considering, this involves taking what appears to be a relatively uninformative statement about someone (a ship's first mate is expected not to be drunk) and inferring something informative from it (namely, that the individual's not being drunk on a particular night is somehow exceptional). This conclusion follows not from the meaning or structure of the original sentence, but rather from the assumption that the captain was trying to be informative when he made the entry in the ship's log. A conclusion that is drawn on the basis of an assumption about how we communicate is called a **conversational implicature**.

Presuppositions

There are other ways in which a speaker's beliefs can be reflected in language use. A familiar example of this involves sentences such as the one in 35.

35. Have you stopped exercising regularly?

Use of the verb *stop* implies a belief on the part of the speaker that the listener has been exercising regularly. No such assumption is associated with the verb *try,* as *36* shows.

36. Have you tried exercising regularly?

The assumption or belief implied by the use of a particular word or structure is called a **presupposition**. The following two sentences provide another example of this.

37. a) Nick admitted that the team had lost.
     b) Nick said that the team had lost.

Choice of the verb *admit* in *37a* indicates that the speaker is presupposing the truth of the claim that the team lost. No such presupposition is associated with choice of the verb *say* in *37b*. The speaker is simply reporting Nick's statement without taking a position on its accuracy.

Still another type of presupposition is illustrated in *38*.

38. a) Abraham Lincoln was assassinated in 1865.
     b) Abraham Lincoln was murdered in 1865.

Whereas use of the verb *assassinate* in *38a* implies that Abraham Lincoln was a prominent political figure, no such presupposition is associated with the verb *murder*.

Speech Acts

Still another set of factors that must be taken into account in semantic analysis involves the type of act associated with the utterance of a sentence. According to one influential proposal, there are three basic speech acts: the **locutionary act**, which corresponds to the utterance of a sentence with a particular meaning; the **illocutionary act**, which reflects the intent of the speaker in uttering that sentence (to praise, criticize, warn); and the **perlocutionary act**, which involves the effect that the speaker has on his or her addressees in uttering the sentence. Suppose, for example, that a teacher who is having trouble maintaining order in the classroom utters the sentence *I'll keep you in after class*. In uttering such a sentence, the teacher is simultaneously producing three speech acts—a locutionary act (involving utterance of a sentence with the meaning 'I'll make you stay in school later than usual'), an illocutionary act (a warning), and a perlocutionary act (silencing the students).

There is no one-to-one relationship between syntactic structure and speech acts. An illocutionary act of warning, for example, could involve (1) a declarative sentence (a statement), (2) an imperative (a command), (3) a *yes-no* question, or (4) a *wh* question.

39. a) There's a bear behind you.
     b) Run!
     c) Did you know there's a bear behind you?
     d) What's that bear doing in here?

Similarly, a perlocutionary act aimed at getting someone to open the window could be expressed in a variety of ways.

40. *a)* I wish you'd open the window.
    b) Open the window.
    c) Could you open the window?
    d) Why don't you open the window?
    e) It's awfully hot in here.

Because of the perlocutionary act associated with these utterances, the appropriate response on the part of the listener should be to open the window. Speakers of English therefore know that *40c* is not to be interpreted as a simple request for information. Only as a joke would someone respond by saying *Yes, I could* and then not do anything about opening the window.

Despite the indirect relationship between sentence structure and speech acts, there is a small set of verbs whose use makes explicit the illocutionary force of a sentence. Common examples of these verbs include *promise, bet, warn,* and *agree.*

41. *a)* I promise that I'll be there.
    b) I bet that the Yankees will lose.
    c) I warn you that's not a good idea.
    d) I agree that you should do it.

The verbs in *41* indicate the type of illocutionary act involved in uttering the sentence—an act of promising, an act of warning, and so on. Such verbs are called **performatives** since the very act of producing them involves the performance of an illocutionary act. Thus, in saying *I promise that I'll be there,* I automatically carry out an illocutionary act of promising. Such is not the case with a sentence like *I'll be there,* which could be a simple prediction, a warning, or a threat.

When a verb is used performatively, it always has a first person subject (*I* or *we*) and occurs in the present tense. Some performative verbs are subject to an additional restriction: they can only be appropriately uttered by speakers with a certain social status or authority. Only a clergyman or a justice of the peace can appropriately utter the sentence *I pronounce you man and wife* while only a judge can properly say *I sentence you to five years in prison.*

6.4 LANGUAGE, MEANING, AND THOUGHT

As we examine the way in which words and structures are used to express meaning, it is natural to wonder about the possibility that language might play a role in shaping how we think. While it is certainly plausible to believe that language facilitates reasoning and problem solving by providing a way to represent complex thoughts, it has sometimes been proposed that linguistic systems might have a considerably more fundamental effect on cognition. Indeed, it has even been suggested that the particular language people speak shapes the way in which they think and perceive the world.

The Sapir-Whorf Hypothesis

The best-known and most influential version of this idea has come to be known as the **Sapir-Whorf Hypothesis** in honor of Edward Sapir and Benjamin Lee Whorf, the two linguists who articulated it most clearly. Sapir, for instance, wrote in 1929:

> Human beings . . . are very much at the mercy of the particular language which has become the medium of expression for their society . . . the 'real world' is to a large extent unconsciously built upon the language habits of the group.

Several years later, Whorf expressed essentially the same sentiment when he made the following claim.

> We dissect nature along lines laid down by our native language. The categories and types that we isolate from the world of phenomena we do not find there because they stare every observer in the face; on the contrary, the world is presented in a kaleidoscopic flux of impressions which has to be organized by our minds—this means largely by the linguistic systems in our minds.

Two types of linguistic phenomena are commonly cited in support of the Sapir-Whorf Hypothesis: cross-linguistic differences in vocabulary, and variation in the type of grammatical contrasts a language encodes. The first type of phenomenon is exemplified by the fact that the Eskimo language has far more words for snow than does English, while Arabic has a far richer vocabulary pertaining to sand. From this, it is sometimes concluded that Eskimo and Arabic allow their speakers to make perceptual distinctions pertaining to snow and sand that English speakers cannot.

A more plausible explanation is that language is shaped by the need to adapt to the cultural and physical environment. According to this alternate view, if a language has a large vocabulary in a particular area, it is because subtle distinctions of that type are important to its speakers. Even speakers of a language without an extensive vocabulary in that area should be able to make the relevant contrasts if they become important to them. This is presumably why skiers, for instance, are able to distinguish among many different types of snow, even though their language may not have a separate word for each. Where necessary, they can then use the resources of their language to describe these distinctions by creating expressions such as *powder snow*.

Consider now cross-linguistic differences in the expression of grammatical contrasts—the type of phenomenon on which Whorf concentrated. Whorf attempted to link the apparent lack of tense contrasts in Hopi (an Amerindian language spoken in the American Southwest) with different cultural attitudes toward time and the future. According to Whorf, time for the Hopi does not consist of the passage of countable units (like days), but rather the successive reappearance of the same entity. There is no 'new day' for the Hopi, Whorf claimed, just the return of the same day. Whorf believed that this is reflected in the Hopi belief that the future is best dealt with by working on the present situation (which will return as the future).

Here again, innumerable problems arise. For one thing, Whorf was apparently mistaken in his belief that Hopi does not have tense; such a category is, in fact, found in this language. Moreover, even if there were no tense contrasts in Hopi or if they were radically different from those found in English, it is unlikely that they could be correlated with speakers' attitudes toward time. There are doubtlessly many individual speakers of English who share the Hopi philosophy for dealing with the future (and some Hopi speakers who do not).

The problem of Hopi tense aside, there are many grammatical phenomena that it would be absurd to correlate with the ability to make distinctions in the real world. Finnish, for instance, has no grammatical contrasts that reflect natural gender (or sex), but one would hardly conclude that the absence of a distinction between *he* and *she* impedes the ability of Finns to distinguish between males and females. Likewise, it is hard to believe that speakers of French believe that women, tents, and shirts are somehow alike even though the words for all three entities (*femmes, tentes,* and *chemises*) are assigned to the same gender class (feminine).

An Experiment There have been various attempts to verify the Sapir-Whorf Hypothesis by experimental means. The most famous of these experiments was conducted in 1958. The basic idea was to determine the effect of English and Navaho on the perception of color, size, and shape. In Navaho, verbs expressing handling actions vary in form depending on the shape of the object being handled. Thus, a long flexible object (a snake) requires the verbal form *šánléh*, a long rigid object (a spear) requires the verbal form *šántúh*, while flat flexible material requires *šánilcóós*. Since there is no such contrast in English, it was thought that children speaking these two languages might group objects in different ways. An experiment was designed to test this.

The children participating in the experiment were presented with a pair of objects such as a piece of rope and a stick, and then shown a third object and asked to tell the experimenter which of the pair went best with the new object. It was thought that the responses of the Navaho-speaking children might reflect the classification imposed by the verb system of their language rather than similarities in size or color. However, it was found that the responses of the forty-seven white English-speaking children (from Boston) were very similar to those of the fifty-nine monolingual speakers of Navaho. Given the differences between the two languages, this is not the result predicted by the Sapir-Whorf Hypothesis.

The repeated failure of experimental attempts to uncover systematic shaping effects for language has drastically reduced the credibility of the Sapir-Whorf Hypothesis. This is not to say that languages do not represent reality in different ways. Clearly, they do. Thus, French distinguishes between knowing someone (*connaître*) and knowing something (*savoir*), a distinction that is not made in the verb system of English. On the other hand, English has an extremely fine set of contrasts involving light (*glimmer, glitter, glow, gleam,* and *glisten*) that are not found in other languages. What is in doubt is whether such differences in the linguistic description of reality reflect deeper, language-induced differences in patterns of thought or perception.

Summing Up

The study of **semantics** is concerned with a broad range of phenomena including the nature of meaning, the role of syntactic structure in the interpretation of sentences, and the effect of **pragmatics** and speaker beliefs on the understanding of utterances. Although serious problems and obstacles remain in all these areas, work in recent years has at least begun to identify the type of relations, mechanisms, and principles involved in the understanding of language. These include the notions of **extension** and **intension** in the case of word meaning, the C-Command Requirement in the case of pronoun interpretation, and **thematic role** assignment in the case of sentence interpretation.

Sources

Various positions on the nature of word meaning and on semantic relations have been outlined and discussed in many books, including those by Fodor and Kempson cited below. The Cooperative Principle is outlined and defended in Paul Grice's important article "Logic and Conversation" in *Syntax and Semantics* 3, edited by P. Cole and J. Morgan (New York: Academic Press, 1975). Speech act theory is introduced in J. Austin's classic work *How to Do Things with Words* (Oxford: Clarendon Press, 1962). The quote from Edward Sapir on language and thought comes from a passage cited in Whorf's article "The Relation of Habitual Thought and Behavior to Language" reprinted in *Language, Thought and Reality,* edited by J. Carroll (Cambridge, Mass.: MIT Press, 1956). The quote from Whorf is taken from his article "Science and Linguistics," also reprinted in *Language, Thought and Reality*. The attempt to verify the Sapir-Whorf Hypothesis experimentally is reported in an article by J. Carroll and J. Casagrande, "The Function of Language Classification in Behavior" in *Readings in Social Psychology,* edited by E. Maccoby et al. (New York: Henry Holt, 1958).

Recommended Reading

Fodor, Janet Dean. 1978. *Semantics: Theories of Meaning in Generative Grammar*. Cambridge, Mass.: Harvard University Press.

Hurford, James and Brendan Heasley. 1983. *Semantics: A Coursebook*. London: Cambridge University Press.

Kempson, Ruth. 1977. *Semantic Theory*. London: Cambridge University Press.

Lyons, John. 1977. *Semantics*. Vols. 1 and 2. London: Cambridge University Press.

McCawley, James. 1981. *Everything That Linguists Have Always Wanted to Know About Logic*. Chicago: University of Chicago Press.

Questions

1. The first part of this chapter noted that a single phonetic form can have two or more meanings. Depending on whether these meanings are related to each other, this phenomenon involves polysemy or homophony. Consider now the following forms. Indicate whether each of these forms exemplifies polysemy or homophony.
   a) [sow]
   b) [græs]
   c) [siy]
   d) [lʌyt]
   e) [siyl]
   f) [riyl]

2. Two other important relations involving word meaning are synonymy and antonymy. Examples of both relations are found in the following data. Indicate whether each pair exemplifies synonymy or antonymy.
   a) car—automobile
   b) fast—slow
   c) young—old
   d) intelligent—smart
   e) intelligent—stupid

3. In our discussion of semantic decomposition, we noted that at least some words have meanings that can be represented in terms of smaller semantic features. Four such words are *dog, puppy, cat,* and *kitten.*
   a) Attempt to provide the semantic features associated with each of these words.
   b) How are the pairs *dog-puppy* and *cat-kitten* different from *man-boy* and *woman-girl*?
   c) Is it as easy to provide semantic features for the words *circle, silver, heavy,* and *three*?

4. In discussing the nature of word meaning, we noted that it is necessary to distinguish between a word's intension and its extension. Describe the difference between the intension and extension of each of these phrases.
   a) the President of the United States
   b) the Queen of England
   c) the capital of Australia

5. Strings of words that can be assigned more than one syntactic tree are structurally ambiguous. Each of the following examples exhibits this type of ambiguity. Use syntactic structure to represent the ambiguity.
   a) foreign car mechanic
   b) The sheriff shot the man with a rifle.
   c) intelligent students and professors
   d) old building committee
   e) Spanish language teacher

6. Each NP in the following sentences has a thematic role that represents the part that its referent plays in the situation described by the sentence. Using the terms described in this chapter, identify the thematic role of each NP in these sentences.
   a) The man spotted the intruder.
   b) The cat jumped onto the table.
   c) Aaron got the letter.
   d) The ball was thrown to Evan by Lorraine.
   e) The table was destroyed in a fire.

7. Two of the NPs in the following sentence must be assigned a thematic role unlike any discussed in this chapter. What roles would you assign to these NPs, and how would you define them?
   Josh painted Kira's boat for the new owner.

7 HISTORICAL LINGUISTICS

Many men sayn that in sweveninges
Ther nys but fables and lesynges;
But men may some swevenes sene
Whiche hardely that false ne bene,
But afterwarde ben apparaunt.
Chaucer, *The Romance of the Rose* (c. 1370)

Language change is both obvious and rather mysterious. The English of the late fourteenth century, for example, is quite unlike that of our times. Without special training, a speaker of Modern English would have great difficulty understanding the opening lines to *The Romance of the Rose* cited above. Not only is the sound pattern of these sentences strange, but words and structures such as *sweveninges, lesynges,* and *false ne bene* are unfamiliar.[1] The existence of such differences between early and later variants of the same language raises questions about the nature, extent, and causes of linguistic change.

Historical linguistics is the branch of our discipline that studies language change. Research in this area is concerned both with the description of language change and with the factors that cause and constrain it. This chapter opens with an examination of the nature and causes of language change. We then survey in more detail phonological, morphological, syntactic, lexical, and semantic change. Finally, we explore some of the techniques used to reconstruct linguistic history. Where practical, examples are drawn from the history of English.

7.1 THE NATURE OF LANGUAGE CHANGE

English has undergone dramatic changes throughout the three major periods of its history: Old English (roughly from 450 to 1100), Middle English (from

---

[1] The translation for these lines is as follows:

Many men say that in dreams
There is nothing but talk and lies
But men may see some dreams
Which are scarcely false
But afterward come true.

1100 to 1500), and Modern English (from 1500 to the present). While Chaucer's Middle English is at least partially comprehensible today, Old English looks like a foreign language. The following is an extract from an eighth-century Old English document, a translation of Bede's Latin history of England. (The letter Þ, called 'thorn', represented the phoneme /θ/ in Old English. Here and elsewhere in this chapter the diacritic ¯ marks a long vowel in the orthography.)

1. And Seaxan Þā sige geslōgan.
   and Saxons the victory won
   'And Saxons won the victory.'

   Þā sendan hī hām ǣrenddracan.
   then sent they home a messenger
   'Then they sent home a messenger.'

These Old English sentences differ from their Modern English counterparts in many respects. In terms of pronunciation, for instance, the word *hām* 'home' was pronounced as [ha:m] in Old English, became [hɔ:m] in Middle English, and then [howm] in Modern English. As the unfamiliar *ǣrenddracan* 'messenger' and *geslōgan* 'won' show, many Old English words have disappeared from use. In terms of morphology too, Old English is quite different from Modern English. The suffix *-an* on the Old English word for 'sent' indicates that the verb is in the past tense and has a third person plural subject (*hī* 'they'). Finally, differences in word order are readily apparent. The Old English verb appears after both the subject and the direct object in the first sentence but before them in the second one.

Systematicity of Language Change

The differences between Old and Modern English have been brought about by a series of regular and systematic changes. The development of a fixed subject-verb-direct object word order in English has affected more than just a few verbs. All verbs in Modern English appear before rather than after the direct object. Similarly, the pronunciation changes that affected the vowel in the word *hām* did not occur in that word only. All occurrences of this vowel in Old English underwent the same changes (see Table 7.1).

Table 7.1 Changes affecting /a:/

Old English	Middle English	Modern English	
/ba:t/	/bɔ:t/	/bowt/	'boat'
/la:nlič/	/lɔ:nli/	/lownliy/	'lonely'
/sta:n/	/stɔ:n/	/stown/	'stone'

All languages undergo change. Language change reflects modifications to the grammar—the system of categories and rules underlying language use. Such changes may affect any part of the grammar, ranging from the rules for sentence formation (syntax) to the pronunciation of individual sounds (phonetics).

Triggers of Linguistic Change

There are numerous causes for linguistic change, and these sometimes interact with each other in complex ways. For this reason, it is often impossible to identify the precise cause of a particular grammatical modification. However, there are specific factors, ranging from articulatory considerations to social pressures, that trigger language change.

Physiological Factors As noted in the chapter on phonetics, articulation is often made easier by modifying a sound so that it is more like or unlike its neighbors. At a very early point in the history of English, for instance, the velar stop /k/, written with the letter *c* in Old English, was palatalized before front vowels under the influence of their more forward place of articulation. The effects of this **palatalization** can be seen in the initial segments of the Old English words in Table 7.2. (The initial segment corresponds to [č] before front vowels but [k] elsewhere.) As these examples show, /k/ was palatalized

Table 7.2 Palatalization in Old English

Old English form	
cinn	'chin'
cēosan	'choose'
cīese	'cheese'
cirice	'church'
ceorl	'churl'
cuman	'come'
cōl	'cool'

[handwritten annotations: "Front unrounded" bracketing cinn through ceorl; "Back Rounded" bracketing cuman and cōl]

only before a front vowel in Old English, giving [č]. This type of modification to the sound pattern of a language can lead both to new types of allophonic variation and to the addition or loss of phonemic contrasts. Detailed examples of such sound changes are presented in Section 7.2.

Analogy Another frequent source of linguistic change is the regularization of exceptional or rare forms by **analogy** with more common forms. Analogy involves the inference that if two elements are alike in some respects (they are both nouns, say), they should be alike in others as well. The development of the plural ending in English has been heavily influenced by analogy. In Old English, nouns belonged to different classes, each with its own way of expressing the plural. The plural of *hand,* for example, was *handa,* the plural of *stān* 'stone' was *stānas*, while the plural of *gēar* 'year' was identical to the singular. Eventually, for reasons that will be discussed in the next section, the suffix -(*e*)*s* became dominant. At this point, analogy took over and speakers of English began to associate the -(*e*)*s* ending with the plural in all but a small class of cases (such as *oxen, men,* and so on). This led to the use of *hands* as the plural of *hand* and *years* as the plural of *year*.

Folk Etymology Sometimes, change originates in the misanalysis of a word by speakers of a language. Typically, this misanalysis reflects the confusion of forms that are phonetically and/or semantically similar. The word *shamefaced,* for instance, was originally *shamefast* (from Old English *sceamfæst* 'bound by shame'). As use of the morpheme *fast* to mean 'bound' became less frequent, the second syllable was reinterpreted as the phonetically similar *faced* to retain its meaningfulness in this compound. Such misinterpretation is known as **folk etymology** (see Table 7.3).

Table 7.3 Folk etymology in English

belfry	from Middle English *berfrey* 'tower'	(unrelated to *bell*)
bridegroom	from Middle English *bridegome* (cf. Old English *brȳd* 'bride' and *guma* 'man')	(unrelated to *groom*)
muskrat	from Algonquian *musquash*	(unrelated to either *musk* or *rat*)
woodchuck	from Algonquian *otchek*	(unrelated to either *wood* or *chuck*)

Borrowing Many linguistic changes can be attributed to **borrowing**, the acquisition of words, sounds, or rules from another language. **Substratum influence** is the effect of a politically or culturally nondominant language on a dominant language in the area. English, for instance, has borrowed vocabulary items from Amerindian languages. In addition to thousands of place names (including the word *Canada*), other familiar borrowings include *moccasin, totem, tomahawk, pemmican, moose,* and *skunk*. **Superstratum influence** is the effect of a politically or culturally dominant language on another language or languages in the area. The Mohawk language (spoken in New York), for example, has borrowed a number of technological terms and expressions from English, including *automobile, thumbtack,* and *wheelbarrow*. Borrowing can also affect the phonological, morphological, and syntactic components of the grammar.

Sociological Factors Speakers may consciously or unconsciously alter the way they speak to approximate what they perceive to be a more prestigious or socially acceptable variety of speech. There have been numerous examples of this in the history of English, notably the loss of postvocalic /r/ along the east coast of the United States. This change, which resulted in the pronunciation of words such as *far* as [fa:], originated in parts of England in the seventeenth and eighteenth century. At that time, postvocalic /r/ was still pronounced throughout English-speaking settlements in North America. Two factors accounted for its loss in parts of this continent. First, the children of the New England gentry picked up the new pronunciation in British schools and subsequently brought it back to the colony. Second, the speech of newly arrived immigrants, including colonial administrators and church officials who enjoyed high social status in the colony, typically lacked syllable-final /r/. As a result, the innovation was widely imitated and ultimately spread along much of the east coast and into the south.

The next sections present examples of phonological, morphological, syntactic, lexical, and semantic change.

7.2 SOUND CHANGE

Although all components of the grammar are susceptible to change over time, some types of change yield more obvious results than others. The area of language where change and variation are most noticeable is its sound pattern. Several common types of sound change can be distinguished.

Phonetically Conditioned Sound Change

Changes in a language's sound pattern often come about under the influence of particular phonetic environments. Such changes are said to be **phonetically conditioned**. The linguistic processes underlying this type of change are identical to the ones found in the phonology of currently spoken languages. Although these processes were presented and discussed in the chapter on phonetics, some are reconsidered here in order to provide examples of their role in language change.

Assimilation Assimilation, the modification of a particular segment to make it more like a neighboring sound, is one of the most frequent sources of sound change. The effect is to increase the efficiency of articulation by requiring fewer articulatory movements. Usually, assimilatory processes bring about changes in place of articulation, nasalization, and voicing. Table 7.4 gives some examples of assimilatory change in Italian in which /k/ was converted to /t/ under the influence of a neighboring /t/.

Table 7.4 Assimilation in place of articulation in Italian

Old Italian	Italian	
/okto/	/otto/	'eight'
/nokte/	/notte/	'night'
/lakte/	/latte/	'milk'

An example of nasalization appears in the history of Portuguese and French. As these two languages evolved from Latin, the vowels occurring before a nasal consonant became nasalized; the nasal consonant was subsequently deleted. (The pronunciation of the vowels in the examples in Table 7.5 underwent additional changes in height and tenseness in French. The

Table 7.5 Nasalization in Portuguese and French

Latin	Portuguese	French	
/bonum/	/bõ/	/bɔ̃/	'good'
/unum/	/ũ/	/œ̃/	'one'

-um ending in the Latin examples was an inflectional affix lost early in the history of both Portuguese and French for independent reasons.)

Voicing frequently occurs between voiced segments. In the examples from Old English in Table 7.6, the stem-final consonant is voiced when the plural suffix *-as* is present since it then appears between voiced segments. Although the vowel of the plural suffix was subsequently lost, the voiced [v] is still found in the Modern English pronunciation of *hooves* and *wolves*.

Table 7.6 Voicing in Old English

Singular		Plural	
[ho:f]	'hoof'	[ho:vas]	'hooves'
[wulf]	'wolf'	[wulvas]	'wolves'

Weakening Consonantal **weakening** (also called **lenition**) involves a lessening in the time or degree of a consonant's closure, often under the influence of a neighboring vowel. A geminate or long consonant can be shortened, a stop can be converted into a fricative, and a consonant can even be weakened to the point where it disappears entirely. Weakening frequently occurs intervocalically, where it is often accompanied by voicing assimilation. The intervocalic stops of Latin, for instance, were systematically weakened in Portuguese (see Table 7.7).

Table 7.7 Lenition in Portuguese

Latin	Portuguese	Change	
cippum	cepo	pp → p	'stump'
abbatem	abade	bb → b	'abbot'
apiculam	abelha	p → b	'bee'
fabem	fave	b → v	'bean'

Dissimilation Dissimilation, which is the opposite of assimilation and considerably less frequent, is a process that makes a sound less like another sound in its environment. Such changes apparently occur where it would be difficult to articulate or perceive two similar sounds in close proximity. The word /anma/ 'soul' in Late Latin, for example, was modified to /alma/ in Spanish and to /arma/ in Provençal to avoid consecutive nasal consonants. Less frequently, dissimilation may be triggered by a nonadjacent sound. For instance, the Latin word /arbor/ 'tree' became /arbol/ in Spanish and /albore/ in Italian to avoid two instances of /r/ in adjacent syllables. No such change occurred in French, where the word for 'tree' /arbrə/ has retained both instances of /r/.

Segment Addition Another widespread type of sound change, called epenthesis, involves the insertion of a consonant or vowel into a particular environment. In some cases, such as those in Table 7.8, epenthesis results from the anticipation of an upcoming sound. In these examples, the epenthetic /b/ or /p/ has the place of articulation of the preceding /m/ (labial) but

Table 7.8 Epenthesis in the history of English

Old English	Modern English	Change	
/timr̩/	/timbr̩/	mr̩ → mbr̩	'timber'
/breml̩/	/bræmbl̩/	ml̩ → mbl̩	'bramble'
/glɪmsian/	/glɪmps/	ms → mps	'glimpse'

agrees with the following segment in terms of voice and nasality. The epenthetic segment therefore serves as a bridge for the transition between the sounds on either side (see Table 7.9). In other cases, epenthesis breaks up

Table 7.9 The nature of epenthesis

/m/	/b/	/r̩/	/m/	/p/	/s/
labial	labial	nonlabial	labial	labial	nonlabial
nasal	nonnasal	nonnasal	nasal	nonnasal	nonnasal
voiced	voiced	voiced	voiced	voiceless	voiceless

a sequence of sounds that would otherwise be difficult to pronounce or even inconsistent with the phonotactic pattern of the language. Some English speakers insert an epenthetic [ə] in the pronunciation of the words in Table 7.10. In Basque, epenthetic vowels break up impermissible consonant clusters in words borrowed from a late form of Latin (see Table 7.11).

Table 7.10 Epenthesis in Modern English

With epenthesis	Without epenthesis	
/æθəliyt/	/æθliyt/	'athlete'
/filəm/	/film/	'film'
/ɛləm/	/ɛlm/	'elm'

Table 7.11 Epenthetic vowels in Basque

Late Latin	Basque	
/astru/	/asturu/	'star'
/libru/	/liburu/	'book'
/fronte/	/boronte/	'front'

Segment Loss Both consonants and vowels are susceptible to deletion. Frequently, segment loss involves the deletion of a word-final vowel (**apocope**) or a word-internal vowel (**syncope**). Examples of each are given in Tables 7.12 and 7.13, respectively. Both processes typically occur in unstressed

Table 7.12 Apocope in English

Old English	Middle English (vowel reduction)	Modern English (apocope)	
/na:ma/	/na:mə/	/neym/	'name'
/lufu/	/luvə/	/lʌv/	'love'

Table 7.13 Syncope in English

Old English	Middle English (vowel reduction)	Modern English (apocope)	
/ba:tas/	/bɔ:təs/	/bowts/	'boats'
/hundas/	/hu:ndəs/	/hawndz/	'hounds'
/sta:nas/	/sta:nəs/	/stownz/	'stones'

syllables and are often preceded historically by **vowel reduction**, a process that converts a vowel into the short, lax segment /ə/. Syncope can be seen in the loss of the unstressed vowel in the plural suffix -*as*. The effects of syncope are also apparent in the loss of the medial vowel in words such as *vegetable, interest,* and *family*, which are frequently pronounced as [véjtəbl̩], [íntrɛst], and [fǽmliy], respectively.

Consonant loss is as much a part of language change as vowel loss. Old and Middle English included /kn/ clusters in word-initial position. The /k/ was later lost, which accounts for the current pronunciation of words such as *knight, knit, knot,* and *knee*. (The spelling of these words reflects their earlier pronunciation.)

The loss of word-final consonants has played a major role in the evolution of Modern French. The final letters in the spelling of the words in Table 7.14 reflect the presence of consonant phonemes at an earlier stage.

Table 7.14 Consonant loss in French

French	Current pronunciation	
bon	/bɔ̃/	'good'
gros	/gro/	'large'
chaud	/šo/	'warm'
vert	/vɛr/	'green'

Segment Movement A change in the relative positioning of sounds has occurred in the history of many languages. In some cases, in a process known as metathesis, sounds may change places. As Table 7.15 shows, this has

Table 7.15 Metathesis in West Saxon

Before metathesis	After metathesis	
/aksian/	/askian/	'ask'
/dʌks/	/dʌsk/	'dusk'

happened in the West Saxon dialect of Old English, where /ks/ has become /sk/. Some Modern English speakers have reversed this change, pronouncing *ask* as [æks]. In some cases, sounds may be transposed over some distance. This has happened in the change from Latin *miraculum* 'miracle' to Spanish *milagro,* in which /r/ and /l/ have changed places although they were not adjacent (see Figure 7.1).

Figure 7.1 Metathesis of nonadjacent sounds

Nonphonetically Conditioned Sound Change

Occasionally, sound changes occur in the absence of any motivation in the phonetic environment. An example of this comes from Oneida (an Amerindian language spoken in Wisconsin), in which /l/ was substituted for /r/. The effect of this substitution can be seen in a comparison of Oneida with Mohawk and Cayuga, two related languages that have not undergone this change. As Table 7.16 shows, Oneida has an /l/ where Mohawk and Cayuga have an /r/. Although the liquids /r/ and /l/ are phonetically similar and alternations between them are not unusual in language, nothing in the phonetic environment explains why /r/ should change to /l/ (or vice versa) in these particular cases.

Table 7.16 The /l/ substitution in Oneida

Mohawk	Cayuga	Oneida	
yoyánere?	oyá:nre?	yoyánle?	'good'
ótskeri?	otskra?	ótskla?	'spit'
oneráhta?	onráhta?	ónlahte?	'leaf'

Similarly, the segments /r/ and /z/ are often involved in sound changes that are not triggered by the phonetic environment. Within the Germanic family of languages, for instance, /z/ became /r/ in English, German, and Swedish but not Gothic. The effects of this change can be seen in the standard spellings of the words in Table 7.17.

Table 7.17 The /z/ to /r/ change in Gothic

English	German	Swedish	Gothic
more	mehr	mera	maiza
deer	Tier	djur	diuzis
hoard	Hort	---	huzd

Phonetic versus Phonological Change

The types of sound change outlined in the preceding section can affect the overall sound pattern of a language in very different ways. In some cases, a sound change may be restricted to the creation of a new allophone of an already existing phoneme. This is called **phonetic sound change**. It is exemplified by the laxing of short high vowels that has developed in Canadian French. This change can be seen in closed word-final syllables, among other contexts. In the examples in Table 7.18, Canadian French has the lax vowels

Table 7.18 Vowel laxing in Canadian French

European French	Canadian French	
[vit]	[vɪt]	'quick'
[libr]	[lɪbr]	'free'
[ekut]	[ekʊt]	'listen'
[pus]	[pʊs]	'thumb'
[vi]	[vi]	'life'
[li]	[li]	'bed'
[vu]	[vu]	'you'
[lu]	[lu]	'wolf'

[ɪ] and [ʊ] in closed final syllables where European French has kept the tense vowels [i] and [u]. Both dialects of French retain [i] and [u] in open syllables. This suggests that Canadian French has developed the rule shown in Figure 7.2. While this rule introduces an allophone not present in European French, it does not create any new phonemes, since there are no mimimal pairs involving [i] and [ɪ] in Canadian French.

$$V \rightarrow [-\text{tense}] / \underline{\hspace{2cm}} C\ (C)\ \#$$
$$\begin{bmatrix} +\text{high} \\ -\text{long} \end{bmatrix}$$

Figure 7.2 Vowel laxing rule in Canadian French

Splits, Mergers, and Shifts Sometimes, sound change can directly affect a language's phonological system by adding, eliminating, or rearranging phonemes. This is called **phonological sound change** and can involve splits, mergers, or shifts.

A **phonological split** is a change in which allophones of the same phoneme come to contrast with each other, creating one or more new phonemes. A phonological split was involved in the creation of the phoneme /ŋ/ in English. Originally, the sound [ŋ] was simply the allophone of /n/ that appeared before a velar consonant. During Middle English, /g/ was lost in word-final position after a nasal consonant, leaving [ŋ] as the final sound in words such as *sing* (see Table 7.19). The loss of the final [g] in words created minimal pairs such as *sin* [sɪn] and *sing* [sɪŋ], in which there is a contrast between [n] and [ŋ]. This allows us to say that the phoneme /n/ split into /n/ and /ŋ/, as shown in Figure 7.3.

Table 7.19 The evolution of /n/

Original phonemic form	/sɪng/
Original phonetic form	[sɪŋg]
Following loss of [g]	[sɪŋ]

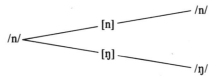

Figure 7.3 A phonological split

A **phonological merger** is a change in which two or more phonemes collapse into a single contrastive unit, thereby reducing the number of phonemes in the language. This has occurred in Cockney, a nonstandard dialect of British English spoken in London. In Cockney, the interdental fricative /θ/ has merged with /f/ as the result of a phonetically unconditioned sound change: /θ/ → /f/ (see Figure 7.4). As the result of this merger, *thin* and *fin* are pronounced alike—as [fɪn].

Figure 7.4 A phonological merger

A **phonological shift** is a change in which a series of phonemes is systematically modified so that their organization with respect to each other is altered. A well-known example of such a change involves the Great Vowel Shift of English (see Table 7.20). Beginning in the Middle English period and continuing into the eighteenth century, the language underwent a series of nonphonetically conditioned modification to long vowels. Figure 7.5 illustrates the effect of these changes on English long vowels. The origin of

Table 7.20 The Great Vowel Shift

Middle English	Great Vowel Shift	Later glide addition	Modern English	
/tiːd/	/iː/ → /ay/		/tayd/	'tide'
/luːd/	/uː/ → /aw/		/lawd/	'loud'
/geːs/	/eː/ → /iː/ → /iy/		/giys/	'geese'
/sɛː/	/ɛː/ → /iː/ → /iy/		/siy/	'sea'
/goːs/	/oː/ → /uː/ → /uw/		/guws/	'goose'
/brɔːkən/	/ɔː/ → /oː/ → /ow/		/browkən/	'broken'
/naːmə/	/aː/ → /eː/ → /ey/		/neym/	'name'

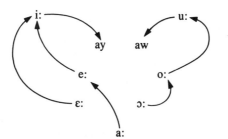

Figure 7.5 Changes brought about by the Great Vowel Shift

the Great Vowel Shift is uncertain. Perhaps the high vowels changed first, and the mid and low vowels were raised to fill the gaps left by the diphthongization of the /i:/ and /u:/. Or perhaps the change began with the low vowels, which pushed the old high vowels out of their former place in the vowel quadrangle, resulting in their diphthongization. Whatever the explanation, it is known that the changes took place gradually and that the diphthongization of /i:/ and /u:/ involved an intermediate stage during which the vowel nucleus in the diphthong was [ʌ] rather than [a]. In some dialects, this pronunciation has been retained before voiceless consonants (in words such as [ʌwt] *out* and [wʌyf] *wife*).

Ordering of Sound Changes

In describing language change, it is often crucial to identify the relative times at which different modifications have occurred. The Old English voicing rule discussed previously and the syncope rule stated in simplified form in Figure 7.6 help illustrate this. Both changes have played a role in the evolution of

Voicing

C → [+ voice] / [+ voice] _____ [+ voice]

Syncope
V → ∅ / _____ C #
[− stress]

Figure 7.6 Old English voicing and syncope rules

many English words, including *hooves* and *wolves,* discussed earlier. The contemporary pronunciation of these forms shows that the voicing change must have occurred before syncope. As Table 7.21 shows, the [v] in the Modern English pronunciation of *wolves* would not have occurred if syncope had preceded voicing, since the former process would have removed the context required by the latter rule. However, if we assume that the voicing change occurred before syncope came into the language, we can explain the presence of [v] in *hooves* and *wolves.*

Table 7.21 Rule ordering in the history of English

Original phonemic form	/wulf + as/
Effect of voicing	wulvas
Effect of syncope	wulvz
Original phonemic form	/wulf + as/
Effect of syncope	*wulfs
Effect of voicing	(cannot apply)

7.3 MORPHOLOGICAL CHANGE

The most widespread morphological changes involve the loss and addition of affixes. Both phenomena have occurred frequently in the history of English, as the following examples illustrate.

Addition and Loss

Modern English has borrowed some of its most widely used affixes from French. During the Middle English period, many French words containing the suffix -*ment* (*accomplishment, commencement*) made their way into the language. Eventually, -*ment* established itself as a productive suffix in English and was used with stems that were not of French origin (*acknowledgment, merriment*). The ending -*able*, which converts a verb into an adjective (*readable, lovable*), followed a similar course. Words with this ending (*favorable, conceivable*) were initially borrowed into English as whole units. Eventually, the suffix became productive and was used with new stems.

Just as affixes can be added to the grammar, so they can be lost. A number of Old English derivational affixes, including -*baere* and -*bora* (see Figure 7.7), are now extinct.

N + *baere* → Adj   (*lustbaere* 'agreeable' from *lust* 'pleasure')

N + *bora* → N   (*mundbora* 'protector' from *mund* 'protection')

Figure 7.7 Extinct Old English affixes

The Loss of Case

Old English had a complex system of case and gender marking. Nouns were divided into three genders—masculine, feminine, and neuter. Assignment to a gender class was not based simply on sex (natural gender); for example, the word for *stone* was masculine and the word for *sun* feminine. Each gender class was associated with a different set of case endings (see Table 7.22). The following Old English sentence contains all four case categories.

2. Se cniht   geaf geif-e Þæs hierd-es   sun-e.
   the youth-Nom gave gift-Ac the shepherd-Gen son-Dat
   'The youth gave a gift to the shepherd's son.'

By the fifteenth century, English case endings had changed radically. The /m/ of the dative plural suffix had been lost, and unstressed vowels in the

Table 7.22 Old English case affixes

	Masculine	Feminine	Neuter
Singular			
	hund 'dog'	gief 'gift'	dēor 'wild animal'
Nominative	hund	gief-u	dēor
Accusative	hund	gief-e	dēor
Genitive	hund-es	gief-e	dēor-es
Dative	hund-e	gief-e	dēor-e
Plural			
Nominative	hund-as	gief-a	dēor
Accusative	hund-as	gief-a	dēor
Genitive	hund-a	gief-a	dēor-a
Dative	hund-um	gief-um	dēor-um

case endings had all been reduced to the short, lax vowel [ə], thus obliterating many of the earlier case and gender distinctions. (The examples in Table 7.23 also include changes to the stem-internal vowels as the result of various processes, including the Great Vowel Shift.) In the loss of case endings, we have an example of how a modification to the morphological component of the grammar was probably triggered by phonological change (final consonant loss and vowel reduction).

Table 7.23 The loss of case affixes in the English word *hound*

Singular	Old English	Middle English	Modern English	
Nominative	/hund/	/hu:nd/	/hawnd/	'hound'
Accusative	/hund/	/hu:nd/	/hawnd/	'hound'
Genitive	/hund-es/	/hu:nd-əs/	/hawnd-z/	'hound's'
Dative	/hund-e/	/hu:nd-ə/	/hawnd/	'hound'
Plural				
Nominative	/hund-as/	/hu:nd-əs/	/hawnd-z/	'hounds'
Accusative	/hund-as/	/hu:nd-əs/	/hawnd-z/	'hounds'
Genitive	/hund-a/	/hu:nd-ə/	/hawnd-z/	'hounds' '
Dative	/hund-um/	/hu:nd-ə/	/hawnd-z/	'hounds'

Analogy

As the preceding examples show, the distinction between singular and plural in Middle English was preserved by the suffix -*s*, which also survived to mark the genitive singular forms. The genitive plural -*s* was added by analogy with the singular. As noted earlier, analogy was also responsible for the development of the plural forms of many English nouns. The Old English feminine noun *hand,* for instance, had the inflectional paradigm shown in Table 7.24. Modern English *hand* clearly developed from the nominative

Table 7.24 The Old English paradigm for *hand*

	Singular	Plural
Nominative	hand	handa
Accusative	hand	handa
Genitive	handa	handa
Dative	handa	handum

and accusative singular form of Old English, but the present-day plural *hands* could not have come from the Old English paradigm. Instead, it was formed on the model of the Old English plural for words such as *hound,* which was *hundas*. Other plural forms that were created on the basis of analogy included *eyes* (*eyen* in Middle English) and *shoes* (formerly *shooen*). Continuing analogy along these lines is responsible for the development of the plural form *youse* (from *you*) in some English dialects. Each generation of English-speaking children temporarily extends the analogy still further by producing forms such as *sheeps, gooses,* and *mouses*. To date, however, these particular innovations have not been accepted by adult speakers of Standard English and so are ultimately abandoned by the language learner.

7.4 SYNTACTIC CHANGE

Like other components of the grammar, syntax is subject to change over time. Syntactic changes can involve modifications to phrase structure rules or transformations, as the following examples illustrate.

Word Order

All languages make a distinction between the subject and direct object. The two most typical ways to represent this contrast are through case marking and word order. Since Old English had an extensive system of case marking, it is not surprising that its word order was somewhat more variable than that of Modern English. The most common word order in clauses was subject-verb-object (SVO).

3. S   V   O
   He geseah Þone mann.
   'He saw the man.'

However, when the clause began with an element such as Þa 'then' or *ne* 'not', the verb remained in second position and preceded the subject.

4.   V   S   O
   Þa sende se cyning Þone disc.
   then sent the king the dish
   'Then the king sent the dish.'

When the direct object was a pronoun, the subject-object-verb order was typical.

5. S   O   V
   Heo hine lærde.
   she him advised
   'She advised him.'

In embedded clauses, the subject-object-verb order prevailed even when the direct object was not a pronoun.

6.   S   O   V
   Þa he Þone cyning sohte, he beotode.
   when he the king visited, he boasted
   'When he visited the king, he boasted.'

During the Middle English period, the loss of case contrasts was accompanied by the adoption of a uniform subject-verb-object order. As Table 7.25 shows, a major change in word order took place between 1300 and 1400, with the verb-object order becoming dominant.

Table 7.25 Word order patterns in Middle English

Year (A.D):	1000	1200	1300	1400	1500
Direct object before the verb	52%	53%	40%	14%	2%
Direct object after the verb	48	47	60	86	98

Inversion   In Old and Middle English, the Inversion transformation involved in the formation of *yes-no* questions could apply to all verbs, not just auxiliaries, yielding forms that would be unacceptable in Modern English.

> 7. Speak they the truth?

During the sixteenth and seventeenth centuries, the Inversion rule was changed to apply solely to auxiliary verbs (see Figure 7.8). With this change, structures such as *Speak they the truth?* fell into disuse.

Inversion   (old form)

NP   V

1   2 → 2 1   They speak → Speak they?

                        They can speak → Can they speak?

Inversion   (new form)

NP   aux

1   2 → 2 1   They speak → *Speak they?

                        They can speak → Can they speak?

Figure 7.8 Inversion in the history of English

7.5 LEXICAL AND SEMANTIC CHANGE

One of the most obvious types of language change involves modifications to the lexicon. Such modifications often reflect cultural changes that introduce novel objects and notions, and eliminate outmoded ones, as illustrated in Table 7.26.

Table 7.26 Some Old English words lost through cultural change

dolgbot	'compensation for wounding'
Þeox	'hunting spear'
eafor	'tenant obligation to the king to convey goods'
flytme	'a blood-letting instrument'

Word formation processes are often employed in response to the need for new lexical items. Some examples are given in Table 7.27.

The next section focuses on the effects of borrowing on English vocabulary.

Table 7.27 Word formation processes in English

Compounding	sailboat, bigmouth
Derivation	uglification, finalize
Acronyms	UNESCO, radar
Blending	smog (from smoke and fog)
Clipping	sci fi, phys ed
Backformation	typewrite (from typewriter)

Borrowing

Borrowing has been a very rich source of new words in English, but it is noteworthy that **loan words** are least common among frequently used vocabulary items, as shown in Table 7.28. This reflects a general tendency for highly frequent words to be relatively resistant to loss or substitution.

Table 7.28 Origin of the five thousand most frequent words in English

Degree of frequency	Source Language			
	English	French	Latin	Other
First 1000	83%	11%	2%	4%
Second 1000	34	46	11	9
Third 1000	29	46	14	11
Fourth 1000	27	45	17	11
Fifth 1000	27	47	17	9

The contribution of French to the vocabulary of English is in large part the result of a historical event—the conquest of England by French-speaking Normans in 1066. As the conquerors and their descendants gradually learned English over the next decades, they retained French terms to refer to political, judicial, and cultural notions. These words were in turn borrowed by native English speakers who, in trying to gain a place in the upper middle class, were eager to imitate the speech of their social superiors. Not surprisingly, borrowing was especially heavy in the vocabulary areas pertaining to officialdom: government, the judiciary, and religion. Other areas of heavy borrowing include science, culture, and warfare (see Table 7.29).

Table 7.29 Some French loan words in English

Government	tax, revenue, government, royal, state, parliament, authority, prince, duke, slave, peasant
Religion	prayer, sermon, religion, chaplain, friar
Judiciary	judge, defendant, jury, evidence, jail, verdict, crime
Science	medicine, physician
Culture	art, sculpture, fashion, satin, fur, ruby
Warfare	army, navy, battle, soldier, enemy, captain

In some cases, French loan words were used in conjunction with native English words to create contrasts of various sorts. For a minor crime, for example, the English word *theft* was employed, but for a more serious breach of the law, the French word *larceny* was used. The English also kept their own words for domesticated animals, but adopted the French words for the meat from those creatures (see Table 7.30).

Table 7.30 French loan words used in conjunction with native English words

English origin	French origin
cow	beef
calf	veal
sheep	mutton
pig	pork

Borrowed words from many other languages attest to various types of cultural contact (see Table 7.31).

Table 7.31 Some lexical borrowings into English

Italian	motto, artichoke, balcony, casino, malaria
Spanish	comrade, tornado, cannibal, mosquito, banana, guitar
German	poodle, kindergarten, seminar, noodle, pretzel
Slavic languages	czar, tundra, polka, intelligentsia, robot
Amerindian languages	toboggan, opossum, wigwam, chipmunk, Alabama, Massachusetts
Dutch	sloop, cole slaw, smuggle, gin, cookie, boom
Hindi	cummerbund, thug, punch, shampoo, chintz
Turkish	yogurt, horde

Semantic Change

Although changes in word meaning take place continually in all languages, words rarely jump from one meaning to an unrelated one. Typically, the changes are step by step and involve one of the following phenomena.

Semantic Broadening is the process in which the meaning of a word becomes more general or more inclusive than its historically earlier meaning (see Table 7.32).

Table 7.32 Semantic broadening

Word	Old meaning	New meaning
bird	'small fowl'	'any winged creature'
barn	'place to store barley'	'any agricultural building'
aunt	'father's sister'	'father or mother's sister'
dog	'a hunting breed'	'any canine'

Semantic Narrowing is the process in which the meaning of a word becomes less general or less inclusive than its historically earlier meaning (see Table 7.33).

Table 7.33 Semantic narrowing

Word	Old meaning	New meaning
hound	'any dog'	'a hunting breed'
mete (meat)	'any type of food'	'flesh of an animal'
fowl	'any bird'	'a domesticated bird'
disease	'any unfavorable state'	'an illness'

Semantic Shift is a process in which a word loses its former meaning and comes to refer to a new, but often related, set of things (see Table 7.34). Sometimes, a series of semantic shifts occurs over an extended period of time, resulting in a meaning that is completely unrelated to the original sense

Table 7.34 Semantic shift

Word	Old meaning	New meaning
immoral	'not customary'	'unethical'
silly	'weak'	'foolish'
bede (bead)	'prayers'	'prayer beads, beads'

of a word. The word *hearse,* for example, originally referred to a triangular plow. Later, it denoted a triangular frame for church candles and later still was used to refer to the device that held candles over a coffin. In a subsequent shift, it came to refer to the framework on which curtains were hung over a coffin or tomb. Still later, *hearse* was used to refer to the coffin itself, before finally taking on its current sense of the vehicle used to transport a coffin.

Metaphor One of the most striking types of semantic change is triggered by **metaphor**, a figure of speech based on a perceived similarity between distinct objects or actions. Metaphorical change usually involves a word with a concrete meaning taking on a more abstract sense. The meanings of many English words have been extended thanks to metaphor (see Table 7.35).

Table 7.35 Some examples of metaphor in English

Word	New meaning
grasp	'understand'
yarn	'story'
high	'on drugs'
down	'depressed'
sharp	'smart'
dull	'stupid'

*7.6 THE SPREAD OF CHANGE

Up to this point, we have been concerned with two major issues in historical linguistics: triggers of linguistic change and types of grammatical change. Still to be dealt with is the question of how linguistic change spreads. The following section focuses on two types of spread: one involving the way in which an innovation is extended through the vocabulary of a language, and the other the way in which it spreads through the population.

Diffusion through the Language

Some linguistic change first manifests itself in a few words and then gradually spreads through the vocabulary of the language. This type of change is called **lexical diffusion**. A well-attested example in English involves an ongoing change in the stress pattern of words such as *present,* which can be used as either a noun or a verb. Originally, regardless of lexical category, the stress fell on the second syllable. However, in the latter half of the sixteenth century, three such words, *rebel, outlaw,* and *record,* began to be pronounced with the stress on the first syllable when used as nouns. As Figure 7.9 illustrates, this stress shift was extended to an increasing number of words over the next decades. This change has still not diffused through the

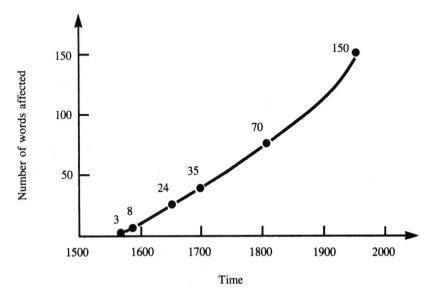

Figure 7.9 Diffusion of stress shift in English

entire vocabulary of English. There are about a thousand nouns of the relevant sort that still place the stress on the second syllable (such as *report, mistake,* and *support*). Table 7.36 illustrates the spread of this change to date. This ongoing change can be observed in action today. The noun *ad-*

Table 7.36 Stress shift in English nouns

Before the sixteenth century	During the sixteenth century	During the eighteenth century	Today
rebél	rébel	rébel	rébel
affíx	affíx	áffix	áffix
recéss	recéss	recéss	récess
mistáke	mistáke	mistáke	mistáke

dress, for example, is pronounced by many people with stress on the first syllable as [ǽdrɛs], although the older pronunciation [ǝdrés] is still heard. This change may continue to work its way through the language until all nouns in the class we have been considering are stressed on the first syllable.

Not all linguistic change involves gradual diffusion through the vocabulary of a language. Some changes apply without exception to all words.

Such an **across-the-board change** is reflected in Caribbean dialects of Spanish, where the phoneme /s/ has developed an [h] allophone in syllable-final position. The relevant allophonic rule can be stated as in Figure 7.10. This rule

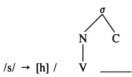

/s/ → [h] /

Figure 7.10 The Spanish [h] allophone rule

has resulted in the change exemplified in Table 7.37. This change appears to be entirely regular, affecting all instances of syllable-final /s/ in the speech of individuals who adopt it.

Table 7.37 The effects of the /s/ to [h] change in Spanish

Standard pronunciation	New pronunciation	
[dos]	[doh]	'two'
[mas]	[mah]	'more'
[es]	[eh]	'is'
[españa]	[ehpaña]	'Spain'

There seem, then, to be two types of language change. One, exemplified by the stress shifts in bisyllabic English nouns, affects individual words one at a time and gradually spreads through the vocabulary of the language. The other, exemplified by the realization of syllable-final /s/ as [h] in some dialects of Spanish, involves an across-the-board change that applies without exception to all words containing the relevant pattern.

Diffusion through the Population

Just as a change sometimes begins with a small number of words, so its effects sometimes appear first in the speech of a small number of people. As noted in Section 7.5, the relative prestige of one group of speakers encourages the imitation of their speech practices by others. Once a change has taken hold in the speech of a high-prestige group, it may gradually spread to other speakers and may ultimately affect the entire linguistic community.

An example of this involves the loss of postvocalic /r/ in English. As noted in Section 7.1, this change originated in England and was subsequently brought to parts of the eastern United States by immigrants and returning students. But a number of factors limited the spread of this innovation. It did not penetrate Pennsylvania or the other Midland states. There, the most prestigious group of settlers were Quakers from northern England, an area that retained the postvocalic /r/.

7.7 LANGUAGE RECONSTRUCTION

When we look at the vocabulary of various languages, we cannot help but notice the strong resemblances certain words bear to each other. By systematically comparing languages, we can establish relationships between them and even discover which languages descended from a common parent. In many cases, it is also possible to reconstruct with some degree of certainty various properties of the parent language.

Cognates

The most reliable sign of family relationships is the existence of systematic phonetic similarities among the vocabulary items of different languages. Many such similarities can be found in Table 7.38, in a sample of vocabulary items from English, Dutch, German, Danish, and Swedish, all of which are members of the Germanic family of languages.

Table 7.38 Some Germanic cognates

English	Dutch	German	Danish	Swedish	
/mæn/	/man/	/man/	/manʔ/	/man/	'man'
/hænd/	/hant/	/hant/	/hɔnʔ/	/hand/	'hand'
/fʊt/	/vuːt/	/fuːs/	/foːʔð/	/foːt/	'foot'
/brɪŋ/	/breŋə/	/brɪŋen/	/breŋə/	/briŋa/	'bring'
/sʌmər/	/zoːmer/	/zomer/	/sɔmər/	/sɔmar/	'summer'

Since the relationship between the form and meaning of a word is arbitrary, the existence of systematic similarities in the forms and meanings of two or more languages must point toward a common source. Conversely, where languages are not related, their vocabulary items fail to show systematic similarities. This can be seen by comparing the words in Table 7.39 from Turkish, which is not a Germanic language, with their counterparts in the languages cited in Table 7.38.

Table 7.39 Some Turkish words not related to the forms in Table 7.38

adam	'man'
el	'hand'
ayak	'foot'
getir	'bring'
yaz	'summer'

Words that have descended from a common source (as shown by systematic phonetic and, often, semantic similarities) are called **cognates**. Cognates are not always as obvious as the Germanic examples in Table 7.38. Where languages from the same family are only distantly related, the systematic correspondence may be considerably less striking. This is exemplified in Table 7.40 with data from English, Russian, and Hindi, all of which are distantly related to each other. Forms from the unrelated Turkish are included to emphasize the similarities among the first three languages.

Table 7.40 Some cognate and noncognate vocabulary items

English	Russian	Hindi	Turkish
two	dva	do	iki
three	tri	tin	üč
brother	brat	bhaya	kardeš
nose	nos	nahī̃	burun

Once the existence of a relationship between two or more languages has been established, an attempt can be made to reconstruct the common source. This reconstructed language, or **protolanguage**, is made up of **protoforms**. These forms are written with a preceding * to indicate their hypothetical character as reconstruction of earlier forms that are not directly observable. Reconstruction can be undertaken with some confidence because the processes underlying language change are systematic. Once uncovered, they can be used to infer earlier forms of the language.

*Techniques of Reconstruction

Reconstruction makes use of two general strategies. The first, the **Majority Rules Strategy**, requires that the phoneme occurring in the largest number of cognate languages be reconstructed in the protolanguage unless it can be ruled out on some other grounds. The second and more important strategy, the **Phonetic Plausibility Strategy**, requires that any process posited to account for the change of the reconstructed phoneme into the sounds observed in the data be phonetically plausible.

Consider the sample cognates in Table 7.41 from members of the Muskogean family of American Indian languages. The data exemplify a corre-

Table 7.41 Muskogean cognates

Choctaw	Koasati	Hitchiti	Creek	
/haši/	/hasi/	/ha:si/	/hasi/	'sun'

spondence between /s/ and /š/ before the vowel /i/. To account for this, we could assume either that Choctaw underwent a change that converted /s/ to /š/ before /i/ or that the other three languages underwent a change converting /š/ to /s/ before /i/. (These hypotheses are shown in Figure 7.11.) Both reconstruction strategies favor Hypothesis A. First, three of the four languages

Hypothesis A
Protoform for 'sun':   */hasi/
Phonetic change (Choctaw only):   *s → š / _____ i

Hypothesis B
Protoform for 'sun':   */haši/
Phonetic change (Koasati, Hitchiti, and Creek):   *š → s / _____ i

Figure 7.11 Two hypotheses

in the data have /s/ before /i/, and second, the phonetic change needed to account for the Choctaw pronunciation involves palatalization before a high front vowel. Since palatalization is a very common phenomenon in human language, it is plausible to assume that it also occurred in Choctaw. It would be much more difficult to argue that the protolanguage contained an /š/ before /i/ and that three languages underwent the change posited by Hypothesis B. Because depalatalization before /i/ would be an unusual phonetic process, it is unlikely to have occurred in the history of the Muskogean languages.

Consider now a slightly more complex example involving the data in Table 7.42, from several languages of the Romance family. (The data are in

Table 7.42 Some Romance cognates

Spanish	Sardinian	Italian	French	Rumanian	
ríba	rípa	rípa	riv	rípə	'embankment'
amíga	amíka	amíka	ami	---	'female friend'
kópa	kúppa	kóppa	kup	kúpə	'cup, goblet'
góta	gútta	gótta	gut	gútə	'drop'

phonemic transcription; the diacritic ′ marks stress.) Our goal here is to establish the protoforms for these words in proto-Romance, the reconstructed language that stands midway between Latin and the modern-day Romance languages.

The reconstructed word for 'embankment' in proto-Romance is */ripa/. The */r/ and */i/ are unchanged in the languages in the data, but there is variation in the second consonant, as shown in Table 7.43. The */p/ posited

Table 7.43 Variation in the second consonant of */ripa/

Spanish	Sardinian	Italian	French	Rumanian
-b-	-p-	-p-	-v-	-p-

in the protoform is retained by Sardinian, Rumanian, and Italian, but in Spanish it undergoes intervocalic voicing, a natural phonetic process, to yield /b/. The same change can be posited for French if we assume the final vowel of the protoform was still present when the consonant changes took place. Subsequent weakening would then account for the change of the voiced stop /b/ to fricative /v/. Finally at some still later stage, the final vowel would have been lost, resulting in the current form of the word. (In its written form, *rive* retains a sign of the earlier reduced vowel /ə/.) The development of the French word *rive* is outlined in Table 7.44. The vowel reduction we

Table 7.44 Evolution of French *rive*

Proto-form	*/ripa/
Voicing	/riba/
Weakening	/riva/
Vowel reduction	/rivə/
Vowel loss	/riv/

have posited for French can be directly observed in Rumanian, where the schwa is retained in word-final position.

For the cognates in the second row of Table 7.42, the protoform */amika/ can be reconstructed. The first three segments remain unchanged in all the languages in the data. The */k/ in /amika/ is intended to account for the correspondences in Table 7.45. Once again, the most commonly occurring

Table 7.45 Variation in the second consonant of */amika/

Spanish	Sardinian	Italian	French
-g-	-k-	-k-	-ø

consonant, */k/, is also the phonetically most plausible choice for the protoform. This consonant is retained in Sardinian and Italian, and voiced intervocalically in Spanish. Weakening accounts for its loss in French. The final vowel of */amika/ is retained in Spanish, Sardinian, and Italian and is lost in French.

Finally, the cognates in the last two rows of Table 7.42 yield the protoforms */kuppa/ 'cup' and */gutta/ 'drop'. All of the languages in the data retain the initial consonant of both protoforms. The vowel */u/ is reconstructed with the help of the Majority Rules Strategy, there being no phonetic grounds for choosing either /u/ or /o/ as the older vowel. (The segment /u/ is retained by three of the five languages in our sample.) As the systematic correspondences in Table 7.46 show, there is also variation involving the intervocalic consonants. Both patterns in Table 7.46 are characterized by

Table 7.46 Variation in the medial consonants of */kuppa/ and */gutta/

Spanish	Sardinian	Italian	French	Rumanian
-p-	-pp-	-pp-	-p	-p-
-t-	-tt-	-tt-	-t	-t-

the presence of a geminate stop consonant in Sardinian and Italian and by a single consonant in Spanish, Rumanian, and French. In order to ensure phonetic plausibility, we assume that the protoforms contained geminate consonants, which were weakened in Spanish, French, and Rumanian. This is an example of a case where the Phonetic Plausibility Strategy overrules the Majority Rules Strategy. Also, if we posited a single consonant in the protoform, we would have to explain why Rumanian /kupə/ did not show the same correspondences as /ripə/, shown in Table 7.43.

As far as the final vowels are concerned, matters are straightforward. The */a/ was retained in Spanish, Sardinian, and Italian, reduced to /ə/ in Rumanian and lost in French, just as happened with the final vowels in the previous examples.

Of the languages exemplified here, historical linguists consider Sardinian and Italian to be the most conservative since they have retained more of the earlier consonants and vowels. (In fact, the Sardinian words in the examples happen to look just like the protoforms, but this degree of resemblance would not be maintained in a broader range of data.) In contrast, Spanish has reduced the geminate consonants and has voiced the simple voiceless consonants. Even more drastic changes have occurred in French, where some stop consonants were converted into fricatives and still others were lost entirely.

*Internal Recon- struction

Sometimes, it is possible to reconstruct the earlier form of a language even though comparative data are not available. This technique, known as **internal reconstruction**, relies on the existence of data on morphophonemic variation from within a single language. The key point is that the sound changes that create allomorphic and allophonic variation can be identified and then used to infer an earlier form of the morpheme. The data in Table 7.47 are from

Table 7.47 A /k/ — /s/ correspondence in French

/mažik/	'magic'	/mažis-iẽ/	'magician'
/ložik/	'logic'	/ložis-iẽ/	'logician'
/müzik/	'music'	/müzis-iẽ/	'musician'

French; because of borrowing, English exhibits a parallel set of contrasts involving /k/ and /š/. The root morpheme in each row exhibits two forms, one ending in /k/, the other ending in /s/. Which is the older form? If a root ending in */s/ is posited, no phonetically plausible change can account for the /k/ in the left-hand column. On the other hand, if a root-final */k/ is posited, the /s/ can be accounted for by assuming that the */k/ was fronted under the influence of the high front vowel of the suffix and then weakened to a fricative—phonetically plausible changes. This internal reconstruction indicates that at an earlier point in the development of French, the root morphemes in Table 7.47 ended in the consonant */k/.

The Discovery of Indo-European

The late eighteenth-century discovery that Sanskrit (the ancient language of India) was related to Latin, Greek, Germanic, and Celtic revolutionized European linguistic studies. Sir William Jones, a British judge and scholar working in India, summed up the nature and implications of the findings in his 1786 address to the Royal Asiatic Society, a part of which follows:

> The Sanscrit language, whatever be its antiquity, is of a wonderful structure; more perfect than the Greek, more copious [having more cases] than the Latin, and more exquisitely refined than either, yet bearing to both of them a stronger affinity, both in the roots of the verbs and in the forms of the grammar, than could possibly have been produced by accident; so strong indeed, that no philosopher could have examined them all three, without believing them to have sprung from some com-

mon source, which, perhaps, no longer exists: there is a similar reason . . . for supposing that both the Gothick and the Celtick . . . had the same origin with the Sanscrit; and the old Persian might be added to the same family. . . .

This discovery led to several decades of intensive historical-comparative work and to important advances in historical linguistics during the nineteenth century. By studying sound correspondences from an ever-increasing number of languages, linguists eventually ascertained that most of the languages of Europe, Persia (Iran), and the northern part of India belong to a single family, which has come to be called Indo-European. By applying the techniques of the comparative method, they even began reconstructing the grammar of the language, now called Proto-Indo-European, from which these languages evolved.

A number of individuals advanced this research. In 1814, the Danish linguist Rasmus Rask carefully documented the relationship among cognates in a number of Indo-European languages, and at the same time established the methods that would govern the emerging science of historical-comparative linguistics. He wrote:

> When agreement is found in [the most essential] words in two languages, and so frequently that rules may be drawn up for the shift in letters [sounds] from one to the other, then there is a fundamental relationship between the two languages; especially when similarities in the inflectional system and in the general make-up of the two languages correspond with them.

Rask worked without access to Sanskrit. The first comparative linguistic analysis of Sanskrit, Greek, Persian, and the Germanic languages was done by the German scholar Franz Bopp in 1816. In 1822, another German, Jakob Grimm, extended Rask's observations and became the first person to explain the relationships among the cognates noted by Rask in terms of a **sound shift**, the systematic modification of a series of phonemes. Some of the correspondences on which Grimm based his work are given in Table 7.48. The

Table 7.48 Some Indo-European sound correspondences

Sanskrit	Greek	Latin	English
pitá	patér	pater	father
tráyas	treîs	trēs	three
śvan	kýon	canis	hound

crucial observation here is that where English has /f/, /θ/, and /h/ (here, in word-initial position), Greek and Latin have /p/, /t/, and /k/ while Sanskrit has /p/, /t/, and /ś/, respectively. Grimm tabulated a series of consonant shifts for the Germanic languages (English, Dutch, German, Swedish, and Danish), which differentiated them from other Indo-European languages. These shifts, which are now known as Grimm's Law, include the changes shown

Table 7.49 The sound shifts underlying Grimm's Law

Non-Germanic	p	t	k	b	d	g	bh	dh	gh
	↓	↓	↓	↓	↓	↓	↓	↓	↓
English	f	θ	h	p	t	k	b	d	g

in Table 7.49. Some additional examples of the relationships expressed by these shifts are given in Table 7.50. In these examples, the Sanskrit, Greek, and Latin consonants either underwent changes different from those found in Germanic or retained the older form.

Table 7.50 Some examples of the consonant shift underlying Grimm's Law

Shift in Germanic	Sanskrit	Greek	Latin	English
p → f	pād-	pod-	ped-	foot
t → θ	tanús	tanaós	tenuis	thin
k → h	śatám	hekatón	centum	hundred
b → p	---	---	lubricus	slippery
d → t	dáśa	déka	decem	ten
g → k	ajras	agrós	ager	acre
bh → b	bhrä́tā	phráter	fräter	brother
dh → d	vidhavā	eítheos	vidua	widow
gh → g	hansá	khḗn	(h)änser	goose

By the middle of the nineteenth century, the study of language had made great strides forward, especially in the field of phonetics, which opened the way for the detailed comparison of linguistic forms. One influential hypothesis at that time was that sound change was regular and even exceptionless. A group of linguists known as the Neogrammarians adopted this idea and made many important contributions to the fledgling science of linguistics by applying it to new and more complicated data. Although we know that factors such as analogy, lexical diffusion, and social pressures can influence the course of sound change, the neogrammarian hypothesis represented an important and daring advance in the development of linguistic theory.

The nineteenth century also saw major advances in the classification of languages. A German scholar, August Schleicher, developed a classification for the Indo-European languages in the form of a genealogical tree. This type of genetic classification is discussed in more detail in the next chapter.

Summing Up

Historical linguistics studies the nature and causes of language change. Language change is triggered by a number of linguistic and sociological factors including **analogy, folk etymology,** and **borrowing**. Change can spread through the language word by word (**lexical diffusion**) or can simultaneously affect all instances of a particular sound or form (**across-the-board change**).

By identifying the changes that a particular language or dialect has undergone, it is possible to **reconstruct** linguistic history and thereby posit the earlier forms from which current speech evolved.

Historical studies of language are of great importance to our understanding of human linguistic competence. Only through such studies can we hope to determine how social, cultural, and psychological factors interact over time to reshape languages. Work in this area of linguistics provides valuable insights into the relationships among languages, shedding light on prehistoric developments in the evolution of language.

Sources

Excellent overviews of historical linguistics as it applies to the development of English are presented in the books by Williams and by Pyles and Algeo cited below.

The data on vowel laxing in Canadian French are from Douglas C. Walker's book *The Pronunciation of Canadian French* (Ottawa: University of Ottawa Press, 1984). The data on word order in Old and Middle English come from the book by Williams cited below. The discussion of borrowing and semantic change in English draws on materials in the book by Williams.

The table depicting lexical diffusion of the stress change in English nouns derived from verbs is taken from the book by Aitchison cited below. Aitchison's remarks are based on the article by M. Chen and W. Wang, "Sound Change: Actuation and Implementation" in *Language* 51: 255-81 (1975). The data on the realization of /s/ as [h] in Spanish were provided by Herbert Izzo of the University of Calgary.

The Germanic cognates used to illustrate family relationships are from Leonard Bloomfield's classic work *Language* (New York: Holt, Rinehart and Winston, 1933). The data on sound change in Muskogean come from Mary Haas's book *The Prehistory of Languages* (Amsterdam: Mouton, 1969). The Romance cognates in this section come from *Proto-Romance Phonology* by Robert A. Hall, Jr. (New York: Elsevier, 1976). The quotes from Jones and Rask are from Holger Pedersen's book *The Discovery of Language: Linguistic Science in the Nineteenth Century* (Bloomington: Indiana University Press, 1959).

Question 2 is based on data provided by Dr. George W. Patterson of Mount St. Vincent's University, whose generosity we hereby acknowledge. The data for Questions 3 and 4 are from F. Columbus's *Introductory Workbook in Historical Phonology* (Cambridge, Mass.: Slavica Publishers, 1974). Question 9 is modeled on a problem proposed in the book by Williams cited below.

Recommended Reading

Aitchison, Jean. 1985. *Language Change: Progress or Decay*. New York: Universe Books.

Arlotto, Anthony. 1972. *Introduction to Historical Linguistics*. Washington, D.C.: University Press of America.

Pyles, Thomas and John Algeo. 1982. *The Origins and Development of the English Language*. 3d ed. New York: Harcourt Brace Jovanovich.

Williams, Joseph. 1975. *Origins of the English Language: A Social and Linguistic History*. New York: The Free Press.

Questions

1. Examine the following data, keeping in mind that Spanish descended from Latin.

   Latin   Spanish
   /ómine/   /ómbre/   'man'

   Three phonological processes have affected the Latin form of the word to give the Spanish form: syncope, dissimilation, and epenthesis. Identify the effect of each of these changes.

2. a) Describe the difference between the two French dialects in the following data. You may assume that the data are in phonetic transcription. (The symbol ü represents a high front rounded vowel, while ö represents a mid front rounded vowel.)

	Standard French	Acadian French	
(1)	ökün	očün	'none'
(2)	kör	čör	'heart'
(3)	ke	če	'wharf'
(4)	kɛ̃:z	čɛ̃:z	'fifteen'
(5)	aküze	ačüze	'accuse'
(6)	ki	čɪ	'who'
(7)	kav	kav	'cave'
(8)	kɔr	kɔr	'body'
(9)	kurir	kurir	'run'
(10)	ãkɔ:r	ãkɔ:r	'again'

   b) What sound change would you posit here? Why?
   c) State the sound change in the form of a rule.

3. a) What sound changes differentiate Guaraní from its parent language, Proto-Tupí-Guaraní, in the following data?

	Proto-Tupí-Guaraní	Guaraní	
(1)	yukɨr	yukɨ	'salt'
(2)	moayan	moayã	'push'
(3)	puʔam	puʔã	'wet'

(4) me ʔeŋ	me ʔē	'give'
(5) tiŋ	čĭ	'white'
(6) póti ʔa	poči ʔa	'chest'
(7) tatátiŋ	tatáčĭ	'smoke'
(8) kɨb	kɨ	'louse'
(9) men	mē	'husband'

b) State these changes in rule form.

4. a) Describe the three changes that took place between Proto-Slavic and Bulgarian in the following data. (The symbol ˘ over a vowel indicates that it is short.) Note that two of these changes took place in a particular order since one created the environment in which the other applies.

	Proto-Slavic	Bulgarian	
(1)	gladŭka	glatkə	'smooth'
(2)	kratŭka	kratkə	'short'
(3)	blizŭka	bliskə	'near'
(4)	žežĭka	žeškə	'scorching'
(5)	lovŭka	lofkə	'adroit'
(6)	gorĭka	gorkə	'bitter'

b) State these changes as rules and indicate the order in which they must have applied.

c) Apply these rules to the Proto-Slavic word for 'adroit' to show how the Bulgarian form evolved.

5. Consider the following lyrics from the Middle English song "Sumer is i-cumen in." Compare the Middle English lyrics with the Modern English translation and answer the questions that follow.

Original text   Transcription
Sumer is i-cumen in;   [sumər ɪs ikumən ɪn
Lhude sing, cuccu!   luːdə sɪng kukːu
Grōweþ sēd, and blōweþ mēd,   grɔːwəθ seːd and blɔːwəθ meːd
And springþ þe wude nū.   and sprɪŋgθ θə wudə nuː]

Translation
'Summer has come in;
Loudly sing, cuckoo!
Seed grows and meadow blooms
And the wood grows now.'

a) What affix converted the adjective *loud* into an adverb in Middle English?

b) What accounts for the difference between the Middle English and Modern English pronunciation of the vowel in *loud*?

c) Are there any other words in this poem that show this change?

d) What words are used for 'grow' in this poem?

e) How has the relative ordering of the subject and verb changed since this was written?

    f)   How has the third person singular present tense suffix changed since Middle English?

6. The following Cree words were borrowed from French as the result of contact between the two groups on the Canadian prairies. (You may notice that the French determiner was not treated as a separate morpheme and was carried along with the borrowed word.) What types of considerations could one plausibly assume played a role in the borrowing of these words into Cree? (*Hint:* Reread the section of this chapter dealing with the factors underlying the borrowing of French words into English.)

	Cree	French	
a)	labutōn	le bouton	'button'
b)	lībot	les bottes	'boots'
c)	lamilās	la mélasse	'molasses'
d)	lapwīl	la poêle	'frying pan'
e)	litī	le thé	'tea'

7. The following line is from "Troilus and Criseyde V" by Geoffrey Chaucer.

His lighte goost ful blisfully is went.

[hɪs lɪxtə gɔːst fʊl blɪsfʊlːi ɪs wɛnt]

'His light spirit has gone very blissfully.'

    a)   How has the meaning of the word *ghost* changed since Chaucer's time?

    b)   Describe the changes that have taken place in the pronunciation of *light* and *ghost*.

8. All of the following English words at one time had meanings that are quite different from their current ones.

	Word	Earlier meaning
a)	moody	'brave'
b)	uncouth	'unknown'
c)	aunt	'father's sister'
d)	butcher	'one who slaughters goats'
e)	witch	'male or female sorcerer'
f)	sly	'skillful'
g)	accident	'an event'
h)	argue	'make clear'
i)	carry	'transport by cart'
j)	grumble	'murmur, make low sounds'
k)	shrewd	'depraved, wicked'
l)	praise	'set a value on'
m)	ordeal	'trial by torture'
n)	picture	'a painted likeness'

o) seduce   'persuade someone to desert his or her duty'
p) box   'a small container made of boxwood'
q) baggage   'a worthless person'

Identify each of these semantic changes as an instance of narrowing, broadening, or shift.

9. The following phonetic transcriptions represent the pronunciation of several words in Old English, Middle English, and Modern English. For each word, determine the possible effects of:
a) the Great Vowel Shift
b) epenthesis
c) diphthongization
d) consonant loss
e) vowel loss

	Old English	Middle English	Modern English	
(1)	spɪnḷ	spɪndḷ	spɪndḷ	'spindle'
(2)	θrɪddua	θɪrdə	θərd	'third'
(3)	ɛmti	ɛmpti	ɛmptiy	'empty'
(4)	havɔk	hawk	hɑk	'hawk'
(5)	θümḷ	θɪmbḷ	θɪmbḷ	'thimble'
(6)	hæːəvɔd	hɛd	hɛd	'head'

10. The following phonetic transcriptions represent some words in six hypothetical languages from the year 2500, all descendants of modern-day Standard English. (Recall that [ɣ] marks a voiced velar fricative.)

	British	American	Canadian	
a)	dri	tri	təri	'three'
b)	dɑp	tɑp	tɑp	'top'
c)	dɪk	stɪk	sədɪk	'stick'
d)	gʊk	kʊk	kʊk	'cook'
e)	gen	ken	ken	'cane'
f)	bost	post	pozət	'post'
g)	moɣər	smogər	səmogər	'smoker'

	Australian	Jamaican	Bermudan	
a)	tre	ri	tri	'three'
b)	tɔp	tɑp	tɑ	'top'
c)	stek	tik	sti	'stick'
d)	kok	kuk	ku	'cook'
e)	kæn	ken	ken	'cane'
f)	pɔst	pos	pos	'post'
g)	smɔkər	mokər	smokə	'smoker'

Indicate the phonetic changes that would have to apply to the current pronunciations of these words to yield the new forms.

11. Consider the following data taken from four languages of the Turkic family. (The symbol q represents a voiceless uvular stop.) The data have been simplified for presentation here.

	Turkish	Uzbek	Tatar	Yakut	
a)	kara	qɔra	kara	xara	'black'
b)	kan	qɔn	kan	xan	'blood'
c)	kar	qɔr	kar	xar	'snow'
d)	kal	qɔl	kal	xal	'remain'
e)	kur	qur	kor	kur	'dry'
f)	kɨz	qiz	kɨz	kɨz	'girl'
g)	kɨzɨl	qizil	kɨzɨl	kɨhɨl	'red'

Using the strategies presented in Section 7.7, reconstruct protoforms for each word on the basis of the data provided.

8 THE CLASSIFICATION OF LANGUAGES

Everything it is possible for us to analyze depends
on a clear method which distinguishes the similar
from the not similar.

— Linneus *Genera Plantarum* (1754)

One of the most striking facts about the linguistic situation in the world today is its diversity. There are thousands of different languages, each with its own sound patterns, vocabulary, and syntactic rules. However, underlying this diversity are important similarities that allow linguists to group languages into a relatively small number of families and types. This chapter is concerned with methods of classification as well as with some of the major findings within this branch of linguistic analysis.

There are essentially two ways to go about classifying languages. One system of classification analyzes languages in terms of their structural characteristics. This results in the grouping together of languages with similar sound patterns and grammatical rules. A second system classifies languages according to their genetic relationships. Languages that developed historically from the same ancestor language are grouped together and are considered to be genetically related. In the first part of this chapter, we describe some of the ways in which languages can be classified structurally, and point out some of the characteristics most commonly found in the languages of the world. We then present the genetic groupings proposed for some familiar languages and conclude by examining some less well-known languages.

8.1 STRUCTURAL VERSUS GENETIC RELATIONSHIPS

Linguists estimate that there are between four thousand and eight thousand different languages presently spoken by the more than five billion people in the world. These figures are imprecise primarily because it is often difficult to determine whether two linguistic communities speak different languages or merely different dialects of the same language. Part of this difficulty arises from the fact that there is simply not enough information about a large number of languages. For example, it is only recently that linguists have come to know a great deal about the indigenous languages of Africa and North

America, and many of the languages of South America, New Guinea, and Australia are still relatively unknown.

One test that linguists use to decide whether two varieties of speech should be considered different languages or different dialects of the same language relies on the criterion of **mutual intelligibility**. Mutually intelligible varieties of a language can be understood by speakers of each variety. According to this criterion, the English of Melbourne, the English of Milwaukee, and the English of London qualify as dialects of the same language. If two speakers cannot understand one another, then linguists normally conclude that they are speaking different languages. The Italian of Florence and the French of Paris are examples of varieties of speech that are not mutually intelligible.

Political, cultural, social, historical, and religious factors often intervene in the determination of linguistic boundaries. For example, Serbians and Croatians often say that they speak different languages. However, even though their history, religion, and spelling systems differ, Serbians and Croatians actually speak mutually intelligible dialects of the same language, which linguists call Serbo-Croatian. In contrast, we often speak of Chinese as if it were a single language, even though it is actually a number of separate, mutually unintelligible languages (Cantonese, Mandarin, Hakka, and so on), each with a host of dialects.

In addition to the problems presented by these nonlinguistic considerations, complications also arise when we try to divide a continuum of mutually intelligible dialects whose two end points are not intelligible. Dutch and German, for example, are mutually intelligible around the border area between Germany and Holland; however, the Dutch of Amsterdam and the German of Munich are not. Similarly, Palestinian Arabic and Syrian Arabic are mutually intelligible, but Moroccan Arabic and Saudi Arabian Arabic are not.

Even if we adopt the conservative estimate that there are only four thousand languages in the world, this is still a very large number. It is therefore desirable to develop a system for classifying languages into smaller groups. This sort of language classification is normally done either in terms of genetic relationships or in terms of structural characteristics.

Languages that are considered to be genetically related are grouped into families whose members are all assumed to have descended from the same ancestor language. This ancestor may be attested (that is, texts written in this language have been discovered or preserved, as in the case of Latin and its descendants), or it may be a reconstructed protolanguage for which no original texts exist (as is the case for Proto-Indo-European). This type of genetic classification is discussed further in Section 8.3.

Although genetically related languages often share structural characteristics, they do not necessarily bear a close structural resemblance. For example, Latvian and English are genetically related (both are descended from Indo-European), but their morphological structure is quite different. An English sentence such as *It has to be figured out* can be expressed in Latvian by a single word.

1. jāizgudro

jā   -iz   -gudro

(one) must out figure (it)

'One must figure it out.'

Of course, Latvian and English are very distantly related, and languages that are more closely related will typically share a larger number of structural similarities. On the other hand, it is also necessary to recognize that even languages that are totally unrelated may share some structural similarities. Thus, English and Swahili, which are unrelated, both employ subject-verb-object word order in simple declarative sentences.

2. Maria anampenda Anna.

'Maria likes Anna.'

The next section examines some of the ways that languages can be grouped together on the basis of structural characteristics.

8.2 STRUCTURAL CLASSIFICATION

The classification of languages according to their structural characteristics is known as **linguistic typology**. A typical study in typology might group together languages that have similar word order patterns, word structure, or phonological systems. An important area of research within the study of linguistic typology involves the search for language universals—structural patterns and traits that occur in all or most human languages. Patterns or traits that occur in all languages are called **absolute universals**, while those that simply occur in most languages are known as **universal tendencies**. Many of the generalizations formulated in the study of linguistic typology involve **implicational universals**—principles that specify that the presence of one trait implies the presence of another (but not vice versa). For instance, languages with fricative phonemes (such as /f/ and /s/) will also have stop phonemes (such as /p/ and /t/), although the reverse is not necessarily true.

The following sections present some of the typological classifications and universals that have been proposed in the areas of phonology, morphology, and syntax.

Phonology

Phonological systems are often classified on the basis of phonemic contrasts rather than by listing entire phonetic inventories. The listing of many allophones can lead to a confused picture of the relationships among phonological systems, but phonemic analysis allows the relevant contrasts to emerge. In this section, all vowel and consonant systems are represented phonemically. However, it should not be forgotten that the phonetic realization of these systems vary a great deal from language to language.

Vowel Systems Languages are often classified according to the size and pattern of their vowel systems. The most common vowel system has five phonemic contrasts, and shows two high vowels, two mid vowels, and one low vowel (see Figure 8.1). The front vowels are unrounded and the back vowels are rounded; the low vowel is unrounded. About half of the world's languages, including Basque, Hawaiian, Japanese, Spanish, and Swahili, have such a system.

```
i       u

e       o

     a
```

Figure 8.1 The most common vowel system

The majority of the world's other languages have vowel systems with three, four, six, or seven different vowels (disregarding contrasts based on length or nasalization, which can double or triple the number of phonemic vowels). Languages with fewer than three, or more than nine distinctive vowels are rare. Some typical vowel systems are presented in Figure 8.2.

```
i   ɨ   u          i                    i        u

e       o          e          o         e    ə   o

    a                   a                    ʌ

                                             a
```

Six vowel   Four vowel   Seven vowel
system   system   system
Gilyak (U.S.S.R.)   Navaho (Arizona)   Geez (Ethiopia)

Figure 8.2 Common vowel systems

Observation of many languages has led to the discovery of a number of universal tendencies in phonological structure. Generalizations about universal tendencies in vowel systems can be made in terms of the phonological characteristics of vowels. Some of these tendencies are listed here along with a description of the most frequently occurring vowels.

- The most commonly occurring vowel phoneme is /a/, which is found in almost all of the languages of the world. Almost as frequent as /a/ are /i/ and /u/.
- Front vowel phonemes (/i, ɛ, æ/) are generally unrounded, while non-low back vowel phonemes (/o, ʊ/) are generally rounded.
- Low vowels (/æ, ɑ/) are generally unrounded.

Although English has an above average number of vowels, these phonemes all comply with the above tendencies. Thus, English has only front unrounded vowels, all the low vowel phonemes are unrounded, and all of the back, nonlow vowels are rounded. The English vowel system can be represented as in Figure 8.3.

iy		uw
ɪ		ʊ
ey	ʌ	ow
ɛ		ɔ
æ	a	ɑ

Figure 8.3 The English vowel system

The relationship among contrasting vowel types (such as oral and nasal vowel phonemes and long and short vowel phonemes) can also be expressed in terms of implicational universals, since the presence of one vowel phoneme type implies the presence of another (but not vice versa).

- If a language has contrastive nasal vowels, then it will also have contrastive oral vowels. For example, French contrasts different nasal vowels (/lɔ̃/ 'long' and /lã/ 'slow'), and contrasts oral vowels with nasal vowels (/la/ 'weary' and /lã/ 'slow'). Predictably, French also contrasts different oral vowels, as in /klo/ 'shut' and /klu/ 'nail'. English shows contrasts among oral vowels but does not contrast nasal vowels with oral vowels. There are no contrasts in English like /bɑt/ and /bɑ̃t/.

- If a language has contrasting long vowels, then it will also have contrasting short vowels. For example, Finnish shows contrasting long vowels and, predictably, contrasting short vowels (see Table 8.1). The reverse is not necessarily the case. English shows contrasting short vowels but does not contrast long vowels with short ones.

Table 8.1 Finnish vowel contrasts

Long versus long	/viːli/	'junket'	/vaːli/	'election'
Short versus short	/suka/	'family'	/suku/	'bristle'
Short versus long	/tuli/	'fire'	/tuːli/	'wind'

Consonant Systems It is not particularly fruitful to classify languages according to the number of consonants that they contain, since the consonant inventories of languages may range from as few as eight consonant phonemes (in Hawaiian, for example) to more than ninety. !Kung, a language spoken in Namibia, has ninety-six consonant phonemes. (The symbol *!k* represents a type of click.) Nevertheless, a number of claims can be made about the consonant systems that occur in human language.

- The most common stop phonemes in language are /p, t, k/. Very few languages lack any one of these, and there are no languages that lack all three. If any one of these three stops is missing, it will probably be /p/; for example, Aleut, Nubian, and Witchita have no /p/ phoneme. The most commonly occurring phoneme of the three is /t/.

- The most commonly occurring fricative phoneme is /s/; few languages lack it. If a language has only one fricative, it is most likely to be /s/; for example, it is the only fricative found in Nandi (a language of Kenya) and Weri (a language of New Guinea).
- Almost every known language has at least one nasal phoneme; in cases where a language has only one nasal phoneme, that phoneme is usually /n/. (The only nasal phoneme in Arapaho is /n/.) If there are two contrasting nasals, they are normally /m/ and /n/.
- The majority of languages have at least one phonemic liquid. However, a small number of languages have none at all (Blackfoot, Dakota, and Efik, which is spoken in Nigeria, and Siona, which is spoken in Ecuador). English, of course, has two: /l/ and /r/.

Consonant phonemes are also subject to various implicational universals.

- If a language has voiced obstruent phonemes (stops, fricatives, or affricates), then it will also have voiceless obstruent phonemes. The reverse is not necessarily true, since Ainu (a language of northern Japan) has only voiceless obstruent phonemes /p, t, k, č, s/.
- Sonorant consonants are generally voiced. Very few languages have voiceless sonorants; those that do always have voiced sonorants as well. For example, Burmese contrasts voiced and voiceless nasals and laterals.
- If a language has fricative phonemes, then it will also have stop phonemes. There are no languages that lack stops; however, there are some languages that lack fricatives. For example, Gilbertese (Gilbert Islands), Kitabal (eastern Australia), and Nuer (southeastern Sudan) have no fricatives.

Prosodic Universals Languages can also be classified according to their prosodic, or suprasegmental type. Languages in which pitch distinctions are phonemic are called tone languages. (The phonetics and phonology of tone were introduced in Chapters 2 and 3.) A great many of the world's languages are tone languages. Mandarin, for instance, has four contrastive tones (see Table 8.2). The other Chinese languages, as well as many Southeast Asian

Table 8.2 Tone contrasts in Mandarin

mā	'mother'	high tone
má	'hemp'	low rising tone
mǎ	'horse'	falling rising tone
mà	'scold'	high falling tone

languages like Burmese and Vietnamese, are also tone languages. A few tone languages are also found in Europe; for example, in one of the dialects of Latvian a three-way tonal distinction is made (see Table 8.3). As noted

Table 8.3 Tone contrasts in Latvian

loks	[lùoks]	'arch, bow'	falling tone
loks	[lūoks]	'green onion'	level (high) tone
loks	[lûoks]	'window'	rising falling (broken) tone

in the chapter on phonetics, tones are of two types, *level* tones and *contour* tones. Tone languages most often contrast only two tone levels (phonologically high and low), although contrasts involving three tone levels (such as high, low, and mid tones) are not uncommon. Hardly any language contrasts more than five levels of tone.

Various suprasegmental universals have been proposed for tone languages. According to one such universal, if a language has contour tones (such as rising tone or falling tone) then it will also have level tones (such as high, mid, or low tone). The reverse is not necessarily true. It is also likely that if a language has complex contour tones (such as rising falling or falling rising), then it will also have simple contour tones (such as rising or falling). Both the Mandarin and Latvian examples fit this pattern.

Differences in stress, discussed in Chapter 2, are also useful in classifying languages. Fixed stress languages are those in which the position of stress on a word is predictable. For example, in Mayan, stress always falls on the last syllable of a word; in Polish, Swahili, and Samoan, stress falls on the penultimate (second to last) syllable of a word, while in Czech, Finnish, and Hungarian, the stressed syllable is always the first syllable of a word. In free stress languages, the position of stress is not always predictable. Free stress is also called phonemic stress because of its role in distinguishing between words. Russian is an example of a language with free stress (see Table 8.4).

Table 8.4 Stress contrasts in Russian

múka	'torture'	muká	'flour'
zámok	'castle'	zamók	'lock'
rúki	'hands'	rukí	'hand' (genitive singular)

Morphology

Both the word and the morpheme are universally valid linguistic categories. However, there are systematic differences in the ways in which individual languages combine morphemes to form words. Four types of systems are usually distinguished, although no language fits any of these types perfectly.

The Isolating Type A language is **isolating** or **analytic** to the extent that its words consist of a single morpheme. Because most words consist only of a root, there are few bound morphemes (affixes). Categories such as number and tense are usually expressed by a free morpheme (a separate word). In Mandarin, for instance, tense is indicated by a free morpheme whose position with respect to other elements is variable.

> *3.* Ta chi fan le.
> he eat   meal past
> 'He ate the meal.'
>
> Ta chi le fan.
> he eat   past meal
> 'He ate the meal.'

Other languages that are predominantly isolating include Cantonese, Vietnamese, Laotian, and Cambodian.

The Agglutinating Type An **agglutinating** language makes extensive use of words containing two or more morphemes (a root and one or more affixes). In such languages, each affix is clearly identifiable and characteristically encodes a single grammatical contrast. Turkish words can have a complex morphological structure, but each morpheme has a single clearly identifiable function. In the words in Table 8.5, for instance, -*ler* marks plurality, -*de* indicates 'in', and -*den* corresponds to 'from'.

Table 8.5 Affixes in Turkish

ev	'house'
ev-ler	'houses'
ev-ler-de	'in the houses'
ev-ler-den	'from the houses'

The Synthetic Type Words in a **synthetic** or an **inflectional language** are also complex. However, in contrast with agglutinating systems, synthetic affixes often mark several grammatical categories simultaneously. In Russian, for example, a single inflectional affix simultaneously marks the noun's gender class (masculine, feminine, or neuter), its number (singular or plural), and its grammatical role (subject, direct object, and so on). The ending -*i*, for instance, can be used to indicate that a noun belongs to the feminine gender class, is plural, and functions as subject. (As noted in Chapter 4, such affixes are called portmanteau morphemes.)

    4. Ptits-i peli.
      'Birds sang.'

If you look again at the noun paradigms for Russian given in the chapter on morphology, you will see that this situation is typical of the entire case system in that language.

The Polysynthetic Type In a **polysynthetic** language, long strings of affixes or bound forms are united into single words, which may translate as an entire sentence in English. The use of portmanteau morphemes is common, although the extent to which this happens varies from language to language. Polysynthetic structures can be found in many native languages of North America, including Inuktitut, Cree, and Sarcee. The following example is from Inuktitut.

    5. Qasuiirsarvigssarsingitluinarnarpuq.
      qasu-iir -sar   -vig   -ssar
      tired not cause-to-be place-for suitable
      -si -ngit -luinar   -nar   -puq
      find not completely someone 3rd sg.
      'Someone did not find a completely suitable resting place.'

Most languages, including English, do not belong exclusively to any of the four categories. English employs analytic patterns in many verbal constructions, where each notion is expressed by a separate word. Future time, for instance, is indicated by a free morpheme, rather than an affix, in structures such as *I will leave*. In contrast, English exhibits considerable agglutination in derived words, such as *unwillingness*, which consist of a series of morphemes, each with a clearly definable meaning and function. The English pronoun system, on the other hand, is largely synthetic since a single form can be used to indicate person, number, gender, and case. The word *he*, for instance, is used to express a third person, singular, masculine subject.

Implicational Universals A variety of generalizations can be made about word structure in human language.

- If a language has inflectional affixes, it will also have derivational affixes. For example, English not only has inflectional affixes such as the past tense *-ed* and possessive *-'s*, but it also contains derivational affixes like *un-*(*unhappy, unwanted*) and *-ly* (*quickly, slowly*).
- If a word has both a derivational and an inflectional affix, the derivational affix is closer to the root (DA = derivational affix; IA = inflectional affix), as illustrated in Table 8.6.

Table 8.6 The ordering of derivational and inflectional affixes

English					
friend-ship-s			*friend-s-ship		
root DA IA			root IA DA		
Turkish					
iš	-či	-ler	*iš	-ler	-či
work	-er	*pl.*	work	*pl.*	-er
root	DA	IA	root	IA	DA

- If a language has only suffixes, it will also have only postpositions. (As noted in Chapter 5, postpositions are the equivalent of prepositions in languages that place the head at the end of the phrase.) Turkish, for example, has only suffixes; as expected, it also has postpositions rather than prepositions. This is illustrated in the following sentence.

6. Ahmet Ayše ičin kitab-i aldi.
   Ahmet Ayše for book-Ac bought
   'Ahmet bought a book for Ayše.'

Syntax

Because we lack detailed descriptions for most of the world's languages, much of the work on syntactic universals has been restricted to the study of word order as it occurs in simple declarative sentences such as *The men built the house*. Patterns are classified in terms of the relative ordering of the subject (S), direct object (O), and verb (V). The three most common word orders (in descending order of frequency) are SOV, SVO, and VSO.

7. SOV (Turkish)
    Hasan öküz-ü aldɪ.
    Hasan ox-Ac bought
    'Hasan bought the ox.'
8. SVO (English)
    The athlete broke the record.
9. VSO (Welsh)
    Lladdodd y ddraig y dyn.
    killed   the dragon the man
    'The dragon killed the man.'

All three of these word order patterns place the subject before the direct object. It has been suggested that the subject appears at a relatively early point in the utterance because it usually encodes the topic; that is, it indicates what the rest of the sentence is about.

While patterns that place the subject before the direct object are by far the most frequent in human language, they are not universal. There are a few VOS languages, the best-known example of which is Malagasy, the language of Madagascar.

10. VOS (Malagasy)
     Nahita ny mpianatra ny vehivavy.
     saw   the student   the woman
     'The woman saw the student.'

As well, there are a very few OVS languages, all of which seem to be spoken in the Amazon basin of South America.

11. OVS (Hixkaryana)
     Toto yahosiye kamara.
     man grabbed jaguar
     'The jaguar grabbed the man.'

To date, there are no known examples of languages whose basic word order is OSV.

Implicational Universals Sometimes, the order of elements within one kind of structure has implications for the arrangement of elements in other structures. Some of these implicational universals are stated here.

- If a language has VSO word order, then it will have prepositions rather than postpositions. Languages of this type include Berber (spoken in Morocco), Classical Hebrew, Maori (spoken in New Zealand), Maasai (spoken in Kenya), Welsh, and Irish.

12. VSO (Irish)
     Fhaca me mo mhátair.
     saw   I my mother
     'I saw my mother.'

     sa teach
     in house
     'in the house'

- If a language has SOV word order, then it will probably have post-positions rather than prepositions. Languages with this structural pattern include Basque, Burmese, Hindi, Japanese, Korean, Quechua, Turkish, and Guugu Yimidhirr, an aboriginal language of Australia.

13. SOV (Guugu Yimidhirr)
Gudaa-ngun yarrga dyinday.
dog-Erg   boy   bit
'The dog bit the boy.'

yuwaal nganh
beach from
'from the beach'

- In languages with VSO word order, adjectives and relative clauses usually follow the noun that they modify.

14. VSO (Hebrew)
wayəxal   ʔĕlohim bayyom   hašševiʕi   məlaʔxto ʔašer ʕosɔh
and-ended God   on-the-day the-seventh his-work that he-did
'And God finished the work that he did on the seventh day.'

- Languages with SOV order will usually place both adjectives and relative clauses before the noun they modify.

15. SOV (Japanese)
atarašii kutsu
new   shoes

[Yamada-ga katte iru] saru
Yamada-N keep pres. monkey
'the monkey which Yamada keeps'

Explaining Universals

At present, linguists are a long way from explaining why linguistic universals exist. Nonetheless, a number of interesting proposals have been made, and it is worthwhile to consider a sampling of them here.

Phonology Perceptual factors play a role in shaping phonological universals. Vowel systems (discussed earlier in the chapter) develop so as to keep vocalic phonemes as different from each other as possible. A three vowel system such as the one in Figure 8.4 allows for plenty of "space" around each vowel, which may make each easier to distinguish from the others. It may also be the case that front vowels are normally unrounded, and back (nonlow) vowels are normally rounded because these vowel types are easier to perceive. Similarly, the fact that /s/ is the most commonly occurring fricative may have to do with its acoustic prominence: varieties of /s/ are inherently louder than other kinds of fricatives.

i   u

a

Figure 8.4 A three vowel system

Morphology Other types of explanations may be appropriate for morphological universals. For example, the fact that languages with suffixes but no prefixes always have postpositions has a historical explanation. In these languages, some postpositions became attached to a preceding word and were thereby converted into suffixes. Because suffixes in such languages have evolved from postpositions, the link between the two elements can be traced to their common origin.

The requirement that derivational affixes occur closer to the root than inflectional affixes has another type of explanation. As noted in the morphology chapter, processes such as derivation form new words, while inflection marks the subclass (plural, past tense) to which a word belongs. Given that a word must be formed before its subclass can be determined, it follows that derivational processes will precede inflection. This is reflected in word structure, where derivational affixes appear closer to the root than inflectional markers. In Figure 8.5, the verbal root *treat* is converted into a noun by the affix -*ment* before the plural inflectional marker is added.

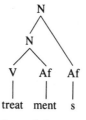

Figure 8.5

Syntax At least some syntactic universals may be explainable in terms of the way that the human brain processes sentence structure. Consider in this respect Table 8.7, which presents a summary of word order patterns based on the implicational universals discussed earlier. In order to explain why

Table 8.7 Word order patterns

Phrase type	Pattern A	Pattern B
VP	*verb*-object	object-*verb*
NP	*noun*-adjective	adjective-*noun*
	noun-relative clause	relative clause-*noun*
PP	*preposition*-NP	NP-*postposition*

the word order properties in each column co-occur in most languages, we must use the notion of head introduced in the chapter on syntax. As you may recall, the head is the obligatory category around which a phrase is organized. Thus, V is the head of VP, N is the head of NP, and P is the head of PP. By re-examining the data in Table 8.7, you will notice an interesting generalization: the word order patterns in the left column place the head (in italics) first while those in the right column place it last. It has been suggested that syntactic structures are easier to produce and understand if the head is always uniformly at the beginning or the end of phrases; this may explain why word order patterns co-occur in the manner illustrated.

This preference cannot be absolute since there are many languages that do not observe a uniform head-first or head-last order. In English, for example, the verb typically comes at the beginning of the VP and the preposition at the beginning of the PP, but nouns occur in the middle of NPs.

16. [NP the new *book* about fitness]

The study of linguistic typology and language universals is a relatively new field within linguistics. There is obviously much still to be learned about linguistic universals, and it must be admitted that some of the current work is speculative and incomplete. No doubt many interesting new facts will eventually come to light.

8.3 GENETIC CLASSIFICATION

The world's languages can be grouped into a relatively small number of language families. However, genetic classification is sometimes difficult for a number of reasons.

Perhaps the biggest problem is simply the amount of data that must be collected before linguists can be confident about the status of a number of groups of languages. It is only in the last two decades, for example, that enough information has been accumulated to propose a detailed classification of the languages of Africa.

In many cases, linguists face the problem of establishing the tests or criteria to be used in proposing genetic relationships. There is some disagreement over the degree of similarity that should exist among languages before a genetic relationship can be proposed. This issue arises because unrelated languages will often share structural characteristics (that is, be typologically similar). This is particularly likely to occur if languages have been in contact long enough to have borrowed a large number of words, sounds, morphemes, or syntactic structures from one another.

Additional difficulties stem from the fact that genetically related languages need *not* be typologically similar. This is especially true if the relationship is a distant one, as is the case with English and Russian. Russian in highly inflectional, has an extensive case system, and has quite free word order, while English is only marginally inflectional, has virtually no case marking, and has fixed word order. Yet, both belong to the Indo-European family.

To complicate matters further still, linguists also disagree as to the number of cognates that must be uncovered before a genetic relationship between languages can be established. The more distant the genetic relationship between languages, the less likely it is that a large number of obvious cognates will be found. Sound changes, for example, can obscure similarities between cognate words. English and Latin are related (though distantly), but the similarity between cognates like Latin *unda*, meaning 'wave', and English *water* is certainly not striking.

Research is hampered as well by the fact that words that may be excellent indicators of a genetic relationship can drop out of the lexicon. For example, Old English had a word *leax* ('salmon') which was cognate with German *Lachs* and Yiddish *lox*, but this lexical item has since been lost from the English lexicon.

Nevertheless, languages that are genetically related do share many similarities, particularly if their common ancestor is not too distant. Some language families contain many hundreds of languages; in other cases, only one language may remain to represent a family; in still other cases, families have become extinct. The following sections present some information about the makeup and membership of a few of the language families represented in the world today.

The Indo-European Family

With only about a hundred languages, Indo-European is not a large family in terms of total number of languages. However, it is the largest language family in the world in terms of total number of speakers: there are about 1.7 billion native speakers of an Indo-European language. Living Indo-European languages can be assigned to one of the nine branches illustrated in Table 8.8.

Table 8.8 Main branches of the Indo-European family

Germanic
Celtic
Italic
Hellenic
Albanian
Armenian
Baltic
Slavic
Indo-Iranian

Germanic The organization of the Germanic family of languages is illustrated in Table 8.9. (In this and other tables, parentheses are used to indicate languages that no longer have any speakers. The tables are intended to exemplify the membership and organization of language families, not to provide

Table 8.9 The Germanic family

(East Germanic)	North Germanic	West Germanic
(Gothic)	Icelandic	German
	Faroese	Dutch
	Norwegian	Frisian
	Danish	English
	Swedish	Afrikaans
		Yiddish

an exhaustive list of the languages in each family.) As Table 8.9 indicates, the Germanic branch of Indo-European can be divided into three sub-branches. The East Germanic branch included Gothic, the oldest Germanic language for which written texts exist (dating from the fourth century A.D.). Gothic and any other languages belonging to this branch of Germanic have long been extinct. The North Germanic (or Scandinavian) branch originally included Old Norse (also known as Old Icelandic), a dialect of which was spoken by the Vikings. From it, descended Icelandic, Faroese (spoken on the Faroe islands, north of Scotland), Swedish, Danish, and Norwegian.

The West Germanic branch includes German, Flemish (spoken in Belgium), Dutch, Afrikaans, Frisian, and English. Afrikaans is descended from the Dutch spoken by seventeenth-century settlers in South Africa (the Boers). Frisian is spoken on the north coast of Holland, and on the Frisian islands just off the coast, as well as on the northwestern coast of Germany. English descended from the speech of the Angles, Saxons, and Jutes, Germanic tribes that lived in northern Germany and southern Denmark (in an area just east of the Frisians) before invading England and settling there in A.D. 449.

Celtic The Celtic branch of Indo-European (see Table 8.10) has two main subbranches: Insular and Continental (now extinct). One representative of

Table 8.10 The Celtic family

Insular		(Continental)
Brythonic	Goidelic	
Welsh	Irish [= Irish Gaelic]	(Gaulish)
Breton	Scots Gaelic	
(Cornish)		

the latter subbranch, Gaulish, was once spoken in France but has long been extinct. The Insular subbranch can be subdivided into two groups of languages: Brythonic and Goidelic. Brythonic languages include Welsh and Breton (which is spoken in northwestern France) as well as Cornish, which was formerly spoken in Britain but is now extinct. The Goidelic branch contains Irish (or Irish Gaelic), which is still spoken natively in the western parts of Ireland, and Scots Gaelic, which is native to some of the northwestern parts of Scotland (especially the Hebrides Islands) and, to a lesser extent, Cape Breton Island in Nova Scotia.

Italic The Italic family originally consisted of a variety of languages spoken in the area corresponding roughly to modern-day Italy. The Italic languages that are presently spoken are all descended from Latin, the language of the vast Roman Empire, and are called Romance languages. It is customary to divide this language family into an Eastern group (consisting of Italian and Rumanian) and a Western group consisting of all the other Romance languages with the exception of Sardinian (which stands alone). The Western group is further divided into Ibero-Romance (Spanish, Portuguese, and Catalan) and Gallo-Romance, which includes the Romance languages spoken in France and Switzerland. These divisions are illustrated in Table 8.11.

Table 8.11 The Romance family

Eastern	Western		
	Ibero-Romance	Gallo-Romance	
Italian	Spanish	French	Sardinian
Rumanian	Portuguese	Occitan	
	Catalan	Romansch	

Hellenic The Hellenic branch of Indo-European has only one living member, Greek. All modern Greek dialects are descended from the classical dialect known as Attic Greek, which was the speech of Athens during the Golden Age of Greek culture (500 to 200 B.C.).

Albanian The Albanian branch of Indo-European has only one member, Albanian, which is spoken not only in Albania, but also in parts of Yugoslavia, Greece, and Italy.

Armenian The Armenian branch also has only one member, Armenian. This language is concentrated in the Armenian S.S.R. (between the Black Sea and the Caspian Sea, in the area known as the Caucasus) and in northeastern Turkey.

Baltic The Baltic branch contains only two surviving languages, Latvian and Lithuanian. Both are spoken in the northwestern U.S.S.R. just northeast of Poland. Lithuanian has an elaborate case system, which resembles the one posited for Proto-Indo-European.

Slavic The Slavic branch of Indo-European can be divided into three sub-branches: East, South, and West. The East Slavic branch is made up of Russian, Ukrainian, and Byelorussian (or White Russian); the latter is spoken in the western U.S.S.R. around Minsk, just east of the northern half of Poland. The South Slavic branch includes Bulgarian, Macedonian, Serbo-Croatian, and Slovenian. The latter three languages are all spoken in Yugoslavia. Both Macedonian and Bulgarian are unlike other Slavic languages in having lost most of their case endings. The West Slavic branch includes Czech, Slovak (the two official languages of Czechoslovakia), and Polish. The organization of the Slavic group of languages is represented in Table 8.12.

Table 8.12 The Slavic family

East Slavic	South Slavic	West Slavic
Russian	Slovenian	Czech
Ukrainian	Serbo-Croatian	Slovak
Byelorussian	Macedonian	Polish
	Bulgarian	

Indo-Iranian The Indo-Iranian branch of Indo-European is divided into Iranian and Indic subbranches. The Iranian subbranch contains about two dozen different languages, including Modern Persian (also called Farsi and spoken in Iran), Pashto (the principal language of Afghanistan), and Kurdish (found in Iran, Iraq, Turkey, and Syria). Other Iranian languages are spoken in Pakistan, the U.S.S.R., and China.

There are about thirty-five different Indic languages. Most of the languages spoken in Pakistan, Bangladesh, and northern India belong to this branch of Indo-European. Some of the most widespread (in terms of number of speakers) are Hindi-Urdu, Bengali, Punjabi, Marathi, and Gujarati. Although Hindi and Urdu are varieties of the same language, they have totally different writing systems and are associated with different cultures; Urdu is spoken principally in Pakistan by Muslims while Hindi is spoken primarily in India by Hindus.

Less well known as an Indic language is Romany, or Gypsy. It is believed that the Gypsies were an entertainment caste in India who were invited to perform in the Middle East sometime in the Middle Ages. They never returned to India, but traveled instead to Turkey and, eventually, Europe. Romany contains many borrowed words—particularly from Greek, which was spoken in Turkey at the time of their stay. Table 8.13 depicts the or-

Table 8.13 The Indo-Iranian family

Iranian	Indic
Persian [= Farsi]	Hindu-Urdu
Pashto	Bengali
Kurdish	Punjabi
	Marathi
	Gujarati
	Romany [= Gypsy]

ganization of Indo-Iranian. The map in Figure 8.6 illustrates the geographic location of the Indo-European families identified in this chapter.

Some Other Families

Although no introductory text could undertake to present a comprehensive survey of the world's language families, some further discussion of this topic is warranted in order to illustrate the extraordinary diversity of human language.

Altaic The Altaic family stretches from Turkey to China in a continuum of languages. Altaic languages are also found in Siberia and East Asia. The membership of the Altaic family (see Table 8.14) is still very much in dispute, but it probably includes at least three branches: Turkic, Mongolian, and Tungusic. Recent scholarship has collected substantial evidence that Korean and Japanese are also members of the Altaic family. However, dissenting scholars argue that the similarities between Japanese, Korean, and the other languages in this proposed family are primarily typological, and that there

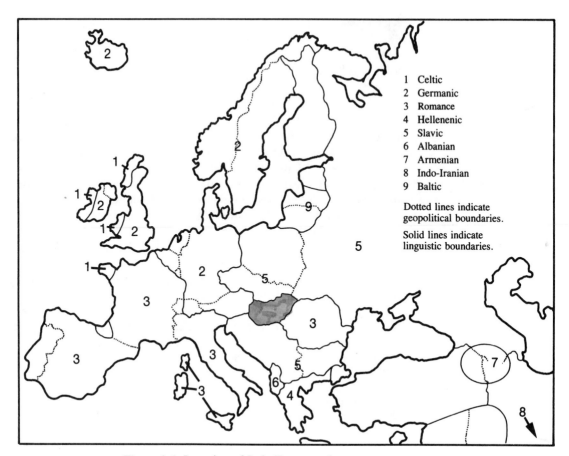

Figure 8.6 Location of Indo-European languages

are few reliable cognates encompassing the complete spectrum of the proposed Altaic family.

The Turkic languages of the Altaic family, spoken by more than eighty million people, include Turkish, Uzbek, Azerbaijani, Tatar, Uighur, Kazakh, and Yakut. The Mongolian languages are spoken by around ten million people, primarily in Mongolia and China, while the Tungusic languages are found in central Siberia and Mongolia. The number of speakers of Tungusic languages probably does not exceed one million people.

Table 8.14 The Altaic family

Turkic	Tungusic	Mongolian		
Turkish	Evenki	Khalkha	Korean	Japanese
Uzbek	Chakar			
Azerbaijani	Buriat			
Tatar [= Tartar]				
Uighur				
Kazakh				
Yakut				

Altaic languages are usually agglutinating, often with several suffixes in the same word. They normally employ SOV word order and typically use postpositions rather than prepositions. Many Altaic languages have vowel harmony, a phonological phenomenon in which all vowels of a word share certain features, such as [round] or [back]. They are usually not tone languages.

Uralic The Uralic family (see Table 8.15) contains about twenty languages and has about twenty-two million speakers. Uralic languages are spoken in a band across the northern part of the temperate zone of Europe, all the way from northern Norway to Siberia. Uralic has two major branches: Samoyedic and Finno-Ugric. The Samoyedic branch contains a handful of languages spoken in the northern U.S.S.R., particularly in areas around the Ural Mountains and also in Siberia.

The most widely spoken Finno-Ugric language is Hungarian. Other Finno-Ugric languages are Finnish, Lapp or Lappish, Estonian, Livonian, Karelian, and Mordvin or Mordva. Uralic languages are primarily agglutinating, and most have postpositions with SOV or SVO word order. The nouns often have many cases (Finnish has fifteen) that appear to have developed historically from postpositions that became attached to nouns as suffixes. Uralic languages are normally not tonal.

Table 8.15 The Uralic family

Finno-Ugric		Samoyedic
Finnic	Ugric	
Livonian	Vogul	Nganasan
Estonian	Ostyak	Selkup
Finnish	Hungarian	Nenets
Vodian	Enets	
Vepsian		
Karelian		
Lapp/Sami		
Mordvin		
Cheremis		
Votyak		
Komi		

Dravidian There are twenty-three Dravidian languages (see Table 8.16), which are primarily found in the southern half of India. About a hundred

Table 8.16 The Dravidian family

North Dravidian	Central Dravidian	South Dravidian
Kurukh	Telugu	Tamil
Malto	Kolami	Malayalam
	Gondi	Kannada
		Toda
		Tulu
		Kodagu

and fifty million people are native speakers of a Dravidian language. The most widely spoken languages in this family are Telugu, Tamil, Kannada, and Malayalam. Dravidian languages are normally SOV. They are agglutinating and nontonal, and usually have initial stress.

Austro-Asiatic The Austro-Asiatic family of languages (see Table 8.17) consists of about a hundred and fifty languages with approximately forty million speakers. The Munda branch of Austro-Asiatic includes languages spoken in central and northeastern India, such as Santali and Mundavi. Mon-Khmer is the largest branch of Austro-Asiatic and contains languages such as Cambodian (also called Khmer) and many other languages of Cambodia, Vietnam, Burma, and southern China. Other Austro-Asiatic languages are spoken in Malaysia and on the Nicobar Islands (northwest of Sumatra). Some Austro-Asiatic languages are tonal (for example, Vietnamese) and some are characterized by large and complex vowel systems. Word order is generally SVO or SOV.

Table 8.17 The Austro-Asiatic family

Munda	Mon-Khmer	Muong-Annam
Santali	Cambodian [= Khmer]	Muong
Mundari	Mon	Vietnamese
Ho	Khasi	
	Car	
	Bahnar	

Sino-Tibetan In terms of numbers of speakers, the Sino-Tibetan family (see Table 8.18) is the largest language family after Indo-European. There are about three hundred Sino-Tibetan languages, with a total of approximately seven hundred million speakers. There are two major branches: the Tibeto-Burman branch and the Sinitic branch. To the first branch belong the Tibetan languages, Burmese, and many other languages spoken in northeastern India, Nepal, Burma, and Tibet. The Sinitic branch contains the languages that we call Chinese. Although a number of these languages are mutually unintelligible, they are usually called "dialects," primarily because the same writing system is used across China and can be understood by speakers of

Table 8.18 The Sino-Tibetan family

Tibeto-Burman	Sinitic		Miao-Yao
	Northern	Southern	
Burmese	Mandarin	Wu	Miao
Tibetan		Cantonese	Yao
Sharpa		Hakka	
		Hsiang	
		Kan	
		Northern Min	
		Southern Min	

different Chinese languages (see Chapter 13). The Sinitic languages can be divided into two groups: Northern and Southern. The Northern branch contains Mandarin, which has dialects spoken in Peking (Beijing), Szechuan, and Nanking. The major Southern Sinitic languages are Wu (with dialects in Shanghai and Suchow), Cantonese, Hakka, Hsiang, Kan, Southern Min, and Northern Min.

The Miao-Yao languages, which are spoken in southern China, Vietnam, Laos, and Thailand, are now often considered to be part of the Sino-Tibetan family as well. There has been considerable disagreement as to this genetic relationship, with some linguists suggesting that the Miao-Yao languages belong to the Austro-Asiatic family or the Austro-Tai family.

Sino-Tibetan languages are usually tonal. They are also normally isolating languages, having many monomorphemic (and usually monosyllabic) words. Consonant clusters are normally avoided; word order is SVO or SOV.

Austro-Tai The Austro-Tai family (see Table 8.19) contains about eight hundred and twenty-five languages, which are spread from Madagascar, off the east coast of Africa, to Hawaii and New Zealand. There are about a hundred and eighty million native speakers of Austro-Tai languages. The two major branches of this family are Kam-Tai and Austronesian. (Not all scholars accept this classification. Some consider Austronesian a separate family.)

The Kam-Tai branch includes Thai (or Siamese), Lao, and several dozen other languages of Laos, Vietnam, and China. The Kam-Tai languages were at one time thought to be Sino-Tibetan because of certain structural characteristics that they share—the use of tone and an isolating morphological structure, to name but two.

The Austronesian branch of Austro-Tai, which contains hundreds of languages, can itself be divided into a Western and an Eastern branch. Western Austronesian languages include Malagasy, Malay (essentially identical to Indonesian), Batak (found on Sumatra), Balinese, Tagalog (the basis for Pilipino, the official language of the Philippines), Chamorro (spoken on Guam), and many other languages spoken in the Philippines, Malaysia, Borneo, Vietnam, Cambodia, Sumatra, Java, and Formosa. The Eastern Austronesian branch contains Tahitian, Samoan, Maori, and Hawaiian (which now has fewer than three hundred native speakers). One feature character-

Table 8.19 The Austro-Tai family

Kam-Tai	Austronesian	
	Western	Eastern
Thai	Malagasy	Fijian
Lao	Malay	Tongan
	Javanese	Tahitian
	Batak	Samoan
	Balinese	Maori
	Tagalog	Hawaiian
	Chamorro	

istic of Austronesian languages is the frequent use of reduplication; many of these languages also use infixes. Word order is usually SVO, although VSO is more prevalent in some Eastern Austronesian languages. Most known VOS languages are Austronesian.

Australian Recent studies have established that all of the aboriginal languages of Australia belong to one Australian family. There are about two hundred such languages, but many have very few speakers. There are currently only about forty-seven thousand speakers of aboriginal Australian languages.

The majority of Australian languages are spoken in Arnhem Land (north central Australia) and the northern part of Western Australia. The languages with the largest number of speakers are Mabuiag (seven thousand speakers on the Torres Straits Islands, north of Australia) and the Western Desert Language (four thousand speakers in Western Australia).

Australian languages are characterized by simple vowel systems, and are not tone languages. Nouns are normally marked for case, sometimes in unusual and intricate ways, and word order is sometimes very free.

Afro-Asiatic Afro-Asiatic languages (see Table 8.20) are spoken primarily across the northern half of Africa and in the Middle East. There are about two hundred and fifty Afro-Asiatic languages and a hundred and seventy-five million speakers of these languages. Afro-Asiatic has five main branches of which one, the Egyptian branch, no longer contains any living languages. Old Egyptian, once spoken by the ancient Pharaohs, has long been extinct. Its descendant, Coptic, is now used only as the liturgical language of the Coptic church. The remaining branches are highly distinct from each other.

Another branch of Afro-Asiatic is Cushitic, whose member languages are spoken in the Sudan, Ethiopia, Somalia, and Kenya. A third branch, Berber, includes several languages of Algeria, Morocco, and Niger, such as Tuareg and Tamazight. Still another branch of Afro-Asiatic, Chadic, contains many of the languages of Chad and Nigeria, such as Hausa. These languages, unlike other Afro-Asiatic languages, are tonal.

The fifth and largest branch of Afro-Asiatic (in terms of number of speakers) is the Semitic branch. Many (now extinct) languages mentioned in the Bible were of Semitic origin, such as Babylonian (also known as Assyrian or Akkadian), (Old) Canaanite, Moabite, Classical Hebrew, and Aramaic.

Table 8.20 The Afro-Asiatic family

(Egyptian)	Cushitic	Berber	Chadic	Semitic
(Coptic)	Somali	Tuareg Tamazight Shilha	Hausa	(Babylonian) (Old Canaanite) Hebrew Aramaic Arabic

Classical Hebrew has not been spoken as a native language for millenia, although it has been maintained as a written language by Hebrew scholars. Modern Hebrew (or Israeli) is not directly descended from Classical Hebrew; rather it was created (or re-created) at the beginning of this century by regularizing some aspects of Classical Hebrew and adding new vocabulary. Modern Hebrew has only had native speakers for the past few decades.

Still another Semitic language, Arabic, has several varieties, not all of which are mutually intelligible. Varieties of Arabic are spoken all across North Africa and throughout the Middle East. All of these are descended from Classical Arabic, which was the language of Mohammed, the founder of Islam, and is the language of the Koran, the holy book of Islam.

The Semitic languages are characterized by a system of consonantal roots. Most roots consist of three (sometimes two) consonants with vowels being inserted to indicate various inflectional and derivational categories. For example, Arabic has the root *k-t-b* (denoting the concept of writing) from which a variety of words can be formed, including *kitab* 'book', *katibun* 'writer', *kataba* 'he had written', and *yaktuba* 'he will write'. The Semitic languages frequently have complex consonant clusters and pharyngeal or pharyngealized consonants.

Niger-Kordofanian Most of the languages spoken in Sub-Saharan Africa, about nine hundred, belong to the Niger-Kordofanian family of languages (see Table 8.21). In all, there are approximately a hundred and eighty million speakers of these languages. Two major branches exist: the Kordofanian branch and the Niger-Congo branch. The Kordofanian branch includes only a handful of languages spoken in the Sudan, such as Koalib and Katla. Niger-Congo, on the other hand, is much larger and can be divided into six smaller branches: West Atlantic, Mande, Gur, Kwa, Adamawa, and Benue-Congo.

The West Atlantic branch of Niger-Congo contains west coast languages such as Wolof (Senegal) and Fulani (Guinea). The Mande branch also contains many West African languages. The Kwa branch contains several Nigerian languages, such as Yoruba, Nupe, and Igbo (or Ibo), as well as Ewe (Ghana and Togo) and Twi (also called Fante, spoken in Ghana). The Adamawa branch includes languages such as Sango and Gbeya, spoken in Nigeria, Zaire, and the Central African Republic.

Table 8.21 The Niger-Kordofanian family

Kordofanian				Niger-Congo		
	West Atlantic	Mande	Gur	Kwa	Adamawa	Benue-Congo
Koalib	Wolof	Mandink	Dogon	Yoruba	Sango	Efik
Katla	Fulani			Nupe	Gbeya	Tiv
				Igbo		Swahili
				Ijo		Zulu
				Ewe		Ganda
				Twi		Shona
				Kru		Kikuyu
						Kongo

The Benue-Congo branch is the largest branch within Niger-Congo. The largest group of languages within this branch is the Bantu group. There are more than a hundred Bantu languages, with more than fifty-five million speakers. Some of the principal Bantu languages are Swahili (Tanzania and Kenya), Zulu (South Africa), Ganda (Uganda), Shona (Zimbabwe), and Kongo (Zaire).

Niger-Kordofanian languages are typically SVO and usually have tone systems (with the notable exception of Swahili). The Bantu languages are usually agglutinating with verb-subject and verb-direct object agreement. Languages in the Bantu group also exhibit a complex system of noun classes, each of which is marked by a distinctive set of prefixes.

Figure 8.7 illustrates the location of the language families we have been considering.

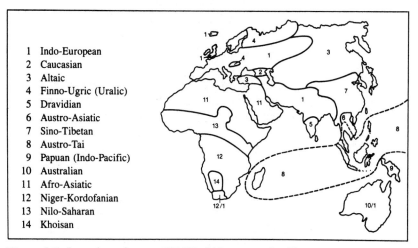

1	Indo-European
2	Caucasian
3	Altaic
4	Finno-Ugric (Uralic)
5	Dravidian
6	Austro-Asiatic
7	Sino-Tibetan
8	Austro-Tai
9	Papuan (Indo-Pacific)
10	Australian
11	Afro-Asiatic
12	Niger-Kordofanian
13	Nilo-Saharan
14	Khoisan

Figure 8.7 Location of some Old World language families

The Americas

Contrary to popular belief, not all native American Indian (or Amerindian) languages belong to the same family. Although many of the relationships are still unclear, it appears that there are a number of different families of Amerindian languages. The major language families found in North and Central America are exemplified in Table 8.22. Their geographic location is indicated in Figure 8.8.

In South America there are presently about eleven million people who speak an Amerindian language. There are at least six hundred different Amerindian languages spoken in South America, but our knowledge of these languages is often minimal. Some linguists estimate that there may be more than a thousand South American Amerindian languages, most of which belong to one of three families: Andean-Equatorial, Ge-Pano-Carib, and Macro-Chibchan.

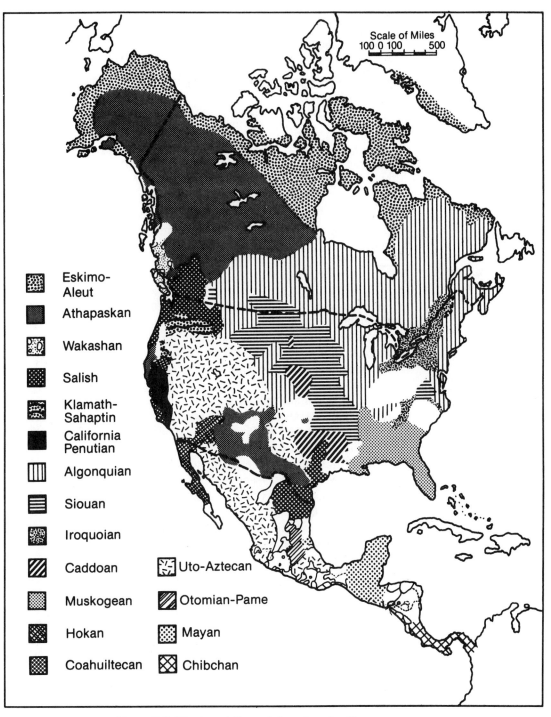

Figure 8.8 North and Central American families

Table 8.22 North and Central American families

Language family	Some member languages
Eskimo-Aleut	Inuktitut
Athapaskan	Navaho, Western Apache, Hupa, Kutchin
Wakashan	Makah, Nootka, Nitinat
Salish	Flathead, Spokan, Kalispel, Coeur d'Alene
Klamath-Sahaptin	Nez Perce, Sahaptin, Klamath
Penutian	Patwin, Wintu, Nomlaki
Algonquian	Cheyenne, Potawatomi, Shawnee, Micmac
Siouan	Crow, Winnebago, Omaha
Iroquoian	Seneca, Mohawk, Oneida, Cherokee
Caddoan	Caddo, Witchita, Pawnee
Muskogean	Choctaw, Koasati, Mikasuti
Hokan	Diegueno, Yuma, Mohave
Coahuiltecan	Comecrudo, Cotoname, Pakawa, Carrizo
Uto-Aztecan	Northern Paiute, Snake, Comanche
Otomian-Pame	Otomi, Pame, Pirinda, Mazahua
Mayan	Huastecan, Cholan, Maya, Tzeltal, Tojolabal
Chibchan	Talamanca, Rama-Corobici, Cueva-Cuna

The Andean-Equatorial family contains languages that are found throughout South America and may have as many as ten million speakers all together. The principal language in this family is Quechua, which has more than six million speakers. Dialects of Quechua are spoken in Peru, Ecuador, and Bolivia. This was the language of the Inca empire, which reached its height in the sixteenth century A.D., before being destroyed by the Spanish conquistadors. Other languages belonging to this family are Aymara (Peru), Arawak (Surinam), and Guarani (the major language of Paraguay). Some Andean-Equatorial languages lack laterals entirely.

The Ge-Pano-Carib family is also spread over much of South America. Some of the languages belonging to this family are Carib (Surinam), Bororo (Brazil), Witotu (Peru), and Mataco (Argentina). Languages of the Ge-Pano-Carib family often lack laterals; the dominant word order in these languages is usually SOV.

Languages of the Macro-Chibchan family are found in Central America and the northwestern part of South America. Some languages belonging to this family are Cuna (Panama), Cayapa (Ecuador), Epera (Columbia), and Warao (Venezuela). Macro-Chibchan languages generally have SOV word order.

Language Isolates

Although linguists have succeeded in placing many hundreds of the world's languages into families, there are still many other languages that cannot be so classified. A language that is not known to be related to any other living language is called an **isolate**. Basque, which is spoken in northern Spain and southern France, is such a language. Examples of other language isolates throughout the world include Ainu (northern Japan), Burushaski (Pakistan), Kutenai (British Columbia), Gilyak (Siberia), Taraskan (California), and Yukagir (Siberia).

Summing Up

The focus of this chapter is on the criteria that linguists use to classify languages and on the enormous linguistic diversity found throughout the world. Linguists sometimes attempt to classify languages solely in terms of their structural similarities and differences (that is, in terms of their **linguistic typology**), without regard for **genetic relationships**. Work in this area is primarily responsible for the discovery of linguistic **universals**, which help to identify the necessary properties of human language. The other major type of classificatory work in linguistics is concerned with establishing language families—groups of languages that are descended from a common source. While research in this area is hampered both by the large number of languages involved and the scarcity of the available data, a sizeable portion of the world's several thousand languages have been placed in families. Although there is little likelihood of ever being able to show that all human languages descended from a common source, work in this area can shed light on the nature of language change as well as on the movement of peoples throughout the world.

Sources

The section on linguistic typology draws on data from the books by Bernard Comrie and Joseph Greenberg cited below. Other material for this section comes from *Tone: A Linguistic Survey,* edited by V. A. Fromkin (New York: Academic Press, 1978); John Hawkins's article "On Implicational and Distributional Universals of Word Order" in *Journal of Linguistics* 16: 193–235 (1980); Merrit Ruhlen's book *A Guide to the Languages of the World* (Language Universals Project: Stanford University, 1976); and the four-volume series *Universals of Human Language,* edited by J. Greenberg (Stanford, Calif.: Stanford University Press, 1978).

The section on language families is based on Bernard Comrie's book *The Languages of the Soviet Union* (London: Cambridge University Press, 1981); Joseph Greenberg's *The Languages of Africa* (Bloomington: Indiana University Press, 1966); the book by Merrit Ruhlen cited previously; and C. F. and F. M. Voegelin's *Classification and Index of the World's Languages* (cited below). The maps used to illustrate the geographic location of language families are adapted from those found in *The Origins and Development of the English Language* by T. Pyles and J. Algeo (New York: Harcourt Brace Jovanovich, 3d ed., 1982). The data for Questions 1 to 3 are found in the book by Merrit Ruhlen, cited above. The data for Question 4 were kindly provided by Dr. Leslie Saxon.

Recommended Reading

Comrie, Bernard. 1981. *Language Universals and Linguistic Typology.* Chicago: University of Chicago Press.

Greenberg, Joseph, ed. 1966. *Universals of Language*. 2d ed. Cambridge, Mass.: M.I.T. Press.

Voegelin, C. F. and F. M. Voegelin. 1977. *Classification and Index of the World's Languages*. New York: Elsevier.

Questions

1. Which tendencies and universals are manifested in the following two vowel systems?
   a) Afrikaans (South Africa) (ü and ö are front rounded vowels)

i	ü		u	
		ə	o	
ɛ	ö		ɔ	
		a		

   b) Squamish (Washington State)

i	u
ə	
a	

2. As noted in Section 8.2, the presence of long and nasal vowel phonemes is governed by implicational universals. Do the following vowel systems comply with the implicational universals that make reference to length and nasality?
   a) Maltese Arabic

i		u	ī	ū
e		o	ē	ō
	a		ā	

   b) Awji (North New Guinea)

i		u		ĩ	ũ
e	ə	o	ẽ	ə̃	õ
	a		ã		

3. Consider the following consonant systems. Do these consonant systems comply with the implicational universals mentioned in this chapter?
   a) Tahitian (Tahiti)

p	t	ʔ
f	h	
v	r	
m	n	

   b) Palauan (Palau Islands)

     t   k   ʔ

     b

       ð

       s

     m   ŋ l r

   c) Nengone (Loyalty Islands, South Pacific)—Stop system only

     p^h t^h $ṭ^h$ k^h ʔ

     b d ḍ   g

     m n   ɲ ŋ

     m̥ n̥   ŋ̥

The diacritic [̣] indicates a retroflex consonant; [̥] marks a voiceless nasal; [ɲ] represents a palatal nasal.

   d) Mixe (South Mexico)

     p t   k   ʔ

        d   g

        t^s č

        s   x h

     v   ɣ

     m n

4. Consider the following data from Dogrib, an Athapaskan language spoken in Canada's Northwest Territories. Does Dogrib comply with all the word order tendencies noted in Section 8.2?

  a) ʔeyi done   mbehčĩ seèle ha.
     that person truck   fix   will
     'That person will fix the truck.'

  b) čeko   se-xè   ʔande ha.
     the child me-with go   will
     'The child will go with me.'

  c) done ǰõ nàdèe
     person here lives-relative clause marker
     'the person who lives here'

5. The following data are from Tongan, spoken on the island of Tonga in the South Pacific (' indicates a glottal stop in this system of representing Tongan). Does Tongan comply with all the word order tendencies noted in Section 8.2?

a) Na'e fana'i 'eSione 'ae pea 'uli'uli.
   past shoot Sione   the bear black
   'Sione shot the black bear.'
b) Na'e lele 'ae ta'ahine ki falekoloa.
   past run the girl   to store
   'The girl ran to the store.'
c) E   siana na'e sio ai'a Sione
   the man past see he Sione
   'the man who Sione saw'

6. Do the following data from Malagasy comply with all the word order
   tendencies mentioned in this chapter?
   a) amin' ny restauranta
      'to   the restaurant'
   b) labiera lehibe
      beer   large
      'large beer'
   c) Entin' ny labiera ny mpiasa.
      brings the beer   the waiter
      'The waiter brings the beer.'

7. To which families do the following languages belong?
   a) Gujarati   i) Yuma
   b) Hakka   j) Korean
   c) Lapp   k) Koasati
   d) Uzbek   l) Arabic
   e) Huastecan   m) Flathead
   f) Faroese   n) Telugu
   g) Twi   o) Javanese
   h) Santali   p) Navaho

9 BRAIN AND LANGUAGE

We speak with the left hemisphere.
Paul Broca (c. 1865)

Up to this point, our discussion of grammatical categories and rules has ignored the question of how this system is represented in the brain, the seat of all cognitive functions. Although **neurolinguistics** (the study of language and the brain) is still in its infancy, progress in recent decades has allowed us to identify the parts of the brain that are concerned with language and to learn something of how linguistic knowledge is represented there.

This chapter provides a brief survey of the organization of the human brain as it pertains to language. We begin with a brief description of the basic structure and functioning of the parts of the brain used for language. Then, we outline the various language disorders caused by damage to different regions of the brain. We conclude by examining the issue of whether there is a critical age for language acquisition.

9.1 THE HUMAN BRAIN

Contrary to popular belief, a human being does not have the largest brain of any creature in the world. This distinction belongs to the blue whale, with an average brain mass of about 9,000 grams (compared to 1,375 grams for humans). Human beings do, however, have the most favorable ratio of brain mass to body mass of any creature (second place belongs to dolphins).

The human brain contains an average of ten billion **neurons**, or nerve cells, each of which is linked with one thousand to ten thousand other neurons. These nerve cells participate in countless electrical microcircuits which make possible thought, perception, communication, and other types of mental activity. The outside surface of the brain, which is known as the **cortex**, consists of a thin wrinkled mantle of grey tissue made up of millions of neurons. This layer of the brain represents a relatively recent evolutionary step in neurological development and is not present to a comparable degree in any other species. Many of the cognitive abilities that distinguish humans from other mammals (including sophisticated reasoning, linguistic skills, and musical ability) reside in the cortex.

The brain is divided into two roughly symmetrical **hemispheres**, sometimes called the right and left brains. The activity of the two cerebral hemispheres is coordinated by a number of interconnecting nerve pathways, the largest of which is the **corpus callosum**. (See Figure 9.1.)

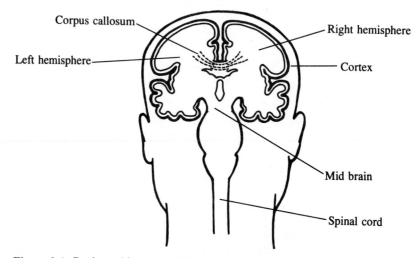

Figure 9.1 Basic architecture of the human brain

Cerebral Dominance

Specialized linguistic and perceptual skills are each associated with a particular hemisphere of the brain. In most individuals, the left hemisphere has primary responsibility for language, while the right hemisphere controls visual and spatial skills as well as the perception of nonlinguistic sounds and musical melodies. The localization of cognitive and perceptual functions in a particular hemisphere of the brain is called **lateralization**. Table 9.1 lists some of the major functions under the control of each hemisphere.

Both hemispheres of the brain are involved in control over muscular activity as well as in sight and hearing. An intriguing fact about the organization of the brain is that each hemisphere controls these activities for the opposite side of the body. Thus, the *right* side of the brain is responsible for movement of the *left* arm and leg, while the *left* hemisphere controls the *right* arm and leg. This is why someone who suffers damage to the right side of the brain (as the result of a stroke, perhaps) will exhibit paralysis on the left side of the body. The control of one side of the body by the opposite side of the brain is known as **contralateralization**.

Table 9.1 Hemisphere dominance

Left hemisphere	Right hemisphere
language	perception of nonlinguistic sounds
analytic reasoning	music
temporal ordering	visual and spatial skills
reading and writing	holistic reasoning
arithmetic	pattern recognition

9.2 BRAIN AND LANGUAGE

The language centers are located in the left hemisphere of the brain in well over 90 percent of right-handed human beings (who themselves make up about 90 percent of the population). Although the figure is somewhat lower for left-handers (perhaps around 60 percent), it is clear that the left side of the brain is somehow special as far as language is concerned.

The Left Hemisphere

Left brain dominance appears to exist even prior to birth. It is now known that a portion of the left brain that is crucial to language is larger in fetuses than is the corresponding portion of the right brain. This asymmetry is maintained throughout life.

Evidence of a different sort for the importance of the left brain to language comes from the study of neurological disorders. In pioneering research conducted in the 1860s, a French surgeon and anatomist named Paul Broca found that damage to specific areas of the left hemisphere resulted in disturbance of spoken language. Comparable damage to the corresponding areas of the right brain typically had no such effect.

Still other evidence for cerebral dominance comes from dichotic listening tasks. This technique involves simultaneously presenting one auditory signal to the left ear and another to the right ear. Thus, a person might be simultaneously presented with the word *pen* in the right ear and the word *sky* in the left, and then be asked to report what he or she had heard. For most people, linguistic stimuli heard in the right ear are more accurately reported than those heard in the left ear. The explanation is found in the way in which auditory information is transmitted from the ear to the brain. Although there are connections between the left ear and the left hemisphere of the brain as well as between the right ear and the right hemisphere, the dominant pathways from each ear lead to the opposite hemisphere (because of contralateralization). As Figure 9.2 shows, the word *pen* presented in the right ear goes directly to the left brain. The word *sky* heard in the left ear,

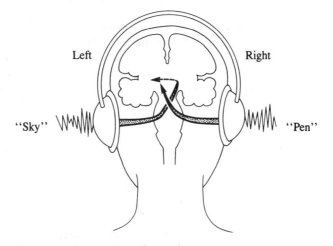

Figure 9.2 Perception of speech

on the other hand, must first go to the right hemisphere, from where it is transferred to the left side of the brain for processing by the language centers. Since stimuli heard in the left ear travel a longer distance before processing, they are reported less accurately than those heard in the right ear.

The Role of the Right Brain The left brain is not dominant for the perception and analysis of all types of sounds. As noted above, nonlinguistic sounds are perceived better through the left ear. If a person hears laughter in the right ear and a siren in the left ear at the same time, he or she is more likely to report having heard the siren. Figure 9.3 illustrates why this is so. As indicated in Figure 9.3, the sound of the siren heard in the left ear will go directly to the right hemisphere, whereas laughter perceived in the right ear will first be transmitted to the left hemisphere and then to the right brain. Since the noise of the siren takes a shorter route to the right brain, it is heard more accurately than the sound of laughter.

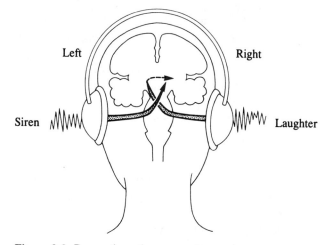

Figure 9.3 Perception of nonspeech sounds

Recent work suggests that certain language-related tasks are carried out by the right brain rather than the left brain. The perception and production of melodies, for instance, is apparently a predominantly right brain activity since patients with damage to the left hemisphere can sing tunes even though their ability to speak is severely impaired. The right brain also seems to be crucially involved in the interpretation of the voice tone and intonation cues that signal emotions such as anger and fear. Thus, a patient suffering from damage to the right hemisphere may be able to understand the literal meaning of a sentence but fail to recognize whether it is spoken in an angry or a fearful way. A parallel phenomenon manifests itself in the area of semantics. Here, it seems that damage to the right hemisphere can interfere with the ability to understand and appreciate metaphorical use of language. It has been found, for example, that patients with this type of brain damage are able to provide only a literal or concrete interpretation of figurative sentences such as *He was wearing a loud tie*.

Coordinating the Two Brains Although most people's language centers are localized in the left brain, both hemispheres are required for the fully natural use of language. Imagine that a person perceives an object (say, a baseball) in only the left visual field. As Figure 9.4 shows, the right brain will first perceive and recognize the baseball on the basis of the visual information it receives. (Recall that because of contralateralization, sensory input from the left visual field will first go to the right brain.) If the pathways connecting the left and right hemispheres are disrupted for some reason, the information will be unable to reach the left side of the brain. A person whose corpus callosum has been severed, as illustrated in Figure 9.4, will be incapable of describing the baseball verbally, although he or she may be able to distinguish it from other objects (say, oranges). This points to the importance of the communication between the two hemispheres.

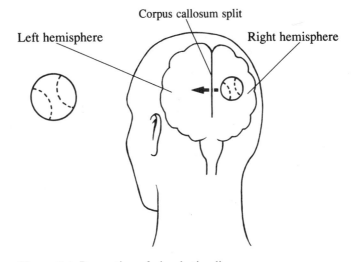

Figure 9.4 Perception of visual stimuli

The Language Centers

The neurological structures involved in language are not situated in a single area of the brain. Rather, there seem to be a number of language centers in the brain, each with its own specialized function. The relative positioning of these areas in the left hemisphere of the brain and the relationships among them are illustrated in Figure 9.5.

Broca's area, named after its discoverer Paul Broca, is located in the front part of the left hemisphere and is responsible for organizing the articulatory patterns of speech. This may have something to do with the fact that it lies very close to the area of the cortex that controls the muscles of the face, jaw, tongue, palate, and larynx. Since the use of inflectional morphemes (plural markers, tense endings) and minor lexical categories (determiners, prepositions) is also governed by Broca's area, this region of the brain has a crucial role in the formation of both words and sentences.

CHAPTER NINE

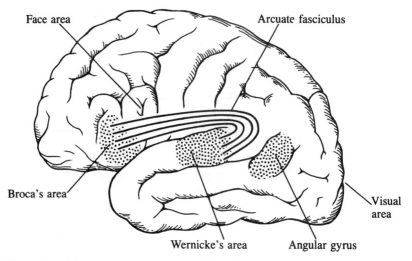

Figure 9.5 The language centers of the brain

Wernicke's area, discovered by the nineteenth-century neurologist Carl Wernicke, is very close to the primary auditory cortex, which is responsible for the reception of auditory input. Wernicke's area plays a major part in the representation of meaning and is involved both in the interpretation of words and in the selection of lexical items for the purposes of sentence production. Broca's and Wernicke's areas are connected by a bundle of nerve fibers known as the **arcuate fasciculus**.

The **angular gyrus**, which lies behind Wernicke's area, is the language center responsible for converting a visual stimulus into an auditory form and vice versa. This area is crucial for the matching of a spoken form with a perceived object, the naming of objects, and the comprehension of written language, all of which require connections between the visual and the speech regions.

When we speak, the words are drawn from Wernicke's area and sent via the arcuate fasciculus to Broca's area, which determines the details of their form and pronunciation. The appropriate instructions are then sent to the adjacent area of the cortex controlling the vocal tract.

Figure 9.6 depicts what happens during the more involved task of uttering a written word. As shown in the model in Figure 9.6, the input from the primary visual area is transferred to the angular gyrus, which associates the visual form of the word with the auditory form stored in Wernicke's area. This word is then transmitted via the arcuate fasciculus to Broca's area, where the articulatory form is stored. The required articulatory instructions are sent to the motor cortex, and the name of the object is finally spoken.

When we try to understand a spoken rather than a written name of an object, the stimulus from the auditory cortex is transmitted to Wernicke's area, where it is then interpreted. In cases where the object can be associated

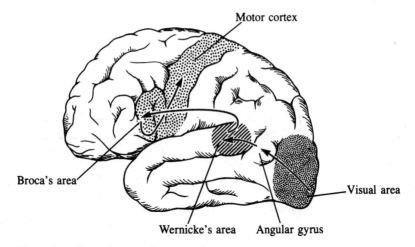

Figure 9.6 Speaking a written word

with an image, a message can be sent to the angular gyrus, where it is converted into a visual stimulus, arousing the appropriate pattern in the visual area. This is illustrated in Figure 9.7. We see, then, that linguistic knowledge is represented in different parts of the brain. Language use—speaking, listening, writing, and reading—requires the coordination of these language centers. If the language centers or the connections between them are damaged, the ability to use language deteriorates. In the next section of this chapter, we consider some of the principal language disorders and what they tell us about the organization of the brain.

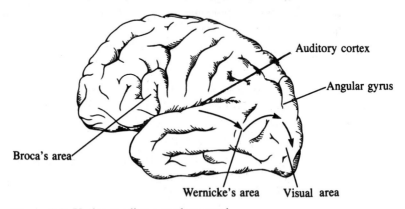

Figure 9.7 Understanding a spoken word

Aphasia

Language disorders resulting from brain damage are grouped together under the general label **aphasia**. Depending upon which region of the brain has been damaged, patients suffer impairment of different language abilities. Brain damage often results in a mixture of symptoms of varying severity and patients with similar brain damage can differ in the precise details of their impairments. Nonetheless, it is possible to identify several major types of aphasia, each with its own characteristic symptoms.

Broca's Aphasia Damage to Broca's area usually results in a disorder with several symptoms, the first and most obvious of which is poor articulation. A second feature of Broca's aphasia is systematic substitution and deletion of sounds, which is termed **phonemic paraphasia**. Consonant clusters may be simplified, as in [sruw] for [skruw] 'screw', and consonant reduplication is also often observed, as in [bæbət] for [æbət] 'abbot'. Substitutions are frequent, especially fronting ([θ] for [s]), devoicing ([t] for [d]), and stopping ([p] for [f]). Despite these articulatory difficulties, the ability to perceive phonemic contrasts remains relatively intact. Thus, a patient with Broca's aphasia might well be able to hear the difference between *ship* and *sip*, without being able to produce it accurately.

It is tempting to think that the impairment of speech production associated with Broca's aphasia is related to the fact that the affected part of the brain is next to the area controlling the facial muscles. The problem with this hypothesis is that damage to Broca's area usually produces only mild weakness of the muscles on the opposite side of the face and no permanent damage. Yet, for some reason, even people who can still control the muscles used in speech cannot use language properly after damage to Broca's area. This suggests that Broca's area must be responsible for planning the patterns of muscle movement in the vocal tract that are specific to speech production (as opposed to those that are used for chewing, swallowing, and so on).

A third feature of Broca's aphasia is an impairment in the ability to form morphological and syntactic patterns. Particularly conspicuous is a symptom known as **agrammatism**, the loss of most minor lexical categories, such as prepositions and determiners, as well as inflectional affixes. The following utterance, from a soldier describing how he was wounded, illustrates the agrammatism associated with Broca's aphasia.

1. Well . . . front . . . soldiers . . . campaign . . . soldiers . . . to shoot . . . well . . . head . . . wound . . . and hospital . . . and so . . .

This patient's speech consists almost entirely of nouns, with very few minor lexical categories or affixes. The absence of these latter elements is a universal characteristic of Broca's aphasia and has been observed in speakers of a variety of languages. This phenomenon is illustrated in the following example of speech by a Turkish patient afflicted with Broca's aphasia. (The omitted elements are indicated in parentheses; the word order used here is normal for Turkish.)

2. a) On parmak (ile) daktilo (bildim)
   Ten finger (with) type (I could)
   'I could type with ten fingers.'

   b) Sivas (-ta) toprak ve iskân müdür (-ü idim)
   Sivas (in) land and housing manager (I was)
   'I was the land and housing manager in Sivas.'

Broca's aphasia is also accompanied by deficits in syntactic knowledge. While patients appear to comprehend well as long as they can rely on their knowledge of word meaning and pragmatics, they are apparently unable to make use of syntactic knowledge to interpret sentences. Thus, passive structures such as *The dog was chased by the cat* are difficult for them to interpret since it is necessary to make use of word order, prepositions, and inflections to determine which animal is doing the chasing and which animal is being chased. Similar problems arise with sentences such as *The boy that the girl is evaluating is tall,* in which word order must be used to determine which person is doing the evaluating and which person is being evaluated.

The pattern of symptoms associated with Broca's aphasia is exactly what we would expect given the responsibilities of Broca's area. As noted earlier, this language center not only controls articulation but also has a crucial role in the formation of words and sentences. Broca's area appears to be largely concerned with organizational and structural aspects of language and is therefore responsible for the articulatory rules that create sound patterns, as well as for the morphological and syntactic rules that form words and phrases.

Wernicke's Aphasia Broca's aphasia stands in sharp contrast to the type of neurolinguistic disorder associated with damage to Wernicke's area. As noted earlier, this language center is responsible for the representation of meaning, as well as the interpretation of words during comprehension and the selection of words during speech production. Patients with Wernicke's aphasia may suffer from some phonemic paraphasia, but the most striking feature of this disorder is an inability to comprehend spoken language and to construct meaningful utterances. Although Wernicke's patients may sound almost normal, their speech is nonsensical. As an example of this, consider the following conversation between an examiner (E) and a Wernicke's patient (P).

3. *E:* How are you today, Mrs. A?
   P: Yes.
   E: Have I ever tested you before?
   P: No, I mean I haven't.
   E: Can you tell me what your name is?
   P: No, I don't I . . . right I'm right now here.
   E: What is your address?
   P: I cud [kʌd] if I can help these this like you know . . . to make it. We are seeing for him. That is my father.

The patient apparently has no understanding of the examiner's questions. Her responses are relatively well-formed structures, although inappropriate as answers to the questions posed by the experimenter. This is the type of disorder we expect, given the role of Wernicke's area in the representation and interpretation of meaning.

A particularly forceful illustration of the difference between Broca's aphasia and Wernicke's aphasia is revealed by a simple test. Patients are presented with pieces of written sentences cut at points corresponding to phrase boundaries (*The girl—from Boston—is musical*). Although patients with Wernicke's aphasia are unable to interpret the sentence, they are able to arrange its parts in the proper order, showing that they have retained some knowledge of syntactic categories and structure. Patients with Broca's aphasia, in contrast, perform very poorly on this type of task. Although they are able to use their understanding of word meaning to interpret simple sentences, they lack the morphological and syntactic knowledge required to reconstruct the sentences in this type of experimental task.

Conduction Aphasia Damage to the arcuate fasciculus affects transmission of information from Wernicke's area to Broca's area. This disorder, which is known as **conduction aphasia**, has several symptoms. First since lexical information from Wernicke's area cannot be transmitted to Broca's area, speech is semantically incoherent. Similarly, because information about bound morphemes and lexical categories cannot be transmitted to Wernicke's area, the comprehension of language is impaired. This is especially true in the case of structures such as *Jill was outwitted by Ashley,* in which elements such as the auxiliary verb, the *-ed* suffix, and the preposition *by* are crucial to comprehension. There is good comprehension of sentences that can be understood on the basis of word meaning alone (*The man washed the car*).

Patients with conduction aphasia do not have articulation problems, because this aspect of speech is controlled by Broca's area, which is undamaged. Their ability to repeat words and sentences, however, is severely impaired. This follows from the fact that while sentences can be heard and interpreted, stored forms cannot be transmitted to Broca's area for production.

Alexia and Agraphia Damage to the angular gyrus impedes the association of visual patterns with auditory forms, thereby interfering with the ability to read and write. Impairment to reading ability is called **alexia**, while loss of the ability to write is known as **agraphia**. Although the two disorders usually accompany each other, alexia sometimes occurs by itself. An alexic patient may therefore be able to write but not to read what he or she has written.

Because damage to the angular gyrus does not affect vision, patients with alexia and agraphia can still see normally. They can even copy letters and words. However, since the angular gyrus contains the information specific to graphic representation of sound patterns, alexic patients perceive the words and letters as meaningless patterns rather than as symbols representing linguistic structures.

The role of the angular gyrus in reading and writing is closely tied to the type of writing system a particular language uses. Because the alphabetic writing system of English represents sound structure, the angular gyrus plays a crucial role in its use. In some societies, the writing system may represent concepts rather than sounds. (As will be noted in the chapter on writing, Chinese employs such a system.) Significantly, damage to the angular gyrus does not impair use of such writing systems. In fact, there are recorded cases of individuals who know both a sound-based writing system and a concept-based one losing the ability to use only the former after suffering damage to the angular gyrus.

Table 9.2 summarizes the three types of aphasia affecting the production and/or comprehension of the spoken language. A plus sign indicates that the ability in question remains largely intact, while a minus indicates severe impairment; an equal sign indicates limited impairment.

Table 9.2 Aphasic disorders

	Broca's aphasia	Wernicke's aphasia	Conduction aphasia
Articulation	−	+	+
Comprehension	=	−	=
Word and sentence structure	−	=	=
Repetition	=	−	−

9.3 THE CRITICAL PERIOD HYPOTHESIS

The human brain is not fully developed at birth. Rather, it matures gradually over a period of several years. There has been some speculation that language and other cognitive skills must be acquired prior to completion of this maturational process. The neurobiologist Eric Lenneberg was a major proponent of the idea that language acquisition must take place during a **critical period** extending from about age two to puberty. Lenneberg hypothesized that the end of the critical period corresponds to the completion of the lateralization process, which results in the location of the language centers in one hemisphere (usually the left). Prior to that time, he suggested, both hemispheres are involved to some extent in language and one can take over if the other is damaged. The term **cerebral plasticity** is often used to refer to this flexibility in neurological organization.

Supporting Evidence

Two observations appeared to support the view that there is considerable cerebral plasticity in the brains of young children. First, it was claimed that preadolescent children suffering damage to the left hemisphere are able to transfer their language centers to the right brain and to reacquire the lost linguistic skills with relatively little disruption. Lenneberg maintained that children suffering aphasia before puberty have a much more rapid and complete recovery than do older children.

Second, young children are known to be excellent second language learners, while their parents can struggle with a new language for years without fully mastering it. (Witness the case of many adult immigrants to the United States who are still less than fluent in English after many years despite great effort.) This has been interpreted as support for the view that there is a critical period for language acquisition in the preadolescent years and that language acquisition cannot be entirely successful after this period has ended.

Counter-evidence

In recent years, new findings have cast doubt both on the extent of cerebral plasticity in young children and on the time at which lateralization occurs. The degree of cerebral plasticity in childhood has been challenged by a study of language acquisition in children who had undergone a hemispherectomy (surgical removal of one of their cerebral hemispheres) before five months of age. It was found that removal of the left hemisphere had serious consequences for language development despite the age of the child. Even in cases where the language function was taken over by the right hemisphere, language acquisition was inferior to that of normal children using the left hemisphere.

Studies involving dichotic listening tasks also suggest that left brain dominance for language is established at a very early age. Indeed, some studies have shown that one-week-old infants have a left hemisphere preference for verbal stimuli. Moreover, as noted earlier, it is now known that a portion of the left brain used for language is larger in fetuses than the corresponding part of the right brain. This suggests that lateralization may be present even before birth.

Still another type of problem for the critical period hypothesis comes from studies of second language learning. As will be noted in more detail in Chapter 11, the widely held view that adults are inferior second language learners is being called into question. While it is true that many adults have difficulty acquiring a second language, it now appears that this is due to a variety of social, cultural, and personality factors rather than merely cerebral maturation. This further jeopardizes the claim that all language learning must occur at a particular period of neurolinguistic development.

The Case of Genie

To construct an ideal test for the critical period hypothesis, it would probably be necessary to raise a child in complete isolation and then observe whether later exposure to speech would trigger language acquisition in the normal way. Such an experiment would of course be unethical and therefore cannot be conducted. Sadly, we know of at least one child who underwent an experience very much like this. This is the girl known as Genie, who first came to the attention of the authorities in Los Angeles in 1970. It was reported that from the age of about twenty months until she was rescued at the age of thirteen years and seven months, Genie had been kept in a small room, with virtually no opportunity to hear human speech. When she was hospitalized for malnutrition, she was suffering from a severe language deficit. Not only was she unable to speak, but also she had little control over her speech organs. Her comprehension skills were very poor, and she could not even respond to simple commands.

Investigators report that after her rescue, Genie began to learn language and that her development was in some ways similar to that of a normal child.

For instance, like other children, she initially tended to simplify consonant clusters such as /sp/, /st/, and /sk/ by deleting the /s/. She also formed two-word utterances. (*Curtiss come, want soup*) and later multi-word sentences such as *Genie love Curtiss*.

Genie also seemed to be using comprehension strategies similar to those of normal children. For example, she interpreted the structure *The boy who is looking at the girl is frowning* by taking the *the girl* to be subject of *is frowning*. This error is also common among your first language learners. Confusion over preposition pairs such as *over* and *under* was also noted.

However, Genie's linguistic behavior was not always identical to that of normal children. For example, her early vocabulary included color words and numbers, which develop late in normal children. Moreover, her early word meanings apparently did not involve the semantic overextensions and underextensions that characterize the speech of young children. Thus, she did not overextend the word *dog* to other four-legged animals as many young language learners do. She also seemed to acquire all *wh* question words at about the same time, in contrast with the developmental pattern for normal children, who learn *why, when,* and *how* later than *what* and *where*.

Still other differences manifested themselves in Genie's syntactic development, which has remained severely retarded. As the following example shows, Genie's sentences are mostly telegraphic and consist largely of NPs.

> 4. See Mama Friday.
>   Mama wash hair in sink.
>   Applesauce buy store.
>   Sick people lady driving ambulance.
>   I supermarket surprise Roy.

While Genie's spontaneous utterances conformed to the usual subject-verb-object pattern of English, she seemed unable to use word order to interpret other people's sentences. Unlike normal children, Genie did not assume that the NP before the verb is the subject. She therefore had difficulty interpreting both active and passive structure types. As will be noted in the chapter on first language acquisition, normal children have little or no difficulty interpreting simple active structures.

Table 9.3 summarizes the linguistic similarities and differences between normal children and Genie.

Table 9.3 Comparison between normal children and Genie

Phenomenon	Normal children	Genie
SVO word order in spontaneous speech	yes	yes
Confusion over prepositions	yes	yes
Simplification of C clusters	yes	yes
Color/number words in early vocabulary	no	yes
Wh words acquired simultaneously	no	yes
Semantic under- and overextensions	yes	no
Comprehension strategy based on word order	yes	no

Genie is one of the few well-studied cases of a child in whom first language acquisition began after the so-called critical period. Unfortunately, few firm conclusions can be drawn. To date, she has still not fully acquired language, and the manner in which she has developed her linguistic skills is similar to language acquisition in normal children in some respects, but not in others. Moreover, dichotic listening tasks suggest that Genie, who is right-handed, is using her right hemisphere for language, the reverse of what generally occurs. Finally, because of the social deprivation, emotional trauma, and malnutrition she suffered early in life, her language deficit may be attributed to factors other than inadequate linguistic experience in the preadolescent years.

For the moment, then, we can only conclude that at least *some* linguistic skills can develop after the critical period. It is hoped that further study will reveal the precise consequences for language and cognition of inadequate exposure to speech in the early years of life.

Summing Up

Understanding the human brain represents one of the great challenges for modern science. The progress that has been made in the last decades has led to the identification of the location and function of the major language centers of the brain—**Broca's area** and **Wernicke's area**. Many difficult issues remain to be resolved. Linguists have as yet little understanding of how specific grammatical rules are represented in the brain, of why the language centers are organized the way they are, and of how biological maturation affects them. In all of these areas, knowledge is growing rapidly and it is possible that there will soon be substantial breakthroughs in the field of neurolinguistics.

Sources

For general overviews of the brain and language, see the items in the rec-ommended reading list. The literature on alexia and agraphia, including its relationship to writing systems, is reviewed by M. Schnitzer in his article "The Role of Phonology in Linguistic Communication: Some Neurolin-guistic Considerations" in *Studies in Neurolinguistics* 1, edited by H. Whi-taker and H. A. Whitaker (New York: Academic Press, 1976). The classic treatment of the relationship between lateralization and aphasia in childhood is found in Eric Lenneberg's *Biological Foundations of Language* (New York: John Wiley & Sons, 1967). Results of the study involving sentences cut at constituent boundaries are reported in the book by Ruth Lesser cited below. The effects of a hemispherectomy on very young children are dis-cussed by M. Dennis and H. Whitaker in "Language Acquisition Following Hemidecortication: Linguistic Superiority of the Left Over the Right Hem-isphere" in *Brain and Language* 3: 404–33 (1976). Evidence for early la-teralization is presented by D. Molfese, R. Freeman, and D. Palermo in "The Ontogeny of Brain Lateralization for Speech and Nonspeech Stimuli" in *Brain and Language* 2: 356–68 (1975). A recent discussion of Genie's linguistic development can be found in Susan Curtiss's article "Developmental Dissociation of Language and Cognition" in *Exceptional Language and Linguistics,* edited by L. Obler and L. Menn (New York: Academic Press, 1982).

Recommended Reading

Curtiss, Susan. 1977. *Genie, a Psycholinguistic Study of a Modern-Day "Wild Child."* New York: Academic Press.

Geschwind, Norman. 1972. "Language and the Brain." *Scientific American* 226, no. 4: 76–83.

Geschwind, Norman. 1974. *Selected Papers on Language and the Brain.* Boston: D. Reidel.

Geschwind, Norman. 1979. "Specializations of the Human Brain." *Scientific American* 241, no. 3: 180–98.

Lesser, Ruth. 1978. *Linguistic Investigations of Aphasia.* New York: Elsevier.

Penfield, Wilder. 1975. *The Mystery of the Mind.* Princeton, N.J.: Princeton University Press.

Springer, Sally and George Deutsch. 1981. *Left Brain, Right Brain.* San Francisco: W. H. Freeman.

Zurif, Edgar and Sheila Blumstein. 1978. "Language and the Brain." *Linguistic Theory and Psychological Reality.* M. Halle, J. Bresnan, and G. Miller, eds. Cambridge, Mass.: MIT Press, pp. 229–46.

Questions

1. Mark the different language centers on the following diagram of the brain.

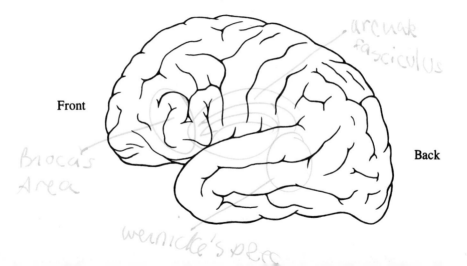

2. Many left-handed people have their language centers in the right side of the brain. What type of results would we expect to obtain from such people on the dichotic listening tasks outlined in this chapter?

3. Consider each of the following samples of speech for aphasics and attempt to identify the precise type of disorder(s) involved.
   a) Well, this is . . . mother is away here working out of here to get her better, but when she's working, the two boys looking in the other part.
   b) Cookie jar . . . fall over . . . chair . . . water . . . empty . . . ov . . . ov. Yeah.
   c) *Experimenter*: What are the days of the week?
      Patient: Six, seven, eight.
      E: What are these? (cherries)
      P: This is apples.
      E: What is this? (ankle)
      P: Feet . . . teeth.

10 LANGUAGE ACQUISITION
The Emergence of a Grammar

*Human brains are so constructed that one brain
responds in much the same way to a given trigger as
does another brain, all things being equal. This is why
a baby can learn any language; it responds to triggers
in the same way as any other baby.*

D. Hofstadter

One of the most intriguing phenomena studied by linguists is children's acquisition of language. Fascination with this issue dates back to at least the seventh century B.C., when the Egyptian Pharaoh Psammetichus had two infants brought up in complete isolation in an attempt to determine the type of language they would learn on their own. The Pharaoh had hoped that the children's utterances would provide some clues about the origin of language. The story is that the children were brought up by an old shepherd couple, who were instructed not to speak to them (or, who were mute, depending on which version you hear). After some years, the children were heard to utter *be*, and the Pharaoh concluded that the original language of humankind was Phrygian, since the Phrygian word for 'bread' is *bekos*. It has been pointed out that it is not surprising that children raised in an environment of sheep cries would produce the syllable *be*.

Fortunately for all concerned, the study of language acquisition has advanced considerably since the Pharaoh's time, and linguists have been able to develop a variety of research strategies that allow linguistic development to be investigated in a more acceptable and fruitful way. Some of these strategies are discussed briefly in Section 10.1. Most of the rest of the chapter is devoted to outlining what has been learned about children's acquisition of the phonological, morphological, semantic, and syntactic systems of their language. We conclude with a brief examination of the contribution of the linguistic environment to language acquisition, the relationship between the emergence of language and cognitive development, and the possible existence of inborn linguistic principles.

10.1 THE STUDY OF LANGUAGE ACQUISITION

It is somewhat misleading to speak of children acquiring a language. In fact what is acquired is a grammar—a set of rules, conditions, and elements that allows people to speak and understand a language. The study of language development is therefore directly related to the type of linguistic analysis with which we have been concerned in preceding chapters. Indeed, linguists look to the study of phonology, syntax, and other components of the grammar for a description of the rules and categories that children acquire during the first years of life.

There are at least two reasons for believing that the development of linguistic skills involves the acquisition of grammatical rules rather than the memorization of words and sentences. First, as noted in Chapters 1 and 5, mature language users are able to produce and understand an unlimited number of novel sentences. This can only happen if they have a system of productive grammatical rules that are applicable to novel cases. It therefore stands to reason that language acquisition involves the development of such rules.

A second indication that children acquire grammatical rules is found in their own utterances. For example, rather than simply memorizing all the regular and exceptional past tense forms for English verbs, children formulate a general rule that adds *-ed* to the verb stem. This rule produces forms such as *doed, leaved,* and *goed* in addition to *washed, walked,* and so forth. Such errors provide clear signs of children's attempts to construct grammatical rules.

Methods

A good deal of research on the acquisition of language is concerned with **developmental** phenomena. These include children's initial and intermediate hypotheses about particular linguistic structures, the kinds of errors they make, and the order in which different forms or structures are mastered. Investigators concerned with these problems draw on two basic methods—naturalistic observation and experimentation. Although both methods provide valuable information about the nature of the language acquisition process, they do so in different ways.

The Naturalistic Approach In the naturalistic approach, investigators observe and record children's spontaneous verbal behavior. One type of naturalistic investigation is the so-called diary study, in which a parent keeps daily notes on a child's linguistic progress. A variant of the diary study involves a trained researcher visiting individual children on a regular basis and recording a sample of utterances (perhaps one hour every second week over a period of five months). In both cases, notes are taken about the context in which children's speech occurs, the toys they are playing with, the pictures they are looking at, and the like.

The Experimental Approach In experimental studies, researchers typically make use of specially designed tasks to elicit linguistic activity relevant to the phenomenon that they wish to study. The children's performance is then used to formulate hypotheses about the type of grammatical system they are employing. Experimental studies usually employ tasks that test children's comprehension, production, and imitation skills.

One widely used method for testing children's comprehension involves supplying them with an appropriate set of toys and then asking them to act out the meaning of a sentence such as *The truck was pushed by the car.* Another method makes use of a question-and-answer format in which a child is read a sentence such as *John promised Tom to go home* and is then asked, *Who is going to go home?* In either case, the child's responses provide insights into the type of grammatical rules being used to interpret sentences.

In a typical production task, the child is shown a picture and asked to describe it. Although production tasks are useful for eliciting individual words, there are many structures, such as passives, which are hard to elicit even from adults. Moreover, because children's ability to comprehend language is often more advanced than their ability to produce sentences of their own, production tasks can provide an overly conservative view of linguistic development.

Both comprehension and production tests are often used in conjunction with imitation tasks. Although one might think that imitation would be excessively easy, it has been found that children's ability to repeat structures reflects the state of their current grammatical knowledge and that a form that has not been mastered will probably not be repeated properly. Thus, a child who has not yet acquired the auxiliary verb *be* will repeat the sentence *Mommy is talking* as *Mommy talking.*

By using naturalistic observation together with experimental techniques, linguists and psychologists have made significant progress in the study of the language acquisition process. Much of this chapter is devoted to a survey of this progress, beginning with the development of speech sounds.

10.2 PHONOLOGICAL DEVELOPMENT

From birth, children are exposed to a variety of noises in their environment. Before they can begin to acquire language, they must first separate non-speech noises from speech sounds. The rudiments of this ability seem to be present at birth, since even newborns respond differently to human voices than to other sounds. Within two months of birth, infants can even recognize their mother's voice.

At about the same age, children also develop the ability to distinguish among certain speech sounds. In one experiment, infants were presented with a series of identical syllables consisting of the string [ba]. These were followed by an occurrence of the syllable [pa]. A change in the children's sucking rate (the normal reaction to a new stimulus) indicated that they perceived the difference between the two syllables and, therefore, were able to distinguish between [p] and [b].

Despite this early sensitivity to distinctions among speech sounds, the ability to distinguish between meaningful words is not yet present. The emergence of this ability has been examined in a task in which children are presented with two toy animals named *bok* and *pok* and are asked to respond to sentences such as *Show me pok*. To respond correctly, children must not only hear the difference between [p] and [b] but also recognize that this difference is linguistically significant—that it is used to distinguish between words in their language. Children under eighteen months have little success in this type of task.

Babbling

Even before children master the phonemic contrasts of their language, they begin to develop the articulatory movements needed to produce these distinctions in speech. The emergence of articulatory skills begins around three or four months of age, when children start to produce cooing and babbling sounds. As Table 10.1 illustrates, there are similarities in the babbling produced by children from different linguistic communities. (The data in the

Table 10.1 Cross-linguistic similarities in babbling

All languages	No languages
p	č
b	ǰ
m	f
	v

table come from a study of children acquiring Hindi, Japanese, English, Arabic, Mayan, and Luo.) Such cross-linguistic similarities suggest that early babbling is independent of the particular language to which children are exposed. In fact, even deaf children babble, although their articulatory activity is somewhat less varied than that of hearing children. Moreover, it is known that children who for medical reasons are unable to babble can later develop normal pronunciation. All of this suggests that babbling precedes but is not actually part of the language acquisition process.

From around age six months or so, children's babbling gradually becomes more similar to the sound pattern of the language they are acquiring. The first sign of this manifests itself in voice pitch. Children learning Chinese, for example, start to produce some of the tonal patterns typical of their language even before they use any genuine words. At this point, their babbling can be distinguished from that of children learning English even though neither group has yet begun to articulate actual words.

Early Phonetic Processes

Babbling increases in frequency until the age of about twelve months, at which time children start to produce their first understandable words. Babbling may overlap with the production of real words for some time before dying out. By the time children have acquired fifty words or so, they begin to adopt fairly regular patterns of pronunciation. These patterns are quite different from those found in the adult language, in terms of both the segments they contain and the phonotactic combinations they allow. Interestingly, these differences seem to be the result of a small number of universal phonetic processes.

The phonetic processes responsible for the speech patterns of young language learners are far from arbitrary. For the most part, these processes simplify phonological structure by creating sound patterns that can be articulated with a minimum of difficulty. Such patterns are typified by syllables consisting of a consonant and a vowel. Stop consonants are preferred to fricatives and alveolars to palatals. Especially difficult are the fricatives [θ] and [ð]; [θ] is frequently pronounced as [f] or [t] and [ð] as [v] or [d]. Liquids too are difficult, and it is not unusual to find [l] and [r] replaced by [w].

Substitution One of the most widespread phonetic processes in child language involves substitution—the systematic replacement of one sound by another. Common substitution processes include **stopping**, the replacement of a fricative by a corresponding stop; **fronting**, the moving forward of a sound's place of articulation; **gliding**, the replacement of a liquid by a glide; and **denasalization**, the replacement of a nasal stop by a nonnasal counterpart. These processes are illustrated with the help of English examples in Table 10.2.

Table 10.2 Substitution in early speech

Process	Example	Change
Stopping (continuant → stop)	sing → [tɪŋ]	s → t
	sea → [tiy]	s → t
	zebra → [diybrə]	z → d
	this → [dɪt]	ð → d, s → t
	shoes → [tuwd]	š → t, z → d
Fronting	shoes → [su:z]	š → s
	John → [dzɑn]	dž → dz
	cheese → [tsi:z]	tš → ts
	goat → [dowt]	g → d
	mouth → [mʌwf]	θ → f
Gliding	lion → [yayn]	l → y
	look → [wʊk]	l → w
	rock → [wɑk]	r → w
	story → [stowiy]	r → w
Denasalization	spoon → [buwd]	n → d
	jam → [dæb]	m → b
	room → [wuwb]	m → b

Syllable Simplification A second type of process in children's speech involves the systematic deletion of certain sounds. In the data in Table 10.3, typical of the speech of two- and three-year-old children, consonant clusters have been reduced by deleting one or more segments. In all of these patterns, the weaker segment in the cluster is deleted. Thus, stops are retained over all other consonants, and fricatives are retained over liquids.

Table 10.3 Reduction of consonant clusters

/s/ + stop — (strategy: delete /s/)
stop → [tɑp]
small → [mɑ:]
desk → [dɛk]

stop + liquid — (strategy: delete liquid)
try → [tay]
crumb → [gʌm]
bring → [bɪŋ]

fricative + liquid — (strategy: delete liquid)
from → [fʌm]
sleep → [siyp]

nasal + stop — (strategy: delete nasal)
bump → [bʌp]
tent → [dɛt]

Another common deletion process in two-year-old children involves the elimination of final consonants. Initial consonants, in contrast, are typically retained if they precede a vowel.

1. dog → [dɑ]
    bus → [bʌ]
    boot → [buw]

Both the reduction of consonant clusters and the deletion of final consonants have the effect of simplifying syllable structure, bringing it closer to the CV pattern that is universally favored by children and that is the most widely found pattern in language.

Assimilation Still another widespread phonetic process in children's language is assimilation—the modification of one or more features of a phoneme under the influence of neighboring sounds. In the following examples, initial consonants have been voiced in anticipation of the following vowel.

2. tell   [dɛl]
    pig   [bɪg]
    push   [bʊs]
    soup   [zuwp]

In the next set of examples, a word-final consonant is devoiced in apparent anticipation of the silence following the end of an utterance.

3. have   [hæf]
    big   [bɪk]
    tub   [tʌp]
    egg   [ɛk]
    bed   [bɛt]

Assimilation is also observed in children's tendency to maintain the same place of articulation for all of the vowels or consonants in a word. This can lead to the pronunciation of *doggy* as [gɑgiy] (with two velar stops) or as [dɑdiy] (with two alveolar stops).

Production versus Perception

All of the examples presented in the previous section involve errors of production. An important question that arises at this point is whether children can perceive phonemic contrasts that they cannot yet make. According to one study, a child who could not produce a distinction in his own speech between *mouse* and *mouth, cart* and *card,* or *jug* and *duck* was, nonetheless, able to point to pictures of the correct objects in a comprehension task. This suggests that this child's ability to perceive the phonemic contrasts in question exceeded his ability to produce them.

Another indication that children's perceptual abilities are more advanced than their articulatory skills comes from their reaction to adult speech that fails to respect the normal phonemic contrasts. The following report describes one such incident:

> One of us, for instance, spoke to a child who called his inflated plastic fish a *fis*. In imitation of the child's pronunciation, the observer said: "This is your *fis*?" "No," said the child, "my *fis*." He continued to reject the adult's imitation until he was told, "That is your fish." "Yes," he said, "my *fis*."

The child's reaction to the adult's imitative pronunciation of *fish* shows that he could perceive the difference between [s] and [š] even though he could not yet produce it himself.

Developmental Order

A major concern of work on phonological development has been the order in which phonemic contrasts emerge in human language. Although it is difficult to tell precisely when a contrast has been acquired and despite a shortage of reliable data from a sufficiently broad range of languages, the general trends in Table 10.4 seem to exist.

Table 10.4 The emergence of speech sounds

- As a group, vowels are acquired before consonants (by age three).
- Nasals are the first nonvocalic segments to emerge, followed with some variation by glides, stops, fricatives, affricates, and liquids.
- In terms of place of articulation, labials are acquired first, followed, with some variation, by velars, alveolars, dentals, and palatals. Interdentals (such as [θ] and [ð]) are acquired last.
- New phonemic contrasts manifest themselves first in word-initial position. Thus, the /p/—/b/ contrast, for instance, will be manifested in pairs such as *pat—bat* before *mop—mob*.

10.3 MORPHOLOGICAL DEVELOPMENT

As is the case with the sound pattern of language, the details of morphological structure emerge over a period of several years. Initially, children's words all consist of a single root morpheme. Gradually, inflectional and derivational morphemes appear, marking an increased capacity for word formation.

A Developmental Sequence

From the early work on language acquisition, it has been clear that the development of bound morphemes and minor lexical categories (such as determiners and prepositions) takes place in an orderly sequence with relatively little variation from child to child. In a pioneering study of this phenomenon, the more or less invariant developmental sequence in Table 10.5 was found in three children between the ages of twenty and thirty-six months.

Table 10.5 Typical developmental sequence for English-speaking children

1. *-ing*
2. *in, on*
3. plural *-s*
4. possessive *-'s*
5. *the, a*
6. past tense *-ed*
7. third person singular *-s*

An interesting feature of this developmental sequence is that it seems to be unrelated to the frequency of the different morphemes in the speech heard by children. As Table 10.6 shows, the determiners *the* and *a* were the most frequent grammatical morphemes in the children's environments, yet were acquired relatively late. The prepositions *in* and *on*, on the other hand, were less frequent than the determiners and the plural ending, but were acquired before either.

Table 10.6 Typical relative frequency of morphemes in parental speech

1. *the, a*
2. *-ing*
3. plural *-s*
4. *in, on*
5. possessive *-'s*
6. past tense *-ed*
7. third person singular *-s*

Determining Factors What determines the order of acquisition of minor lexical categories and bound morphemes? Research on a variety of languages suggests that several factors are involved.

1. Occurrence of the morpheme in utterance-final position Children show a greater tendency to notice and remember elements that occur at the end of the utterance than those found in any other position. All other things being equal, this favors the learning of suffixes over prefixes.

2. Syllabicity Children seem to take greater notice of morphemes such as -*ing* and *on,* which constitute syllables, than the plural or possessive suffix -*s*, which is a single consonant.

3. Susceptibility to stress The fact that morphemes such as English *the* or *in* can be stressed apparently increases their salience and facilitates their acquisition. Many morphemes (-*ing*, -*ed*, and nonsyllabic affixes such as -*s*) cannot be stressed in natural speech.

4. Obligatoriness All other things being equal, a morpheme that is obligatory in a particular context will be easier to acquire than one that is optional. For example, case markers for the subject and direct object in Turkish are obligatory, while those in Korean are optional. Turkish children can use case markers to interpret sentences before age two—over a year before Korean children can.

5. A straightforward relation between form and meaning Whereas the English inflectional suffix -*ed* marks only past tense, the portmanteau verbal ending -*s* simultaneously represents three linguistic categories: third person, singular, and present (nonpast) tense. This latter type of morpheme is more difficult for children to acquire.

6. Lack of exceptions Whereas all singular nouns form the possessive with -'*s*, not all verbs use -*ed* to mark the past tense (*saw, read, drove*). Such exceptions hinder the language acquisition process.

7. Lack of allomorphic variation Whereas the affix -*ing* has the same form for all verbs, the past tense ending -*ed* has three major allomorphs—/t/ for verbs such as *chase*, /d/ for forms such as *crave*, and /əd/ for verbs such as *recite*. This type of allomorphic variation, which also occurs with the plural, possessive, and third person singular affixes in English, slows morphological development.

8. Absence of homophones In English, three separate morphemes (the plural, the possessive, and the third person singular) have the form -*s*. This apparently creates confusion and interferes with language acquisition.

9. Clearly discernible semantic function Whereas morphemes such as *in, on,* and the plural -*s* appear to express easily identifiable meanings, some morphemes (such as the third person singular -*s*) appear to make no contribution to the meaning of the sentence. Acquisition of this latter type of morpheme is relatively slow.

The status of the English morphemes whose developmental order we have been considering is indicated in Table 10.7; as before, morphemes are listed in order of emergence. (A morpheme is considered obligatory if it

Table 10.7 Factors facilitating development

Morphemes	Factors								
	1	2	3	4	5	6	7	8	9
–ing	+	+	–	+	+	+	+	–	+
in, on	–	+	+	+	+	+	+	+	+
plural *-s*	+	–	–	+	+	–	–	–	+
possessive - *'s*	+	–	–	+	+	+	–	–	+
the, a	–	+	+	+	+	+	–	+	+
past tense *-ed*	+	±	–	+	+	–	–	–	+
third person singular *-s*	+	±	–	+	–	–	–	–	–

cannot be deleted without changing the meaning of the sentence.) As you can see, the morphemes that are acquired first generally exhibit more of the properties just discussed than those that emerge at a later point.

Morpho-phonemic Rules

As children's productive and perceptual abilities improve, they start to gain command of morphophonemic rules, including those responsible for allomorphic variation of the sort associated with the English plural (/s/ in *hats*, /z/ in *pens*, /əz/ in *judges*) and the past tense (/d/ in *played*, /t/ in *taped*, /əd/ in *hunted*). Initially, even allomorphic variation as straightforward as the *a/ an* alternation in English can cause difficulty for language learners, and it is not unusual to hear children aged two to three produce utterances such as *an cucumber*.

A well-known technique for studying the development of morphophonemic rules is to present children with nonsense words and then ask them to form plurals or past tense forms. If the children have mastered rules for allomorphic variation, they ought to be able to add appropriate endings even to words they have never heard before. In a classic experiment, children were shown a picture of a strange creature and told "This is a wug." A second picture was then presented and the children were given the following type of question.

> 4. Now, there's another wug. There are two of them.
> Now, there are two . . . ?

Children who knew the plural formation rule were able to respond with the form /wʌgz/. Table 10.8 indicates the average scores attained by preschoolers (aged four to five) and first graders (aged five and a half to seven) on specific nonsense words in this experiment. As you can see, the various allomorphs of the plural are acquired at different times. Particularly problematic is the /əz/ allomorph, which is needed in the last four nonsense words in the table. Even first-grade children fail to produce the correct form of the plural here in well over half the cases studied.

Table 10.8 Percentage of correct responses on wug test

		Preschoolers	First graders
/s/	heafs	79%	80%
/z/	wugs	76	97
	luns	68	92
	tors	73	90
	cras	58	86
/əz/	tasses	28	39
	gutches	28	38
	kashes	25	36
	nizzes	14	33

Word Formation Rules

Like inflectional morphemes, derivational affixes and compounding appear to be acquired in a more or less fixed order. This was illustrated in a study of the six word formation processes in Table 10.9. Children were given

Table 10.9 Word formation processes

Type	Example
Agentive -er	teacher (= one who teaches)
Noun-noun compounds	bird house
Adjectival -y	dirty
Instrumental -er	eraser (= something to erase with)
Adverbial -ly	quickly, quietly
Diminutive -ie or -y	Johnny, doggie

sentence frames that required the formation of a new word for a real or made-up root. For the agentive -er, for example, a typical frame would be *A person who teaches is called a. . . .* As Table 10.10 shows, not all word formation processes were equally easy for the children. The crucial factor in determining the order of emergence of these word formation processes seems to be productivity. The two processes that apply most freely in English (the formation of a noun by the addition of the agentive affix -er to a verb and compounding) were the first to emerge. On the other hand, morphemes such as -ly that can apply to only a restricted set of adjectival roots (*quiet/quietly* but **red/redly, *fast/fastly*) seem to be mastered at a much later age.

Table 10.10 Percentage correct for made-up roots

Construction	Preschool	Early school	Middle school
Agentive -er	7%	63%	80%
Compound	47	50	65
Adjectival -y	0	30	55
Instrumental -er	7	35	45
Adverbial -ly	0	13	20

10.4 DEVELOPMENT OF WORD MEANING

By age eighteen months or so, the average child has a vocabulary of fifty words or more. Over the next months this vocabulary grows rapidly, sometimes by as much as ten or twelve words a day. The words in a typical vocabulary of a two-year old are in Table 10.11. As Table 10.11 shows,

Table 10.11 Typical vocabulary of a two-year-old child

Objects

body parts: cheek, ear, foot, hand, leg, nose, toe
food: cookie, cereal, drink, egg, fish, jam, milk
clothes: boot, clothes, dress, hat, shirt, shoes, socks
household: bag, bath, bell, bottle, box, brush, chair, clock, soap, spoon, water, watch
animals: bear, bird, cat, cow, dog, horse, sheep

Properties

bad, dirty, fat, good, more, nice, poor, sweet

Actions and events

bring, burn, carry, catch, clap, come, cut, do, dry, fall, get, give, go, kick, kiss, knit, look, meet, open, pull, push, ring, shut, sit, sleep, speak, sweep, tickle, wag, warm, wash

Other

away, down, now, up, no, yes, thank you, goodbye

noun-like words are predominant in the child's early vocabulary, with verb- and adjective-like words being the next most frequent category types. Among the most frequent individual words are expressions for displeasure or rejection (such as *no*) and various types of social interaction (such as *give* and *bye-bye*). Over the next few years, continued rapid expansion of this vocabulary takes place so that by age six most children have mastered about five thousand different morphemes. These developmental trends are found in all linguistic communities and therefore appear to be universal.

Acquisition of Word Meaning

A major factor in lexical development is the child's ability to use contextual clues to draw inferences about the category and meaning of new words. From around seventeen months of age, for instance, children can use the presence or absence of determiners to distinguish between proper nouns (names) and common nouns. Two-year-old children who are told that a new doll is a *dax* will identify a similar doll as a *dax* as well. However, if they are told that the new doll is *Dax*, they will restrict use of the new word to the doll they have actually been shown.

Children are also able to use the meaning of other words in the sentence as well as their understanding of the nonlinguistic context to form hypotheses about new words. In one experiment, for example, three- and four-year-old children were asked to act out the meaning of sentences such as "Make it so there is *tiv* to drink in this glass (of water)." The only clues to the interpretation of the nonsense word *tiv* come from the meaning of the sentence and from the child's understanding of the types of changes that can be made to a glass of water. Not only did more than half the children respond by either adding or removing water, some even remembered what *tiv* "meant" two weeks later!

Initially, children sometimes fail to identify the concept conveyed by a new word or phrase. For example, after one child was told sternly by his mother, "Young man, you did that on purpose," he was asked what *on purpose* meant. He replied, "It means you're looking at me." In another case, an adult was so bothered by his son's demands for some beer that he finally said, "Let's have some peace in the house." The next day the father was asked by his thirsty son for some "peace-in-the-house." These are examples of a relatively rare phenomenon: the use of words whose meanings do not overlap at all with those of their counterparts in adult speech. Two far more typical error types involve overextension and underextension of the meanings of adult words.

Overextension In cases of **overextension**, the meaning of the child's word overlaps with that of the corresponding adult form, but also extends beyond it. The word *dog*, for example, is frequently overextended to include horses, cows, and other four-legged animals. Similarly, *ball* is sometimes used for any round object, such as a balloon, an Easter egg, a small stone, a plastic egg-shaped toy, and so on.

The Basis for Overextension A major issue in the study of language acquisition is whether children's overextensions are the result of similarities in the appearance (shape, size, texture) or the function of the objects to which the overextended word refers. The evidence collected to date suggests that perceptual properties are the critical factor in children's first hypotheses about word meanings. As a result, children often overextend a word to include a set of perceptually similar objects that they know to have diverse functions. One child, for example, used the word *moon* for the moon, grapefruit halves, a crescent-shaped piece of paper, a crescent-shaped car light, and a hangnail. Another child used the word *money* for a set of objects ranging from pennies to buttons and beads. If you reconsider the examples of overextension given in Table 10.12, you will see that they too are more plausibly explained in terms of perceptual similarities than a shared function.

Children seem to overextend more in their production than in their comprehension. A child who overextends the word *dog* in his or her own speech, for example, may well point only to dogs when asked by an adult to find the dogs in the picture shown in Figure 10.1. This suggests that children sometimes deliberately overextend words in production to compensate for their limited vocabulary.

Table 10.12 Examples of overextension

Word	First referents	Subsequent extensions
tick tock	watch	clocks, gas-meter, fire hose on a spool, scale with round dial
fly	fly	specks of dirt, dust, small insects, child's toes, crumbs of bread
quack	duck	all birds and insects, flies, coins (with an eagle on the face)
candy	candy	cherries, anything sweet
apple	apples	balls, tomatoes, cherries, onions, cookies
turtle	turtles	fish, seals
cookie	cookies	crackers, any dessert
kitty	cats	rabbits, any small furry animal
box	boxes	elevators

Figure 10.1 Picture used for animal identification tasks

Underextension While overextensions are the most frequent type of word-meaning error in early language, children also frequently employ **underextension** by using lexical items in an overly restrictive fashion. For example, at the age of nine months, one child restricted her use of the word *car* to a particular situation. She used it only for cars moving on the street as she watched out of the window, not for cars standing still, for cars in pictures, or for cars she rode in herself.

Another type of underextension is the use of a word to name a specific object without extending it to other members of that class. Thus, *kitty* might be used to refer to the family pet, but not to any other cats. Still another type of underextension involves limiting the use of words to a subset of the entities for which an adult would use a particular lexical item. For example, the word *dog* might be used for collies, spaniels, and beagles, but not for Chihuahuas.

Spatial and Dimensional Terms

English has many prepositions that are used to express spatial relations (such as *in, on,* and *under*). These prepositions differ from each other in terms of the complexity of the relation they express. Consider in this respect prepositions such as *in* and *on* versus *behind*. The relation expressed by the former class of prepositions does not depend on the speaker's viewpoint: if two marbles are on a box, then they are on it no matter what the speaker's viewpoint. This is not true for the relations expressed by *in front of* and *behind*. We can say that the marbles are behind the box only if the box is between us and the marbles. If we were to place ourselves on the opposite side of the box, we would then be able to say that the marbles were in front of the box. Further complications arise when the object with respect to which the marbles are situated has an inherent front and back (such as a television). In this case, we can say that the marbles are behind the television regardless of our own perspective. Given this complexity in the use of prepositions such as *in front of* and *behind*, it is not surprising to find that they are mastered after elements such as *in* and *on*.

Dimensional terms describing size are also acquired in an order that reflects their inherent semantic complexity (see Table 10.13). The adjectives *big* and *small* are the least complex of the dimensional adjectives since they can be used for talking about any aspect of size (height, area, volume, and so on). The adjectives *tall, high, long,* and *short,* on the other hand, can only be used for a single dimension (height/length). *Thick/thin, wide/narrow,* and *deep/shallow* are still more restricted in their use since they describe

Table 10.13 Order of acquisition for dimensional adjectives

big-small
tall-short, long-short
high-low
thick-thin
wide-narrow, deep-shallow

the secondary or less extended dimension of an object. For instance, the dimension of a stick that we describe in terms of width or thickness is almost always less extended than the dimension that we describe in terms of height or length. As Table 10.13 shows, the order of acquisition of these dimensional adjectives closely reflects their relative complexity.

10.5 SYNTACTIC DEVELOPMENT

Like phonological and morphological development, the emergence of syntactic rules takes place in an orderly sequence. Beginning with the production of one-word utterances near the end of the first year of life, children gradually master the rules for sentence formation in their language. Some of the milestones in this developmental process are considered here.

The One-Word Stage

As noted earlier, children begin to produce one-word utterances between the ages of twelve and eighteen months. A basic property of these one-word utterances is that they can be used to express the type of meaning that would be associated with an entire sentence in adult speech. Thus, a child might use the word *dada* to assert (among other things) 'I saw daddy's hat', *more* to mean 'Give me more candy', and *up* to mean 'I want up'. Such utterances are called **holophrases**.

A striking feature of holophrastic utterances is children's skill in communicating complex messages with a single word. This skill seems to be based on a strategy of choosing the most informative word that applies to the situation being commented upon. A child who wanted a candy, for example, would say *candy* rather than *want* since the former word is more informative in this situation. Similarly, a child who notices a new toy would be more likely to say *toy* than *see*, thereby referring to the most novel feature of the situation he or she is trying to describe.

Table 10.14 lists some of the semantic relations that children commonly try to express during the one-word stage.

Table 10.14 One-word utterances

Semantic relation	Utterance	Situation
Agent of an action	dada	as father enters the room
Action or state	down	as child sits down
Object of an action	door	as father closes the door
Location	here	as child points
Recipient	mama	as child gives mother something
Recurrence	again	as child watches the lighting of a match

The Two-Word Stage

Within a few months of their first one-word utterances, children begin to produce two-word utterances of the sort shown in Table 10.15.

It is unclear whether children in the two-word stage have acquired syntactic categories such as noun, verb, and adjective. As the following utter-

Table 10.15 Patterns in two-word speech

Child's utterance	Adult form	Semantic relations
Baby chair	The baby is sitting on the chair.	agent-location
Doggie bark	The dog is barking.	agent-action
Ken water	Ken is drinking water.	agent-object
Hit doggie	I hit the doggie.	action-object
Daddy hat	Daddy's hat	possessor-possessed

ances show, words that belong to separate categories in the adult language (the adjective *busy* and the verb *push*) can occur in identical patterns in the two-word stage. This makes it difficult to determine whether the child is treating them as separate categories.

> *5.* Mommy busy.
> Mommy push.

Another problem is that the inflectional affixes that distinguish among syntactic categories in adult English (such as the plural and the past tense) are absent from the speech of children in the two-word stage. While this does not show that children lack lexical categories, it makes it very difficult to demonstrate that they possess them. For this reason, many linguists and psychologists prefer to describe children's utterances in terms of the semantic relations that they express (as in Table 10.15) rather than the syntactic categories of adult speech.

The Telegraphic Stage

After a period of several months during which their speech is limited to one- and two-word utterances, children begin to produce longer and more complex grammatical stuctures. Some representative utterances from the first part of this period are given in the following example.

> *6.* Chair all broken.
> Daddy like this book.
> What her name?
> Man ride bus today.
> Car make noise.
> Me wanna show Mommy.
> I good boy.

At first, these utterances lack bound morphemes and most minor lexical categories. Because of their resemblance to the style of language found in telegrams, this acquisitional stage is often dubbed **telegraphic**. Over a period of several months, affixes, determiners, and auxiliary verbs emerge.

A noteworthy feature of the telegraphic stage is that children make virtually no word order errors. As the previous examples illustrate, adult word order patterns are employed even though individual words may not have the appropriate endings. In languages with variable word order (such as Korean and Russian), children use the various word order patterns in roughly the same proportion as adults do.

Later Development

In the years following the telegraphic stage, children continue to acquire the complex grammar that underlies adult linguistic competence. To date, acquisition studies have dealt with only a few aspects of this later development. Some of the findings on particular English constructions are reviewed in this section.

Negation Children seem to acquire basic patterns of negation involving *no* and *not* in three stages during the second and third years of life.

Stage 1 (approximately eighteen to twenty-five months) The use of *no* at the beginning of the sentence.

> 7. No the sun shining.
> No sit there.
> No dog bite you.
> No money.
> No Mom sharpen it.
> No Fraser drink all tea.

Stage 2 (approximately twenty-six to forty-two months) Negative elements (usually *no*) now occur sentence-internally, but children still do not have productive mastery of auxiliary verbs. Forms like *can't* and *don't* occur occasionally, but *can* and *do* are not found. This suggests that children do not yet have command of auxiliary verbs and are treating *can't* and *don't* as simple negative morphemes.

> 8. I no singing song.
> The sun no shining.
> Don't sit there.
> Dog no bite you.
> We can't talk.
> I no want envelope.
> I no taste them.

Stage 3 (after forty-two months) The forms *not* and *n't* now appear sentence-internally with auxiliary verbs, as in adult speech.

> 9. I'm not singing a song.
> The sun isn't shining.
> The dog won't bite you.
> It's not cold.
> I don't have a book.

Interrogative Sentences Like negative constructions, interrogative structures emerge gradually between the ages of two and four. For many children, the following three stages are involved.

Stage 1 Children produce both *yes-no* questions and *wh* questions, but without the help of Inversion. Intonation and/or the presence of a *wh* word signals that the utterance is a question.

> 10. See hole?
>   I ride train?
>   Ball go?
>   Sit chair?
>   Where that?
>   What we think?
>   Why you smiling?
>   Why not me drink it?

During this period, *wh* words are quite restricted in their occurrence. It is only after a period of several months that *what, where,* and *why* are used with a broad range of verbs.

Stage 2 Auxiliary verbs make their appearance and undergo Inversion, but only in *yes-no* questions. *Wh* questions continue to be formed without Inversion.

> 11. *Yes-no* questions (with Inversion):
>   Did Mommy pinch her finger?
>   Can't you fix it?
>   Do I have it?
>   Will you help me?
>   Is Mommy talking to Robin's grandmother?
> 12. *Wh* questions (no Inversion):
>   What I did yesterday?
>   Why kitty can't stand up?
>   Where I should put it?
>   Where I should sleep?
>   Why you are smiling?

Stage 3 Inversion is applied in *wh* questions as well as *yes-no* questions.

> 13. Where did my mitten go?
>   Where should I sleep?
>   Why are you smiling?

For some children, Inversion in *wh* questions develops in two substages, appearing first in affirmative structures and later in negative ones. In these cases, children who are able to produce the affirmative constructions in *13* above will still use ill-formed negative sentences such as the following.

> 14. Why you can't sit down?
>   Why kitty can't stand up?

Even after children have learned subject-verb Inversion, they often make mistakes involving tense and agreement, such as those in *15*.

15. Did I caught it?
    What did you doed?
    Does lions walk?

Passivization As noted in the chapter on syntax, it is possible to use a transformational rule to relate the passive structure to its active counterpart.

16. a) The truck bumped the car. (*active*)
    b) The car was bumped by the truck. (*passive*)

The passive form is a relatively late acquisition. As the data in Table 10.16 show, children have a great deal of difficulty with passive constructions up

Table 10.16 Comprehension of passive constructions

Group	Percentage correct
Nursery school	20%
Kindergarten	35
Grade 1	48
Grade 2	63
Grade 3	88

to age seven or so. The most common error made by children is to assume that the first NP is the agent and the second NP the thing acted upon. This simple word order strategy works for active sentences, but it fails for passive constructions since a sentence like *16b* is treated as if it had the meaning of *17.*

17. The car bumped the truck. (*active*)

As the foregoing data show, this word order strategy is applied very generally by preschool children with the result that they misinterpret most passives. Around age five or six, children realize that this strategy is not always appropriate, but they are confused about how they should interpret passive structures. The scores for this period (around 50 percent correct) suggest that responses are based on guessing. Finally, around age seven, children's scores begin to rise dramatically, indicating that they have begun to acquire the passive construction.

10.6 DETERMINANTS OF LANGUAGE ACQUISITION

In the preceding sections, we have seen that children acquire the grammar for their language over a period of several years. While it is relatively easy to describe the order in which children acquire various phonemic contrasts, morphemes, and syntactic rules, it is much more difficult to explain *how* they do this. The sections that follow outline some of the skills and abilities that may help children acquire the categories and rules that make up the grammar of their language.

The Role of Imitation and Correction

At one time, it was widely believed that children learn language by simply imitating the speech of those around them. We now know that this cannot be true, since many utterance types produced by children do not closely resemble structures found in adult speech. Plural forms such as *foots* and negative constructions such as *No the sun shining* are obvious examples of structures that are unique to child language. As noted earlier, such utterances reflect children's attempts to construct grammatical rules, not the imitation of adult speech.

The importance of imitation to language acquisition is placed in further doubt by the fact that children are typically unable to imitate structures that they have not yet learned. Thus, a child who has not yet acquired the Inversion rule for *wh* questions will "imitate" sentence *18a* by producing *18b*.

18. *a*) What have you seen? (*model*)
    b) What you have seen? (*child's imitation*)

Findings like these suggest that children process the speech they hear in terms of their current grammatical system.

This is not to say that imitation plays no role in language learning. While many children rarely attempt to repeat the utterances they hear, some language learners do seem to make selective use of imitation. They imitate new words in constructions they have already learned and repeat novel constructions that contain words already familiar to them. Such selective imitation suggests that children do not blindly mimic adult speech, but rather exploit it in very restricted ways to improve their linguistic skills.

Another common belief is that parents provide children with direct linguistic training by correcting ill-formed utterances. This belief has not been supported by studies of actual interactions between parents and children. Instead of correcting children's speech, parents react to the meaning of children's utterances. In one case, a parent reacted to the utterance *Mama isn't boy, he's a girl* by responding *That's right*.

Even when adults do attempt to correct children's grammatical errors, their efforts seem to have little effect. The following actual exchange between a child and his mother is typical in this regard.

19. *Child:* Nobody don't like me.
    Mother: No, say "Nobody likes me."
    Child: Nobody don't like me.
    [*Exchange is repeated eight times.*]
    Mother: No, now listen carefully; say "Nobody likes me."
    Child: Oh! Nobody don't LIKES me.

A more subtle form of correction occurs when adults repeat a child's immature utterance, making the adjustments needed for it to be grammatical in the adult language.

20. *Child:* Daddy here.
   Mother: Yes, Daddy is here.
   Child: Boy chasing dog.
   Mother: Yes, the boy is chasing the dog.
   Child: Him go.
   Mother: Yes, he is going.

A recent study of upper-middle-class families in the United States suggests that mothers are more likely to revise their children's utterances if they are ungrammatical. It is not yet known whether this practice is common in other groups or whether it actually helps in children's acquisition of language.

The Role of Parental Speech

Linguistic development obviously depends in crucial ways on the child's linguistic experience. Children who are exposed to English learn to speak English, those exposed to Spanish learn Spanish, and so on. Moreover, children who are not exposed to language do not develop linguistic skills beyond the babbling stage.

A good deal of recent work has been devoted to the search for a possible relationship between language acquisition and the type of speech that is typically addressed to young language learners. Such speech is often called **caretaker speech** or **Motherese**. A valuable product of this research has been the discovery that speech addressed to young children has special properties that could well heighten its comprehensibility. Phonologically, for example, caretaker speech is known to consist of clearly articulated utterances with pauses between phrases and exaggerated intonation contours to signal questions, imperatives, and statements. Parental speech also tends to concentrate on the here and now, consisting primarily of statements relating to the child's current surroundings, activities, and needs. The following examples help illustrate this.

21. That's right, pick up the blocks. *(said as the child is picking up a box of building blocks)*
   That's a puppy. *(said as the child is looking at a young dog)*
   The puppy's in the basket. *(said as the child is examining a puppy in a basket)*

It seems reasonable to suppose that exposure to this type of language makes it easier for children to match forms (morphemes, words, and phrases) with meanings, and thereby to acquire the vocabulary and structure of their language.

On the other hand, we know that the amount of linguistic interaction required to trigger language development need not be large. In some cultures, for instance, children are not considered to be potential conversational partners until they are fluent speakers. Little speech is addressed directly to them, although they do spend a lot of time with their mothers and are exposed to a good deal of conversation among adults. The fact that these children seem to learn language in a normal fashion indicates that exposure to the speech style typical of middle-class mothers in North American society is not necessary for language acquisition.

We also know that parental speech has highly selective effects on child language. In one widely cited study, the speech of fifteen mothers to their daughters (aged one year to two years and three months) was analyzed. It was found that there were correlations between only some aspects of caretaker speech and child speech. For instance, the number of *yes-no* questions in parental speech was positively correlated with the rate at which auxiliary verbs developed. This was presumably because auxiliaries occur in the salient sentence-initial position in *yes-no* questions (*Can Jennifer go?*). However, many other features of parental speech seem not to influence child language. For example, the relative frequency of bound morphemes in parental speech apparently has no direct effect on their order of acquisition.

Although there is now an extensive literature on caretaker speech, researchers working in this field have not yet succeeded in explaining precisely how properties of parental speech contribute to language acquisition. Even granting the value of a language input consisting of short, clearly articulated sentences whose meaning can be deduced from context, important issues remain unresolved. How, for example, do these short, clearly articulated sentences help the child learn the phrase structure rules discussed in the chapter on syntax? How do properties of parental speech help the language learner discover the Particle Movement transformation?

In and of itself, parental speech cannot explain how language acquisition occurs. However, research into caretaker speech may contribute to this goal in less direct ways by helping determine the types of linguistic experience that are most valuable to children. This in turn will help identify the types of mechanisms and strategies involved in language acquisition.

The Role of Cognitive Development

One of the most puzzling problems in child psychology revolves around the relationship between language acquisition and cognitive development. Because there are dramatic changes in children's linguistic abilities and in their other cognitive skills during the first years of life, it is tempting to think that the two are somehow linked. Indeed, prominent psychologists have suggested both that cognitive development shapes language acquisition (a view put forward by the Swiss psychologist Jean Piaget) and that language acquisition is crucial to cognitive development (a position associated with the Russian psychologist Lev Vygotsky).

There are many suggestive similarities between language acquisition and cognitive development. During the first two years of life, for example, several cognitive advances that could facilitate language acquisition take place. One of these involves the development of **object permanence**, the ability to recognize that objects have an existence independent of one's interaction with them. Prior to the development of this ability, children seem to assume that an object ceases to exist when it moves out of sight, and that it is a different entity when it reappears. They therefore do not know where to look for an object that they observe being hidden. From their perspective, it has apparently simply ceased to exist. The emergence of object permanence around age eighteen months generally coincides with the beginning of a period of rapid growth in the child's vocabulary. The relative timing of these two events suggests a possible connection: children do not learn the names for objects until they understand that those objects have an independent existence.

During the first twenty-four months of their lives, children also acquire the ability to classify objects and actions. They seem to understand that certain things are eaten, others can be sat upon, still others serve as toys, and so on. It is conceivable that these classification skills are also used to create linguistic categories such as noun and verb. It has also been suggested that a general ability to arrange and order elements with respect to each other plays a role in children's attempts to organize words into sentences.

Still another link between cognitive development and language acquisition involves seriation, the ability to arrange elements (such as sticks) in order of increasing or decreasing size. Children who are unable to perform this type of task typically describe the objects on which they are working simply as *long* or *short*. In contrast, children who are capable of seriation (aged five and older) use comparative terms such as *longer* and *shorter*. Here again, there is an apparent connection between an aspect of language (the comparative suffix for adjectives) and a more general cognitive skill (seriation).

Although examples like these can be easily multiplied, there are many features of linguistic development that cannot be tied to cognitive development in any specific way. For instance, there is no apparent cognitive explanation for why children's early negations involve sentence-initial negative elements. Nor is there an obvious explanation for why *Wh* Movement is acquired before Inversion.

It is also important to recognize that just as cognitive development may influence language acquisition, so may the emergence of linguistic skills have an effect on cognition. At the very least, language seems to provide its users with an enhanced capacity for complex reasoning. It is also conceivable that language may help draw children's attention to certain conceptual distinctions that would otherwise develop more slowly. For instance, in the course of being exposed to words such as *father, mother,* and *brother,* children may make discoveries about family relationships that might otherwise develop more slowly.

*The Role of Inborn Knowledge

Although both cognitive development and exposure to the speech of others are clearly crucial to language acquisition, other factors must also be involved. Apes have many of the cognitive skills of two-year-old children, but they do not acquire language even when they are exposed to speech. This suggests that there is something about the human mind that equips it to acquire language. A very influential view among linguists is that children are born with advance knowledge of the type of categories and rules that are found in the grammar of any human language. They would therefore know, for example, that the words in the language they are acquiring will belong to a small set of syntactic categories (N, V, and so on), and that there will be rules of a certain sort to create larger phrases (NP, VP, S). However, they would have to learn from experience the precise order of elements within each phrasal category. The set of inborn categories and principles common to all human languages is called **Universal Grammar**.

The view that certain grammatical knowledge is inborn is known as **nativism**. Although nativism has roots in philosophy that date back thousands of years, its popularity in linguistics is due largely to the theories of Noam Chomsky, a linguist at the Massachusetts Institute of Technology. Chomsky's basic claim is that the grammars for human language are too complex and abstract to be learned on the basis of the type of experience to which children have access. He therefore concludes that significant components of the grammar must be inborn.

To illustrate this, we must consider a relatively complex example involving the notion of c-command introduced in the chapter on semantics. As you may recall, c-command is defined as follows.

22. The NP x c-commands the NP y if every category dominating x also dominates y.

The c-command relation plays a crucial role in the statement of a number of linguistic principles, including the following constraint on reflexive pronouns (in English, pronouns ending in *self*).

23. The C-Command Requirement: A reflexive pronoun must be c-commanded by its antecedent.

The C-Command Requirement is responsible for the interpretation of sentences such as *24*.

24. The boy's father hurt himself.

The antecedent for *himself* in *24* is *the boy's father,* not *the boy*; that is, the sentence must be taken to mean that the father of the boy is both the person who was hurt and the person who did the hurting. This fact follows from the C-Command Requirement provided that we assume that sentence *24* has the structure depicted in Figure 10.2. In Figure 10.2, there is only one category that dominates the NP *the boy's father*—namely S. Since this category

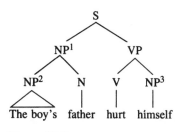

Figure 10.2

also dominates the reflexive pronoun, NP¹ c-commands *himself* according to our definition and can therefore serve as its antecedent in accordance with the C-Command Requirement. The same is not true of *the boy* (NP²). Of the two categories that dominate it—S and NP¹—only the first also dominates the reflexive. This means that NP² does not c-command the reflexive and cannot serve as its antecedent.

There are two major reasons for believing that the C-Command Requirement must be inborn. First, the notion of c-command is quite abstract. It is not the type of concept that we would expect young children to discover simply by listening to sentences. Since we also know that parents do not give children formal language lessons, it makes sense to think that c-command is an inborn notion that does not have to be discovered or taught.

Second, the C-Command Requirement seems to be universal. There appear to be no languages in which the equivalent of English *himself* can refer to the boy rather than the boy's father in structures such as *24*. The universality of this principle would be explained if it were innate and hence part of the advance or inborn linguistic knowledge of all human beings.

Other types of evidence for the innateness of the C-Command Requirement are possible. We might find, for instance, that this principle appears at about the same time in children acquiring different languages. The emergence of a principle at a uniform time across language groups is what we would expect if it were genetically determined. Although nothing definitive can be reported here, some preliminary work on languages as varied as English, Japanese, and Korean suggests that children in all three linguistic communities develop the ability to interpret sentences such as *The boy's father hurt himself* around age four or five.

The claim that children are born with abstract linguistic principles is controversial, and research on alternatives continues. However, the hypothesis that the grammar is genetically structured is an exciting and intriguing development in linguistics. It is one of the many areas in the field of language acquisition where important breakthroughs remain to be made.

Summing Up

This chapter has been concerned with the problem of how children acquire the grammatical rules of their first language. Research in this area deals with two major issues: the nature of the **developmental** sequence leading to the emergence of mature linguistic competence and the factors that make it possible for children to acquire complex grammatical rules. We have seen that over a period of several years children gradually acquire different subsystems of the grammar (**phonology**, **morphology**, **syntax**, and so on). In many cases, acquisition will involve a number of intermediate stages, each of which marks a successively closer approximation to the adult grammar. A number of factors are known to contribute to the child's acquisition of language, including the properties of parental speech, the effects of general cognitive development, and (possibly) inborn linguistic knowledge. We look to future research for deeper insights into the precise role of these and other factors.

Sources

Pioneering work on infant perception is reported in "Developmental Studies of Speech Perception" by P. Eimas in *Infant Perception*, edited by L. Cohen and P. Salapatek (New York: Academic Press, 1975). The cross-linguistic data on babbling are summarized and discussed in *Phonological Acquisition and Change* by J. Locke (cited below). Differences between children's production and perception of speech sounds are discussed in *The Acquisition of Phonology: A Case Study* by N. Smith (London: Cambridge University Press, 1973); the "*fis* phenomenon" is reported in "Psycholinguistic Research Methods" by J. Berko and R. Brown in *Handbook of Research Methods in Child Development*, edited by P. Mussen (New York: John Wiley & Sons, 1960). David Ingram's *Phonological Disability in Children* (cited below) contains many useful examples of early phonetic processes.

The pioneering work on the developmental order for English bound morphemes and lexical categories was done by R. Brown and reported in his book *A First Language: The Early Stages* (Cambridge, Mass.: Harvard University Press, 1973). The cross-linguistic data on the factors determining morphological development come from "Universal and Particular in the Acquisition of Language" by D. Slobin in *Language Acquisition: The State of the Art,* edited by E. Wanner and L. Gleitman (London: Cambridge University Press, 1982). The original "*wug* test" was done by J. Berko and is reported in her article "The Child's Learning of English Morphology" in *Word* 14: 150–77 (1958). The work on the development of derivational affixes and compounding in English is from "Recent Research on the Acquisition of English Morphology" by B. Derwing and W. Baker in *Language Acquisition,* edited by P. Fletcher and M. Garman (London: Cambridge University Press, 1979).

The "*dax* experiment" on proper and common nouns is reported by N. Katz, E. Baker, and J. Macnamara in their article "What's in a Name? A Study of How Children Learn Common and Proper Nouns" in *Child Development* 45: 469–73 (1974); the "*tiv* experiment" is from "The Child as Word Learner" by S. Carey in *Linguistic Theory and Psychological Reality,* edited by M. Halle, J. Bresnan, and G. Miller (Cambridge, Mass.: MIT Press, 1978). The literature on spatial and dimensional terms is reviewed in *Psychology and Language* by H. Clark and E. Clark (cited below).

The data on the acquisition of passive structures come from a study by E. Turner and R. Rommetveit, reported in their article "The Acquisition of Sentence Voice and Reversibility" in *Child Development* 38: 650–60 (1967). The data on the development of negatives and question structures are based on the classic article by E. Klima and U. Bellugi, "Syntactic Regularities in the Speech of Children," in *Psycholinguistic Papers,* edited by J. Lyons and R. Wales (Edinburgh: Edinburgh University Press, 1966).

The role of correction in language development is examined in "Derivational Complexity and the Order of Acquisition in Child Speech" by R. Brown

and C. Hanlon in *Cognition and the Development of Language,* edited by
J. Hayes (New York: John Wiley & Sons, 1970) and in "Brown and Hanlon
Revisited: Mothers' Sensitivity to Ungrammatical Forms" by K. Hirsh-
Pasek, R. Treiman, and M. Schneiderman in *Journal of Child Language* 11:
81–88 (1984). The relationship between *yes-no* questions in parental speech
and the development of auxiliaries is discussed by E. Newport, H. Gleitman,
and L. Gleitman in their article, "Mother, I'd Rather Do It Myself: Some
Effects and Noneffects of Maternal Speech Style" in *Talking to Children,*
edited by C. Snow and C. Ferguson (London: Cambridge University Press,
1977).

Recommended Reading

Clark, Herbert and Eve Clark. 1977. *Psychology and Language.* New York:
Harcourt Brace Jovanovich.

De Villiers, Jill and Peter de Villiers. 1978. *Language Acquisition.* Cambridge, Mass.: Harvard University Press.

Ingram, David. 1976. *Phonological Disability in Children.* London: Edward
Arnold.

Locke, John. 1983. *Phonological Acquisition and Change.* New York: Academic Press.

Owens, Robert. 1984. *Language Development: An Introduction.* Columbus,
Ohio: Charles E. Merrill.

Piattelli-Palmarini, Massimo, ed. 1980. *Language and Learning: The Debate
between Jean Piaget and Noam Chomsky.* Cambridge, Mass.: Harvard University Press.

Wanner, Eric and Lila Gleitman, eds. 1982. *Language Acquisition: The State
of the Art.* London: Cambridge University Press.

Questions

1. The following transcriptions represent the pronunciation of a two-year-
   old child. Indicate which phonetic processes have applied in each case.
   a) Smith   [mɪt]
   b) skin   [kɪn]
   c) spoon   [buwn]
   d) zoo   [duw]
   e) John   [dɑn]
   f) bath   [bæt]
   g) other   [ʌdə]
   h) tent   [dɛt]
   i) teddy   [dɛdiy]
   j) brush   [bʌt]
   k) bump   [bʌp]

2. Drawing on the phonetic processes posited for the preceding exercise, predict one or more plausible immature pronunciations for each of the following words.
   a) show
   b) please
   c) spit
   d) under
   e) juice
   f) thumb
   g) zebra

3. Consider the following two speech samples. Determine the stage of development of this child in terms of his acquisition of negative constructions and question structures. What do we expect to happen next in the development of each structure?

   Sample A   Sample B
   a) no more noise   f) Who will read the book?
   b) no go in   g) What Evan will read?
   c) no fit   h) Where Evan will read?
   d) no it won't fit i) Why you see seal?
   e) no ready go   j) Why she want to?

4. Considering children's tendency to overgeneralize morphological rules, what might we expect a young child to use in place of the following adult words? Justify your choice in each case.
   a) fish (plural)
   b) went
   c) mice
   d) ate
   e) has
   f) geese
   g) brought
   h) hit (past tense)
   i) himself
   j) women

5. Consider the following examples of overextensions, all of which have actually been observed in children's speech. What is the basis for each of these overextensions?

	Word	First referent	Overextensions
a)	sch	sound of a train	music, noise of wheels, sound of rain
b)	bow-wow	dog	sheep, rabbit fur, puppet
c)	baby	baby	people in pictures
d)	sizo	scissors	nail file, knife, screwdriver, spoon

e)	policeman	policeman	mailman, sailor, doctor
f)	strawberry	strawberry	grapes, raspberry
g)	fireworks	fireworks	matches, light, cigarette

6. Each of the following utterances is from the speech of a child in the two-word stage. Identify the semantic relation expressed by each of these utterances.

	Child's utterance	Intended meaning
a)	Jimmy swim	Jimmy is swimming.
b)	Ken book	Ken's book.
c)	Daddy work	Daddy is at work.
d)	push baby	You push the baby.
e)	Mommy read	Mommy is reading.

7. The allomorphic variation associated with the third person singular verbal ending -*s* is identical to that found with plural -*s*. Make up a test parallel to the one discussed in Section 10.3. If possible, give your test to children between the ages of three and seven. Are your results similar to the ones discussed in the chapter?

11 SECOND LANGUAGE ACQUISITION

*The study of languages . . . should be joined to that
of objects, that our acquaintance with the objective
world and with language . . . may progress side by
side. For it is people we are forming and not parrots.*

Comenius, 1657

In the last chapter, we introduced some of the theories about how children acquire a first language and outlined the different stages through which children pass during the language acquisition process. Unlike the first language (L1) learner, the second language (L2) learner already has an established language system for communicating. Cognitively more mature, L2 learners do not approach a second language in the same manner as they do a first. These facts alone justify setting L2 acquisition apart from L1 acquisition and treating it as a separate field of study. The term **applied linguistics** is often used to refer to L2 research, in that it is directly concerned with the application of linguistic theory to second language teaching and learning.

At the outset, it is necessary to define some of the terminology indispensable to a discussion of L2 acquisition. The term **second language** is used to mean a language that is learned after the first or native language is relatively established. It is not applicable to the case of a child learning two languages simultaneously during a bilingual upbringing. The L2 acquisition process also includes learning a new language in a foreign language context (studying English in Japan) as well as learning a new language in the host environment (learning French in France). The term second language may refer to a second, third, fourth, or even fifteenth language.

Some L2 researchers make a strong distinction between L2 learning and L2 acquisition. They define *learning* as a deliberate, conscious attempt to master a language. In contrast, they define the term *acquisition* as a less deliberate, subconscious process of mastering language, and often associate it with the manner in which children acquire language. Other researchers maintain that learning and acquisition are distinct types of cognitive behavior, and that learned and acquired knowledge are totally unrelated. In this chapter, however, the two terms will be used interchangeably. Second language acquisition is taken here to involve both conscious and subconscious processes regardless of the age of the learner and the language learning environment.

11.1 QUESTIONS AND ISSUES

Is learning a second language at all similar to the way we learn a first language? What is the effect of age on the language learning process? How is the L2 learner's progress affected by the language learning environment and the type of linguistic input he or she receives? These are just a few of the many questions to which L2 researchers are committed to finding answers. The results of some of their efforts will be discussed in this section.

The Optimal Age Issue

It has long been claimed that the older the learner, the less successful he or she will be at learning a second language. The role of age in learning second languages is a controversial issue in L2 research.

Critical Period Hypothesis Among the traditional conceptions of L2 learning is the idea that children learning second languages in natural environments learn more easily and more proficiently than do adults under similar circumstances. This widely held belief has led to the idea that there is an optimal age or a critical period for L2 acquisition, which ends around the age of puberty. There are basically three considerations that are relevant to this idea: biological, cognitive, and affective.

The biological argument has already been introduced in Chapter 9. Proponents of this argument believe that a child's brain is more ''plastic'' and, consequently, should be more receptive to certain aspects of language acquisition, especially in the area of pronunciation. Some researchers claim that a basic linguistic process such as pronunciation is dependent on early maturing neural circuits that control the brain and organs used for speech, while higher-order language functions, such as the development of semantic relations, are more dependent on late maturing neural circuits. This is in part why some researchers claim that after puberty, languages have to be learned through a conscious, labored effort, and that foreign accents cannot be overcome easily after this time. This idea continues to be controversial, however, since the biological evidence is too scanty to support a satisfactory explanation for the alleged superiority of children over adults in L2 learning.

The cognitive argument is that the adult's superiority in the domain of abstract thought should give adults the edge over children in L2 acquisition. This has implications for adolescents and adults, who generally learn the second language in a formal setting where the emphasis is on the conscious learning of language structures and grammatical rules. However, dependence on conscious rule knowledge may also impede the natural process of L2 acquisition.

Affective or emotional differences between children and adults are also reputed to have a crucial influence on second language learning. While adolescents are learning to think more abstractly, they are also experiencing the familiar adolescent feelings of self-consciousness and anxiety. Children are generally less inhibited about mimicking sounds than are adults, and this may positively affect their pronunciation. Normally, children do not have negative attitudes toward the second language culture, and they usually have a strong desire to be part of a group or community, which enhances their desire to learn the language.

While "the younger the better" is still a popular recommendation for potential L2 learners, it is still being investigated. The biological, cognitive, and affective arguments conflict regarding the optimal time for learning a second language. Nevertheless, studies support the idea that the number of years of exposure to the second language and the starting age of the learner affect the ultimate level of success, especially regarding pronunciation. Although young children may initially learn more slowly than adults, they eventually surpass them.

The Role of Linguistic Input

Two factors crucial to L2 acquisition are the kind of language and the type of language learning environments to which an L2 learner is exposed. The language that learners hear serves as their learning model, and the environment in which they hear it affects how they view the second language and how they learn it.

Foreigner Talk and Teacher Talk As pointed out in Chapter 10, a great deal of attention has been concentrated on the language heard by the child and the way in which this language becomes more complex as the child matures. L2 researchers maintain that a special type of language input, not unlike caretaker speech, also exists for L2 learners. They have labeled this language **foreigner talk** or **teacher talk** depending on the situation. Both caretaker speech and foreigner or teacher talk are characterized by simplification of the linguistic code.

When speaking to L2 learners, native speakers choose simple word order and more common vocabulary items. They usually word explanations or questions carefully and attempt to produce well-formed utterances by avoiding false starts, slips of the tongue, unfinished sentences, and hesitations. They modify vocabulary by employing frequently used words, and avoiding idiomatic expressions such as *He flew off the handle* in favor of *He got angry*. Vocabulary that might be unfamiliar is often paraphrased, such as *hold on very tightly* for the verb *cling*.

The excerpt in *1a* exemplifies language that might be used by a teacher to native speakers of English in a classroom. The excerpt in *1b*, by way of comparison, illustrates what happens when the same teacher speaks to nonnative speakers of English in an ESL (English as a second language) situation.

1. a) (non-ESL situation) . . . I didn't recognize her at first sight.
   b) (same teacher in ESL situation) . . . I didn't know who she was when I first saw her.

While it is clear that many native speakers employ similar kinds of foreigner talk, it is not clear how such modifications affect the L2 learner's developing grammar, or whether the effects are positive or negative.

Some researchers maintain that the best way to improve an L2 learner's linguistic ability is through **comprehensible input**, input a little beyond the learner's linguistic competence. Such input is indispensable for language acquisition since, in order to acquire language most effectively, learners must understand a large portion of the language presented to them and must also be challenged by a more difficult structure. They can acquire the latter within the communicative context by using their extralinguistic knowledge. From this perspective, it appears that oversimplification of the linguistic code might have a negative effect on the L2 learner's progress. More research is needed before we can understand the precise effects of foreigner or teacher talk on L2 acquisition and the exact nature of comprehensible input.

The Language Learning Environment

L2 learning can take place in different environments: natural, formal, or a combination of both. Learning a second language in the host country or in an immersion program involves natural environments because the focus is on communication. Learning a second language in a classroom situation or in any situation where a prescribed course of study is followed involves formal environments. The combination of a formal and a natural environment might entail studying the second language in a classroom in the host country.

Language learners who return from studying a second language in the host country generally outperform students who have been exposed only to formally structured classroom situations. Living in the L2 country provides a natural environment for communicating that is rarely found in a classroom. Contacts with native speakers can also help to break down social and cultural barriers.

In the classroom or formal environment, L2 learners focus on formal aspects of the language and do not have much time for spontaneous conversation about daily events. They are usually occupied with drills, translation, and grammar, while only part of the class time is free for conversation and language games.

Natural and formal language learning environments offer different benefits to the L2 learner. While natural environments enhance communication skills, formal environments allow for learning of explicit rules that the student may apply accurately in certain linguistic situations. Allowing for formal language study tends to satisfy curiosity about language at the same time as it caters to individual language learning strategies. Such strategies can be strongly pronounced in adults who have developed specific learning styles over the years. As well, adults usually express a preference for structured language learning as opposed to the more natural environment, at least in the initial stages. Once they have established a solid base in the second language, they often choose an immersion program as the next step.

Comparing
L1 and L2
Acquisition

L2 researchers are divided over whether L1 and L2 acquisition are similar. There are numerous factors that must be considered when making such a comparison: age (cognitive, physiological, and affective maturity), the language learning environment, and the respective characteristics of the L1 and L2 systems being compared.

L1 and L2 Morpheme Acquisition Both L1 and L2 learners appear to acquire morphemes in specific orders. When the L1 and L2 orders are compared, however, several differences are apparent. In spite of these, some researchers claim that since there seems to be a universal order of acquisition for morphemes, both L1 and L2 acquisition are guided by universal cognitive mechanisms. Other investigators are more skeptical. They point out that the bulk of evidence on L2 grammatical morpheme acquisition is based on learners of English as a second language in North America. There is very little cross-linguistic evidence to support claims regarding natural acquisition orders for learners of other languages. To date, insufficient research has been done to explain similarities or differences between L1 and L2 acquisition orders.

Transitional Constructions In the domain of English syntactic development, specifically the learning of negation and interrogatives, L1 and L2 acquisition appear to share similar characteristics. Both L1 and L2 learners tend to negate externally at first (*No smoke*), then to negate internally (*I no smoke*), ultimately followed by the correct form (*I don't smoke*).

The acquisition patterns for *wh* questions and *yes-no* questions are also similar. Question acquisition begins with repeating an utterance with rising intonation (*I ride car?*), followed by use of *wh* words sentence-initially without inverting the auxiliary. Finally, verbs are inverted correctly for both *wh* and *yes-no* questions. Both L1 and L2 learners continue for some time to make mistakes in tense and agreement.

These different stages of syntactic development consist of **transitional constructions** and are said to make up **developmental sequences**. While many of the stages in L1 and L2 acquisition appear to be similar, some researchers have found that L2 learners produce a wider variety of forms in a single developmental phase. Other have noted that the transitional constructions produced by L2 learners do not necessarily exist in their native language. Some researchers use these findings to support the idea that there are universal mental mechanisms involved in learning a second language, although more cross-linguistic evidence is needed to confirm these claims.

Researchers have also discovered that **routines** and **patterns** are employed by both L1 and L2 learners in the early stages of language acquisition. In L1 research, it has been noted that children often produced unanalyzed stretches or chunks of speech that are considerably beyond their developing rule system in terms of complexity. Routines are defined as whole utterances that are error free and appear to be learned as unanalyzed wholes, similar to the way a single word is learned. For instance, a child may say *Lookit* or *It's my turn* in order to participate in play activities. Patterns are partially analyzed utterances with open slots for a word or phrase such as *Gimme* _____or *D'you wanna* _____? The child may not segment the words correctly at first, not realizing that *Gimme* ('Give me') is in fact two words and not one.

It appears that L2 learners rely more heavily on routines and patterns than L1 learners. Thrust into the communicative situation, the L2 learner needs these devices to allow social interaction despite minimal linguistic competence. Routines such as *How do you do* or *Happy to meet you* are typical of the chunks learned in the initial L2 learning stages. By using routines and patterns, L2 learners can begin communication in the second language before acquiring the structures of that language. Some linguists even believe that the early memorization of routines and patterns is central to the acquisition of rule-governed language.

*11.2 THE STUDY OF SECOND LANGUAGE ACQUISITION

The field of L2 research, as we know it today, is less than twenty years old. To a great extent, it has followed a pattern of research similar to that of L1 acquisition, borrowing and adapting many of the L1 research techniques. Like L1 research (see Chapter 10), L2 research employs both naturalistic and experimental studies. When conducting experimental studies, researchers typically make use of several kinds of tasks.

The **structured communication task** involves testing L2 learners' knowledge of a specific second language structure such as negation or *wh* questions. For example, hoping to elicit a negative construction, the researcher asks *Do you have a pet elephant?* and the subject may answer *No, I don't.* Such a task is commonly used in experimental studies. A **nonstructured communication task** is simply natural conversation between the researcher and L2 learner, with no special focus on a particular language structure. It is most often used in longitudinal studies, in which large amounts of dialogue data are collected from the same subject or group of subjects over an extended period of time.

In a **linguistic manipulation task**, the subject's attention is directed to the language forms themselves. For example, asking an L2 learner to change the proper nouns to a pronoun in the sentence *Jeremy and Jessica competed for first place* requires the subject to manipulate certain elements.

The results from these different tasks may not be directly comparable. Communicative tasks require a less conscious approach than do linguistic manipulation tasks, which require a conscious focus on a linguistic detail, a process rarely engaged in when conversing naturally.

In order to obtain a complete picture of the L2 acquisition process, it is necessary to combine the findings from both naturalistic and experimental studies, keeping in mind that differences in the tasks may affect the results. Studies conducted on a wide range of different languages are also needed in the quest for universals of second language acquisition. For example, in order to discover more about the universal processes involved in the acquisition of complex sentence structures such as relative clauses, many languages and language types must be considered.

In the sections to follow, we will examine several aspects of the L2 learner's development as investigated by recent studies. The research findings we present concentrate on learning English as a second language, a reflection of the current focus of L2 research.

Phonological Development

Many studies have been done in the area of L2 phonological development. Children acquiring a language in the second language environment are likely to achieve a nativelike pronunciation whereas adults are not. While it is possible for adults to acquire a nativelike accent, it is more often the exception than the rule.

The phonological domain is an area where a learner's first and second language clearly interact. It has been postulated that the L2 elements that are similar to those in the L1 repertoire will be replaced by those elements in the early stages. However, L2 sounds that do not exist in the L1 will follow their own course of development, in much the same way as sounds develop in the native language. While L2 phonological acquisition may be similar to L1 acquisition in this regard, it is very different in other respects. L2 learners must produce complex phonetic sequences from the very beginning. Their first attempts at pronunciation are not restricted to labial and alveolar stops and low vowels, which are predominant in the early stages of L1 acquisition.

As a result of the L1 and L2 phonological interactions, pronunciation errors may systematically reflect the structure of each learner's respective native language. For example, a German speaker using English may say *I am sat* instead of *I am sad,* applying the final consonant devoicing rule of German. Korean speakers may tell you that they saw a *ship in the field* when they actually saw a *sheep*, since Korean has a rule that laxes vowels in closed syllables. These examples are cases of **interference** or **negative transfer**, the inappropriate use of an L1 structure in the L2 system.

Such errors usually arise in the early stages of L2 acquisition in the phonological, syntactic, and morphological domains. Instances of transfer from the phonological domain are generally not as easily modified as those in the areas of syntax and morphology. Many people who come from various L1 backgrounds and have lived in the second language culture for a long time master the second language syntax and lexicon, but may not lose their accents.

Morphological Development

In their efforts to study the L2 acquisition of grammatical morphemes, L2 researchers were inspired by Roger Brown's classic longitudinal study of child L1 learners. They wanted to determine whether there also exists a common order of acquisition among L2 learners of various language backgrounds. The performance of child and adult L2 learners has been investigated independently, as age is considered a crucial factor.

Child L2 Morpheme Acquisition Data have been obtained from both cross-sectional and longitudinal studies of children learning English from more than twenty-two language backgrounds, including Afghani, Arabic, Chinese, Greek, Hebrew, Italian, Japanese, Korean, Persian, Spanish, Thai, Turkish, and Vietnamese. It has been found that these children showed a similar order of acquisition regardless of their first language. The emphasis in some research of this type has been on establishing a developmental order for groups of morphemes, rather than for the individual morphemes themselves. Figure 11.1 indicates the groups of morphemes that some researchers have found to make up different developmental stages.

Group 1	Case contrasts in pronouns *(he-him, they-them, she-her)*	

Group 2	Singular copula *('s / is)*	Singular auxiliary *('s / is)*
	Plural auxiliary *(are)*	Progressive *(-ing)*
	Plural *(-s)*	

Group 3	Past irregular *(went)*	Conditional auxiliary *(would)*
	Possessive *('s)*	Plural *(-es)*
	Third person singular *(-s)*	

Group 4	Perfect auxiliary *(have)*	Past participle *(-en)*

Figure 11.1 Child L2 grammatical morpheme acquisition

Adult L2 Morpheme Acquisition Using many of the same morphemes, L2 researchers decided to investigate the possibility that adults, like children, acquired these morphemes in an invariant order. With the help of structured oral communication tasks, another study concluded that adults from at least sixteen different language groups acquired eleven grammatical morphemes in more or less the same order. When we compare the order of acquisition for adults and children for eight of the grammatical morphemes in question, it is obvious that, in spite of some differences, the acquisition sequence is remarkably similar, regardless of the subject's age or language background (see Figure 11.2). (The groupings for child L2 learners correspond to those illustrated in Figure 11.1.) Many researchers have suggested that frequency of occurrence in the speech of native speakers may explain the order of morpheme acquisition, but to date this claim has not been substantiated. An alternative explanation involves the notion of communicative impact, which

	Child L2 learners	Adult L2 learners
Group 2	Plural (-s) Progressive (-ing) Singular copula ('s/is) Singular auxiliary ('s/is) Articles (the, a)	Progressive (-ing) Singular copula ('s/is) Plural (-s) Articles (the, a) Singular auxiliary ('s/is)
Group 3	Past irregular (went) Third person singular (-s) Possessive ('s)	Past irregular (went) Third person singular (-s) Possessive ('s)

Figure 11.2 L2 acquisition patterns for children and adults

predicts that L2 learners will learn morphemes according to their relative importance for understanding a message. For example, the plural affix -s is one of the first morphemes learned. This morpheme marks plural number, which is very important to the meaning of an utterance such as *The girls came over*. (Many girls are coming as opposed to only one.) This plural marker is learned prior to the possessive *'s* (for example, *Jed's car*), perhaps because the possessive relation can be inferred from the word order and so need not be marked morphologically. When learners are communicating, they usually focus on content and not on form. Therefore, only the semantically more important items receive priority in the initial stages of grammatical morpheme acquisition.

These explanations are still speculative. However, many researchers prefer to interpret the invariant order of morpheme acquisition as evidence for universal processing strategies among children and adults similar to those observed in L1 acquisition.

Syntactic Development

Recently, the focus of attention has shifted from the acquisition of certain morphological structures to include studies on specific syntactic structures, especially negation and interrogatives.

Negation Regardless of native language background, L2 learners appear to learn basic English sentence negation in four steps, as shown in Table 11.1.

The most common first attempt at negating in English is to place the negative particle *no* (or occasionally *not*) before the phrase to be negated.

It must be noted that the steps toward the mastery of negation are not so clearly delineated for every L2 learner. To some degree, variation depends on the native language of the L2 learner. Spanish L1 speakers, for

Table 11.1 Negation structures

Stage 1	External negation	No your sitting here. No smoke. No happy. Not cold.
Stage 2	Internal negation: *No* occurs inside the negated phrase. *Don't* may appear but is considered as an unanalyzed unit or chunk. (The learner is not conscious of the two units *do* and *not*.)	I no can sing. She no come tomorrow. I don't can explain.
Stage 3	Auxiliary verbs may be used. *No* or *not* are used correctly with main and auxiliary verbs.	You not doing it. I won't try. No, I didn't.
Stage 4	The target language structure is acquired: the use of auxiliaries is consistently correct, and the construction (*no* + verb) disappears. Tense and agreement are marked, but not always perfectly.	He doesn't know he won. I didn't felt it.

instance, tend to spend more time on the first step of external negation since their language contains many sentences structurally similar to those used in the first stage. For example, *No estudio mucho,* which translates as 'I don't study a lot', literally means 'not (I) study much'. Some L2 learners also exhibit a preference for either *no* or *not* in the initial stages.

Questions Research on the development of *wh* questions and *yes-no* questions is based on studies of children, adolescents, and adults with different language backgrounds. The acquisition of these two question types will be discussed together.

The *wh* question in English requires the speaker to perform two operations. First, the speaker is required to place a *wh* word (*what, why, who, where, when,* or *how*) at the beginning of the sentence. Second, it is necessary to invert the auxiliary verb and the subject. For example, in order to form a *wh* question in response to the statement *Henrietta will sing a song,* the speaker will make the following changes.

2. *a*) Prepose *wh* word. (What Henrietta will sing?)
   b) Invert subject and auxiliary verb. (What will Henrietta sing?)

During the first stage in the development of questions, the learner's first interrogative structure is often a sentence with rising intonation with no inversion or fronted *wh* words. The acquisition of *wh* questions and *yes-no* questions is a gradual process, and the stages given in Table 11.2 may overlap. They do not always emerge in this order, and some L2 learners, depending on their native language, may linger at one stage longer than at others or may develop a different stage. German L1 speakers, for example, often invert the main verb, producing questions such as *Sing you those*

Table 11.2 Question structures

Stage 1	Rising intonation, no inversion. Some *wh* questions such as *What this?* appear at this stage but they seem to be learned as chunks.	Mickey is painting?
Stage 2	True production of *wh* questions begins. The auxiliary is usually omitted, so there is no subject-auxiliary inversion.	What you study? What the time? What you doing?
Stage 3	Auxiliaries such as *is*, *are*, and *was* appear, but are not yet inverted systematically with the subject.	Where is the woman? Are you a teacher? What she is singing?
Stage 4	For *wh* questions, the verbs *is*, *are*, and *was* tend to be regularly inverted. The auxiliaries *do* and *am* are still omitted at this stage, although inversion with *do* may begin for *yes-no* questions.	Who are they? What he saw? Do you work in the school?
Stage 5	The auxiliaries *do*, *am*, and *has* are acquired and correctly inverted with subjects in *wh* questions. However, the *do* in *yes-no* questions may still be misformed.	Where do you live? When are you leaving? Do he see that?

songs? until they learn to insert *do*. This is probably because main verbs as well as auxiliaries may undergo inversion in German.

11.3 METHODS OF ANALYSIS

We have seen how L2 learners follow a clear developmental route, making errors at different stages as they experiment and revise their linguistic knowledge. Achieving fluency in a second language is evidently a creative process, one of trial and error, revision and reconstruction.

Contrastive Analysis

Seeking to improve L2 teaching methodologies, early researchers came to believe that by comparing and contrasting the learner's native language with the second language, new insights could be gained into the language learning process. This approach is known as **contrastive analysis (CA)**. It was claimed that the errors produced by the learner would occur at those points at which the two languages were dissimilar.

Consider, for example, the English-speaking L2 learner who wants to say *I am ten years old* in French. The correct structure is *J'ai dix ans* (literally, 'I have ten years'). It can be predicted that many students will produce *Je suis dix ans* ('I am ten years'), substituting the verb *être* ('to be') for *avoir* ('to have'), a direct translation of the English form. This illustrates the idea behind comparing L1 and L2 language structures so that potential trouble spots can be predicted and focused on in the L2 lesson.

In time, many researchers questioned the theoretical and practical relevance of CA. They discovered that not all errors could be predicted from the source language. Some errors were unique and did not reflect the L1 structure. The L2 learner's language could be quite variable according to context and situation, and CA did not take this into account. Moreover, the anticipated improvements in teaching methodology were not forthcoming. Whether or not teachers could predict errors seemed to have little to do with the effectiveness of their teaching.

Error Analysis

From the CA perspective, any errors in L2 production, especially those that evidently involved negative transfer, were viewed as evidence of the L2 learner's incompetence with the second language. In time, however, L2 researchers and teachers began to view the learner as a creative participant in his or her language development. This, in turn, affected their view of the L2 learner's errors. An approach known as **error analysis (EA)** saw errors as indicators of the learner's current underlying knowledge of the second language, or as clues to the hypotheses that a learner may be testing about the second language. In this sense, errors provide us with insights into the language system that L2 learners are acquiring and using at a particular period. Such an L2 system is called **interlanguage**.

Interlanguage is viewed as a dynamic system since it changes constantly as the learner progresses through a theoretically infinite number of states of grammatical development along a continuum. The learner starts with the native language and continuously revises and extends rules until fluency in the second language is attained. Each L2 learner's interlanguage is unique. As learners progress toward nativelike proficiency in the second language, their interlanguage is characterized by fewer and fewer errors.

Proponents of EA claim that a careful study of a large corpus of spoken and written errors committed by L2 learners provides data that can help teachers determine the L2 learner's development. They therefore concentrate their efforts on the description and classification of various kinds of errors, with an explanation of these errors as their ultimate goal.

Error Types Research on L2 learners' interlanguages has resulted in the identification of several types of errors. Such errors fall roughly into two categories: interlingual and developmental. **Interlingual** errors are the result of L1 interference, implying that some structure from the native language has been transferred to the second language, as in the example above of English speakers learning how to talk about their age in French.

When L2 errors cannot be accounted for on the basis of the first language, they are considered to be **developmental**; that is, to result from the manner in which the language acquisition mechanisms themselves operate. These errors arise from a mismatch between the L2 learner's grammar and that of the native speaker. Such errors are considered developmental because they represent evidence of the learners' attempts to acquire language based upon their hypotheses about the language they are learning.

A comparison of adult and child L2 learners shows that adults tend to exhibit more first language influence in their errors than do children. The adult errors that reflect the L1 structure generally comprise about 30 percent of the total number of errors, the remainder being developmental. Allowing for problems in identifying the causes of errors, the percentages suggest that L1 interference is not the prime cause of learner errors.

It must be noted that because of the ambiguous nature of many errors, the distinction between interlingual and developmental errors is not always clear. When an L2 learner uses the double negative in English (*I don't know nothing about it*), there is no way of knowing whether this is a developmental error or whether the learner has picked up a structure from a nonstandard dialect.

Within the interlingual and developmental categories, errors can also be classified according to the grammatical subsystem involved: phonology, syntax, morphology, and semantics. Errors can be further classified as errors of omission, addition, or substitution (the L2 learner may omit certain items, add unnecessary ones, or exchange one element for another). Items may also be misordered or misformed either phonologically or morphologically. Table 11.3 provides one example of how errors may be classified by creating an error taxonomy. Whether these errors are classifiable as interlingual or developmental can be determined only by comparing the relevant L1 and L2 structures and by examining the errors within the corpus of the data from which they were extracted, namely, the discourse produced by the L2 learner.

Many researchers argue that comparative taxonomies focus too much on the error tokens themselves and not enough on the communicative effect

Table 11.3 Taxonomy of interlanguage errors

Grammatical subsystem	Sample error	Description	Category
Morphology	He was call.	Omission	Developmental: past participle form not acquired
	Why didn't you came to work?	Addition	Developmental: double marking of past tense
Syntax	What this is?	Misordering	Developmental: misordering of the verb
Phonology	Man is eborubing. (evolving)	Substitution and addition (/b/ substituted for /v/, /r/ substituted for /l/ ; /u/ added)	Interlingual: phonological interference from Japanese
Semantics	She is a sensible person.	Substitution (*sensible* for *sensitive*)	Interlingual: French lexical interference (French *sensible* = English *sensitive*)

of these errors. What effects do certain types of errors have on a reader or listener? What kinds of errors result in total miscommunication between the L2 learner and the native speaker?

The Communicative Effect Taxonomy Several communicative effect taxonomies have subsequently been developed by having native English speakers make judgments about the comprehensibility of sentences with different types of errors. Apparently, errors that significantly hinder communication involve word order as in *3*, connectors as in *4*, and other features of sentence organization.

> 3. *a*) Marcella amused that movie very much. (produced utterance)
>   *b*) That movie amused Marcella very much. (intended utterance)
> 4. *a*) She will be rich until she marries. (produced utterance)
>   *b*) She will be rich *when* she marries. (intended utterance)

However, in the sentence *My husband not here,* communication is not impeded even though the verb is missing. Nor does the following error in verb complement affect intelligibility: *My doctor suggests me to take a vacation.* It is understood that the speaker meant 'My doctor suggests that I should take a vacation'.

Determining the effect of learners' errors is a complex and problematic task. The way in which native speakers respond to these errors will vary according to their age, their educational level, and the extent of their communication with foreigners. Also, perceptions of errors may vary according to the context in which they are presented (informal or formal), and whether the errors are being read or heard.

Although the development of taxonomies is important in error analysis, merely describing an error does not provide an explanation that would lend insight into the strategies an L2 learner might be using. The EA field is presently moving in the direction of error explanation but, so far, with little success.

11.4 THE LEARNER

During the past decade of L2 studies, researchers have realized that there is a need to focus more sharply on how L2 learners master the complexities of a new grammatical system. They have subsequently examined in greater detail the kinds of strategies learners may use as well as their personality characteristics. Both are crucial to the development of L2 theory and teaching methodologies.

Language Learner Strategies

At present, there are numerous definitions of the term **strategy**. In this chapter, we define strategies as the mental processes involved (1) in forming and testing hypotheses about linguistic input, and (2) in using linguistic knowledge in communicative situations. Although an elaborate taxonomy of learner strategies has been developed, we will consider only three types that are particularly relevant to language learning: learning strategies, production strategies, and communication strategies.

Learning Strategies are the ways in which language learners process language input and develop linguistic knowledge. These processes may be subconscious (unplanned) or conscious (deliberate). Recall the overgeneralization shown by children when learning to form the past tense (as when the past tense of *go* is produced as *goed*). This is also evidenced in L2 acquisition, as was illustrated in the section on error analysis. The process of overgeneralization is considered to be a subconscious one; the L2 learner is unwittingly relying on prior knowledge and extending it to create new language forms.

The memorization of prefabricated or formulaic speech, such as the routines and patterns employed by L1 and L2 learners (*I dunno, I can't speak English*), is another subconscious learning strategy. The learner frequently hears these patterns used in a communicative situation and absorbs them without analyzing the separate components. Although the process is unobservable, the patterns themselves are the observable products of the related and conscious strategy of pattern imitation. The imitation of certain language patterns is often encouraged in L2 classrooms as a teaching technique.

Production Strategies are employed by L2 learners when attempting to use their learned linguistic knowledge in communication. Production strategies may include the preplanning or rehearsing of utterances as well as the correction of utterances.

Preplanning in production involves choosing the components of the utterance (nouns, verbs, adjectives and adverbs, affixes and inflections, and their corresponding phonetic realizations) with a communicative objective in mind. Correcting or monitoring strategies are a part of the rehearsing aspect of production. Learners use a monitoring strategy when they correct what they want to say just before they say it or immediately afterwards.

Communication Strategies, like production strategies, serve communicative needs. However, they differ in that they are used when L2 learners lack the appropriate linguistic knowledge to say what they want to say. A communication strategy is usually a conscious plan instigated to fulfill an immediate communicative need. For example, an L2 learner may want to say *The teacher made the child go home,* but he or she does not know the causative form *make*, and therefore uses his or her available knowledge to say *She asked the child to go home*. In many cases, the result may be a slight modification of the original intent of the message, but the central idea is conveyed.

Communication strategies encompass a host of substrategies, which involve paraphrasing, substituting one word for another (such as *animal* for *giraffe*), borrowing from the native language (transfer), or avoiding certain structures altogether by changing the topic of conversation. L2 learners make use of such strategies to keep a conversation going. Understandably, the use of communication strategies is more prevalent in a natural environment than in a formal environment. The memorization of tourist ''survival language'' for on-the-spot communication is a familiar example of a popular communication strategy.

L2 versus L1 Learner Strategies Language learner strategies include learning, production, and communication strategies, among many others. Many L2 learners employ similar strategies: they overgeneralize, they transfer certain aspects of their native language, and they simplify various L2 structures as they subconsciously or consciously test their hypotheses about the second language. We have seen that some of these strategies are similar to those applied by children during the L1 acquisition process as they infer rules and draw conclusions about the language they hear. Not unlike children, L2 learners often need a **silent period** (a period of aural exposure to the language) so that incoming information may be processed and stored in memory. Once stored, it is ready for use in spontaneous production, and ultimately becomes a permanent part of the L2 repertoire.

L2 strategies, however, differ from those employed by L1 learners due to the L2 learner's cognitive maturity, longer attention span, and greater memory capacity. L2 learners may have a different drive to communicate depending on their language learning environment. Strategies will also vary according to the cognitive makeup and personality of the learner.

Cognitive Style

The term **cognitive style** refers to the way in which we are predisposed to process information in our environment. Whether we are trying to learn calculus or a new language, we need to perceive and develop concepts, to organize them, to store them in memory, and to be able to recall them. The manner and speed with which we do all of these things is believed to depend on our particular cognitive or learning style.

Currently, L2 researchers are examining several cognitive styles in order to determine their relationship to the way in which we learn languages. The styles that have received the most attention in recent research are **field independence** and **field dependence**.

It is assumed that an individual will have a tendency to be either predominantly field independent or field dependent to varying degrees along a continuum. A person who tends to be field independent is characterized as a highly rational, analytic personality. A field independent cognitive style enables a person to separate the components of a whole picture or idea to focus on one component without being distracted by the neighboring components. Such a person could probably study for a biology exam in a noisy college cafeteria.

The dominantly field dependent person, on the other hand, relies on the whole picture or total field to the point where the separate components of the picture are not easily perceived. Instead, this person perceives the picture as a total experience or a unified whole.

It has been hypothesized that the more successful language learners are the ones who can focus on the language stimuli relevant to the language learning task at hand and disregard inappropriate ones. This supposedly relates to the ability to isolate and identify single words. Less successful learners will be more easily distracted by irrelevant cues, as they are dependent on the entire stimulus field and cannot select the proper cues for attention. This might lead one to conclude that field independent types would make better L2 learners than field dependent types. Field dependence, however, is associated with empathy and openness, qualities that characterize people who would be highly motivated to communicate and to integrate into the L2 community.

Recent research indicates that both styles may be equally important for L2 learning depending on the L2 learning context. Field independent people are purportedly more successful in the traditional classroom setting where the focus is usually on analytical oral and written activities, whereas field dependent people are expected to do well in a natural setting where communication is the focus.

We must keep in mind that tests that label students as one type or another ignore the possibility that an individual may approach different tasks in different ways. For example, solving a mathematical problem as opposed to learning new L2 vocabulary will require people to adapt their cognitive styles. It is a misconception to think that field independence or field dependence is invariable within one person. Instead, most people have general inclinations one way or another, and when given certain contexts, they will rely on the most appropriate style for the problem at hand, as well as the most effective strategy.

Personality

A person who appears hopeless at language is not necessarily lacking in the appropriate intellectual ability; it may be a personality trait that inhibits him: he may be resisting what seems to him an encroachment on his personality.

W. E. Lambert

Many psychologists argue that personality is inseparably related to our cognitive or learning style. L2 researchers have tried to isolate and investigate several personality traits that they believe to have implications for success or failure in learning a second language. Aptitude, motivation, attitude, and empathy are a few of the many traits studied for their potential effects on the language learning process.

Aptitude Whether an L2 learner is an adult or a child, it is assumed that some people have a special talent, a knack, or an aptitude for learning a second language. Aptitude involves having verbal intelligence (familiarity with words and the ability to reason analytically about verbal materials). Questions remain concerning the effect of aptitude on L2 success and the accuracy with which varying degrees of aptitude can be measured to account for the rate of development or eventual success or failure in L2 learning.

Motivation In L2 acquisition, motivation is described as the need or desire the learner feels to learn the second language. Two kinds of motivation have been cited with respect to how they affect language acquisition: integrative motivation and instrumental motivation.

Integrative motivation is defined as a desire to achieve proficiency in a new language in order to participate in the life of the community that speaks the language. Someone motivated in this sense exhibits a sincere and personal interest in the people and the culture represented by the group.

Instrumental motivation is identified as the desire to achieve proficiency in a new language for utilitarian reasons, such as getting a job or a promotion. Thus, it reflects the practical value and advantages of learning a new language.

Both types of motivation may influence the rate and quality of L2 acquisition, each being more effective under specific conditions. In fact, most situations involve both types of motivation. For example, English-speaking civil servants working in New York City might be motivated to improve their Spanish proficiency by the prospect of a salary increase. In addition, working in a predominantly Spanish-speaking community, they might be motivated by the desire to understand better the people they serve. In this case, they are both instrumentally and integratively motivated.

There is no doubt that motivation plays a critical role in determining the success or failure of L2 learners. Still unresolved are the problems of measuring motivation and its different manifestations to determine its exact effects.

Attitude L2 learners' attitudes are said to reflect their beliefs or opinions about the second language and culture, as well as their own culture. Some researchers believe that attitude and motivation are closely related. They claim that integrative and instrumental motivation reflect the basic attitude of the language learner toward learning languages and toward the second language culture. For example, an English-speaking American's positive attitude and desire to understand Hispanic Americans will lead to high integrative motivation to learn Spanish. The extent to which learners prefer their own language over the one they are learning is an important attitudinal factor.

Negative attitudes may lead to decreased motivation and in all likelihood failure to attain proficiency. In an L2 learning situation, projecting a positive attitude is also a necessary ingredient for keeping communication lines open, which in turn inevitably leads to the acquisition of better communication skills.

Empathy Empathy has been defined as the ability to put oneself in someone else's shoes. An empathic L2 learner has the capacity for participation in another's feelings or ideas, to project his or her personality into the personality of another. Some researchers propose that empathic people will be favorably predisposed to learning languages in a natural environment. They may more easily emulate a nativelike pronunciation since they are purportedly less inhibited than others. Furthermore, because of their sensitivity to others, empathic people may be better at picking up nuances of word meaning and their implications in different linguistic contexts. While these suppositions are not unreasonable, they remain as suppositions since their implications are extremely difficult to quantify.

11.5 TEACHING METHODOLOGIES

The field of applied linguistics has been influenced by theoretical trends in linguistics, psychology, and sociology. This influence is reflected in the various methodologies and approaches in second language teaching over the years. A brief look at some of the approaches prevalent before the 1960s as well as the most recent developments will help to outline the often divergent directions of L2 teaching and learning philosophies and to focus on what can be expected in the future.

Grammar Translation Method

The most traditional method for L2 teaching is the **grammar translation method**, which has its roots in the way in which Latin and Greek have been taught for centuries. This method emphasizes reading, writing, translation, and the conscious learning of grammatical rules. Its primary goal is to develop literary mastery of the second language. Memorization is the main learning strategy and students spend their class time talking "about the language" instead of "in the language." The curriculum requires the memorization of paradigms, patterns, and vocabulary, with translation being used to test the acquired knowledge. Consequently, the role of L1 is quite prominent.

Such an approach satisfied the needs of traditional humanist education for many years, until World War II created a greater demand for L2 speakers with highly developed speaking and listening skills. Today, the grammar translation method is still popular in many education systems and makes up some part of many L2 curricula.

Direct Method

The **direct method**, which originated in the seventeenth century, was revived in the 1900s as an alternative to grammar translation. Advocates of this method believe that adult L2 learners can learn a second language in essentially the same manner as a child. Therefore, if possible, the teacher should try to create a natural learning environment within the classroom. Instead of explicit grammar instruction, the major emphasis is on communicating. Classes are carried out totally in the second language with absolutely no reliance on the first language or on any form of translation. The expectation is that through question and answer dialogues, the second language will gradually be acquired. Problems have arisen with such an approach because adults do not in fact learn exactly like children, and they express the need for explicit instruction in grammar and other aspects of the second language.

Audiolingual Method

Neither grammar translation nor the direct method was based on any particular linguistic or psychological theory. Searching for an alternative to these two approaches, preferably one with a strong theoretical foundation, L2 teachers and researchers turned to the linguistic and behaviorist learning theories of the 1950s. These two theories provided the foundation for the **audiolingual method**.

The audiolingual method in some sense represents a return to the direct method, as its main goal is to develop nativelike speaking ability in its learners. Translation and reference to L1 are not permitted. Underlying this approach, however, is the notion that L2 learning should be regarded as a mechanistic process of habit formation.

In classrooms and language laboratories, students are conditioned to respond correctly to either oral or written stimuli. Since proponents of this method assume that language is a set of conditioned habits, students are not granted time to think about their responses but are required to respond immediately to a model utterance. Language learning is not viewed as a creative, cognitive process but as mechanical mimicry.

Audiolingual learning comprises dialogue memorization and pattern drills, thus ensuring careful control of responses. None of the drills or patterns are to be explained, since knowledge of grammatical rules would only obstruct the mechanical formation of habits. The audiolingual method enjoyed a long period of popularity, but is rarely used today in its entirety.

Eventually, work in cognitive psychology and transformational grammar undermined the view that linguistic behavior was based on habit formation and could be effectively learned through rote memorization exercises. Cognitive psychologists maintain that the mind is an active agent in the language learning process, and is not just passively influenced by environmental factors. Language must be taught and learned as a functional system applicable in communicative contexts, and not as a series of drills or abstract rules. This approach is presently manifested to some degree in communicative language teaching.

Communicative Language Teaching

During the past decade, the development of **communicative language teaching methods**, an approach that seeks to produce communicatively competent language learners, has been heralded as the future direction for L2 researchers and teachers. While it appears that the notions behind communicative competence are replacing the underpinnings of audiolingualism and grammar translation, the transition has not been entirely smooth.

Misinterpretation of the concept of **communicative competence** itself is in part responsible for the confusion. Becoming communicatively competent does not simply entail having the ability for spontaneous self-expression. While it includes having grammatical knowledge of the system, it also extends into a more abstract domain: knowledge of the appropriateness of language use. This domain includes sociocultural knowledge, paralinguistic (facial and gestural) and proxemic (spatial) knowledge, and sensitivity to the level of language use in certain situations and relationships, depending on whether they are formal or casual. Merely knowing how to produce a grammatically correct sentence is not enough. A communicatively competent person must also know how to produce an appropriate, natural, and socially acceptable utterance in all contexts of communication. *Hey, buddy, you fix my car!* is grammatically correct but not as effective in most social contexts as *Excuse me, sir, I was wondering whether I could have my car fixed today*.

In the past, most methodologies have concentrated on grammar, vocabulary, and pronunciation. Now, with the focus shifted to the learners and how they might learn to use language, many teachers are at a loss to understand the exact constituents of a communicative language teaching approach or method. Communicative language teaching has become an umbrella term to cover many approaches that purport to be communicative in design. In many cases, this approach emphasizes content and not form. By providing the student with authentic communicative activities involving relevant themes and topics, the experiential aspect of L2 learning is emphasized. It is assumed that if the students interact with second language speakers using real-life subject matter, the language will be acquired subconsciously.

Since language always operates within a sociocultural context, many people also believe that such a context should be an integral part of any communicative method. L2 researchers and teachers have realized too that any L2 method must be founded on psycholinguistic insights about the cognitive processes involved in acquiring a second language. More research is needed in the area of learner strategies in order to improve our current understanding of the language learning process and to develop better teaching methods.

The Role of the Teacher The teacher who chooses a communicative methodology must be prepared to play a new part in the classroom. Throwing out a one-way communication line is no longer sufficient. Rather, the teacher must adopt several roles: a mediator in a group-dynamic situation, a catalyst for ideas, a facilitator of communication, an advisor and organizer. The teacher must cultivate an awareness of individual learner differences, which vary with the L2 learner's age, sex, background, and socioeconomic status. This awareness must extend to choosing teaching materials that are truly communicative in nature. Students need real-life problems to solve in the second language, such as calling an airline and asking for flight times or having dinner at someone's home in the L2 culture. These activities can be simulated in the classroom or can actually be carried out in the community. Role-playing (with specific instructions) as well as self-awareness activities that concentrate on personal feelings, opinions, and attitudes of the L2 learner are invaluable stimuli for productive communication.

Multiple Methodologies L2 teachers and researchers are realizing that one method alone will not satisfy the demands of language learners of different ages, different learning styles, diverse backgrounds, and varying degrees of motivation. Today we see the emergence of a variety of new communicative approaches that are being used primarily in adult L2 education. These recent approaches take into consideration that more than cognitive factors need attention in the L2 acquisition process. Their orientations are subsequently more holistic or humanistic. They attempt to provide a nonthreatening environment where teacher and classmates provide support to each L2 learner. In this manner, one can deal with the complex affective aspect of the learner's personality, an aspect that has often been overlooked in the past.

Total physical response is the most widely publicized of these approaches. It takes into consideration the silent period deemed necessary for some L2 learners. During the first phase of total physical response, students are not required to speak. Instead, they concentrate on obeying simple commands in the second language. These commands eventually become more complex. For example, *Walk to the door* becomes *Scratch your head while you walk to the door at the back of the classroom.* Students later become more actively involved, verbally and creatively. The objective of this approach is to connect physical activity with meaningful language use as a way of instilling concepts. Proponents claim that it is very effective in the initial to early intermediate stages of L2 acquisition.

In the **community counseling** classroom, L2 learners are told that they are part of a group and not a class. This group identification supposedly reduces potential anxieties and provides a great deal of emotional support to the learner. The teacher is seen in the role of a counselor, while the students are clients. A client begins communication in his or her native language, the counselor translates, and the client repeats the utterance. Then another client picks up the conversation, which is then continued by another, and so forth. The conversation proceeds in this fashion with the counselor intervening to translate. The session is taped so that linguistic rules and certain utterances may be explained later.

Students who learn via the **natural approach** are also not expected to communicate verbally in the second language from the outset. They spend class time involved in communicative activities such as problem-solving tasks and language games, often working in pairs. Students may, however, respond using their native language and can decide for themselves when they are ready for the second language. Errors are ignored unless communication is impaired. Formal explanations and grammar exercises are completed outside the classroom environment. Teachers using this approach claim that rapid acquisition of listening and speaking skills is enhanced, as there is a tremendous amount of comprehensible input available to the students during their silent period.

11.6 THE IMMERSION APPROACH

Over the last decade, **immersion** programs have become increasingly popular as a way of teaching children a second language, especially for Spanish in the United States and French in Canada. In this context, immersion means that students are instructed in most of their courses and school activities in the second language. Instruction is usually begun in the second language and eventually incorporates the native language.

The main objective of any immersion program is that all students acquire a high level of proficiency in oral, listening, and literacy skills. Attempts to achieve literacy in the second language prior to achieving literacy in the native language have been quite successful in both the United States and Canada. Moreover, immersion has exerted a positive influence on the L2 learner's attitude toward the L2 culture.

Fundamental to an immersion program is the belief that normal children have the inherent capacity to learn a second language without jeopardizing their native language expertise. The success rate of immersion programs to date has convinced parents and educators that such a belief is valid.

Total Immersion

Total immersion involves the instruction of all subjects in the second language, including physical education and extracurricular activities. Early total immersion begins in kindergarten with no in-class use of the native language until the second or third year in school. At that time, treated as any other subject, L1 language arts in the native language may be taught for one hour a day. As the grade level increases, so does the degree to which the native language is used. In the case of French immersion in Canada, instruction in English language arts is eventually increased to a maximum of 35 percent of total daily instruction time, the remaining instruction being in French.

Both native and second language skills are carefully monitored during the immersion program. In the beginning stages, immersion students may experience some problems with their native language, particularly in spelling and reading (in which they have received less instruction). Eventually, they catch up with monolingual speakers in all subject areas.

Partial Immersion

Partial immersion involves instruction in the second language for half the school day and in the native language for the other half. Early partial immersion begins in kindergarten. The language of instruction in the morning or afternoon may differ with each grade from year to year. Compared with their monolingual peers, partial immersion students' performance in the native language is generally poorer for several years into the immersion program. When their L2 skills are compared with those of the total immersion students at the same grade level, partial immersion students are also less proficient.

Since immersion programs provide greater exposure to the second language than any other type of language teaching program, it is not surprising that they produce better results. For the same reason, early total immersion programs have a higher success rate than do early partial programs. Students from early total immersion programs invariably develop a more nativelike command of the second language than do students from other immersion programs.

Even though immersion students become highly proficient in listening and literacy skills, their production skills are often flawed, since many immersion students develop a type of interlanguage with their classmates. In a situation where communication among nonnative speakers of a second language is the primary goal, many errors are unheeded and uncorrected, thereby becoming a part of the immersion students' L2 system. This deficiency need not persist, however. If immersion is complemented by more formal instruction and drill of complex language structures, production skills may be greatly enhanced.

Summing Up

This chapter focuses on some of the major issues and questions that concern L2 researchers, linguists, and teachers in the field of **second language acquisition**. L2 acquisition may take place in a **natural** or **formal environment** or a combination of both. In their attempts to discover more about the L2 acquisition process, researchers have compared various L1 and L2 processes, relying to a great extent on L1 research methods. Findings in the areas of morpheme acquisition and syntactic development suggest that both L1 and L2 learners share similar **transitional constructions** and **learner strategies**. Learner strategies include **learning**, **production**, and **communication** strategies and substrategies.

Contrastive analysis and **error analysis** have both contributed to the attempt to learn more about the L2 learner's **interlanguage**. The study of interlanguage promises to provide greater insight into the L2 acquisition process.

Over the past decade, there has been a great deal of research in the areas of personality and **cognitive style**. Attitude and motivation are considered to be important requisites for success in L2 acquisition. The cognitive styles of **field independence** and **field dependence** may also affect an L2 learner's approach to L2 learning.

L2 teaching methodologies have, to varying degrees, been influenced by linguistics and psychology. The shift in focus to the learner as a communicator has spawned numerous teaching methodologies and approaches within the domain of **communicative language teaching**. The contributions of many source disciplines, including linguistics, neurolinguistics, psychology, sociology, and pedagogy are needed before we are able to understand fully the mystery of what happens inside the L2 learner's mind.

Sources

Research reported on morpheme acquisition and syntactic development is drawn from Bailey et al. in H. Dulay, M. Burt, and S. Krashen (cited below), R. Ellis (cited below), and B. van Patten's "Processing Strategies and Morpheme Acquisition" in *Universals of Second Language Acquisition,* edited by F. Eckman, L. Bell, and D. Nelson (Rowley, Mass.: Newbury House, 1985).

Discussions of contrastive analysis, error analysis, and interlanguage are based on S. P. Corder's *Error Analysis and Interlanguage* (Oxford: Oxford University Press, 1981) and T. van Els et al. (cited below). Examples of communicative effect errors were adapted from H. Dulay, M. Burt, and S. Krashen (cited below) and S. Johannson's "Problems in Studying the Effect of Learner's Errors" in *Studies in Second Language Acquisition* 1: 41–52 (1975).

Arguments for the critical period hypothesis come from S. Krashen, M. Long, and R. Scarcella's *Child-Adult Differences in L2 Acquisition* (Rowley, Mass.: Newbury House, 1982) and T. van Els et al. (cited below). Research on foreigner talk and teacher talk is drawn from *Classroom Oriented Research in Second Language,* edited by H. Seliger and M. Long (Rowley, Mass.: Newbury House, 1983). The notion of comprehensible input is presented in detail in S. Krashen's *Principles and Practices in Second Language Acquisition* (Oxford: Pergamon Press, 1982).

The presentation of learner strategies is drawn largely from R. Ellis (cited below). The literature on personality and cognitive styles is reviewed in H. Brown's *Principles of Language Learning and Teaching* (Englewood Cliffs, N.J.: Prentice-Hall, 1980). The quote on personality is taken from W. E. Lambert's "Psychological Approaches to the Study of Language, Part II: On Second Language Learning and Bilingualism" in *Modern Language Journal* 47: 114 (1963).

Language teaching methodologies are reviewed in T. van Els et al. (cited below) and in H. Hammerly's *Synthesis in Second Language Teaching* (N. Burnaby, B.C.: Second Language Publications, 1982).

Information on immersion is drawn from M. Swain's "French Immersion: Early, Late, Partial" in *Canadian Modern Language Review* 34: 577–85 (1978), F. Genesee's "Bilingual Education of Majority-Language Children: The Immersion Experiments in Review" in *Applied Psycholinguistics* 4: 1–46 (1983), and M. A. Snow and R. Shapira's "The Role of Social-Psychological Factors in Second-Language Learning" in M. Celce-Murcia (ed.) (cited below).

Recommended Reading

Celce-Murcia, M., ed. 1985. *Beyond Basics: Issues and Research in TESOL.* Rowley, Mass.: Newbury House.

Dulay, H., M. Burt, and S. Krashen. 1982. *Language Two.* Oxford: Oxford University Press.

Ellis, R. 1985. *Understanding Second Language Acquisition.* Oxford: Oxford University Press.

Hatch, E. M. 1983. *Psycholinguistics: A Second Language Perspective.* Rowley, Mass.: Newbury House.

van Els, T., T. Bongaerts, G. Extra, C. van Os, and A-M. Janssen-van Dieten, 1984. *Applied Linguistics and the Learning and Teaching of Foreign Languages.* R. R. van Oirsouw, trans. London: Edward Arnold.

Questions

1. In Spanish, sentences are negated by placing *no* 'not' before the (first) verb. As well, subject pronouns may be omitted. Given these facts, predict what types of errors a Spanish speaker in the early stages of learning English might make in negating the following utterances.
   a) I can see.
   b) The children like cookies.
   c) She is standing by the window.
   d) Fred likes to play the piano.

2. Tape record a conversation (at least thirty utterances) with an L2 learner with his or her permission. Write down everything said in the conversation, eliminating imitations and repetitions. Choose one specific aspect of the data, such as tense, pluralization, or articles, and describe it.
   a) Identify the errors made.
   b) Determine which errors can be considered interference errors, and which can be considered developmental errors.
   c) What percentage (approximately) of the errors can be attributed to interference?
   d) What other types of errors remain, and what do they suggest?
   e) Discuss the implications of your findings in terms of what you know about learner strategies.

3. The following data were elicited through a nonstructured communication task (natural conversation) from intermediate-level L2 learners of different language backgrounds who were learning English as a second language. Explain how the italicized forms differ from standard English usage. Do you see a predictable relationship between these interlanguage forms and standard usage? Can you determine any strategies these learners appear to employ with respect to word use?
   a) I had a *discuss* with my teacher.
   b) You get sick very *easy*.
   c) Martin is a *physics*.
   d) The dog is stopped to *breath*.
   e) You have to *trip* to Canada.
   f) She can't finish her *educated*.

4. Discuss some of the advantages and disadvantages of natural and formal language learning environments for adult L2 learners.

5. Your friend has decided to study Russian as a second language. She is twenty-four years old and lives in Chicago. What factors would you recommend that she consider when undertaking such a venture?

6. Think of people you know who have successfully learned a second language and those who have earnestly tried and failed. Consider their personalities. In your opinion, what are the most important characteristics for learning a second language?

7. If you were to design a second language program whose goal was to teach adult immigrant students basic communication skills (sometimes referred to as ''survival English''), what would be the main features of your program? Which teaching methodology or combination of methodologies would you choose? Justify your choices.

8. If you were planning an immersion program for a school system, at what age would you recommend that it begin? Defend your decision on the basis of what you know about child and adult differences and similarities in learning a second language.

9. The following data represent a conversation between native speakers of English (NS) and beginning non-native speakers (NNS). Note any instances of what you perceive to be foreigner talk. In what ways do the native speakers ask non-native speakers questions? Do you think that asking questions in this way provides a good model for L2 learners? Why or why not?
   a) *NS:*   Did you like Atlanta?
              Did you like Atlanta? Atlanta, did you like it?
      NNS: Yes, I like.
   b) *NS:*   When do you go to, uh, Montana? You say you fish in Montana, right?
      NNS: Yeah, right.
      NS: When? When do you go there?
   c) *NS:*   Do you know anyone in Maine?
      NNS: (silence)
      NS: Do you know anyone in Portland?
      NNS: Sorry?
      NS: Do you have a friend in Portland?
      NNS: Oh! Yeah, I have.

12 LANGUAGE IN SOCIAL CONTEXTS

> *. . . it is clear that*
> *the causes on which*
> *linguistic facts depend*
> *must be social in nature . . .*
> Antoine Meillet

This chapter treats a variety of social contexts in which one can examine both the use of language and the impact of extralinguistic factors on language. The topics range from regional variation in language through social variation in language to studies of language use in interaction. The goal is to convey the fact that a speech community is highly complex and structured. A reading of this chapter should leave an awareness that the reality of language in social contexts is not one of proper speech versus all other speech but of a set of complementary speech varieties that constitute the structured speech community. In promoting this awareness, the chapter also reveals the analytical techniques and theoretical assumptions that underlie the topics examined.

12.1 FUNDAMENTAL CONCEPTS

The subdiscipline of linguistics that treats the social aspects of language is called **sociolinguistics**. In this chapter, this label will be used to refer to all research about language in social contexts. Such research ranges from the very limited and localized context of a single conversation to studies of language use by whole populations. Given these quite diverse areas of research interest, it might be assumed that many sociolinguists do not share the same fundamental concepts or goals. This is to some extent true.

Despite the fact that there are a number of ways of approaching the study of language in social context, there are nevertheless certain terms and concepts that are common to most of them. All sociolinguistic studies concern language in a social context, treating speakers as members of social groups. The group isolated for study is called the **speech community**. Depending on the study, the speech community may have as few members as a family or as many members as China. The important characteristic is that the members of the speech community must, in some reasonable way, interact linguistically with other members of the community; they may share closely related language varieties, they may share attitudes toward linguistic norms, or they may be part of a single political entity.

The term **speech variety** or **language variety** refers to any distinguishable form of speech used by a speaker or group of speakers. The distinguishing characteristics of a speech variety may be lexical, phonological, morphological, or syntactic; usually they are a combination of all of these. We will be interested in speech varieties of three types: social speech varieties (also called **social dialects** or **sociolects**), regional speech varieties (or **regional dialects**), and functional speech varieties (or **registers**). Sociolects are again subdivisible into several smaller categories, largely as a function of the type of social group that shares the particular speech variety. Most often, one thinks of sociolects in terms of the socioeconomic status of speakers. Other sociolects, however, may be associated with ethnic, sex, occupational, or age groups. In most speech communities, there is a single speech variety called the **standard**, which is perceived by members of the community to be higher in status and more correct than the others.

While sociolects are defined by the linguistic differences associated with definable social groups in a single geographic area, regional dialects are associated with the linguistic traits shared by social groups in a single geographical area. Clearly the variety spoken by any single speaker, the **idiolect**, will be jointly determined by the sociolect and regional dialect appropriate to that individual.

Besides the interspeaker differences in speech associated with the geographical area and the social characteristics of the speaker, there are intraspeaker differences associated with the speech situation: who is being spoken to, the subject of the conversation, who else may be listening, and so on. Thus, while most speakers are limited to a single sociolect and geographical dialect, a fluent speaker must employ a variety of registers.

12.2 DIALECTOLOGY

The term **dialectology** is used to refer to the study of regional dialects. Modern dialectology got its start in Europe about a century ago as a result of the interest of historical linguists in observing the spread of sound change. This early work was principally concerned with phonology. Later work has considered other aspects of language, but phonology is still the greatest area of concentration, with the lexicon in second place. Dialectologists have been comparatively less interested in morphology and syntax.

Methods

The work of dialectologists is often published in the form of articles, but the most characteristic form for the results of their investigations is the dialect atlas. A dialect atlas contains numerous maps that exhibit regional variation in a language. The boundaries between dialects (and subdialects) are represented on these maps by means of lines called **isoglosses**. The latter are generally drawn with respect to one feature (usually phonological or lexical).

These lines are meant to indicate that with respect to the feature or features in question, people on one side share one variant while those on the other share a different one.

The two maps in Figure 12.1 illustrate how this technique is applied with respect to some items of everyday vocabulary in the state of Pennsylvania. In the first map, this region is divided with respect to the words *curtains* and *blinds,* and in the second with respect to *pail* and *bucket.* As the maps show, people in the northern and eastern parts of Pennsylvania call certain objects *curtains* and *pail* while people in the southern and western parts of the state called the same objects, respectively, *blinds* and *bucket.* Of course, isoglosses are idealizations. Not everybody on one side of the line says *curtains*, and not everybody on the other side says *blinds*. An isogloss is an approximation of where dominant tendencies change.

Early dialectologists typically surveyed large areas. They also believed that isolated rural speech was likely to be purer and of more interest than urban speech. They therefore emphasized rural and small-town speakers

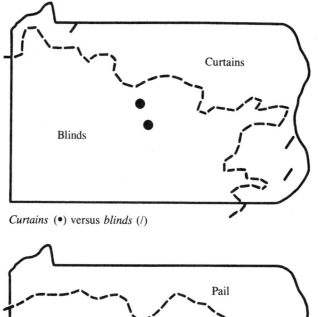

Curtains (•) versus *blinds* (/)

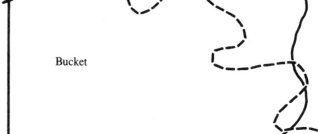

Pail versus *bucket*

Figure 12.1 Dialect areas in Pennsylvania

over urban ones. Thus, the *Linguistic Atlas of the Eastern United States,* with more than 2,500 informants, had only twenty-five from New York City. More recently, a number of sociolinguists have been interested in intensive studies of urban areas. William Labov interviewed well over 100 speakers from a single area of New York City. Similarly, there has been a change of emphasis from the written questionnaires of the early dialect studies to attempts to record speech in the most natural possible form.

The questions in Table 12.1 are taken from a survey that explored certain lexical peculiarities of the English spoken in the Canadian province of Prince Edward Island. Respondents were asked to circle the form they ordinarily used in each instance or, where appropriate, to supply their own form.

Table 12.1 Sample questions from a Prince Edward Island dialect survey

Definitions for the terms sought	Possible responses
Name for loud sound made by cow when calf is taken away	bawl, beller, bellow, loo, cry, low, mew, moo
Call to chickens at feeding time	bee, biddie, chick-chick, chickie-chickie, chuck-chuck, co-chee, coo-chick, kip-kip, kit-kit, kut-kut, widdie
Freshwater fish with claws (swims backward)	crab, craw, crawdad, crawdaddie, crawfish, crayfish
Insect that glows at night	fire bug, firefly, glow worm, June bug, lightning bug
Piece of playground equipment	dandle, ridy horse, seesaw, teeter, teeter board, teetering board, see horse, tilt(s), teeter-totter, tilting board, tinter, tinter board, hicky horse, cock horse, cocky horse

English in North America

Dialect differences in Europe often have hundreds of years of history. By the time of Alfred the Great (ninth century A.D.), there were already several distinct varieties of Old English, and some of these distinctions can be followed through to distinctions in Modern English varieties in Great Britain. Dialect differences in North America originated much more recently. Although there was some tendency for speakers of a single English dialect to settle together in North America, the net effect of immigration was a geographical mixing of English dialects and thus a leveling of dialect differences. The major geographical dialects of North American English, therefore, have histories of only a few hundred years of separation at most.

Within the United States alone, there are several major regional dialects. These are illustrated in Figure 12.2. The main dialect areas in the eastern United States are the Northern, Midland, and Southern regions. They are distinguished from each other primarily in terms of particular phonological and lexical features. The distinctions among these regions tend to become

Figure 12.2 North American English: dialects and development

less obvious as one moves to the west. This reflects the historical pattern of migration from east to west in North America in which dialectal differences have become blended.

American English Generally speaking, the study of American dialectology has proceeded like the settlement of the United States itself, from east to west. The most extensively published studies and the most certain generalizations concern the Eastern Seaboard and adjoining states. Here we find three major dialect areas: Northern, encompassing the area north of a line running westward from central New Jersey through northern Pennsylvania; Southern, including those areas south and east of a line starting at the Atlantic at the southern border of New Jersey and heading westward almost to West Virginia, and then heading south through North Carolina and South Carolina; and Midland, including the area between the Northern and Southern areas. The Northern dialect area contains Eastern New England (Maine, New Hampshire, Rhode Island, and eastern Massachusetts and Connecticut) as a major sub-area. The Midland dialect is divided into Northern Midland (Pennsylvania, southern New Jersey, northern Maryland, and northern West Virginia) and Southern Midland (southern West Virginia, western Virginia, western North Carolina, and northwestern South Carolina). Studies have been made of the westward extensions of these dialects, but the situation is more complicated and less well studied than along the Eastern Seaboard.

Northern English The Northern dialect is set off by the use of such vocabulary terms as *pail* rather than *bucket*, *angleworm* for *earthworm,* and *pit* rather than *seed* in a cherry. Phonologically it has a phonemic distinction between the vowels in *morning* and *mourning*, /s/ in *greasy*, and /u/ in *root*. Eastern New England is set off from the rest of the Northern dialect by the loss of postvocalic /r/ (i.e., /r/ when not before vowels in such words as *barn, four,* and *daughter*) and the use of /a/ for /æ/ in words such as *aunt, bath,* and *half.*

Midland English The Midland dialect is distinguished by vocabulary items such as *skillet* for frying pan, *blinds* for window shades, and *poke* for a paper sack. Phonologically it retains postvocalic /r/ and has /θ/ finally in *with*. Northern Midland is distinguished by *run* for a small stream and /a/ in *frog, hog,* and *fog*, which do not rhyme with *dog*. Southern Midland has *redworm* for *earthworm*, *pack* for *carry*, and /a/ for /ay/ in words such as *write* and *ride*.

Southern English Southern English is marked by the loss of postvocalic /r/, /z/ in *Mrs.*, and the use of *tote* for *carry* and *snap beans* for *string beans*. It shares with Southern Midland the use of *you-all* for the second person plural pronoun, /yuw/ in words such as *news* and *due*, *shucks* rather than *husks* for the coverings of corn, and *might could* for *might be able to*.

12.3 SOCIAL DIFFERENTIATION OF LANGUAGE

The emphasis in the foregoing sections was on dialectology, or the horizontal variation of language. The following sections deal with the vertical variation of language. The varieties of language examined here are assumed to be arranged in a kind of a hierarchy in that one of them has a higher status than the others. Many of the others are limited to small social groups. Studies of this type of variation treat what is referred to as the **social stratification** of language. It is probably fair to say that most sociolinguistic studies are concerned with this vertical variation of language.

Many of the principal working notions that underlie stratificational studies have been introduced in Section 12.1. It is important to point out that certain concepts are taken from sociology, including the notions of stratification and socioeconomic class. We will assume that these notions are valid for purposes of discussion in this chapter—with some caveats. Labels such as *working class* and *middle class* are not terms with universal meaning. They are relativistic. The same labels can be used when describing the sociolinguistics of the United States and, for example, Britain. The concept of socioeconomic class is, however, quite different in these two societies. Moreover, it is entirely irrelevant in a description of tribal societies in countries such as Papua-New Guinea. Stratification of language, while widespread in the world, is probably not universal. Perhaps the only real sociolinguistic universal introduced so far in this chapter is social differentiation. The claim underlying this universal is that there are always differences in speech communities and that these differences correlate with the existence of social groups within the community. These social groups might be functions of the socioeconomic, sexual, age, ethnic, educational, occupational, or other characteristics of their members.

In modern, developed societies there is one language variety that stands above the others. This superposed variety is usually called the standard language; it is the variety that is employed by the government and communications media, is used and taught in educational institutions, and is the main or only written language. It is more fixed and resistant to change than any other variety in the community and is something of a yardstick against which other varieties are measured. It is to the written standard that prescriptivists, those who seek to regulate how others use language, usually appeal when they condemn some usage as incorrect, improper, or even barbarous.

The Social Stratification of English

The United States is distinctive in that, instead of a national standard there are a small number of regional varieties that are regarded as correct in their areas. We term this variety or varieties *Standard English*. These varieties differ principally in their phonology, and hardly at all in their written form. It is relatively easy to tell an educated Bostonian from an educated Charlestonian by listening to even their most careful speech; it is virtually impossible to distinguish the two on the basis of written works. Varieties other than the standard are termed *nonstandard*. This term is to be preferred to the designation *substandard*, which suggests some inherent inferiority of these varieties. In fact, the selection of standard and nonstandard varieties of English and other languages has to do with historical facts about who spoke which variety when; it has nothing to do with anything intrinsic to the varieties. Were English history a bit different, Cockney English might be standard English in Great Britain, and prescriptivists would have great fun criticizing those speakers who actually pronounce written *h*'s.

Nonstandard Grammatical Features Certain features of nonstandard varieties of English are often singled out by prescriptivists as demonstrating the inherent illogic or lack of systematicity of nonstandard varieties. An oft-cited grammatical feature of this sort is the so-called double negative, seen in sentence *1a*.

> *1. a*) He don't know nothing.
>   *b*) He doesn't know anything.
>   *c*) He knows something.

A prescriptivist asserts that the two negations in the first sentence (-*n't* and *no*-) cancel each other out. Thus, the speaker in *1a* has supposedly uttered an affirmative sentence with the meaning of *1c*. Anyone who hears the sentence in *1a*, however, knows that its meaning is the same for the nonstandard speaker as the meaning of *1b* is for the speaker of the standard. (Of course, proponents of this view refuse to carry it to its logical conclusion and accept *He don't never know nothing* as a negative sentence because of its three negatives.) The nonstandard and standard negative sentences differ from the affirmative sentence in the same two ways: both verbs are marked as negative and both indefinite pronouns are marked differently from the pronoun in the affirmative sentence. When the verb is negated in Standard English, an indefinite pronoun in the verb phrase is also negated, by changing *some*- to *any*-. In the nonstandard variety, negating the verb causes the pronoun to be negated by changing *some*- to *no*-. Both varieties mark negation twice and thus are equally logical.

There is another nonstandard feature in *1a*—the verb *do*, which co-occurs with the subject pronoun *he*. This sort of usage and the similar one seen in nonstandard *He know* are also condemned by prescriptivists. These two sentences violate the Standard English subject-verb agreement rule, which requires present-tense English verbs with third person subjects to have a special ending (-*s*). An examination of the morphology of Standard English verbs and a look at the historical development of these forms, however, show that over time all but the third person singular ending -*s* has been lost in the present tense. A nonprescriptivist view of those nonstandard varieties that lack a special ending in this form would hold that they have simply carried this particular linguistic change to its logical conclusion by eliminating the last remaining inflectional ending in the present tense.

Double negation, subject-verb agreement, and a number of other grammatical features are, of course, fairly superficial aspects of language. Trivial as some of these features may seem to some, the following letter (which appeared in numerous North American newspapers) attests to their enduring importance for others.

Dear Ann Landers:
I have been dating a young man for several years. Dan is everything a girl could want. Well, almost. He is kind, nice looking, considerate, fun

to be with, and he makes good money. The only drawback is Dan's grammer. For example, he says, "I seen," "youse," and "have went." I bite my tongue when he makes these awful mistakes, especially in front of my friends. I don't want to be ashamed of him, Ann, and I don't want to embarrass him either, but I'm afraid one day I might.

Is there a chance that we can have a good marriage in spite of this? I am 26 and a college graduate. Dan is 27 and attended trade school. I do love him, but I fear I'll be a nagging wife—or worse yet, a silent wife who is ashamed of her husband's grammer. Please hurry your answer. He is waiting for mine.

—York, Pennsylvania

Dear York:
Dan sounds too good to discard. Ask him if he wants to be corrected—when the two of you are alone, of course. Incidentally, you misspelled the word grammar throughout your letter. It is AR, dear. Perhaps you and Dan are not so far apart as you think.

Nonstandard Phonological Features The entities of interest to sociolinguists are called sociolinguistic **variables**. These variables are speech sounds that do not occur uniformly across a speech community or, occasionally, even in the speech of an individual. For instance, a particular variable may be realized one way in one speech variety and a different way in another speech variety. Similarly, a variable might be rendered one way by speakers when they are speaking carefully and another way in a more casual speaking style.

Perhaps the most widespread phonological variable in English is (ng). We use parentheses to set off sociolinguistic variables, thus distinguishing them formally from phonemes and phones. Since (ng) is a variable, it is not always realized the same way in speech. Its two realizations are [n] and [ŋ]. The same word might be pronounced with one or the other realization by the same speaker or by different speakers: *swimming* might thus be realized as [swɪmɪn] or as [swɪmɪŋ]. These realizations do not occur randomly in speech. There are well-established correlations between the two realizations of (ng) and such extralinguistic factors as the socioeconomic status and sex of speaker, the relative formality (or informality) of the speech situation, its physical location, and the nature of the particular lexical item. The variable tends to be realized as [ŋ] by speakers of higher socioeconomic status, by females, and in formal situations. Words such as *analyzing* (in general, formal vocabulary) are pronounced more frequently with [ŋ] than with [n], while words such as *chucking* are more often heard with [n] than with [ŋ]. One study even showed that in school situations, more [ŋ]'s were heard in the classroom and more [n]'s were heard on the playground.

Other English sociolinguistic variables often discussed in the literature are listed in Table 12.2 with their realizations. These three variables differ from the variable (ng). Use of the nonstandard varieties of (th) and (dh) will bring highly negative judgments of the speakers. Use of the nonstandard variety [n] for (ng), while not approved, will not result in such severe judg-

Table 12.2 Some English sociolinguistic variables

Variable	Phonetic realization
(th)	[θ], [t^θ], or [t]
(dh)	[ð], [d^ð] or [d]
(r)	[r] or [Ø] (*zero*)

ments. The status of postvocalic [r], the (r) variable, varies radically by geographic area, as we have seen. No single realization is standard in all areas of the United States. Use of the [r] will be regarded as correct in Los Angeles and stigmatized in Maine.

Often the existence of competing realizations of a single variable is indicative of a sound change in process. Thus, black speakers in Hillsborough, North Carolina, exhibit variation in the realization of (r); the community is in the process of change from non-[r] pronouncing to [r] pronouncing.

Language and Sex

Social differentiation of language is not limited to variation associated with socioeconomic class. Variation may also be a function of the sex of individuals. There is a considerable literature on the general topic of language and sex. This label is used here in a broad sense, covering all of the following:

- Differences in language use associated with the sex (or sexual orientation) of the speaker or the person spoken to.
- Differences in language use associated with the sex of the referent (person spoken about).
- Attempts to alter the language with respect to the ways sex is or is not encoded.

Researchers in this field have identified two ways in which language is differentiated according to sex of speaker: sex-exclusive differentiation and sex-preferential differentiation.

Sex-Exclusive Differentiation refers to the radically different speech varieties men and women possess in a particular society. In some societies, a woman or a man may not normally be allowed to speak the variety of the other sex. It is in this sense that the varieties are sex-exclusive. A society in which this is the norm is typically one in which the roles assigned the sexes are rigid, and in which there is little social change.

This phenomenon has been observed in some Amerindian societies but is no longer as widespread as it probably was in the remote past. A study of Koasati (a Muskogean language spoken in Louisiana) showed that members of this speech community possess different verb forms based on the sex of the speaker. Two of these differences are described in Table 12.3. If

Table 12.3 Sex-exclusive verb forms in Koasati

W	M	
kā	kas	'he is saying'
lakawhôl	lakawhós	'lift it!'

the women's form ends in a nasalized vowel, the men's form has final [s] and no nasalization. Where the women's form has falling pitch-stress (marked ˆ) on its final syllable and ends in a short vowel followed by [l], the men's form shows high pitch-stress (marked ´) and [s] for the [l]. (W stands for woman and M for man.) In traditional Koasati society, women and men normally used the forms appropriate to their sex, but they were not forbidden the use of forms associated with the other sex. In quoting a member of the opposite sex, a Koasati used the form appropriate to the person being quoted.

Sex-exclusive differentiation has assumed an even more radical form in some societies. The most extreme form, and a rarity, is one in which the sex of the speaker and that of the addressee are both encoded in the language. In Biloxi (an extinct language of the Siouan family), all of the forms (each meaning 'carry it!') were found (see Table 12.4). Singular and plural refer to the number of addressees.

Table 12.4 Examples of sex-exclusive differentiation in Biloxi

	Singular	Plural
M to M	kikankó	kítakankó
M or W to W	kitkí	kítatkí
W to M	kitaté	kítatuté

Sex-Preferential Differentiation is much more common in the languages of the world than is sex-exclusivity. This phenomenon is reflected in the relative frequency with which men and women use the same lexical items or other linguistic features. If, as is often asserted, female English speakers use words such as *lovely* and *nice* more often than do male speakers, we can claim that English speakers exhibit sex-preferential differentiation. Women have also been shown to possess a greater variety of specific color terms than men in North American society. If this is true, it is probably due to the tasks traditionally performed by women. There is no evidence to show that women have more acute color perception than do men. Men are reputed to possess larger lexicons in areas associated with traditional male activities (such as particular occupations and sports). These examples may appear stereotypical, but they do reflect the sometimes subtle, sometimes blatant, differences between the activities of members of the two sexes. It is not the language that is sexist but the attitudes of its speakers.

Other differences between men's and women's language in North American society are seen in women's more frequent use of politeness formulas. There are a number of ways in which requests (or commands) can be mitigated in English. Instead of simply saying to someone *Open the window!* we might say *Please open the window! Would you please open the window? Could you open the window? Would you mind opening the window? Do you fid it stuffy in here?* and so on. These are all less direct ways of requesting than the straightforward command and, it is claimed, would more likely be employed by women. Since we are discussing sex-preferential usage here, we must emphasize that all of the above ways of phrasing a request are available to all speakers but, it is asserted, are not equally selected by male and female speakers.

In another areas, studies have shown that women accompany speech by smiling more often than do men. Smiling is an example of paralanguage, as it may accompany speech but is not a part of the stream of speech. Other investigations have demonstrated that men in North American society apparently interrupt the speech of women more than do women that of men. Apparently, women more often than men use a conversational device termed the *ingressive affirmative,* the somewhat inhaled *yeah* heard from speakers of British and Canadian English. Its function may be to imply agreement with another speaker or to pass up a turn at speech—perhaps to avoid assertive behavior. This feature, taken together with the others discussed above, shows how the second-class status of women has been and continues to be reflected in our language.

Grammatical Gender The most obvious way in which sex differences with respect to a referent are manifested in English is through grammatical gender. The use of English pronouns is instructive in this regard. We do not employ *he*, for instance, to refer only to males. In Standard English, it is used as a generic third person singular pronoun when the sex of the referent is unknown or irrelevant. Thus, we occasionally still hear sentences such as *Did everyone turn in* his *assignment today?* even if the entire group of referents consists of women. However, we more often hear utterances such as the following: *No one can with impunity take the law into* their *own hands* (asserted by Mayor Koch of New York City) and *Why don't we go to our first caller and see what* their *concerns are?* (from a television talk-show host). In these sentences, we have instances of singular (sex-indefinite) *they*, which is widespread in colloquial English and which denotes an indefinite individual of unspecified sex. For speakers who utter sentences of this sort, the pronouns *she* and *he* are reserved for reference to individuals whose sex is known.

English nouns, though not overtly marked for gender like those in Latin, Russian, or many other languages, do distinguish between women and men. Generally in English, nouns referring to occupations are at once both masculine and generic. There occasionally are female forms for the names of occupations (*sculptress, actress, usherette*) but these have evolved to connote more than just the sex of the practitioner of the occupation. Many observers feel that these and similar forms trivialize the women so labeled. A woman who acts in films pointedly identified herself as an *actor* in an interview, not as an *actress*. She said that *actor* connoted for her someone who was serious about the craft, while *actress* did not.

The term *man* has come under considerable scrutiny in the recent past with respect to its reference. The pervasiveness of male-referential forms used generically (as in *chairman, postman,* and *mankind*) disturbs many observers, who feel that such language not only reflects discriminatory historical values but also perpetuates them.

This concern has resulted in moves to eliminate discriminatory forms from the language. In many instances, the suffix *-man* has been changed to sex-neutral -*person*. Other morphological processes have resulted in the creation of new forms (a *postman* becomes a *letter carrier,* and a *fireman* becomes a *fire fighter*). Changes have also come about in the use of pronouns. In many cases, regulations, laws, and the like have been rewritten to eliminate discriminatory masculine forms, replacing them with forms such as *he/ she* or generic *they*. Whatever the future holds, many people's sensitivity to the ways in which the sex of referents is (or is not) encoded in language has been heightened over the past few years.

Taboo and Euphemism Taboo is both a technical term and an everyday vocabulary item. It was borrowed from the Tongan language and, in its most general sense, refers to a prohibition on the use of, mention of, or association with particular objects, actions, or persons. As originally used in Polynesia, *taboo* had religious connotations, but in sociolinguistics it now denotes any prohibition on the use of particular lexical items. Where it is necessary to refer to tabooed items, speakers are often allowed to employ an indirect expression called a **euphemism**. Taboo and euphemism are thus two faces of the same coin.

In the English-language speech community, the most obvious taboos are not religious but sexual. Despite a recent tendency toward the relaxation of some prohibitions on the use of explicit terms relating to sex, many such taboos still exist. These long ago gave rise to the use of euphemisms (often technical terms of Latin and Greek origin) in ordinary conversation. They enabled speakers to avoid the more earthy colloquial lexical items.

The first item in the taboo list in Table 12.5 is an example of the lengths to which Victorians went in order to avoid mention of anything they felt to be suggestive. *Leg* was seen to be too explicit a reference to the body,

Table 12.5 Taboos and euphemisms relating to sex

Tabooed word	Euphemism
leg	limb
cock	rooster
breast	bosom
fuck	copulate, make love

particularly the female body, and thus was replaced by the more generic term *limb*. This was the language fashion during an age when women wore floor-length dresses and piano legs were covered out of modesty on the part of their owners. *Rooster* is a North American euphemism for older *cock*. It is derived from the verb *roost* and replaced a word that had come to be used to denote 'penis'.

Another set of taboos in the English-speaking world have to do with excrement (see Table 12.6). The word *toilet* is an interesting example of a euphemism that, after long use, has itself come to be taboo. It came to be used in French in the past as a euphemism for the word meaning *restroom*.

Table 12.6 Taboos and euphemisms relating to excrement

Tabooed item	Euphemism
shit	poop
fart	break wind
piss	pee
toilet	convenience, facility, commode

It originally meant 'little towel'. English speakers who avoid a word such as *toilet* in the late twentieth century might be deemed prudish, but they do nevertheless exist.

Politics and Language

In countries with substantial populations speaking different languages, there may be a need for more than one standard language. Such countries often have designated official languages, which are recognized by the government for national or regional use. In Canada, French and English are official languages; in Finland, Finnish and Swedish are official languages; in Belgium, French and Flemish (Dutch) are similarly recognized. Countries with numerically significant localized minorities sometimes assign quasi-official status to the languages of these peoples. In such situations, the local language may be used on street signs, in the local media and, occasionally, even in local schools and administrative bodies. Examples of this type of limited local linguistic autonomy abound—in, for instance, the Inuit language in Canada, the Sámi (Lapp) language in Norway, and the Romansch language in Switzerland.

On a global scale, English has increasingly become the chief international language of communication. In many countries, this is perceived to present a threat to indigenous languages. English is by far the most common second language in the world. The more English is used for communication between persons who speak it as a second language, the less their own languages are used, and the less useful they may become for modern communication. It is to avoid the loss of their indigenous languages that many governments take action either by limiting the use of foreign languages (such as English) or by requiring the use of some indigenous language. Thus, we have the examples of both France and Quebec restricting the use of English and encouraging the use of French in business and technology. A more extreme example is Ireland, where the use of the Irish language is promoted, although it is spoken by only about five percent of the country's population.

Multilingualism There is a great deal of variation in nations of the world with regard to language situations. At one extreme are countries such as Iceland and Portugal in which almost everybody speaks the same language. (Although this situation is limited to a very few relatively small countries, most Americans seem to think of this as the normal situation.) Next are countries such as the United States and Spain in which there is one dominant language spoken by a good-sized majority of the nation, but in which there are notable linguistic minorities. Then there are countries such as Canada and Belgium in which the great bulk of citizens are speakers of one of two major languages. At the other extreme are countries such as India, which had twenty-four major languages and hundreds of minor ones. (The designations *major* and *minor* are determined by number of speakers and legal position in the nation.)

Just as there are many language situations among the nations of the world, so there are many language policies adopted by these nations. One such policy, much favored, is to recognize only a single language for most official and educational purposes. This is the policy in East Germany, Malaysia, and Senegal, among many others. It is important to note that the connotations of this policy may be very different depending upon the existing linguistic situation. Thus, in East Germany, the national language, German, is spoken natively by the vast majority of the population. In Malaysia, the national language, Bhasa Malay is spoken natively by the largest single ethnic group in the country, but there are significant minorities whose languages, Chinese and Tamil, have little official status. This creates the potential for tension between speakers of Chinese and Tamil on one side and Bhasa Malay on the other. In Senegal, more than 90 percent of the population speaks Wolof natively, but the national language is French, spoken natively by almost none of the population. This situation reflects the relative prestige of the two languages and the legacy of French colonial rule of Senegal.

In the United States, the preponderant portion of the population speaks English natively, and this is the *de facto* national language. However, the Supreme Court decision in *Lau* vs. *Board of Education* and policies emitting from both the legislative and executive branches of the government have established safeguards for speakers of minority languages. Thus, voting materials must be made available in significant minority languages, and school boards must plan for the education of non-English-speaking children in ways that take into account their differing native languages.

Canada, Belgium, and Czechoslovakia, among others, follow a policy of absolute legal equality between two languages. While this sometimes is better followed in theory than in practice, it does provide a method by which two ethnic groups may live in a single political entity without either imposing its language on the other. In Canada and Belgium, this policy has provided a framework for continued political unity, which would have been seriously endangered if a single language policy had been pursued. The Republic of South Africa follows an unusual version of this policy in that the two official languages, Afrikaans and English, are each spoken natively by a small minority of the country's population. Switzerland is the only nation to attempt the policy of legal equality with more than two languages, German, French, and Italian all having equal status in Switzerland. Romansch, a Romance language, also has a legal status, albeit more restricted.

Nations such as the Soviet Union, India, and the Philippines, in which a large variety of languages are spoken by significant groups, have opted for a national language-regional languages policy. In this arrangement, a single language, often the largest single language (e.g., Russian in the Soviet Union) is chosen as the national language. All citizens of the country are expected to be able to function in that language. At the same time, other languages are recognized as official in specific geographical areas of the country (e.g., Ukrainian in the Ukraine). India follows this policy but has two national languages, Hindi and English; twelve other languages have official status in particular states, while Sanskrit and Sindhi have official status but no designated territory.

12.4 SPECIAL LANGUAGES

The term *special language* is meant to cover a set of loosely related types of sociolects. These have traditionally been labeled with the somewhat overlapping terms *slang, argot, jargon,* and *cant.* The major relevant concepts here are secret language, occupational sociolect, and nonstandard, fleeting usages. We will use *argot* in the sense of secret language. Occupational sociolect (occasionally termed jaron or cant in the literature) will be denoted here by the more current term *sublanguage,* and slang will be used in its conventional sense to denote faddish, nonstandard usages.

Slang

Slang is a label that is frequently used to denote certain informal usages of nearly anyone in the speech community. The term was first attested in English in the mid-eighteenth century, used in reference to "special vocabulary used by any set of persons of a low or disreputable character; language of a low and vulgar type" (according to the *Oxford English Dictionary*). In the twentieth century, it is often applied to aspects of the language of adolescents.

While there are always many new features developing in the language of teenagers, certain words may persist in the teenage lexicon for long periods or may appear almost cyclically from time to time. Words denoting enthusiastic approval (such as *super, great, neat, neato, keen, cool, groovy, awesome, radical, beauty, bad, boss, right on,* and *excellent,* all accompanied by appropriately exaggerated paralinguistic effects) are at any given time either definitely in or definitely out. Aside from terms denoting approval, there are also those reflecting disapproval (*nerd* and *bogus*), greetings (*sup!*—from *What's up?*), and leave-takings (*later!*).

Argots and Play Languages

The term **argot** was borrowed from French. It first appeared in print in the early seventeenth century when it was used as the label for the secret language of beggars and street merchants. As the original argot developed, it came to include some usages borrowed from Romany, the language of the Gypsies. Later still, it became the secret language of the French underworld. Since argot is now used as a label for any secret language, it may be applied to the language or sociolect of any social group whose members evidence a desire to conceal the content of their communication from some other group or from the majority community generally. In this sense, it can be applied to the sociolect of sexual minorities, to Romany in the case of the

Gypsies, to the language of pre-World War II Jewish communities in eastern Europe (Yiddish), as well as to the other social groups already mentioned.

On the extreme end of the spectrum of speech varieties covered by argot (or perhaps a bit beyond) are the secret play languages of children and the codes and ciphers of governments and industry. Insofar as these are linguistic and are used to make in-group communication unintelligible to an outsider, they can qualify as argots. A number of children's secret languages exist in the world. Perhaps the most familiar to English speakers is *Pig Latin*, which derives its lexicon from English by moving a word-initial syllable onset to the end of a word and adding a suffix /ey/ (*school* becomes /uwlskey/). Pig Latin is typical of play languages, which make regular phonological (or phonotactic) modifications to existing vocabulary in the standard language but do not create new lexical items. Another such language is Cat's Elbow (from the German *Katzenellenbogen*). It works by adding the vowel *o* after each consonant in a word and then repeating the consonant, leaving existing vowels unchanged. Thus, English *drink* would become *dodrorinonkok*. Play languages such as these serve their main function in making the speech of one group of children inaccessible to younger children. They are transparent to older children and adults, and cumbersome to use.

Boontling (also referred to as Boonville lingo) is an example of a more elaborate play language used by adults as well as children. It arose in Boonville, California, in the late nineteenth century and is still in use. It has been the subject of a number of articles in popular magazines and of at least one serious study. Some lexical items are formed by the application of morphological rules (for example, *pleeble* from a blend of *play ball* and *buzz chick* onomatopoetically from the sound of a baseball flying through the air and landing in a glove). Most, however, seem to be the product of the imagination of Boontling speakers (*spilldukes* 'a fistfight' and *fence jumpin* 'adultery'). By one count, some 15 percent of its vocabulary are euphemisms for items taboo in Standard English. Besides being a source of amusement to its speakers, Boontling serves legitimate functions of any argot when, for example, members of the local baseball team are able to communicate openly in the presence of an opposing team.

Cockney Rhyming Slang An early and still-attested example of an English argot is Cockney rhyming slang. This secret language, associated with the less advantaged social strata of London, arose in the nineteenth century among the navvies, relatively unskilled day-laborers. The navvies, faced with unemployment, drifted into the underworld and took their argot with them. From there, it spread more broadly in the speech community. Rhyming slang is an extremely good example of an argot in that its utterances are produced by application of particular rules to the basic language, and its speakers' goal is to communicate with each other while being unintelligible to an outsider. Rhythming slang, like other argots, thus sounds like gibberish to the uninitiated. To perform adequately, a potential "rhymester" must know established usages in the argot and must be skilled enough to be able to coin new rhymes that can be understood by another. For the most part, only nouns are rhymed, but occasionally verbs are as well. Quite ordinary English words are replaced by individual words or entire phrases with which they rhyme. For example, the word *wife* has had the following rhyming slang equivalences: *bit of tripe, carving-knife, drum and fife, joy of my life, storm and strife, struggle and strife, trouble and strife, war and strife,* and *worry and strife.* Some rhymes are more obscure than these, such as *bottle of spruce* (a cheap beer), which means 'twopence' because it rhymes with *deuce.* Conventionalized rhymes can also be abbreviated, thus making the argot even more inaccessible—*Aristotle,* which stands for 'bottle', is usually heard in the abbreviated form *Arry.* The following sentence is concocted from known rhyming slang vocabulary: *The old pot got an Arry for his trouble and strife,* meaning 'The old man got a bottle for his wife.' (*The old pot* is an abbreviated form for *the old pot and pan,* rhyming slang for 'old man'.)

Sublanguages

The speech varieties associated with particular professions (occupational sociolects) have traditionally been called either **jargons** or **cants**. *Jargon* is a loanword from French. It first appeared in print in the thirteenth century with the meaning 'unintelligible language'. It is now used in English to denote 'obscure, specialized language' or 'vocabulary peculiar to some field'. The term *cant* appeared in English in the early sixteenth century and originally referred to the singing style of beggars. It is assumed to have arisen (probably in medieval France) as a verb describing the chanting of mendicant (begging) monks. It later came to be used in an overlapping sense with both jargon and argot. The confusion and ambiguity associated with these terms in popular usage is responsible for the coinage of the new term **sublanguage** to denote 'occupational sociolect'.

Sublanguages, far from being designed to obscure matters, are essential to their users. They provide a necessarily specialized lexicon by means of which members of a group can communicate efficiently. They are highly structured speech varieties with precise communicative functions. Sublanguages are different from the standard in their lexicons but often display syntactic differences as well. Another important aspect of sublanguages is that their appropriate use is based on an assumption of shared knowledge among interactants. If speakers share knowledge of a field and the sublanguage associated with it, they can communicate with a maximum level of efficiency and a minimum of redundancy.

As particular fields make an increasing impact on the majority society, their sublanguages may also supply the standard language with new lexical items or with new senses of existing forms. The computer, for example, has recently enriched Standard English with a number of lexical items. Among these are the terms *boot, bit, byte, firmware, software, throughput, crash,* and *program. Condominium,* a term previously limited to legal and political discourse and meaning 'a type of co-ownership', has recently entered Standard English with a somewhat different meaning (in addition to those it previously had): 'a single unit in a collectively owned multi-unit complex of apartments or townhouses'.

12.5 MIXED LANGUAGES

In the past, when explorers or merchants went out into the world to find new lands or markets or sources of raw material, they often did not share a language with the people with whom they came into contact. When this situation was encountered, one of three solutions was adopted: (1) the foreigners learned the language of their hosts (or vice versa), (2) they used some third language commonly employed in the region for trading purposes, or (3) a new language emerged, made up of elements from the various native languages of its users. Languages that are used for communication among speakers of different languages are called **lingua francas**. This name derives from a medieval trade language used in the Mediterranean region and based largely on Romance languages (Italian, French, and Spanish) but also containing elements of Greek, Arabic, and Turkish. In the modern world, it is fair to say that English is the most important lingua franca, since it is used as a means of communication between large numbers of people who do not otherwise share a common language.

Pidgins

A lingua franca may be the native language of a people (as in Modern English) or it may be a language that has arisen as a mixture of two or more languages (as in the case of the original lingua franca). Such a mixed language is called a **pidgin**. In many cases, pidgins reflect the influence of the higher (or dominant) language in their lexicon and that of the lower language in their phonology (and occasionally syntax). The etymology of the word *pidgin* is disputed, although traditionally it has been assumed to have arisen from a pidgin form of the English word *business*. Linguists now use pidgin as a label for any language that is historically a mixture of two or more languages and that serves as a lingua franca for groups of speakers but is not the first language of any people. In parts of the world where pidgins are still employed, their use is often confined to the marketplace.

Wes-Kos In Cameroon, in West Africa, there still exists a functioning English-based pidgin, called variously Wes-Kos, West-African Pidgin-English, Broken-English, Coast-English, Kitchen-English, Bastard-English, and Bush-English, among others. A survey of some of the features of Wes-Kos gives an idea how the structure of a donor language (here English) can be modified in a pidgin:

- English interdental fricatives and voiced fricatives are missing ('bath' is /baf/ and 'nose' is /nows/).
- Consonant clusters are simplified by dropping a consonant or inserting an epenthetic vowel ('camp' is /kam/, 'stranger' is /trenja/, and 'school' is /sikul/).
- English bound morphemes (affixes) have been replaced by reduplication and compounding (/was-rum/ 'washroom' pluralized becomes /was-rum-was-rum/, /tif/ 'to steal' intensified becomes /tif-tif/ 'to steal repeatedly', and /dokta-kau/ 'veterinarian' is compounded from words meaning 'doctor' and 'cow').
- Syntax is heavily dependent upon fixed word order, and there is no inflection (/i bin gow mit king-boi/ 'he went to meet the prince' and

/wi masa i tu wuman, dem now fit gow josna/ 'our boss's two wives can't go now').

North American Lingua Francas In the past, in order to facilitate trading and communication among linguistically diverse people, various lingua francas were employed by the Native peoples of North America. Among these was the North American Plains Indian Sign Language (see Figure 12.3), which was at one time used in an area between the Mississippi River and the Rocky Mountains and from northern Mexico to the Canadian prairies. It was an unusual example of a nonverbal lingua franca.

Another North American lingua franca was the *Chinook Jargon,* once used in an area extending from Oregon to the Alaska panhandle. It was a pidgin that owed its lexicon to a number of languages, among them the indigenous Chinook and Nootka languages as well as French and English. The English element in this pidgin is rather limited. French loans are more numerous—*lemooto* 'sheep' from *le mouton,* and *lalang* 'language, tongue' from *la langue.* As seen in these examples, the French determiner was taken over along with the noun and incorporated into it. Chinook Jargon arose in

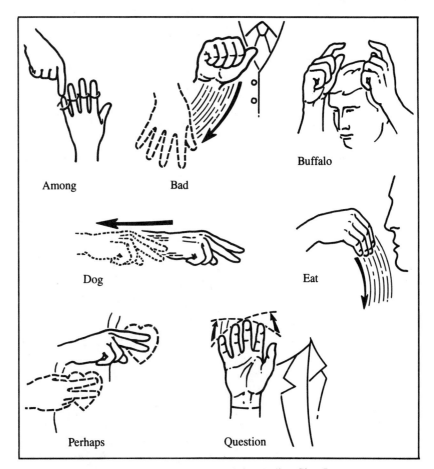

Figure 12.3 Examples of signs used in Plains Indian Sign Language

an area in which numerous mutually unintelligible languages were spoken. At that time, the need for a lingua franca in such a region would have been great. With the rise of English as the dominant language, however, the need for any other lingua franca vanished.

Creoles

Creoles differ from pidgins in that they are the first language of some group. They do, however, share a common mode of origin with pidgins. Creoles are, in fact, pidgins that have become established as a first language in some speech community. The term *creole* came into being as a label for people of Spanish or Portuguese descent born and brought up in South America. It later came to mean persons of mixed race or (black) slaves. Even later, it was a label for the language of these slaves, especially the mixture of French and other languages spoken in Haiti. This mixed language came to be the first language of the Haitian population, and eventually linguists ap-

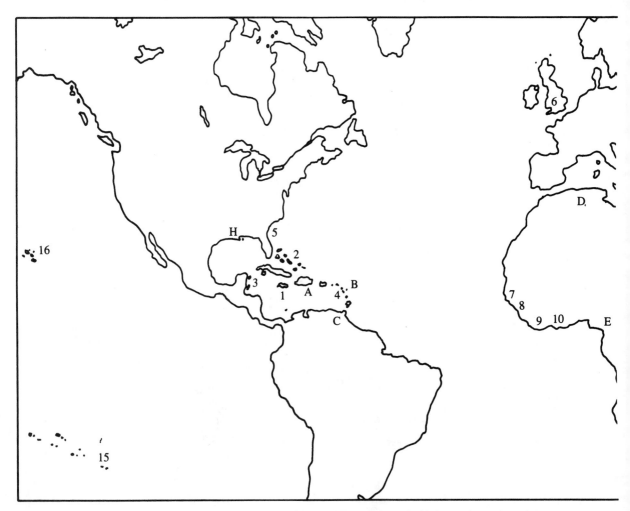

Figure 12.4 Some English- and French-based pidgins and creoles of the world

propriated the term as a generic label for any previously pidginized language that became a first language.

In most instances, creoles that have become established as first languages in particular countries continue to exist alongside the standard language that was originally pidginized. The standard language usually serves as the language of education and administration. The creole, not having the stabilizing base of a written tradition and likely subject to the influence of the standard, tends to change more rapidly over time. Typically, different varieties of the creole emerge, some resembling the standard more than others. In such situations, those creole varieties that least resemble the standard are called **basilects**. That variety most similar to the standard is labeled the **acrolect**. Varieties between these two extremes are called **mesolects**.

Along with most pidgins, most creoles have existed in a relatively narrow belt between the Tropics of Cancer and Capricorn (see Figure 12.4).

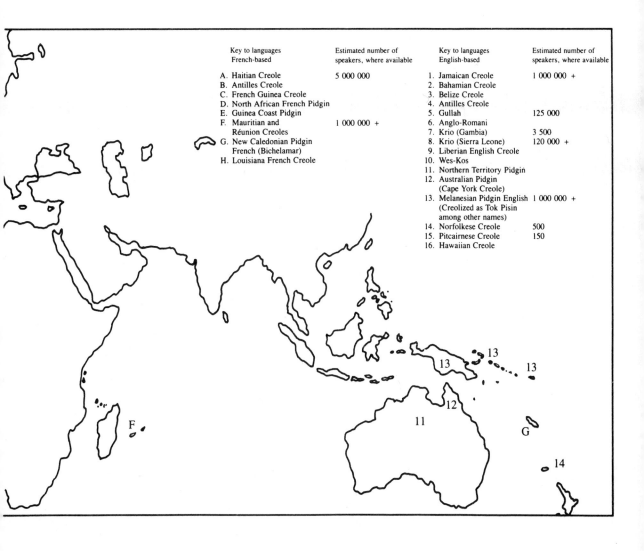

Key to languages French-based	Estimated number of speakers, where available
A. Haitian Creole	5 000 000
B. Antilles Creole	
C. French Guinea Creole	
D. North African French Pidgin	
E. Guinea Coast Pidgin	
F. Mauritian and	1 000 000 +
Réunion Creoles	
G. New Caledonian Pidgin French (Bichelamar)	
H. Louisiana French Creole	

Key to languages English-based	Estimated number of speakers, where available
1. Jamaican Creole	1 000 000 +
2. Bahamian Creole	
3. Belize Creole	
4. Antilles Creole	
5. Gullah	125 000
6. Anglo-Romani	
7. Krio (Gambia)	3 500
8. Krio (Sierra Leone)	120 000 +
9. Liberian English Creole	
10. Wes-Kos	
11. Northern Territory Pidgin	
12. Australian Pidgin (Cape York Creole)	
13. Melanesian Pidgin English (Creolized as Tok Pisin among other names)	1 000 000 +
14. Norfolkese Creole	500
15. Pitcairnese Creole	150
16. Hawaiian Creole	

There are a number of them in the West Indies, the East Indies, and West Africa.

Cape York Creole Among the English-based creoles of the world is Cape York Creole (CYC), spoken in the northern tip of Australia opposite Papua-New Guinea. The data from this creole in Tables 12.7 to 12.9 will help to illustrate the fact that creoles are not simply deformed or bastardized languages but, in fact, have interesting characteristics of their own that are not shared with the standard.

Table 12.7 Singular pronouns in Cape York Creole

First person	ai, mi
Second person	yu
Third person	i, im

CYC has developed categories of pronouns not seen in Standard English. Differences from Standard English include the fact that in the third person there is no three-way gender distinction and that all of these pronouns can serve as a subject. Only *mi, yu,* and *im,* however, can serve as objects. This is reminiscent of the Standard English pronouns *me* and *him,* which serve only as objects. The main difference between the CYC pronominal system and that of Standard English lies in the nonsingular forms. CYC exhibits two nonsingular categories: dual and plural. The forms for second and third person are shown in Table 12.8. The form *-pela* derives from En-

Table 12.8 Dual and plural pronouns in Cape York Creole (second and third person)

Dual, second person	yutu(pela)
Dual, third person	tupela
Plural, second person	yu(pela)
Plural, third person	ol, dempela

glish *fellow*. It occurs in several realizations, *-fela* being the acrolectal form. In the first person, a further distinction is made between *inclusive* and *exclusive* pronouns. Inclusive pronouns *include* the speaker and addressee ('you and I'), while exclusive pronouns *exclude* the addressee but include the speaker and someone else. These pronominal categories are realized in CYC in the forms in Table 12.9, all of which are first person, nonsingular.

Table 12.9 Dual and plural pronouns in Cape York Creole (first person, nonsingular)

Dual, inclusive	yumi, yumtu	(speaker plus one addressee)
Dual, exclusive	mitu	(speaker plus one other, not the addressee)
Plural, inclusive	mipela, wi	(speaker plus addressees)
Plural, exclusive	mitupela, wi	(speaker plus others, not addressees)

The following example illustrates the semantic differences among some of these categories. Assume that they are uttered in a situation in which three persons (A, B, and C) are present.

> 2. *a*) If A says to B *yumi go nau,* A is saying that the two of them will go but not C.
>
> *b*) If A says to B *mitu go nau,* A is saying that A and C will go but not B.
>
> *c*) If A says to B and C *mipela go nau,* A is saying that all three of them will go.

It should be apparent from these few examples that creoles, far from being less than a standard, are capable of distinctions not found in the standard. The existence of a dual category of number alongside those of plural and singular, for example, affords CYC speakers a precision not available to speakers of Standard English. The dual is often seen in languages spoken in small-scale, mainly agricultural societies in which it is useful to be able to designate items as occurring in pairs. The distinction between inclusive and exclusive pronouns is widespread in languages of the world, being present in many Amerindian languages, for example. Note how, in the foregoing translations, English can only somewhat clumsily paraphrase the ideas expressed by these CYC pronouns. These distinctions are, however, important to CYC speakers—and probably to speakers of neighboring indigenous languages—and thus are incorporated into the pronominal system. Like other English-based creoles, CYC shares a number of features with Standard English but has its own linguistic system and its own history.

12.6 SPEECH SITUATIONS

Speech situations are social situations in which there is use of speech. They are the main locus for research by interactional sociolinguists. The methods of description and analysis of speech situations differ markedly from the techniques we have previously examined in this chapter. A speech situation consists of a number of components. In analyzing a speech situation, the sociolinguist seeks to specify how each of these components is realized. Once this has been done, an understanding of the how, what, and why of the interaction is achieved.

In Table 12.10, the components of the speech situation have been mnemonically arranged to form the acronym SPEAKING. These notions become more concrete in the context of a specific example. Consider the following situations, which might occur in a university.

Setting, Scene A classroom could be the setting and might accommodate a number of scenes, among them a lecture, tutorial, club meeting, or conversation.

Participants The different scenes provide for a number of possible relationships between interactants: teacher-student, leader-member, addresser-addressee, among others.

Table 12.10 Components of the speech situation arranged mnemonically

S	The setting and scene of a speech situation, distinguishing between the physical locale and the type of activity
P	The participants, often characterized by terms such as addresser, addressee, speaker, performer, audience, questioner, answerer, caller, interviewer, interviewee, and so on
E	The ends, including both functions and outcomes
A	The act sequence, including the content and form of speech
K	The key, tone, mood, or manner, distinguishing among serious, facetious, formal, sarcastic, and so on
I	The instrumentalities, including the "channel" (verbal, nonverbal, face to face, written) and "code" (the language and/or variety used)
N	The norms of interaction and interpretation (the basic rules that seem to underlie the interaction)
G	The genre, any one of a class of named speech acts (greeting, leave-taking, lecture, joke, and so on)

Ends Among the numerous possible functions might be the instructional (in a lecture), the consultative (in a tutorial), and the interactional (in a friendly conversation). The outcomes could include whatever has been learned in the lecture or tutorial, the plans for a party in the club meeting, or the sharing of gossip in the conversation.

Act sequence The content and form might vary from the structured lecture material, to the question and answer or problem solving of the tutorial, to the agenda of the meeting, to the small talk of the conversation.

Key The mood would range from the comparative formality of the lecture to the relative informality (even jocularity) of the conversation.

Instrumentalities All the situations would be face to face, mostly verbal (aside from appropriate nonverbal aspects such as the raising of a hand for recognition and the performance of written tasks). The variety of English would likely be Standard English in the lecture but might contain significantly more nonstandard features in the conversation. Recalling the sociolinguistic variable (ng) from Section 12.3, we might expect to hear it realized as [ŋ] in the lecture but as [n] more often in the conversation.

Norms The norms would vary considerably from situation to situation. The rights (or status) of participants would differ markedly. In the lecture, tutorial, and, perhaps to a lesser extent, the club meeting, the teacher (or leader) would control the situation. He or she might do most of the talking and generally determine the course of the interaction. Other participants would normally be required to secure the permission of the leader in order to speak. In the conversation, there would be greater equality between participants.

Genre A lecture can be termed a genre in itself. It is recognizable by its form, limited number of topics, speaker-audience format, and relative formality. A tutorial would include questions and answers, among other acts. A conversation consists of a number of possible speech acts (or genres). Among these might be an initial greeting (*Hi!*), a concluding leave-taking

(*Bye!*), and intervening narratives (including perhaps a joke). Thus, it can be seen that genre is a component that can be understood on more than one level. A lecture can be a genre but so can a greeting or a joke, which is included in the lecture.

As we can see from these examples, speaking in social contexts involves more than simply being able to form grammatical sentences. Sociolinguists claim that speakers possess communicative competence, or underlying knowledge of the linguistic system combined with knowledge of the rules (or norms) for the appropriate use of language in speech situations. In interactional sociolinguistics, the concern is not so much with the grammaticality of utterances but rather with their appropriateness. The next section treats this matching of language with situation in its discussion of the concept of functional speech variety, or register.

Register

The form that talk takes in any given context is called a register. Different registers may be characterized in phonological, syntactic, or lexical terms. A register is also a function of all the other components of a speech situation discussed in the previous section. A formal setting may condition a formal register, characterized by particular lexical items, greater adherence to the rules of Standard English, absence of stigmatized sociolinguistic variables, and so on. An informal setting may be reflected in a less formal register that exhibits casual vocabulary, more nonstandard features, greater instances of stigmatized variables, and so on. Registers can also be categorized in terms of their relative explicitness.

Two good friends discussing a matter well known to both do not need to make every detail of their conversation explicit. Each may correctly assume that the other knows basically what the conversation is about. Such an assumption can result in the appropriate use of pronouns and elliptical sentences, both of which are less explicit (more implicit) than nouns or full sentences. The speakers' shared background knowledge will fill in the blanks. Similarly, shared knowledge in an ongoing situation, such as experienced by spectators at a hockey game, means that one fan can refer to the goalie as *he* (perhaps pointing as well) and be understood by another. A university lecture (or a textbook) is, on the other hand, a scene that requires both a formal and an explicit register, since new and unfamiliar concepts are being introduced and explained.

The following examples of some registers of spoken and written language are mainly differentiated from each other in terms of relative formality and explicitness.

> *3.* "This is close to a charge. Call it yourself. No, he did move over on him!"

This was uttered by a color commentator describing an instant replay in a basketball game. It was understandable in context and appropriately implicit. Only one noun was used in the quotation, and it is a technical term in basketball. The referents of the pronouns (other than the audience-directed "yourself") were entirely context-bound. It was reasonable to assume that anyone who could see the telecast could interpret their meanings.

    4. "That's what I ought to look like is like that."

This sentence is again entirely context-bound (and maximally implicit) in its meaning. It was appropriate, however, when uttered. Its speaker and addressee both understood what *that* refered to. Its syntax is also consistent with its informality.

    5. "In those pants you really look like a zhlub."

Again, the interpretation of the precise reference is limited to the context in which the sentence was uttered. Also, the use of an ethnic slang term *zhlub* (meaning 'gauche or coarse person' in Yiddish) signals an informal register.

    6. "Wilt thou have this man to be thy wedded husband. . . ."

Lexical, morphological, and syntactic archaisms signal this formal (and ritualized) register.

    7. "Pellagra is characterized by cutaneous, mucous membrane, CNS, and gastrointestinal symptoms."

This quotation from a medical handbook illustrates features of a formal register (in the written channel) by its fully formed sentence, high degree of explicitness, use of the passive, and the presence of medical sublanguage.

    8. "Bruins Harpooned"

This appeared as a caption to a graphic on a television newscast. Its elliptical form is obviously derived from the style of newspaper headlines. It is appropriate to the written channel of communication and illustrates the importance of shared knowledge in the interpreting of elliptical utterances. A hockey fan would know that the caption refers to the defeat of the Boston Bruins by the Hartford Whalers.

    The preceding quotations are a small sample of the variety of registers available to English-speakers. All competent speakers of the language are able to produce at least a few registers, thereby making their speech appropriate for particular speech situations.

Forms of Address

One aspect of speech that has been productively analyzed by interactional sociolinguists is that of address term usage. This phenomenon has been observed in a variety of languages and cultures. It seems clear that all languages have address forms and specific rules that determine their appropriate use. Every time speakers call someone or refer to him or her by name, they indicate something of their social relationship to or personal feelings about that individual. A person might be on first-name terms with a friend but not with an uncle or a mother. A grandparent might be addressed by a pet name coined in childhood, but an employer might be called "Ms. Costello" and might address the employee by first name. There is nothing unusual about these examples. Not everyone functions with precisely this assortment of address forms, but they are probably quite representative of general usage in our society.

Compared to most of the world's languages, English has a relatively simple system of address terms, such as those shown in Table 12.11. Address

Table 12.11 Types of address terms in English

Term	Example
First name (FN)	Jane!
Title + last name (TLN)	Mr. Simpson!
Title alone (T)	Nurse!
Last name (LN)	Smith!
Kinterms (KT)*	Granny!

*Alone or with FN or LN, as appropriate

terms can be used reciprocally or nonreciprocally. In the first case, speakers address each other with the same type of term (FN or TLN). This is a sign of a symmetrical social relationship in which both parties have the same status (friends, colleagues, and so on). In the case of nonreciprocal usage, there is an asymmetrical relationship, one in which the difference in status between participants is marked. Thus, one person might use FN, and the other TLN. This is typical of a doctor-patient or teacher-student relationship.

In English, and other languages as well, it is also possible to avoid address terms altogether when participants are unsure which term to use. This practice is called **no-naming**. In the case of English speakers, it results in participants using *you* while scrupulously avoiding terms such as FN or TLN. A familiar example of this occurs in the university setting when students no-name an instructor if unsure whether to call him or her by a more specific address term.

Other European languages have one complication that has been largely missing from our language since the seventeenth century: the choice of two pronouns in the second person. On one level in the grammars of these languages, choosing between these two pronouns (*tu* and *vous* in French) is a function of the number of people being addressed—singular versus plural. These pronouns, however, also encode the sociolinguistic dimensions mentioned above. Thus, the form *tu* is like our FN in connoting friendship or intimacy when used mutually and in connoting lower status of the addressee when used nonreciprocally. The form *vous* used with a singular addressee is similar to our TLN in these respects. The details of these usages vary from language to language, but these broad outlines are indicative of the general tendencies.

Outside Europe and other areas where European languages dominate, these overall patterns still hold but often in complex systems with vast numbers of address forms. In many instances, we also have to take into account not only the second person pronouns, but first and third person pronouns as well. In many languages (especially those in highly traditional, stratified societies), there are a number of first person singular pronouns. In Thai, for example, there are seventeen different forms that translate English *I*. Their appropriate use is based on the status of the speaker, that of the addressee, and the relationship between the two. In the same language, there are a further seventeen second person forms and eleven third person forms. In addition, there are numerous categories of nouns that can be used in direct address. The rules for deciding which form is appropriate are complex and require the participants to have some knowledge about each other's status. Given these complications and the possibility that selecting an inappropriate form might be rude or insulting, there is also a provision for no-naming. The forms in Table 12.12, all equivalent to English *you*, are but a small sample of the set of address terms available in the Bangkok speech community.

Table 12.12 Some Thai address terms

Speaker	Addressee	Term
friend/kin/spouse	friend/kin/spouse	/nii/
adult/superior	child/inferior	/nuu/
Buddhist monk	superior monk	/pradeedprakhun/
inferior/non-monk	superior/monk	/tʰan/

Summing Up

The field of **sociolinguistics** treats the social aspects of language use. This chapter focuses on three principal types of **speech variety**: **regional dialects**, **sociolects**, and **register**, along with a number of related phenomena. **Dialectology** deals with regional variation in language. All varieties of a language are dialects, but in all communities, one variety, the **standard**, has more prestige than the others. In many countries, the linguistic picture is complicated by the existence of multilingualism. Sociolects of any language may reflect **social stratification** and **social differentiation**, as well as the age and sex of their users. Among many speakers, **taboo** forms are replaced by **euphemisms**. Some segments of any population develop secret languages or **argots**, while **sublanguages** are associated with specialized professions, and **play languages** with children. The interaction of different linguistic groups may give rise to **pidgins**, mixed languages without native speakers. **Creoles** arise when pidgins are learned as native languages. Finally, speech situations are reflected in the use of registers, linguistic variants that are appropriate in a given situation.

Sources

The dialect maps of Pennsylvania are adapted from Carroll E. Reed's article "Double Dialect Geography" in *Readings in American Dialectology,* edited by H. Allen and G. Underwood (New York: Appleton Century Crofts, 1971). The map in Figure 12.2 is adapted from C. V. Baeyer's *The Ancestry of Canadian English* (Hull: Canadian Government Publishing Centre, Minister of Supply and Services, 1980).

An important source and, indeed, underlying inspiration for sections dealing with the social stratification of English is William Labov's article "The Logic of Nonstandard English" in *Report of the Twentieth Annual Round Table Meeting on Linguistics and Language Studies,* edited by James E. Alatis (Washington: Georgetown University Press, 1970), pp. 1–43. The sociolinguistic (phonological) variables are dealt with in William Labov's *Sociolinguistic Patterns* (Philadelphia: University of Pennsylvania Press, 1972).

The underlying organization and some of the terminology used in the language and sex section derive from Anne Bodine's article "Sex Differentiation in Language" in *Language and Sex: Difference and Dominance,* edited by Barrie Thorne and Nancy Henley (Rowley, Mass.: Newbury House, 1975), pp. 130–51. The Amerindian examples in this section are taken from Mary Haas's article "Men's and Women's Speech in Koasati" in *Language* 20: 142–49 (1944). The reference to the ingressive affirmative comes from Francis J. Peters' work *The Paralinguistic Ingressive Affirmative in English and the Scandinavian Languages* (Dissertation: New York University, 1981).

Material on play languages is in part derived from Alvin Schwartz's book *The Cat's Elbow and Other Secret Languages* (New York: Farrar Straus Giroux, 1982). A further source on Boontling is Charles C. Adams' *Boontling: An American Lingo* (Austin: University of Texas Press, 1971). Data on Cockney Rhyming Slang are from J. Franklyn's *A Dictionary of Rhyming Slang* (London: Routledge and Kegan Paul, 1975). The major source for sublanguage is *Sublanguage: Studies of Language in Restricted Domains,* edited by Richard Kittredge and John Lehrberger (Berlin: Walter de Gruyter, 1982).

The data on Wes-Kos were taken from G. D. Schneider's *West African Pidgin-English* (Athens, Ohio: published by the author, 1966). Material on Cape York Creole is derived from the article "Cape York Creole" by Terry Crowley and Bruce Rigsby in *Languages and Their Status,* edited by Timothy Shopen (Cambridge, Mass.: Winthrop Publishers, 1979), pp. 153–207. The discussion of Plains Indian Sign Language and the accompanying illustrations are adapted from Allan Taylor's article "Indian Lingua Francas" in the Ferguson and Heath volume cited below, pp. 175–95. Chinook Jargon lexical items come from E. H. Thomas's *Chinook: A History and Dictionary of the Northwest Coast Trade Jargon* (Portland: Binfords and Mort, 1970). The map showing the distribution of some English- and French-based creoles and pidgins is from Ian F. Hancock's article "A Survey of the Pidgins and Creoles of the World" in *Pidginization and Creolization of Languages,* edited by Dell Hymes (Cambridge, Mass.: Cambridge University Press, 1971), pp. 509–23 and from Ian F. Hancock's article "Repertory of Pidgin and Creole Languages" in *Pidgin and Creole Linguistics,* edited by Albert Valdman (Bloomington: Indiana University Press, 1977).

The components of SPEAKING and the inspiration for the section in which they appear derive from Dell Hymes's article "Models of the Interaction of

Language and Social Life'' in *Directions in Sociolinguistics: The Ethnography of Communication,* edited by J. Gumperz and D. Hymes (New York: Holt, Rinehart and Winston, 1972), pp. 35–71. An underlying source for the section on address terms is the article by Roger Brown and Albert Gilman, ''The Pronouns of Power and Solidarity'' in *Style in Language,* edited by Thomas A. Sebeok (Cambridge, Mass.: MIT Press, 1960), pp. 253–76. The discussion and examples of Thai address terms are taken from Angkab Palakornkul's work *A Sociolinguistic Study of Pronominal Strategy in Spoken Bangkok Thai* (Dissertation: University of Texas, 1972).

Recommended Reading

Chambers, J. K. and Peter Trudgill. 1980. *Dialectology.* London: Cambridge· University Press.

Ferguson, Charles A. and Shirley Brice Heath, eds. 1981. *Language in the USA.* London: Cambridge University Press.

Hudson, R.A. 1980. *Sociolinguistics.* London: Cambridge University Press.

Saville-Troike, Muriel. 1982. *The Ethnography of Communication.* Oxford: Basil Blackwell.

Questions

1. Based on knowledge of your speech community, design a simple questionnaire (along the lines of the sample from Prince Edward Island given in the chapter) testing for particular lexical items. If you live in a rural community, you might explore items similar to those in the chapter. If you live in a city, look, for example, at names for types of buildings, streets, sidewalks, the spaces between streets and sidewalks, and so on.

2. Choose a particular field of endeavor (farming, computers, weaving) and describe the unique features of its sublanguage.

3. Examine the speech in your community, and determine whether there are any sociolinguistic variables such as the (ng), (dh), and (th) discussed in the chapter. If so, how are they reflected in speech? (*Hint:* You might examine the realizations of the phonemes /t/ and /d/ in words such as *sitting* and *reading*.)

4. Test some of the assertions of this chapter's section on language and sex. Can you observe differential rates of interruption by men and women in conversations?

5. List and classify semantically as many slang words from your community as you can. Do all groups of adolescents in a particular community or school share the same slang? How do their ways of speaking differ? How are they alike?

6. Each of the following words is formed using the rules of some play language. Examine the words and state the rule that underlies the formation of each set.
   a) egelegephagant, higippogopogotagamugus
   b) nutsbuts, raibaisinsbins, icebicecreambeam
   c) bed and brutter, trimb a clee, chamb lop, sli skope

7. In early Modern English, there were two functioning second person pronouns: *thou* and *ye*. *Thou* was used by social superiors to inferiors (including parents to children) and *ye* was used by the inferior in addressing the superior. *Thou* has been lost from general use in our language. Only *ye* (in the form *you*) has survived. In view of the discussion of address terms in this chapter, what has caused this change?

13 WRITING SYSTEMS

> *The invention of writing . . . has had a greater influence in uplifting the human race than any other intellectual achievement.*
>
> James Breasted, *The Conquest of Civilization*

Writing and talking are different in both origin and practice. Our ability to use language is as old as humankind, and reflects the biological and cognitive modification that has occurred in the evolutionary history of our species. **Writing, the symbolic representation of language in storable graphic form, is a comparatively recent cultural development, having occurred over only the past five thousand years.** We have no idea where speech began, but we know that writing originated only in certain areas of the world. The contrast between talking and writing comes into sharper focus when we consider that any normal child acquires spoken language without specific formal instruction, while writing must be taught and learned through deliberate effort. There are entire groups of people in the world today, as well as individuals in every literate society, who are unable to write. While language comes naturally to human beings, writing does not.

13.1 TYPES OF WRITING

Just as spoken language shows an arbitrary link between sound and meaning, written language shows an arbitrary link between symbol and sound. Writing systems can be grouped into three basic types, called logographic, syllabic, and alphabetic. The symbols used in each of these types of writing correspond to three principal units of linguistic representation: words, syllables, and segments.

Logographic Writing

The term **logographic** (from Greek *logos* 'word') refers to a system of writing in which a sign may represent an entire word. For example, imagine that the English word *house* was represented by a stylized drawing of a house: ⌂. If this symbol was read as [háws], we could say that English had a logographic writing system. Most logographic signs represent root morphemes. It is rare to find a logographic symbol for an inflectional ending like the plural.

Syllabic Writing

As the name suggests, **syllabic** writing employs signs to represent syllables (a set of syllabic signs is called a **syllabary**). Languages with relatively simple syllabic structures such as CV or CVC (Japanese and Cree, for example) are well suited to this type of writing, since they contain a very limited number of syllable types. In Japanese, the word *kuruma* 'car' can be written with three syllabic signs, 〈 *ku*, ろ *ru*, and ま *ma*.

Alphabetic Writing

Alphabetic writing represents consonant and vowel segments. Generally, alphabets do not indicate allophonic details of pronunciation and so are largely phonemic in nature. This is illustrated by the English spelling of the words *pat, tap,* and *apt,* which represent three arrangements of the phonemes /p/, /t/, and /æ/ without indicating (allophonic) aspiration on the consonants. The International Phonetic Alphabet is a specialized alphabet devised expressly to represent details of pronunciation. As we shall see in Section 13.4, some spelling systems also reflect morphology.

Like logographic and syllabic writing, alphabetic writing emerged and spread around the earth over a long period of time. The next sections trace the development of these writing systems from their pictorial ancestry.

13.2 THE HISTORY OF WRITING

The antecedents of writing are buried in the distant past. Figures and scenes depicted on cave walls and rock faces in Europe and Africa twelve thousand years ago or perhaps even earlier may have been forerunners of writing. Such rock painting is not limited to those continents. The petroglyphs (scenes painted on stone) of the North American Indians may represent a type of protoliterate stage that did not evolve into a full-fledged writing system.

We are not sure these drawings represent steps toward writing or were even intended for purposes of linguistic communication. Perhaps they were forms of esthetic expression, perhaps they were employed as a form of magic to guarantee a successful hunt or other benefits, or perhaps they were the product of religious activity. Some illustrations, such as those depicting the phases of the moon, may have been part of some form of record keeping. Figure 13.1 shows a pair of elk from a rock-wall drawing in Sweden dating from the Old Stone Age (early paleolithic) period, perhaps as far back as 20,000 B.C.

Figure 13.1 Drawings: Sweden, early paleolithic

Pictograms

Whatever their intent, there is no doubt that pictures were among the precursors of the written word. Pictures from later periods were clearly drawn for purposes of communication. These representations are generally referred to as **pictograms** or picture writing. Each pictogram was an image of the object it represented, and, as far as we know, offered no clues to pronunciation. Each situation depicted could be understood by the viewer independent of language. This kind of communication has been found among people throughout the ancient and modern world; it has been used by American native peoples, by African tribes, by natives of Siberia, and by ancient peoples of the Middle East. Figure 13.2 shows Inuit picture writing, and

▬ [gone away to hunt — no food here]

Figure 13.2 Inuit picture writing

Figure 13.3 illustrates pictograms that date back to the fourth millennium B.C. in the Middle East and around fourteen hundred B.C. in China. Picto-

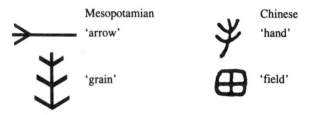

Figure 13.3 Early pictograms

grams are still used today. Signs indicating roadside services or information in parks are all pictographic in nature. The International Olympic Committee has developed a standardized set of pictograms to indicate sporting events (see Figure 13.4).

Figure 13.4 Contemporary pictograms: Olympic signs for sporting events

From Pictogram to Ideogram

The earliest-known pictographic writing came from Sumeria, from where it spread to surrounding areas about five thousand years ago. The inadequacy of such a system became obvious when it was necessary to portray abstract notions such as courage, love, hatred, and willingness, or to indicate grammatical categories such as person and number. Making pictograms was also laborious, and the results could be ambiguous.

The users of early pictograms dealt with the problem of representing more abstract notions by extending the use of a particular pictogram to include abstract concepts felt to be associated with it. A pictogram of the sun could also mean 'light' or 'heat' or even 'energy'; an arrow, 'to run'; and a foot, 'to go'. Pictograms that represent ideas rather than concrete objects are called **ideograms** (see Figure 13.5).

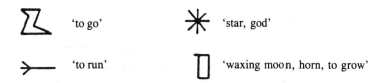

'to go'	'star, god'
'to run'	'waxing moon, horn, to grow'

Figure 13.5 Sumerian ideograms

Ideograms represented an important step toward a true writing system, which involves the use of arbitrary symbols to represent linguistic units. The shape of the symbol and the meaning it represented were no longer directly linked. Users of the signs had to associate them with linguistic forms, and not directly with meaning, a development that led to the type of writing discussed in the next section.

A contemporary and very sophisticated development of both pictographic and ideographic writing, **Blissymbolics** (originally called semantography), was developed by Charles K. Bliss. It makes use of a number of

person   forward   building   visitor

recombinable symbols that represent basic units of meaning, as the following example illustrates. Though Blissymbolics was intended as a means of international, cross-linguistic communication by its inventor, its primary use today is as a means of augmentative communication for nonspeaking individuals.

From Pictogram to Logogram

We cannot say with certainty at what date pictures began to be read as words, but there can be little doubt that by the time they were no longer recognizable as pictures, they were truly logographic or word writing.

It has been suggested that the idea of writing had its origin in small clay tokens and counters that were used in record keeping and business transactions in the ancient Middle East. These small, fire-baked pieces of clay were apparently used for this purpose for thousands of years before writing emerged. Counters representing cattle and other goods were stored on shelves or in baskets. Eventually, people began to make an impression of the tokens on soft clay tablets rather than storing and shipping the tokens themselves. This may have led to the idea that other objects and events in the world could be represented symbolically.

Logographic writing represents the oldest kind of genuine writing system. Ancient Mesopotamian cuneiform inscriptions, Egyptian hieroglyphics, and primordial Chinese characters were all logographic systems in their early stages (see Figure 13.6). In fact, all writing systems maintain some logo-

Figure 13.6 Logograms

graphic writing. Conventional abbreviations such as &, %, $, and the like are logographic, as are the symbols for numerals. Logographic writing can be "read" independently of its language of origin. For example, the Arabic numbers 1, 2, 7, 10, and so on can be read in any language, and the symbol for 'house' shown in Section 13.1 can be read as *maison* in French or *casa* in Italian. This can be an advantage in certain cultures. Chinese speakers of diverse linguistic backgrounds can read the same books and newspapers even though their dialects are mutually unintelligible, since even today Chinese writing is highly logographic. The character 火 means 'fire' whether it is pronounced as [xwo] in Peking or [fɔ] in Canton (tones are omitted throughout). A major disadvantage of logographic writing lies in the fact that extensive memorization is needed to use it; one must learn several thousand Chinese characters to read even a newspaper.

Cuneiform Over the centuries, Sumerian pictograms were simplified and eventually produced with the use of a wedge-shaped stylus, which was pressed into soft clay tablets. This form of writing, initiated in the fourth millennium B.C., has come to be known as **cuneiform** (from Latin *cuneus* 'wedge').

In time, a change in writing practices led the cuneiform signs to be rotated ninety degrees to the left. This resulted in their bearing even less resemblance to their pictographic origins than before. Figure 13.7 illustrates this development in two forms. Cuneiform signs were read for their sound value alone. The **rebus** principle was important in this development. A rebus is a string of pictorial symbols read for their phonetic value. For example, if the word *sea* was represented in English by the pictogram 〰, the word *see* could also be represented by this same sign. Similarly, the words

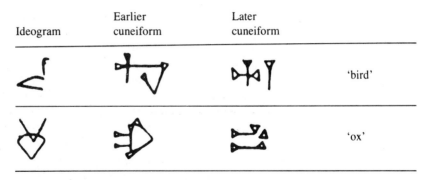

Ideogram	Earlier cuneiform	Later cuneiform	
			'bird'
			'ox'

Figure 13.7 Changes in cuneiform writing

I and *son* could be represented by ⟨eye symbol⟩ and ⟨sun symbol⟩, respectively. Using these forms, a whole sentence could be written, as in Figure 13.8.

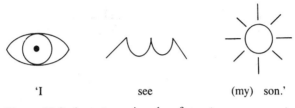

'I   see   (my) son.'

Figure 13.8 A sentence in rebus form

The rebus principle emphasizes a relationship between sound and symbol that has its origin in logograms. The word symbols of logographic writing can be read for their phonetic value, and so can be used to represent either words or syllables with the same pronunciation.

A shift in the use of symbols to represent sounds rather than words happened in several different logographic systems. Sumerian signs could be read as rebuses. The sign for the word *ti* 'arrow' →— was also used for the word *ti* 'life', and the sign for the word *mu* 'tree' ⊳◇ could also stand for the word *mu* 'name' and the suffix *-mu* 'my'. Cuneiform script maintained this practice, so that, for example, the sign for the word *an* 'sky' ⊳⊳⫪ could also represent any word or syllable with that pronunciation.

The cuneiform system was borrowed by the Elamites and Akkadians in the third millennium B.C., a little later by the Persians, and in the second millennium B.C. by the Hittites far to the North in the ancient region of Anatolia (modern Asian Turkey). In time, the borrowers employed the signs of this script as a syllabic writing system. Figure 13.9 shows an example of

hi   [person]   kam   ma   ad   da

'This person Kamada'

Figure 13.9 Elamite syllabic cuneiform

Elamite cuneiform. Cuneiform writing persisted to the first few centuries of the Christian era in some areas, and then disappeared from use, not to be rediscovered until the nineteenth century. It was first deciphered from Old Persian texts, a breakthrough that led to the decipherment of Akkadian, Sumerian, and Hittite, among other languages that employed it.

Hieroglyphics At about the time Sumerian pictography was flourishing, a similar system of pictorial communication was in use in Egypt. The Egyptian signs have become known as **hieroglyphics** (meaning 'sacred inscriptions' in Greek). The earliest texts display about five hundred such symbols.

Like Sumerian pictograms, the hieroglyphic signs at first represented objects, but later they became logographic in that they began to be associated with words. Egyptian hieroglyphics developed into a mixed system of both word writing and syllabic writing. For example, the sign for a lute was a picture of a lute: ♀ ; this represented the word itself: *nfr*. (Only the consonants of words represented by hieroglyphics are known with certainty. The Egyptians did not represent the vowels, and they can only be partially reconstructed from transcriptions in Greek and other languages that were made much later.) Eventually, the sign came to be disassociated from the word it represented, and was used to transcribe other words that consisted of or included these sounds, such as the word for 'good', whose consonants were also *nfr*. As with cuneiform writing, the association between symbol and sound came to be more important than a direct symbol and meaning association. Figure 13.10 shows some hieroglyphics. Hieroglyphics contin-

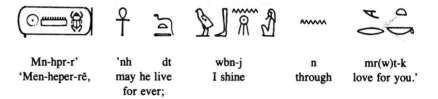

Mn-hpr-r'	'nh	dt	wbn-j	n	mr(w)t-k
'Men-heper-rē,	may he live		I shine	through	love for you.'
	for ever;				

Figure 13.10 Egyptian hieroglyphics (c. 2000 B.C.)

ued in decreasing use to Christian times. By the second century A.D., Egyptian began to be written with Greek letters. By the third century A.D., hieroglyphics had been replaced by the Greek alphabet.

From Logogram to Syllabary

We have seen how pictographic systems historically evolved into sound-writing systems as symbols for words began to be read for their sound value alone. A further development occurred when symbols came to represent syllables rather than words. Syllabic writing is more efficient than logographic writing, since a relatively small number of signs are needed to represent the possible sound combinations of a language.

Japanese Syllabics Modern Japanese is written with two syllabaries. These systems, known as **katakana** and **hiragana**, were developed by using modified Chinese signs for their approximate phonetic value.

Figure 13.11 shows the two syllabaries and their phonetic values. Katakana evolved from standard Chinese script, and hiragana from a less formal form of the same Chinese script. This difference in origin is reflected in their appearance. Katakana is more blocklike, and hiragana is more rounded.

Katakana chart

COLUMN LINE	A	I	U	E	O
SINGLE VOWEL	ア A	イ I	ウ U	エ E	オ O
K	カ KA	キ KI	ク KU	ケ KE	コ KO
S	サ SA	シ SHI	ス SU	セ SE	ソ SO
T	タ TA	チ CHI	ツ TSU	テ TE	ト TO
N	ナ NA	ニ NI	ヌ NU	ネ NE	ノ NO
H	ハ HA	ヒ HI	フ HU	ヘ HE	ホ HO
M	マ MA	ミ MI	ム MU	メ ME	モ MO
Y	ヤ YA		ユ YU		ヨ YO
R	ラ RA	リ RI	ル RU	レ RE	ロ RO
W	ワ WA		ン N		ヲ O

Hiragana chart

COLUMN LINE	A	I	U	E	O
SINGLE VOWEL	あ A	い I	う U	え E	お O
K	か KA	き KI	く KU	け KE	こ KO
S	さ SA	し SHI	す SU	せ SE	そ SO
T	た TA	ち CHI	つ TSU	て TE	と TO
N	な NA	に NI	ぬ NU	ね NE	の NO
H	は HA	ひ HI	ふ HU	へ HE	ほ HO
M	ま MA	み MI	む MU	め ME	も MO
Y	や YA		ゆ YU		よ YO
R	ら RA	り RI	る RU	れ RE	ろ RO
W	わ WA		ん N		を O

Figure 13.11 Hiragana and katakana syllabaries and their phonetic values (Voicing and vowel length are indicated with diacritics not presented here.)

Figure 13.12 shows the development of corresponding Japanese hiragana and katakana symbols from the original Chinese characters.

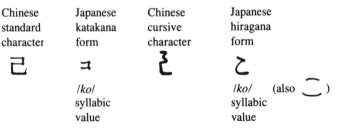

Chinese standard character	Japanese katakana form	Chinese cursive character	Japanese hiragana form

/ko/ syllabic value   /ko/ (also ⌣) syllabic value

Figure 13.12 Evolution of a pair of Japanese katakana and hiragana signs

Although Japanese can be written exclusively with the syllabaries, literary Japanese employs Chinese characters (called **kanji** in Japanese), in addition to hiragana and katakana. The Chinese characters are used to represent word roots. Since they are essentially logographic, they are read as Japanese. For example, the Chinese character 人 (*man*) represents *rən* in Mandarin but is read as *hito* in Japanese. Hiragana when used together with kanji spells out grammatical morphemes. The phrase *the man's car* may be represented as in Figure 13.13, with the roots 'man' and 'car' written with

hito   no   kuruma

man   poss.   car
kanji   hiragana   kanji

Figure 13.13 Phrase in kanji/hiragana

kanji, and the possessive morpheme *no* written with hiragana. The same phrase could just as well be written entirely with hiragana (see Figure 13.14).

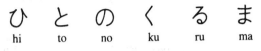

hi   to   no   ku   ru   ma

Figure 13.14 Hiragana phrase

Katakana is used to write non-Japanese words and is also widely employed in advertising (see Figure 13.15).

A disadvantage of syllabic writing is its unsuitability for languages such as English that have many syllable-initial or syllable-final consonant clusters. When syllabic writing is employed for such languages, either an unwieldy number of symbols must be devised since so many phonotactic combinations are possible, or (as has historically been the case) symbols that represent CV sequences are occasionally used to represent consonants alone.

Figure 13.15 Chinese characters (kanji), hiragana, and katakana in Japanese advertisement

From Syllabary to Alphabet

Alphabetic scripts are used to write English, French, Russian, Vietnamese, German, Turkish, and many other languages. These systems typically require fewer signs than syllabic writing since most languages have fewer phonemes than they have syllable types. Between twenty and thirty symbols for a language would not be uncommon. Such systems are readily applicable to any language, but the universal applicability of alphabetic writing has been inhibited by long-established local traditions, as in China and Japan, where millions of people would require re-educating in order to read and write with an unfamiliar alphabetic system.

The First Alphabet During the second millennium B.C., the Semites of ancient Phoenicia (modern Lebanon) devised a writing system of twenty-two consonantal signs, some of which may have developed from Egyptian hieroglyphics. This was the most successful of the various efforts of Semitic peoples to create a writing system, and was ultimately to lead to the development of many alphabetic writing systems, including both the Greek and Latin alphabets. Vowels were not written by the Phoenicians but had to be supplied by the reader, as would be necessary in English if signs for vowels were lacking in sentences such as *whr r th vwls? Wh hs thm?*

The Phoenicians were a trading people who carried their products abroad by land and sea. Their use of writing spread to adjacent countries and beyond, along with their commercial enterprises. Greece was one of the recipients of this new method of writing. The first true alphabet arose in the process of adapting the Phoenician system for the representation of the Greek language. Each Phoenician letter had a name, and the first sound of that name was the sound for which the letter stood. So, for example, the letter whose name was *bet* stood for the sound [b], while the letter whose name was *nun* stood for the sound [n]. All Phoenician letters stood for consonants, but some of these consonants did not exist in Greek. Thus, the letter *?alep* stood for the glottal stop, which the Greeks did not have in their language. On the principle that the first sound of the letter's name was the sound of the letter, they apparently concluded that this particular letter stood for the vowel sound [a], and they called it *alpha*. By making the same mistake with several other consonant letters, they arrived somewhat by accident at a complete alphabet marking all the phonemes of their language.

In the hands of the Greeks, the Phoenician writing system thus became a true alphabet: each sign represented one phoneme and all phonemes were recorded by a sign. Figure 13.16 illustrates the evolution of the Classical Greek and ultimately the Latin alphabet from the original Phoenician con-

Phoenician		Classical Greek	Latin
Sign	Phonetic value		
ⵣ	?	A	A
ⴳ	b	B	B
ⵑ	g	Γ	C,G
△	d	Δ	D
ⴽ	h	E	E
Y	w	Y	F
Ⅰ	z	Ⅰ	Z
目 目	ḥ	H	H
⊕	ṭ	θ	—
ⵥ	j	Ⅰ	I
ⵏ	k	K	K
㇄	l	Λ	L
ⵕ	m	M	M
ⵗ	n	N	N
ⵣ	s	Ξ	—
○	ʕ	O	O
ⵉ	p	Π	P
ⵔ	ṣ	—	—
Φ	q	—	Q
ⵇ	r	P	R
W	š	Σ	S
Ⅹ +	t	T	T

Figure 13.16 Evolution of the Latin alphabet

sonantal signs. Among other major changes, the Greeks discarded some unneeded consonant symbols, and added others to the system, namely, Φ, X, and Ψ. They also converted some symbols into vowel signs, and invented the sign Ω [ō]. The Phoenician names for the letters *aleph, bēth, gīmel, dāleth, hē,* and so on often reflected the pictorial origin of the sign: *aleph* 'ox' and *dāleth* 'door', for example. The Greeks maintained the names of the letters (as *alpha, beta, gamma,* and so on) but the names carried no other meaning.

Other Alphabets When Greek colonists occupied southern Italy in the eighth and seventh centuries B.C., they took their alphabet with them. It was in turn passed to the Etruscan inhabitants of central Italy. It is thought that they in turn passed it on to the small but growing Roman state. As the Romans grew in power and influence during the following centuries, first as masters of Italy and later of Europe, the Roman alphabet spread throughout the Empire.

Under the Romans, the Greek alphabet was again modified, this time with some signs influenced by the Etruscans. The Γ in Greek writing developed into both *C* for the phoneme /k/ and *G* for /g/. The oldest inscriptions also retained *K* for /k/ in some words, but it was generally replaced by *C*. Similarly, *Q* was retained before /u/. Roman script also employed Greek *U*, *V*, *X*, *Y*, and *Z* and moved *Z* to the end of the alphabet. Discarded were Φ, θ, Ψ, among others, and the vowel sign Ω. *H* was converted back to a consonant sign.

Some subsequent changes were made in the alphabet as it was adapted by various peoples of the Roman Empire. In English, we find *J* becoming a consonantal variant of *I* and *W* developing from juxtaposing two *V* signs. Spanish employs a tilde (˜) over *n* (ñ) to signify a palatal nasal, as in *año* [año] 'year', and French uses a cedilla under the *c* (ç) to indicate a dental fricative as in *français* [frãsɛ] 'French'.

An offshoot of the Greek script was created by Slavic peoples in the ninth century A.D. The brothers Constantine (Cyril) and Methodius introduced a writing system for the translation of the Bible that is now known as **Glagolitic** script. A later development, which combined adaptations of Glagolitic letters with Greek and Hebrew characters, has come to be known as the **Cyrillic alphabet**. The current Russian, Byelorussian, Ukrainian, Serbian, Macedonian, and Bulgarian alphabets, as well as those used to represent many non-Slavic languages spoken in the Soviet Union, have evolved from this early Cyrillic script. Some examples of its development and adaptation are given in Figure 13.17, followed by a short passage in contemporary Russian Cyrillic, which is transliterated for its letter values.

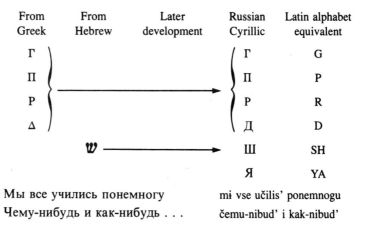

From Greek	From Hebrew	Later development	Russian Cyrillic	Latin alphabet equivalent
Γ			Γ	G
Π			Π	P
Ρ			Р	R
Δ			Д	D
	ש		Ш	SH
			Я	YA

Мы все учились понемногу   mɨ vse učilis' ponemnogu
Чему-нибудь и как-нибудь . . .   čemu-nibud' i kak-nibud'

'We all pick up our education
In bits and pieces as we can . . .'   Pushkin, *Eugene Onegin, I.5*

Figure 13.17 Contemporary Russian Cyrillic transliterated

ΙϮSΑΥΙ◊ΑϞ = harigasti ['a god's name'(?)]

Figure 13.18 Runic script

A still earlier offshoot of the Greco-Etruscan tradition of writing was adopted by Germanic tribes in the north of Italy. The script, referred to as Runic (from Old Irish *rúin* 'secret') writing, developed about the beginning of the Christian era, worked its way nothward as far as Scandinavia, and persisted until the sixteenth century in some areas before succumbing to the Roman script. Figure 13.18 illustrates some of these signs in one of the oldest Runic inscriptions from about the second century B.C. The angular style of the letters arose because the alphabet was carved in wood or stone, neither

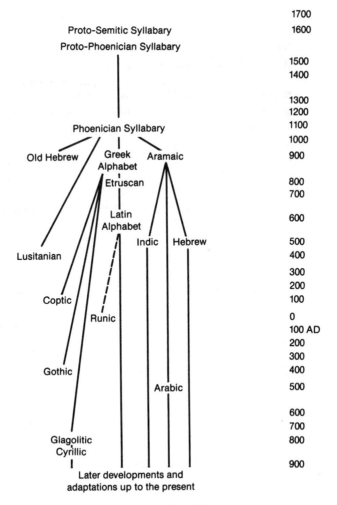

Figure 13.19 Development of alphabets
(Dotted lines indicate that the line of development is hypothetical.)

of which readily lends itself to curved lines. The script is read from right to left.

Other Developments The script used by the Phoenicians also gave rise to the Aramaic, Old Hebrew, and South Arabic scripts, which, in turn, led to a host of further writing systems eventually stretching across the Near East and North Africa from India to Morocco. Figure 13.19 illustrates this widespread diffusion on a time scale.

*13.3 SOME NON-EUROPEAN WRITING SYSTEMS

While writing systems that originated in the ancient Middle East have spread all over the world, other writing systems have emerged as well. This section examines some of these.

Chinese Writing

The Chinese system of writing developed out of picture forms that came to represent words, and has since remained largely a word writing, or logographic, system. The oldest inscriptions are the oracle texts, written on animal bones and tortoise shells and dating back to about fourteen hundred B.C. These include many recognizable drawings, such as ⊙ 'sun' and ☽ 'moon'. A change toward more symbolic signs began at an early date as more abstract notions were symbolized, such as ⌣ 'above' and ⌢ 'below'. Signs were also combined to extend meanings metaphorically. For example, the sign for 'to tend' 牧 is composed of 牛 'cow' and 攴 'hand and whip'. The word 'east' 東 is said to consist of 日 'sun' rising behind a 木 'tree'. 'To follow' 从 is two men in sequence, and so on. These complex forms were not read as combinations of the sounds of the joined symbols; they were—and still are—logographic signs in their own right. 'Tree', for example, is pronounced [šu] and 'sun' is [rɪ] in Mandarin, while 'east' is [dʌŋ].

Chinese writing has evolved away from a straightforward symbol-sound correspondence. Due to historical change, there are many homophonous forms in modern Chinese. Consequently, numerous Chinese characters are now composed primarily of two parts, a nonphonetic **determinative** (also called the **specifier** or **radical**) and a phonetic component, which we will simply refer to as the **character**. The character indicates the segmental pronunciation, while the determinative indicates which of the numerous meanings a given character's sound may be associated with. For example, the character 多, pronounced [duə] and written in combination with the determinative for 'eye' 目 as 眵 means 'dim', but written together with the determinative for 'grain' 禾 as 移 means '(to) transport'. In speech, one can determine from the phonemic word tone and context which meaning of [duə] is appropriate. In writing, the determinatives make this clear.

The determinative may precede, follow, or be located below the character. A second example of the determinative-character relationship involves the symbol 方. This character may stand alone, in which case it is pronounced [faŋ] and means 'square' or 'place'. When combined with various determinatives, it represents different meanings and has correspondingly different forms (see Figure 13.20). It can be seen that Chinese writing is not mere "picture writing" as is sometimes believed.

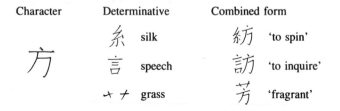

Character	Determinative		Combined form	
方	糸	silk	紡	'to spin'
	言	speech	訪	'to inquire'
	⺿	grass	芳	'fragrant'

Figure 13.20 Character-determinative combinations in Chinese

Calligraphy is an ancient and respected art in China, and Chinese writing exists in a number of styles. In recent times, the script has been written from left to right along a horizontal axis, although older texts begin in the right-hand margin and are read downwards. Modern governments have attempted to introduce simplified characters as a way of promoting literacy. At the same time, a system of writing Mandarin with a modified Latin alphabet, called **pinyin**, has also been introduced in the People's Republic of China.

American Scripts

Of the three major civilizations that developed on the American continents, the Incas in western South America, the Aztecs of Mexico, and the Mayans of the Yucatan, only the latter two made any significant advances in the realm of writing. Both saw the evolution of pictograms that leaned toward phonetic word signs, just as did the Egyptian hieroglyphics illustrated earlier. The Aztecs wrote the word *teocaltitlan* 'temple people' with the sign for 'lips' *te-n-tli,* 'road' *o-tli,* 'house' *cal-li,* and 'teeth' *tlan-tli,* rendering *te-o-cal-tlan* (omitting the syllable *ti*) (see Figure 13.21).

Teocal(ti)tlan 'temple people'

Figure 13.21 Aztec hieroglyphics

Some writing systems do not date back to a distant ancestor but have simply been invented, often by an individual who was familiar with the general process of writing. Some were developed in this way after the colonization of North America in order to furnish native peoples with a form of written communication. Professional linguists have often played a role in such developments. In other cases, the work was done by missionaries to facilitate the reading of the scriptures. In one well-known case, the Cherokee leader Sikwayi (Sequoia) devised a script for the use of his tribe. Each symbol in the syllabic script he invented was either based on the shapes of English letters or newly invented (see Figure 13.22). Eventually, the orthography was reduced to eighty-five signs, and books and a newspaper of the Cherokee nation were published in it.

D	a	R	e	T	i	ꭿ	o	Oʻ	u	i	a
f	ga	h	ge	y	gi	A	go	J	gu	E	ga
Oʼ	ha	?	he	ꭷ	hi	F	ho	Γ	hu	ꭹ	ha

Figure 13.22 Some Cherokee syllabic symbols

The syllabic script of the Cree Indians was the creation of a missionary, J. Evans, in the nineteenth century. It was employed primarily for religious literature, and by 1861, the entire Bible appeared in the Cree syllabary. Today, in somewhat modified form, the same script is used by Cree speakers across Canada. These symbols, with some modification, are also used by the Eskimos of northern Canada to represent their language, which is unrelated to Cree (see Figure 13.23).

ᐱᒡ ᑐᕆᒃ ᑖᑦᐁ ᐅᔧᕿ ᑭᑦᐱ ᑭᒃ

Figure 13.23 Eskimo script

Alphabetic scripts based upon modified Roman letters were also used among the Algonquian tribes for various periods of time. Occasionally, some Roman letters were assigned new phonetic values.

Alaskan Eskimos also developed a word-writing system in the form of pictures toward the end of the nineteenth century. In time, this developed into a partially syllabic system, although it did not achieve full syllabic status. Several types of systems are in use in different regions of Alaska, and in some, tendencies toward alphabetization are discernible.

Korean Writing

The invention of writing systems was not limited to North America. Korean was once written with Chinese characters, which had been introduced in the first centuries A.D. However, Korean suffixes could not be easily represented by Chinese writing. Various devices were tried to alleviate this problem, but inadequacies persisted. Finally, King Sejong (1419–1452) commisioned an alphabetic script consisting of eleven vowels and seventeen consonants that, after some modifications over the centuries, became the standard Korean writing system. The uniqueness of Hangul lies in the fact that the shapes of the letters are not completely arbitrary, but instead incorporate a kind of distinctive feature analysis. Figure 13.24 presents a chart of the symbols for individual consonants. The first row contains the ''basic'' consonants. In each subsequent row of consonants, a line is added to the basic symbol, first one line to mark a stop, then another line to mark aspiration. Each column thus corresponds to a place of articulation, except for the sibilant column. Also, the shape of the basic consonant symbols is to some extent pictorial. The symbol for *m* resembles the lips, the symbol for *n* shows the tongue tip touching the teeth, and so on.

	bilabial	apical	sibilant	velar
lax continuant	ㅁ m	ㄴ n	ㅅ s	
lax stop	ㅂ b	ㄷ d	ㅈ ɟ	ㄱ g
tense aspirant stop	ㅍ pʰ	ㅌ tʰ	ㅊ cʰ	ㅋ kʰ

Figure 13.24 Some Korean Hangul obstruent symbols

The vowel symbols shown in Figure 13.25 are also systematic. The two ''basic'' vowels, *i* and *ɯ*, are each written with a single line. The remaining back vowels are all *t*-shaped, while the remaining front vowels consist of the symbol for *i* combined with the symbol for the corresponding back vowel.

In writing Korean, consonant and vowel symbols are grouped into syllables, so that the resulting groups resemble Chinese characters visually, although the system is actually entirely alphabetic.

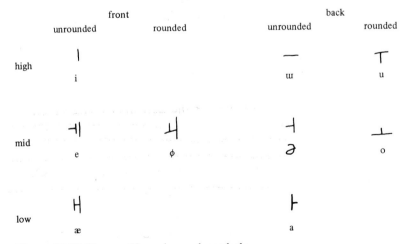

| | front | | back | |
	unrounded	rounded	unrounded	rounded
high	ㅣ i		ㅡ ɯ	ㅜ u
mid	ㅔ e	ㅚ φ	ㅓ ə	ㅗ o
low	ㅐ æ		ㅏ a	

Figure 13.25 Korean Hangul vowel symbols

African Scripts

In the past several centuries, societies in Central Africa have also produced syllabic scripts, which have either developed through stages from pictograms to refined syllabaries or have been invented by one or several individuals. Although the idea of writing appears to have been imported into these societies, the development of the various systems was indigenous.

The first Sub-Saharan African writing seems to have been that of the Vai peoples in the region of Sierra Leone and Liberia, where a native of the area developed a syllabary from a picture communication system in the nineteenth century. In the final stage, the cumbersome system consisted of 226 syllabic signs plus a few word signs. Vai writing appears to have spawned a number of imitations throughout the area. More recent is the writing of the Bamum in the Cameroons, invented at the end of the nineteenth century by a native leader. The current seventy syllabic signs show tendencies toward alphabetization.

The only sure example of alphabetic writing developed in modern times among African peoples is the Somali alphabet. The originator, acquainted with Arabic and Italian, devised an alphabet composed of nineteen consonants and ten vowels. The letter symbols appear to have been freely invented, but when the alphabet is listed or recited, the letter names follow the order of those of Arabic.

Indian Scripts

A pictorial script appears to have had an independent origin in Northern India, where inscribed seals, pottery, and copper tablets dating back to the third millennium B.C. have been unearthed. The system seems to have consisted of about 250 signs such as 𐎛, ▦, and ▲, but died away long before another writing system, seemingly derived from Semitic (see Figure 13.26), was employed in the middle of the first millennium B.C. to record the ancient Sanskrit language.

आसीद् राजा नलो नाम

| ā | sid | rājā | nalo | nāma |

'There was (a) king Nalo (by) name'

Figure 13.26 Sanskrit writing: Ramayana, Nala episode, line 1

The date of the first appearance of Indian Sanskrit signs cannot be ascertained, but they resemble Aramaic and appeared as a full system of writing in the edicts of Aśoka (who ruled from 272 to 231 B.C.). They were set down in two types of writing: Kharosthi and Brahmi. The former continued in use until about the fifth century A.D. in Northern India. The Brahmi script gave rise to all later varieties of Indian writing.

One of these varieties, a cursive type called the Gupta script, was later employed to write Tocharian, Saka, and Turkish manuscripts discovered in eastern Turkestan. In India, it evolved into the Devanagari script, which became the most widespread type of writing in the subcontinent and which was used to record the voluminous literature of the Sanskrit language. Inscriptions in Devanagari are found throughout Southeast Asia, Indonesia, and as far afield as the southern Philippines.

Varieties of Indian writing were carried abroad by Buddhist missionaries and influenced writing systems in Tibet and Central and Southeast Asia. The Dravidian peoples of Southern India also developed a number of scripts under the influence of the Northern varieties.

13.4 ENGLISH SPELLING

English employs an alphabetic system of writing in which symbols are used to represent individual consonants and vowels rather than syllables or words. The set of conventions for representing language in written form is called an **orthography**. In this section, we will consider the nature of English orthography. We will then use the following section to examine the relationship between writing and reading.

Irregularities

A frequently expressed complaint about English orthography is that it does not establish a one-to-one relationship between symbols and sounds. Table 13.1 lists some well-known examples of this. The following excerpt from a

Table 13.1 Some problems with English orthography

Problem	Example
1. Some letters do not represent any sound in a particular word.	through, sign, give, palm
2. A group of two or more letters can be used together to represent a single sound.	think, [θ], chip [č], ship [š]
3. A single letter can represent a cluster of two or more sounds.	Saxophone [ks], exile [gz]
4. The same letter can represent different sounds in different words.	on [ɑ], bone [ow], one [wʌ]
5. The same sound can be represented by different letters in different words.	rude, loop, soup, new, sue, to, two [uw]

poem by Richard Krogh vividly illustrates the extent to which English orthography departs from the principle of one symbol, one sound.

> Beware of heard, a dreadful word
> That looks like beard and sounds like bird.
> And dead; it's said like bed, not bead;
> For goodness sake, don't call it deed!
> Watch out for meat and great and threat
> (They rhyme with suite and straight and debt).
> A moth is not a moth in Mother,
> Nor both in bother, broth in brother.

There are a number of reasons for the irregularities in English spelling. Foremost among these is the fact that much of our orthography was in place in the fifteenth century before sound changes such as the Great Vowel Shift were complete. Because only some instances of the sounds represented by each letter changed, the relationship between spelling and sound was complicated. This has led to the use of the letter *i* to represent [ay] (*hide*) and [ɪ] (*hid*), the letter *a* to represent both [ey] (*opaque*) and [æ] (*opacity*), and so on.

Another complicating factor stems from the fact that words borrowed from other languages were often written in accordance with the spelling conventions of the source language. Many of the scribes responsible for the establishment of the original orthographic conventions were influenced by the French, Latin, and Greek spellings of borrowed words. For example, they maintained the Latin *t* rather than substitute a more phonetic spelling to represent the final segment of the root in words such as *reaction, oration, junction,* and so on. They also retained the initial *p* in Greek words such as *psyche,* and the convention of using *ph* to represent the [f] in words such as *philosophy*. Under the influence of French-speaking scribes, the digraph *th* was introduced for the sounds [θ] and [ð], replacing the Old English letters Þ and ð.

Other conventions arose as guides to pronunciation. The "silent *e*" of some words was introduced in the fifteenth century to indicate that the preceding syllable contained a long vowel. Today, these vowels have become diphthongs, as in *pine, irate, flute,* and *note*.

Obstacles to Reform

Over the years, there have been numerous proposals for the reform of English orthography. Indeed, such well-known people as Benjamin Franklin, George Bernard Shaw, and Noah Webster have been advocates of orthographic reform. However, far-reaching changes are both unlikely and undesirable for at least two reasons. First, any attempt at serious reform of English orthography would require a long and difficult period of transition. As the following letter to *The Economist* from M. J. Shields illustrates, reform would not be painless even if it took place over a period of many years.

> For example, in Year 1 that useless letter 'c' would be dropped to be replased either by 'k' or 's', and likewise 'x' would no longer be part of the alphabet. The only kase in which 'c' would be retained would be the 'ch' formation, which will be dealt with later. Year 2 might reform 'w' spelling, so that 'which' and 'one' would take the same konsonant, wile Year 3 might well abolish 'y' replasing it with 'i' and Iear 4 might fiks the 'g-j' anomali wonse and for all.
>
> Jenerally, then, the improvement would kontinue iear bai iear with Iear 5 doing awai with useless double konsonants, and Iears 6–12 or so modifaiing vowlz and the rimeining voist and unvoist konsonants. Bai Iear 15 or sou, it wud fainali be posibl tu meik ius ov thi ridandant leterz 'c', 'y' and 'x'—bai now jast a memori in the maindz of ould doderers— tu replais 'ch', 'sh' and 'th' rispektivli.
>
> Fainali, xen, after sam 20 iers ov orxogrephkl riform, we wud hev a lojikl, kohirnt speling in ius xrewawt xe Ingliy spiking world. . . .

People who knew only the reformed spelling system proposed in this letter would have difficulty reading books written in the current orthography. Ultimately, it would be necessary to translate billions of books, newspapers, and other manuscripts currently in libraries into the new spelling system.

A second factor militating against serious orthographic reform has to do with the dialectal variation found within English. Because English is spoken in more parts of the world than any other language, it has many different dialects. Any attempt to establish an orthography based on a principle of one sound, one symbol would result in serious regional differences in spelling. For instance, speakers of Boston English would write *car* as *ca* (or *ka*) since they do not pronounce syllable-final [r]. Speakers of some dialects would write both *tin* and *thin* as *tin,* and *day* and *they* as *day* since they have no [t] and [θ] or [d] and [ð] distinction. Moreover, while many Americans would have identical spellings for *cot* and *caught* (since these words are homophonous in their speech), others would spell the words differently to reflect the fact that they pronounce them differently.

Even if practical considerations did not rule out major reforms to our orthography, there might still be linguistic arguments for retaining at least some of the current irregular spelling conventions. In many cases, for example, our present spelling system allows us to distinguish homophones from each other.

1. to, too, two   threw, through
   bare, bear   so, sew
   no, know   blue, blew
   flea, flee   or, oar
   sore, soar   their, there

If our orthography followed the one sound, one symbol principle, each set of words in *1* would have the same spelling, thereby creating the potential for confusion and ambiguity.

Another advantage of our current orthography is that it often indicates derivational relationships among words. For instance, if the words *logic* and *logician* or *sign* and *signature* were spelled phonetically, it would be difficult to perceive the relationship between them since the root is pronounced differently in each case.

2. logic   [lajɪk]
   logician   [ləjɪšən]
   sign   [sayn]
   signature   [sɪgnəčər]

There are many other such cases where English orthography ignores differences in pronounciation so that a morpheme can have the same or nearly the same spelling in different words (see Table 13.2). Examples such as these show that English orthography does not simply try to represent phonemic contrasts. In some cases at least, it ignores morphologically conditioned alternations among phonemes to provide a single representation for the variants of a morpheme. This has led some people to conclude that English orthography is a type of morphological spelling system, in that it is more

Table 13.2 Some pronunciation differences not represented by English

electric — electricity	[k] and [s] represented as *c*
insert — insertion	[t] and [š] as *t*
right — righteous	[t] and [č] as *t*
bomb — bombard	Ø and [b] as *b*
damn — damnation	Ø and [n] as *n*
impress — impression	[s] and [š] as *ss*
allege — allegation	[j] and [g] as *g*; [ɛ] and [ə] as *e*
resign — resignation	Ø and [g] as *g*; [ay] and [ɪ] as *i*
chaste — chastity	[ey] and [æ] as *a*
produce — productive	[uw] and [ʌ] as *u*
please — pleasant	[iy] and [ɛ] as *ea*

sensitive to morphological factors than phonemic ones. Once this fact is taken into account, it is possible to see the usefulness of orthographic conventions that allow *c* to stand for either /k/ (*electric*) or /s/ (*electricity*) and *t* to represent /t/ (*react*) or /š/ (*reaction*).

13.5 IMPACT ON READING

The three types of writing systems described earlier in this chapter each represent different types of linguistic units—words in the case of logographic systems; syllables in the case of syllabaries; and consonants and vowels in the case of alphabets. Because of these differences, each orthography places different demands on readers. We know that different parts of the brain are used for reading word-based writing systems and sound-based orthographies (syllabaries and alphabets). Because phonological structure is largely irrelevant to logographic writing, people suffering from Broca's aphasia (see Chapter 9) typically do not lose the ability to write and read logograms. However, the use of syllabaries and alphabets can be severely disrupted by this type of brain disorder. There are reports of Japanese patients suffering from Broca's aphasia who are unable to use hiragana or katakana (the Japanese syllabaries), but retain mastery of kanji (the word-writing system that is also in use in Japan).

Further information about the relationship between language and writing systems comes from the study of the congenitally deaf. Because such people have never heard speech, they have little or no understanding of the phonological units that alphabets represent. Significantly, congenitally deaf individuals have a great deal of difficulty learning to read English. Even after many years of instruction, their reading remains poor and few attain college-level skills in this area.

The type of linguistic unit represented by an orthography has an effect on how children with normal hearing learn to read. Each system has its own advantages and disadvantages. Children learning Chinese characters, for instance, have little difficulty understanding what each symbol represents, but it takes them many years to memorize enough symbols to be able to write and read all the items in their vocabulary. (As noted earlier, knowledge of several thousand separate symbols is required just to read a newspaper.)

Even educated people typically know only a few thousand characters and must use dictionaries for new or unfamiliar words.

This problem does not arise in syllabic and alphabetic orthographies. Because languages have far fewer syllables and phonemes than words, the entire inventory of symbols can be learned in a year or two and then used productively to write and read new words. This is the major advantage of sound-based orthographies over word-based writing systems.

There is reason to think that children find syllabaries easier to master than alphabets. Children learning syllabaries (such as Japanese) are reported to have fewer reading problems than children learning alphabetic orthographies. Although at least some difficulties encountered by children learning to read English may be due to the complexity of English spelling conventions, Italian and German children learning to use their relatively regular alphabetic orthographies also have reading problems.

The advantage of syllabaries over alphabets for young readers apparently stems from the fact that children have less difficulty identifying syllables than phonemes. One study revealed that 46 percent of four-year-olds and 90 percent of six-year-olds can segment words into syllables In contrast, virtually no four-year-olds and only about two-thirds of all six-year-olds can segment words into phoneme-size units. Since learning to read involves an understanding of the types of units represented by written symbols, it therefore stands to reason that syllabaries will generally be easier for young children to learn.

Of course, it must be remembered that syllabaries may have disadvantages of other sorts. While syllabic writing is feasible for languages such as Japanese that have a small number of syllable types, it would be quite impractical in English where there are dozens of different syllable structures. Ultimately, an orthography must be judged in terms of its success in representing language. There is no doubt that an alphabetic orthography is superior to a syllabary for representing the phonological structure of English.

Summing Up

The development of writing is one of humanity's greatest intellectual achievements. From **pictograms**, **ideograms**, and **logograms**, the graphic representation of language has developed through **syllabic** writing to the **alphabet**. This was achieved through the discovery of the relationship of sign to sound, first on the word level, then on the syllabic level, and finally on the level of the individual segmental unit. All this resulted in the reduction in the number of signs required to symbolize a language in written form. In a few areas of the world, such as China, the lack of efficiency in signs is offset by wide readability of the script among diverse peoples of differing languages.

Many, if not most of the large number of writing systems found throughout the modern world owe their origin directly or indirectly to the Semitic writing of the eastern Mediterranean, and perhaps ultimately to Egyptian writing.

As the idea of writing spread, new forms of the signs were freely invented and sound-symbol correspondences were altered in accordance with language structures. Some writing systems derived from the Greco-Phoenician tradition are today scarcely recognizable as such, since so little remains of the original signs. In cases where the entire system was invented, perhaps only the idea of writing is traceable to the early traditions.

Sources

Comprehensive surveys of the development of writing and of the world's writing systems are found in Jensen and Gelb (both cited below). The idea that writing may have originated in record keeping with clay tokens is taken from Schmandt-Besserat (cited below). The following figures are adapted from Jensen: 13.1–13.3, 13.5–13.7, 13.9, 13.10, 13.12, 13.16, 13.18, 13.21, and 13.23. The hiragana and katakana charts are from Len Walsh's *Read Japanese Today* (Rutland, Vt.: Charles E. Tuttle, 1971). Presentation of the Cree syllabary is adapted from D. Pentland, *Nēhiyawasinahikēwin: A Standard Orthography for the Cree Language* (Saskatoon: Saskatchewan Indian Cultural College, 1977). Figure 13.19 is adapted from Gelb (cited below). The examples of Northern Indian pictorial script are from John Marshall, *Mohenjo-Daro and the Indus Civilization* (London, 1931). The discussion of Chinese writing is based on Newnham (cited below) and Dr. R. L. Fisher (personal communication). Chinese characters were kindly provided by Lin Zhiqiu. Data on children's ability to segment words into syllables and phonemes comes from I. Y. Liberman, reported in Gibson and Levin (cited below).

Recommended Reading

Gelb, I. J. 1952. *A Study of Writing*. Chicago: University of Chicago Press.

Gibson, E. and H. Levin. 1975. *The Psychology of Reading*. Cambridge, Mass.: MIT Press.

Gleitman, L. and P. Rozin. 1977. "The Structure and Acquisition of Reading I: Relations between Orthographies and the Structure of Language." Reber, A. and D. Scarborough, eds. *Toward a Psychology of Reading*. Hillsdale, N.J.: Erlbaum Associates, pp. 1–53.

Jensen, H. 1970. *Sign, Symbol and Script*. G. Unwin, trans. London: George Allen and Unwin.

Newnham, R. 1980. *About Chinese*. Baltimore, Md.: Pelican Books.

Sampson, Geoffrey. 1985. *Writing Systems: A Linguistic Introduction*. Stanford: Stanford University Press.

Schmandt-Besserat, Denise. 1971. "The Earliest Precursor of Writing." *Scientific American* 238, no. 6:51–59.

Questions

1. Suppose you are the user of a pictographic writing system that can already represent concrete objects in a satisfactory way. Using the pictographic symbols of your system, propose ideographic extensions of these symbols to represent the following meanings.
   a) hunt
   b) cold
   c) fast
   d) white
   e) strength
   f) cook
   g) tired
   h) wet
   i) angry
   j) weakness

2. Construct a syllabary for English that can be used to spell the following words. What problems do you encounter?
   a) foe   law   shoe
   b) slaw   slow   slowly
   c) lee   day   daily
   d) sue   pull   shop
   e) ship   loop   food
   f) lock   shock   unlock
   g) locked   shocked   pulled
   h) shops   locker   shod
   i) float   splint   schlock

3. How does English orthography express the morphophonemic alternations in the following words? Begin your analysis with a phonemic transcription of the forms.
   a) hymn   hymnal
   b) part   partial
   c) recite   recitation
   d) reduce   reduction
   e) design   designation
   f) critical   criticize   criticism
   g) analogue   analogous   analogy

4. After discussing the forms in Question 3, consider the following forms. Does the spelling system treat all cases of allomorphic variation the same way?
   a) invade   invasion
   b) concede   concession
   c) assume   assumption
   d) profound   profundity

5. Briefly outline the advantages and disadvantages of the three major types of writing that have evolved throughout history.

14 ANIMAL COMMUNICATION

As I listened from a beach-chair in the shade
To all the noises that my garden made,
It seemed to me only proper that words
Should be withheld from vegetables and birds.

W. H. Auden

D o animals communicate among themselves as humans do? Can animals communicate with humans? Linguists take such questions seriously, since language is often said to be something that sets humans apart from all other animals. If animals do communicate with a system that is structured like human language, then language as we know it is not the unique property of our species, and we will have to look for other ways of defining humanness. In this chapter, we investigate the ways in which animal communication is like human language and the ways in which it is different.

14.1 NONVOCAL COMMUNICATION

One of the most striking things about animal communication is the variety of means by which it is carried out. Animals communicate not only with sounds but with scent, light, ultrasound, visual signs, gestures, color, and even electricity. From the slime mold to the giant blue whale, all animals appear to have some means of communication. Some nonvocal modes of communication are described here.

Scent Chemically based scent communication is used by species as different as molds, insects, and mammals. Chemicals used by animals specifically for communicative purposes are called **pheremones**. The slime mold signals its reproductive readiness through the release of a pheremone. Dogs and other canines leave a urine-based pheremone as an identification mark to stake out their territory, and many nonhuman primates have specialized scent glands for the same purpose.

Light Probably the most well-known light user in North America is the firefly or lightning bug. This small flying beetle uses light flashes in varying patterns to signal its identity, sex, and location.

Electricity Certain species of eels in the Amazon River basin communicate their presence and territoriality by means of electrical impulses at various frequencies. Each species signals at a specific frequency range, and the transmitting frequencies, like those of radio and television stations, do not overlap.

Color The color—or color patterns—of many animals plays an important role in their identification by members of their own species and other animals. The octopus changes color frequently and this coloring is used for a wide range of messages, including territorial defense and mating readiness.

Posture This is a common communicative device among animals. Dogs, for example, lower the front part of their bodies and extend their front legs when they are playful. They lower their whole bodies to the ground when they are submissive. Postural communication is found in both human and non-human primates as well.

Gesture A gesture may be defined as active posturing. Humans wave their arms in recognition or farewell, dogs wave their tails in excitement, and cats flick their tails when irritated. Many birds perform elaborate gestures of raising and lowering the head or racing back and forth across the water in their mating rituals.

Facial expression These are specific types of gesture that communicate meaning. When a male baboon yawns, bares its fangs, and retracts its eyebrows, it is indicating a willingness to fight. When humans draw back the corners of their mouths into a smile, they are generally indicating cooperation. A nonhuman primate's smile also indicates nonaggressiveness (see Figure 14.1).

Figure 14.1 Smiles

14.2 COMMUNICATION STRUCTURE

Underlying this bewildering variety of communicative methods are certain common features. An understanding of these is necessary for comparing the differences and similarities among communicative systems.

Organization

All communication relies on the existence of a **sign**, which is a unit of communication structure that consists of two parts: a **token**, be it a word, a scent, a gesture, or an electrical frequency, and a **referent** that exists in the "real world." The real world can be thought of as either external, mental, or emotional, and so a referent can be a tree, an abstract idea, a perception, or a feeling. All signs are associated with some **meaning**, such as 'danger', or 'item of furniture with legs and a flat top'. Figure 14.2 illustrates these distinctions.

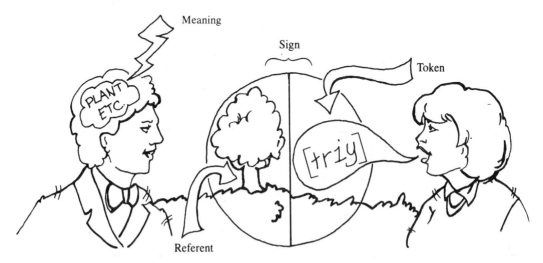

Figure 14.2 The structure of communication

Token A token is that part of a sign that stimulates at least one sense organ of the receiver of a message. The phonetic transcription of the word *tree* [triy] represents the sounds of the word as uttered by speakers of English. It is a typical linguistic token. A token can also be a picture, a photograph, a sign-language gesture, or one of the many other words for *tree* in different languages.

Referent A token's referent or extension (Chapter 6) corresponds to the thing or things the token designates in the real world. In our example, the referent is represented by a drawing since there is no room to include a real tree between the pages of this book. (Of course, the token [triy] could also have a picture of a tree as its referent.) It is easiest to think of referents as persons or things, but as noted above, they may be ideas or feelings as well.

Meaning The meaning of a sign is its intension, or the concepts it evokes to users of the system in question (Chapter 6). A word for 'tree' evokes concepts that probably include 'plant', 'having a trunk', and 'bearing leaves or needles' in the minds of speakers of any language.

We will assume that all communication has some real-world referent, and that this feature of communication is shared by animals and humans alike. What we must ask is what kinds of tokens are employed in communication, how they are structured, and what kinds of meanings are conveyed.

Kinds of Tokens

Tokens can be divided into three basic kinds, depending on (1) whether they naturally resemble their referents, (2) whether they are arbitrarily associated with their referents, or (3) whether they are directly linked with their referents in a physical or mechanical sense.

Iconic Tokens Iconic tokens, or **icons**, always bear some resemblance to their referent. A photograph is an iconic token; so too is a stylized silhouette of a man or a woman on a restroom door. A baboon's open-mouth threat is iconic, resembling as it does the act of biting. Onomatopoeic words like *buzz, splat,* and *squish* in English and their counterparts in other human languages are also iconic in that they somewhat resemble the referent they represent. Some examples of iconic tokens are given in Figure 14.3.

Figure 14.3 Some iconic tokens

Symbolic Tokens bear an arbitrary relationship to their referents. Human language is highly symbolic in that the vast majority of its tokens bear no inherent resemblance to their referents, as the words in Figure 14.4 show. No phonological property of these words gives any hint as to their possible meaning. (*Hana* means 'flower' or 'nose' in Japanese, *prozor* is 'window' in Serbo-Croatian, *talo* is 'house' in Finnish, *kum* means 'sand' in Turkish, and *berat* means 'heavy' in Indonesian.)

hana = ?
prozor = ?
talo = ?
kum   = ?
berat = ?

Figure 14.4 Arbitrary sound-meaning correspondence in language

We encounter many other symbolic tokens in everyday life. The hexagonal shape of a stop sign is symbolic; it bears no inherent connection with the message it helps to communicate. The colors used in traffic signals are symbolic as well. Red has no more inherent connection with the act of stopping than yellow.

Symptomatic Tokens spontaneously convey the internal state or emotions of the sender. For example, the fact that our body temperature rises when we are ill is a spontaneous reflection of our internal state. When someone steps on our foot and we cry out, that too is a spontaneous reflection of our internal state. Symptomatic tokens need not be associated with organic life. Even the popping of toast out of a toaster is a symptomatic token, since it directly reflects the fact that the machine has reached a certain internal state.

Since symptomatic tokens are spontaneous, we do not consider them to be deliberately selected by the sender for purposes of communication. We do not choose to cry out in pain in the same way as we might, for example, decide to call our dwelling place a *house, home, dwelling,* or *residence* in the appropriate circumstances. As forms of communication, symptomatic tokens are used primarily by the receiver of a message to assess the internal state of the sender. Since senders do not deliberately choose to send the signal, the message is assumed to be essentially out of their control. Among humans, this fact about symptomatic tokens can be turned on its head, and these tokens can be feigned. The result is deception, trickery, or lying.

Tokens are not always exclusively of one type or another. Symptomatic tokens, for example, may be iconic, as when a dog opens its mouth in a threat to bite, or they may be symbolic, as in the case of traffic lights. Finally, all tokens can act as **signals** when they trigger a specific action on the part of the receiver, as do traffic lights, many words in human language, warning cries of birds, or even toast popping out of the toaster.

Token Structure

No matter what their type, tokens show different kinds of structure. A basic distinction is made between **graded** and **discrete** tokens.

Graded Tokens Graded tokens convey their meaning by changes in degree. A good example of a gradation in communication is voice volume. The more you want to be heard, the louder you speak along an increasing scale of loudness. There are no steps or jumps from one level to the next that can be associated with a specific change in meaning.

Gradation is common in many forms of communication. The hands of most clocks move in a graded manner, as does the needle of an automobile speedometer. Many animal signals, such as the barking of dogs, are graded as well. A dog has essentially one type of bark, which may become louder and faster, but does not become another kind of barking. Figure 14.5 contains some examples of graded tokens.

Figure 14.5 Some graded tokens

Discrete Tokens Discrete tokens are distinguished from each other by "step-wise" differences. There is no gradual transition from one token to the next. The phonemes of human language are good examples of discrete tokens. Contrasting stop and fricative phonemes in English are perceived as either voiced or voiceless—there is no intermediate category. The digital displays of watches are discrete as well, since they progress from one minute (or even second) to the next with no gradation. Traffic lights, too, are discrete tokens; there is no gradual shifting from green to yellow to red. Some examples of discrete tokens are given in Figure 14.6.

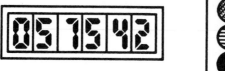

/ p /
/ b /
/ m /

Figure 14.6 Some discrete tokens

All three kinds of tokens—*iconic, symbolic,* and *symptomatic*—may be graded or discrete. The gradual baring of its fangs by a threatening canine is iconic and graded. A photograph is iconic and discrete. Morse code is symbolic and discrete, but a slowly dimming light that signals the beginning of a theatrical performance is symbolic and graded. Symptomatic tokens, too, may be discrete (the traffic light again) or graded (the crying of a child or the act of blushing).

A View
of Animal
Communication

Most animal language, it is claimed, shows little arbitrariness. It is said to be largely symptomatic and not deliberate, conscious, or symbolic. For example, if a monkey gives a certain cry in the presence of danger, it is assumed that the monkey is spontaneously signaling its fear by vocalizing but is not deliberately warning other group members of the danger. The vocalization is interpreted and used by other members of a group for their own benefit.

It is further claimed that animal communication is neither conscious nor deliberate. It is not widely believed, for example, that a monkey assesses a situation and then deliberately chooses to warn members of danger by selecting a token from a repertoire of meaningful sound symbols at its disposal. The term **stimulus-bound** is also used to describe animal communication, since it is often claimed that animal communication occurs only when it is triggered by exposure to a certain stimulus or for certain specific ends. Animals do not communicate about anything but the here and now. As the philosopher Bertrand Russell noted, "No matter how eloquently a dog may bark, it cannot tell you that its parents were poor but honest."

With respect to structure, animal communication is said to show few traces of discrete structuring beyond the obvious fact that one group of symptomatic, graded signals may sound very different from another. Whining in dogs, for example, is clearly different from barking, but both are assumed to be symptomatic. Combining and recombining of discrete units of structure such as phonemes, morphemes, and words are not characteristic of the way animals communicate. Dogs do not combine whines and barks to make novel messages.

This does not mean that animal communication consists of random emotional outbursts. Nor does it mean that animal communication does not show structure. Animal communication is both complex and organized. Evolutionary pressure has guaranteed that animal communication is optimally in tune with the survival requirements of each species. The electrical communication of Amazonian eels is an excellent means of communication in muddy waters. The danger whistle of a small, tree-dwelling primate is ideal for nocturnal communication in dense forest. Small jungle frogs in South America communicate by sticking out their long and colorful legs, ideal for sending messages in the dim and noisy jungle. But jungle frogs do not try new combinations of leg movements in order to come up with an original message, any more than the electric eel recombines frequencies in order to signal something it has never conveyed before. Animal communication appears to be severely limited in the messages it can convey.

Recent work on animal communication has often focused on its relationship to human linguistic communication. The next sections examine communication among several kinds of animals and compare it with human language.

14.3 THE BEES

I have no doubt that some will attempt to "explain" the performances of the bees as the results of reflexes and instincts. . . . for my part, I find it difficult to assume that such perfection and flexibility in behavior can be reached without some kind of mental processes going on in the small heads of the bees.

August Krogh, *Scientific American*

The System

Forager bees display a remarkable system of communicating the location of a food source to other bees in their hive. When a food source has been discovered, the forager flies back to the hive and communicates information about it by performing special movements (which humans call *dancing*) before other members of the hive. The dancing conveys information about the location of the food source, its quality, and its distance from the hive.

Distance Distance is conveyed by one of three different dances performed on the wall or floor of the hive (some species have only two different dances, and so may be said to have a different "dialect"). In doing the round dance, the bee circles repeatedly. This indicates a food source within five meters or so of the hive. The sickle dance indicates a food source from five to twenty meters from the hive. It is performed by the bee dancing a curved figure-eight shape. The tail-wagging dance indicates distances further than twenty meters. In this dance, the bee wags its abdomen as it moves forward, circles to the right back to its starting point, repeats the wagging forward motion, and circles left. The cycle then begins again.

Direction The round dance does not communicate direction, presumably since the food source is so close to the hive. The direction of more distant food sources is indicated in the other two types of dance.

As the bee performs the sickle and tail-wagging dances, it is simultaneously indicating the direction of the food source. Bees orient themselves in flight relative to the angle of the sun. When the dancing is performed on the vertical wall of the hive, it is apparently "understood" that the top of the hive wall represents the current position of the sun in the sky. During the sickle dance, the angle of the open side of the figure eight relative to the hive's vertical alignment indicates the direction of flight toward the food source relative to the sun. When the bee performs the tail-wagging dance, the angle of its wagging path relative to the hive's vertical angle indicates the path of flight toward the food source relative to the sun. Figure 14.7 illustrates the dances and their manner of indicating the direction of the food source.

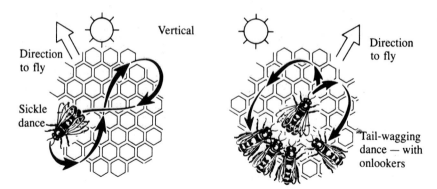

Figure 14.7 Bee dancing

Quality Quality of the food source is indicated by the intensity of the dancing and the number of repetitions of the circling movements. As the food source is depleted, the dance is performed with less vivacity.

Other Factors These messages are not communicated with perfect accuracy, nor are they the only ones involved in bee communication. Bees also leave a hive-specific pheremone trace at the site of the food source, thereby directing their fellow foragers to the precise location. The bees also carry back traces of the food source odors, which further aid other bees in the search. A whole complex of communicative modes operating on different channels—a **constellation**—is employed in bee communication.

Bees and Humans

How does bee communication compare with human language? The three patterns that the bees dance are in no way inherently connected with the messages they communicate and so are symbolic in nature. The communication of direction is iconic, and in this sense may be comparable to a human gesture. It is, however, a very sophisticated iconicity mixed with a symbolic element, since the bees are able to transfer the horizontal flight path to a vertical representation on the hive wall. The expression of food source quality is, in all probability, symptomatic: the more stimulated a bee is by the quality of the food source, the faster it dances.

The total communicative constellation involves other passive sources of communication as well, such as pheremones and food source samples. The performance even involves audience participation. During its dancing, the returning bee is expected to provide samples from the food source. If it fails to, it may be stung to death.

Bee communication, then, like human language, shows symbolic, iconic, and symptomatic traits, as well as interaction between sender and receiver of the messages. But there is a major difference between the two systems of communication. The topic of bee communication is severely constrained. Bees communicate only about food sources. Furthermore, their potential for communication is very limited. Only certain locations of food sources can be conveyed. Bees cannot communicate the notion of up or down. They can be easily tricked into communicating the wrong direction of the food if a strong light source is placed in an incorrect position with relation to the food. They can also be tricked into giving the wrong information about distance to the food source if they are forced to walk or stop several times on route. This indicates that they gauge distance by time. The bees show no means of assessing varying information and of communicating this fact. Their system of communication appears to be closed ended and limited to a specific number of facts about a specific type of information.

It also appears that bee language is largely innate—that is, there is very little need for a new forager bee to be exposed to the system in the presence of other bees. Foragers on their first flight perform the appropriate dances, although they refine their performance to some extent with time and exposure to other dancing. Their flight orientation to the sun is imperfect at first, but it develops within a few hours.

The innateness of bee dancing has been tested by cross-breeding Austrian bees, which do not perform the sickle dance to express intermediate distance of the food source from the hive, with Italian honeybees, which do. The results of such experiments further support a genetic interpretation of bee communication. In a cross-breeding experiment, the bees that bore a physical resemblance to their Italian parent performed the sickle dance to indicate intermediate distance 98 percent of the time. The bees that bore a physical resemblance to their Austrian parent performed the round dance to indicate intermediate distance 96 percent of the time; they did not perform the sickle dance at all. The dance pattern used in a specific situation appears to be inherited from a certain parent along with other more obvious genetic traits.

In 1948, when the Danish physiologist August Krogh made the statement quoted at the beginning of this section, he struck at the widely accepted notion that animal behavior was either the result of some kind of conditioning or, in some ill-defined way, instinctive. Much has been learned since then about the enormous quantity of information imparted by genetic transfer. It is now possible to state with a fair degree of certainty that the complex and sophisticated behavior of bees and other equally remarkable insects is in all probability largely genetically predetermined and, unlike human language, it relies very little on exposure to the mature system in order to be acquired.

14.4 THE BIRDS

How intelligent is a creature that can amuse himself for fifteen minutes by uttering, over and over, the following sounds: uhr, uhr, uhr, Uhr, URH, URH, Wah, Wah, wah, wah, wah.

Jake Page (on his Amazon Parrot)

The System

Birds, as Jake Page later found out, can do a lot more than utter sounds over and over. Even the parrot, which has been labeled for years as nothing but a stimulus-bound mimic, has been shown to have some capacity for meaningful labeling (although it took a test parrot four years to acquire a vocabulary of eighteen nouns). The parroting of trained birds is nothing more than a nonintentional response to an external stimulus arrived at through repetitive conditioning. Natural communication among birds is far more interesting than the performances of trained ones, and efforts to understand how birds communicate have shed light on parallels in human linguistic communication.

Bird vocalization can be divided into two types, **call** and **song**. Calls are typically short bursts of sound or simple patterns of notes. Songs are lengthy, elaborate patterns of mostly pitched sounds.

Calls Calls serve very specific functions in the bird community. They typically warn of predators, coordinate flocking and flight activity, express aggression, or accompany nesting or feeding behavior. The cawing of crows is a typical call. It seems to convey a generalized mobilization to possible danger. When a crow hears cawing, it flies up to a tree if it is on the ground, or flies higher in a tree—or to another tree—if it is already in one. (If there are crows in your neighborhood, you can test this yourself, as cawing is easy to imitate.)

In some birds, individual calls are associated with specific activities; a danger call is quite different from a call given when birds are grouped in flight. A flight call is generally short, crisp, and easy to locate by other group members. The honking of geese in flight is a typical example of this sort of call. Because it is loud and easy to locate, it is well suited to enable the bird flock to stay together. The call given by small birds when larger avian predators threaten them is very different. It is typically thin and high-pitched. This kind of sound is difficult to locate, and so can be given as a warning without revealing the position of the caller. Such functional utility is typical of bird calls, and in fact, calls that serve the same communicative purpose are often remarkably similar among different species of birds.

Songs Birdsong is different from calling. Although calls are produced year round, singing is largely seasonal. Furthermore, it is generally only male birds that sing.

The main purposes of song are, as far as we know, to announce and delimit the territory of the male and to attract a mate. Birds establish territory for breeding purposes and defend it vigorously. Across the United States, it is a common sight in the spring to see a pair of red-winged blackbirds (*Agelaius phoeniceus*) team up to drive away a male of their species that has strayed into their territory. The use of song enables male birds to establish and maintain this territory without constant patrolling and fighting. Moreover, once a bird has established its territory, its song serves to attract and maintain contact with a mate. It follows that birdsong is unique from species to species, and even varies to some degree from bird to bird within the same species, since its purposes require species and individual recognition.

In some species, songs are nothing more than a successive repetition of calls. In others, songs consist of complex patterns of pitches—sometimes called syllables—that form longer repeated units or themes. The sometimes elaborate complexity of song structure reflects individual variation among the singers, and, as pointed out previously, serves a specific purpose. Figure 14.8 shows a **spectrograph** (an acoustic recording that shows pitch and intensity of sound) of the song of the European robin (*Erithacus rubecula*). Note how the different subsections of the song are distinct and recognizable. There is also some evidence that sections of a song are combined in different orders by certain birds. There is no evidence that recombination is associated with different meanings.

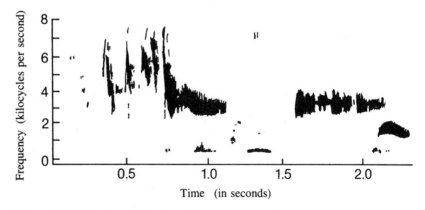

Figure 14.8 Spectrograph of a robin song

Avian Dialects There is evidence for both song and call dialects among bird species. Researchers even speak of avian isoglosses, lines that can be drawn on a map to indicate shared characteristics among dialects, and that are based on variations in the melody of song syllables or themes (see Figure 14.9). The reason for the existence of dialects is still unclear; it may be no more than a reflection of individual avian variation in song and call learning.

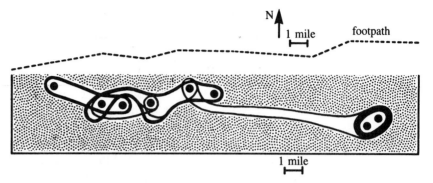

Figure 14.9 Avian isoglosses: call patterns of male Hill Mynas (Shaded area indicates forested hills; unshaded is open plain.)

If it is, we are led to an intriguing issue in the relationship of bird vocalization to human language—the question of how bird vocalizations are acquired.

Birds and Humans

The acquisition of call and song by birds shows interesting parallels with recent hypotheses about the acquisition of language by human children (see Chapter 10). Though a great deal of bird vocalization—particularly calls—appears to be innate, there is much that appears to be acquired. Studies of avian dialects have shown that birds reared in the same nest acquire different song dialects when they live in different dialect areas. It also appears to be the case that singing ability is lateralized in the left brains of birds, as is linguistic ability in humans. Still more significant for linguistic study is the fact that some birds must acquire the species-specific characteristics of their song within a certain time-span or critical period.

A number of bird species do not develop fully characteristic songs if they are deprived from hearing them during the early stages of their lives. The chaffinch (*Fringilla coelebs*) is one such bird. If chaffinches are reared in isolation, they sing, but replicate only in a general way the typical song of the species. If young chaffinches are reared away from fully developed singers, but with other young chaffinches, the entire experimental "community" develops an identical song. Finally, chaffinches that have been exposed to only some part of the fully developed song (those that are captured in the autumn of the first year of life) will, the following spring, develop a song that is partially typical but not completely well formed.

These experiments indicate that there are some songbirds that have both an innate and a learned component in their song. The innate component predisposes them to perform a general song that is extremely simplified. This has been called a **template** or a blueprint. Only exposure to the fully formed song of the species will enable them to produce the correct song. (Exposure to other song causes some species to imitate in this direction; other species simply do not acquire anything they are exposed to unless it is their own species-characteristic song.) Finally, it is clear that certain birds do not acquire their characteristic song in a brief span of time, but that several seasons of exposure are required. The evidence from songbird studies, while not transferable directly to humans, gives strong support to the idea that a combination of innate and learned components is one way that the acquisition of complex behavior takes place in nature.

14.5 NONHUMAN PRIMATES

Some animals share qualities of both man and the four-footed beasts, for example, the ape, the monkey, and the baboon.

Aristotle, *On Animals*

Fascination with nonhuman primates goes far back in human history. Their social behavior has long been seen as an amusing (and sometimes instructive) parody of human behavior. Since the establishment of the fact that we are closely related genetically to these animals, the resemblance of their behavioral, social, and communicative traits to ours has been seen as more than an amusing counterpart to human activity. Recently, the question of our shared cognitive, and especially linguistic ability, has become more important; it is thought that a better understanding of nonhuman primates may shed light on the evolution of human social and cognitive abilities.

Nonhuman primates form a large class of mammals, which range from the tiny tarsier to the imposing mountain gorilla. They cannot be described by resorting to one simple characteristic. Some are nocturnal, some diurnal in their activity cycle. Some are solitary, some form part of complex social groups. Many are tree-dwelling, but many are ground-dwelling. Some are quadrupeds, and some show periods of bipedal locomotion. Figure 14.10

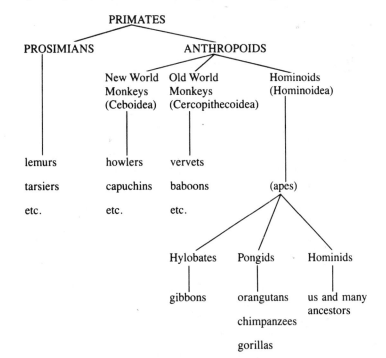

Figure 14.10 The primates

shows one widely accepted classification of nonhuman primates. The prosimians are an evolutionarily primitive group found on the island of Madagascar. New World Monkeys are the only primates with prehensile (grasping) tails. Old World Monkeys include the many tree-dwelling species of Africa and the Far East. The larger nonhuman primates—baboons, chimpanzees, and gorillas—are not native to North and South America. Baboons—large, mainly ground-dwelling primates—are found from central to northern Africa. They show a high degree of social organization, intelligence, and aggressiveness. The hominoids include the large but gentle gorillas, chimpanzees, and humans. Recent genetic testing suggests that chimpanzees are our closest genetic relatives.

In the next section, we turn our attention to nonhuman primate communication in the wild. It is there that we can gain an understanding of how forms of nonhuman primate communication resemble or differ from our own. One way of comparing nonhuman primate communication with human language is to see how the systems of communication are structured.

Prosimian Communication

Prosimian communication shows a small repertoire of sounds that are patterned into discrete groups. The lemur (*Lemur catta*) of Madagascar is a typical prosimian with respect to its vocal communication system. It has been described as making essentially two types of vocalization, noises and calls, each of which shows some grading. The vocalizations appear to be symptomatic. They are classified in Table 14.1; quasi-phonetic descriptions like *spat* should be interpreted as onomatopoeic. Each graded set of sounds is used in a circumscribed range of situations. The calls, in particular, are limited to threat or fear encounters. They seem to form a graded series, ranging from the *light spat* to the *bark* in intensity.

Table 14.1 Lemur vocalization

Noises		Calls	
Sound	Context	Sound	Context
single click	in response to strange objects	light spat (yip)	when driving off threatening inferiors
clicks, grunts	during locomotion, or for friendly greeting	spat	when crowded or handled roughly
purr	while grooming	bark	when startled

Monkeys

The study of communication among the many varieties of New and Old World Monkeys is too vast for this chapter. An oversimplified picture reflects what most researchers agree is primarily a symptomatic system, but one that shows even more gradation in the signals than does the communication of prosimians. The study of one small monkey, however, suggests that not all monkey vocalizations are symptomatic.

The East African vervet monkey (*Cercopithecus aethiops*) is said to have three distinctive and arbitrary calls that announce the presence of either eagles, snakes, or large mammals posing a threat. These calls are associated with different responses by the monkeys. When they hear the eagle call, the monkeys look up or run into the bushes. The snake call causes them to look down at the ground near them. The mammal alarm sees them run up into the trees, or climb higher in a tree if they are already in one. These findings, which appear to have been well established by experimentation since they were first reported in 1967, suggest that not all nonhuman primates rely strictly on symptomatic signals to communicate or to trigger behavior in other monkeys. It is claimed rather that the vervets assess the potential danger situation and then choose a specific call with a clearly defined referent to announce the danger. Furthermore, each call is a vocalization token that is arbitrarily linked with its referents. Other monkeys respond appropriately to the calls without necessarily observing the danger themselves. All this taken together suggests a cognitive ability for classification of objects in the world and an ability to link this classification system to arbitrary sounds for purposes of intentional communication (see Figure 14.11).

The acquisition of these signals is interesting. Infant vervets appear to distinguish innately among broad classes of mammals, snakes, and birds, but they also give the "eagle call" when other birds appear and the "leopard call" when other terrestrial mammals appear. Adults distinguish between leopards and less dangerous mammals, and eagles and less dangerous birds (as well as between snakes and sticks), and it is claimed that this ability must be perfected through experience. This once again suggests that a mixture of innate components and learning is typical of the way in which some communication systems are naturally acquired.

Gibbons, Baboons, and Chimpanzees

Since the higher primates are close genetic relatives of humans, it is natural to expect their vocal communication to resemble that of humans. Surprisingly, communication among the higher primates does not show much indication of arbitrary sound tokens. Rather, the communication systems of these animals are made up of a number of graded calls.

Gibbons Gibbons display an interesting form of vocal interaction known as duetting. Duetting, the interchange of calls in a patterned manner between two members of a species, is found among certain birds, bats, and even antelopes. Duetting is, however, atypical of primate communication—among the hominoids, only gibbons perform it. It appears to signal the territoriality of an established mating pair, and to be essentially symptomatic.

Baboons The baboon communication system, illustrated in Figure 14.12, shows a number of clear-cut types of sound and correlated meaning, all of which can be interpreted as symptomatic. These systems consequently require each member of a species to pay a great deal of attention to the situation

African hawk eagle   Black-chested snake eagle   Martial eagle

Eagle alarm

Leopard alarm

Snake alarm

Figure 14.11 Response of vervet monkeys to specific predators

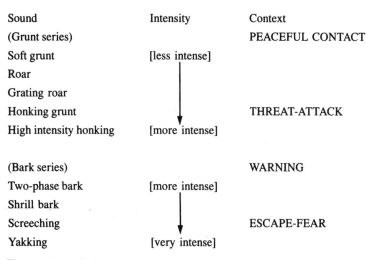

Sound	Intensity	Context
(Grunt series)		PEACEFUL CONTACT
Soft grunt	[less intense]	
Roar		
Grating roar		
Honking grunt		THREAT-ATTACK
High intensity honking	[more intense]	
(Bark series)		WARNING
Two-phase bark	[more intense]	
Shrill bark		
Screeching		ESCAPE-FEAR
Yakking	[very intense]	

Figure 14.12 Baboon vocalization structure

in which the utterances are given—not surprising among such socially developed species. These baboon vocalizations can be interpreted as part of a single graded series, which rises in intensity according to the situation in which a sound is used.

Chimpanzees Chimpanzees vocalize with a number of graded calls. As many as sixteen types have been reported. Some of these appear to show rather specific referents. Chimps typically hoot to signal location (a sound that carries well in dense forest). Hooting is also used in greeting or when chimps are excited about something. Another typical vocalization is known as rough grunting and is given in the presence of a favorite food source.

Baboon, chimpanzee, and gorilla vocalizations all show a great deal of variation. There is every indication that their vocalizations form part of a constellation of communicative acts including gesture, posture, gaze (eye "pointing"), and the expression of affect, all of which must be interpreted by other troop members. There is very little evidence for arbitrary relationships between sound and meaning in baboon, chimpanzee, or gorilla vocalizations, despite the high degree of intelligence and social organization these animals demonstrate. Even more significantly, there is no evidence of recombining various sections of a message to form new messages. Nothing that parallels the phonemic or morphological recombination of human language has been discovered in the natural communication systems of non-human primates.

Many primatologists believe that the lack of linguistic parallels in closely related species may be due to their social organization. The small groups or family units typical of chimps and gorillas may not have required the development of any other mode of communication. What has evolved is suited to their needs. This does not mean, however, that our near-relatives do not possess any of the cognitive abilities necessary for using a system of communication akin to human language. There is some evidence, for example, of left-hemisphere development of the type associated with human linguistic ability. A number of recent experiments with nonhuman primates have attempted to determine the extent—if any—of their linguistic abilities.

14.6 TESTING NONHUMAN PRIMATES FOR LINGUISTIC ABILITY

Much attention has been paid in recent years to nonhuman primates that are supposedly able to communicate with humans through the use of sign language.

Controlled testing of the possible shared linguistic abilities of nonhuman primates and humans goes back to 1948, when two psychologists attempted to train Viki, a young chimpanzee, to say meaningful words in English. With great effort, Viki learned to approximate the pronunciations of a few words like *cup* and *papa* over a period of fourteen months,. But the experiment was doomed to failure from the start, because the vocal fold structure and supralaryngeal anatomy of the chimpanzee is unsuited for producing human sounds.

Chimpanzee vocal folds are fatty and less muscular than those of humans, and the neurological pathways between the brain and vocal folds are less developed than in humans. The chimpanzee's epiglottis extends well up into the throat cavity, which lessens the range of sounds it can produce. Finally, the whole larynx-tongue linkage rests higher in the chimpanzee throat, which results in limitations on its humanlike sound production as well. In short, the chimpanzee is unsuited for human speech, and concentrating effort on teaching it to articulate words was distracting from the more provocative question: to what extent is the chimp capable of linguistic behavior?

Some Experiments

An experiment conducted from 1965 to 1972 by Allen and Beatrice Gardner with a young female chimpanzee named Washoe created a new perspective on nonhuman primate linguistic abilities. The Gardners attempted to raise Washoe much as a human child would be raised, and to teach her American Sign Language (Ameslan), on the assumption that it was a genuinely linguistic form of communication (of which there is no doubt). Given the known manual dexterity of chimpanzees, it was felt that sign language might provide a window on chimpanzee linguistic abilities.

Washoe The Gardners' reports claim that Washoe communicates intentionally with arbitrary signs in a creative manner, and thus shows the rudiments of human linguistic ability. Washoe learned to produce approximately 130 signs over a period of three years. (She recognized many more.) Most significantly, it is claimed that Washoe spontaneously combined these signs to form novel utterances. She is reported to have signed *water bird* on seeing ducks. Washoe also is said to have spontaneously produced *baby in my cup* when her toy doll was placed in her drinking cup and she was asked "What's that?"

Washoe was the first but not the only chimpanzee to be taught sign language. The results have suggested to some linguists that chimpanzees show greater ability to associate arbitrary tokens with referents than was believed earlier, and that they demonstrate rudimentary syntactic behavior. Other chimps, gorillas, and an orangutan that have been taught Ameslan since the pioneering Washoe experiment are reported to have performed even better.

Nim Still other experiments in teaching chimpanzees sign language have produced contradictory results. The achievements of a chimpanzee named Nim have been interpreted by his teachers as consisting of frequent repetitions of a small number of all-purpose signs (*Nim, me, you, eat, drink, more,* and *give*) that were largely appropriate to any context. These signs are said to have made up almost 50 percent of Nim's production. Furthermore, there are no reports of his engaging in creative combining of signs. It is also claimed that all of the signing chimps and gorillas are unconsciously cued by their trainers (there is more on this phonemenon in a later section).

Nonsigning Experiments

Much of the criticism leveled at Washoe's performance centered on the relative informality of her training and claims that Ameslan is a loose communicative system that does not require a strict adherence to syntactic rules. Two very different experiments with chimpanzees attempted to forestall such criticism.

Lana, Sherman, and Austin A chimpanzee called Lana was trained to fulfill her needs for food, fresh air, grooming, and entertainment (in the form of slide shows) by requesting these from a computer-controlled apparatus. Communication with the computer was carried out by means of a simple but syntactically rule-governed language of nine arbitrary symbols. The symbols were on buttons that lit up and activated the computer when pressed. Any deviation from the syntactic rule system invented for the experiment failed to get the desired responses from the computer. Human experimenters communicated directly with the chimpanzee through use of the same symbols. Lana learned to label and to request food and other amenities through the computer.

The experiment with Lana was criticized because she was said to have learned simple reflex associations among symbol, sequence, and reward, and was consequently not displaying linguistic abilities. The experiment was later broadened to include two other chimps, Sherman and Austin. The trainers claimed that Sherman and Austin showed abilities to refer to abstract classes that reflect humanlike linguistic capacity. They were able to categorize items as either *food* or *tool.* After three training sessions, one of the chimps (Sherman) showed a 90 percent success rate on first viewing. The chimpanzees' trainers claimed that these animals could categorize objects on the basis of their function—just as human children can—and that the animals also showed the ability to categorize symbols as well as objects.

Sarah Another now-classic experiment involved training a <u>young female</u> <u>chimp named Sarah to manipulate arbitrary plastic symbols in a predeter-</u> <u>mined manner in order to obtain rewards.</u> Sarah had to learn to use word order correctly, since only the order in Figure 14.13 would obtain a banana.

Figure 14.13 Arbitrary symbols used in experiments with the chimpanzee Sarah

She also seemed to show sensitivity to more abstract words such as *if/then* in sentences like the one in Figure 14.14.

Figure 14.14 A "sentence" understood by Sarah

But was Sarah learning aspects of human language or was she, too, trained? Humans who are taught similar skills perform them as well as Sarah but find it difficult to translate them into human language. They approach the exercise of moving plastic symbols around to obtain a reward as a puzzle that is not necessarily associated with language. It has been suggested that Sarah was performing the same kind of puzzle-solving and not demonstrating humanlike linguistic capacities.

These studies have led to a resurgence of interest in human-animal communication. Language-using dogs, cats, pigs, and even turtles have been reported for thousands of years. The basis of much of the current criticism of all of these experiments rests on the performance of a horse in Germany at the turn of this century.

The Clever Hans Controversy

When I play with my cat, who is to say that my cat is not playing with me?
Michel de Montaigne, *Essays*

In 1904, a Berlin school teacher named Wilhelm von Osten claimed to possess a horse that showed evidence of a humanlike capacity to think. His horse, Clever Hans (*der kluge Hans*), could supposedly calculate and convey messages by tapping out numbers or numbered letters of the alphabet with a front hoof or by nodding his head. Experimentation by a skeptical scientist, Oskar Pfungst, eventually showed that Clever Hans was not so much a creative thinker as a careful observer. The horse perceived cues that indicated he had performed correctly. For example, von Osten involuntarily moved his head very slightly when a correct answer had been reached. This movement was outside the normal perceptual range of human observers (less than five millimeters), but the horse had learned to associate it with the correct answer. When observers did not know the answer to a question, or when Clever Hans was blindfolded, he failed to perform his miracles.

Clever Hans's performance resulted from **dressage**, a type of interaction between trainer and animal that depends on the animal's interpreting subtle cues given by the trainer. The Clever Hans phenomenon is an excellent example of dressage, which need not involve conscious communication on the part of humans. The highly developed perceptual ability displayed by Clever Hans is common to many animals. Many scientists believe that chimpanzees and gorillas that use sign language and perform other languagelike tasks are demonstrating nothing more than the Clever Hans phenomenon.

The position is explained as follows. Human trainers want very much for their animal charges to succeed. This desire is translated into involuntary actions, which can be seized on by the animal due to its keen perceptual abilities; it is these cues that determine the animal's performance. A typical example of this is pointed out in Washoe's signing of *baby in my cup*, which has been recorded on film (*First Signs of Washoe*). A careful examination of this interchange shows that the human repeatedly holds out the object to be signed and then points rapidly at the cup. Probably none of this cueing was intentional on the human's part.

Some so-called linguistic activity may be the result of factors other than the Clever Hans effect. Some reports of creative signing, such as Washoe's *water bird,* are dismissed as reflex signing that shows no intention of forming combination on the part of the chimp. Reports of the gorilla Koko's wit (she occasionally produces the opposite sign of the one requested, such as *up* for 'down') are also considered exaggerated or simply wishful thinking.

Some reports of linguistic behavior are attributed to inaccurate or non-systematic observing. (If Washoe answered *what's that* with any noun sign, the answer was considered correct.) Other reports are attributed to over-optimistic interpretation of signs. (Koko is reported to intentionally produce "rhyming" signs—those that are very similar to the one asked for or expected.) In short, those who do not view chimpanzee signing and symbol manipulation as linguistically relevant claim that this behavior is more simply explained as arising from straightforward response-reward association and/ or from dressage, and not a reflection of linguistic competence. As one researcher noted, training two pigeons to bat a ping-pong ball across a net does not mean that the birds know the rules of ping-pong.

The Great Ape Debate

We believe that . . . there is no basis to conclude that signing apes acquired linguistic skills.

Mark S. Seidenberg and Laura Petitto

When these projects [Washoe, Lana, Sarah, and Nim] are taken together, it can be seen that chimpanzees are within the range of language behavior of humans and therefore have the capacity for language.

Roger Fouts

Researchers involved with the chimpanzees and gorillas who are being taught to sign attest to the emotional bonds they form with them. They also emphasize that even in human language, such bonds are a prerequisite to normal communication. They strongly insist that apes do communicate spontaneously and creatively with humans. Roger Fouts, who has spent many years in close contact with Washoe and other chimpanzees, puts the case this way.

> I reject the notion that there is some ultimate cut-and-dried criterion that distinguishes language from all other social and cognitive behaviors, or that distinguishes human communication and thought from that of all other species.

It is important to emphasize that most researchers sympathetic to the idea that apes show human linguistic abilities employ a broader definition of language than many of their critics. For these researchers, language use includes socialization and the use of communicative constellations. For many linguists critical of these projects, linguistic ability can, by definition, be tested only if the animals show—at the very least—spontaneous and intentional symbolic and syntactic behavior.

Symbol Use All researchers who support the claim that nonhuman primates can employ intentional symbolic communication deny that cueing is a major factor in the apes' abilities, although most admit that it might be present on occasion. In order to refute charges of the Clever Hans effect, researchers employ a strict form of experimentation.

Primate sign-language researchers try to avoid cueing by the use of a **double-blind test**. In this test, the ape is shown objects or pictures of objects that are invisible to a second human researcher. The ape's signing is then recorded by this researcher, and interpreted by a third one. In this way, unintentional cueing is said to be avoided.

Critics of this research claim that even double-blind tests can be affected by human-animal interaction. First, the apes must be taught to perform the task. During this process they may be conditioned to provide certain responses. Secondly, it is difficult to avoid any human-animal interaction during these tests, and this could lead to subliminal cueing. As we have also seen, many claims for symbolic behavior on any ape's part have been dismissed as stimulus-response conditioning—the mere aping of behavior in order to obtain a reward. Even some linguists who allow that a level of symbolic signing has been achieved now say that this is not a critical feature for defining language. Rather, syntactic behavior is said to be the critical feature.

Is There Syntax? Claims for syntactic behavior are also made. Most researchers claim that the general syntax of Ameslan is copied by the apes, though Koko is said to have developed her own word order in noun phrases—the adjective consistently follows the noun it modifies. In general, syntactic behavior is harder to identify in signing, not because it is not present, but because signing forms constellations with facial expression and gestures and so may be said to reduce the need for rigorous syntax. Koko, for example, can sign a meaning like 'I love Coca-Cola' by hugging herself (the sign for 'love') while signing *Coca-Cola* at the same time with her hands.

It is certain that apes do not show syntactic behavior to the degree that humans do (for example, embedding is completely lacking), and many linguists claim that without such behavior, the apes cannot be said to be using language. Syntax, in the strict linguistic sense, means a system of rules capable of producing a sentence of potentially infinite length (even though in practice this is never required). There is no evidence that primates have shown this ability.

Creative Signing? Another feature of language that sets it apart from most animal communication is its creativity—the fact that humans can use language to create novel messages. Sign researchers claim that such creativity is present in the many instances of novel combinations signed by the animals. Some of Koko's novel combinations are provided in Table 14.2. Critics say either that these are accidental or that the ape produces the two signs independently of each other and thus does not display true compounding.

Table 14.2 Some sign combinations produced by Koko

Compound	Referent
milk candy	rich tapioca pudding
fruit lollipop	frozen banana
pick face	tweezers
blanket white cold	rabbit-fur cape
nose fake	mask
potato apple fruit	pineapple

Implications

At this time, supporters of the apes have not yet proved to the satisfaction of their critics that genuine symbolic behavior is occurring, much less anything resembling syntactic patterning or creative linguistic use. These researchers claim that their opponents keep raising the stakes every time a chimp or a gorilla accomplishes something that could be interpreted as linguistic, and that the critics are motivated by a long tradition of viewing animals as "organic machines" that can only respond automatically to a given situation with a narrow repertoire of signs. Their own view, they claim, is at once more ancient and more modern in granting animals a certain as yet unknown degree of intentionality and cognitive ability in their behavior.

Even if only limited symbolic communication is being achieved, the significance of these ape-human interaction experiments goes far beyond popular enthusiasm about what an ape might say to us if it could "talk." It has often been pointed out that an animal's view of the world must be totally unlike our own. It is perhaps not surprising that apes appear to communicate largely about basic needs such as food and play, and the expression of emotion. What is viewed by some as important about this research is that it may help illuminate what is truly unique about human linguistic ability, and that it may ultimately shed light on the evolutionary origins of human language by demonstrating the degree of shared cognitive abilities.

14.7 COMPARING COMMUNICATION SYSTEMS: DESIGN FEATURES

Confusion occasionally arises when comparing animal and human behavior due to the failure to make a distinction between communication and language. Unquestionably, animals communicate among themselves and with other species, including humans. The question is, do animals communicate among themselves and with humans with a system akin to human language? In the final section of this chapter, we will compare human linguistic communication with what we have learned about systems of animal communication.

The Features

Differences and similarities between human language and natural animal communication systems can be highlighted by comparing essential characteristics of the systems. These characteristics are called **design features** and are set up (perhaps unfairly) with reference to human language. Since this book emphasizes the essentially mental nature of linguistic ability, the design features that follow do not include the traditional references to vocal-auditory transmission. What is emphasized is the nature of the semantic and organizational structuring of each system.

1. *Interchangeability* All members of the species can both send and receive messages.

This is obviously true of human language. It is not the case with bee dancing (performed only by foragers) or birdsong (performed only by males). Nonhuman primate vocalizations appear to be interchangeable.

2. *Feedback* Users of the system monitor what they are transmitting.

Humans monitor their linguistic output and correct it. It is debatable whether bees do so when they dance, or whether birds monitor their calls. It is not known whether birds monitor their song; it is likely that they do.

3. *Specialization* The communication system serves no other function but to communicate.

Human language represents reality—both external (real world) and internal (states, beliefs)—symbolically in the mind. Speech serves no purpose other than to convert language into sound for transmission purposes. Symptomatic tokens are unspecialized. Crying is a symptomatic signal that may be interpreted by someone else and thus function communicatively, but its primary purpose is physiological (the clearing of foreign matter from the eye, the release of emotional tension). Bee dancing and birdsong, on the other hand, appear to be specialized communicative activity. Alarm calls of any species may be symptomatic but at the same time are specialized for different types of predators.

4. *Semanticity* The system conveys meaning through a set of fixed relationships among tokens, referents, and meanings.

Human language conveys meaning through arbitrary symbols. Bee dancing conveys meaning, but within a very limited range, as do bird calls and song, along with nonhuman primate vocalizations. (See feature 8.)

5. *Arbitrariness* There is no natural or inherent connection between a token and its referent.

This is overwhelmingly true of human language, with the possible exception of a few onomatopoeic terms. Bee dancing shows some arbitrariness, since there is no obvious connection between the form of the dance and the distance from the hive. Expressions of food source quality and direction are not arbitrary, however. Many bird calls are highly suited for their purpose, such as danger calls, which are difficult to locate, and in this sense are not arbitrary. Most nonhuman primate vocalization appears to be equally adaptive. Arbitrariness has, however, been claimed for vervet alarm calls.

6. *Discreteness* The communication system consists of isolatable, repeatable units.

Human language shows distinctive features, phonemes, syllables, morphemes, words, and still larger combinations. Bee dancing may be thought of as consisting of two (or three) discrete types, but these dances are not recombinable. There is some evidence for subunits in birdsong. They are also present in primate call systems.

7. *Displacement* Users of the system are able to refer to events remote in space and time.

Bee dancing shows displacement. No evidence for displacement is found in bird calls or songs. Baboons occasionally produce threat and fight vocalizations long after an aggressive encounter, but there is no evidence that this is reflecting displacement; it probably reflects a slow winding down of the animal's affective state.

8. *Productivity* New messages on any topic can be produced at any time.

This is obviously true of human language. Bees show limited productivity. Bird calls show none. Birdsong shows evidence of recombination (the songs of laughing gulls are well documented in this respect), but it is doubtful whether these recombinations transmit novel messages. This is also true of recombination in the calls of certain monkeys (such as macaques).

9. Duality of patterning Meaningless units (phonemes) are combined to form arbitrary signs. These signs in turn can be recombined to form new, meaningful larger units. In human language, phonemes can be combined in various ways to create different symbolic tokens: *spot, tops, opts,* and *pots.* These tokens in turn can be combined in meaningful ways: *Spot the tops of the pots.*

There is no evidence of this type of patterning in any known animal communication system.

10. Tradition At least certain aspects of the system must be transmitted from an experienced user to a learner.

This is obviously a factor in the acquisition of human language. It is possibly present in a very limited way in bee communication, and it is definitely present in the acquisition of birdsong for some species. The situation for nonhuman primates is unclear.

11. Prevarication The system enables the users to talk nonsense or to lie.

Undoubtedly, this property is found in human language. There are specialized mimics found among birds, fishes, and even insects. The question of intentionality is crucial here. Current work with birds suggests that some species learn as many songs as possible and use this repertoire to maintain territorial advantage by "impersonating" other species. This may well be purely genetically determined behavior, but, in any event, it is highly complex.

12. Learnability A user of the system can learn other variants.

Humans can learn a number of different languages. Bees are limited to their own genetically specified dialect. Bird calls are apparently limited in this same way. As noted previously, some birds learn songs of other species,

Table 14.3 Summary of design features for bees and birds

Design feature	Bees	Birds
1. Interchangeability	no; foragers only	no; only males sing
2. Feedback	?	?
3. Specialization	yes	yes
4. Semanticity	yes — very limited	yes — limited
5. Arbitrariness	yes, for expressing distance	yes, though highly adaptive
6. Discreteness	in a limited way	yes, in song
7. Displacement	yes	no
8. Productivity	yes — very limited	possibly
9. Duality of patterning	no	no
10. Tradition	possibly, but highly limited	yes, limited
11. Prevarication	no	possibly
12. Learnability	no	possibly
13. Reflexiveness	no	no

but this may well be simply mimicry. Nonhuman primates seem restricted to their own systems.

13. *Reflexiveness* The ability to use the communication system to discuss the system itself.

No evidence exists that any other species writes grammars or linguistics textbooks.

Tables 14.3 and 14.4 summarize this survey of design features.

Table 14.4 Summary of design features for nonhuman primates and humans

Design feature	Nonhuman primates	Humans
1. Interchangeability	yes	yes
2. Feedback	probably	yes
3. Specialization	in part	yes
4. Semanticity	yes	yes
5. Arbitrariness	limited confirmation; selectively adaptive	yes
6. Discreteness	in call systems	yes
7. Displacement	no	yes
8. Productivity	possibly	yes
9. Duality of patterning	no	yes
10. Tradition	possibly	yes
11. Prevarication	possibly	yes
12. Learnability	no	yes
13. Reflexiveness	no current evidence	yes

Summing Up

This brief overview of animal communication systems emphasizes that human language is one communication system among the many that life forms on this planet employ. Communication can be described with reference to the **sign**, which is composed of a **token**, a **meaning**, and a **referent**. Tokens may be **iconic**, **symbolic**, or **symptomatic**, and classified as **graded** or **discrete** types. Most animal communication has traditionally been viewed as symptomatic, though studies of communication among birds and bees suggest symbolic signs are used. A significant innate component may interact with some exposure to the communication system, especially among birds. Nonhuman primate communication consists of graded series of vocalizations and appears to show little arbitrariness.

Experiments with nonhuman primates have created controversy over whether chimpanzees and gorillas have shown symbolic behavior and a capacity for linguistic behavior. Many researchers have dismissed the work as an example of **dressage** or the Clever Hans phenomenon.

Though human language shares certain **design features** with other communication systems, it lacks many that they possess. Humans, for example, are hopelessly inadequate at following scent trails, a feat the prosimians accomplish with ease; cannot change color for communicative purposes with the facility of an octopus; and are not as gifted as horses and many other mammals at assessing and interpreting subtle body gestures. Humans do possess an ability to symbolize that far exceeds that of bees and even (allowing for the most generous interpretation possible of recent experiments) our nearest relatives, chimpanzees and gorillas. Human language is also more flexible and productive in manipulating these symbols than any known animal communication system. Language is as suited for—and indeed as much a part of—human life patterns as the communication systems of our fellow creatures are for their modes of existence.

Picture Credits

Iconic tokens in Figure 14.3 are from the following sources: the baboon open-mouth threat is taken from I. DeVore, ed., p. 66 (cited in sources); park information signs are courtesy of Alberta Provincial Parks; canine threat-fear gradation is from M. W. Fox's *Behavior of Wolves, Dogs and Related Canids*; bee dancing (Figure 14.7) is adapted from K. von Frisch's *The Dance Language and Orientation of Bees*, p. 57 (cited in sources); spectrograph of the robin song is from Thorpe (cited in sources); avian isoglosses in Figure 14.9 are from Paul Mundinger's "Microgeographic and Macrogeographic Variation in Acquired Vocalizations of Birds" in *Acoustic Communications in Birds* 2, pp. 147–208, edited by D. E. Kroodsma, E. H. Miller, and H. Ouellet (New York: Academic Press, 1982). The figure illustrating the response of vervet monkeys to predators is taken from Michael Bright's *Animal Language* (cited in recommended reading). Tokens used in the Sarah experiments are taken from D. Premack and A. J. Premack as cited in E. Linden's *Apes, Men, and Language,* p. 179 (Baltimore, Md.: Pelican Books, 1974).

Sources

The theory of semiotics outlined in this chapter is based on the work of Thomas A. Sebeok in *Contribution to the Doctrine of Signs,* Studies in Semiotics 5 (Bloomington: Indiana University Press, 1976), who is not responsible for what has been made of it here. Bee communication is drawn from K. von Frisch's "Dialects in the Language of the Bees" in *Scientific American* 202, no. 2: 78–87 (1962) and his work *The Dance Language and Orientation of Bees,* translated by C. E. Chadwick (Cambridge, Mass.: Harvard University Press, 1967). Bird vocalization is based largely on W. H. Thorpe's *Bird-Song* (Cambridge, Mass.: Cambridge University Press, 1961). Jake Page's parrot is reported in *Science* (1982). Lemur vocalizations in Table 14.1 are drawn from A. Jolly's *Lemur Behavior* (Chicago: University of Chicago Press, 1966). Vervet communication is drawn from R. M. Seyfarth and D. L. Cheney's "How Monkeys See the World," edited by Snowden et al. (cited below), and baboon communication from K. R. L. Hall and I. DeVore's "Baboons Social Behavior" in *Primate Behavior,* edited by I. DeVore (Toronto: Holt, Rinehart and Winston, 1965), pp. 53–110. Creative signing by Koko is reported in F. Patterson and E. Linden's work *The Education of Koko* (New York: Holt, Rinehart and Winston, 1981). Some exercise material is drawn from various articles in *How Animals Communicate*, edited by Thomas A. Sebeok (Bloomington: Indiana University Press, 1977).

Recommended Reading

Bright, Michael. 1984. *Animal Language*. London: British Broadcasting Corporation.

de Luce, Judith and Hugh T. Wilder, eds. 1983. *Language in Primates: Perspectives and Implications*. New York: Springer-Verlag.

Hockett, Charles. 1960. "The Origin of Speech." *Scientific American* 203, no. 3:88–96.

Lieberman, Philip. 1984. *The Biology and Evolution of Language*. Cambridge, Mass.: Harvard University Press.

Sebeok, Thomas A. and Jean Umiker-Sebeok. 1980. *Speaking of Apes*. New York: Plenum Press.

Sebeok, Thomas A. and Robert Rosenthal, eds. 1981. *The Clever Hans Phenomenon: Communication with Horses, Whales, Apes, and People*. Annals of the New York Academy of Sciences 364. New York: The New York Academy of Sciences.

Snowden, C. T., C. H. Brown, and M. R. Petersen, eds. 1982. *Primate Commmunication*. London: Cambridge University Press.

Thorpe, W. H. 1974. *Animal Nature and Human Nature*. Garden City, New York: Doubleday.

Questions

1. Are the following examples relatively more *iconic, symbolic,* or *symptomatic*? Classify each one according to the type that you believe is most predominant, and comment on what other type you find present.
   a) Dogs wag their tails when happy; cats flick their tails when irritated.
   b) An octopus, when showing aggressive behavior, becomes bright red.
   c) The Canada goose shows aggressive intentions by opening its mouth, coiling its neck, and directing its head toward an opponent. When it is unlikely to attack, its mouth is closed, its neck is horizontally extended, and its head is directed away from an opponent.
   d) Tree leaves change color in the fall.
   e) A certain species of spider taps her web briskly to signal her young to go back into the web funnel when she is disturbed.

2. Find three examples each of *icons, symbols,* and *symptoms* you encounter in the course of a day. Is it possible to classify unambiguously each token as to type? If not, state why in each case.

3. Review the alarm calls of the vervet monkey presented in this chapter. Not everyone agrees that vervets show the cognitive ability to classify the world in terms of predatory birds, snakes, and mammals. At least two different interpretations of the vervet alarm calls have been proposed. Can you suggest what they might be?

4. Add two columns to the list of design features presented in Tables 14.3 and 14.4. For one column, take the perspective of a researcher who believes that apes show true linguistic ability in their signing, and fill in the column from this point of view. Fill in the other column from the perspective of a researcher who does not believe such ability has been shown. Be sure to comment on each design feature.

5. In your opinion, what kind or kinds of evidence would provide conclusive proof that animals communicate with a system like human language? In other words, what feature or features of human language separate it from other communicative systems found in nature? Is it possible to state this in terms of difference in kind or type, or is human linguistic communication only different in degree?

15 COMPUTATIONAL LINGUISTICS

Contrary to popular belief, computers are not smart. In fact, they are only as smart as the human beings that teach them, no more and no less. Computers have no magical powers to do anything they are not explicitly told to do. They cannot guess, except when told how to guess. They cannot think, except when human programmers tell them very explicitly how to reason. But they can remember, and this they do exceptionally well. Furthermore, they can count. This they do remarkably well and remarkably fast too.

One of the central questions in computational linguistics is this: what would a computer program have to contain to enable the computer to analyze or create sentences and paragraphs correctly? These sentences could be either spoken or written. This is something that we humans achieve effortlessly. However, consider the amount and type of information that a computer would have to know about language in order to understand a simple sentence like this:

1. Many elephants smell.

First, the computer would have to understand the meaning and use of each of the words. For example, the word *many* can occur only with countable nouns, as in *many elephants*. The word *many* cannot occur with uncountable nouns, as in **many money*. A countable noun can appear in such phrases as *one elephant* or *two elephants,* whereas an uncountable noun cannot, as in **one money* or **two moneys*. Some words of this type, such as *most*, can appear both with countable nouns, as in *most elephants,* and uncountable nouns, as in *most money*. A computer would have to know that the *-s* at the end of *elephants* means that the word is plural. This being the case, the verb *smell* has to be in the plural form. The sentences **Many elephants smells* and **Many elephant smells* are not grammatical English sentences.

In addition to this grammatical knowledge about *many* and about agreement between subject and verb, there is a great deal of other information people have about sentence *1*. We know that elephants are animals and we know that animals smell, so we know that elephants are likely to be smelly. This is called *real world knowledge* as distinct from *grammatical knowledge*.

For example, although flies are animals too, they do not smell with the same intensity as elephants. Furthermore, when analyzed carefully, the verb *smell* has two uses. One is the intransitive use in which the subject of the sentence, in this case *elephants,* is what is smelly, as in *Many elephants smell bad.* The other is the transitive use, in which the elephants are doing the smelling, as in *Many elephants smell their food.* The meaning of the two verbs is different even though they are spelled the same, and the function of the subject *elephant* is different in the two interpretations.

What sort of knowledge about pronunciation would a computer need to know to utter this sentence? The rules of pronunciation, like the rules of grammar, are different for each language. They are likely to vary within the same language depending on many factors. For example, the word *elephant* has the letters *ph* in the middle. English speakers know that this *ph* is to be pronounced with the phoneme /f/, as in *telephone* or *emphatic.* However, what about the words *upholstery* or *upheaval*? Why are these words not pronounced with an /f/ for the letter *ph*? Both words consist of the prefix *up-* and a base. In the case of *upholstery,* the word came from Old English *up-* and *-holden,* and it appears that this internal structure continues to determine the phonemes in pronunciation, even in Modern English. Of course, there is more to pronunciation than just converting letters to sounds, as shown in Chapters 2 and 3, and in later sections of this chapter.

These examples are sufficient to illustrate the quantity and variety of information that humans know about language. We take this knowledge for granted. Until we try to write computer programs to understand or generate even the most simple sentences, there is no need to pick apart the knowledge about language that we possess. However, computers are only as capable as the humans that program them, so it is the task of the linguist to spell out this knowledge for the computer. This is a major undertaking, involving all aspects of knowledge of language.

Computational linguistics is a relatively new discipline that lies in the intersection of the fields of linguistics and computer science. It is but one of many new hybrid disciplines involving computers that require computational expertise as well as a background in another field. The term *computational linguistics* covers many subfields. It sometimes refers to the use of computers as a tool to understand or implement linguistic theories. This means that linguists and computer scientists can gain a better understanding of the scientific and research questions by using computers. On the other hand, the term is sometimes used to refer to working systems or applications in which linguistic knowledge is needed. In this case, the questions and issues are usually ones of software engineering as well as of theory.

This chapter is organized around subfields of linguistics that are discussed in other chapters in this book: phonetics and phonology, morphology, syntax, and semantics. There is also a section on computational lexicology. The first part of the chapter shows how each *linguistic* subfield is used as the basis for a *computational linguistic* subfield. The second part of the chapter shows some ways in which these various subsystems are combined to create computer systems that use language.

15.1 COMPUTATIONAL PHONETICS AND PHONOLOGY

The Talking Machine: Speech Synthesis

At the 1939 World's Fair in New York, a device called a vocoder was displayed. The machine, developed by scientists at Bell Laboratories, reconstructed the human voice by producing a sound source which was then modified by a set of filters. The values for the filters were derived from the analysis of human speech. The vocoder system consisted of a source of random noise for unvoiced sound, an oscillator to give voicing, a way to control resonance, and some switches to control the energy level. This was to simulate the vowel sounds and fricatives (see Chapter 2). Then there were controls for the stop consonants /p,b/, /t,d/, and /k,g/. An amplifier then converted the modified source signal into sound that resembled the human speech it was originally modeled after.

The vocoder was nicknamed the Talking Machine. It was a crude device, but it demonstrated that good speech synthesis could indeed be achieved, given the right values for the major frequencies, and the right methods of concatenating and modifying adjacent values. Early systems used different technology from that used today, but the principles remain the same. The goal is to replicate the wave forms that correctly reflect those of human speech in order to produce speech which, at the very least, will be intelligible and aesthetically pleasing and, in the ultimate, could not be distinguished from the speech of a human being.

Chapter 2 gave a summary of articulatory phonetics, that is, how sounds are made when humans speak. Chapter 3 covered some aspects of sound systems. Speech recognition and speech synthesis rely on a detailed knowledge of acoustic phonetics as well as articulatory phonetics, although there are correlations between the acoustic and articulatory properties of sounds. Acoustic phonetics is the study of the structure of the wave forms that constitute speech. As explained in Chapter 2, the lungs push a stream of air through the trachea. The air stream is modified first at the glottis and then by the tongue and lips.

Each sound can be broken down into its fundamental wave forms, as shown in Figure 15.1. The figure shows a spectrographic analysis or **spectrogram** of the words *heed, hid, head, had, hod, hawed, hood,* and *who'd* as spoken by a British speaker. The diagrams give a visual representation of the duration of the utterance on the horizontal axis, and the different frequencies in the wave form on the vertical axis. The main frequencies, or **formants**, show up because they have more intensity than other frequencies. Note the different locations of the formants along the frequency dimension for the different vowels. The sound /h/ is only slightly visible as fuzzy lines across the spectrum because /h/ is a voiceless fricative with little or no glottal constriction (see Chapter 2, Section 2.5). The acoustic effect is weak "white

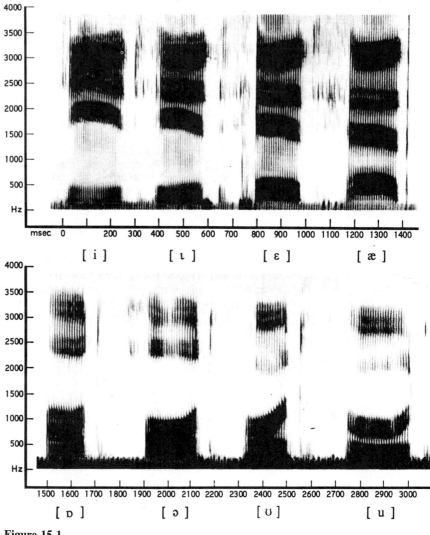

Figure 15.1

noise" resembling fuzz or static. The /d/ is a stop, so there is just a low frequency "voice bar" resulting from the vibrations in the glottis, but there are no vowel formants for the period of closure since the air flow is blocked. This shows up as blank space on the spectrogram. For speech synthesis, the first three formants are the most critical for identifying different vowels. The others add some refinement to the sound, but they do not determine intelligibility or naturalness with the same significance as the first three formants.

Since different vowels are composed of different frequencies, in theory all a speech synthesizer would have to do is replicate those vowel sounds, put in a few consonants, and string them together just as letters are strung together to make words and sentences. Unfortunately, the matter is not so simple, since sounds are not fixed. Rather, they vary according to the segments that surround them. Effects occur on adjacent segments and across groupings, sometimes as far as six phonemes away. For example, Figure 15.2 shows the same phonemic vowel /æ/, but notice the rises and slumps in the formants. The figure shows how adjacent consonants can modify vowels. Similarly, vowels modify consonants. Nasal sounds modify entire chunks of speech. On top of these local changes, there are changes to entire phrases based on suprasegmental features such as stress and intonation (see Chapter 2, Section 2.9).

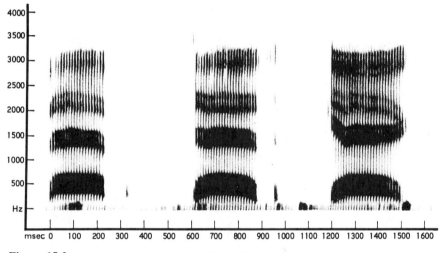

Figure 15.2

Many steps are involved in achieving speech synthesis, and there are many different choices in ordering these steps. The text to be spoken has to be analyzed syntactically, semantically, and orthographically. Pronunciations for exceptional words such as *have* /hæv/ or *four* /for/ must be found. These words do not follow the predictable phonological rules of English: *have* does not rhyme with *nave* or *rave*, and *four* does not rhyme with *sour* or *glamour*. Contrastive sounds need to be assigned based on the letters and based on other information about the word. After the correct phoneme is chosen, a system must look at the environment to see which allophone of the phoneme to choose. For example, to return to Figure 15.2, if the system were trying to pronounce *bab* /bæb/, the vowel /æ/ corresponding to the labial onset and labial offset would be chosen, since labials tend to lower adjacent formants.

A syntactic analysis of a sentence permits a system to identify words that might go together for phrasing. This is particularly important for noun compounds in English. As many as six nouns can be strung together, and the pronunciation of the compound can change the listener's interpretation of the meaning. For example, the phrase *Mississippi mud pie* could have two interpretations, depending on the syntax of the phrase. The most likely interpretation is shown in Figure 15.3, where the mud pie is Mississippi style.

CHAPTER FIFTEEN

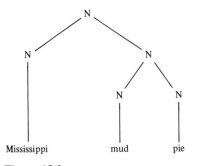

Figure 15.3

Alternatively, the pie could be made of mud from Mississippi, in which case the syntax of the phrase is different, as shown in Figure 15.4, and so is the pronunciation. Syntactic analysis can also determine the part of speech for

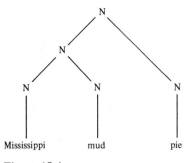

Figure 15.4

noun/verb pairs that are spelled the same but pronounced differently, such as the verb *record* /rəkɔ́rd/ and the noun *record* /rékərd/. Finally, parentheticals will be identified, as in these sentences:

    2. Here are the apples, as you can see.
    3. He said, although I don't believe it, that he was a good driver.

Parentheticals are typically pronounced at a lower pitch and loudness. When pronounced with main phrase intonation, they are difficult to understand. Finally, a semantic analysis of a sentence, and of a text, gives an idea of focus and stress. These features must be translated into duration (length), pitch, and loudness in order for synthetic speech to sound completely natural.

Given advances in computer technology, along with advances in electronics and acoustics, intelligible speech synthesis has already been achieved. However, everyone who has seen popular science fiction films knows that even now, synthetic speech still sounds synthetic. In addition to the syntactic and semantic issues raised above, a number of difficult problems remain, such as incorporating intonational variety into the rules to eliminate the droning quality of synthesized speech, and improving individual sounds.

Speech Recognition or Speech Analysis

As we have seen, speech consists of very complex wave forms changing rapidly across time and in subtle ways, which can affect the perception of a message. The task of speech recognition is to take these wave forms as input and decode them. This is exactly what we humans do when listening to speech. The wave form that reaches the ear is a continuous stream of sound; we segment the sound into words, phrases, and meaningful units so we can determine the meaning of the utterance. The task of a speech recognition system is to teach a computer to understand speech, whether the system models human mechanisms or not.

Even though human beings have no trouble decoding speech wave forms, computers do. The problems are immense. First of all, as shown in Chapter 2, Section 2.10, speech sounds are modified by adjacent sounds in natural speech. The faster and more informal the speech, the more sounds are merged and dropped. Guessing what sounds have been dropped based on faulty and limited input is an extremely difficult task. Knowledge of context, of syntactic structure, of probabilities of occurrence are helpful, but the problem is still not solved.

Since decoding of continuous speech presents such problems, some systems impose the requirement that words be pronounced slowly, and separated by a slight pause. The pause gives a clear cue that the word has ended, so a system has much less guesswork to do. Also, if the speech is said more slowly, fewer sounds will be dropped. In addition to the constraint of pronouncing words in isolation, limiting a system in its vocabulary means that the recognition machine will have less guesswork to do. Finally, yet another way to reduce the guesswork is to require that an individual user "train" the system to be tailored to his voice alone. Anyone who is skilled at recognizing voices can attest to the fact that no two people sound alike. The purpose of "training" a computer is to familiarize it with the unique and distinguishing features of the user's voice.

Another very difficult problem for speech recognition is what is called the "cocktail party effect," such as that of being in a crowded room. Even though there is much noise from other people, from music, or from the street, humans manage to filter out the background noise and pick out a particular sound or conversation to listen to. Everyone has had the experience of not hearing a sound, such as a leaking faucet, until someone points out the sound, and the annoying sound then becomes the only one to be heard. Whatever mechanisms were used to suppress the noise of the faucet were deactivated when brought to the listener's attention. Computer recognition systems cannot distinguish the speech signal from the noise, so they perform poorly in noisy environments. Thus, another condition—a reasonably quiet environment—must be imposed on systems in order for them to function adequately.

Each of these constraints can be imposed to result in more reliable systems, but the overall research problem still remains: how can humans be so adept at decoding speech yet computers cannot be easily taught to do so?

15.2 COMPUTATIONAL MORPHOLOGY

Morphology is the study of the internal structure of words, covering such topics as affixation, compounding, and infixation (see Chapter 4). Most research in computational morphology arose as a by-product of developing natural language processing systems. Looking up words in a computational dictionary for these systems turned out to be more complicated than met the eye, precisely because of morphological processes that can conceal the base word. For example, if a dictionary has the word *book,* the word *books* would not be found by a simple search. Unless a system is explicitly told that *book* is related to *books* by a productive and regular rule of inflectional morphology, it would not be able to infer that those words are related. Thus, a program needs to include the rule of pluralization in English as well as other rules in order to recognize or generate the morphological permutations of words.

Morphological Processes

Most morphologically conditioned changes in written English involve spelling, with some changes in stems, and some truncation rules. Examples are *stop/stopped, sing/sang,* and *tolerate/tolerant.* In general, morphological variations in English are not as opaque as in other languages. Some languages, such as German, have very productive compounding, whereas others have infixation and reduplication, or complex stem changes. Words altered by morphological processes cannot be easily recognized by a natural language processor unless they are properly related to their bases for lexical lookup.

Implementing Morphological Processes: Method One Broadly speaking, there are two approaches to computational morphology. Historically, the first was called a stemming or stripping algorithm. An algorithm is a set of rules for solving a problem; the term was first used in mathematics to describe the rules for solving mathematical problems. Since algorithmic procedures usually involve a sequence of repeated steps, the term is naturally suited to computer programs in general, and to programs for computational linguistics in particular. In the stemming or stripping algorithm, affixes are recursively stripped off the beginnings and ends of words, and base forms are proposed. If the base form is found in the base-form dictionary, then the word is analyzable. Successful analyses provide information about the internal structure of the words as well as whatever other information is produced by the rule for a given affix, such as part of speech change, inherent semantic changes (e.g., *-ess* is +feminine), or other information (e.g., abstract, Latinate, singular, plural). Most of these systems are sensitive to constraints on affix ordering such as described in the chapter on morphology. Inflectional affixes occur outside of derivational affixes, and there may be some derivational affixes that occur outside of other derivational affixes.

Two different types of dictionaries are possible with the stemming method: word-based and stem-based. A word-based system has a dictionary with words only. For word generation, all input to morphological rules must be well-formed words, and all output will be well-formed words. For word analysis, all proposed bases will be words. The word-based system has proven to be very useful for projects that use large machine-readable dictionaries, since dictionaries list words, not stems. A machine-readable dictionary is a dictionary that appears in computer form, such as that available in spelling checkers or thesauruses. Machine-readable dictionaries have definitions, pronunciations, etymologies, and other information, not just the spelling or synonyms. (See Section 15.4 for more on machine-readable dictionaries.)

Table 15.1 presents an example of the type of analyses given by a word-based stemming system. To analyze *conceptualize* as an infinitive verb

Table 15.1 Input word: conceptualize

Analysis	Part of speech	Features
concept	n	num(sing)
-ual	adj	
-ize	v	form(inf)

(v form(inf)), first *conceptual* must be analyzed as an adjective (adj). This would be done by a rule stating that the suffix *-ize* can attach to certain adjectives to create verbs. *Conceptual* can be analyzed as an adjective if *concept* can first be analyzed as a singular noun (n num(sing)). This would be done by a rule for *-ual* stating that the suffix *-ual* can attach to certain nouns to create adjectives. *Concept* is stored in the dictionary as a singular noun, so this lexical lookup serves as the final step of the analysis. The analyses shown here actually result from recursive calls to the morphological rules. Each rule has conditions that restrict its operation. In this example, the *-ual* rule states that the base must be a singular noun. The condition for the *-ize* rule is that the base must be an adjective. Since each condition is met, an analysis is possible. The word *conceptualize* is deemed a well-formed infinitive verb.

How would the system analyze a more complex form? Consider the analyses in Table 15.2 of the word *conceptualizations,* which is based on

Table 15.2 Input word: conceptualizations

Analysis	Part of speech	Features
concept	n	num(sing)
-ual	adj	
-ize	v	form(inf)
-ation	n	num(sing)
-s	n	num(plur)

the previous example. In this example, the suffix *-ation* attaches to infinitival verbs. Notice that when *-ation* attaches to *conceptualize,* there is a spelling change. If no spelling rules were written, then the word **conceptualizeation* would be allowed by the system. Finally, the plural marker *-s* is attached at the outside of the noun. For the plural suffix -*s*, there is no change in the part of speech, but only in the number feature of the word from singular to plural. Observe that these examples illustrate a word-based system. Both the dictionary entry, in this case *concept,* and the complex words *conceptualize* and *conceptualizations* are well-formed words of English.

How would this system differ if it were stem-based? For this example, the morpheme -*cept* might be listed in a stem dictionary, due to its presence in other words in English, such as *reception, conception, inception,* and *perception.* Since -*ceive* and -*cept* are related in a regular way, this relationship might also be given in the stem dictionary, or the words could be related by rule. Consider again *conceptualizations,* analyzed down to a stem in Table 15.3. In this example, the prefix *con-* attaches to -*cept.* The point

Table 15.3 Input word: conceptualizations

Analysis	Part of speech	Features
con-		
-cept	n	num(sing)
-ual	adj	
-ize	v	form(inf)
-ation	n	num(sing)
-s	n	num(plur)

was made earlier that a word-based morphology system can use a regular dictionary as its lexicon, but no such convenience exists for a stem-based system. In order for stem-based morphology to get wide coverage, a large dictionary of stems is required. (More on this topic is found in the section on computational lexicology later in this chapter.)

Implementing Morphological Processes: Method Two The other common approach to computational morphology, the two-level approach, is fundamentally different from the stemming approach. This results in basic differences in computational properties. Both systems contain a lexicon or dictionary, although two-level morphology *requires* a stem-based lexicon. Both systems have rules, but the rules are very different. In two-level morphology, the rules define correspondences between surface and lexical representations; they specify if a correspondence is restricted to, required by, or prohibited by a particular environment. *Lexical* roughly corresponds to *underlying,* whereas *surface* usually means *orthographic* but sometimes *phonemic.* In Figure 15.5, the lexical representation of *try* followed by the +*s* is compared with a surface representation *tries*.

Lexical and surface representations are compared using a special kind of rule system called finite-state transducer. Simply put, the rules would decide whether the lexical *y* could correspond to the surface *i* based on information the rules have already seen. The rules that compare lexical and surface form move from left to right, so when a successful correspondence is made, the rule moves along. One of the claimed strengths of this method is that, since the procedure moves from left to right, it accurately reflects

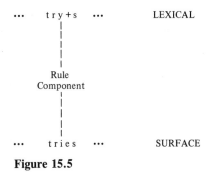

Figure 15.5

the way that people process words. Since people hear and read English from left to right (i.e., the beginning of the word is heard before the end), a system that incorporates this directionality might be an actual model of performance. The primary drawback of the two-level system is that it requires a specialized stem dictionary, complete with restrictions on the stems so that not all affixes attach without restrictions. For example, a dictionary would need to include -*cept* or -*mit* (for *transmit, submit, permit,* and so on).

Some Problems in Computational Morphology

Compounding is a particularly thorny problem since it tends to be so productive that compounds are often not listed in a dictionary. The word *bookworm,* for example, does not appear in Webster's Seventh New Collegiate Dictionary. A good morphological analyzer should be able to analyze *bookworm* as shown in Table 15.4. However, what about a word like *accordion*?

Table 15.4 Input word: bookworm

Analysis	Part of speech	Features
book	n	num(sing)
worm	n	num(sing)

The analysis in Table 15.5 shows *accordion* to be composed of the noun *accord* plus the noun *ion*. This is obviously incorrect because *accordion* is not a compound analogous to *bookworm*. Since *accordion* does not ever have this analysis, it might be marked as an exception to morphological decomposition.

Table 15.5 Input word: accordion

Analysis	Part of speech	Features
accord	n	num(sing)
ion	n	num(sing)

A related problem arises due to overenthusiastic rule application. Table 15.6 presents an analysis of *really*. Here *really* is analyzed as [*re-* [*ally-*

Table 15.6 Input word: really

Analysis	Part of speech	Features
re-		
ally	v	form(inf)

verb]verb], meaning "to ally oneself with someone again." This analysis is correct, although highly improbable. Cases like *really* bring up a difficult issue. Should a word like *really* be specially marked in the dictionary as a nonanalyzable word, an exception to the rules that would apply to regular formations like *reapply, redo,* and *reduplicate*? Or should the rules be allowed to apply freely? What about a word like *resent,* which could either be [*re-*[*sent*verb]verb] as in *He didn't get my letter, so I resent it* and [*re-sent*verb] as in *Did he resent that nasty comment*? The spelling of this word is truly ambiguous, so a decision about its analyzability requires knowledge of syntactic and semantic features in the sentence and context. Usually the decision is driven by practical concerns. A system that is designed to implement a theory, but that does not need to perform well on a task that applies the theory would probably allow the rules to apply freely. A system that needs to perform accurately on large texts would probably mark *really* and *resent* as nonanalyzable words, even though strictly speaking they are not.

15.3 COMPUTATIONAL SYNTAX

Research in computational syntax arose from two sources. One was the practical motivation resulting from attempts to build working systems to analyze and generate language. Some of these systems, such as machine translation and database query systems, are discussed in Section 15.6. The other source was a desire on the part of theoretical linguists to use the computer as a tool to demonstrate that a particular theory is internally consistent. In this case, less value was given to efficiency or broad coverage since this was not the goal. The emphasis was instead on theory testing and on formal issues in natural language analysis. Ideally, builders of practical systems should take more advantage of theoretical insights, and linguistic theoreticians should pay more attention to practical problems. This has been the case in recent research on parsing, although this is a fairly new friendship.

Natural
Language
Analysis

Parsers and Grammars Chapter 5 showed how sentences can be analyzed by rules into substructures such as noun phrases, verb phrases, prepositional phrases, and so on, as shown in Figure 15.6. Given a system of rules, an analyzer will be able to break up and organize a sentence into its substruc-

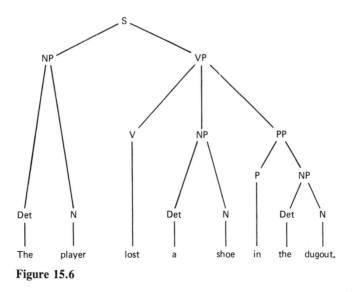

Figure 15.6

tures. A grammar can be viewed as the set of rules that define a language. These rules can be of different shapes or formats, which give them different properties. A **parser** is the machine or engine that is responsible for applying the rules. A parser can have different strategies for applying rules. Chapter 5, Section 5.10 showed how the rules for sentence structure differ between languages. These differences are reflected in the grammars for these languages, although the parser that drives the grammars can remain constant.

Determinism vs. Nondeterminism Any time a syntactic parser can produce more than one analysis of the input sentence, the problem of backtracking is raised. For example, if the beginning of the sentence in Figure 15.7 is read word by word, there is more than one possible ending. In choice (a), the

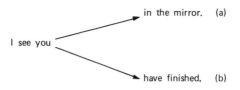

Figure 15.7

word *you* is the object of the main verb *see*. For (b) the word *that* has been left out, as is permitted in English, so the word *you* is the subject of the clause *you have finished*. If the parser follows path (a), and if that path turns out to be the wrong one, how can the situation be rectified to get the right analysis? Or can choices be controlled so that a parser never has to undergo the time-consuming task of going back and starting over?

The term **nondeterministic** may refer to going back or backtracking if the first analysis turns out to be impossible. It may also mean following multiple paths in parallel, meaning that both analyses are built at the same time but on separate channels. The term **deterministic** means that the parser has to stick to the path it has chosen. There have been many proposals about controlling the backtracking of parsers. The problem is a serious one since the number of alternatives increases as the coverage of a system increases. The result is that as an analyzer improves, it also becomes more and more cumbersome because each time it is presented with more and more options.

Top-Down vs. Bottom-Up Parsing Consider the following phrase structure rules for English:

4. *a)* S → NP VP
   b) NP → (Det) (AdjP) N (PP)
   c) VP → V (NP) (PP)
   d) PP → P NP

There are two ways to build an analysis of a sentence, using just these rules. This section illustrates the principles of what is called *top-down* and *bottom-up* parsing. Working systems may not be built to function exactly like this, but the principles are the same.

In addition to the rules in *4*, we also need to give some lexical items, or **terminal nodes**, for each category or **nonterminal**.

5. N → Curly
   V → sat
   P → on
   det → the
   N → grass

Generally speaking, a nonterminal is not a word in the language. Rather, it is a category or a phrase, such as N or NP. A terminal can be thought of as a word (although sometimes a terminal is a part of a word or several words). In top-down parsing, the analyzer always starts with the topmost node, in this case S, and finds a way to expand it. The only rule in the set *4* for S is shown in Figure 15.8. Both NP and VP are nonterminal nodes.

NP   VP

Figure 15.8

The next rule to apply is the NP expansion rule and then the VP expansion rule. The results are shown in Figure 15.9. Although N is a nonterminal, it

Figure 15.9

has no expansions, so the next rule to apply would be the VP rule. If the subject of the sentence had been *the batter,* then the NP would have been expanded to Det and N. This process continues until no more expansions could apply, and until all the lexical items or words in *5* occur in the correct position to match the input sentence *Curly sat on the grass.* Top-down parsers suggest a hypothesis that a proposed structure is correct until proven otherwise.

In contrast, bottom-up parsers take the terminals (words) of a sentence one by one, replace the terminals with proposed nonterminal or category labels, and then reduce the strings of categories to permissible structures. For the same example, the analysis would be built as follows: first the word *Curly* would be assigned the category N; then *sat* would be assigned to V, and so on. The partial analysis up to this point is shown in Figure 15.10.

Figure 15.10

None of the rules in *4* permit the combination of N and V; none permit V and P nor P and Det to combine. But the NP rule does combine Det and N to build up a structure, as shown in Figure 15.11. This continues until the

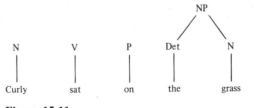

Figure 15.11

structure of a sentence is built. It has been proposed that the building of the structure from the terminal nodes up to the topmost S node from left to right reflects the way human beings process sentences more accurately than the top-down approach, but this is a controversial issue.

*****Generative Capacity** The term *generative* in this context refers to formal properties of grammars as mathematical systems. It does not refer to language generation, which is discussed below. Recall that a grammar consists of a set of rules that describe a language. Assume also some finite set of symbols, *V*, the vocabulary of a language. For English, examples of *V* would be:

    6. V_L = [*player, shoe, child, lost, a* . . .]

In the vocabulary *V* are other symbols and categories, such as *N* and *Det.* Formally, a language *L* over *V* is a finite set of strings of symbols taken from *V*. Informally, a language consists of strings from the vocabulary. Of course, a sentence is more than just a string of words, as shown in Chapter 5. Furthermore, the set of strings is greater than the set of well-formed sentences, as sentences *7* to *9* show. Even though the vocabulary *V* may be a finite list, the language *L* may be finite or infinite. This is because of recursion, a very powerful property of natural languages. (Chapter 5, Section 5.1, contains a discussion of recursive rules.) The application of a finite number of recursive rules results in languages that can contain an infinite number of well-formed strings.

The following sentences consist of vocabulary from the set in *6*. While *7* is a well-formed sentence in English, *8* and *9* are not.

    7. A child lost a shoe.
    8. *child shoe a.
    9. *Lost a shoe a child.

Although *9* is not in the language *L* for English, it could be found in the language *L* for Spanish, given the same vocabulary.

    10. Perdió un zapato un niño.
         lost   a   shoe   a   child

The grammar of English would give a correct description of *7*, but not *8* or *9*. On the other hand, the grammar of Spanish would allow both *7* and *9*, but not *8*. The goal of an implemented grammar is exactly the same. An **implementation** is simply a practical system. The grammar rules are programmed into a computer, and the computer program then decides if the string is permitted in the language. If the string is permitted, it then has the task of giving the sentence the correct description.

Natural languages (as opposed to computer languages) are highly complex, so discovering the correct grammar for a given language is an extremely difficult task. The complexity and subtlety of natural languages continue to present a challenge to linguists. There are many competing theories of what the "correct" grammar of natural languages will be like. Even the grammar for English, a very well-studied natural language, is not at all well-understood. One issue that all theories agree upon, however, is that a grammar should have certain properties. Grammars should give a correct description of the following:

    A. The strings of a language *L*
    B. The structures corresponding to the strings in *L*

Property A is called **weak generative capacity**. Property B is called **strong generative capacity**. (Generative here does not mean "create" but rather "describe.")

To explain, Figure 15.6 shows an analysis in which the first two words *the* and *player* are joined into a noun phrase (NP). The verb phrase (VP) is described by the grammar as consisting of a verb (V), followed by a noun phrase (NP), followed by a preposition phrase (PP). These three constituents are immediately dominated by the VP node. What if a different grammar were to claim a different structure for this sentence? Consider the structure in Figure 15.12. This analysis makes different claims about the structure of

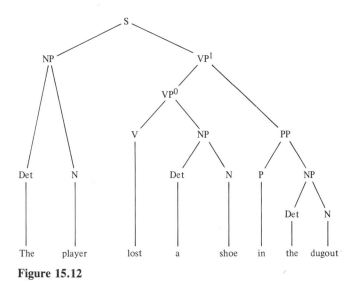

Figure 15.12

the sentence, but the actual string of words stays the same. The tree in Figure 15.12 has two levels of verb phrase. One is VP^1, which dominates everything in the predicate of the sentence. The other is VP^0, which dominates only the main verb and the direct object. The grammar generating the structure in Figure 15.12 differs in strong generative capacity from the grammar for Figure 15.6. However, both grammars may have the same weak generative capacity since they both have the ability to describe the string *The player lost a shoe in the dugout*.

Role of Syntax and Semantics The preceding section dealt with syntactic analyzers, but it is important to note that the division between what should be handled by the syntactic component of a system and what is properly in the semantic component is a matter of great debate. For example, some systems might claim that selections of prepositions by verbs, often considered a syntactic property, is actually dependent on the semantic category of the verb. For example, not all verbs can take the instrumental, as in the reading of *11* in which *the stick* was used to hit the dog.

    11. He hit the dog with a stick.

If a different verb is substituted for *hit*, would the sentence be semantically or syntactically ill-formed?

    12. ?He told his story with a stick.

Some systems assume that a syntactic analysis precedes a semantic one, and that the semantics should be applied to the output of syntactic analyses. This is the position of the earliest transformational models, which was incorporated into many computational systems. Some systems perform syntactic and semantic analyses hand-in-hand. Other systems ignore the syntactic, viewing it as a second-step derivative from semantic analyses.

Natural Language Generation

What Is Generation? To utter a sentence, a speaker first must decide on goals, plan the information to be included, and then express that information in a sentence of his or her language. The language generation problem is often viewed as the reverse of the language analysis problem, but this is not accurate. In the same way, the generation of speech, discussed in Section 15.6, is in no way simply the reverse of speech recognition. Certain problems are the same, but many are not.

Language generation has been the underling of computational linguistics. The reason for this may be that it is a more difficult area to work in than language analysis. For language analysis, the linguist is given a set of data (i.e., strings of the language) with which to work. For language generation, the linguist has ideas and plans that need to be turned into language. A language generator must be able to make decisions about the content of the text, about issues of discourse structure, and about cohesion of the sentences and paragraphs. In contrast, a language analyzer might be invoked to make proposals about discourse and content, but the raw material upon which guesses are based is already there. For the language generator, only concepts and ideas are available to work with. Choices of words (lexical items) and syntactic structures are part of decisions to be made in building a text.

As with syntactic analyzers, there are two approaches to generation: top-down and bottom-up. In the top-down approach, first a very high-level structure of the output text is determined, along with very abstract expressions of meaning and goal. Then lower levels are filled in progressively. Subsections are determined, and examples of the verbs with their subjects and objects, if any, are proposed. This is refined, until the prefinal stage when lexical items are chosen from the dictionary. After all sentences have been decided upon, and after all lexical items have been inserted, there is a component to "smooth" and provide low-level coherence to the text. This component makes sure that pronouns are used correctly, for example, and that connecting phrases such as *in the preceding paragraph* or *on the other hand* are used correctly. In contrast, the bottom-up approach builds sentences from complex lexical items. First, words to achieve the goals are hypothesized. Then sentences are composed, and finally high-level paragraph and text coherence principles are applied.

The Generation Lexicon The lexicon is just one link in many difficult steps involved in generating natural and cohesive text for an underlying set of goals and plans. Imagine that you have determined an underlying message, plan, or goal. In order to figure out how to translate the underlying message into some actual words in a language, your generation system will have to figure out such matters as what verbs to pick and how to pick the subjects and objects, if any, for those verbs.

Suppose you want to express how fast time is going by in your life. You might use the verb *elapse*. *Elapse* is said to be a one-place predicate or a one-place verb. It is intransitive, so it takes just one argument, the subject. (The term *argument* here refers to grammatical dependents of a verb.) If you want to talk about baseball, you need to describe the action. You might use the verb *hit*. *Hit* is transitive; it takes two arguments. *Hit* is also often used with an instrumental, a phrase that tells what the subject hit *with*, as in *with a stick* in sentence *11*. In this case, *hit* can take three arguments. Finally, a verb like *give* takes a subject, object, and indirect object, and those three arguments can be expressed as a subject, object, and a recipient, indicated by *to* as in *13*. Alternatively, *give* can undergo what is called Dative Movement, as in *14*, in which case the indirect object *dog* appears next to the verb and is not preceded by the preposition *to*.

13. He gave a stick to the dog.
14. He gave the dog a stick.

Often verbs with very close meanings take different numbers of arguments and in different order. For example, *give* can also mean *donate*, but *donate* does not permit the same alternations as *give*.

15. He donated a stick to the dog.
16. *He donated the dog a stick.

A system must be capable of deciding what the meaning to be conveyed is, and then it must be capable of picking very similar words to express that meaning. The lexicon or dictionary must supply items to instantiate the link between meaning and words.

The design and content of the generation lexicon is one of the most difficult areas in language generation. The lexicon needs to contain many different types of information, such as syntactic facts about verbs, facts about usage and focus, and facts about types of modifiers. Building lexicons for generation is one of the goals of computational lexicology, as discussed in the following section.

15.4 COMPUTATIONAL LEXICOLOGY

Since phrases, sentences, and paragraphs are composed of words, computer systems need to contain detailed information about words. The section on morphology dealt with the structure and analyses of word forms, but there is more to know about words than this.

Computational linguists are realizing that an analyzer or generator is only as good as its dictionary or lexicon. The lexicon is the repository of whatever information a particular system needs. The individual words in the lexicon are called lexical items. Chapter 5, Section 5.3, shows how lexical insertion occurs in syntactic structure. For example, in order for a bare structure such as Figure 15.13 to be "filled out" with real words, a program would need to have a match between a word marked Det in the lexicon and the slot in the tree requiring a Det. The same goes for any part of speech,

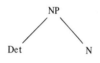

Figure 15.13

such as noun, verb, or adjective. Given the items in *5*, a valid match for Figure 15.13 would be Figure 15.14. Figure 15.15 would not be a valid match. Notice that the preposition *on* occurs under the determiner node, and the verb *sat* occurs under the noun node. At the very least, the condition of matching part of speech has to be met.

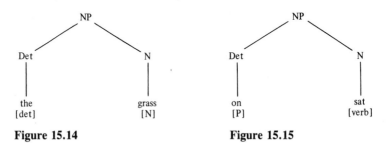

Figure 15.14   **Figure 15.15**

A computer program would need to know more than just part of speech to analyze or generate a sentence correctly. Subcategorization, that is, the number of arguments a verb can take, must be considered (see Chapter 5). Knowledge of thematic roles, such as agent, patient, and goal, is also needed (see Chapter 6, Section 6.2). A syntactic analyzer would also need to know what kinds of complements a verb can take.

17.   I decided to go.
18.   *I decided him to go.
19.   *I persuaded to go.
20.   I persuaded him to go.

The verb *decide* can take the infinitive *to go* as in *17*, but it cannot take an NP object and then the infinitive, as in *18*. The verb *persuade* is the opposite. It cannot take the infinitive *to go* as in *19*, but it must have an NP object before the infinitive, as in *20*.

The lexicon needs to know about the kinds of structures in which words can appear, about the semantics of surrounding words, and about the style of the text. For example, sentence *21* is strange in meaning, but the structure is fine.

21.   I broke the concept.

The verb *break* is transitive and so can take an object, but the problem here is the type of noun; *concept* is [+ abstract], but *break* requires a [+ concrete] noun. Only concrete objects are breakable, unless the meaning is metaphorical as in *The disease broke his will to live*. (See Chapter 6 for more discussion of semantics.)

What does a computational lexicon look like? So far the list of information includes:

22. Lexical Item
   1. Part of Speech
   2. Sense Number
   3. Subcategorization
   4. Semantic Restrictions

Keeping in mind that a computational lexicon has to contain as much information as possible in order to correctly analyze and generate phrases, sentences, and text, the following are also needed:

22. (continued)
   5. Pronunciation
   6. Context and Style
   7. Etymology
   8. Usage (e.g., taboos)
   9. Spelling (including abbreviations)

The task of collecting all the important information for every existing word in the English language is awesome. In addition, given that the kind of information needed cannot be found in conventional dictionaries, how are computational lexicons built? There are several approaches. One is to hand-build a lexicon specifying only those features that a given system needs and using only the lexical items that are most likely to occur. For example, assume that an analyzer is reading the *Wall Street Journal,* and assume that the sentence to be analyzed is *His interest is high this month.* If the analyzer is to assign a meaning to this sentence, it has to know at least the information below.

   Word: interest-1
   1. Part of Speech: Noun
   2. Inherent Semantic Features: [+concrete], . . .
   3. Context: Financial

In just this usage, there is no reason to know about the abstract meaning of *interest* as "attention" or "concern." The lexical entry for this other sense would include the information below.

   Word: interest-2
   1. Part of Speech: Noun
   2. Inherent Semantic Features: [+abstract], . . .
   3. Context: Emotional

Most words have many different senses, and sometimes the different senses have very different grammatical behavior. Every time a new word is added to the lexicon, if a new feature is also added, then the dictionary builder has to go back through the lexicon and modify every word to match the new expanded word. When *interest-2* was added to the dictionary, new features had to be added, namely that *interest-1* does not have a context "Emotional" and that *interest-2* does not have a context "Financial." One of the major problems in building computational dictionaries is extensibility. The problem is how to add new information, and modify old information, without starting over each time.

Another option in building large lexicons is to use two resources: the power of the computer and the data of machine-readable dictionaries. A machine-readable dictionary (MRD) is a conventional dictionary, but it is in machine-readable form (i.e., on the computer) rather than on the bookshelf. MRDs are useful in building large lexicons because the computer can be used to examine and analyze automatically information that has already been organized by lexicographers, the writers of dictionaries. Unfortunately, the type of information that is needed by a computational dictionary is not always easy to find in a conventional dictionary. However, with some clever approaches to exploiting the hidden information in conventional MRDs, it appears that many important facts can be pulled out and put into a computational lexicon. This work is still in its earliest stages, so it is uncertain how far it can be pushed, but it is an important line of research in computational linguistics.

For example, the knowledge that a word has a sense that is [+human] is needed in a computational lexicon for both syntactic and semantic reasons. Webster's Seventh New Collegiate Dictionary, which has about seventy thousand headwords, has just over a thousand nouns that are defined in terms of the word *person*. Some examples are given below:

> *accessory*
>> a *person* not actually or constructively present but contributing as an assistant or instigator to the commission of an offense—called also accessory before the fact
>
> *acquaintance*
>> a *person* whom one knows but who is not a particularly close friend
>
> *intellectual*
>> a very intelligent or intellectual *person*
>
> *scatterbrain*
>> a giddy heedless *person*: FLIBBERTIGIBBET
>
> *unbeliever*
>> one that does not believe: an incredulous *person* : DOUBTER, SKEPTIC

Notice that each word can have other senses. *Accessory,* for example, can mean an object or device that is not essential but that enhances the main object. A program has been written to extract these words. The headwords are then marked [+human], and synonyms such as *flibbertigibbet, doubter,* and *skeptic* can also be marked as [+human] in one sense.

Although this approach is appealing, caution is in order. In the first place, lexicographers are people, and dictionaries are huge undertakings written by many different contributors. Therefore, there is less internal consistency than would be ideal. Finally, and most seriously, there is the problem that most words have more than one sense. Keeping track of which senses have which features is not an easy task. Furthermore, the decision on what is a sense is also not clear-cut. The problem of extensibility enters into play again. Even with all these restrictions, however, using machine-readable dictionaries as a resource for constructing large lexicons looks very promising.

Another approach to building large lexicons for natural language analysis and generation is **corpus analysis**. The larger the corpus, or text, the more useful it is, since the chances of covering the language as it actually is used increase. In addition to size, a good corpus should include a wide variety of types of writing, such as newspapers, textbooks, popular writing, fiction, and technical material. As an example of the way large corpora (the plural of corpus) are useful, consider the verb of movement *flounce*. The definitions given for the verb in Webster's Seventh New Collegiate Dictionary are:

> *flounce* 1
> to move with exaggerated, jerky motions
> to go with sudden determination
> to trim with flounces

These definitions tell nothing about likely subjects. Looking at corpus data will yield this information. From a large corpus, about twenty occurrences of the verb *flounce* were extracted. Thirteen had subjects that were female, as in sentences *23* and *24*.

> *23.* Carol flounced out to the kitchen for an apron.
> *24.* She flounced off with a following of hens behind her.

Four had subjects that were clothing:

> *25.* The white cashmere dressing-gown flounced around her.

One had *horses* as the subject, and the other subjects were pronouns. The point is that, given a good parser, it would be possible to extract automatically all the subjects of a given verb, and then to look for properties of those subjects. For *flounce,* that information would appear in the lexicon as:

> *Word: flounce-1*
> *1.* Part of Speech: Verb
> *2.* Subcategorization: Intransitive
> *3.* Semantic Restrictions: female human subject

> *Word: flounce-2*
> *1.* Part of Speech: Verb
> *2.* Subcategorization: Intransitive
> *3.* Semantic Restrictions: clothing subject

Using computers to extract linguistically useful information from dictionaries and texts for the purpose of constructing large lexicons is a new field within computational linguistics. It holds great promise in providing a solution to the difficult but fundamental problem of building computational lexicons out of already existing resources. At this point, clever programs give large and comprehensive lists of words with a potential characteristic, but human judgments are still necessary. If the computer is viewed as a tool to be used in collecting lists of words, then the endeavor is successful. If the goal is to view the computer as the only tool, and to eliminate the human judge, then computational lexicon builders still have a long way to go.

15.5 COMPUTATIONAL SEMANTICS

So far in this chapter, we have focused on structure: the structure of sentences and words. However, in order to understand what a word, sentence, or text means, a computer program has to know the semantics of words, sentences, and text. This section treats briefly some of the semantic representations and processes that have been proposed in computational linguistics.

Semantic issues were touched on in the preceding section. The lexical item contains a field for semantic information, including such information as what kind of semantic features a verb requires for its subject or which thematic roles a verb requires or permits. The semantic fields for the two senses of *flounce* are:

> *Word: flounce-1*
> Semantic Restrictions: female human subject
> *Word: flounce-2*
> Semantic Restrictions: clothing subject

Although the semantics of words is an important component of any language system, there is yet a broader issue: the semantics of sentences and paragraphs.

Two approaches to semantics and language analysis have been proposed: syntactically based systems and semantically based systems. Considering for the moment the analysis of sentences, in the first approach the sentence is assigned a syntactic analysis, much in the way outlined in Chapter 5 and earlier in this chapter. A semantic representation is built after the syntactic analysis is performed (see Figure 15.16). The problems arise in

Syntactically Based Systems

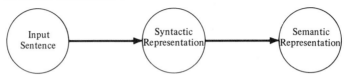

Figure 15.16

getting from one representation to the other. This is sometimes called the mapping problem. However, in the semantically based system, first a semantic representation is built. Sometimes there is no syntactic analysis at all (see Figure 15.17). Consider a response to the question *Who got the coffee today?*

26. The new student went.

Semantically Based Systems

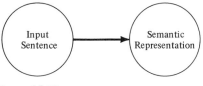

Figure 15.17

A syntactic analysis of the sentence would show that *the new student* is the first NP directly dominated by S (see Figure 15.18). From there, the parser

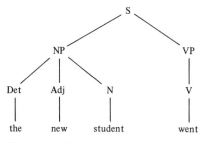

Figure 15.18

might guess that the subject is *the new student*. This is often true in English, although it is not always the case. Still, nothing is said about the fact that the subject is the actor (i.e., the one who performs the action) with a verb like *go*. Compare this to the intransitive version of the verb *open*.

> 27. The door opened.

In this case, the subject *door* is not performing an action. Something or someone opened the door. A syntactically based system obtains this knowledge about a sentence after a structure is built.

In contrast, a semantically based system builds a semantic representation first. For sentence *26*, it might look something like the one in Figure 15.19.

```
Go  −  Actor
          NP
went      the new student
```

Figure 15.19

The word order is not important. The semantic representation of related sentences might be the same.

> 28. John gave the book to Mary.
> 29. John gave Mary the book.
> 30. The book was given to Mary by John.

The mapping into the various syntactic forms of what is basically the same sentence occurs after the semantic representation is decided upon. Semantically based systems have been used for text and discourse analysis, such as for understanding stories.

Both approaches still need to accomplish the same goal, namely that of assigning word meaning, sentence meaning, and text meaning. The problem of semantic representation will not be covered here. However, it must be mentioned that determining matters like reference, as in *31*, and scope, as in *32* to *34*, are part of what needs to be achieved.

31. I saw him in the bookstore.
32. Pregnant women and children get out first.
33. Ripe apples and peaches make a good fruit salad.
34. Every person speaks two languages.

For *31*, is this a specific bookstore or just some bookstore? For *32*, what is the scope of *pregnant*? Is it *pregnant women and pregnant children*? This is unlikely. But in *33*, the likely interpretation is *ripe apples and ripe peaches*. Finally, in *34*, does every person speak the same two languages? Or different languages?

Pragmatics

The word *meaning* itself has many meanings. In addition to word meaning, logic, paragraph meaning, and so on, it has also been loosely applied to the field of **pragmatics**. Pragmatics is the study of how language is used in communication. Consider the following telephone conversation.

35. Caller: Is George at home?
Answer: Yes.

This dialogue is amusing because the answerer has broken some basic conversational principles. The caller is not really asking the literal question *Is George at home?* although the semantic analysis of the sentence would indicate that this is a request for information about whether or not George is at home. The syntactic form of the question requires the answers *yes* or *no*, but nothing else. The dialogue in *36* does not have the amusing quality of *35*.

36. Caller: Are you tired?
Answer: Yes.

Conversational principles require that an answer be as informative as possible. This is not the case in *35*. Another example of conversational principles is illustrated in *37* and *38*.

37. Sue got on the horse and rode into the sunset.
38. Sue rode into the sunset and got on the horse.

Why is *38* strange? The coordinating conjunction *and* should just be a simple joining of two like parts. The nouns from *33*, for example, could be reversed with no strange result (the scope problem remains unsolved, however):

39. Ripe peaches and apples make a good fruit salad.

The reason for the problem in *38* is that the word *and* is often given a temporal interpretation. This may not be part of the meaning of *and* but rather a matter of how it is used.

Whether pragmatics is a subfield of semantics is controversial, but there is no disagreement on the fact that knowledge of pragmatic principles is necessary to understanding and generating language.

15.6 PRACTICAL APPLICATIONS OF COMPUTATIONAL LINGUISTICS

The previous sections of this chapter have shown how the use of computers has forced linguists to formulate rigorous statements of theory and facts, because all of the implicit knowledge that humans have about language has to be made explicit. Theories become testable in a concrete way. Implementations of practical systems tend to force researchers (and students) to understand a particular language process in very detailed terms. Since related skills are needed both for linguistic analysis and for programming, the field of computational linguistics has flourished. This section discusses some specific types of computer systems that involve using linguistically sophisticated programs.

An **application** can be defined as the use to which a program or set of programs is put, for example, a payroll application, an airline reservation application, or a word processing application. Most early applications in computational linguistics fell into three categories: indexing and concordances, machine translation, and information retrieval. Other applications included speech synthesis and recognition and database applications.

Indexing and Concordances

Indexing means finding, identifying, and usually counting all occurrences of a certain word in large texts. This application of computers to language study does exactly what computers are best at doing: locating a word, recording the location by line or sentence number, and counting how many times it appears. The examples of the use of the word *flounce* in the lexicology section were extracted from text using an indexing program. The program searched text on the computer to find any occurrence of the string *flounce, flouncing, flounced,* or *flounces.* When the string was found, the computer program took out the sentence and saved it in a separate file. A tally was kept of each time a targeted word was found.

A concordance tells which words occur near other words. Concordance and indexing programs are used widely in literary analysis. Some authors seem to favor using certain words in the context of other words. Concordance programs can find these relationships. A concordance program could tell, for example, how many times the word *she* occurred next to *flounce.*

Perhaps the most widely used word count was performed by Henry Kucera and Nelson Francis in 1962 on a corpus of one million words. The corpus is referred to as the Brown corpus since the work was completed at

Brown University. Kucera and Francis took fifteen different texts and wrote a program to count the number of times each word appeared. The ten most frequent words of English are:

the	69,971
of	36,411
and	28,852
to	26,149
a	23,237
in	21,341
that	10,595
is	10,099
was	9,816
he	9,543

The numbers after the words indicate how many times they appeared in the one million words. Word frequency lists such as this have been useful to psycholinguists who need to pay attention to frequency when designing experiments.

These early applications are still very useful, but they are not linguistic in nature. They used the power of the computer to count and categorize words, so the results were of use to the linguist, but they did not rely on any linguistic knowledge. For example, to find *flounce,* the related words *flounced, flounces, flouncing* also had to be looked for. Early systems were not endowed with morphological knowledge, so they could look only for the exact string given. The program could not figure out that *flounce* and *flouncing* were related forms. Furthermore, all occurrences of the strings *flounce, flounces,* and so on were pulled out, without regard to part of speech. Since the goal was to look at subjects of verbs, it was necessary to distinguish between the verb *flounce* and the noun *flounce* as in *The women always flounce out* and *The chair had a lacy flounce around the bottom.* Notice the implications of this: two of the top ten most frequent words are forms of the verb *be,* but since the system counts only strings, the forms *is* and *was* are counted separately. The inability of early systems to relate words had other problems. For example:

Minute	53
Min	5
Min.	1
Min,	1

are probably all variations of the word *minute,* although this would have to be verified by checking the original text. The count of *minute* is 53, but it really should be 60.

Most current concordance and indexing programs have solved some of the easier problems such as abbreviations, but most of the harder problems still remain. First of all, morphological knowledge is needed in order to relate various forms of the same word to just one base word. Second, syntactic knowledge is needed in order to figure out the part of speech of the word in the sentences and in order to figure out the arguments of the verbs, such as subject and object. Finally, semantic knowledge is needed to know the thematic roles of the arguments and to know which meaning of a word is intended.

Text Retrieval

Most libraries have abstracts of articles available by computer. Anyone who has ever tried to search for articles on a particular topic has had the frustrating experience of having to wade through masses of irrelevant material to find what was wanted. For example, when the word *morphology* was searched in the Library Index of Book Titles, the following titles were among those returned:

> Principles of Polymer Morphology
> Image Analysis and Mathematical Morphology
> Drainage Basin Morphology
> French Morphology

If a linguistically sophisticated program had been used to retrieve these titles, it is likely that they would have been divided according to the semantic subject field. Thus a chemist would not get titles on French, just as a linguist would not get titles on chemistry.

What linguistic expertise could text retrieval systems use? Again, as with indexing and concordance, the three critical subareas are computational morphology, syntax, and semantics. For example, someone wanting to know about the theory of light might want to find all references to the word *light* in an encyclopedia. This is not an unreasonable request, since there are now several encyclopedias available on compact disc, which can be read by a disc attached to a personal computer. The user can search through the text in ways that cannot easily be done with encyclopedias in book form. Searching for the string *light* anywhere in the text might give *lightening, enlightenment,* and *lighthearted,* but also *delight* and *candlelight.* On the other hand, if the user searches only for *light* surrounded by blanks, then words like *lighting* or *lights* would be missed. Without a parser and semantics, there is no clue about the nature of the word *light* when it is found in the text. The problem appears simplistic, but it is far more complex than meets the eye.

Machine Translation

The purpose of a machine translation system is the same as that of any translation system: taking text written or spoken in one language and writing or speaking it in another (see Figure 15.20). Translation poses challenging problems both for the human translator and for the machine attempting to do what the human does. Projects in machine translation in the 1940s and

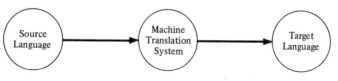

Figure 15.20

1950s spawned much of the early research in computational linguistics. Consider the written case first, and think of a single institution like the United Nations. Every day millions of words need to be translated from one language to another. Add to that other political and scientific institutions, plus businesses and publishers. This results in an overwhelming need for help in translation since the process, when done correctly, is time-consuming and mentally demanding. Since computers are suited to tasks requiring memory, it would seem that, with careful programming, the problem of translating by computer could be solved.

This was the thinking of computer scientists and linguists, but the problems turned out to be far more difficult than was imagined. Much government money was poured into the machine translation task from the late 1940s to the early 1960s, but results were slow to emerge due to the complexity of unforeseen problems. The subtlety of language, the nuances and lack of precision, caused problems because computers are suited to mathematical computation where subtleties do not prevail. Funding agencies became disillusioned, and although most researchers were still hopeful, they were humbled by the difficulties encountered in early years.

Researchers are now more realistic about their goals. Rather than attempting to build full-fledged machine translation systems that automatically convert a text from one language to another, some projects are aiming toward machine-assisted translation. In these projects, the computer is viewed as a tool to aid the translator. The computer makes suggestions, but the human translator makes final decisions. Other projects are developing ways to take texts and pass them through a preprocessor. A preprocessor is a system that looks at sentences and figures out which ones might present problems. The computer can identify the problem, and then ask the original writer to clarify. Take the first example in this chapter:

40. Many elephants smell.

Since this sentence is ambiguous as explained earlier, it might be sent back to the writer to be clarified.

Machine translation applications encompass many aspects of computational linguistics. For this reason, the venture is one of the more challenging to researchers. In addition, the notion of a machine that is capable or nearly capable of mimicking a very complex and subtle human activity constitutes an intriguing enterprise.

The source language needs to be analyzed syntactically and semantically. Lexical items need to be matched. This is a particularly difficult task. Not only do words in one language often not exist in another, but sometimes several words are used for one. One example involves the German words *essen* and *fressen*. Both words mean *eat* in English, but the verb *essen* is used for humans, whereas *fressen* is used for animals. If the system made the mistake of using *fressen* for people, it would be an insult. An example from Spanish concerns a missing word, as shown in *41* and *42*. Sentence *43* gives the word-by-word translation of the Spanish in *42*.

41. The elephants slept but didn't snore.
42. Los elefantes durmiéron pero no roncaron.
43. *The elephants slept but not snored.

The word-by-word translation of *42* is not English. What's wrong? In English, if the subject of a negative sentence is omitted, then the properly inflected form of the verb *do* needs to be inserted. Since *41* is in the past tense, and since the subject is plural, the correct form is *did*. There is no word for *did* in the Spanish version of the same sentence. Just as the human translator has to know this fact, so does the machine translation system. If the input language were Spanish and the input sentence were *42*, then the English generation system would need to know to insert the verb *do*, properly inflected, and not to inflect the main verb. The difficulties increase with languages that are fundamentally different in nature, such as English and Japanese, or Spanish and Finnish, or French and Chinese.

If the machine translation system is required to take spoken language as input and give spoken language as output, then the system becomes even more complex, as shown in Figure 15.21.

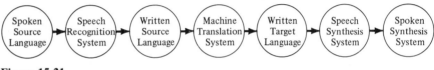

Figure 15.21

Speech Recognition

A speech recognition system takes spoken language as input and understands it (see Figure 15.22). The result could be the written text of what was said, or it could be orders to another machine. For example, a smart typewriter equipped with a recognition device will take orders to delete a line. The typewriter follows orders, but the words *delete line* will not be written. Speech recognition is a process that humans perform effortlessly, but teaching computers to recognize speech has turned out to be more difficult than was originally thought. Some of the linguistic problems involved were outlined in the sections on computational phonetics and phonology.

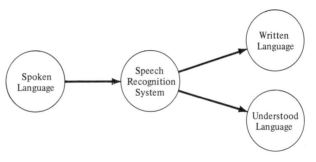

Figure 15.22

What are some applications that would benefit from a speech recognition system? One that has been explored is in the area of medical record keeping. Writing down details of examinations is time-consuming; often doctors leave out critical information due to these time pressures. With a speech recognition system, the doctor would simply talk while doing an examination. The speech would automatically and instantly be translated into text, which could be printed out immediately. In this way, the doctor could examine the report with the patient there to make sure everything has been covered. Medical terminology is fairly controlled, so the computer would have an advantage in guessing words. The examination room is relatively quiet, reducing the problem of background noise. Finally, a speech recognition system would allow the doctor to use both hands while speaking. Medical records could immediately go into a central library, which could be referred to by researchers studying symptoms and diagnoses. Last but not least, no one would ever have to struggle to read the doctor's illegible handwriting!

Such a system would have to be absolutely perfect. However, it is easier to correct an error in a report than to write one. Other applications that have been explored include quality control devices for inspecting assembly lines. For example, a worker would be able to say words like *pass* or *fail,* and the machine would then know whether to accept the part or refuse it. A very important application of speech recognition is in developing aids for the physically disabled. These include devices such as voice-operated appliances, machines, and tools. Applications such as these have great promise.

Speech Synthesis

A speech synthesis system has the opposite goal from a speech recognition system (see Figure 15.23). Applications for speech synthesis systems abound. One of the most important uses is "reading" to the visually im-

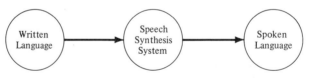

Figure 15.23

paired. Previously this required a human either to do the actual reading or to pre-record books and other material. This is not only expensive but also limiting, since what the person wants or needs to read may not be available on tape. Another important application is as a talking aid for the vocally handicapped. Communication boards and talking typewriters show the need for converting text to spoken language.

Another fairly common application is in an area called *database query*. A database is a large source of information, such as bank records, billing records, airline schedules, and theater and movie schedules. Imagine wanting to find out about ticket availability for the theater, movies, or other cultural events. This information is constantly changing as people buy tickets and as agencies release tickets. When you call, the text-to-speech machine can read the information aloud directly out of the database. No one has had to record it, which is time-consuming and expensive. Furthermore, the information is completely up-to-date. Other applications include use in machine translation systems, for robots, for expert systems, and for novel medical applications.

Summing Up

This chapter has covered the relatively new field of **computational linguistics**, which is the application of computers to the study of linguistic problems. There are two goals in computational linguistics. One is to use the computer as a tool to build programs that model a particular linguistic theory or approach. For this goal, the computer becomes a testing ground for the theory. The other goal is to build working systems that use linguistic information. The chapter covers the fields of computational phonetics and phonology, morphology, syntax, lexicology, and semantics and pragmatics. A section on **applications** presents some of the devices that have incorporated linguistic tools, such as *machine translation* systems and *reading machines* for the visually impaired.

Recommended Reading

Allen, James. 1987. *Natural Language Understanding*. Benjamin/Cummings: Menlo Park, California.

Grishman, Ralph. 1986. *Computational Linguistics: An Introduction*. Cambridge University Studies in Natural Language Processing. Cambridge University Press: Cambridge.

Journal of the Association for Computational Linguistics. 1987. Volume 13, Numbers 3–4.

King, Margaret, ed. 1983. *Parsing Natural Language*. Academic Press/Harcourt Brace Jovanovich: London.

Klatt, Dennis. "Review of text-to-speech conversion for English." *Journal of the Acoustical Society of America*. Vol. 82:3:1987.

Levinson, Stephan E. and Mark Y. Liberman. "Speech Recognition by Computer." *Scientific American*. April 1981.

Savitch, Walter J, Emmon Bach, William Marsh and Gila Safran-Naveh, eds. 1987. *The Formal Complexity of Natural Language*. New York: D. Reidel/Kluwer.

Questions

1. What kinds of problems might a computer have with these sentences?
   a) Sue bought red apples and plums.
   b) It was a large animal house.
   c) Susan baked in the kitchen.
   d) Susan baked in the sun.
   e) Susan baked.

2. What are the main uses of a text-to-speech system? What information does the computer need to know in order to pronounce these sentences in informal style?
   a) What are you doing tonight?
   b) The woman was delighted.
   c) That article misled me.
   d) That's a new car, isn't it?
   e) It was a tough test, although I did well.
   f) Can't you sing better?

3. What rules are necessary for a computer program to analyze these words? (*Hint:* First figure out the prefixes and suffixes. Refer to the chapter on morphology if necessary.)
   a) kindness
   b) kindly
   c) kindnesses
   d) nationalism
   e) countability
   f) nontransformational
   g) reusable

4. What different structures might a syntactic analyzer propose for the following sentences?
   a) She saw the man with a telescope.
   b) Watch dogs bark.
   c) Broadcast programs like 60 Minutes.

5. Think of a word that has many different meanings, such as *bank* or *interest*. Then give information about that word using the categories in Section 15.4. Give at least two senses for each part of speech. The following example has one sense for the noun part of speech, and two senses for the verb part of speech.

   WORD: bank
   a) Part of Speech: Noun
   b) Sense Number: 1
   c) Semantic Restrictions: of a river
   d) Pronunciation: /bæŋk/
   e) Context and Style: normal
   f) Example: The bank of the river was grassy.

   WORD: bank
   a) Part of Speech: Verb
   b) Sense Number: 1
   c) Subcategorization: transitive, requires the preposition *on*
   d) Semantic Restrictions: object of preposition is either a person or thing
   e) Pronunciation: /bæŋk/
   f) Context and Style: informal
   g) Example: I can't bank on him to do it.

WORD: bank
a) Part of Speech: Verb
b) Sense Number: 2
c) Subcategorization: transitive
d) Semantic Restrictions: object is money
e) Pronunciation: /bæŋk/
f) Context and Style: normal
g) Example: She banks her money at the local branch.

6. Give three applications of computational linguistics. How can these systems improve the quality of life for people with physical disabilities?

GLOSSARY

Affix (Af) A bound morpheme that modifies the meaning and/or syntactic (sub)category of the stem in some way (e.g., *un-* and *-able* in *unreadable*).

Affricate A non-continuant consonant characterized by a slow release of its closure (e.g., [č] and [ĵ].

Agglutinating (language) A language that makes extensive use of polymorphemic words (i.e., words containing a root and one or more affixes) and in which each grammatical contrast is typically encoded by a separate, clearly identifiable morpheme (e.g., Turkish).

Agrammatism A language disorder involving the loss of minor lexical categories and affixes, usually associated with Broca's aphasia.

Agraphia Loss of the ability to write caused by brain damage.

Algorithm A set of rules for solving a problem. The term was first used in mathematics to describe the rules for solving mathematical problems.

Alexia Loss of the ability to read due to brain damage.

Allomorph A variant form of a morpheme (e.g., In English /-əz/, /-z/, and /-s/ are allomorphs of the plural morpheme /z/).

Allophone A variant of a phoneme (e.g., [t] and [tʰ] are allophones of the phoneme /t/ in English).

Alphabetic (writing) A system of writing in which symbols represent consonant and vowel segments.

Alveolar ridge A small ridge that protrudes from just behind the upper front teeth within the oral cavity (also called the *alveolum*).

Alveopalatal (sound) A sound produced in the area between the palate and the alveolar ridge where the roof of the mouth rises sharply (also called **Palatoalveolar**) (e.g., [š], [ž]).

Amerindian (language) A indigenous language of North America (e.g., Cree, Haida).

Analogy An inference that if two things are alike in some respects they must be alike in others (e.g., Since *mow* and *know* are alike in that they are both verbs, by analogy with *mowed*, the past tense of *know* should be *knowed*).

Analytic (language) A language in which words are typically made up of a single morpheme (also called an **Isolating language**) (e.g., Cantonese).

Angular gyrus A language center in the brain that lies behind Wernicke's area and is responsible for converting a visual stimulus into an auditory form and vice versa.

Animate In some languages, a class consisting of nouns, most of which have living referents.

Antecedent The NP on which a pronoun depends for its interpretation (e.g., *John* in *John hurt himself*).

Antonyms Words or expressions that have opposite meanings (e.g., *hot* and *cold*).

Aphasia Language loss caused by damage to the brain.

Apocope The loss of a word-final vowel (e.g., Middle English [na:mə] → Modern English [neym]).

Archaisms Lexical items that are survivors of forms previously more widely used (e.g., Newfoundland English *drite* meaning 'dryness in the air').

Arcuate fasciculus The bundle of nerve fibers connecting Wernicke's area and Broca's area.

Argot The language of any social group whose members want to conceal the content of their communication from some other group (sometimes called **Cant**).

Articulatory phonetics The study of the physical production of speech sounds.

Aspiration The release of air through the oral cavity caused by a delay in the voicing of a vowel following the release of a voiceless stop.

Assimilation The modification of one or more features of a sound under the influence of neighboring elements (e.g., *Banff* is often pronounced [bæmf]).

Association lines Lines that link a phonetic or phonological representation on one tier to representations on another tier (e.g., the lines connecting a tonal representation to the vowel pronounced on that tone).

Audiolingual method A method of second language teaching based on the notion that second language learning should be regarded as a mechanistic process of habit formation.

Auxiliary verb (Aux) A verb that occurs with a regular or main verb (also called a **Helping verb**) (e.g., *has* in *He has left*).

Back (a) **(sound)** A sound made with the tongue retracted. (b) **(of the tongue)** The hindmost part of the tongue that lies in the mouth.

Backformation A word formation process that occurs when a word whose structure is apparently similar to that of a derived form undergoes a process of "deaffixation" (e.g., *resurrection* → *resurrect*).

Basilect The creole variety that is least similar to the standard.

Bilabial (sound) A sound made with both lips (e.g., [p], [b]).

Binary (features) Features that are considered to be either wholly present or wholly absent in the articulation of a sound (e.g., [±voice], [±coronal], etc.).

Blade (of the tongue) The part of the tongue that lies just behind the tip.

Blend A new word that is created from parts of two already existing lexical terms (e.g., *breakfast* + *lunch* → *brunch*).

Blissymbolics A contemporary development of both pictographic and ideographic writing, intended as a means of international, cross-linguistic communication for non-speaking individuals.

Body (of the tongue) The main mass of the tongue.

Borrowing The acquisition of words, sounds, or rules by one language from a language with which it has contact (e.g., English has borrowed the words *government, religion,* and *science* from French).

Bound (morpheme) A morpheme that must be attached to another element (i.e., it cannot constitute a word by itself) (e.g., *-s* in *books*).

Boustrophedon A style of writing in which lines are written alternately right to left, left to right, and so on.

Broca's area An area in the frontal lobe of the left hemisphere that plays a crucial role in organizing the articulatory patterns of speech and the formation of words and sentences.

C-command A notion that is relevant to the interpretation of a reflexive pronoun and is formulated as follows: A category *A* c-commands a category *B* when every category dominating *A* also dominates *B*.

Call (bird) Short bursts of sound produced by birds that typically serve to warn predators, co-ordinate flocking and flight activity, and so on.

Cant See **Jargon** and **Argot**.

Caretaker speech See **Motherese**.

Case An inflectional category that marks the grammatical function of an NP (i.e., subject, object, etc.) (e.g., nominative, accusative, genitive).

Cerebral dominance The control of cognitive and perceptual functions by a particular hemisphere of the brain.

Cerebral plasticity Flexibility in neurological organization that is supposedly characteristic of children in the critical period for language acquisition.

Character The part of a Chinese logogram that indicates the segmental pronunciation.

Clause A structure consisting of an NP and a VP; also called S.

Clipping A word formation process whereby a new word is created by shortening a polysyllabic word (e.g., *advertisement* → *ad*).

Coda The segments of a syllable that follow the nucleus (e.g., /n/ and /l/ in *central*).

Cognates Words that have descended from a common source (e.g., English *father*, German *Vater*, and French *père*).

Cognitive style The way in which we are predisposed to process information in our environment.

Communication strategy A strategy that serves the communicative needs of an L2 learner; a conscious plan instigated to fulfil an immediate communicative need.

Communicative competence A speaker's underlying knowledge of the linguistic system and the norms for the appropriate use of language in particular speech situations.

Communicative language teaching method (CLT) Second language teaching methods that are communicative in design, emphasizing functional language in the attempt to attain the goal of communicative competence.

Community counselling (teaching method) A method of second language teaching in which the L2 learner is considered part of a group rather than a class, and the teacher assumes the role of counsellor, allowing the student to begin communication in his or her own language.

Complement clause A sentence-like construction that is embedded as a sister of V (e.g., *I wonder* whether he has left).

Complementary distribution The distribution of allophones in their respective phonetic environments such that one never appears in the same phonetic context as the other (e.g., the distribution of long and short vowels in English).

Complementizer (Comp) A word that introduces an embedded clause (e.g., *that, if, whether*).

Complex (word) A word that consists of two or more morphemes (e.g., *gentle-man-ly*).

Compounding The combination of two or more free morphemes to form a new word (e.g., *lighthouse*).

Comprehensible input The linguistic input to which the L2 learner is exposed that is slightly beyond his or her competence in the target language.

Conduction aphasia A language disorder resulting from damage to the arcuate fasciculus and characterized by severe difficulty in repeating auditory forms.

Conjugation The complete set of inflected forms associated with a verb (also called a **Verbal paradigm**).

Conjunction (C) A minor lexical category whose members serve to join categories of the same type (e.g., *and, or*).

Consonant Sounds made with a narrow or complete closure in the vocal tract; the airflow is either completely blocked momentarily or restricted so much that noise is produced.

Constellation A complex of communicative modes operating on different channels.

Continuant A sound produced with continuous airflow through the mouth (includes vowels, glides, fricatives, and some liquids).

Contour tone A tone that changes pitch on a single syllable.

Contradiction A relationship between two sentences wherein the truth of one sentence entails the falsity of the other (e.g., *Harry is a bachelor; Harry is married*).

Contralateralization Control of one side of the body by the brain hemisphere on the opposite side.

Contrast To show difference(s) in form that may be related to difference(s) in meaning (e.g., The sounds [k] and [p] contrast in the words *cane* and *pain*).

Contrastive analysis (CA) An approach to L2 acquisition research that involves the comparison of the linguistic structures of the L2 learner's native language and the target language to determine their similarities and differences.

Conversational implicature A conclusion about the speaker's intended meaning based on "rules" for conversation such as the Co-operative Principle.

Conversion A morphological process that creates a new word by assigning a stem to a new lexical category without affixation (e.g., *ship* (noun) → *ship* (verb)).

Co-operative Principle A principle used in communication and according to which an utterance is assumed to be informative and relevant in the context of the communicative situation.

Corpus callosum A bundle of nerve fibers connecting the two hemispheres of the brain.

Cortex The outside surface of the human brain (also called *grey matter*) that provides the basis for the cognitive abilities distinguishing humans from other mammals.

Cranberry morpheme A morpheme that is neither an affix nor a free morpheme and that occurs in extremely restricted contexts (e.g., *cranberry, huckleberry*).

Creative (use of language) A characteristic of human language that allows novel and innovative responses to new experiences and situations.

Creole A language that has developed from a pidgin to become established as a native language in some speech community.

Critical period According to some theorists, a period extending from about age two to puberty during which language must be acquired.

Cuneiform A form of writing used by the Sumerians in the fourth millenium B.C. and produced with a wedge-shaped stylus pressed into soft clay tablets.

Cyrillic (alphabet) A writing system that combines adaptations of Glagolitic letters with Greek and Hebrew characters.

Dative (Dat) The case marker used for the noun heading an indirect object or recipient NP.

Declension The complete set of inflected forms associated with a noun (also called a **Nominal paradigm**).

Deep structure A level of syntactic representation that results from insertion of lexical items into the tree structure generated by the phrase structure rules.

Degree specifier (Spec) A minor lexical category whose members combine with an adjective or adverb and describe the extent to which the property designated by the adjective or adverb is present (e.g., *very, quite*).

Deletion A phonetic process that removes a segment from certain phonetic contexts (e.g., *Parade* is often pronounced [preyd]).

Denasalization In child language, the replacement of a nasal stop by a non-nasal counterpart (e.g., [suwd] for [suwn]).

Dental (sound) A sound made with the tongue placed against, between, or near the teeth.

Derivation (a) In morphology, a word formation process by which a new word is built from a stem, usually through the addition of an affix, that changes the word class and/or basic meaning of the word. (b) The set of steps or rule applications that results in the formation of a sentence in syntax and of a phonetic representation from an underlying form in phonology.

Design features Essential characteristics of communication systems that have been established with reference to human language.

Determinative A non-phonetic symbol that indicates a composite character's meaning; used in Chinese writing and historically also found in other logographic systems, such as Egyptian and Sumerian (also called a **Radical** or a **Specifier**).

Determiner (Det) A minor lexical category whose members combine with nouns to form noun phrases and specify whether the noun is definite or indefinite (e.g., *the, a*).

Deterministic parsing A type of automatic computer parsing of language in which no backtracking is permitted.

Developmental (approach) An approach to language acquisition research that focuses on the stages children go through as they make hypotheses about particular linguistic structures.

Developmental (errors) Errors that occur in language acquisition and provide evidence of the learner's attempts to create a grammatical system based on his or her hypotheses about the target language (e.g., *Why didn't he came to work?*).

Developmental sequences The stages of linguistic development that are relatively invariant across language learners.

Dialectology A branch of linguistics concerned with the analysis and description of regional varieties of a language.

Diaphragm The large sheet of muscle that separates the chest cavity from the abdomen and helps to maintain the air pressure needed to keep the speech mechanism functioning steadily.

Diphthong Vowels that exhibit a change in quality within a single syllable (e.g., [ey], [ow], [aw]).

Direct method (DM) A method of second language teaching that is based on the belief that an adult L2 learner can learn language in the same manner as a child and therefore involves no grammar instruction but rather concentrates on communicating.

Direct object The NP immediately dominated by VP; the sister of V (e.g., *the budgie in Kate fed the budgie*).

Discrete (tokens) Tokens that are distinguished from each other by "stepwise" differences (e.g., the digital display of a clock).

Dissimilation A process in which a sound is modified so that it becomes less like another neighboring sound (i.e. the opposite of assimilation) (e.g., *fifths* may be pronounced as [fɪfts]).

Distinctive feature A feature that serves to distinguish contrastive forms (e.g., The feature [voice] is distinctive in English because it underlies the contrast between /p/ and /b/, /t/ and /d/, etc.).

Dominate A structural relation in which there is a path in the tree from a node *A* to a node *B* (e.g., S dominates NP and VP).

Double-blind test A test in which a subject's responses are interpreted independently by someone other than the administrator of the test.

Downdrift A tonal phenomenon in which each high tone is lower than the preceding high tone, but higher than the low tone that immediately precedes it.

Dressage An interaction between a trainer and an animal in which the animal responds to very slight (sometimes subconscious) cues communicated by the trainer.

Entailment A relation between two sentences wherein the truth of the second necessarily follows from the truth of the first, but the reverse is not necessarily the case (e.g., The truth of *The wolf killed the bear* entails the truth of *The bear is dead*).

Environment The phonetic context in which a segment occurs.

Epenthesis The phonetically motivated insertion of a sound between segments (e.g., *Film* may be pronounced as [fɪləm]).

Ergative (Erg) In ergative languages, a case marker used for the subject of a transitive verb but not the subject of an intransitive verb.

Error analysis (EA) An approach to L2 research that involves the listing and classification of the learner's errors in an attempt to discover developmental patterns.

Euphemism A word or phrase that is less direct than the taboo word it replaces and is considered to be more socially acceptable (e.g., *passed away* for *died*).

Exclusive A type of first person plural pronoun whose referents do not include the addressee.

Extension The set of entities that a word picks out in the world (e.g., The extension of the current *Queen of England* is Queen Elizabeth II).

Feature (a) (**Phonetic**) The smallest non-reduceable building block of linguistic structure. (b) (**Phonological**) See **Distinctive feature**. (c) (**Semantic**) See **Semantic feature**.

Field dependence A learning style in which the learner operates holistically, perceiving the "field" as a whole rather than in terms of its component parts.

Field independence A learning style in which the learner operates analytically, perceiving the "field" in terms of its component parts rather than as a whole.

Flap A sound made by striking a point of articulation as an articulator passes across it (as in the alveolar flap of English).

Flapping A phonetic process in which an alveolar stop is pronounced as a voiced flap between vowels, the first of which is generally stressed (e.g., [bʌtər] → [bʌDər]).

Folk etymology The misanalysis of a word by the speakers of a language, typically reflecting the confusion of forms that are phonetically and/or semantically similar (e.g., *berfrey* → *belfry*).

Foreigner Talk The speech used by native speakers in communicating with L2 learners, characterized by the use of relatively simple structures and common lexical items.

Formants The main frequencies of a sound. Formants show up as black bands on a spectrogram because they have more intensity than other frequencies.

Free form An element that may occur in isolation and/or whose position with respect to neighboring elements is not entirely fixed.

Free (morpheme) A morpheme that constitutes a word by itself (e.g., *book*).

Free rule application Unordered application of rules in a derivation.

Free variation The free alternation of allophones and/or phonemes in a given environment (e.g., *sto*[pʔ], *sto*[p]; /ɛ/*conomics*, /iy/*conomics*).

Fricative A consonant produced with a continuous airflow through the mouth and with a narrowed oral passage such that there is audible friction (e.g., [s], [z], [f], [v], etc.).

Front (sound) A sound made in front of the palatal region.

Fronting The moving forward of a sound's place of articulation (e.g., [šuw] → [suw]).

Gender classification A grammatical category dividing nouns into classes often based on shared semantic and/or phonological properties (also called **Noun class**).

General Canadian The variety of English spoken by educated, urban, middleclass people in the provinces west of the Maritimes (also called **Inland Canadian**).

Generate To form a linguistic representation by a system of rules.

Generative grammar A systen of rules capable of forming or generating the potentially infinite set of sentences in a language.

Genitive (Gen) The case marker used for nouns bearing the possessive relation.

Glagolitic A writing system introduced among Slavic peoples for the translation of the Bible by the brothers Constantine (Cyril) and Methodius in the ninth century A.D.

Glide A type of sound that is produced with an articulation like that of a vowel, but that moves quickly to another articulation or quickly terminates (e.g., [y], [w]).

Gliding In child language acquisition, the replacement of a liquid by a glide (e.g., [wayd] for [rayd]).

Glottal (sound) A sound made with a special modification of the vocal folds besides that needed for voicelessness, voicing, and whispering (e.g., [ʔ] and [h]).

Glottis The space between the vocal folds.

Graded (tokens) Tokens that change in quantity or degree without steps or jumps from one level to the next (e.g., voice volume).

Grammar The system of elements and rules needed to form and interpret sentences.

Grammar translation method (GTM) A method of second language teaching that emphasizes reading, writing, translation, and the conscious learning of grammatical rules, its primary goal being to develop a literary mastery of the target language.

Grammatical (sentence) A sentence that speakers judge to be a possible sentence in their language.

Hangul The standard Korean alphabetic script.

Head The lexical category around which a phrasal category is built and that is invariably present in the phrase (e.g., N is the head of NP).

Helping (verb) See **Auxiliary verb**.

Hemispheres The two roughly symmetrical sides of the brain, sometimes called the right and left brains.

Hieroglyphics Egyptian pictograms that developed through logographic, syllabic, and even partially alphabetic stages.

High (sound) A sound made with the tongue raised (e.g., [i], [k], [u]).

Hiragana One of the two Japanese syllabic writing systems.

Holophrase One-word utterances that are endowed with a sentence meaning and that characterize an early stage of first language acquisition.

Homophones Two words that have an identical phonetic form but are each associated with an entirely different meaning (e.g., *sail/sale*).

Icon A token that bears some resemblance to its referent (e.g., a photograph).

Ideogram A pictogram that represents an idea rather than a concrete object.

Illocutionary act An act that is performed by the speaker by virtue of producing an utterance (e.g., promising, commanding, arresting).

Immersion A method of second language teaching in which the students are instructed in most of their courses and school activities in the second language.

Implicational universals Principles that stipulate that the presence of one linguistic trait implies the presence of another, but not vice versa (e.g., Languages with fricative phonemes (/s/, /z/, etc.) will also have stop phonemes (/p/, /t/, etc.) although the reverse is not always true).

Inanimate In some languages, a class consisting of nouns, most of which have non-living referents.

Inclusive A type of first person plural pronoun whose referents include the addressee.

Infix An affix that occurs within another morpheme.

Inflection A morphological process that modifies a word's form in order to mark the grammatical subclass to which it belongs (e.g., sg. *wolf* → pl. *wolves*).

Inflectional language See **Synthetic language.**

Inland Canadian See **General Canadian.**

Instrumental motivation The desire to achieve proficiency in a new language for utilitarian reasons, such as getting a job or a promotion.

Integrative motivation A desire to achieve proficiency in a new language in order to participate in the life of the community that speaks the language.

Intension A word or expression's inherent sense, the concepts that it evokes (e.g., The intension of *Prime Minister of Canada* is 'leader of the majority party in Parliament').

Intercostals The muscles between the ribs.

Interdental (sound) A sound made with the tongue placed between the teeth (e.g., [θ], [ð] as in *bath* and *bathe*, respectively).

Interfaces The interactions among the various components of grammar.

Interference The inappropriate use of an L1 structure in the L2 system.

Interlanguage The dynamic language system unique to an L2 learner as he or she passes through a number of states of grammar along a continuum, starting with the native language and ultimately approaching the target language.

Interlingual (errors) Errors made by L2 learners that are the result of L1 interference.

Internal reconstruction A technique used to reconstruct an earlier form of a language by relying on the current morphophonemic variation within that language.

International Phonetic Alphabet (IPA) A system for transcribing the sounds of speech that attempts to represent each sound of human speech with a single symbol.

Intonation Movement of pitch that is not related to contrastive differences in the meanings of forms.

Intransitive (verb) A verb that cannot take a direct object NP (e.g., *sleep, exist*).

Isogloss In a linguistic atlas, a line that separates an area in which a particular feature of pronunciation, grammar, or vocabulary is found from surrounding areas where that feature is absent.

Isolate A language that is not known to be related to any other living language (e.g., Ainu).

Isolating (language) See **Analytic (language)**.

Jargon Obscure specialized language or vocabulary peculiar to some field (see **Sublanguage**).

Kanji Chinese characters used to represent word roots in Japanese.

Katakana One of the two Japanese syllabic writing systems; it is widely used in advertising and in spelling non-Japanese words.

Labial (sound) Any sound made with closure or near-closure of the lips (e.g., [w], [b], [m], etc.).

Labiodental (sound) A sound produced with the lower lip near or touching the upper teeth (e.g., [f], [v]).

Labiovelar (sound) A sound made with the tongue raised near the velum and the lips simultaneously rounded (e.g., [w]).

Larynx A box-like structure made of cartilage and muscle in which the vocal cords are located, commonly known as the voice box.

Lateral fricative A lateral sound made with a narrow enough closure to be classified as a fricative.

Lateral (sound) A sound made with the sides of the tongue lowered (e.g., varieties of [l]).

Lateralization The localization of a neurological function in one side of the brain (cf. cerebral dominance).

Lax (vowel) A vowel that is made with a relatively less constricted tongue body or root (e.g., [ɪ], [ə], [ʊ]).

Learning strategies The ways in which L2 learners process language input and develop linguistic knowledge (e.g., generalization).

Length The subjective impression of time occupied by the duration of a phone.

Lenition See **Weakening**.

Lexical ambiguity A situation in which a single form has two or more meanings (e.g., A *trunk* is a 'piece of luggage' or an 'elephant nose').

Lexical category A class of words distinguished on the basis of its semantic and combinatorial properties (e.g., noun, verb, preposition).

Lexical diffusion The process whereby a linguistic change manifests itself first in a few words and then gradually spreads through the vocabulary of the language.

Lexical insertion The insertion of words into tree structures under the appropriate lexical category label.

Lexicography A branch of linguistics concerned with the principles and practice of dictionary-making.

Lexicon The speaker's mental dictionary; it contains a lexical entry for each item in his or her vocabulary as well as a set of word formation rules.

Lingua franca A language that enables communication to take place when two or more groups of people come into contact who do not share a common native language.

Linguistic competence The linguistic knowledge that enables the speaker of a language to produce and understand an unlimited number of familiar and novel utterances.

Linguistic manipulation task An experimental task in second language acquisition research in which the subject's attention is directed to the language forms themselves.

Linguistic typology The classification of languages according to their common structural characteristics (e.g., word order patterns).

Linguistics The study of how language is organized and used.

Liquid A consonant made with a continuous flow of air through the oral cavity but with an obstruction less than that of fricatives (e.g., [l], [r]).

Loan words Words that are borrowed from one language into another (e.g., The words *poodle* and *kindergarten* were borrowed into English from German).

Locative (Loc) A case marker used to signal that an NP indicates place or location.

Locutionary act A speech act consisting of the utterance of a sentence with a particular meaning.

Logogram A sign that represents an entire word and is not recognizable as a picture.

Logographic (writing) A system of writing in which a sign represents an entire word.

Loudness The subjective impression of a phone's volume relative to the sounds around it.

Low (sound) A sound made with the tongue lowered (e.g., [a], [ɑ], [æ]).

Machine-readable dictionary A dictionary that appears in computer form, such as that found in spelling checkers or thesauruses.

Machine translation Translating from one language, such as English, to another, such as French, using a computer.

Main (verb) A verb other than an auxiliary (*They may* win).

Major lexical categories Lexical classes in which membership is "open" in the sense that new words are constantly being added (e.g., noun, verb, adjective).

Majority Rules Strategy A strategy used in comparative reconstruction requiring that the phoneme occurring in the largest number of cognate languages be reconstructed in the proto-language unless it can be ruled out on some other grounds.

Manner of articulation The manner in which airflow is modified by the speech organs in the production of a sound.

Matrix (clause) The larger clause in which an embedded clause occurs (e.g., the entire bracketed sentence in [*John said* that he was leaving]).

Meaning The intension of a sign in a communication system.

Mesolect A creole variety that falls between a basilect and an acrolect.

Metaphor A figure of speech containing an implied comparison based on the perception of a similarity between distinct objects or actions (e.g., *He grasped the idea*).

Metathesis A change in the relative positioning of sounds (e.g., *Ask* may be pronounced as [æks]).

Mid (vowel) A vowel for which the tongue is neither raised nor lowered (e.g., [ɛ], [ʌ], [o]).

Minor (lexical category) A lexical class in which membership is "closed" in the sense that it is restricted to a fixed set of elements already in the language (e.g., preposition and pronoun).

Non-deterministic parsing A method of automatic parsing by computer in which either the computer is permitted to backtrack when an analysis fails or in which more than one analysis may be built in parallel.

Non-phonetically conditioned sound change A sound change that has no motivation in the immediate phonetic environment.

Non-standard (language) A variety of language that differs from the standard language in systematic ways.

Non-structured communication task A task used in L2 research in which the researcher and the L2 learner are involved in natural conversation with no special focus on a particular language structure.

Non-terminal symbol The parts of a structure which are not lexical items, for example, VP, NP, det, N. Compare with *terminal* symbol.

Noun (N) A major lexical category whose members typically name entities, or concrete or abstract things (e.g., *key, Jean, honesty*).

Noun class See **Gender classification**.

Noun phrase (NP) A phrase built around a noun head (e.g., *the black shroud*).

Nucleus The [+syllabic] segment that forms the core or basis of a syllable.

Number A grammatical category marking distinctions between singular, plural, and (where appropriate) dual.

Object permanence The child's realization that objects in the environment exist as independent entities with their own inherent properties—a milestone usually reached in the sensori-motor stage of development.

Obviative A form that is used in some languages for referring to an entity (other than the speaker or the addressee) that has not been chosen as the focus of the conversation.

Onomatopoeic (word) A word whose phonetic shape resembles its referent in some sense (e.g., *buzz, splash, cock-a-doodle-doo*).

Onset The portion of a syllable that precedes the nucleus (e.g., /spl/ in *spleen*).

Oral (sound) A sound produced with a raised velum allowing airflow only through the oral cavity (e.g., [o], [p], [h]).

Orthography The set of conventions for representing language in written form.

Overextension A developmental phenomenon in which the meaning of a child's word overlaps with that of the equivalent adult word, but also extends beyond it (e.g., *Dog* is used to refer to other animals as well as dogs).

Palatal (sound) A sound produced with the tongue touching or nearly touching the palate (e.g., [y]).

Palatalization A process of assimilatory change whereby a consonant anticipates a front vowel or consonant and takes on a palatal or alveopalatal place of articulation.

Palate The highest part of the roof of the mouth.

Palatoalveolar (sound) See **Alveopalatal (sound)**.

Paraphrase The relationship between two sentences with identical meanings (e.g., *The wind is tearing the canopy* and *The canopy is being torn by the wind*).

Parse (verb) To give a grammatical description of words, phrases, and sentences.

Partial reduplication A morphological process in which part of a stem is repeated to form a new word.

Particle (Prt) A minor lexical category whose members are attached to VP and can occur either before or after a direct object (e.g. *He took* out *the garbage; He took the garbage* out).

Passive (voice) A grammatical device that indicates that the subject does not denote the agent of the action described by the verb (e.g., *The film was produced by the NFB*).

Patterns In L2 learning, partially analysed utterances with open slots for a word or phrase (e.g., *D'you wanna _____?*).

Performative (verb) A verb whose utterance involves the performance of an illocutionary act (e.g., *promise, warn,* etc.).

Perlocutionary act A speech act that has a particular effect on the listener (e.g., an utterance that frightens, ridicules or insults).

Person A grammatical category that typically distinguishes among the first person (speaker), second person (addressee), and third person (anyone else).

Pharyngeal (sound) A sound made by modifying airflow in the pharynx.

Pharynx The tube of the throat between the larynx and the oral cavity.

Pheremones Chemicals used for specific communicative purposes by animals.

Phone Any human speech sound.

Phoneme A contrastive segmental unit with predictable phonetic variants.

Phonemic paraphasia A language disorder involving the systematic substitution and deletion of phonemes (e.g., *Wrench* may be pronounced as *kench*).

Phonemic (representation) A level of representation in which the predictable features of sound are left unspecified.

Phonetic Plausibility Strategy A strategy used in comparative reconstruction that requires that any process posited to account for the change of the reconstructed phoneme into the sounds observed in the data be phonetically plausible.

Phonetic sound change A sound change that affects the allophones of an already existing phoneme, but does not result in the addition, deletion, or rearrangement of phonemes.

Phonetically conditioned (sound change) A change in a language's sound pattern that stems from the modification of a segment under the influence of a particular phonetic environment.

Phonetics The various phenomena related to the sounds of speech; the study of speech sounds.

Phonological merger A historical change occurring in cases where two or more phonemes collapse into a single contrastive unit, resulting in a net reduction in the number of phonemes in the language.

Phonological rules Rules that relate the underlying forms of words to their phonetic forms.

Phonological shift A historical change in which a series of phonemes is systematically modified so that their organization with respect to each other changes (e.g., the Great English Vowel Shift).

Phonological sound change A sound change that results in the addition, deletion, or rearrangement of phonemes.

Phonological split A historical change in which allophones of the same phoneme come to contrast with each other, creating one or more new phonemes in the language.

Phonology The various phenomena related to linguistic sound systems; the study of the organization of sounds and sound patterns in language.

Phonotactics The system and study of the arrangement of phonemes in sequence.

Phrase structure rules The grammatical devices used to specify the dominance and word order relationships that are found in sentences (e.g., NP → (Det) (Adj P) N).

Phyla In language classification, a group of related stocks of language families.

Pictogram A symbol that is an image of the object it represents and that is drawn for the purpose of communication.

Pidgin A lingua franca with a highly simplified grammatical structure that has emerged as a mixture of two or more languages and has no native speakers.

Pinyin A system of writing Mandarin with a modified Latin alphabet.

Pitch The auditory property of a sound that enables us to place it on a scale that ranges from low to high.

Place of articulation The point at which the airstream is modified in the vocal tract to produce a phone (also called *point of articulation*).

Plural An inflectional category associated with nouns with more than one referent.

Polysemy A phenomenon in which a word has two or more meanings that are at least vaguely related to each other (e.g., A *diamond* is a 'jewel' or a 'baseball field').

Polysynthetic (language) A language that makes extensive use of polymorphemic words (i.e., words made up of a root and one or more affixes) but that is more complex than an agglutinating or synthetic language in terms of the number of morphemes it can combine and the type of allomorphic variation it exhibits (e.g., Chipewyan, Inuktitut).

Portmanteau (morpheme) A single morpheme that is used to encode more than one grammatical contrast (e.g., The affix *-a* in Russian *dom-a* 'house' simultaneously marks genitive case, singular number, and masculine gender).

Postposition In some languages (e.g., Korean), a minor lexical category whose members typically designate relations in space or time; they follow the NP with which they combine to form a PP.

Pragmatics The speaker's and hearer's background attitudes, beliefs, and understanding of the context of an utterance and the knowledge of the way in which language is used to communicate information.

Prefix An affix that occurs in front of its stem (e.g., *re-* in *redo*).

Preposition (P) A minor lexical category whose members typically designate relations in space or time (e.g., *in, before*); they precede the NP with which they combine to form a PP.

Prepositional phrase (PP) A phrase built around a preposition head (e.g., *in the zoo*).

Presupposition The assumption or belief implied by the use of a particular word or structure (e.g., The verb *admit* in *Nell admitted that the team had lost* indicates that the speaker is presupposing the truth of the claim that the team lost).

Primary (stress) The most prominent stress in a word (e.g., The first syllable in *telegraph* has primary stress).

Processes (phonetic) Articulatory adjustments that occur during the production of speech.

Production strategy A strategy employed by L2 learners when attempting to use their learned linguistic knowledge in the communication process (e.g., rehearsing, pre-planning of utterance).

Productivity In morphology, the relative freedom with which an affix combines with stems of the appropriate category (e.g., The English plural suffix *-s* is more productive than the adjectival suffix *-ous*).

Progressive assimilation The modification of one or more features of a sound due to the influence of a preceding segment (so called because the direction of the influence is "forward" to a following segment).

Pronoun (Pro) A minor lexical category whose members can replace a noun phrase and that can look to another element for its interpretation (e.g., *he, herself, it*).

Prosodic See **Suprasegmentals**.

Proto-form The form that is reconstructed as the source of cognate words in related languages.

Proto-language The reconstructed language that is presumed to be the common source for two or more related languages (e.g., Proto-Indo-European).

Proximate A form that is used in some languages for referring to the entity (other than the speaker or the addressee) that has been chosen as the focus of the conversation.

Quality (of a vowel) The characteristic sound of a vowel.

Radical See **Determinative**.

Rebus A string of pictorial symbols read for their phonetic value.

Recursive A property of a rule or rules that allows indefinite reapplication.

Reduced (vowel) The vowel schwa [ə], so called because it often appears as a weakly articulated, unstressed variant of stressed vowels.

Reduplicative (affix) An affix that repeats all or part of the stem to which it is attached.

Referent The entity to which a word or phrase refers.

Reflexive pronoun A pronoun that must have a c-commanding antecedent in the same clause; in English, a pronoun ending in the morpheme *self*.

Regional dialect A speech variety associated with a particular geographical area.

Register A speech variety used in a specific social situation.

Register tone A tone that has a stable pitch over a single syllable.

Regressive assimilation A phonological process in which one or more features of a sound are modified due to the influence of a following sound (so called because the direction of the influence is "backward" to a preceding segment).

Relative clause A sentence-like construction that is embedded within an NP and provides information about the set of entities denoted by the head noun (e.g., *The meteor* that she saw).

Retroflex Sounds produced by curling the tongue tip back into the mouth (e.g., Canadian English [r]).

Root (a) **(of the tongue)** The part of the tongue contained in the upper part of the throat. (b) In a complex word, the morpheme that belongs to a lexical category such as noun, verb, adjective, and so on (e.g., *ash* in *ashes*).

Rounded (sound) A sound that is made with the lips protruding (e.g., [u], [w]).

Routines In L2 learning, whole utterances that are error-free and appear to be learned as unanalysed wholes, similar to the way a single word is learned.

Rule A formal statement of a linguistic process.

Sapir-Whorf Hypothesis The hypothesis articulated by Edward Sapir and Benjamin Whorf that the particular language people speak has a shaping influence on the way in which they think and perceive the world.

Schwa The lax, mid, unrounded vowel [ə].

Second language A language that is learned after the first or native language is relatively established.

Secondary (stress) The second most prominent stress in a word (e.g., The third syllable in the word *solitary* has secondary stress).

Segment An individual speech sound.

Semantic broadening A process whereby the meaning of a word becomes more general or inclusive (e.g., *Barn* used to mean 'a place to store barley').

Semantic feature The components of meaning that make up a word's intension (e.g., *Man* has the feature [+human]; *dog* has the feature [−human]).

Semantic narrowing A process whereby the meaning of a word becomes less general or inclusive (e.g., *Meat* used to mean 'any type of food').

Semantic role The role that the referent of an NP plays in the event described by a sentence (also called **Thematic role**) (e.g., agent, patient).

Semantic shift A process whereby the meaning of a word changes in such a way that the word comes to refer to a new, but related, set of objects (e.g., *Silly* used to mean 'weak').

Semantics The various phenomena pertaining to the meaning of words and sentences; the study of meaning in human language.

Sentence (S) A syntactic unit consisting of a noun phrase and a verb phrase.

Sex-exclusive differentiation A type of sexual differentiation of language in which certain forms are used only by men and other forms are used only by women.

Sex-preferential differentiation A type of sexual differentiation of language in which certain forms tend to be used more by men and other forms tend to be used more by women (e.g., In English, the word *lovely* is more likely to be used by a woman).

Sibilant A strident sound that is relatively higher in pitch than other stridents and has a hissing quality (e.g., [s], [z]).

Sign A unit of communication structure that consists of two parts, a token and a referent.

Signal A token that triggers a specific action on the part of the receiver (e.g., a traffic light).

Silent period In second language learning, a period of aural exposure to the language during which the learner does not attempt to use the language orally.

Simple vowel A vowel that does not show a noticeable change in quality within a single syllable (e.g., [ɪ], [æ], [ʌ]).

Simple (word) A word that consists of a single morpheme (e.g., *flea*).

Singular An inflectional category associated with nouns with a single referent.

Sisters Two or more categories that have the same node immediately above them in a tree structure (e.g., V and the direct object NP).

Slang An informal non-standard speech variety characterized by newly coined and rapidly changing vocabulary.

Social dialect See **Sociolect**.

Social stratification The differentiation of language varieties along social parameters.

Sociolect A speech variety spoken by a group of people who share a particular social characteristic (e.g., ethnicity, sex, age, occupation) (also called **Social dialect**).

Sociolinguistics The study of the various phenomena pertaining to the social use of language.

Song Lengthy patterns of sounds produced only by male birds for territorial and mating purposes.

Sound shift The systematic modification of a series of phonemes.

Specifier See **Determinative**.

Spectrograph The graphic representation of an acoustic analysis of sound produced by a machine.

Speech community A group whose members share both a particular language or variety of language and the norms for its appropriate used in social context.

Speech sounds See **Phone**.

Speech variety The language or form of language used by any group of speakers on any one occasion.

Standard (language) The superimposed language variety of a country that is generally employed by the government and the media, and that is taught in schools and is often the only or main written language.

Stem The unit to which an affix is added (e.g., In the word *statements* the root *state* is the stem for *-ment* while the complex form *statement* is the stem for *-s*).

Stimulus-bound (response) A response that is triggered by exposure to a particular external event.

Stock In language classification, a group of related language families.

Stop A consonant produced with a complete and momentary closure of airflow through the vocal tract (e.g., [p], [t], [k]).

Stopping In child language acquisition, the replacement of a fricative with a corresponding stop (e.g., [tuwp] for *soup*).

Strategy The mental processes involved in forming and testing hypotheses about linguistic input and in using linguistic knowledge in communicative situations.

Stressed (syllable) A syllable that is relatively prominent in an utterance, often due to the combined effects of pitch, loudness, and length (e.g., In the word *college*, the first syllable is stressed).

Strident A fricative that is distinctly noisier than other fricatives made at or near the same place of articulation (e.g., [s] vs. [θ], [z] vs. [ð]).

Structural change The output, or right side, of a transformational rule.

Structural description The input, or left side, of a transformational rule.

Structurally ambiguous The property of a string of words that is assigned to more than one syntactic structure (e.g., *I took a picture of the tourist with the camera*).

Structured communication task A task used in L2 research that involves testing an L2 learner's knowledge of a specific second language structure such as negation or interrogatives.

Subcategorization frame Features that divide lexical categories into subcategories by indicating their compatibility with different types of sisters (e.g., *put*: +[___ NP PP]).

Subject The NP immediately dominated by S; the sister of VP (e.g., *Backpacks* in *Backpacks are comfortable*).

Sublanguage A speech variety associated with a particular profession that facilitates communication among members of that profession (sometimes used in an overlapping sense with **Jargon** and **Cant**).

Substitution test The replacement of a group of words by a single word to test whether the group of words is a syntactic unit (e.g., The gang *robbed the bank*; They *robbed the bank*).

Substratum influence The influence of a less politically or culturally dominant language on a more dominant language (e.g., the influence of the speech of the indigenous population in a colonial country on the language of the conquering power).

Suffix An affix that occurs after its stem (e.g., *-s* in *tapes*).

Superstratum influence The influence of a more politically or culturally dominant language on a less dominant language (e.g., the influence of the English language on the native speech of former colonial territories such as India).

Suppletion The replacement of one root by another to express an inflectional contrast (e.g., the past tense of *go* is *went*).

Suprasegmentals The intrinsic aspects of phones, such as pitch, loudness, and length.

Surface structure A level of syntactic representation that results from the application of whatever transformations are needed to yield the final syntactic form of the sentence.

Syllabary A set of syllabic signs, each of which represents a syllable.

Syllabic liquid A liquid that functions as a syllabic nucleus (e.g., the [l̩] in *rubble*).

Syllabic nasal A nasal that functions as a syllabic nucleus (e.g., the [ṇ] in *button*).

Syllabic (writing) A system of writing in which each sign represents a syllable.

Syllable A unit of phonological organization composed of one or more segments and minimally containing a nucleus, usually a vowel, a syllabic liquid, or a syllabic nasal.

Symbolic (tokens) Tokens that bear no inherent resemblance to their referents (e.g., the word *hair*).

Symptomatic (tokens) Tokens that spontaneously convey the internal state of the sender (e.g., a yelp of pain).

Syncope The loss of word medial vowels, often due to their appearance in an unstressed syllable next to a stressed syllable (e.g., *Police* may be pronounced as [pḷiys]).

Synonyms Two words or expressions with identical meanings (e.g., *select* and *choose*).

Syntax The various phenomena pertaining to the form and organization of sentences; the study of sentence formation.

Synthetic language A language that makes extensive use of polymorphemic words (e.g., words containing a root and one or more affixes) and often uses portmanteau morphemes (also called an **Inflectional language**) (e.g., Spanish).

Systematic gaps Non-occurring forms that would violate the phonotactic constraints of a language (e.g., in English **mtlow*).

Taboo Any social prohibition on the use of particular words or phrases.

Tap A sound made by rapidly touching the tongue tip to the back of the teeth or the alveolar ridge.

Teacher Talk The linguistic input received by L2 learners from their second language teachers, often characterized by simplification of the linguistic code.

Telegraphic The speech that is usually produced by children aged two-and-a-half to four years and is characterized by a lack of minor lexical categories and affixes.

Template The innate component that predisposes birds to perform a rudimentary version of their species-specific song.

Tense In syntax and morphology, an inflectional category indicating the time of an event or action relative to the moment of speaking.

Tense (vowel) A vowel produced with a relatively tense tongue and vocal tract musculature (e.g., [i], [e], [u], etc.).

Terminal symbol The lexical items or prefixes, suffixes, stems, and words of a language. Compare with *non-terminal* symbol.

Thematic role See **Semantic role**

Tier A level of phonological description in which only certain phonological elements are represented (e.g., a syllabic tier, a tonal tier).

Tip (of the tongue) The narrow area at the front of the tongue.

Token That part of a sign that stimulates at least one sense organ of the receiver of a message.

Tone Pitch differences that signal differences in meaning.

Tone language A language in which differences in word meaning can be signaled by differences in pitch.

Total physical response (TPR) A method of L2 teaching in which the student is initially not required to speak, but rather carries out simple commands in the second language (e.g., *Close the door*).

Trace (*t*) An empty category that is left behind when an NP is moved.

Trachea The tube through which air flows between the lungs and the larynx, commonly known as the windpipe.

Transformation A rule that moves a category within a syntactic structure to create a new syntactic structure (e.g., *Wh*-**Movement**).

Transitional constructions The structures characteristic of different stages in the developmental sequence during L2 acquisition.

Transitive (verb) A verb that takes a direct object NP (e.g., *hit, use*).

Tree structure The hierarchical representation of a phrase or sentence.

Trill A sound made by passing air over the raised tongue tip and allowing it to vibrate for several cycles.

Underextension A developmental phenomenon in which a child uses a lexical item to denote only a subset of the items it denotes in adult speech (e.g., *Cat* is used to refer to only one specific cat).

Underlying (form) In phonology, a form from which phonetic forms are derived by rule.

Universal Grammar The proposed set of genetically transmitted categories and principles common to all human languages.

Universal tendency Structural patterns or traits that are found in most languages (e.g., Most languages have fricative phonemes).

Uvula The small flap of tissue that hangs from the velum.

Uvular (sound) A sound made with the tongue touching or near the uvula (e.g., [q], [G]).

Variable (sociolinguistic) Sounds that are realized in different ways in speech, depending on sociolinguistic factors (e.g., The progressive ending *-ing* is realized as either [ɪŋ] or [ɪn]).

Velar (sound) A sound made with the tongue touching or near the velum (e.g., [k], [g], [ŋ]).

Velum The soft area toward the rear of the roof of the mouth (also called the *soft palate*).

Verb (V) A major lexical category whose members designate actions, sensations, and states (e.g., *run, feel, seem*).

Verb complement A clause within the VP portion of a sentence (e.g., *He said* [he would leave]).

Verb phrase (VP) The phrase built around a verb head (e.g., *Shoot the puck*).

Verbal paradigm See **Conjugation.**

Vocal cords See **Vocal folds.**

Vocal folds A set of muscles that line the inner wall of the larynx and flare outward forming paired folds (also called **Vocal cords**).

Vocal tract The speech organs above the larynx (i.e., the oral cavity, the throat or pharynx, and the nasal cavity).

Voice In syntax and morphology, an inflectional category used to indicate the role of the subject's referent in the action described by the verb (e.g., passive versus active).

Voiceless (sound) Any sound made with the vocal folds not vibrating (e.g., [p], [s], [h]).

Voicing A state during which the vocal folds are brought close together, but not tightly closed, allowing air to pass between them causing them to vibrate.

Vowel A resonant, syllabic sound produced with less obstruction in the vocal tract than that required for glides.

Vowel reduction A process that converts a vowel into the short, lax segment [ə].

Weakening A type of assimilation in which a lessening in the time or degree of a consonant's closure occurs (also called **Lenition**).

Wernicke's area The area of the brain involved in the interpretation and the selection of lexical items.

***Wh* question** A question beginning with a *wh* word such as *who, what, where* (e.g., *Who did it?*).

Whisper A glottal state in which the vocal folds are adjusted so that the front portions are pulled close together while the back portions are apart.

Word A minimal free form.

Writing The symbolic representation of language in storable, graphic form.

LANGUAGE INDEX

Afrikaans, 236, 237, 340
Afro-Asiatic, 244–46
Ainu, 228, 248
Albanian, 238, 240
Aleut, 227
Algonquian languages, 247, 248
Altaic languages, 239–41, 246
American English, 25, 26, 31–32, 42, 58, 63–64, 192, 224, 329–31, 335–37. *See also* American English *in Subject Index*
American Sign Language (Ameslan), 400–1
Amerindian (American Indian languages), 34, 206. *See also specific languages*
Arabic, 184, 224, 244, 245, 272, 342–43, 362, 371, 375
Aramaic, 244, 371, 375
Arapaho, 228
Arawak, 248
Armenian, 238, 240
Athapaskan languages, 36, 247, 248
Australian English, 29, 224
Australian languages, 244, 246
Austro-Asiatic, 242, 246
Austro-Tai, 243–44, 246
Aymara, 248
Azerbaijani, 240

Babylonian (Assyrian; Akkadian), 244
Bahnar, 242
Balinese, 243
Baltic languages, 238, 240
Basque, 113, 195, 226, 233, 248
Batak, 243
Bemba, 158
Bengali, 239
Berber, 232, 244
Bhasa Malay, 340
Biloxi, 336
Bini, 37
Black English, 335
Blackfoot, 228
Boontling (Boonville lingo), 342
Bororo, 248
Boston English, 378
Breton, 237

British English, 25, 29, 99, 199, 224, 329, 332–33, 337
Bulgarian, 238, 369
Buriat, 240
Burmese, 228, 233, 242
Burushaski, 248
Byelorussian (White Russian), 238, 369

Caddoan languages, 247, 248
California Penutian languages, 247, 248
Camodian (Khmer), 230, 242
Canadian English, 25, 29, 63–64, 329, 337, 339
Canadian French, 32, 198
Cantonese, 224, 230, 242, 243
Cape York Creole (CYC), 347–49
Car, 242
Carib, 248
Catalan, 237–38
Cat's Elbow, 342
Caucasian languages, 246
Cayapa, 248
Cayuga, 197
Celtic, 215, 237, 240
Chakar, 240
Chamorro, 243
Cherokee, 373
Chibchan languages, 247, 248
Chinese, 262, 272, 340, 365–67, 371–72, 379–80
Chinook, 345
Chinook Jargon, 345–46
Choctaw, 211–12
Coahuiltecan languages, 247, 248
Cockney, 199
Cockney English, 332
Cockney rhyming slang, 342–43
Coptic, 244
Cornish, 237
Cree, 39, 230, 359, 373
Creek, 211
Cuna, 248
Czech, 229, 238

Dakota, 228
Danish, 210, 215, 236, 237

Dogon, 245
Dravidian languages, 241–42, 246
Dutch, 42, 206, 210, 214, 224, 236, 237
Duwai, 42

Efik, 228, 245
Egyptian, Old, 244
Enets, 241
English. *See, in this index,* Australian English; British English; Middle English; Modern English; New Zealand English; Old English; South African English; Standard English; *and, in Subject Index,* American English; Canadian English; English language
Epera, 248
Eskimo, 184
Eskimo-Aleut languages, 247
Estonian, 241
Evenki, 240
Ewe, 245

Faroese, 236, 237
Fijian, 243
Finnish, 27, 39, 80, 101, 105, 113, 114, 185, 227, 229, 241, 339
Flemish (Dutch), 237, 339
French, 101, 105, 110, 159, 162–63, 185, 193–94, 196, 201, 205, 212–14, 224, 227, 238, 321, 339, 340, 342–43, 345, 346, 353, 369, 377. *See also* French *in Subject Index*
  Canadian, 32, 198
Frisian, 236, 237
Fulani, 245

Ganda, 245, 246
Gaulish, 237
Gbeya, 245
Geez, 226
Georgian, 113
German, 101, 103, 105, 110, 113, 197, 206, 210, 214–16, 224, 236, 237, 340, 380, 420, 442. *See also* German *in Subject Index*
Germanic, 214–16, 236–37, 240
Gilbertese, 228
Gilyak, 226, 248
Gondi, 241

Gothic, 197, 215, 236, 237
Greek, 40, 56, 214–16, 238, 239, 317, 342–43, 364, 367–69, 377
Guarani, 248
Gujarati, 239
Guugu Yimidirr, 233

Hakka, 224, 242, 243
Halkomelem, 113
Hare, 93
Hausa, 158, 244
Hawaiian, 226, 227, 243
Hebrew, 233, 244–45, 369, 371
  classical, 232
Hellenic, 238, 240
Hindi, 30, 206, 210, 211, 233, 272, 341
Hindi-Urdu, 239
Hitchiti, 211
Hixkaryana, 232
Ho, 242
Hokan languages, 247, 248
Hopi, 184–85
Hsiang, 242, 243
Hua, 5, 158
Hungarian, 229, 241, 374

Icelandic, 236, 237
Igbo (Ibo), 245
Ijo, 245
Indian English, 341
Indo-European languages, 214–16, 224, 235–40, 246
Indo-Iranian languages, 239, 240
Inuit, 339
Inuktitut, 33, 230
Irish (Irish Gaelic), 232, 237, 239
Iroquoian languages, 247, 248
Italian, 33, 39, 110, 193, 194, 206, 212–14, 224, 237, 238, 340, 344, 375, 380
Italic languages, 237–38, 240

Japanese, 33, 44, 62, 72, 79–80, 107, 113, 158, 226, 233, 239–40, 272, 294, 359, 365–67, 379, 380
Javanese, 243

Kan, 242, 243
Kannada, 241, 242
Karelian, 241
Katla, 245
Kazakh, 240
Khalkha, 240

Khasi, 242
Khmer, 65–66
Khoisan languages, 246
Kikuyu, 245, 246
Kitabal, 228
Klamath-Sahaptin languages, 247, 248
Koalib, 245
Koasati, 335–36
Kodagu, 241
Kolami, 241
Kongo, 245, 246
Korean, 159–60, 162, 233, 239–40, 285, 294, 373–74
Kosati, 211
Kru, 245
!Kung, 227
Kurdish, 239
Kurukh, 241
Kutenai, 248

Lao, 243
Lapp/Sámi, 241, 339
Latin, 99, 193–96, 214–16, 235, 237, 317, 337, 368, 369, 377
  Pig, 342
Latvian, 224–25, 228, 229, 238
Lithuanian, 238
Livonian, 241
Luo, 272

Maasai, 232
Mabuiag, 244
Macedonian, 238, 369
Malagasy, 232, 243
Malay, 65, 67, 77–78, 243
Malayalam, 241, 242
Malto, 241
Mandarin, 36–37, 93, 101, 105, 165, 224, 228, 229, 242, 243, 371, 372
Mandink, 245
Maori, 232, 243
Marathi, 239
Mataco, 248
Mayan languages, 229, 247, 248, 272
Mazateco, 36
Mende, 69
Miao, 242, 243
Middle English, 189–90, 195–96, 198, 201, 204
Midland English dialect, 331
Modern English, 189–90, 194–96, 199, 201–4, 329. *See also* Standard English

Mohawk, 192, 197
Mon, 242
Mordvin (Mordva), 241
Mundavi, 242
Muong, 242
Muskogean languages, 211–12, 247, 248

Nancowry, 110
Nandi, 228
Navaho, 185, 226
Nenets, 241
New Zealand English, 29
Nganasan, 241
Niger-Kordofanian, 245–46
Nilo-Saharan languages, 246
Nootka, 345
Norse, Old (Old Icelandic), 237
North American Plains Indian Sign Language, 345
Northern English dialect, 331
Northern Min, 242, 243
Norwegian, 236, 237
Nubian, 227
Nuer, 228
Nupe, 245

Occitan, 238
Old Canaanite, 244
Old English, 189–92, 194–96, 200–4, 236, 329
Old Norse (Old Icelandic), 237
Omeida, 197
Ostyak, 241
Otomian-Pame languages, 247, 248

Papuan (Indo-Pacific) languages, 246
Pashto, 239
Persian (Farsi), 215, 239
Phoenician, 367–68
Phrygian, 269
Polish, 31, 229, 238
Portuguese, 30, 31, 193–94, 237–38
Proto-Indo-European, 215, 224
Provençal, 194
Punjabi, 239

Quechua, 233, 248

Romansch, 238, 339, 340
Romany (Gypsy), 239, 341–42
Rumanian, 32, 113, 212–13, 237, 238
Russian, 14, 32–34, 55, 57, 110–13, 210, 211, 229, 230, 235, 238, 285, 337, 340–41, 369

Salish languages, 247, 248
Sámi (Lapp), 241, 339
Samoan, 229, 243
Sango, 245
Sanskrit, 214–15, 341, 375–76
Santali, 242
Sarcee, 230
Sardinian, 212–14, 237, 238
Saudi Arabian Arabic, 224
Scots Gaelic, 42, 65, 237
Selayarese, 160–61
Selkup, 241
Semitic, 375
Serbian, 369
Serbo-Croatian, 33, 34, 59, 224, 238
Sharpa, 242
Shilha, 244
Shona, 245, 246
Sindhi, 341
Sino-Tibetan, 242–43, 246
Siouan languages, 247, 248
Slavic languages, 206, 238, 240. *See also specific languages*
Slovak, 238
Slovenian, 238
Somali, 244, 375
South African English, 340
Southern English dialect, 331
Southern Min, 242, 243
Spanish, 110, 115, 162–63, 194, 196, 206, 209, 212–14, 226, 237–38, 316, 342–43, 369. *See also* Spanish *in Subject Index*
Standard English, 202, 332, 334, 337, 342, 348–51
Swahili, 80–81, 226, 229, 245, 246
Swati, 111
Swedish, 197, 210, 215, 236, 237, 339

Tagalog, 96, 101, 105, 107, 113, 243
Tahitian, 243
Tamazight, 244
Tamil, 113–14, 161–62, 241, 242, 340
Taraskan, 248
Tatar (Tartar), 240
Telugu, 158, 241, 242

Thai, 243, 353–54
Tibetan, 242
Tiv, 245
Toda, 241, 242
Tongan, 243
Tuareg, 244
Tulu, 241
Turkish, 14, 32, 39, 59, 92, 96, 111–13, 116, 206, 210, 211, 230, 231–33, 240, 260, 342–43
Twi (Fante), 245
Tzotzil, 165

Uighur, 240
Ukrainian, 238, 341, 369
Uralic languages, 241, 246
Uto-Aztecan languages, 247, 248
Uzbek, 240

Vepsian, 241
Vietnamese, 228, 230, 242
Vodian, 241
Vogul, 241

Wakashan languages, 247, 248
Walbiri, 4–5
Warao, 248
Welsh, 34, 232, 237
Weri, 228
Wes-Kos, 344–45
Western Desert language, 244
Wichita, 227
Witotu, 248
Wolof, 245, 340
Wu, 242, 243

Yap, 39
Yakut, 240
Yao, 242, 243
Yiddish, 236, 342
Yidin, 113
Yoruba, 245
Yukagir, 248

Zulu, 245, 246

INDEX

Ablative case, 112
Ablaut, 98
Absolute universals, 225
Absolutive case, 113
Accidental gaps, 56
Accusative case, 112–14, 201–2
Acoustic phonetics, 13
Acrolect, 347
Acronyms, 106
Across-the-board-change, 209
Active sentences, 164
Active voice, 116
Act sequence, speech situation and, 350
Address, forms of, 352–54
Adjective phrases (AdjPs), 130–33
Adjectives, 89, 127, 128, 158–59
   word formation and, 100–2
Adverbial clauses, 149–51
Adverbial phrases (AdvPs), 131, 142
Adverbs, 89, 127, 128
Affixes, 94–98
   definition of, 94
   derivational, 100–1, 108–9, 231, 234
   inflectional, 107–12, 115, 231, 260
   loss and addition of, 200–2
   types of, 95–96
   word formation and, 100–1, 103, 106
Affricates, 23, 34
Agglutinating language, 230, 241, 242, 246
Agrammatism, 257, 260
Agraphia, 262
Agreement
   subject-verb, 333
   of verbs, 287–88
-al, as affix, 94
Alexia, 262
Allomorphic, 277
Allomorphs, 278
   conditioned, 117–19
   definition of, 92
   deriving, 117
   identifying, 92
Allophones, 60–66, 198
   definition of, 60
   language-specific patterns of, 64–66

   nasal vowels and, 63–65
   syllabic phonology and, 73–75
   vowel raising and, 63–64
Allophonic rules, 116, 120
Alphabetic writing, 359, 363–67, 373, 375, 379, 380
Alpha notation, assimilation and, 78–79
Alveolar ridge, 19, 20
Alveolars, 19–21, 47
   affricates, 34
   fricatives, 22–23, 34
   laterals, 25, 34–35
   liquids, 25, 34, 35
   stops, 21, 33
Alveopalatal (palatoalveolar) area, 19, 20
Alveopalatals
   affricates, 23, 34
   fricatives, 22–23, 34
Ambiguity, 141–42
   lexical, 172–74
   structural, 135–36, 174–76
American English, 29, 192, 224, 329–32, 335–37
   assimilation in, 42
   consonants in, 25
   glides in, 26
   transcription of consonants and vowels in, 31–32
   vowel contrasts in, 58
   vowel raising and, 63–64
Analogy, 191, 202
Analytic (isolating) language, 229–30
Angular gyrus, 258–59, 262–63
Animal communication, 383–412
   bees, 389–92, 408–9
   birds, 392–95, 408–9
   Clever Hans controversy and, 403–4
   great ape debate and, 404
   human language compared to, 389–92, 394–95, 402
      design feature, 406–9
   nonhuman primates, 395–406, 409
      testing for linguistic ability, 400–6
   nonvocal, 383–84

organization of, 385
structure of, 384–89
Antecedents, 179
Anterior feature, 47
Antonyms, 172
Aphasia, 259–63
Apocope, 195
Application, definition of, 439
Applied linguistics. *See also* Second
    language acquisition
definition of, 299
Aptitude, second language acquisition
    and, 315
Arbitrariness, as design feature, 407
Arcuate fasciculus, 258
Argots, 341–43
Aristotle, 169, 395
Articulation, manners of. *See*
    Manners of articulation
Articulators, use of term, 24–25
Articulatory phonetics, 13. *See also*
    Phonetics
Aspirated feature, 48
Aspiration, 67, 68, 73–74
definition of, 24
Assimilation(s), 77–79, 119
alpha notation and, 78–79
definition of, 77
language acquisition and, 274–75
sound change and, 193–94
types of, 42–43
Association lines, 69
Attitude, second language acquisition
    and, 316
Auden, W. H., 383
Audiolingual method, 318
Auxiliary verbs, 127, 139, 143, 262,
    286, 287
Aztec hieroglyphics, 372

Babbling, 272
Baboons, communication among,
    398–99
Backformation, 106
Back sounds, 47
Bamum writing system, 375
Bases, 94, 98–99
Basilects, 347
Bede, 190
Bees, communication among, 389–92,
    408–9
Bell Laboratories, 415

Bilabials, 19
fricatives, 33, 34
stops, 21, 33
Binary properties of language, 45–47
Birds, communication among, 392–
    95, 408–9
Blends, 106
Bliss, Charles K., 361
Blissymbollics, 361
Bopp, Franz, 215
Borrowed forms, phonotactics and,
    56
Borrowings, 192, 204–6, 377
Bound morphemes, 93–94, 262, 276–
    78, 344
Bound stems, 99
Brackets, sentence structure
    represented by, 94–95
Brahmi script, 375
Brain, 253–68
of children, 300
critical period hypothesis and, 263–
    66
hemispheres of, 254–57, 263, 264,
    266
language centers of, 255, 257–59
specialization of, 9, 10
structure of, 253–54
syntax and, 234
Brain damage, 255, 256, 259
aphasia and, 259–63
in children, 263, 264
Breasted, James, 358
Breathing, survival vs. speech, 9–10
Broca, Paul, 253, 255, 257
Broca's aphasia, 379
Broca's area, 257–63
Brown, Roger, 305
Brown corpus, 439–40

Calls, bird, 392–94
Canadian English, 329, 337, 339
consonants in, 25
vowel raising and, 63–64
vowels in, 29
Cants (jargons), 343
Caretaker speech (motherese), 290
Carroll, Lewis, 106
Case, noun, 111–14, 241, 244
loss of, 201–2
C-command requirement, 179–80,
    293–94
ceive, as morpheme, 99

Cerebral plasticity, 263
Change, language and, 7–8
Characters, Chinese, 371–72
Chaucer, Geoffrey, 189, 190
Children. *See also* Language acquisition
  metathesis and, 44
  reading and, 379–80
  second language acquisition and, 300–1, 305–7, 311
Chimpanzees, communication of, 399–406
Chomsky, Noam, 142, 293
Clarity, 8
Class, noun, 110–11
Classification of languages, 223–52
  genetic, 223–25, 235–48
    Americas, 246–48
    Indo-European, 235–40, 246
    isolates, 248
    other families, 239–46
  structural, 223–35
    explaining universals, 233–35
    genetic classification compared to, 223–25
    morphology, 229–31, 234
    phonology, 225–29, 233
    syntax, 231–35
Clauses
  complement, 148
  embedded, 148–51, 153, 203
  matrix clauses, 148
  relative, 154–55
Clever Hans controversy, 403–4
Clippings, 106
Closed words (function words), 89
Coarticulation, 40–44
  ease of articulation, 40–41
  processes, 41–44
"cocktail party effect," 419
Cognates, 210–11, 213, 240
Cognitive development, language acquisition and, 291–92
Cognitive style, 314–15
Color, animal communication and, 384
Comenius, 299
Communication, 126
  animal. *See* Animal communication
  creativity and, 1–3
Communication strategies, 313–14
Communicative competence, 318–19
Communicative effect taxonomy, 312

Communicative language teaching methods, 318–19
Community counseling, second language acquisition and, 320
Complementary distribution, 59–60
Complement clauses, 148
Complementizers (COMPs), 148
Complex words, 91
Compounding, 100, 103–5
Comprehensible input, 302
Computational linguistics, 413–46
  lexicology and, 431–36
  morphology and, 420–24
  phonetics and phonology and, 415–19
  practical applications of, 439–45
  semantics and, 436–39
  speech recognition or speech analysis and, 419
  speech synthesis and, 415–18
  syntax and, 424–31
    natural language analysis, 424–30
    natural language generation, 430–31
Concordances, 439–41
Conduction aphasia and, 262, 263
Conjugation (verbal paradigm), 114–15
Conjunctions, 89, 127
Consonantal feature, 46
Consonants, 17–26, 31–35, 344
  articulation of, 18–20
  aspirated vs. unaspirated, 24–25
  contrasts of, 57
  features of, 46–49
  in foreign languages, 33–35
  fricatives, 22–23
  language acquisition and, 273–74
  language classification and, 227–28
  liquids, 25–26
  nasal, 21, 30, 42, 46
  sound change and, 194–96
  transcription of American English, 31–32
  vowels compared to, 18
  weakening of (lenition), 194
Constantine (Cyril), 369
Constellation, in bee communication, 390, 391
Continuants, 22, 48, 57
Contour tones, 36–37
Contractions, 8

Contradiction, 174
Contralateralization, 254, 257
Contrastive analysis, second language
     acquisition and, 309–10
Contrasts, 65
  in English language, 57–58, 65–66
  features and, 67–68
  language-specific, 59
  minimal pairs and sets and, 57, 61
  segments in, 57–59
Conversational implicature, 181
Conversion (zero-derivation), 97–98
Cooperative principle, 181
Coronal feature, 47
Corpus analysis, 435
Corpus callosum, 254, 257
Correction, language acquisition and,
     289–90
Cortex, 253, 254, 257–59
Cranberry morphemes, 99
Creativity, 1–3, 405
Creoles, 346–49
Critical period hypothesis, 263–66
  second language acquisition and,
     300–1
Cuneiforms, 362–64
Cyrillic alphabet, 369

Dances of bees, 389–91
Database query, 444–45
Dative case, 112, 201–2
de-, as affix, 94, 99
Deafness, reading and, 379
Declension (nominal paradigm), 112,
     113
Deep structure, 146, 147, 151–53,
     155–56
  ambiguity and, 176
  meaning and, 178
Degree specifiers (specs), 130–31
Delayed release feature, 48
Deletion, 43–44, 79
Denasalization, 273
denationalization, structure of, 93–94
Dentals, 20, 25, 47
  affricates, 34
  liquids, 25, 35
  stops, 21, 33
Derivation, 100–4, 146
Design feature, 406–9
  definition of, 406
Determinative, in Chinese, 371–72
Determiners, 89, 127, 257, 260

Determinism vs. nondeterminism
     computational syntax and, 425–27
Devanagari script, 375–76
Development, 270–88. See also
     Language acquisition
  cognitive, 291–92
  errors in, 310–11
  morphological, 276–79
  phonological, 271–75
  second language acquisition and,
     305–10
  syntactic, 284–88
  word meaning and, 28–84
Developmental sequence, 303
Devoicing, 42
Dialectology, 327–31
  definition of, 327
  methods, 327–29
  North American English and, 329–
     31
Dialects. See also Dialectology
  avian, 393–94
Diaphragm, 15
Dictionaries, machine readable, 434–
     35
Dimensional terms, language
     acquisition and, 283
Diphthongs, 27, 30, 82
Direct method, 317
Direct objects, 113–14, 135, 140, 203
  word order and, 231–35
Discreteness, as design feature, 407
Discrete tokens, 388
Displacement, as design feature, 407
Dissimilation
  definition of, 42
  sound change and, 194
Diversity, linguistic, 223
Dominance, 135
Double-blind tests, 404–5
Double negatives, 333
Downdrift, 38–39
Duality of patterning, as design
     feature, 408

Electricity, animal communication
     and, 384
Embedded clauses, 203
Empathy, second language acquisition
     and, 316–17
Ends, speech situation and, 350
English language. See also, in this
     index, American English;

Canadian English; *and, in the Language Index,* Australian English; British English; Middle English; Modern English; New Zealand English; Old English; South African English; Standard English
  affixes in, 95–96
  articulatory processes and, 41–44
  coarticulation in, 41
  complementary distribution in, 59–60
  contrasts in, 57–59, 65–66
  features of, 45–49, 67–68
  free vs. bound morphemes in, 93
  French compared to, 5, 20
  Hua compared to, 5
  Khmer compared to, 65–66
  nasalization in, 77–78
  phonemes and, 61–63, 65–66
  phonetics and, 14
    manners of articulation, 21–26
    places of articulation, 19
    vowels, 27–33
  phonetic transcription, 14
  phonological rules in, 76, 77, 79, 81–82
  phonotactics and, 55–56
  pitch in, 36
  stress in, 39–40, 80
  syllabic phonology and, 73–75
  syllables in, 70, 73–75
  voicing in, 67–68
  vowels in, 74–75
  Walbiri compared to, 4–5
  word structure in, 93–98
Entailment, 173–74
Environment
  second language acquisition and, 302
  of segments, 59
Epenthesis, 79–80, 119, 194–95
  definition of, 44
Ergative case, 113
Error analysis, second language acquisition and, 310–12
Eskimo script, 373
Esophagus, 19
Euphemism, 338–39
Evans, J., 373
Evolution, language and, 9–10
Experimental studies of language acquisition, 270–71
Extension, 170

Facial expression, animal communication and, 384
Features of natural classes, 44–49, 54–55
  as binary properties, 45–47
  distinctive, 67
  major, 46–47
  manner, 48
  phonological rules and, 77
  in phonology, 67–69
  place, 47
  vowel, 46, 49
Feedback, as design feature, 406
Field dependence, 314
Field independence, 314–15
Flapping
  definition of, 42
  rule application and, 81–82
Flap sound, r and, 25, 34
Folk etymology, 192
Foreigner talk (teacher talk), 301
Formants, 415–17
Fouts, Roger, 404
Francis, Nelson, 439–41
Free forms, definition of, 90
Free morphemes, 93–94
Free rule application, 81, 82
Free variation, definition of, 66
French, 99. *See also* French *in Language Index*
  Canadian, 32
  consonants in, 33, 35
  grammar of, 5
  phonetics and, 20
  voicing in, 78–79
  vowels in, 30–32
Fricatives, 22–23, 228, 233, 273, 344
  definition of, 22
  in foreign languages, 33–35, 42
  lateral, 34
  strident vs. nonstrident, 23
Fronting, 273
Functional speech varieties (registers), 327
Function words (closed words), 89

Gardner, Allen, 400
Gardner, Beatrice, 400
Gender classification, 110–11, 113
Gender marking, 201
Generative capacity, computational syntax and, 427–29
Genie, case study of, 264–66

Genitive case, 112–14, 201–2
Genre, speech situation and, 350–51
German language, 32. *See also*
    German *in Language Index*
  assimilation in, 42
  consonants in, 33–35, 42
  vowels in, 39
Gesture, animal communication and,
    384
Gibbons, communication among, 398
Glagolitic script, 369
Glides, 27, 42, 273
  allophones of, 62
  in American English, 26
  contrasts and, 57
  definition of, 17, 18
  features of, 46
  in foreign languages, 35
  nasal, 46
Glottals, 19–21, 47
  fricatives, 22–23, 34
  stops, 21, 33
Glottis (glottal states), 16–17, 19
*Good English; or, Popular Errors in
    Language* (Gould), 8
Gould, Edward S., 8
Graded tokens, 387
Grammar, 270. *See also* Morphology;
    Phonetics; Phonology;
    Semantics; Syntax
  components of, 4
  computational syntax and, 424–25
  definition of, 4
  fallacies about, 4–9
    deterioration, 7–8
    lack, 4–5
    logical rules, 6–8
    primitive, 5
    teaching, 6
    unpredictability, 8–9
  generative, 142
  linguistic competence and, 4–9
  nonstandard, 333
  translation method, 317
Grammatical gender, 337–38
Grateful, 99
Great vowel shift, 199–200, 202, 376–
    77
Grimm, Jakob, 215
Grimm's law, 215–16
Gupta script, 375

Hangul script, 373–74
Heads of phrases, 133–34

Hemispheres, cerebral, 254–57, 263,
    264, 266
Hieroglyphics, 364, 367, 372
High sounds, 47
Hiragana, 365–67, 379
Historical linguistics, 189–222
  language reconstruction and, 210–
    16
  lexical and semantic change and,
    204–7
  morphological change and, 200–2
  nature of language change and,
    189–93
  phonetically conditioned change
    and, 193–97
  phonological change and, 197–200
  sound change and, 193–200
  spread of change and, 207–9
  syntactic changes and, 203–4
Hofstadter, D., 269
Holophrases (one-word utterances),
    284
Homophones, 172, 277, 378
Horrible, 98–99
Huckleberry, word structure of, 99

-ible, as affix, 98–99
Iconic tokens (icons), 386–88
Ideograms, 360–61
Illocutionary act, 182, 183
Imitation, language acquisition and,
    289
Immersion approach, 320–22
Implementation, 428
Implicational universals, 225, 227,
    228, 231–33
Inborn knowledge, language
    acquisition and, 292–94
Indefiniteness, morphemes and, 92
Indexing, 439–41
induction, phonological representation
    of, 54–55
Infixes, 96, 244
Inflection, 107–16
  nominal, 107–8, 110–14
  properties of, 108–9
  verbal, 107–8, 114–16
Inflectional (synthetic) language, 230
Ingressive affirmative, 337
Innate factors, animal communication
    and, 391–92, 394–95
Instrumental motivation, 316
Instrumentalities, speech situation
    and, 350

Intension, 170
Integrative motivation, 316
Interchangeability, as design feature, 406
Intercostal muscles, 15
Interdental sounds, 20
Interference (negative transfer), 305
Interlanguage, 310–11
Interlingual errors, 310–11
Internal reconstruction technique, 214
International Phonetic Alphabet (IPA), 14, 23, 26, 35, 359
Interrogative sentences. *See* Questions
Intonation, 36–39
Intransitive verbs, 113–14, 141
Inversion transformation, 143–44, 146, 147, 152, 153, 161–63, 287
   changes in, 204
IPA (International Phonetic Alphabet), 14, 23, 26, 35, 359
Islands, 155–58
Isoglosses, 327–28, 394
Isolating (analytic) language, 229–30

Jargons (cants), 343
Jones, Sir William, 214–15

Kanji, 379
Katakana, 365–67, 379
Key, speech situation and, 350
Kharosthi script, 375
Krogh, August, 389, 391–92
Krogh, Richard, 376
Kucera, Henry, 439–41

Labials, 19, 47
Labiodentals, 19
   affricates, 34
   fricatives, 22–23, 34
Labiovelar, 20
Labov, William, 329
Lag, critical period and, 263–66
Lambert, W. E., 315
Language. *See also specific topics*
   brain and. *See* Brain
   classification of. *See* Classification of languages
   linguistic change spread through, 207–8
   minimal meaningful units of, 90–91
   preview of, 1–12
   in social contexts. *See* Social contexts, language in
   sounds of. *See* Phonetics; Phonology
Language acquisition, 269–98, 394
   determinants of, 288–94
   formal vs. informal, 6
   methods for study of, 270–71
   morphological development and, 276–79
   phonological development and, 271–75
   production vs. perception in, 275
   second. *See* Second language acquisition
   word meaning and, 28–84
Language variety (speech variety), 327
Larynx, 9, 15–17
Lateral feature, 48
Lateral fricatives, 34
Lateralization, 254
Laterals, 25
Lau vs. Board of Education, 340
Lax vowels, 29–30
Learnability, as design feature, 408–9
Learners, second language acquisition and, 312–17
   cognitive style, 314–15
   personality of, 315–17
   strategies, 312–14
Learning strategies, 313
Length, 35, 39
Lenition (consonantal weakening), 194
Lenneberg, Eric, 263
Lexical ambiguity, 172–73
Lexical categories, 94, 127–28, 257, 260, 262
   major, 89
Lexical change, 204–6
Lexical diffusion, 207–8
Lexical insertion, 139–42, 147
Lexical item, definition of, 89
Lexicology, computational, 431–36
Lexicon, 89
   generation, 430–31
Light, animal communication and, 383
Lingua francas, 244–46
Linguistic Atlas of the Eastern States, 329
Linguistic change. *See* Historical linguistics

Linguistic competence
    definition of, 4
    grammar and, 4–9
Linguistic manipulation task, 304
Linguistics. *See also specific topics*
    computational. *See* Computational
        linguistics
    definition of, 1
    historical. *See* Historical linguistics
Linneus, 223
Lips, 18
    articulators and, 24–25
    dual functions of, 9, 10
    rounded, 49
    vowels and, 26–27
Liquids, 25–26, 42, 273
    contrasts and, 57
    definition of, 25
    in foreign languages, 34–35
    phonemes and, 62
    syllabic, 26
List of Adrian Messenger, The
        (MacDonald), 64
Lives of a Cell, The (Thomas), 1
Loan words. *See* Borrowing
Locative case, 112
Locutionary act, 182
Logic, grammar and, 6–8
Logographic writing, 358, 361–64,
        371–72, 379
Long distance movement, 153
Loudness, 35
Low sounds, 47
/l/ phoneme, in English language, 62
Lungs, 15
    dual functions of, 9, 10

MacDonald, Philip, 64
Machine readable dictionary (MRD),
        434–35
Machine translation system, 441–43
Majority rules strategy, 211, 213
Manners of articulation, 20–26
    affricates and, 23, 34
    definition of, 20
    features of, 48
    fricatives and, 22–23, 33–34
    liquids and, 25–26, 34–35
    oral vs. nasal, 21
    stops and, 21–22, 33, 35
    voice lag and aspiration and, 24–25
Matrix clauses, 148

Meaning. *See also* Semantics
    creativity and, 2
    of sign, 385
    specialization and, 10
Meillet, Antoine, 326
Mesolects, 347
Metaphors, 207
Metathesis, 44, 196–97
Methodius, 369
Mid vowels, definition of, 28
Minimal pairs, 66
Minimal pair test, 57–58, 61
Minimal sets, 58
Mit, as morpheme, 99
Mixed languages, 344–49
Modal auxiliary verbs, 139
Monkeys, communication among,
        396–98
Montaigne, Michel de, 403
Morphemes (signs), 91–96, 214
    arbitrary, 91
    bound, 262, 276–78, 344
    free vs. bound, 93–94
    identifying, 92
    inflectional, 257
    language acquisition and, 276–78,
        303
    language classification and, 229–31
    portmanteau, 113, 230
    second language acquisition and,
        306–7
    variant forms of. *See* Allomorphs
    word structure and, 93–99
Morphology, 89–125, 260. *See also*
        Word formation
    changes in, 200–2
    computational, 420–24
    definition of, 4, 89
    general theory of, 89–90
    inflection and, 107–16
    language acquisition and, 276–79
    language classification and, 229–31,
        234
    of particular languages, 90
    phonology and, 116–21
    second language acquisition and,
        305–7
    specialization and, 10
    spelling and, 378–79
    word-based, 98–99
    word formation and, 100–7
Morphophonemic rules, 116–21, 278–
        79

Motherese (caretaker speech), 290
Motivation, 315–16
Movement test, 130
Multilingualism, 339–41
Mutual intelligibility, 224

Nasal cavity, 15, 19
Nasal feature, 46
Nasalization, 193–94, 226
Nasal sounds, 68
    allophones and, 63–65
    assimilation and, 42
    coarticulation and, 40–41
    consonants, 21, 30, 33, 42, 46
    definition of, 21
    in Malay, 77–78
    vowels, 21, 30–31, 42, 46, 47, 63–
        65
Native speakers, definition of, 1
Nativism, 293
Natural approach to second language
        acquisition, 320
Natural classes of sounds
    definition of, 44
    features of, 44–49, 54–55
        as binary properties, 45–47
        distinctive, 67
        major, 46–47
        manner, 48
        phonological rules and, 77
        in phonology, 67–69
        place, 47
        vowel, 46, 49
    phonemes and, 62–63
Naturalistic approach to language
        acquisition, 270, 271
Natural language analysis, 424–30
Natural language generation, 430–31
Near-minimal pairs, 58, 66
Negation, second language acquisition
        and, 286, 307–8
Negatives
    double, 7, 333
    word order in, 8–9
Negative transfer (interference), 305
Neogrammarians, 216
Neural pathways, 9–10
Neurolinguistics, 253. *See also* Brain
Neurons (nerve cells), 253
Newman, Edwin, 8
Nodes, 135, 139–40
Nominal paradigm (declension), 112,
        113

Nominative case, 112–14, 201–2
No-naming, 353
Nondeterminism vs. determinism,
        computational syntax and,
        425–27
Nonstandard language, 332–35
Nonstructured communication task,
        304
Nonvocal communication of animals,
        383–84
Norms, speech situation and, 350
Noun class, 110–11
Noun phrases (NPs), 128–29, 131–33
    reflexive pronouns, 179–80
    rule, 137
    thematic roles and, 176–78
Nouns, 89, 127–28
    case of, 111–14, 201–2, 244
    cases of, 241
    inflection and, 107–8, 110–14
    number of, 110, 113
    plural forms of, 6–7
    stress shifts and, 98
    verbs created from, 1–2
    word formation and, 102–4
Number. *See also* Plural forms;
        Singular forms
    of nouns, 110, 113
    of verbs, 114–15

Object permanence, 291–92
Obstruents
    contrasts and, 57
    definition of, 45
One-word utterances (holophrases),
        284
Onomatopoeic words, 107
Open words, 89
Oral cavity, 15
Oral sounds, 21
    vowels, 63, 65, 227
Ordered rule application, 81–82
Orthography, English, 376–79
Osten, Wilhelm von, 403
Overextension, 281–82
Oxford English Dictionary, 341

Page, Jake, 392
Palatalization, 191, 212
Palatals, 19, 20, 47
    fricatives, 33, 34
    glides, 26
    liquids, 35
    stops, 21, 33

Palate, 9, 19, 20
Paralanguage, 337
Paraphrase, 173
Parental speech, language acquisition
    and, 290–91
Parsers, 425–27
Partial immersion approach, 321–22
Partial reduplication, affixes and, 96
Participants, speech situation and,
    349
Particle movement, 144–45, 147
Passive structures, 163–65
Passive voice, 116
Passivization, 163–65
  language acquisition and, 288
Past tense, morphemes and, 93
Patterns, 303–4
Performatives, 183
Perlocutionary act, 182–83
Personality, second language
    acquisition and, 315–17
Person number agreement, 114–15
Petitto, Laura, 404
Pfungst, Oskar, 403
Pharyngeals, 19, 20
Pharynx, 15, 19, 20
Pheremones, 383
Phonemes, 60–66
    contrast and, 67–68
    definition of, 60
    language classification and, 226–28
    language-specific patterns of, 64–66
    minimal pair test and, 61
    natural classes and, 62–63
    reality of, 61–62
Phonemic paraphasia, 260, 261
Phones (speech sounds)
    number of, 13
    oral vs. nasal, 21
    segments, 14
Phonetically conditioned, definition
    of, 193
Phonetic forms (PFs), 118
Phonetic plausibility strategy, 211,
    213
Phonetics, 13–53
    acoustic, 13
    articulatory, 13, 415
    classes and features in, 44–49
    coarticulation in, 40–44
    computational, 415–19
    consonant articulation in, 18–20
    definition of, 4, 13
    language acquisition and, 272–75

manners of articulation, 20–26, 33
    affricates, 23, 34
    American glides, 26
    features of, 48
    fricatives, 22–23, 33–34
    glides, 35
    liquids, 25–26, 34–35
    oral versus nasal, 21
    stops, 21–22, 33, 35
    syllabic liquids and nasals, 26
    voice lag and aspiration, 24–25
  segments and, 14
  sound change and, 193–97
  sound classes in, 17–18. See also
      Consonants; Glides; Vowels
  sound-producing system in, 15–17
  suprasegmentals in, 35–40
    length, 35, 39
    loudness, 35, 36
    pitch, 35–39
    stress, 39–40
  transcription of, 14, 26, 35, 66–67
    American English consonants
      and vowels, 31–32
Phonological merger, 199
Phonological shift, 199
Phonological split, 198
Phonology, 54–88
  definition of, 4, 54
  derivations and rules, 75–82
    application, 81–82
    form and notation, 76–77
    processes, 77–81
  features and tones in, 67–70. See
      also Features of natural classes
  language acquisition and, 271–75
  language classification and, 225–26,
      229, 233
  morphology and, 116–21
  nonstandard, 334
  phonetic variation and, 59–66
    complementary distribution, 59–
      60
    environment, 59
    free variation, 66
    phonemes and allophones, 60–66
  phonotactics and, 55–57
  sound change and, 197–200
  second language acquisition and,
      305
  transcription of, 66–67
  units of analysis in, 54–55. See also
      Features of natural classes;
      Segments, sound; Syllables

Phonotactics, 55–57
  accidental vs. systematic gaps and, 56
  borrowings and, 56–57
  definition of, 55
  English, 55–56
Phrases
  adjectival, 130–33
  adverbial, 131, 142
  in foreign languages, 159–61
  heads of, 133–34
  intermediate structures, 131–33
  nominal, 176–78
  noun, 128–29, 131–33
  prepositional, 129–30
  verb, 130
Phrase structure rules, 136–39, 147
Physiological factors in linguistic change, 191
Piaget, Jean, 291
Pictograms, 360–61, 372, 375
Pidgins, 244–46
Pinyin, 372
Pitch, 35–39
Places of articulation, 19–20, 47
Plato, 169
Play languages, 342
Plural forms, 119
  allomorphs, 117–18
  case and, 201–2
  formation of, 6–7
  inflection and, 107–8, 110
  irregular, 119–20
  language acquisition and, 278–79
  morphemes and, 92
Politeness formulas, male vs. female use of, 336–37
Politics, language and, 339–41
Polysemy, 172
Polysynthetic language, 230–31
Population factors in linguistic change, 209
Portmanteau morphemes, 113, 230
Postpositions, 159
Posture, animal communication and, 384
Pragmatics, 181, 438–39
Prefixes, 95, 97
  inflection and, 111
  word formation and, 100–2
Prepositional phrases (PPs), 129–30
Prepositions, 111, 127, 257, 260–62, 283

Presuppositions, 181–82
Prevarication, as design feature, 408
Primates, nonhuman, communication among, 395–406
  design features for, 409
  gibbons, baboons, and chimpanzees, 398–406
  monkeys, 396–98
  prosimians, 396
  testing for linguistic ability, 400–6
Process, articulatory, 41–44
  assimilation, 42–43, 77–79
  deletion, 43–44, 79
  dissimilation, 42
  epenthesis, 44, 79–80
  metathesis, 44
  phonological rules and, 77–81
  stress as, 80–81
Production strategies, 313
Productivity, as design feature, 407–8
Progressive assimilation, 42–43
Pronouns, 6, 89, 114, 127–29, 203, 231
  reflexive, 179–80
Pronunciation, 6. *See also* Phonetics; Sounds
  allomorphic variation and, 92
  changes in, 190
Prosimian communication, 396
Prosodic properties. *See* Suprasegments
Prosodic universals, 228–29
Protoforms, 211, 213
Protolanguage, 211
Psammetichus, Pharaoh, 269

Questions
  language acquisition and, 286–87
  second language acquisition and, 308–9
  wh, 151–55, 287, 308
  yes-no, 143–44, 147, 161–62, 204, 287

r
  in English, 25
  in foreign languages, 34–35
Radicals (specifiers), 371
Rask, Rasmus, 215
re-, as affix, 98–99
Reading, writing systems and, 379
Rebus principle, 362–63

Reconstruction, 210–16
  cognates and, 210–11
  Indo-European, 214–16
  internal, 214
  techniques of, 211–14
Recalcitrant, 98–99
Recursion, 134
Reduced feature, 49
Reduced vowels, 29
Reduplicative affixes, 96
Referents, 169–70, 385, 386
Reflexiveness, as design feature, 409
Reflexive pronouns, 179–80
Regional speech varieties (regional
    dialects), 327. *See also*
    Dialectology
Registers (functional speech
    varieties), 327
  speech situation and, 351–52
Register tones, 36–37
Regressive assimilation, 42–43
Relative clauses, 154–55
Requests (commands), male vs.
    female use of, 336–37
Respiration, survival vs. speech, 9–10
Retroflex *r*, 25, 34
Retroflex stops, 33
Romance of the Rose, The (Chaucer),
    189
Roots, definition of, 94
Round feature, 49
Routines, 303–4
/r/ phoneme, in English language, 62
Runic script, 370–71
Russell, Bertrand, 169, 388

Sapir, Edward, 184
Sapir-Whorf Hypothesis, 184–86
Scent, animal communication and,
    383
Schleicher, August, 216
Schwa, 29, 35, 43, 79, 118
Second language acquisition, 299–325
  environment for, 302
  first language acquisition compared
    to, 303–4
  immersion approach to, 320–22
  learners and, 312–17
  learning vs., 299
  methods of analysis and, 309–12
  morphological development and,
    305–7
  optimum age for, 300–1

phonological development and, 305
questions and issues in, 300–4
role of linguistic input and, 301–2
study of, 304–9
syntactic development and, 307–9
teaching methodologies for, 317–20
Secret languages, 341–42
Segments, sound, 15, 54–59
  in contrast, 57–59
  diphthongs and, 27
  environment of, 59
  features of, 45, 67–68
  phonological rules and, 77
  phonotactics and, 55–57
Seidenberg, Mark S., 404
Sejong, King, 373
Self-expression, problems of, 8
Semantic broadening, 206
Semantic features, definition of, 170–
    71
Semanticity, as design feature, 407
Semantic narrowing, 206
Semantic roles (thematic roles), 176–
    78
Semantics, 169–88, 258, 261–62
  changes in, 206
  computational, 436–39
  computational syntax and, 429–30
  conduction aphasia and, 262
  definition of, 4, 169
  language acquisition and, 28–84
  sentences and, 173–83
    other factors, 180–83
    syntactic structure, 174–80
  thought and, 183–86
  words and, 169–73
Semantic shift, 206–7
Sentence formation. *See* Syntax
Sentences
  definition of, 135
  semantic relations involving, 173–
    83
    other factors, 180–83
    syntactic structure, 174–80
  structure of. *See* Syntax
Setting, scene, speech situation and,
    349
Sex, language and, 335–39
Sex-exclusive differentiation, 335–36
Sex-preferential differentiation, 336–
    37
Shaw, George Bernard, 377
Shields, M. J., 377

Sibilants, definition of, 23
Signals, tokens as, 387
Sign language, chimpanzees' use of, 400–1, 403, 405
Signs. *See also* Morphemes; Referents; Tokens
  definition of, 385
Sikwayi (Sequoia), 373
Simon, John, 8
Simple vowels, definition of, 27
Simple words, 91
Singular forms, 110
  case and, 201–2
Sisterhood, 135
Social contexts, language in, 326–57
  dialectology and, 327–31
  fundamental concepts, 326–27
  mixed languages and, 344–49
  social differentiation and, 331–41
  special languages and, 341–43
  speech situations and, 349–54
Social dialects (sociolects), 327
Social differentiation of language, 331–41
  politics and, 339–41
  sex and, 335–39
  social stratification and, 332–35
Sociological factors in linguistic change, 192
Social stratification of language, 332–35
  definition of, 332
  English and, 332–35
Sociolinguistics. *See also* Social contexts, language in
  definition of, 326
soleme, words created from, 3
Songs, bird, 392–94
Sonorant feature, 46
Sounds. *See also* Phonetics; Phonology
  rule-governed creativity and, 2–3
Sound shift, 215
Spanish language. *See also* Spanish *in Language Index*
  consonants in, 33–35
  negation in, 7
  phonetic transcription, 14
Spatial terms, language acquisition and, 283
Specialization
  as design feature, 407
  language and, 9–10

Special languages, 341–43
Specifiers (radicals), 371
Spectrograms, 415–17
Spectrographs, of bird songs, 393
Speech acts, 182–83
Speech community, 326–27
Speech organs. *See also specific organs*
  dual functions of, 9–10
Speech recognition, computational linguistics and, 419, 443–44
Speech situations, 349–54
  forms of address and, 352–54
  register and, 351–52
Speech sounds. *See* Phones
Speech synthesis, computational linguistics and, 415–18, 444–45
Speech variety (language variety), 327
Spelling, English, 376–79
S rule, 136–37, 143
Standard language, 332, 343, 347
Standard speech, 327
Stems, 95, 98
Stevens, Wallace, 13
Stimulus-bound, 388
Stopping, 273
Stops, 21–22, 65–66
  definition of, 21
  in foreign languages, 33, 35
Strategies of language learners, 312–14
Stress, 39–40, 120, 229, 242, 277
  diffusion of shifts in, 207–8
  primary, 40
  as process, 80–81
  secondary, 40
  word formation and, 104–5
Stress shift, 98
Stridents, 23, 48
Structural change, definition of, 143
Structural description, definition of, 143
Structured communication task, 304
Subcategorization frames, 140–41, 151
Subjects, 135, 203
  word order and, 231–35
Subject-verb agreement, 333
Sublanguages, 343
Substandard language, 332
Substitution, language acquisition and, 273
Substitution test, 128–29, 131

Substratum influence, 192
Suffixes, 95, 97, 99, 102–3, 231, 234
  inflection and, 109
Superstratum influence, 192
Suppletion, 116
Suprasegments (prosodic properties),
    35–40, 228–29
  length, 35, 39
  loudness, 35, 36
  pitch, 35–39
  stress, 39–40
Surface structure, 146, 147, 151–53,
    155–58
  ambiguity and, 174–76
Swift, Jonathan, 8
Syllabic feature, 46
Syllabic nasals, 26
Syllabic sounds, 26
Syllabic writing, 359, 363–67, 373,
    375, 379, 380
Syllables, 54–55, 70–75, 277
  definition of, 17, 18, 54, 70–71
  nucleus of, 17, 26, 46, 70
  phonological rules and, 77
  as phonological structure, 73–75
  setting up, 71–73
  simplification of, language
      acquisition and, 273–74
  vowels and, 17, 18
Symbolic tokens, 386, 388
Symptomatic tokens, 386–88
Syncope, 195, 200
Synonyms, 171–72
Syntax, 126–68
  animal communication and, 405
  Broca's aphasia and, 260–62
  categories, 127–36, 158–59
  changes in, 203–4
  clauses
      embedded, 148–51, 153
      relative, 154–55
  computational, 424–31
  cross-linguistic variation in, 158–65
  definition of, 4, 126
  generative grammar, 142
  islands, 155–58
  language acquisition and, 284–88
  language classification and, 231–35
  lexical insertion and, 139–42, 147
  phrase structure rules, 136–39, 147
  in pidgins, 344–45
  second language acquisition and,
      307–9

sentences interpretation and, 174–
    80
  specialization and, 10
  structural ambiguity and, 135–36
  transformational rules and, 143–47
  wh questions and, 151–55
Synthetic (inflectional) language, 230
Systematic gaps, definition of, 56

Taboos, euphemism and, 338–39
Talking Machine, 415
Tap, definition of, 34–35
Teacher talk (foreigner talk), 301
Teaching
  grammar, 6
  second language acquisition and,
      317–20
Teeth
  dentals and, 19, 20
  dual functions of, 9, 10
Telegraphic stage, 285
Template, 394
Tense of verbs, 107, 109, 115–16,
    287–88
Tense feature, 49
Tense vowels, 29–30
Text retrieval, 441
Thematic roles (semantic roles), 176–
    78
Thomas, Lewis, 1
Thought, semantics and, 183–86
Time expressions, 131
  verbs created from, 2
Tokens, animal communication and,
    385–88
Tone(s), 36–39
  assimilation of, 70
  contour, 36–37
  intonation and, 38–39
  register, 36–37
  representation of, 69–70
Tone languages, 243, 228–29
Tonge, Israel, 126
Tongue
  back of, 19
  blade of, 18, 19, 47
  body of, 19
  consonant articulation and, 18–19
  dual functions of, 9, 10
  root of, 19
  tip of 18, 19, 47
  vowels and, 26–27
Total immersion approach, 321

Total physical response method, 320
Trachea (windpipe), 16, 19
Tradition, as design feature, 408
Transformational rules, 143–47
Transitional constructions, language
    acquisition and, 303–4
Transitive verbs, 113–14, 141
Tree configurations, 156–57
Tree diagrams, 94–95
Tree structures, ambiguity and, 174–
    76
Trills, 35
Two-word utterances, 284–85
Typology, linguistic, 225

Uncouth, 98–99
Underextension, 283
Underlying, use of term, 75
Underlying representation (UR), 117–
    18
    abstract, 120–21
Universality, features and, 49
Universals, language, 225–29, 231–35
    implicational, 225, 227, 228, 231–33
Universal tendencies, 225, 226
Universal grammar, 293
Uvulars, 20
    liquids, 35
    stops, 21, 33

Vai writing system, 375
Variables, sociolinguistic, 334–35
Velars, 19–21, 47
    affricates, 34
    fricatives, 33, 34
    stops, 21, 33
Velum, 19, 20, 40–41
Verbal paradigm (conjugation), 114–
    15
Verb phrases (VPs), 130, 138
Verbs, 89, 127–28, 203
    agreement of, 287–88, 333
    auxiliary (helping), 127, 139, 143,
        262, 286, 287
    complements of, 148–49
    complements of *wh* movement in,
        152–53
    English vs. French, 5
    inflection and, 107–9, 114–16
    intransitive, 113–14, 141
    from nouns, 1–2
    number of, 114–15
    past tense of, 93

performatives, 183
stress shift and, 98
subcategorization of, 140, 141
tense of, 107, 109, 115–16, 287–88
transitive, 113–14, 141
voice of, 116
word formation and, 102, 103
word order and, 231–35
Vocal folds (vocal chords), 16
dual functions of, 9, 10
Vocal tract, 15, 19
Vocorder, 415
Voice, of verbs, 116
Voiced sounds, 16, 21–23, 33–35, 60,
    67–68
allophones and, 61–63
definition of, 16
in French, 78–79
laterals, 25
long vs. short vowels and, 74–75
Voice feature, 48
Voice lag, 24–25
Voiceless sounds, 16, 21–24, 33–35,
    60, 65–66, 68
allophones and, 61–63
definition of, 16
fricatives, 22–23, 33–34
Voicing, 194, 200
Vowels, 17–18, 26–33
consonants compared to, 18
contrasts of, 58
definition of, 26–27
description of, 27–29
diphthongs, 27, 30
epenthesis and, 44, 79–80
features of, 46, 49
Great Vowel Shift, 199–200, 202,
    376–77
language classification and, 225–27,
    233, 241, 242
long vs. short, 74–75
mid, 28
nasal, 21, 30–31, 42, 46, 47, 63–65
oral, 63, 65
oral vs. nasal, 227
raising of, 63–64
reduced, 29
rounded, 32
sound change and, 194–96, 198–200
simple, 27
stress of, 39–40
syllabic liquids and nasals
    compared to, 26

syllables and, 17
tense vs. lax, 29–30
transcription of, in American
    English, 31–32
Vygotsky, Lev, 291

Weakening, consonantal (lenition),
    194
Webster, Noah, 377
Wernicke, Carl, 258
Wernicke's area, 258–59, 261, 263
Whispers, 16–17
Whitman, Walt, 54
Whorf, Benjamin Lee, 184–85
wh questions, 151–55, 287, 308
Word-based morphology, 98–99
Word formation, 100–7. *See also*
    Morphology
  compounding and, 100, 103–5
  derivation and, 100–4
  language acquisition and, 279
  lexical change and, 204–6
  other types of, 106–7
Word order, 111
  changes in, 203
  language classification and, 231–33,
      241–44, 246
  negation and, 8–9
  predictability and, 8–9
  in Walbiri vs. English, 4–5

Words
  closed vs. open, 89
  definition of, 90
  meaning of, 169–71
  semantic relation among, 171–73
  simple vs. complex, 91
  sound patterns in, 2–3
Word structure, 93–99, 231, 234
  without affixes, 97–98
  affixes and, 94–97
  problematic cases and, 99
  representation of, 94–95
  stems and, 95
Writing systems, 262–63, 358–82
  English spelling and, 376–79
  history of, 359–71
    alphabetic writing, 367–71
    ideograms, 360–61
    logograms, 361–64
    pictograms, 360–61
    syllabic writing, 364–67
  non-European, 371–76
  reading and, 379
  types of, 358–59

Yes-no questions, 287
  inversion in, 143–44, 147, 161–62,
      204

Zero-derivation (conversion), 97–98